A Documentary
History of
Religion in
America

A DOCUMENTARY HISTORY OF RELIGION IN AMERICA

since 1865

Edited by EDWIN S. GAUSTAD

WILLIAM B. EERDMANS PUBLISHING COMPANY•GRAND RAPIDS

Copyright © 1983 by William B. Eerdmans Publishing Co.
255 Jefferson Ave., S.E., Grand Rapids, Mich. 49503
Printed in the United States of America

Reprinted, June 1986

Library of Congress Cataloging in Publication Data

Gaustad, Edwin Scott.
  A documentary history of religion in America.

  Includes bibliographies and index.
  Contents: [1] To the Civil War—[2] Since 1865.
  1. United States—Religion—Sources.
BL2530.U6G38 1982   291'.0973   82-7398
ISBN 0-8028-1871-4 (pbk. : v. 1)
ISBN 0-8028-1874-9 (pbk. : v.2)

For Evan Scott

CONTENTS

CHAPTER TEN
RELIGION AND THE LIFE OF THE MIND   308

PREFACE

As in the case of Volume One (*To the Civil War*), this second and concluding volume enables the reader to be his or her own historian. Using the many original sources here provided, the reader can construct a narrative, offer an analysis, arrive at an individually tailored synthesis. On the other hand, one may — in somewhat more relaxed fashion — simply enjoy the plethora of voices, now and then taking sides (or issue) with those who vigorously defend a given point of view.

Few of the documents that follow stand outside the stream of America's religious history. Most are written or spoken or hurled by persons planted firmly within that stream, by those drawing from the water's source and vitally concerned about its future direction. Disinterested documents are, in other words, the exception and not the rule. Which is just as well, for a large volume given over to authors who cared neither one way nor another about the outcome would make for a very dull book. Partisan voices have more flavor, if not always a perfect balance of piquancy and spice. An editorial aim has been to offer enough balance in introductions, documents, and suggested readings to set a table sufficient for virtually any taste. Naturally, it is never possible to empty the entire storehouse at any one time, however desirable in theory that might appear to be. In the long run, it is probably better to know that men and women have cared (and cared deeply) about a wide range of "faith and order" options than to know that every affirmation has its alternative or even its negation.

An explicit intent of Volume One, to be faithful to America's religious pluralism, persists in Volume Two. At times, however, the task has been not so much to be faithful to pluralism as to avoid being drowned by it. That is, one could concentrate so heavily on giving every novelty its due, granting to every marginal group its moment on center stage, that the major traditions, the large constituencies, the long-lived denominations would be shoved aside. The effort, especially in the twentieth century, has been to avoid both extremes: neither wholly ignoring the new and small nor wholly ignoring the old and large. Of course, both reader and editor must know that no single simple principle explains every inclusion or justifies each omission.

Finally, here as before, personal exultation or exasperation has been preferred over the cool and generally clumsy prose of the committee. Rabbi Samuel Mayerberg's fight against municipal corruption in Kansas City or Pastor Washington Gladden's similar battle in Columbus, Ohio, make better reading than any Report on Measures for Consideration and Possible Adoption by the City Council. And candidate Alfred Smith's personal plea in Oklahoma during a tough presidential campaign may tell us more about American religion than any heavy-handed analysis of the Origins and Expressions of Protestant Nativism in Selected Communities of Pre-Depression United States.

The courtesy of publishers and journal editors is acknowledged elsewhere. Here I express sincerest appreciation to the University of California, Riverside, for intramural grants; to graduate student Jim German for tireless and efficient sleuthing in pursuit of elusive documents; and to Eerdmans editor Charles Van Hof for alert, discerning, and even good-humored direction of both volumes of this *Documentary History*. The nation's religious history is a full one: a drama with an enormous cast of characters, a story still being told.

E.S.G.

ILLUSTRATIONS

ACKNOWLEDGMENTS

With much gratitude I acknowledge the helpfulness of publishers, editors, and private individuals who have agreed to the use of materials under their control.

Abingdon Press © 1968. Walter Rauschenbusch, *The Righteousness of the Kingdom*.
American Mercury. J. B. Matthews in Vol. 77 (July, 1953).
Asch, Moses. Sholem Asch, *The Nazarene* (1939).
Atlantic Monthly. H. P. Van Dusen in Vol. 154 (August, 1934).
Beacon Press. © 1976 Philip E. Slater, *Pursuit of Loneliness*.
Bloch Publishing Co. S. S. Mayerburg, *Chronicle of an American Crusader* (1944).
James T. Burtchaell, C. S. C. Advertisement in *Christian Century*, Vol. 94 (Nov. 16, 1977).
Center for Migration Studies. S. J. La Gumina, *The Immigrants Speak* (1979).
University of Chicago Press. Paul Tillich, *Systematic Theology*, Vol. I (1951); © 1951 by the publisher. Josiah Royce, *Problem of Christianity* (1968 [1913]), © 1918 by MacMillan Co., 1968 by the publisher.
Christian Century Foundation. Billy Graham in Vol. 77 (Feb. 17, 1960).
Christianity Today. Carl Henry in July 8 and July 22, 1957, issues; J. A. O. Preus in Oct. 25, 1974, issue; John Tietjen in April 11, 1975, issue.
Crossroad Publishing Co. © 1981 Martin E. Marty, *The Public Church*.
Joan Daves. © 1963 Martin Luther King, Jr., excerpt from "I Have a Dream."
Mrs. Virginia Douglas Dawson. Lloyd C. Douglas, *The Robe* (1942).
Dial Press © 1971. T. C. Wheeler, *The Immigrant Experience*.
Doubleday & Co. © 1981 Sonia Johnson, *From Housewife to Heretic*. © 1949 Fulton Oursler, *The Greatest Story Ever Told*. © 1947 Fulton J. Sheen, *Peace of Soul*.
Farrar, Straus & Giroux, Inc. Thomas Merton, *Seasons of Celebration*, © 1950, 1958, 1962, 1964, 1965 by the Abbey of Gethsemani. Xavier Rynne, *Letters from Vatican City*, © 1963 by the publisher.
Forward Movement Publications (412 Sycamore St., Cincinnati). *Reports from Four Meetings* (n.d.).
Harcourt Brace Jovanovich, Inc. Thomas Merton, *The Sign of Jonas* (1953), © Abbey of Our Lady of Gethsemani, renewed 1981 by Trustees of the Merton Legacy Fund.
Harper & Row, Publishers. © 1929, 1956 Reinhold Niebuhr, *Leaves from the Notebook of a Tamed Cynic*. © 1932 Laymen's Foreign Missions Inquiry, *Re-Thinking Missions*. Anton T. Boisen, *The Exploration of the Inner World*, © Willet, Clark & Co. © 1970 James H. Cone, *A Black Theology of Liberation*. © 1963 Martin Luther King, Jr., *Why We Can't Wait*. Dorothy Day, *The Long Loneliness*, © 1952 by the publisher. E. J. Goodspeed, *As I Remember*, © 1953 by the publisher. G. B. Oxnam, *I Protest*, © 1954 by the publisher.
Horizon Press © 1955. T. Friedman and R. Gordis, *Jewish Life in America*.
Raymond G. Hunthausen, Archbishop. Pastoral Letter, January 28, 1982.
Institute for Ecumenical and Cultural Research. D. E. Harrell, Jr., in *Occasional Paper* No. 15 (May, 1981).

Jewish Publication Society of America. C. H. Voss, ed., *Stephen Wise* (1969). Blu Greenberg, *On Women and Judaism* (1981).

Jewish Theological Seminary of America (Melton Research Center for Jewish Education). Nahum Sarna, *Understanding Genesis* (1966).

McGraw Hill Book Co., © 1981. Kenneth Wooden, *Children of Jonestown*.

MacMillan Publishing Co. H. F. Ward, *Our Economic Morality and the Ethic of Jesus*, © 1929 by the publisher, © 1957 by the author. Rufus Jones, *Pathways to the Reality of God*, © 1931 by the publisher, © 1959 by Mary H. Jones. A. N. Whitehead, *Process and Reality*, © 1929 by the publisher, © 1957 by Evelyn Whitehead. H. R. Niebuhr, *The Meaning of Revelation*, © 1941 by the publisher, © 1969 by Florence Niebuhr, C. M. Niebuhr, R. R. Niebuhr. © 1957 Walter J. Ong, *Frontiers of American Catholicism*.

Methodist Church (Board of Church and Society). *Concern*, Vol. 7 (Dec. 1, 1965).

New Directions Publishing Corp. © 1980 Gary Snyder, *The Real Work*.

New York Times. © Special Report, September 8, 1928.

W. W. Norton © 1979. Christopher Lasch, *The Culture of Narcissism*.

Paulist Press. Frank Ponce in *New Catholic World*, July/August, 1980, © 1979, Missionary Society of St. Paul the Apostle in the State of New York.

University of Pennsylvania Press. Jacques Maritain in *Religion in the Modern World* (1941).

Random House, Inc. Alan Watts, *The Way of Zen* (1957). Etienne Gilson, *The Philosopher and Theology* (1962). *The Autobiography of Malcolm X* (1964). Sam J. Ervin, Jr., *The Whole Truth* (1980).

Religious Humanism. W. S. Fisk in Vol. I (Winter, 1967).

Fleming H. Revell Co. © 1946, 1974. C. S. Macfarland, *Pioneers for Peace Through Religion*.

Schocken Books. © 1978 Emil L. Fackenheim, *The Jewish Return into History*. Arthur Hertzberg, *Being Jewish in America*, © 1979 by the publisher.

Charles Scribner's Sons. Reinhold Niebuhr, *Reflections on the End of an Era*, © 1934 by the publisher, © 1962 by the author.

Seabury Press. R. N. Bellah, *The Broken Covenant* (1975). P. L. Berger and R. J. Neuhaus, eds., *Against the World/For the World* (1976).

Sheed and Ward (Andrews and McMeel, Inc.). R. S. Lecky and H. E. Wright, eds., *Black Manifesto* (1969). C. E. Currant and R. E. Hunt, eds., *Dissent In and For the Church* (1969).

Simon & Schuster. © 1970, 1971 C. H. Voss, ed., *A Summons Unto All Men*.

Union of American Hebrew Congregations. Julian Morgenstern, *The Book of Genesis* (1965 [1919]).

Unity. Charles Fillmore in Vol. 106 (June, 1947).

Upper Room. Meditation, April 2, 1935, © The Upper Room, P.O. Box 189, Nashville, TN 37202.

Viking Penguin, Inc. © 1979 Margot Adler, *Drawing Down the Moon*.

University of Washington Press. H. S. Lucas, *Dutch Immigrant Memoirs*, Vol. 2 (1955).

Watch Tower Tract and Bible Society. Excerpt from *1974 Yearbook*.

Westminster Press © 1967. William Hamilton in J. L. Ice and J. J. Carey, *The Death of God*.

Wilson Quarterly (Hoover Institution Press). Nathan Glazer in Vol. 5 (Autumn, 1981).

Yale University Press. John Dewey, *A Common Faith* (1934).

SEVEN:

Reconstructions
and Reaffirmations

In the decade before the Civil War, German Reformed theologian Philip Schaff had spoken of God's power "to call forth from the chaos a beautiful creation" (see Vol. I, p. 518). A decade after that remark, chaos had become catastrophe, and any notion of a beautiful creation seemed a tragic illusion. A nation not yet a century old had gnawed away at its own body, weakening, poisoning, threatening everything capable of supporting healthy life. A wasted, devastated South reeled like a drunk that could not stand. A wearied, bloodied North found itself hardly more ready to cope with "victory." This "terrible war," in Lincoln's words, had gone on and on, seemingly without end. Churches too were casualties: wounded, sick, dismayed. Had God's arm been shortened that he could not reach, his ears deafened that he could not hear?

TO BIND UP THE NATION'S WOUNDS
So it seemed for a time. Gradually, however, Schaff's optimism gathered substance. Connecticut's Horace Bushnell found in all that shedding of blood a kind of national atonement. We have been told, Bushnell observed, that "without the shedding of blood, there is no remission of sins" (Hebrews 9:22). So, too, "without the shedding of blood, there is almost nothing great in the world, or to be expected for it. For the life is in the blood — all life. . . ." And Schaff himself, the year after Appomattox, proclaimed that America's "impregnable faith in a great future is daunted by no obstacle. . . ." Thus began the task of ecclesiastical and theological reconstruction, of binding up wounds, ministering to the sick and afflicted, educating the unskilled and unlearned, putting back together the scattered fortunes and furnishings of many a household of faith. Not always were those tasks sensitively undertaken or successfully concluded. But both churchmanship and theological leadership were called upon to wrest a more beautiful creation out of war's cruel chaos.

1

"WELCOME TO THE RANSOMED"

For one important body of Americans, the Civil War had already wrought a momentous as well as a beautiful creation: namely, freedom. The Emancipation Proclamation (January 1, 1863), though far from having an immediate effect everywhere and far from curing all the ills of the black experience, gave to freed men and women new opportunity and new aspiration. For either to be realized, the Constitution had to be amended and consciences had to be altered. The latter took longer than the former. But even in the midst of war and in the heart of the nation's capital, black Methodist Daniel Payne celebrated the Emancipation, "yea, rather the *Redemption* of the enslaved people of the District of Columbia . . .": "Welcome to the Ransomed."

While emancipation could be seen as the end of one long road, most understood it as the beginning of another. Northern churches called for helpers to hurry to their side; for every thousand freed slaves, we require "at least one able, experienced, faithful missionary to preach to them, to teach, to organize and counsel them." Each missionary, moreover, required several teachers as assistants. And if a million should be emancipated, then a thousand missionaries will be required, with thousands more to be recruited as assistants. Schools did spring up, churches did gather monies and deploy personnel, blacks did — in gratifying numbers — join existing churches or set about creating their own. Not all was achieved that had been hoped; on the other hand, more was done for the sake of the newly ransomed than some had wished.

BOUND FOR THE PROMISED LAND

For all the blood that had soaked into the battlefields of Antietam, Gettysburg, and Petersburg, the ultimate healing came in the form of many transfusions of new blood. In the half-century following the Civil War, hundreds, then thousands, then millions of new immigrants arrived. From 1865 to 1915, about twenty-five million hopefuls reached America's shores. They came from western and northern Europe, from eastern and southern Europe, and even from Russia and the Far East. A pervasively Protestant America watched Roman Catholicism, already by 1850 the largest single denomination, grow by giant increments as new national groups arrived in wholesale lots. For its own part, this large church found the sudden surge in membership both enheartening and overwhelming. How to feed and house? to educate or mollify? to maintain in harmony as part of the one universal and apostolic Church? In New York City, for example, Archbishop John Hughes grappled with problems that daunted, even before the numbers swelled — and swelled.

In that same half-century (1865– 1915), Judaism mushroomed from a modest and predominantly German minority to a large and visible presence. As with Roman Catholicism, the numerical growth among Jews brought with it a wondrous variety in liturgy, political attitude, and national origin. Most of the new arrivals reveled in the discovery that "in this great glorious and free country," as Solomon Schechter declared in 1904, "we Jews need not sacrifice a single iota of our Torah; and, in the enjoyment of absolute equality with our fellow citizens, we can live to carry out those ideals for which our ancestors so often had to die."

WOMEN'S WORK?

One group of fellow citizens in the half-century after 1865 felt that equality continued to elude them. The emancipation of women, like the emancipation of the slaves, required reform of both Constitution and conscience. Not until 1920 did women win the right to vote, and more than half a century after that, full Constitutional equality remained ambiguous at best. The late nineteenth century, however, did see religious doors being opened more widely to women. Women entered pulpits, led reforms, edited and translated the Bible, although none of this was accomplished without stern opposition. Arguments — whether for or against the broader participation of women — came from history and tradition, from biblical direction and social need, from common sense and common hope. Little common ground could be found, however, between those who on the one hand held that "woman is not designed by God . . . to all the franchises in society to which the male is entitled," and those who on the other hand concluded that "the masculine and feminine elements, exactly equal and balancing each other, are as essential to the maintenance of the equilibrium of the universe as positive and negative electricity. . . ." Depending on the perspective of the antagonists, cosmic equilibrium in the 1880s and 1890s was either being badly upset or more nearly achieved.

THE WEST

The nation's effective dominion over a vast continent, interrupted by a costly war, resumed its reach in the postwar period. Religious forces continued then, as they had earlier, to be instruments of civilizing and of Christianizing, those two processes being seen as complementary if not synonymous. Once the Mississippi River had been crossed, the lands to be reached were of greater expanse, the Indians to be instructed of profounder distrust. Roman Catholic Pierre Jean De Smet and Presbyterian Sheldon Jackson left St. Louis and kept walking westward and northward, Jackson continuing all the way to Alaska. Neither Catholics nor Presbyterians, however, managed to send the first missionaries into Alaska; that priority belonged to the Russian Orthodox Church. Well before the Civil War, that ancient church had entered the American West — not by crossing mountains, plains, and rivers, but the Pacific Ocean itself. Writing in 1840, Father John Veniaminov, Orthodoxy's most famous missionary to "Russian America," described with pleasure "the dissemination and consolidation of Christ's Faith in one of the most remote territories of our Society, where through God's pleasure I had the opportunity of spending many years." Also before the Civil War, mainland American missionaries had penetrated another outpost of empire: the Sandwich or Hawaiian Islands. After that war, Japanese emigrating to Hawaii filled those islands with a faith even more ancient than Russian Orthodoxy: namely, Buddhism. By this means, the Asiatic East was moving toward the American West at the same time that Atlantic seaboard easterners migrated toward the Pacific West. In the nineteenth century, East and West did meet; the twain were joined, even if they failed to become one.

THE WORLD

In 1893 East and West met with more deliberate intent in mid-America's great metropolis of Chicago. The occasion, the World Parliament of Religions, emerged as a sort of "side exhibit" of Chicago's Columbian Exposition of that year. But this side exhibit, brainchild of Congregationalist John Henry Barrows, appeared to the religiously minded to be as striking as the main show, and perhaps even more instructive. Now not only Buddhism but Hinduism, Confucianism, Shinto, and Islam had their own spokesmen. If Americans had heard anything at all of these religions, they had heard from Christian missionaries; now, a differing point of view made itself known. Judaism had its spokeswomen, Catholicism — both Greek and Roman — its apologists, Protestantism its participants as well as its sometimes anxious observers. And apart from the adherents of specific institutional forms of religion, many came to probe that slippery entity called "religion." The Parliament stood as an augury of the nation's future: pluralistic, adventuresome in dialogue, defensive in structure, persuaded that somehow men and women of goodwill could play a role in promoting peace on earth.

Yet confronted with diversity so flamboyant, so indelible, some wondered if this coat of many colors was religion's most impressive garment as it moved forward to solve humanity's problems or to offer solace for problems that had no solution. If, moreover, one looked at the world of religions in broadest terms — Hindu, Buddhist, Moslem, Christian, etc. — did this not suggest that those large divisions ought to present a united front to a restless world? Could not badly divided Christendom, for example, put its own house in order, the better to compete against other religious options, now seen as genuine and alive?

If Parliament dramatized diversity in religion, the Eleventh Census (1890) documented it so far as the United States was concerned. The Christian faith seemed a fractious, brawling collection of competing sects, too busy distinguishing themselves from their fellows to worry about the advances of Buddhism or Islam. "The external divisions of Christendom," said Lutheran seminary president Francis Pieper in 1893, "are a most deplorable state of things . . . contrary to the will of God." And the Methodist layman who had conducted the religious census, H. K. Carroll, thought that, at the very least, denominational families ought to be able to overcome their minor differences.

By the dawn of the twentieth century, the United States was a showplace of religious freedom. Some feared, however, that it might turn out to be the graveyard of sect, schism, and separation, of religious faith reduced to the most casual choice, the most insignificant option. Before many decades had passed, the nation's churches and synagogues might, like Samson without his hair, "become weak" and "not know that the Lord had left" them. Should that occur, the theological and ecclesiastical reconstructions and reaffirmations of the nineteenth century could be judged only as failures.

1. TO BIND UP THE NATION'S WOUNDS

The Scene

Military Rule

In the closing days of the Civil War and for some years thereafter, the South was a conquered country, subject to military rule and military occupation. So also, the South's churches bowed before military might and arbitrary order. Liberties, whether civil or religious, always suffer in time of war as the urgencies of the moment override the niceties which, in calmer times, would be conceded as the rights of all. Three separate orders given in three Confederate states reveal the temper of those abnormal times, two of the orders issued during the war, the third some five months after the surrender. That third order, directing (Episcopal) Bishop Richard H. Wilmer (1816– 1900) of Alabama to include prayers for the president of the United States in all regular services, resulted in the temporary closing of all Episcopal churches in the state. Wilmer protested directly to President Andrew Johnson who ordered that the churches be reopened forthwith and Bishop Wilmer fully reinstated.

1.

SPECIAL ORDER, NO. 31

Headquarters U. S. Forces
Natchez, Miss., June 18, 1864

II. The Colonel commanding this district having been officially notified that the pastors of many churches in this city neglect to make any public recognition of allegiance under which they live, and to which they are indebted for protection, and further, that the regular form of prayer for "the President

[Source: Walter L. Fleming, ed., *Documentary History of Reconstruction* (Cleveland: Arthur H. Clark, 1906), I, pp. 221–26.]

of the United States, and all others in authority," prescribed by the ritual in some churches, and by established custom in others, has been omitted in the stated services of churches of all denominations, it is hereby

Ordered, That hereafter, the ministers of such churches as may have the prescribed form of prayer for the President of the United States, shall be read at each and every service in which it is required by the rubrics — and that those of other denominations, which have no such form — shall on like occasions pronounce a prayer appropriate to the time, and expressive of the proper spirit toward the Chief Magistrate of the United States. Any minister failing to comply with these orders, will be immediately prohibited from exercising the functions of his office in this city — and render himself liable to be sent beyond the lines of the United States forces.

2.

GENERAL ORDER NO. 3

Norfolk, Va., Feb. 11, 1864

All places of public worship in Norfolk and Portsmouth are hereby placed under the control of the provost marshals of Norfolk and Portsmouth respectively, who shall see the pulpits properly filled by displacing, when necessary, the present incumbents, and substituting men of known loyalty and the same sectarian denomination, either military or civil subject to the approval of the commanding general. They shall see that all churches are open free to all officers and soldiers, white or colored, at the usual hour of worship, and at other times, if desired; and they shall see that no insult or indignity be offered to them, either by word, look, or gesture on the part of the congregation. The necessary expenses will be levied as far as possible, in accordance with the previous usages or regulations of each congregation respectively.

3.

GENERAL ORDER NO. 38

Headquarters Department of Alabama
Mobile, Ala., Sept. 20, 1865

The Protestant Episcopal Church of the United States has established a form of prayer to be used for "the President of the United States and all in civil authority." During the continuance of the late wicked and groundless rebellion the prayer was changed for one for the President of the Confederate States, and so altered, was used in the Protestant Churches of the Diocese of Alabama.

Since the "lapse" of the Confederate government, and the restoration of authority of the United States over the late rebellious States, the prayer for the President has been altogether omitted in the Episcopal Churches of Alabama.

This omission was recommended by the Rt. Rev. Richard Wilmer, Bishop of Alabama, in a letter to the clergy and laity, dated June 20, 1865. The advice of the bishop to omit this prayer, and its omission by the clergy, is not only a violation of the canons of the church, but shows a factious and disloyal spirit, and is a marked insult to every loyal citizen within the department. Such men are unsafe public teachers, and not to be trusted in places of power and influence over public opinion.

It is, therefore, ordered, pursuant to the directions of Major-General Thomas, commanding the military division of Tennessee, that said Richard Wilmer, bishop of the Protestant Episcopal Church of the Diocese of Alabama, and the Protestant Episcopal clergy of said diocese be, and they are hereby suspended from their functions, and forbidden to preach, or perform divine service; and that their places of worship be closed until such time as said bishop and clergy show a sincere return to their allegiance to the government of the United States, and give evidence of a loyal and patriotic spirit by offering to resume the use of the prayer for the President of the United States and all in civil authority, and by taking the amnesty oath prescribed by the President.

This prohibition shall continue in each individual case until special application is made through the military channels to these headquarters for permission to preach and perform divine serice, and until such application is approved at these or superior headquarters.

District commanders are required to see that this order is carried into effect.

By order of MAJOR-GENERAL CHAS. R. WOODS.

Theological Reflection

At the same time that such orders were being given in the South, theological reflection in the North attempted to put into perspective all the suffering and dying —on both sides. The Hartford, Connecticut, pastor, Horace Bushnell (1802–76), returned to his alma mater, Yale, to deliver a commencement oration in July of 1865. But no college in America could think of honoring its graduates in that year without also honoring —and mourning —its dead. In the American Revolution the nation was born; in the Civil War the nation was reborn. The rebirth was even bloodier than the birth, but it is important for us all to remember, Bushnell noted, that now our unity as a nation has been "cemented and forever sanctified."

[Source: Horace Bushnell, "Our Obligations to the Dead," in *Building Eras in Religion* (New York: Charles Scribner's Sons, 1910), pp. 325–28.]

According to the true economy of the world, so many of its grandest and most noble benefits have and are to have a tragic origin, and to come as outgrowths only of blood. Whether it be that sin is in the world, and the whole creation groaneth in the necessary throes of its demonized life, we need not stay to inquire; for sin would be in the world and the demonizing spell would be upon it. Such was, and was to be, and is, the economy of it. Common life, the world's great life, is in the large way tragic. As the mild benignity and peaceful reign of Christ begins at the principle: "without shedding of blood, there is no remission," so, without shedding of blood, there is almost nothing great in the world, or to be expected for it. For the life is in the blood, — all life; and it is put flowing within, partly for the serving of a nobler use in flowing out on fit occasion, to quicken and consecrate whatever it touches. God could not plan a Peace-Society world, to live in the sweet amenities, and grow great and happy by simply thriving and feeding. There must be bleeding also. Sentiments must be born that are children of thunder; there must be heroes and heroic nationalities, and martyr testimonies, else there will be only mediocrities, insipidities, common-place men, and common-place writings, — a sordid and mean peace, liberties without a pulse, and epics that are only eclogues [country poems].

And here it is that the dead of our war have done for us a work so precious, which is all their own, — they have bled for us; and by this simple sacrifice of blood they have opened for us a new great chapter of life. We were living before in trade and commerce, bragging of our new cities and our census reports, and our liberties that were also consciously mocked by our hypocrisies; having only the possibilities of great inspirations and not the fact, materialized more and more evidently in our habits and sentiments, strong principally in our discords and the impetuosity of our projects for money. But the blood of our dead has touched our souls with thoughts more serious and deeper, and begotten, as I trust, somewhat of that high-bred inspiration which is itself the possibility of genius, and of a true public greatness. Saying nothing then for the present of our victors and victories, let us see what we have gotten by the blood of our slain.

And first of all, in this blood our unity is cemented and forever sanctified. Something was gained for us here, at the beginning, by our sacrifices in the fields of our Revolution, — something, but not all. Had it not been for this common bleeding of the States in their common cause, it is doubtful whether our Constitution could ever have been carried. The discords of the Convention were imminent, as we know, and were only surmounted by compromises that left them still existing. They were simply kenneled under the Constitution and not reconciled, as began to be evident shortly in the doctrines of state sovereignty, and state nullification, here and there asserted. We had not bled enough, as yet, to merge our colonial distinctions and make us a proper

Julia Ward Howe (1819–1910), author of the "Battle Hymn of the Republic" and leader in woman's suffrage movement. Picture taken in Newport, Rhode Island, in 1905. *(Keystone-Mast Collection, University of California, Riverside)*

nation. Our battles had not been upon a scale to thoroughly mass our feeling, or gulf us in a common cause and life. Against the state-rights doctrines, the logic of our Constitution was decisive, and they were refuted a thousand times over. But such things do not go by argument. No argument transmutes a discord, or composes a unity where there was none. The matter wanted here was blood, not logic, and this we now have on a scale large enough to meet our necessity. True it is blood on one side, and blood on the other, — all the better for that; for bad bleeding kills, and righteous bleeding sanctifies and quickens. The state-rights doctrine is now fairly bled away, and the unity died for, in a way of such prodigious devotion, is forever sealed and glorified.

American Hope

A nation of no long history, of no single culture, of varied race, language, and religion had spent four years tearing itself apart. Was there any reason whatsoever to expect greatness from such a land, such a people? Answers to that question had to come more from faith and religious hope than from experience and worldly calculation. The answer of Philip Schaff (1819 – 93), theologian and church historian of the German Reformed seminary in

[Source: "Dr. Schaff's Lectures on America Delivered in Europe, 1865" (trans. C. C. Starbuck), in the *Christian Intelligencer*, 38, no. 9 (Mar. 1, 1866), unpaged.]

Mercersburg, Pennsylvania, was delivered in Europe in 1865. America is not a moral and spiritual chaos, Schaff argued, though he admitted that much would suggest the contrary. Rather, America is "a sound and robust national organism" which, as it faces a great future, is "daunted by no obstacle," not even by this prolonged and cruel conflict itself.

I am, it is true, very well aware that in every country all healthy conditions and institutions must assume a form agreeable to the natural development of its history, and that it is an idle undertaking to transplant foreign manners and customs, unmodified, to our own soil. But on the other hand, you will not deny, that not only the past but also the present is a book of instruction, warning, and encouragement for all that are willing to read it. Ought America, the land of the West, whither points the course of the sun and of civilization, to be an exception to this? The nations and churches of the old and of the new world are now, through a thousand channels of intercourse, continually drawing nearer together, and ought more and more to learn to understand, to value and to love each other better, and thereby advance the coming of that great crowning era, where there shall be one flock and one Shepherd, in the fullest sense of that prophetic word.

Among all the countries of the earth, America appears least of all to present the image of a harmonious whole. . . . Viewed cursorily and from without, it appears an impenetrable spiritual, moral, and religious chaos, a veritable *Tohuwhabohu* [Hebrew, a great void]. It is a land of antitheses and antagonisms, like no other, and affords sufficient material for the most diverse impressions and judgments, from enthusiastic eulogy to the most utterly scornful censure. It is an arena and smelting crucible of all nationalities, churches, and sects, where the noblest and basest elements of the old world ferment confusedly together. New York, for instance, is as much Irish, German, and French, as an Anglo-American city, and in heterogeneousness of composition more cosmopolitan than even London or Paris.

But the very fact that America can not only endure without harm such an uninterrupted stream of the immigration of nations from the East, but can, without difficulty and with incredible rapidity, denationalize it and assimilate it unto itself; and that, in cases innumerable, out of men who, in Europe, had appeared pecuniarily or morally lost beyond hope, it makes useful citizens and earnest Christians — this very circumstance bears witness to the existence of a sound and robust national organism, which in impregnable faith in a great future is daunted by no obstacle, and welcomes immigrants from all lands to the development and administration of its inexhaustible resources for the good of mankind.

The Task

Territory Conquered

Even before the war ended, northern churchmen called for the conquered South to become the converted South: converted by the "free churches" and the "full gospel" of northern religion —especially Congregationalism. Lyman Abbott (1835 – 1922), editor, lecturer, and popular Congregational preacher, was to dominate much northern Protestant thinking for half a century. Here, as a twenty-nine-year-old contributor to a New Haven periodical, Abbott declared that the war's terrible devastation must be followed by a moral and ecclesiastical reconstruction. It is clear, however, that Abbott saw such reconstruction as primarily a northern, not a southern responsibility. "We cannot trust those that have preached their congregations into rebellion to preach them back again."

At the commencement of this war we were often sneeringly asked the question — "Suppose you conquer the South, what are you going to do with it?" This question, impertinent then, becomes pertinent now. A considerable part of the South is conquered. The Federal flag floats in triumph over the principal parts of Missouri, Arkansas, Tennessee, and Louisiana. United States laws are enforced, United States Courts administer justice, United States authority is recognized and submitted to. And now the question does arise, full of perplexity, what are we going to do with the conquered territory?

For it is apparent to the dullest of vision that we must do something. To conquer alone is not enough. It is impossible permanently to substitute military rule for civil authority, or make the President a permanent autocrat of the subjugated territory. All military governorships are temporary expedients; — doubtful ones at that. Where the Confederate authority has been destroyed, there the Federal authority must be restored in its *legitimate* and *constitutional* forms. Where the political and social despotism of the slave oligarchy has been destroyed, a permanent republicanism must be reorganized. Destruction must be followed by reconstruction. The history of liberty teaches us this necessity. . . .

Let us learn then a lesson from the experience of the past. To fight, to die even, for liberty, is not enough. When the enemies of the Republic have been conquered in battle, the *preparation* for the nation's work has been done; that is all. It then remains to enter upon the territory emancipated by the sword, and there establish in a permanent form the living institutions of freedom. We have not only to conquer the South, — we have also to convert

[Source: Lyman Abbott, "Southern Evangelization," in *The New Englander*, 23 (1864), 699, 700–702, 702–3, 706–7.]

it. We have not only to occupy it by bayonets and bullets, — but also by ideas and institutions. We have not only to destroy slavery, — we must also organize freedom. If we fail in our second task, success in the first will be of little use. The political problems involved in the delicate and difficult work of reconstruction are already engaging the attention of our wisest statesmen, as well they may. But, as we hope to show, there are religious problems connected with this subject which demand the attention of the church and ministry. To these we desire briefly to advert; — rather to provoke attention to the problem than to offer any satisfactory solution of it. . . .

Two conditions are absolutely essential to the perpetuity of republican institutions: popular intelligence and popular morality. In other words, before any people are competent to govern themselves successfully, they must possess intelligence and sound morals. Hence two institutions are essential to their preservation: common schools and Christian churches. Free institutions without general intelligence can exist only in name. There is no despotism so cruel and remorseless as that of an unreasoning mob. Men who do not know how to govern themselves cannot know how to govern a great country. The ignorance of the masses, and the consequent power of the few, alone made this rebellion possible. The power has been taken from the few. It remains to give knowledge to the masses. But knowledge alone is not enough. For, while intelligence tends to make *men* free, it does not suffice to constitute a free *State*. And it is not enough to emancipate individuals from iniquitous thraldom. That liberty may be permanent, it must be organic. Heads, legs, arms, trunks, gathered in an indiscriminate pile from the battle-field, cannot make a single man. They must be united by sinews and ligaments, inspired with life, and governed by one dominant head. So a mass of individuals, however free, gathered together, do not constitute a free Republic. Individualism is the characteristic of simple barbarism, not of republican civilization. They must be bound together by ties of interest and affection, inspired with one common national life, and possessed of one central government. How to harmonize individual liberty with the cohesion necessary to secure the preservation of the State, is the problem of republicanism. It is a problem which can never be solved without the aid of the Christian religion.

Thus to constitute a permanently free State, men must be taught not only their rights, but also their duties and their obligations. Submission must be inculcated, conscience must be educated, a generous love must be inspired. To establish liberty it is not enough to strike in sunder with the sword the chains which bind men. They must be bound together not, indeed, with handcuffs, as in a chain-gang, but with bands more enduring, because wrought of God, — bands of duty and affection. Thus the gospel is needed to prepare the way for true freedom. In truth, the principles of religion underlie republicanism. Religion teaches man that he is a son of God, and thus makes him unwilling to be a slave of man. She educates him to yield a willing submission to the sovereign power of God, and so renders it more easy for him to obey the reasonable requirements of his earthly superiors. And she inspires him with a universal affection for the human race, and so makes it possible for him to administer government in peace and amity with his fellows. . . .

We have thus endeavored to show, that to perpetuate Republicanism in the South we must follow the terrible devastations of war, with the more grateful, though no less difficult, work of reconstruction. And that to this reconstruction, the establishment of free churches and the proclamation of a full gospel is absolutely essential. Let us add that the Christian churches of the North alone can do this indispensable work. Government cannot. For though religious institutions are essential to the Republic, the Republic cannot establish religious institutions. Church and State are forever divorced in America. And God forever avert the day when the churches of America shall lapse into the hands of the politicians! Then *all* will be gone. Nor can we trust to the return of the exiled ministry, and the resurrection of the dead churches. We cannot transform the old schools of slavery and treason into schools of loyalty and liberty. We cannot trust those who have preached their congregations into rebellion to preach them back again. . . .

Now too is the time to commence this work. While society is fermenting, and institutions are being created, and customs are being established, and public opinion is forming, and governments are in process of organization, is the time to impress upon this new organization its permanent character. While nature was in chaos God fashioned and formed it as it is. While the metal is molten is the time to stamp and mold it. The Egyptian husbandman, while the waters still overflowed the banks of the Nile, was accustomed in olden times to go out in his boat and drop the seed upon the surface of the waters, that it might enter the softened and prepared soil. While the deluge of waters still overflows the fair fields of the South, is the very time for the Christian husbandman to sow the good seed, that when the waters shall retire it may be found already germinating — its growth beginning.

Unity Maintained

As a denomination primarily of the northeastern United States, Congregationalism easily avoided any division along political or sectional lines. But what of denominations with major memberships in both South and North? When a nation divided, must not a church suffer schism also? Remarkably, the Protestant Episcopal Church managed to keep its organizational integrity intact. Meeting in a national or General Convention every three years, Episcopalians in 1859, in 1862, and in 1865 avoided rupture, even while

[Source: "The Next General Convention," in *The American Quarterly Church Review, and Ecclesiastical Register*, 17, no. 3 (Oct., 1865), 452 – 53, 454.]

the "Sects about us are falling to pieces." In the excerpt below, the editor of an Episcopal journal reviews in 1865 the two previous conventions as he offers hope for the approaching one.

It is a great point, and let it never be forgotten, that up to the breaking out of the Civil War in 1861, no sectional feuds or animosities had disturbed our peace, or alienated the hearts of brethren. Even at the General Convention of 1859, held in the city of Richmond, when the mutterings of the storm began to be heard, and when sagacious men saw the cloud in the distant horizon, already bigger than a man's hand, and knew what it meant, unless God, in His mercy, should avert the awful judgment, still the members of that Convention, from the East and the West, the North and the South, only clung the closer to each other, and religiously vowed fidelity to one another, and to Christ, and to His Church, with a deeper solemnity. And, in the last General Convention, in this city of New York, in 1862, when the vials of wrath were pouring out their fury, and the brethren came together once more, to counsel and pray for the peace and prosperity of Israel, who can ever forget the impressiveness of that scene, when the seats appointed for the Southern brethren were found to be vacant? And yet the names of the absent Tribes were, as usual, officially called. Eyes wet with tears, and faces filled with sorrow, told unerringly where all hearts were, at that Convention. As little was done as possible, even in the legislation of the Church. Every thing was left undone that could be, in testimony of the hope and the belief that these broken ranks would be filled again; at any rate, that the bonds of Unity were not as yet hopelessly broken. . . .

And now, another Convention is close upon us. Whatever fears we may have formerly entertained as to its results, and as to its influence on the welfare of the Church and the well-being of the Nation, those fears are passing away. As this mighty nation is to be One Nation, and as we are to be One People and not many peoples, so, unless God's wrath is to be visited upon us for our unfaithfulness, we are to be yet again One Church, knit more firmly than ever before together, to do one great blessed work, for CHRIST, for this nation, and for the world. The Sects about us are falling to pieces. Even the most conservative of them are rending to fragments with their internal feuds and animosities, their mutual criminations and recriminations, their fierce and angry fanatical passions. So, for GOD'S sake, and the Church's sake, and for the souls of men, let it not be among us.

Division Hardened

Methodists, on the other hand, did divide along geographical lines in 1844, the critical issue being sharply divergent attitudes toward slavery among Methodists in the North from those in the South. But since slavery was officially abolished by the Emancipation Proclamation during the war, what now prevented Methodists North and South from coming together again? The answer, of course, is that much prevented such a reunion, including a deep bitterness which many southern Methodists felt against what they viewed as northern intrusion, condescension, and radicalism. The following document, a pastoral letter from the bishops of the Methodist Episcopal Church, South, shows the lines of separation hardened and any loving reconciliation a distant dream.

[1865] The abolition, . . . of the institution of domestic slavery in the United States does not affect the question that was prominent in our separation in 1844. Nor is this the only difference or principal one between us and [the Northern Methodist Church]. While testifying with pleasure to the nobler conduct and sentiments of many brethren among them, we must express with regret our apprehension that a large portion, if not a majority, of Northern Methodists have become incurably radical. They teach for doctrine the commandments of men. They preach another gospel. They have incorporated social dogmas and political tests into their church creeds. They have gone on to impose conditions upon discipleship that Christ did not impose. Their pulpits are perverted to agitations and questions not healthful to personal piety, but promotive of political and ecclesiastical discord. . . . Without such a change as we see no immediate prospect of, in their tone and temper and practice, we can anticipate no good result from even entertaining the subject of reunion with them. . . . Preach Christ and Him crucified. Do not preach politics. You have no commission to preach politics. The divinity of the Church is never more strikingly displayed than when it holds on its even, straightforward way in the midst of worldly commotions. . . .

The conduct of certain Northern Methodist bishops and preachers in taking advantage of the confusion incident to a state of war to intrude themselves into several of our houses of worship, and in continuing to hold these places against the wishes and protests of the congregations and rightful owners, causes us sorrow and pain, not only as working an injury to us, but as presenting to the world a spectacle ill calculated to make an impression favorable to Christianity. They are not only using, to our deprivation and exclusion, churches and parsonages which we have builded, but have proceeded to set up a claim to them as their property; by what shadow of right, legal or moral, we are at a loss to conceive. We advise our brethren who

[Source: Walter L. Fleming, *Documentary History of Reconstruction* (Cleveland: Arthur H. Clark Co., 1907), II, pp. 233 – 34.]

suffer these evils to bear them patiently, to cleave closely together and not indulge in any vindictive measures or tempers. A plain statement of the case, and an appeal to the justice of those in authority cannot fail to defeat such scandalous designs, and secure us the full restoration of all our rights.

While some talk of the reunion of the two Churches, we forewarn you of a systematic attempt, already inaugurated, and of which the foregoing is only an instance, to disturb and if possible disintegrate and then absorb our membership individually. In the meeting [1864] of their bishops and missionary secretaries, alluded to, it was resolved to send preachers and plant societies in our midst wherever there is an opening. Their policy is evidently our division and ecclesiastical devastation. Against all this be on your guard.

Faith Rebuilt

Before the decade of the 1860s ended, Horace Bushnell, ever the theological mediator and "comprehensive" thinker, offered a fresh understanding of the theological enterprise itself. He did so, not chiefly to heal the wounds of the war, but to mend or even to forestall the repeated tendency of America's religious bodies to quarrel, castigate, and separate. We are all literalists, Bushnell argued, whether liberal or conservative, acting as though our particular theological formulation were a precise and authoritative description of concrete reality. We pretend that theology is a science, but this it is not, nor can it ever be. For our very language makes this impossible: "the whole web of speech is curiously woven metaphor." Recriminations, divisions, and "general uncharitableness" will pass away once we recognize that the gospel is, in truth, a "gift to the imagination."

I shall endeavor to exhibit . . . the fact that our Christian gospel is a Gift more especially to the human Imagination. It offers itself first of all and principally to the interpretative imaginings and discernings of faith, never, save in that manner, to the constructive processes of logic and speculative opinion. It is, in one sense, pictorial; its every line or lineament is traced in some image or metaphor, and by no possible ingenuity can it be gotten away from metaphor; for as certainly as one metaphoric image is escaped by a definition, another will be taken up, and must be, to fill its place in the definition itself. Mathematical language is a scheme of exact notation; all words that are names of mere physical acts and objects are literal, and even animals can, so far, learn their own names and the meaning of many acts done or commanded. But no animal ever understood a metaphor; that belongs

[Source: "Our Gospel a Gift to the Imagination," in *Hours at Home,* 10 (Dec., 1869), 160, 161, 166, 167–68.]

to intelligence, and to man as a creature of intelligence; being a power to see, in all images, the faces of truth, and take their sense, or read [*intus lego*] their meaning, when thrown up in language before the imagination.

Every word is a figure called in to serve a metaphoric use, in virtue of the fact that it has a physical base naturally significant of the spiritual truth or meaning it is used metaphorically to express. Physical bases are the timber, in this manner, of all mental language, and are generally traced in the etymologies of the dictionaries; though sometimes they are lost and cannot be traced. And it is not merely the verbs, nouns, adjectives, that carry these metaphoric uses, but their very grammar of relationship, as they are found originally in space themselves, is also framed in terms of space by the little words called prepositions.

But we must look into language itself and see how the great revelation of God is coming and to come. First of all, it is impossible, as we have seen already, that any terms of language for mental notions, things of the spirit, unseen worlds, beings invisible, should ever exist, save as there are physical images found to serve as metaphoric bases of the necessary words; for we cannot show them to the eye, and then name them, as we do acts or objects visible; we can only hint them by figures, or objects, metaphorically significant of them. And so we see beforehand, that all the truths of religion are going to be given to men by images; so that all God's truth will come as to the imagination. Hence the necessity of the old physical religion to prepare draperies and figures for the new. Hence, also, when we come to the new, we are constantly met, we perhaps know not why, or how, by images taken from the old, in a way that seems half fanciful and curiously mystical. Adam is the figure of him that was to come, the second Adam, because he (Christ) was to be the head, correspondently, of a spiritual generation. Christ is David, Melchizedek, high priest, the spiritual Rock, a prophet like unto Moses, and I know not what beside. John the Baptist is Elias that was to come. In the same manner, heaven is a paradise or garden, or a new Jerusalem, or a state of glorious city life in God, and the new society of grace is to be the kingdom of God, or the kingdom of heaven, and Christ himself, Messiah, that is, king. All the past is taken up as metaphor for all the future. All these things, we are to say, happened unto us for ensamples, that is, types for the expression of our higher truth.

And so we are questioning often about the credibility of a double meaning in Scripture; as if it were a thing fanciful beyond belief. Whereas the meanings double and redouble as often as new typologies are made ready. The spiritual comes out of the physical, and the more spiritual out of the less; just because one thing is ready for the expression of another, and still another. There is nothing fantastical in it, but it comes to pass under a fixed law of language — all language, even the most common — even as a stalk of corn pushes out leaf from within leaf, by a growth that is its unsheathing. . . .

But we must have a theology, some will say; how can religion or religious truth get body, or any firm hold of the world, without a theology? And what is theology? It is very commonly supposed to be a speculated system of doctrine, drawn out in propositions that are clear of all metaphor, and are stated in terms that have finally obtained a literal and exact sense. But no such system is possible, for the very plain reason that we have no such terms. We have a great many words that have lost their roots, or have come to be so far staled by use that the figures in their bases do not obtrude themselves on our notice. But if we suppose, as we very commonly do, in all the logical uses of speculation, that they have become exact coins, or algebraic notations for the ideas represented by them, we are in a great mistake. . . .

But we must have science, some will remember — is there any hope for theologic science left? None at all, I answer most unequivocally. Human language is a gift to the imagination so essentially metaphoric, warp and woof, that it has no exact blocks of meaning to build a science of. Who would ever think of building up a science of Homer, Shakespear, Milton? And the Bible is not a whit less poetic, or a whit less metaphoric, or a particle less difficult to be propositionized in the terms of the understanding. Shall we then have nothing to answer, when the sweeping question is put, why philosophy and every other study should make advances, and theology be only spinning its old circles, and revising and re-revising its old problems? It must be enough to answer that philosophy, metaphysical philosophy, having only metaphor to work in, is under exactly the same limitation; that it is always backing, and filling, and turning, and returning, in the same manner; that nobody can name a single question that has ever been settled by all the systems it has built and the newly contrived nomenclatures it has invented. Working always in metaphors, and fooling itself how commonly by metaphor, it gets a valuable gymnastic in words, and prepares to a more full and many-sided conception of words. So far it is fruitful and good, and just so far also is the scientific labor of theology. After all it is simple insight in both, and not speculation, that has the true discernment. Words give up their deepest, truest meaning, only when they are read as images of the same.

But we must have definitions, it will be urged, else we cannot be sure what we mean by our words, and when we have the definitions, why can we not have science? But if we mean by definitions an exact literal measurement of ideas, no such thing is possible. In what we call our definitions, whether in theology, or moral philosophy, we only put one set of metaphors in place of another, and, if we understand ourselves, there may be a certain use in doing it, even as there is in shifting our weight upon the other leg — perhaps we make ourselves more intelligible by doing it. And yet there is a very great imposture lurking almost always in these definitions. . . . Nothing makes infidels more surely than the spinning, splitting, nerveless refinements of theology. This endeavor, always going on, to get the truths of religion away from the imagination, into propositions of the speculative understanding, makes a most dreary and sad history — a history of divisions, recriminations, famishings, vanishings, and general uncharitableness. Lively, full, fresh, free as they were, the definitions commonly cut off their wings and reduce them to mere pebbles of significance. Before they were plants alive and in flower, now the flavors are gone, the juices dried, and the skeleton parts packed away and classified in the dry herbarium called theology.

2. "WELCOME TO THE RANSOMED"

Emancipation Celebrated

*The Emancipation Proclamation issued on January 1, 1863, had no im-
mediate effect, of course, in those areas still under Southern control or still
being contested by opposing armies. In the District of Columbia itself, however, emancipation was immediate. Daniel A. Payne (1811–93), of black
and Indian ancestry, moved briefly in Lutheran and Presbyterian circles
before becoming in 1852 a bishop in the African Methodist Episcopal Church.
From 1863 to 1876 Payne also served as president of Wilberforce University
(Ohio), this position reflecting his strong commitment to an educated black
clergy. In the excerpt below, the AME bishop loses no time in urging freed
fellow blacks to make their emancipation from slavery also the occasion for
an emancipation from sin.*

We are gathered to celebrate the emancipation, yea, rather, the *Redemption*
of the enslaved people of the District of Columbia, the exact number of whom
we have no means of ascertaining, because, since the benevolent intention of
Congress became manifest, many have been removed by their owners beyond
the reach of this beneficent act.

Our pleasing task then, is to welcome to the Churches, the homesteads,
and circles of free colored Americans, those who remain to enjoy *the boon of
holy Freedom.*

Brethren, sisters, friends, we say welcome to our Churches, welcome to
our homesteads, welcome to our social circles.

Enter the great family of Holy Freedom; not to *lounge in sinful indolence,*
not to *degrade yourselves by vice,* nor to *corrupt society by licentiousness,* neither
to *offend the laws by crime,* but to the *enjoyment of a well regulated liberty,* the
offspring of generous laws; of law as just as generous, as righteous as just —
a liberty to be *perpetuated* by equitable law, and sanctioned by the divine; for

[Source: "Welcome to the Ransomed," in Daniel A. Payne, *Sermons and Addresses
1853–1891* (New York: Arno Press, 1972), pp. 6–7 of this sermon.]

law is never equitable, righteous, just, until it harmonizes with the will of Him, who is *"King* of kings, and *Lord* of lords," and who commanded Israel to *have but one law for the home-born* and the *stranger.*

We repeat ourselves, welcome then *ye ransomed ones;* welcome *not* to indolence, to vice, licentiousness, and crime, but to a well-regulated liberty, sanctioned by the Divine, maintained by the Human law.

Welcome to habits of industry and thrift — to duties of religion and piety — to obligations of law, order, government — of government divine, of government human: these two, though not one, are inseparable. The man who refuses to obey divine law, will never obey human laws. *The divine first,* the *human next.* The latter is the consequence of the former, and follows it as light does the rising sun.

We invite you to our Churches, because we desire you to be religious; to be more than religious; we urge you *to be godly.* We entreat you to never be content until you are emancipated from sin, from sin without, and from sin within you. But this kind of freedom is attained only through the faith of Jesus, love for Jesus, obedience to Jesus. As certain as the American Congress has *ransomed* you, so certain, yea, more certainly has Jesus redeemed you from the guilt and power of sin by his own precious blood.

As you are now free in body, so now seek to be free in soul and spirit, from sin and Satan. The *noblest freeman is he whom Christ makes free.*

Aid Solicited

Committed to both an evangelical and an abolitionist stance, the American Missionary Association —largely Congregational in membership —took the welfare of the freed black as its major concern. Both during the Civil War and after, the Association understood "welfare" in the broadest terms: food, clothing, shelter, education, and a surrounding, sustaining Christian community to help the newly "ransomed" reach their full potential. Only then could the lie be given to the many who contended "that the negroes are an improvident race, unfit to take care of themselves."

APPEAL FOR THE FREEDMEN

By a Committee appointed at the Annual Meeting of the American Missionary Association, October 16, 1862

In the providence of God, tens of thousands of freed slaves are now waiting, in various parts of the South, for the privileges which freedom confers, and slavery has denied them. The number is constantly increasing, and within a few months, or weeks, it is probable that hundreds of thousands will be

[Source: *The American Missionary,* ser. 2, 7 (Jan., 1863), 13.]

looking to their friends for aid. And what class of people ever presented a better claim to charity? Indeed it hardly deserves the name of charity, to supply their wants. They only ask a little interest on a long standing debt. We have all reaped the fruits of their unpaid toil.

Their first wants are physical. Many of them have escaped, and will escape from their bondage in a very destitute condition. They need clothes, and bedding, and some shelter from the storm. This want will be temporary: they will soon be able to supply themselves. But for a few months they must have help.

They need education. Few of them can read, and still fewer can write. They need day schools and evening schools, for children and adults. Every family should at once be supplied with the Bible, and the mass of them should be taught to read it.

They need the preaching of the Gospel. Many of their own number are exhorters and preachers: but need teachers who can "expound unto them the way of God more perfectly."

They need assistance in organizing themselves into schools, Sabbath schools, congregations and churches. And they need intelligent friends and counselors, to guard them against the insults, impositions, immoralities and various abuses of those who hate them, and are interested to prove that the negroes are an improvident race, unfit to take care of themselves.

For every thousand of these emancipated people there should be at least one able, experienced, faithful missionary, to preach to them, to teach, to organize, and counsel them; and he should be assisted by several subordinate teachers. If a million should be emancipated within a few months, a thousand teachers will be needed, besides the requisite clothing, houses, school-houses, books and churches. Very inferior accommodations will satisfy them at first, but in some shape these must be provided.

These wants should be met at once. Never again will they welcome so heartily, appreciate so gratefully, and improve so satisfactorily these advantages, as on their first escape from the house of bondage. Such an inviting, promising field has rarely, if ever, been open to the Christian world. No time should be lost; already our work lags behind the demand. The missionaries and the teachers will be found when the call is made, if they can be sustained; and to support a thousand missionaries and the requisite number of teachers will cost less than the support of a single regiment of cavalry. Shall it be said that the good people of the United States cannot do so much in this important work, without diminishing their contributions to other benevolent objects? We dare not ask for less. To say nothing of our obligations to these oppressed people, we owe it to ourselves, and to our country, if the President's proclamation is to be carried out, to see to it that it does not work disastrously, or fail of its legitimate fruits, for want of efficient co-operation on the part of the christian community.

Education Offered

In addition to the religiously-sponsored American Missionary Association, the Freedmen's Bureau, sponsored by the federal government, came into existence in 1865 and lasted until 1872. Its first and only head, General Oliver O. Howard (1830–1909), played a leading role in the creation of Howard University in Washington, D. C.; he also served as its first president, from 1869 to 1874. In his autobiography, Howard reveals the extent to which religion was involved here, just as it was in virtually every other effort to educate America's postwar blacks. Religion not only helped bring the educational institutions into being but also provided the leadership, the funding, and the curricular direction, the latter often being heavily theological in character.

Each denomination desired to have, here and there, a college of its own. Such institutions the founders and patrons were eager to make different from the simple primary or grammar schools; these, it was hoped and believed, would be eventually absorbed in each State in a great free school system. The educators naturally wished to put a moral and Christian stamp upon their students, especially upon those who would become instructors of colored youth. My own strong wish was ever to lay permanent substructures and build thereon as rapidly as possible, in order to give as many good teachers, professional men, and leaders to the rising generation of freedmen as we could, during the few years of Governmental control.

One of the institutions for the higher education of the negro which has maintained ample proportions and also bears my own name, warrants me in giving somewhat in detail its origin and my connection with it.

The latter part of 1866, a few gentlemen, at the instance of Rev. F. B. Morris, who held an important Governmental office at the capital, and was a benevolent and scholarly man, came together at the house of Mr. A. Brewster, on K Street, Washington.

There had been two or three of such informal meetings, consisting mainly of residents of Washington, when Senators Wilson and Pomeroy, B. C. Cook, Member of the House, and myself were invited to this respectable self-constituted council, November 20, 1866. Nearly all of the dozen or more gentlemen who were present, and among them Rev. Dr. C. B. Boynton, the pastor of the Congregational Church of the city, were Congregationalists. A preliminary organization was already in existence. The subject under discussion for this time was a place for a theological school for the colored preachers and those who were to become such, that their teachings should be of value. Mr. H. D. Nichols moved that the new institution be entitled "Howard

[Source: *Autobiography of Oliver Otis Howard* (New York: Baker & Taylor Co., 1907), II, pp. 395–97.]

Theological Seminary." That name was adopted. Mr. Morris and some others were in the outset in favor of connecting with the seminary some industrial features; and, to show my good will, I made the same offer, being authorized by the law, that I had been making to other educational associations, that if they would furnish a proper lot, I would cause to be erected thereon, by the [Freedmen's] Bureau, a suitable building. I believed it wiser not to use my name, but it was remarked sportively "there are other Howards."

At a meeting December 4, 1866, there was in ideas and proposals considerable progress manifested. At first, I had desired delay, thinking that the time was hardly ripe for a large institution at the capital; but, seeing the enthusiasm and fixed purpose of this body of some fourteen gentlemen, a few of whom I now observed were Presbyterians and two or three of other persuasions, I participated in their discussions. "Howard Normal and Theological Institute for the Education of Teachers and Preachers," was the new title adopted.

On January 8, 1867, at another gathering, Dr. Boynton was elected the president of the preliminary board. At this session my brother, General C. H. Howard, then assistant commissioner of the district and vicinity, moved a committee to plan a law department — a medical department having already been favorably canvassed. Thus, little by little, the idea of a university grew upon the preliminary board, the project of an institution which should

School for freedmen, Vicksburg, Mississippi, 1866
(Library of Congress)

have many separate departments acting together under one board of trustees. At this January sitting, an important committee was named to obtain a charter. . . . The charter was easily obtained, having seventeen charter members. The incorporation title was: "An Act to incorporate the Howard University in the District of Columbia." It was approved by the President of the United States March 2, 1867.

Optimism Tempered

Some denominations created their own agencies or bureaus to assist and nurture those Americans suddenly left to fend for themselves. The Freedmen's Aid Society, organized by the Methodist Episcopal Church (North) in 1866, saw its challenge in these terms: "The emancipation of four million of slaves has opened at our very door a wide field calling alike for mission and educational work. It has devolved upon the Church a fearful responsibility." In assuming that fearful responsibility, white northern Methodists reported their early efforts (1868) in optimistic and confident terms. Eight years later (1875), however, the enormity of the tasks weighed more heavily as the sad realization dawned that "we have been able to contribute so little. . . ."

1. 1868

The South being thrown open to a loyal and liberty-loving ministry, Christians who had remembered those in bonds, who had prayed for, and in all proper ways labored for the overthrow of slavery, could carry or send to the millions degraded by it the means of mental and moral elevation. The Church, called to give the Gospel to every creature, must, if faithful to her trust, enter the open door, and use every efficient means to hasten the evangelization of the South. The school was found to be invaluable as an auxiliary to the missions among the Freedmen. They were every-where found anxious to have the Gospel preached to them by missionaries from the North, and to have Churches planted among them, but they were more anxious to have schools for themselves and their children.

The dawn of their freedom kindled within them a passion to learn to read and write, and a people whose incapacity to learn had been urged as a plea for their servitude, welcomed the teacher as first among their benefactors. The efforts of the undenominational commissions could not directly promote the missionary work; their agents and teachers were not chosen with reference to evangelical sentiments and experimental godliness; their schools were not

[Source: *Reports of the Freedmen's Aid Society of the Methodist Episcopal Church* . . . (Cincinnati: Western Methodist Book Concern, 1893), pp. 6, 11 (1868); pp. 3–4 (1875).]

designedly located so as to favor the spread of the Gospel; even where they had Sunday schools they were conducted so as to insure only temporary results. The control of the educational work connected with missions was as necessary to success as the work itself, and this necessity, seen alike by every denomination that entered the inviting field presented by the South, was the chief cause of the organization of denominational societies. . . .

It is a gratifying fact, and one that indicates the missionary character of our enterprise, that nearly a score of our teachers are ministers of the Gospel, who have been drawn to this field of labor because it furnishes such rare facilities for doing good both to the bodies and the souls of men. These teach school during the week and preach on the Sabbath, and thus carry forward in harmony this great movement for the intellectual and moral elevation of the race. All our teachers labor in the Sunday as well as in the day schools, and are preparing the thousands of ignorant and degraded children for usefulness on earth and happiness in heaven. We have been exceedingly fortunate in the selection of our laborers, for they have almost invariably been good scholars and successful teachers, and have been drawn to this work by love to Jesus and fallen humanity. The school-house, occupied as a meeting-house for religious worship as it usually is by our missionaries, and also by our teachers for Sunday school and the instruction of the children during the week, becomes to the South, as elsewhere, the true symbol of a high Christian civilization. These humble buildings in which the children are taught, are scarcely less the temples of the living God than the temples of science — for in them immortals pass into a higher spiritual as well as intellectual life.

2. 1875

The retrospection of our past efforts in behalf of this injured people awakens mingled emotions of gratitude and sadness: gratitude, that we have been enabled to accomplish so much in an enterprise so intimately connected with the safety of the nation, the elevation of man, and the prosperity of the Church; sadness, that, amid such general desolation, resulting from ignorance, superstition, crime, and slavery, we have been able to contribute so little to the relief and elevation of millions in our midst, suffering the accumulated wrongs of ages.

The work upon which this Society has entered is a gigantic one, and taxes to the utmost the energies and the benevolence of the nation. It is the Christian training of five millions of people, one-eighth of our entire population, and through these the elevation of hundreds of millions of incoming generations. They are now freemen and citizens, endowed with the rights and privileges of citizenship. It must not be forgotten that they were emancipated in ignorance, degradation, and poverty, and are what centuries of wrong and oppression have made them; and it is equally clear that the act of emancipation conferred no preparation for this new condition of life, into which, totally disqualified, they have been thrust. President Lincoln, with a dash of his pen, struck the fetters from the bodies of these four millions of slaves, but their minds were still left in the chains of ignorance, and the iron of slavery had entered into their souls. Emancipation was one of the grandest acts of the nineteenth century, and thrilled with joy the hearts of the people; and forever honored will be the noble men that participated in its achievement; but emancipation is not complete in itself; it presupposes and demands preparation. The nation has emancipated this people; but it has done it at its peril, unless it pushes more vigorously the work of Christian education. We insist upon it that the part we took in emancipation binds us with solemn obligations to educate, for education is the only completion of emancipation; and we are urged to complete this work by every consideration that induced us to commence it. To have emancipated and left these millions in ignorance and degradation would have been a work of doubtful philanthropy, and would have partaken more of the character of crime than of charity. To neglect the preparation of this people would be to perpetuate the wrongs inflicted by slavery, increase the peril of the nation, bring disgrace upon the Church, and provoke the just judgments of heaven. Giving freedom, and preparing its recipients for it, must go hand in hand, else this blood-bought boon is not worth the terrible price it cost.

Baptists Multiplied

Only after the Civil War did denominations predominantly or exclusively black in their membership experience great growth. Three Methodist bodies, African Methodist Episcopal and African Methodist Episcopal Zion (both essentially northern in origin) along with the Colored Methodist Episcopal Church (essentially southern), made significant strides in the second half of the nineteenth century. But the greatest number of blacks by far became Baptists. An 1890 sermonic survey, excerpted below, reviews the spectacular growth since 1865 among the "colored Baptists." Taking a text from Hebrews 11:34, editor E. M. Brawley exulted in the unmistakable evidence that "out of weakness we were made strong."

Our past was that of weakness, but our present is that of strength.

Twenty-five years ago we had, except in a few instances, no churches in the South. Now (1890) we have nearly twelve thousand church organizations,

[Source: E. M. Brawley, ed., *The Negro Baptist Pulpit* . . . (Philadelphia: American Baptist Publication Society, 1890), pp. 287–89.]

and connected with nearly every one of them is a Sunday-school. Then we had practically no ordained ministers; now we have fully eight thousand. Then there were but two or three colored associations; now there are nearly four hundred. Then we numbered a few hundred thousands; now we are more than a million and a quarter. Then we had not even one institution of learning; now we have forty, ranging from high-grade normal schools to colleges and universities. Then it was not possible for our young people to get a liberal or professional education in the South; now any young man or woman can get it, whether in the arts or sciences, in theology, law, or medicine. And he can get his training under Baptist auspices; for we now have schools of theology, law, and medicine, in addition to those which are purely literary. Then there was no education among our ministry, but few being able to read, and the masses were in the same condition; now we have hundreds of educated ministers, many of them having received their training in the best institutions of the North. Some of these men have taken high rank as scholars and orators. Then we had no educators; now we have college presidents and professors, and many thousand school teachers. One-third of all the professors employed in the educational work of the American Baptist Home Mission Society are colored. Then such a thing as a colored trustee of a college was unheard of; now all our colleges and seminaries have colored members on their boards. Then there was no general officer of a national organization; now we have one district secretary. Then we did practically no literary work, and could produce but few books; now we have a number of authors among us, and their books are read. Then we did not have any newspapers; now there are forty, edited by colored Baptists. Then we had no professional and but few business men; now we have a large number of lawyers, physicians, and merchants. Then our forces were not organized; now they are organized, and have reached a reasonable degree of efficiency. Then we did no mission work; now we are doing mission work in every State, and even in Africa. Then we had comparatively no church property; now we have considerable, some buildings costing between fifty thousand and one hundred thousand dollars, and the total valuation being millions. Then we had no personal property, scarcely so much as "a vine and fig tree" under which to worship God; now our total wealth is estimated to be many millions. Then we were regarded as being in character and in intellect children; now we are recognized as men. Such growth is without precedent in the history of mankind. Truly we were once weak; but out of weakness we are made strong.

But we have by no means attained the strength which we will have and must have. What we have attained is but the earnest of what we should seek after in the next quarter of a century. Our large numbers will even prove to be a source of weakness to us, unless we elevate them in point of efficiency and in moral and mental character. A tremendous work is yet on our hands. May God help us to realize it!

Missions Encouraged

Indeed, so swift was the growth of black Baptists in America that soon their leaders began to look beyond the borders of the United States to members of their own race abroad. How peculiarly fitting, it seemed, that the progeny of blacks brought generations earlier from "darkest Africa" should now return as Christian missionaries to that great continent "to save and elevate. . . ." In the story of the conversion of the Ethiopian eunuch (Acts 8:27 – 39), blacks found all the New Testament sanction they required for both the universality of the Christian religion and the remarkable eagerness "with which the race has accepted the Gospel."

The Christian religion is the exponent of the highest civilization, the highest moral and social condition of the race to-day. Where it has been accepted, and its faith and doctrines incorporated into the life and character of any people, it has in a very potential manner affected the moral, intellectual and social condition of such people. . . .

No people or race is excluded from its all-embracing provisions, nor from its divinely uplifting power when it is embraced. It should produce in the race in America, or in Africa, worthy examples of its power to save and elevate in proportion to individual or race conformity to its spirit and precepts. Its light shone early in the soul of one of the race when the Ethiopian eunuch accepted it through the preaching of Philip the evangelist, and "believed that Jesus Christ is the Son of God." He asked Baptism and was immersed by Philip, "and when they were come up out of the water the eunuch went on his way rejoicing." The large number of the [Negro] race in America who are Baptists is a living evidence of the readiness with which the race has accepted the Gospel and conformed to its doctrines and ordinances as did the eunuch of the race in the apostolic period of planting and training of Christian churches. A larger percentum of the race in America are members of evangelical Churches than of any other race in the land; and a large number of them are members of Baptist churches than of all other evangelical bodies. National Statistician for 1900 gives the number of the race members of Baptist churches in this country as 1,854,600. To this number must be added members of Baptist churches in the States not enumerated in the reports, which make a total of about 2,000,000. To this must be added the members of various other evangelical bodies in this country and we have a grand total of about 3,123,000 Negro Christians in the United States.

These should be a power as a missionary force for the evangelization of the world. They should, by their numerical strength, give to the race a distinctive character in active and effective missionary work among Christian

[Source: R. D. Baptist, in L. G. Jordan, *Up the Ladder in Foreign Missions* (Nashville: National Baptist Publishing Board, 1903), pp. 160– 62.]

evangelizing workers. The aggressive character of those workers who went out from the churches at Jerusalem and Antioch for the conversion of the world to Christ was marked by the strong opposition they aroused from jealous, unbelieving Jews and stolid heathen devotees, and were stigmatized as "These that have turned the world upside down." To drink in the same spirit and follow their example should produce like results of success in the same work. The world will look for results, and the great Head of the Church will hold the large number of Baptists responsible, in all work of the gospel, in proportion to their numbers, other things being considered. Some of the things to be considered are, the "talents" given, and culture, and right training in the use of the talents intrusted, including the resources vouchsafed as visible means of accomplishing the work Christ has given them to do. But in these things, as necessary accompaniments for efficiency, the responsibility of individual study is involved that they may be approved of God, workmen that need not be ashamed. This large number of Christian workers of the race owe it to Christ, who has called them into His service, to the world in which they live, the field in which Christ instructs them work, and to Africa in particular, "The rock from which they have been hewn," the original home of the race, whose benighted millions still grope in darkest heathenism, outraged and neglected, to individually measure up to the fullest possibility of resources and effort in the work of human redemption. A great work remains to be done for the race in this and other lands, and every Baptist should therefore be intensely a missionary Baptist. The command is "lift up your eyes and look on the fields, they are white already to harvest." And again, "go work to-day in my vineyard."

3. BOUND FOR THE PROMISED LAND

The Ocean's Bounty

Europe
In the half-century between the end of one war and the beginning of another (1865 – 1914), the sources of European immigration tended to shift from northern and western Europe to the eastern and southern portions of that continent. The comparable shift, in religious terms, was away from Protestantism toward Roman Catholicism and Judaism. Nonetheless, the Protestant stream did not altogether cease. The following three excerpts reflect the flow from: (1) Russia (Mennonite); (2) Holland (Reformed); and (3) Norway (Lutheran). The Dutch recollection is provided by Lucy Klooster (d. 1941), a life-long resident of a Reformed community in Michigan, while the Norwegian account comes from Eugene Boe, a Minnesota native and later professional writer living in New York City.

1.

Eugene Schuyler U.S. Legation, St. Petersburgh, to Hamilton Fish, No. 168, March 30, 1872.

I have the honor to enclose you a copy of a letter I have received from Mr. [Timothy] Smith, the Consul at Odessa, on the subject of the contemplated emigration of the Mennonite colonies in the South of Russia to America, and also a copy of my answer thereto.

The Mennonites first came to Russia from Prussia in 1789 in answer to an invitation of Catherine II who gave them land, means with which to establish themselves and temporary relief from taxes and contributions, and

[Sources: (1) *Mennonite Quarterly Review*, 24 (Oct., 1950), 338 – 39. (2) Lucy Klooster, in H. S. Lucas, *Dutch Immigrant Memoirs and Related Writings* (Seattle: University of Washington Press, 1955), II, pp. 280 – 81. (3) Eugene Boe, in Thomas C. Wheeler, *The Immigrant Experience* (New York: Dial Press, 1971), pp. 68, 70.]

promised them religious freedom and exemption for ever from every form of military service. They settled in the South of Russia, in what is now the Government of Taurid, on a tract of land between the rivers Dnieper, Molotschna and Tokmak, and in 1855 numbered some 17,000 souls (male).

The Mennonites are good agriculturists but are particularly noted for their plantations of fruit, forest and mulberry trees. This culture they have followed with great success on steppes that were formerly perfectly bare.

The Mennonites are intelligent, industrious and persevering, and in addition very clean, orderly, moral, temperate and economical. As may be judged from their application they are excessively religious. Petzholdt in his travels in 1855 says, that it is his "firm conviction that Russia can not show any more diligent and more useful citizens." There are schools in every village and education is universal amongst them.

The details of the Law of Universal Compulsory Military Service* have not yet been decided on, but it is not proposed to exempt any individuals or classes of the community from its operation.

I do not think it would be possible to find in Europe any better emigrant than these Mennonites, and should the whole colony go to the United States they would rapidly develop into good and useful citizens.

As I have stated in my letter to Mr. Smith, it is a crime for Russian subjects to emigrate, and a crime to induce them to emigrate without permission. If therefore it is thought desirable that these people should go to the United States, it will probably be necessary for our Government to assist them in obtaining from the Imperial authorities the requisite permission to emigrate. I desire also to call your attention to the question of the Mennonites as to whether any aid in money can be given them for their expenses.

2.

The sound of wagon wheels grinding steadily over dusty trails, bumping over corduroy roads, splashing into mudholes became quite common in this part of Northern Michigan in the early 1880's. The occupants of such a wagon might have been a young man and woman seated upon two or three boxes containing all their worldly goods. A few hours before they very likely had arrived by train at Traverse City or Mancelona. Weary and worn by the many days' journey from the Netherlands and a several days' train trip from New York City, how good it would have seemed to have rested for a day or two! Why had they come? Money was scarce and land here was very cheap. Should they stay down in the Dutch settlements farther south, the only work for many of them might be that of hired help to other farmers. On the other hand, perhaps some relative or friend had come up to this territory before

---

* It was this Russian law, promising exemption to none, which prompted the pacifist Mennonites to seek refuge elsewhere.

them and had written in glowing terms of the country, the springs, and the lakes. . . .

By the year 1886 several clearings had been made and new families were moving in quite regularly. They felt one handicap greatly, the distance to church. Many families walked the four or five miles to the church in Atwood, for on Sunday, if at all possible, they must be in the House of the Lord. Feeling the need of weekday services, in which they might present to Him their prayers and petitions, a new type of meeting was begun, upon which we may surely believe God looked with gladness of heart. Many of the settlers of the community, Dutch and English alike, gathered at the little schoolhouse on the corner every Thursday evening and despite handicaps of language and difference of denomination, together brought their prayers and petitions before the throne of Grace. This is the way an attendant, who lives in Kalamazoo, describes it: We had good times in those olden days when that good man of God, Martin van der Schouw, led in prayer — meetings to the glory of God. After reading and explaining a portion of Scripture he led us in prayer. Then everybody who wanted to pray or testify could do so. The audience in the old schoolhouse consisted of Reformed, Christian Reformed, Methodists, Presbyterians, etc., but they were united around the Cross of Calvary. The road to the meeting place was not so smooth as it is these days. We drove in ox wagons, came over drifting logs, through marsh and swamp. It happened some nights that there were more mosquitoes in the schoolhouse than people, but I for one must confess, that afterwards we could say, "It was good for us to be there, for the Lord was in our midst."

As the Dutch settlers arrived in the community, the talk of organizing a church became common. More children were coming, and the walk was almost too much for them. How wonderful it would be to have a church in the community which would make possible regular Sunday services for all the members of the family. Finally, in 1889 the request for organization was made and heard by the Grand River Classis and on September 10, . . . eight families joined together as a nucleus of the church. . . .

3.

The settlements [in Minnesota] were all homogeneous and self-contained. The immigrant invasion of that part of the country was overwhelmingly Scandinavian, but the separate components of Scandinavia did not become a melting pot in the New World. A township like Aastad remained exclusively Norwegian. The Swedes and Danes and Finns kept to themselves in communities that had names like Swedish Grove and Dane Prairie and Finlandia. The different groups could have made themselves understood to one another and might have found they had much in common. But these exchanges did not occur.

Even those first settlers who eventually left their farms to live in town — as did my grandparents after thirty-four years — managed to reestablish this separateness in a new community. The county seat, Fergus Falls [Otter Tail County], in the early 1900s was a polyglot village of Poles, Germans, Irish, Scotsmen, New England Yankees, and Dutch, as well as Scandinavians. But the various Scandinavian populations touched no other group but themselves. Each had its own Lutheran churches, newspapers, and social fraternities, with little or no cross-pollination. My grandfather and my grandmother lived more than sixty and eighty years, respectively, in this country, but there's no evidence they had more than glancing contact with anyone who was not Norwegian. . . .

They could still articulate the twenty-third Psalm and believe it. "The Lord is my shepherd, I shall not want. . . ." Even when poverty, disease, or death overtook them, they could see divine purpose being fulfilled. They must thank God, for God governed best. He sent them suffering and tribulations only to test their faith.

Their faith was their abiding comfort, and that faith alone enabled them to endure the perversities of fate. This time on earth was but a preparation for the heavenly home which would be their eternal abode. While they struggled through this mortal phase, a welcome was being prepared for their arrival in heaven. Ultimately they would assemble with God in the eternal mansion, where they would find everlasting joy and contentment in beholding God's face.

In the years before the first church was built, the little colony of settlers gathered each Sunday in one another's dugouts. The host would read a passage from the Bible and give his interpretation of it. Then there would be prayers and hymns. When the group came to my grandparents' hut, there was always the singing of . . . [a] favorite hymn, "Den Store Kvede Flok" ("The Big White Flock," signifying angels).

As years passed, the growing community had the services of a *klokker*. The *klokker* was not an ordained minister but a kind of peddler of spiritual wares who carried the Good Word from farm to farm. He knew the Bible, he could give sermons, and he had the authority to baptize.

The coming of the *klokker* was a great event. This was God's emissary on earth. Nothing was too good for him. The devoutness and hospitality of the family must shine forth so that God would receive a good report of them. They might be living on *grot* (a mixture of flour and water) and eggs, but one of the laying chickens must be killed to feed the *klokker*. Taking his leave, he would often say, "I'll be at your house next Friday if not Providentially detained." The coy reference suggested that at any moment God might see fit to recall him for some heavenly mission. But the *klokker's* gift for survival on this planet proved quite as remarkable as that of his flock's.

Asia

By the middle of the nineteenth century, Chinese emigrants began in large numbers to leave the hunger and wars of their homeland for the United States. With an annual emigration to the West Coast of some fifteen to twenty thousand Chinese, their numbers had risen to over three million by 1882 when the nation took steps to halt further emigration from China. Despite strong anti-Oriental prejudices and open wonderment at the cultural-religious-racial peculiarities of the Chinese, America's churches did launch missionary efforts among these "heathen." The first excerpt indicates the concern of a Chinese Baptist concerning evangelization; the second tells of the experience in San Francisco's Chinatown of newly converted Chinese Methodists.

1.

Letter of Missionary Fung Chak

[Portland, Oregon]

There is much, very much to do, but who shall perform the labor? When shall there be workers, and when shall there be means to carry on the work for the Chinese on this Coast? There are many here, and many more on the way to this country; but where, and how, and by whom are they to hear the Gospel?

The Chinese, in coming to America, meet with all its vices, but very few of its virtues. They see the worst side of all classes and very little of the better. The Baptists have so far accomplished very little for the Chinese on this Coast, but the need of work to be done is oh, how great! In Oregon, Washington Territory, and Idaho Territory, there are now thousands of Chinese. I have no means at hand of knowing accurately just how many there are, but there is no place for them to hear the Gospel with the exception of Portland. There are thousands of Chinese now employed on the construction of the railroad. Seattle is another centre in Washington Territory from whence many Chinese separate into the surrounding country.

But what can we do? We can only with aching hearts see these thousands of precious souls sinking into hell, with never a hand to save or a voice to warn. Oh, is there no money for the Chinese, however much there may be for others?

Must they be despised and hated themselves, and also the salvation of their souls utterly ignored? The Chinese are generally willing to hear the Gospel, and will gather and listen attentively to its preaching; but we have no wealthy converts yet, and so we cannot by ourselves carry on any great work, or

[Sources: (1) *Baptist Home Missions in North America 1832–1882* (New York: Baptist Home Mission Rooms, 1883), pp. 98–99. (2) Jade Snow Wang in Thomas C. Wheeler, *The Immigrant Experience* (New York: Dial Press, 1971), pp. 113–14.]

employ missionaries. We are deeply grateful for the assistance that has been granted us by the Board thus far, and we pray that such assistance may be continued in time to come. Portland is a centre through which all the travel of Oregon and the upper country passes, so that not only many of the resident Chinese hear the Gospel here, but many who go out to work in various directions are also to a greater or less extent benefited. We trust and pray that the Board will fully sustain the mission here. We feel that the mission here must be sustained. The Chinese must not be wholly left without the Gospel. Whatever may be, do not think of helping the Chinese less. Think of thousands of souls without the Gospel, without one voice to warn them from the vortexes that yawn on every side to engulf them, and drag them down to endless ruin.

If such work is neglected not only are souls lost, but there is a reaction against those who refuse them the Gospel, by creating darkness where there should be light. It can hardly be realized in the East, what a strong arm of the work in China is the work on this Coast.

We have converts in China, while many have been to China and returned to this country.

There are also many who have heard the Gospel through this mission, and though they are not yet openly Christians, yet an impression has been made that can never be wholly effaced, and ideas have been introduced that will never be forgotten. Yet, comparatively, we can reach but a few of the many.

There is an immediate necessity for the appointment of another missionary; there should be two—one to look after the work in Washington Territory, making his home at Seattle, while the Chinese on the railroad and in the towns springing up in eastern Oregon, Washington and Idaho Territories, should have someone to tell them of the better way. The mission at Salem should not be allowed to come to nought. One of our mission scholars has had a little school at Astoria since last Summer. The scholars have paid room rent, bought some books, etc., but they are in nowise able to sustain a mission, and the effort must sooner or later be discontinued. Thus there seems opportunity to extend the work for the Chinese, if means could be granted for that purpose; and we trust the Board will in the future find it possible to more fully improve this needy and important field,

With great respect and Christian regards, I am, truly your Brother in the Lord Jesus Christ,

FUNG CHAK

2.

On Sundays, we never failed to attend the Methodist Church, as my father's belief in the providence of God strengthened with the years, and his wife and family shared that faith.* My father's faith in God was unwavering and

* The father as a young man left southern Canton for San Francisco in 1903.

unshakable. (Some day, we were to hear his will, which he wrote in Chinese, and which began, "I believe in God, Jehovah. . . .") I have no statistics on the percentage of Christians in Chinatown at that time, but I am sure they were a minority. Our Methodist branch could not have had more than a hundred adult members, with less than fifty regular Sunday attendants. Many of Daddy's contemporaries scoffed at or ridiculed Christians as "do-gooders" who never gambled, when Mah-Jongg games were Chinatown's favorite pastime. Father used to chase lottery peddlers away from his factory; cards were never allowed in our home. I suppose that for him, the Christian faith at first comforted him far from his loved ones. Secondly, it promised him individual worth and salvation, when all his life in China had been devoted only to his family's continuity and glorification. Third, to this practical man who was virtually self-taught in all his occupations, Christianity suggested action on behalf of others in the community, while Confucianism was more concerned with regulating personal relationships. Daddy seldom hesitated to stick his neck out if he thought social action or justice were involved. For instance, he was on the founding board of the Chinese YMCA and fought for its present location, though he was criticized for its being on a hill, for being near the YWCA, for including a swimming pool.

Group singing and community worship in a church must have been dramatically different from the lonely worship of Chinese ancestral tablets at home. He listened to weekly sermons, expounding new ideas or reiterating old ones, and sometimes they were translated from the English spoken by visiting pastors. His daughters learned to sing in the choir and were permitted to join escorted church visits to Western churches — their only contact with a "safe" organization outside of Chinatown.

If my father had one addiction, it was to reading. He eagerly awaited the delivery of each evening's Chinese newspaper — for there had been none where he came from. His black leather-bound Testaments, translated into Chinese, were worn from constant reference. Before our Sunday morning departure for Sunday School, he conducted his own lessons at our dining table. No meal was tasted before we heard his thankful grace.

Roman Catholicism

Education

Among the alluring promises that America extended to its new arrivals was that of a free and public education —surer and safer than bread or shelter, as immigrant Mary Antin had written. But for Roman Catholics, the promise contained a joker. That "free and public" education possessed a distinctly Protestant cast. Given that circumstance, some Catholics wondered if public monies could not also be used to support an education with a distinctly Catholic cast. Archbishop John Hughes (1797 – 1864) thought that a not unreasonable request, but his battle in New York was lost. The only alternative remaining, the Catholic hierarchy concluded, was to provide —at whatever cost —a separate and private system of education for the thousands of Catholic children already in America and for the thousands arriving annually upon its shores. Two documents shed light on this important development: (1) Hughes's strong protest in 1840 against a system unfair and unworthy "of our just and glorious constitution"; and (2) a Pastoral Letter of 1884 revealing the depth of both conviction and commitment of the nation's Catholic leadership.

1.

Besides the introduction of the Holy Scriptures without note or comment, with the prevailing theory that from these even children are to get their notions of religion, contrary to our principles, there were in the class-books of those schools false (as we believe) historical statements respecting the men and things of past times, calculated to fill the minds of our children with errors of fact, and at the same time to excite in them prejudice against the religion of their parents and guardians. These passages were not considered as sectarian, inasmuch as they had been selected as mere reading lessons, and were not in *favor* of any particular sect, but merely *against* the Catholics. We feel it is unjust that such passages should be taught at all in schools, to the support of which we are contributors as well as others. But that such books should be put into the hands of *our own* children, and that in part at our own expense, was in our opinion unjust, unnatural, and at all events to us intolerable. Accordingly, through very great additional sacrifices, we have been obliged to provide schools, under our churches and elsewhere, in which to

[Sources: (1) John R. G. Hassard, *Life of the Most Reverend John Hughes* . . . (New York: D. Appleton & Co., 1866), pp. 230– 32. (2) Peter Guilday, ed., *The National Pastorals of the American Hierarchy, 1792–1919* (Washington: National Catholic Welfare Conference, 1923), pp. 244– 47.]

educate our children as our conscientious duty required. This we have done
to the number of some thousands for several years past, during all of which
time we have been obliged to pay taxes; and we feel it unjust and oppressive
that while we educate our children, as well we contend as they would be at
the public schools, we are denied our portion of the school fund, simply
because we at the same time endeavor to train them up in principles of virtue
and religion. This we feel to be unjust and unequal. For we pay taxes in
proportion to our numbers, as other citizens. We are supposed to be from
one hundred and fifty to two hundred thousand in the State. And although
most of us are poor, still the poorest man among us is obliged to pay taxes,
from the sweat of his brow, in the rent of his room or little tenement. Is it
not, then, hard and unjust that such a man cannot have the benefit of education
for his child without sacrificing the rights of his religion and conscience? He
sends his child to a school under the protection of his Church, in which these
rights will be secure. But he has to support this school also. In Ireland he
was compelled to support a church hostile to his religion, and here he is
compelled to support schools in which his religion fares but little better, and
to support his own school besides.

Is this state of things, fellow-citizens, and especially Americans, is this
state of things worthy of *you*, worthy of our country, worthy of our just and
glorious constitution? Put yourself in the poor man's place, and say whether
you would not despise him if he did not labor by every lawful means to
emancipate himself from this bondage. He has to pay double taxation for the
education of his child, one to the misinterpreted law of the land, and another
to his conscience. He sees his child going to school with perhaps only the
fragment of a worn-out book, thinly clad, and its bare feet on the frozen
pavement; whereas, if he had his rights he could improve the clothing, he
could get better books, and have his child better taught than it is possible in
actual circumstances.

Nothing can be more false than some statements of our motives which
have been put forth against us.

It has been asserted that we seek our share of the school funds for the
support and advance of our religion.

We beg to assure you with respect, that we would scorn to support or
advance our religion at any other than our own expense. But we are unwilling
to pay taxes for the purpose of destroying our religion in the minds of our
children. This points out the sole difference between what we seek and what
some narrow-minded or misinformed journals have accused us of seeking.

If the public schools could have been constituted on a principle which
would have secured a perfect NEUTRALITY of influence on the subject of
religion, then we should have no reason to complain. But this has not been
done, and we respectfully submit that it is impossible. The cold indifference
with which it is required that all religion shall be treated in those schools —
the Scriptures without note or comment — the selection of passages, as reading

lessons, from Protestants and prejudiced authors, on points in which our creed is supposed to be involved — the comments of the teacher, of which the commissioners cannot be cognizant — the school libraries, stuffed with sectarian works against us — form against our religion a combination of influences prejudicial to our religion, and to whose action it would be criminal in us to expose our children at such an age.

2.

Few, if any, will deny that a sound civilization must depend upon sound popular education. But education, in order to be sound and to produce beneficial results, must develop what is best in man, and make him not only clever but good. A one-sided education will develop a one-sided life; and such a life will surely topple over, and so will every social system that is built up of such lives. True civilization requires that not only the physical and intellectual, but also the moral and religious, well being of the people should be promoted, and at least with equal care. Take away religion from a people, and morality would soon follow; morality gone, even their physical condition will ere long degenerate into corruption which breeds decrepitude, while their intellectual attainments would only serve as a light to guide them to deeper depths of vice and ruin. This has been so often demonstrated in the history of the past, and is, in fact, so self-evident, that one is amazed to find any difference of opinion about it. A civilization without religion, would be a civilization of "the struggle for existence, and the survival of the fittest," in which cunning and strength would become the substitutes for principle, virtue, conscience and duty. As a matter of fact, there never has been a civilization worthy of the name without religion; and from the facts of history the laws of human nature can easily be inferred.

Hence education, in order to foster civilization, must foster religion. Now the three great educational agencies are the home, the Church, and the school. These mould men and shape society. Therefore each of them, to do its part well, must foster religion. But many, unfortunately, while avowing that religion should be the light and the atmosphere of the home and of the Church, are content to see it excluded from the school, and even advocate as the best school system that which necessarily excludes religion. Few surely will deny that childhood and youth are the periods of life when the character ought especially to be subjected to religious influences. Nor can we ignore the palpable fact that the school is an important factor in the forming of childhood and youth, — so important that its influence often outweighs that of home and Church. It cannot, therefore, be desirable or advantageous that religion should be excluded from the school. On the contrary, it ought there to be one of the chief agencies for moulding the young life to all that is true and virtuous, and holy. To shut religion out of the school, and keep it for home and the Church, is, logically, to train up a generation that will consider religion good for home and the Church, but not for the practical business of real life. But a more false and pernicious notion could not be imagined. Religion, in order to elevate a people, should inspire their whole life and rule their relations with one another. A life is not dwarfed, but ennobled by being lived in the presence of God. Therefore the school, which principally gives the knowledge fitting for practical life, ought to be pre-eminently under the holy influence of religion. From the shelter of home and school, the youth must soon go out into the busy ways of trade or traffic or professional practice. In all these, the principles of religion should animate and direct him. But he cannot expect to learn these principles in the work-shop or the office or the counting-room. Therefore let him be well and thoroughly imbued with them by the joint influences of home and school, before he is launched out on the dangerous sea of life.

All denominations of Christians are now awaking to this great truth, which the Catholic Church has never ceased to maintain. Reason and experience are forcing them to recognize that the only practical way to secure a Christian people, is to give the youth a Christian education. The avowed enemies of Christianity in some European countries are banishing religion from the schools, in order gradually to eliminate it from among the people. In this they are logical, and we may well profit by the lesson. Hence the cry for Christian education is going up from all religious bodies throughout the land. And this is no narrowness and "sectarianism" on their part; it is an honest and logical endeavor to preserve Christian truth and morality among the people by fostering religion in the young. Nor is it any antagonism to the State; on the contrary, it is an honest endeavor to give to the State better citizens, by making them better Christians. The friends of Christian education do not condemn the State for not imparting religious instruction in the public schools as they are now organized; because they well know it does not lie within the province of the State to teach religion. They simply follow their conscience by sending their children to denominational schools, where religion can have its rightful place and influence.

Two objects therefore, dear brethren, we have in view, to multiply our schools, and to perfect them. We must multiply them, till every Catholic child in the land shall have within its reach the means of education. There is still much to do ere this be attained. There are still thousands of Catholic children in the United States deprived of the benefit of a Catholic school. Pastors and parents should not rest till this defect be remedied. No parish is complete till it has schools adequate to the needs of its children, and the pastor and people of such a parish should feel that they have not accomplished their entire duty until the want is supplied.

But then, we must also perfect our schools. We repudiate the idea that the Catholic school need be in any respect inferior to any other school whatsoever. And if hitherto, in some places, our people have acted on the principle that it is better to have an imperfect Catholic school than to have none, let them now push their praise-worthy ambition still further, and not relax their efforts till their schools be elevated to the highest educational excellence. And we implore parents not to hasten to take their children from school, but to give them all the time and all the advantages that they have the capacity to profit by, so that, in after life, their children may "rise up and call them blessed."

Ethnicity

From Ireland and Germany, from Italy and Portugal, from Spain and all of its once great empire, Roman Catholics came to America. They were still Roman *Catholics, not* Irish *Catholics, nor* German *Catholics, nor* Italian *Catholics —or was this really the case? If, as noted above (pp. 34—35), Scandinavian Lutherans did not find a great deal of community with each other, how much more plausible that Catholics of widely separated geography and ethnicity might have difficulty —especially in a strange and threatening land —in seeing themselves in terms other than those of national origin. The problem was easy to understand, difficult to alleviate. Three documents follow: (1) a defense by James Cardinal Gibbons of the heavy Irish emigration to America; (2) an 1886 memorial of a Milwaukee priest, P. M. Abbelen, on behalf of Catholic Germans; and (3) a recollection from the early twentieth century of problems plaguing Catholic Italians.*

1.

Perhaps someone will ask what I think of Irish immigration in general. Ought the Irish to stay at home, or ought they emigrate very largely, and especially to the United States? It is a grave problem. Ireland is a very ancient nation, with a very glorious history, and her race of men is pre-eminently adapted to the soil on which they live. Divine Providence seems to have matched the lovely fertile island with a population of brave and industrious men, and pure and beautiful women. Surely this has not been in order to tear them roughly from the farm and the hamlet, the mill and the forge, the cradle and the spinning wheel, to scatter them like the leaves of the forest or the sands of the sea. . . .

Yet this same history shows us the Irish race as possessed beyond all others with the spirit of the world-wanderer. The earliest reliable utterances of their history bear witness that they were seafaring, adventurous people; and since their conversion to Christianity there can be no doubt that this spirit has been

[Sources: (1) James Gibbons, *A Retrospect of Fifty Years* (Baltimore: John Murphy 1916), I, pp. 280—83. (2) Colman J. Barry, *The Catholic Church and German Americans* (Milwaukee: Bruce Publishing Co., 1953), pp. 289—90, 294—95. (3) Julian Miranda, in S. J. LaGumina, *The Immigrants Speak* (New York: Center for Migration Studies, 1979), pp. 131—32.]

heightened and consecrated by religious ardor for the propagation of Christianity. Willingly and unwillingly, wittingly and unwittingly, they have been
a people of missionaries longer than any other race. No other people ever
gave themselves *en bloc* to Christian missions as they; no other people ever
suffered for their Catholic faith as they. And when, with the dawn of this
century, the remarkable movements began which have today produced some
130,000,000 of English-speaking people, and been the chief element in the
renaissance of Catholicism from its Continental tomb, it was the Irish who
were the pioneers, they being then almost the only English-speaking Catholics, and devoting themselves the world over to the planting of the Catholic
faith, the support of its claims and its missionaries, and the sustenance of the
Papal authority. They are no longer the only English-speaking Catholics,
though they are yet nearly everywhere in the majority; but we would be base
and ingrate to forget that it was they who bore the brunt of the struggle for
many decades of this century.

I would not, therefore, discourage Irish immigration, because there are
at stake more than economic considerations. There are at stake the interests
of the Catholic religion, which in this land and in this age are largely bound
up with the interests of the Irish people. God's hand is upon them, going
and coming; and I prefer to believe that He who harmonizes the motion of
the planets and the flow of the tides, is also First Agent and Prime Mover
in those no less mysterious movements by which peoples pass from one land
to another. . . .

2.

1. The question concerns the relation of non-English to English parishes,
and especially the relation of German to Irish parishes in the United States
of North America.

2. We ask of the Sacred Congregation de Propaganda Fide that it so define
this relation that German parishes shall be entirely independent of Irish parishes, or on a par with them; that rectors of Irish parishes shall not be able
to exercise any parochial jurisdiction over Germans enrolled in any German
church, or who by right should be thus enrolled, whether they be newcomers
from Germany or born in America of German parents. . . .

Nearly everywhere the opinion prevails that Irish rectors are truly and by
right the parish priest of all those who were born in America, as if having
over them an eminent domain; that German priests are, of course, necessary
to take care of the souls of Germans while they speak the German language,
but that it cannot fail to happen that they shall in the course of time lose their
language and learn English, and that the sooner this happens the better; that
the ecclesiastical status of the Germans is therefore a transitory one, and that
German parishes should not be put on an equal footing with English parishes.
There are also some who think that it is contrary to canon law that there

should be two independent parishes in the same territory, and for this reason also that the English should be the only parish. . . .

In all this controversy, besides a difference of language, we must not by any means make light of the difference and discrepancy of Catholic customs as they are to be found among Germans and Irish. The Irish, on account of the oppression and persecution which they suffered for religion's sake in their own land, love simplicity in divine service, and in all the practice of religion, and do not care much for pomp and splendor. But the Germans, from the liberty which as a rule they have enjoyed in the exercise of their religion from the earliest times, and the traditions of their fathers, love the beauty of the church edifice and the pomp of ceremonies, belfries and bells, organs and sacred music, processions, feast days, sodalities, and the most solemn celebration of First Communion and weddings. These and other like things, although not essential to Catholic faith and life, foster piety and are so dear and sacred to the faithful that not without great danger could they be taken away from them.

Then, again, Germans differ very much from the Irish in the administration of ecclesiastical goods and affairs. For nearly everywhere the former so manage their temporal affairs that the rectors, with a body of laymen, or even laymen alone, properly elected, carry on the administration, while the Irish leave all these things in the hands of the priests. It must be confessed, it sometimes happens among the Germans that the laymen meddle too much in such affairs, but this rarely happens; nearly everywhere the temporal affairs in German parishes are administered exceptionally well.

Finally, even manners and social customs of the two nationalities differ exceedingly. Thus it happens that scarcely ever will you find Germans and Irish united in matrimony. All this is here said neither to favor the Germans nor to disparage the Irish. Rather, these things are told by way of a narrative and as matters of fact, that it may be made clear how vastly one differs from the other, these two nationalities which are the principal parts of the Church in the United States, and how necessary it is that each should have its own priests and churches co-ordinate and independent. With the lapse of time, by a certain natural formative process one will become more assimilated to the other. But, God forbid that any one should dare, and most of all, that bishops and priests should endeavor to accelerate this assimilation by suppressing the language and customs of the Germans. The German temperament and a most sad experience demonstrate that their effort is not conducive to edification, but for the destruction and ruin of souls.

3.

On the topic of the church, it must be remembered that Southern Italian men were not so church scrupulous as the women although they were Catholic. I think no one should mistake their non-church attendance for a lack of belief in the Roman Catholic faith. The seeming lack of scrupulosity in Italians should not delude anybody about their lack of commitment to Christianity and its central ideas. I think there is a great paradox, and a great ambivalence there. Basically they dislike the clergy, and if they dislike the Italian clergy they despise the American clergy. They were very cruelly treated by this group. I remember when I was a child going for my First Communion and, I was asked by one of the nuns to recite the Our Father. I had only known it in either Sicilian or Latin (dog Latin). I knew what was going to happen but I got up and recited it and of course the class guffawed and the nun made fun of me. In a rage, I left the class. It was a Sunday and my grandfather was coming to the house, saw my face and said *che succedio?* (what happened?). At first, I did not want to tell him because of the *omerta* (you did not whine) but I finally told him that I said my prayer in Sicilian and they laughed at me. Inside of thirty seconds he had me by the arm and had propelled me up to the church. There, he got hold of Fr. Fitzsimmons and the nun and verbally laid them out. Nevertheless, this affected my church attendance. The lack of concern by the church for the immigrants and the cultural difference between the Italian and Irish Catholicism was responsible for a lot of the movement of Italians out of the Church toward Protestantism. This was also, however, a way to upward mobility. Had there been Italian clergy there is no question but that it would have made a difference. First of all the mere fact of being able to converse with the priest in your own language is important, but the role of the priest has been limited until very recently. The priest was not really a social agent by and large. I do not think priests gave social assistance beyond the performance of their strictly religious functions.

Liberty

While the heavy immigration of Catholics presented enormous problems of administration and education to the Church, it raised once again widespread fears on the part of many who were not members of that Church. Nativism erupted once again in the 1880s and 1890s as it had prior to the Civil War (see Vol. I, pp. 459–60). (1) Congregationalist Josiah Strong (1849– 1916), though progressive in matters of social reform, saw Roman Catholicism as the enemy of America's liberties and the perverter of her grand destiny. In 1885 he wrote a book entitled Our Country *(the "our" being understood as Anglo-Saxon):* Its Possible Future and Its Present Crisis. *A major contributor to the present crisis, in Strong's view, was the peril of "Romanism." (2) Cardinal Gibbons, archbishop of Baltimore from 1877*

[Sources: (1) Josiah Strong, *Our Country* . . . (New York: Baker & Taylor, rev. ed., 1891), pp. 73–75. (2) James Gibbons, *A Retrospect of Fifty Years* (Baltimore: John Murphy, 1916), I, pp. 263–64.]

to 1921, found it necessary time and again to explain, to those willing to listen, the compatibility of Catholic theology with American democracy.

Emigrants after clearing inspection on Ellis Island in New York, 1907
(Keystone-Mast Collection, University of California, Riverside)

1.

We have made a brief comparison of some of the fundamental principles of Romanism with those of the Republic. And,

1. We have seen the supreme sovereignty of the Pope opposed to the sovereignty of the people.

2. We have seen that the commands of the Pope, instead of the constitution and laws of the land, demand the highest allegiance of Roman Catholics in the United States.

3. We have seen that the alien Romanist who seeks citizenship swears true obedience to the Pope instead of "renouncing forever all allegiance to any foreign prince, potentate, state or sovereignty," as required by our laws.

4. We have seen that Romanism teaches religious intolerance instead of religious liberty.

5. We have seen that Rome demands the censorship of ideas and of the press, instead of the freedom of the press and of speech.

6. We have seen that she approves the union of church and state instead of their entire separation.

7. We have seen that she is opposed to our public school system.

Manifestly there is an irreconcilable difference between papal principles and the fundamental principles of our free institutions. Popular government is self-government. A nation is capable of self-government only so far as the individuals who compose it are capable of self-government. To place one's conscience, therefore, in the keeping of another, and to disavow all personal responsibility in obeying the dictation of another, is as far as possible from *self*-government, and, therefore, wholly inconsistent with republican institutions, and, if sufficiently common, dangerous to their stability. It is the theory of absolutism in the state, that man exists for the state. It is the theory of absolutism in the church that man exists for the church. But in republican and Protestant America it is believed that church and state exist for the people and are to be administered by them. Our fundamental ideas of society, therefore, are as radically opposed to Vaticanism as to imperialism, and it is as inconsistent with our liberties for Americans to yield allegiance to the Pope as to the Czar. It is true the Third Plenary Council* in Baltimore denied that there is any antagonism between the laws, institutions and spirit of the Roman church and those of our country, and in so doing illustrated the French proverb that "To deny is to confess." No Protestant church makes any such denials.

History fully justifies the teaching of philosophers that civil and political society tends to take the form of religious society. Absolutism in religion cannot fail in time to have an undermining influence on political equality. Already do we see its baneful influence in our large cities. It is for the most part the voters who accept absolutism in their faith who accept the dictation of their petty political popes, and suffer themselves to be led to the polls like so many sheep.

2.

No constitution is more in harmony with Catholic principles than is the American. And no religion can be in such accord with that constitution as

---

* This important council had met in 1884, with fourteen archbishops and sixty American bishops in attendance.

the Catholic. While the State is not absorbed in the Church, nor the Church in the State, and thus there is external separation, they both derive their life from the same interior principle of truth, and in their different spheres carry out the same ideas, and thus there is between them a real internal union. The Declaration of Independence acknowledges that the rights it proclaims come from God as the source of all government and all authority. This is a fundamental religious principle in which the Church and State meet.

From it follows the correlative principle that as God alone is the source of human rights, so God alone can efficaciously maintain them. This is equivalent to Washington's warning that the basis of our liberties must be morality and religion. Shall, then, the various Christian churches have influence enough with the millions of our people to keep them in morality and religion? No question can equal this in importance to our country. For success in this noble competition the Catholic Church trusts in the commission given her by her Divine Founder to teach and bless "all nations, all days, even until the end of the world." For guarantee of the spirit in which she shall strive to accomplish it, she points confidently to history's testimony of her unswerving assertion of popular rights, and to her cordial devotedness to the free institutions of America constantly manifested, in word and in work, by her Bishops, her clergy and her people.

Judaism

Education

*The commitment of America's Jews to education was matched only by their commitment to keep sectarian worship or instruction out of the public schools. Bible-reading, for so long an unquestioned tradition in the Protestant-dominated public schools, was often the crux. (1) In a famous case (*Minor v. Board of Education*) which reached the Superior Court of Cincinnati in 1869, the Court's majority upheld the ritual reading of the Bible in the local public schools. A persuasive dissent, however, delivered by Judge Alphonso Taft (1810−91; father of the president) led to a reversal by the Ohio Supreme Court the following year. (2) In San Francisco in 1875, the Lord's Prayer, urged upon the schools by a local Protestant clergyman, became the issue; a Jewish respondent to the "Rev. Mr. Hemphill" proclaimed as the American ideal "free thought and free, unsectarian education."*

[Sources: (1) *The Bible in the Public Schools* (New York: Da Capo Press, 1967 [1870]), pp. 408−9, 410−11, 414−15. (2) L. P. Gartner, ed., *Jewish Education in the United States: A Documentary History* (New York: Teachers College Press, 1969), pp. 91−93. (3) Abram S. Isaacs, "What Shall the Public Schools Teach?", *Forum*, 6 (Oct., 1888), 207−8.]

*(3) And in 1888, Abram S. Isaacs (1851 – 1920) made the case before
the general public that the state —and therefore the state's schools —has "nothing to do with religion."*

1.

Dissenting Opinion of Judge Alphonso Taft

I can not doubt, therefore, that the use of the Bible with the appropriate
singing, provided for by the old rule, and as practiced under it, was and is
sectarian. It is Protestant worship. And its use is a symbol of Protestant
supremacy in the schools, and as such offensive to Catholics and to Jews.
They have a constitutional right to object to it, as a legal preference given by
the State to the Protestant sects, which is forbidden by the Constitution.

And here, I again refer to the obvious distinction between the use of the
Bible by way of worship, and its use as a reading book. . . . The question,
whether the Board of Education under our Constitution could make the Bible
a reading book in the schools, contrary to the conscientious scruples of the
people, does not, in my opinion, arise in this case. For it is, as a form of
worship and religious instruction only, and not as a reading book, that it is
used in our schools, and as *such,* those who object to it, have a right to regard
it; and that is the ground, as I have understood these proceedings, on which
this suit has been brought.

The answer states that the children of Roman Catholic parents, equal to
at least half the entire number of children who attend the common schools,
are kept away by reason of this rule; that a large number of Jews, who have
children in the schools, object to the rule from conscientious reasons.

The counsel for the plaintiffs insist, that the Bible can, in no just sense,
be regarded as sectarian, and that the conscientious scruples alleged, are not
to be regarded.

The facts on which this question turns, are simple. The Roman Catholic
uses a different version of the Bible and includes the Apocrypha, as part of
it, which are excluded from the Protestant Bible. The Protestant Bible, is the
King James' version, which the Catholics regard as not only not a correct
translation, but as distorted in the interest of the Protestant, as against the
Roman Catholic Church. They object, therefore, on conscientious grounds,
to having their children read it or hear it read. They say and believe, that
it is a source of fatal religious error.

Nor is the incorrectness of the translation the only objection they entertain
to the reading of the Bible in these schools. They hold, that the Bible is
entrusted to the Church, and that it is not a suitable book to be read by, or
to, children without explanation by persons authorized by the Church and of
sufficient learning to explain and apply it.

We are not at liberty to doubt the conscientious objections, on the part of the Catholic parents to placing their children in the schools, while the schools are opened by the reading of the Protestant Bible and singing. . . .

It is said that the Catholic clergy demand their share of the fund, to be used in carrying on schools under their control. That can not be done under the Constitution. But this affords no reason why the Board of Education should not grant to the Catholic people, what the Bill of Rights guarantees to every sect, that their rights of conscience shall not be violated, and that they shall not be compelled to attend any form of worship, or to maintain it against their consent, or be compelled to submit to religious preferences, shown by the government to other religious societies.

It is not for a court to anticipate, before judgment, that any party will not be satisfied with what the law gives him, nor are courts accustomed to withhold what is due because something else is asked.

Another numerous class of heavy tax-payers, the Jews, object to the old rule. But it is claimed on behalf of the plaintiffs, that the Jews have met with something like a conversion, and have become reconciled to the New Testament. That they held out for a while, but afterward came in, and there was no further difficulty with them, and that their case need not to have been further regarded. There is too much evidence of dissent on their part, from the old rule, to permit us to conclude that they have ever intended to waive their rights of conscience and of religious liberty. Like the majority of us, the Jews have received their faith from their ancestors, and according to that historic faith, the assertion in the New Testament that Jesus of Nazareth is God, is blasphemy against the God of Israel. If a Protestant Christian would object to have the common schools daily opened with the forms of worship peculiar to the Catholic Church, which worships the same triune God with him, how much more serious must be the objection of the Jew, to be compelled to attend, or support, the worship of a being as God, whose divinity and supernatural history he denies?

The truth in this matter undoubtedly is, that the Jews, like many others, have found out that our common schools are munificently endowed, and, in general, well conducted, so that the privilege of attending them is inestimable, and they have wisely concluded to secure for their children the secular education of the common schools, and attend to their religious nurture at home and in their own organizations. A faith which had survived so much persecution, through so many centuries, they may well have risked in the common schools of Cincinnati, though at some cost of religious feeling.

It is in vain to attempt to escape the force of the clauses of the Bill of Rights by assuming that the Protestant Christian religion was intended in the Bill of Rights, and that the sects of Protestant Christians *only* were, therefore, entitled to protection. Between all forms of religious belief the State knows no difference, provided they do not transgress its civil regulations—a mighty contrast to some times and some countries, which have boasted of their religious liberality, because the ruling sects have tolerated the dissenting mi-

nority, as a nuisance, which they have magnanimously forborne to abate.
. . .

While the Court will take cognizance of the existence of the Christian
religion and of the Protestant religion, it is only for the purpose of preserving
civil peace and order, and the welfare of the State; and for the same purpose,
it will take cognizance of the existence of every sect. The State protects every
religious denomination in the quiet enjoyment of its own mode of public
worship. It protects them from blasphemy, when the public peace and order
require it.

It is, therefore, an entire mistake, in my opinion, to assert, that the Protestant Christian religion has been so identified with the history and government of our State or country, that it is not to be regarded as sectarian under
our Constitution; or, that, when the Bill of Rights says that "religion, morality
and knowledge being essential to good government," it means the Protestant
Christian religion. That would be a preference, which the same section expressly disclaims, and emphatically forbids.

To hold otherwise, and that Protestant Christians are entitled to any control
in the schools, to which other sects are not equally entitled, or that they are
entitled to have their mode of worship and their Bible used in the common
schools, against the will of the Board of Education, the proper trustees and
managers of the schools, is to hold to the union of Church and State, however
we may repudiate and reproach the name. Nor is it to be presumed, that the
cause of genuine religion, or of the Bible, can be permanently advanced by
a struggle for this kind of supremacy. The government is neutral, and, while
protecting all, it prefers none, and it *disparages* none. The State, while it does
not profess to be Christian, exercises a truly Christian charity toward all. Its
impartial charity extends to all kinds of Protestants, Roman Catholics, Jews
and Rationalists alike, and covers them with its mantle of protection and
encouragement; and no one of them, however numerous, can boast of peculiar
favor with the State.

2.

Joseph R. Brandon's Reply to the Reverend Mr. Hemphill

Mr. Hemphill, in his cry about Godless schools, evidently represents that
class of men who must see the name of God stamped upon everything; who
are uneasy because it does not appear in the Constitution of the United States,
and are continually agitating to get it there, as the first step to sectarianizing
the Government. What doctrine is this? Cannot things speak of God to the
soul of man without the letters of His name being graven upon them? Do
flowers speak to us of Him? — yet we find not His name on them. Do we see
the lightning assume the form of the letters of His name, or hear the thunder
pronounce the sound? — yet, *they* speak to us of Him. Does the wind shriek
His name to us in the tempest, or whisper it in the zephyr? — yet they speak

to us of Him. Do the heavens declare His glory, and the earth His handi-
work? — "There is no speech, there is no language, yet their voice is heard."
And if the name of God does not appear in the Constitution of the United
States, surely to him who has God in his heart His hand is seen therein, and
he may exclaim with the magicians of Egypt, "The finger of God is here." . . .

The hope of all thinking men as the means to this end is education —
education of the highest order — the cultivation of science, the exercise of
reason, *unlimited* in its objects; but to this end it must be UNSECTARIAN.
None must be shut out from that light, which is to dissipate the clouds of
bigotry and prejudice, and hasten the appearance of the cloudless sky of which
we have spoken, and whence the heavenly dew distils.

Education — unsectarian education is the hope and salvation of the Jew, as
of all who have passed through religious persecution; for it is from the deep,
dark clouds of ignorance, which bespeak its absence among men, that the
direst shafts of bigotry and persecution which have fallen upon our people
and others have proceeded. Well, indeed, and earnestly may we labor for its
diffusion, and seek not to drive children from, but to persuade and invite
them to the common schools by removing all obstacles in the way.

Let our education be of the widest kind. Let reason and religion, too long
divorced, too long at enmity, be reconciled. Let all of us, with free thought
and free, unsectarian education, seek to lift ourselves and our fellows above
the clouds of ignorance, sectarianism and prejudice, until these clouds can be
dissipated; . . .

No, reader; because sectarian prayer has not been permitted in the schools,
the friend of true education and true religion need not wail with Mr. Hemphill — that a battle has been lost — that Rome has conquered. He may rather
rejoice that free thought, free education, free religion has gained a victory
over the churchmen of all denominations; that the great principle has at last
been enunciated, that the State, which should be the common parent and
protector of all its children — majority or minority — few or many — will not
lend its aid to dispense the particolored light of any particular sect, but only
that colorless, illuminating principle which is common to all; and let us
fervently hope, and at the same time be vigilant, that sectarianism, whether
in the garb of Catholic priest, or Protestant minister, rob us not of the
victory.

3.

Abram S. Isaacs, "What Shall the Public Schools Teach?"

I have been general in suggestions as to what the schools should teach, leaving
to specialists a more detailed answer. Upon one subject, however, a more
precise reply is necessary. What is the relation of the schools to religion? Shall
they teach religion in any form?

The answer was very simple decades ago, when the population was smaller and more homogeneous. But to-day, with diverse religious and non-religious elements on every side, there can be but one answer: the state has nothing to do with religion, its schools are not to instill religious teachings. Such work is for the churches and the synagogues. A godless school is not necessarily an ungodly school; the omission of the name of the Deity from the book of Esther did not interfere with its place in the canon. If your school develops character, intelligence, modesty, strength, helpfulness in the pupil, it can safely leave the distinctly religious element to other teachers and influences. The absence of any positive religious teachings, however, should not be made a pretext for the inculcation of positive irreligious teachings and the deification of the sneer. But the entire subject should be omitted from the programme. It is none of the school's business, as long as the state has no established church.

The evils in the present method are many. It is true, the law is opposed to sectarian teaching in the schools, yet it favors the reading of the Bible. Usually hymns are added of a sectarian character, suitable for a Protestant Sunday School, and admirable in their way, but in this connection out of place. Then the Lord's Prayer is repeated; on the lovely and sublime character of which I make no criticism, for I recognize its rabbinical spirit in every line. But it has become a distinctly Christian prayer, and is usually followed by Christian allusions, which are excellent in the Sunday school, but not in the public school, which is supported by hosts of tax-payers who are non-Christians. In most cases, the selections from the Bible are made without tact and contain doctrinal references. Under such circumstances, the only remedy is to withdraw religion entirely from the schools. The treatment which the Bible receives, the monotonous and perfunctory readings of disconnected chapters, is enough to make it, like Milton's "Paradise Lost," with its parsing reminiscences, a closed book to the scholars for all time.

Organization

In dealing with the public school system or with a suspicious Gentile majority, America's Jews stood together in unity. In dealing with each other, however, tensions and dissensions soon appeared. In the latter years of the nineteenth century, religious divisions emerged as observant Jews adopted varying attitudes toward Jewish law (Torah) and its interpretation (Halakah). (1) Reform Judaism, led by Isaac Mayer Wise (1819–1900), moved farthest

[Sources: (1) I. M. Wise, *Selected Writings* (Cincinnati: Robert Clarke Co., 1900), pp. 260–62. (2) Solomon Schechter, *Seminary Addresses and Other Papers* (Cincinnati: Ark Publishing Co., 1915), pp. 83, 84–86. (3) Emanuel Rackman, "American Orthodoxy: Retrospect and Prospect," in Theodore Friedman and Robert Gordis, eds., *Jewish Life in America* (New York: Horizon Press, 1955), pp. 23–25.]

to the left, seeing much of the ancient Mosaic or Rabbinical legislation as "altogether foreign to our present mental and spiritual state" —to quote from the 1885 Declaration of Principles. (2) Conservative Judaism, with Solomon Schechter (1847–1915) as its eloquent spokesman, would remain loyal to that which was uniquely Jewish at the same time that it avoided a "moribund rationalism" and took cognizance of an American environment and a modern world. (3) And then there was Orthodox Judaism —the faith of Abraham, Isaac, and Jacob —maintained without alteration or compromise. As a Yeshiva University professor explains below, Orthodoxy would presumably be the first "to meet the challenge of the American scene. . . . In fact, it was the last to do so."

1.

REFORMED JUDAISM
(1871)

Change, universal and perpetual, is the law of laws in this universe. Still there is an element of stability, the fact of mutation itself; the law of change changes not. This law lies in the harmony of the spheres; the mystery of truth in nature's variegation; the manifestation of the wisdom of the Immutable Deity. Progress and perfectibility are the effect, and, as far as reason penetrates, the conscious aim of this cause. The geologist, as he comes away from the lowest stratum into which his researches have gone along the crust of this planet, and the historian, who returns from the study of the life of humanity from the cradle of its birth to the nineteenth century, see the chain of conscious progress in form and idea, from the lowest to the highest known to man, see the promise of perfectibility everywhere, and see permanent retrogradation nowhere. Wisdom, boundless and ineffable, and the revelations of Deity lie in this law of laws "which God hath created to do."

Therefore, Reformed Judaism, the subject of this essay, acknowledges no necessary stability of the form, but also no change of the principle. All forms change, adapting themselves to new conditions, and all changes proceed from the same principle, which is not subject to change. This is the central idea of Jewish reasoners on Judaism in the nineteenth century.

Before following this idea in its sequence, it must be understood that the term "Reformed" in connection with "Judaism," does not imply restoration to an older form; it is intended to convey the idea of putting into a new and improved form and condition. Judaism, from this standpoint admits no retrogression, and maintains that all forms which the principle has developed and crystallized, were necessarily beneficial for each respective time or locality. But the civilization of the nineteenth century, being the sum and substance of all previous phases, has produced conditions unknown in former periods of history. Therefore, the principle of Judaism also must develop new forms corresponding to the new conditions which surround its votaries who live among the civilized nations; forms, too, which were neither necessary nor desirable in former periods of history, and would not be such now to other Israelites, although adhering to the same principle, who live among semi-barbarous, or even less enlightened nations. Again, as civilization progresses, the principle of Judaism will always develop new forms in correspondence with every progressive state of the intelligence and consciousness, until the great day when one shepherd and one flock will unite the human family in truth, justice and love. As an illustration of this, it is to be remembered that the Israelite of the reformed school does not believe in the restoration of the ancient mode of worship by the sacrifice of animal victims and by a hereditary priesthood. He considers that phase was necessary and beneficial, in its time and locality, but that it would be void of all significance in our age when entirely different conceptions of divine worship prevail, and it would appear much more meaningless to coming generations. The divine institutions of the past are not obligatory on the present generation or on coming ages, since the conditions which rendered them necessary, desirable and beneficial have been radically changed. Therefore, Progressive Judaism would be a better designation than Reformed Judaism. But, on account of common usage, the latter term has been adopted as the caption of this essay, and should be understood in this spirit alone.

2.

ALTAR BUILDING IN AMERICA

(1904)

The first settlers in this country were mostly men who had left their native land for conscience' sake, despairing of the Old World as given over to the powers of darkness, despotism and unbelief. And I can quite realize how they must have gloried in the idea of being chosen instruments of Providence who were to restore the spiritual equilibrium of the world by the conquest of new spheres of religious influence and their dedication to the worship of Almighty God.

As a Jew coming from the East of Europe, where my people are trodden down, where seats of Jewish learning and Jewish piety are daily destroyed, I am greatly animated by the same feelings and am comforted to see the New World compensating us for our many losses in the Old. I rejoice, therefore, at the privilege of being with you on this solemn occasion. . . .

We are now prepared for the minuter consideration of our text.

"And thou shalt write upon the stones all the words of the Torah very plainly." The stones are erected, and at this moment have been dedicated to the service of God. But bricks and mortar, marble pillar and gilded domes do not make an altar. What constitutes an altar are the words of the Torah, which are engraved on the very stones, which influence the lives of the worshipers and convert their homes into places of worship. The verse in Exodus 20:24, also containing injunctions regarding the altar, is paraphrased by the great Hillel as if God were saying to man, "If thou wilt come unto My house, I will come into thy house." "The word of our Lord endureth forever." This is a divine promise. But if after frequent visits to places of worship, you have experienced nothing of the nearness of God in your houses, then you may safely doubt whether you have really been in a house of God. It is the home which is the final and supreme test of the altar. A synagogue, for instance, that teaches a Judaism which finds no reverberating echo in the Jewish home, awakens there no distinctive conscious Jewish life, has failed in its mission, and is sure sooner or later to disappear as a religious factor making for righteousness and holiness. It may serve as a lecture hall or a lyceum, or as a place to which people in their *ennui* repair for "an intellectual treat;" but it will never become a place of worship, a real altar for acceptable sacrifices, bestowing that element of joy in God . . . which is the secret and strength of Judaism.

This is a test applicable to all ages and to all countries; to the New World as well as the Old. There is nothing in American citizenship which is incompatible with our observing the dietary laws, our sanctifying the Sabbath, our fixing a Mezuzah on our doorposts, our refraining from unleavened bread on Passover, or our perpetuating any other law essential to the preservation of Judaism. On the other hand, it is now generally recognized by the leading thinkers that the institutions and observances of religion are part of its nature, a fact that the moribund rationalism of a half century ago failed to realize. In certain parts of Europe every step in our civil and social emancipation demanded from us a corresponding sacrifice of a portion of the glorious heritage bequeathed to us by our fathers. Jews in America, thank God, are no longer haunted by such fears. We live in a commonwealth in which by the blessing of God and the wisdom of the Fathers of the Constitution, each man abiding by its laws, has the inalienable right of living in accordance with the dictates of his own conscience. In this great, glorious and free country we Jews need not sacrifice a single iota of our Torah; and, in the enjoyment of absolute equality with our fellow citizens we can live to carry out those ideals for which our ancestors so often had to die.

3.

AMERICAN ORTHODOXY: RETROSPECT AND PROSPECT
(1955)

The earliest Jewish settlers on American soil brought with them the only Judaism they knew — Orthodox Judaism. Two centuries later Reform Judaism took root and fifty years thereafter Conservative Judaism was born. Under

Jewish market, East Side, New York City, 1900
(Library of Congress)

the circumstances, one would have expected that Orthodox Judaism would be the first to meet the challenge of the American scene, both ideologically and institutionally. In fact, it was the last to do so. Paradoxically enough, it is only in the last few decades that Orthodoxy seriously came to grips with the problem of its own future.

For too long a time Orthodoxy relied upon the fact that the preponderant number of American Jews professed to be its adherents. Majorities supporting the status quo in many social situations often rely upon the force of their numbers and their inertia, while well organized and dedicated minorities make gains or change. The Orthodox Jewish community once was such a majority. It was slow to realize the extent to which it was losing its numerical advantage. Also, the ranks of American Orthodoxy were constantly replenished with thousands of immigrants from abroad. The new arrivals more than compensated for the defections to other groups. Now the loss of the European reservoir of Jews has caused American Orthodoxy to become concerned. It had to find the way to command the loyalty of American-born Jews. Finally, Orthodoxy by its very nature compromises less easily with new environments and new philosophies, so that it could not avail itself of that flexibility which aided the growth of the Reform and Conservative movements. The challenge of the American scene had to be met differently and the solution came later. Nonetheless, the contributions of Orthodoxy to our dual heritage as Americans and as Jews were many and significant.

It fell to the lot of Orthodoxy to establish the legal status of Jews and Judaism in American democracy. To the everlasting credit of our pioneering forbears it must be said that they were not content with second-class citizenship in the United States. George Washington confirmed this attitude in his now famous letter to the Orthodox congregation in Newport, Rhode Island. However, the false dictum that America is a "Christian state" must be challenged again and again, even in the twentieth century, and while the battle is now waged by all Jews, and especially by the defense agencies, it is usually one Orthodox Jew or another who creates the issue. The right of Sabbath observers to special consideration where "Blue Sunday" laws are in effect; their right to special treatment in the armed forces; their right to unemployment insurance benefits when they decline employment because of religious scruples — these are typical of many problems that Orthodox Jews raise in the hope that their resolution will insure maximum expansion of the American concept of equality before the law. In many instances, bearded Orthodox Jews who retain their Eastern European dress are also a challenge to the sincerity of most Americans who boast that their way of life spells respect for differences. The resistance of many of our co-religionists to the levelling character of American mores, and its inevitable discouragement of diversity, is a healthy contribution to our understanding and practice of democracy. Altogether too often American Jews require the reminder even more than American Christians.

In the same spirit it was American Orthodoxy that bore, and still bears, the burden of resistance to world-wide calendar reform. Though all Jewish groups have cooperated, it is Orthodoxy alone that regards any tampering with the inviolability of the Sabbath day fixed at Creation as a mortal blow to Judaism and in the name of the religious freedom of minorities it seeks to alert the American conscience to desist from prejudicial action.

It was, however, in the establishment and construction of thousands of synagogues throughout the country that Orthodox Jews made manifest not only their loyalty to their ancestral heritage but their appreciation of their grand opportunity in this blessed land of freedom. How truly pauperized immigrants managed, in cities large and small, to rear beautiful edifices for worship is a saga worthy of more attention than it has heretofore received.

What is particularly noteworthy is that no central agency guided or financed the movement. In every case it was individual Jews who banded together and performed the feat, a remarkable tribute to the effectiveness of our tradition in inducing in individual Jews the capacity to act on their own initiative for the greater glory of God.

4. WOMEN'S WORK?

Pulpit

If women wanted to enter into the pulpit, this often meant that they must create their own church (as Ann Lee and Ellen White, for example, had done; see Vol. I, pp. 369, 375). The older, more established denominations saw the introduction of females into their ministry as radical, unbiblical, and unsuitable to the "weaker" sex. When Antoinette Brown Blackwell (1825 – 1921) accepted ordination in the Congregational church in 1853, she broke a barrier by becoming the first woman to be ordained by a major denomination. Yet, other barriers of resistance remained as Blackwell was obliged to defend the capacity and propriety of women entering professional life. (1) In 1875, she took issue, on physiological and psychological grounds, with a recent (1873) Boston publication by E. H. Clarke, Sex in Education; Or, A Fair Chance for the Girls. *(2) Among those not convinced by Blackwell's argumentation or example was R. L. Dabney (1820 – 98), a Presbyterian minister, theologian, and professor in Virginia. Writing in 1879, Dabney explained that the Bible clearly shows woman's position in the church to be subordinate to man's.*

1.

Dr. Clarke has given voice and tangibility to many of the floating suggestions of years, insisting that women are physically incapacitated for habitual study, that growing young girls should not be allowed to compete with boys in an identical course of education, and leading us squarely up to the inference that the strain of persistent mental work can never be successfully borne by average womanhood: The Dr. pronounces our national, rapidly growing method of co-education in schools and colleges "a crime before God and humanity, that physiology protests against, and that experience weeps over." The entire community, therefore, has a most vital interest in this book, which maintains that co-education is more than a mistake; that it imperils the health of the girls,

[Sources: (1) A. B. Blackwell, *The Sexes Through Nature* (New York: G. P. Putnam's Sons, 1875), pp. 162 – 63, 163 – 67. (2) R. L. Dabney, "The Public Preaching of Women," *Southern Presbyterian Review*, 30 (Oct., 1879), 689 – 90, 695 – 96, 711 – 13.]

curtailing their hope of posterity, and threatening their few possible children with greatly unfeebled constitutions. . . .

Many of us have felt for years that the "Woman question" must be met just here, upon a comparative physiological and psychological basis. . . .

That every-day question is, does study, a few hours of regular daily application to mental work, impair or tend to impair the vigor of the feminine constitution? Are the daily lessons which are fitting and healthful for a school boy so exacting that they must draw the blood to nurture the brain of the school girl to the detriment of her appropriate womanly growth? Does moderate study, on any day and at any period of a healthy woman's life, tend to exhaust her natural strength, or to produce a reaction so violent that it must become a direct promoter either of weakness or of disease? These questions are all one; they apply to the girl of fifteen or to the woman of thirty alike. They must be answered as bearing not only on her own welfare, but also on that of the rising generation.

There are many ways of reaching the same conclusion, but the first and best method is based upon experience. . . . It is fitting that I add personal testimony to enforce my position, that study is as healthful to women as to men, and, as society now is, that it must prove to be relatively much more so.

In the days when mothers sent their babies for early instruction, I was a little school-girl in prompt and regular attendance at three years. I remained at school, averaging from a half to two-thirds of every intervening year, until I was twenty-four; so that I have literally "come of age" under a system of joint education for the sexes, for I never attended a girls' school. During this whole period I studied as continuously as an average boy studies, was not conspicuously deficient at recitations, and for years together did more real brain work outside of all class exercises than in connection with them; yet my health was generally good, and it continued good for years after I left the Theological Seminary,* though I was engaged in work more health-trying than anything in my previous experience. Once, not from ordinary overwork, but in passing through an ordeal not uncommon in modern days, in which the faith of one's fathers is shaken to the foundations, and when forced to meet the added struggle of continuing to teach many things which were no longer believed, or dropping out from a profession chosen conscientiously in the face of untold obstacles, my health was seriously impaired. But I speedily gained both a broader faith and a firmer health, which remain unimpaired to this day. I am the mother of six children, five of whom enjoy a vigor of constitution above the average; and one, in the midst of apparently perfect health, was swept off by one of those scourges of infancy against which Omniscience alone could always guard effectively. . . .

We may regard this as an exceptional instance of a woman's ability to

---

*Oberlin in 1850; she left without being allowed to receive a theological degree.

endure persistent brain work unharmed in health; but I believe it to be simply one illustration of human power to thrive on habitual daily exercise of both mind and body, alternated with sufficient rest and relaxation.

2.

In this day innovations march with rapid strides. The fantastic suggestion of yesterday, entertained only by a few fanatics, and then only mentioned by the sober to be ridiculed, is to-day the audacious reform, and will be to-morrow the recognised usage. Novelties are so numerous and so wild and rash, that in even conservative minds the sensibility of wonder is exhausted and the instinct of righteous resistance fatigued. A few years ago the public preaching of women was universally condemned among all conservative denominations of Christians, and, indeed, within their bounds, was totally unknown. Now the innovation is brought face to face even with the Southern churches, and female preachers are knocking at our doors. We are told that already public opinion is so truckling before the boldness and plausibility of their claims that ministers of our own communion begin to hesitate, and men hardly know whether they have the moral courage to adhere to the right. These remarks show that a discussion of woman's proper place in Christian society is again timely.

The arguments advanced by those who profess reverence for the Bible, in favor of this unscriptural usage, must be of course chiefly rationalistic. They do indeed profess to appeal to the sacred history of the prophetesses, Miriam, Deborah, Huldah, and Anna, as proving that sex was no sufficient barrier to public work in the Church. But the fatal answer is: that these holy women were inspired. Their call was exceptional and supernatural. There can be no fair reasoning from the exception to the ordinary rule. . . .

The argument then, whether any woman may be a public preacher of the Word, should be prevalently one of Scripture. Does the Bible really prohibit it? We assert that it does. And first, the Old Testament, which contained, in germ, all the principles of the New, allowed no regular church office to any woman. When a few of that sex were employed as mouth-pieces of God, it was in an office purely extraordinary and in which they could adduce a supernatural attestation of their commission. No woman ever ministered at the altar as either priest or Levite. No female elder was ever seen in a Hebrew congregation. No woman ever sat on the throne of the theocracy except the pagan usurper and murderess, Athaliah. Now Presbyterians at least believe that the church order of the Old Testament Church was imported into the New, with less modification than any other part of the old religion. The ritual of types was greatly modified; new sacramental symbols replaced the old; the temple of sacrifice was superseded, leaving no sanctuary beneath the heavenly one, save the synagogue, the house of prayer. But the primeval presbyterial order continued unchanged. The Christianised synagogue became the Christian congregation, with its eldership, teachers, and deacons, and its women invariably keeping silence in the assembly. The probability thus raised is strong.

Secondly, if human language can make anything plain, it is that the New Testament institutions do not suffer the woman to rule or "to usurp authority over the man." See 1 Tim. ii. 12; 1 Cor. xi. 3, 7– 10; Eph. v. 22, 23; 1 Peter iii. 1, 5, 6. In ecclesiastical affairs at least, the woman's position in the Church is subordinate to the man's. . . .

The woman is not designed by God, nor entitled to all the franchises in society to which the male is entitled. God has disqualified her for any such exercise of them as would benefit herself or society, by the endowments of body, mind, and heart he has given her, and the share he has assigned her in the tasks of social existence. And as she has no right to assume the masculine franchises, so she will find in the attempt to do so only ruin to her own character and to society. For instance, the very traits of emotion and character which make woman man's cherished and invaluable "helpmeet," the traits which she must have in order to fulfil the purpose of her being, would ensure her unfitness to meet the peculiar temptations of publicity and power. The attempt would debauch all these lovelier traits, while it would leave her still, as the rival of man, "the weaker vessel." She would lose all and gain nothing.

One consequence of this revolution would be so certain and so terrible that it cannot be passed over. It must result in the abolition of all permanent marriage ties. Indeed, the bolder advocates do not scruple to avow it. The destruction of marriage would follow by this cause, if no other; that the unsexed politicating woman, the importunate manikin-rival, would never inspire in men that true affection on which marriage should be founded. The mutual attraction of the two complementary halves would be forever gone. The abolition of marriage would follow again by another cause. The rival interests and desires of two equal wills are inconsistent with domestic union, government, or peace. Shall the children of this unnatural connexion be held responsible to both of two sinful but coördinate and equally supreme wills? Heaven pity the children! Again, who ever heard of a perpetual copartnership in which the parties had no power to enforce the performance of the mutual duties nor to dissolve the tie made intolerable by violation? It would be as iniquitous as impossible. Such a copartnership of equals, with coördinate wills and independent interests, must be separable at will, as all other such copartnerships are.

This common movement for "women's rights" and women's preaching must be regarded then as simply infidel. It cannot be candidly upheld without attacking the inspiration and authority of the Scriptures. We are convinced that there is only one safe attitude for Christians, presbyters, and church courts to assume towards it. This is utterly to discountenance it, as they do any other assault of infidelity on God's truth and kingdom. The church officer who becomes an accomplice of this intrusion certainly renders himself obnoxious to discipline, just as he would by assisting to celebrate an idolatrous mass.

We close with one suggestion to such women as may be inclined to this new claim. If they read history they find that the condition of woman in Christendom, and especially in America, is most enviable as compared with her state in all other ages and nations. Let them ponder candidly how much they possess here which their sisters have enjoyed in no other age. What bestowed those peculiar privileges on the Christian women of America? The Bible. Let them beware then how they do anything to undermine the reverence of mankind for the authority of the Bible. It is undermining their own bulwark. If they understand how universally in all but Bible lands the "weaker vessel" has been made the slave of man's strength and selfishness, they will gladly "let well enough alone," lest in grasping at some impossible prize beyond, they lose the privileges they now have, and fall back to the gulf of oppression from which these doctrines of Christ and Paul have lifted them.

Society

The reform of society, many freely argued in the nineteenth century, was a man's job. But what if men were in fact a major source of the social problem? Could the leopard change his spots? (1) With regard to the overindulgence in alcohol, men indeed were the problem, and women —perhaps —the solution. Women, if organized and dedicated and vocal, could make, would make an enormous difference. This was the conviction and firm purpose of Frances E. Willard (1839—98) who led the Women's Christian Temperance Union from modest beginnings in Ohio to world-wide organization and influence. At the first convention of the W.C.T.U. in Cleveland in 1874, the following "Plan of Work" was adopted. (2) On the Roman Catholic side, Alice Toomy argued for women to take a more active role in the "public sphere" than they had traditionally done —not just in temperance concerns but in many other social arenas as well. Toomy made her argument in the pages of the Catholic World, *and in those same pages she was answered by Katherine E. Conway: ". . . it seems settled beyond question that woman, as woman, can have no vocation in public life" (p. 681).*

1.

PLAN OF WORK.

I. —of Organization.

Since organization is the sun-glass which brings to a focus scattered influence and effort, we urge the formation of a Woman's Temperance Union in every

[Sources: (1) Frances E. Willard, *Women and Temperance* . . . (New York: Arno Press, 1972 [1883]), pp. 636—37, 638, 640. (2) Alice T. Toomy, *Catholic World,* 57 (Aug., 1893), 674—76.]

State, city, town, and village. We will furnish a Constitution for auxiliaries, with all needed information, to any lady applying to corresponding secretary.

II. —of Making Public Sentiment.

The evolution of temperance ideas in this order: the people are informed, convinced, convicted, pledged. With these facts in view we urge:

First. — Frequent temperance mass meetings.

Second. — The careful circulation of temperance literature in the people's homes and in saloons.

Third. — Teaching the children in Sabbath-Schools and public schools, the ethics, chemistry, physiology, and hygiene of total abstinence.

Fourth. — Offering prizes in these schools for essays on different aspects of the subject.

Fifth. — Placing a copy of the engraving known as "The Railroad to Ruin," and similar pictures, on the walls of every school-room.

Sixth. — Organizing temperance glee clubs of young people to sing temperance doctrines into the peoples' hearts as well as heads.

Seventh. — Seeking permission to edit a column in the interest of temperance in every newspaper in the land, and in all possible ways enlisting the press in this reform.

Eighth. — Endeavoring to secure for pastors everywhere frequent temperance sermons, and special services in connection with the weekly prayer-meeting and the Sabbath-School at stated intervals, if they be only quarterly.

Ninth. — Preserving facts connected with the general subject, and with our work, in temperance scrap-books, to be placed in the hands of a special officer appointed for this purpose. . . .

IV. —of the Pledge.

If nobody would drink, then nobody would sell.

First. — We urge the circulation of the total abstinence pledge as fast and as far as facilities permit, life signatures being sought, but names being taken for any length of time, however brief.

Second. — We have a special pledge for women, involving the instruction and pledging of themselves, their children, and as far as possible their households; banishing alcohol in all its forms from the sideboard and the kitchen, enjoining quiet, persistent work for temperance in their own social circles.

Third. — We earnestly recommend ladies to get permission to place a pledge-book in every church and Sabbath-school room, where it shall be kept perpetually open in a convenient place, indicated by a motto placed above it. Also that each member of our unions keep an autograph pledge-book on her parlor table, and carry one in her pocket. . . .

VII. —of Temperance Coffee Rooms.

If we would have men forsake saloons, we must invite them to a better place, where they can find shelter, and food, and company. We would open small, neat coffee-rooms, with reading-rooms attached, which the ladies might supply with books and papers from their own homes, and by solicited friends. When practicable, there should also be Friendly Inns, connected with which there might be provided for those willing to compensate by their labor for their food and lodging, a manufacturing shop, comprising many trades. . . .

Conclusion.

Dear sisters, we have laid before you the plan of the long campaign. Will you work with us? We wage our peaceful war in loving expectation of that day "when all men's weal shall be each man's care," when "nothing shall hurt or destroy in all my holy mountain," saith the Lord; and in our day we may live to see America, beloved mother of thrice grateful daughters, set at liberty, full and complete, from foamy King Gambrinus* and fiery old King Alcohol.

2.

THERE IS A PUBLIC SPHERE FOR CATHOLIC WOMEN

The Catholic Women's Congress held in Chicago, May 18 [1893], gave an outline sketch of the work of Catholic women, beginning with a paper on "The Elevation of Womanhood through the Veneration of the Blessed Virgin," and closing with the life-work of Margaret Haughery,** of New Orleans, the only woman in America to whom the public have raised a statue.

The enthusiasm awakened by this Congress drew a large body of Catholic women together, who organized a National League for work on the lines of education, philanthropy, and "the home and its needs" — education to promote the spread of Catholic truth and reading circles, etc.; philanthropy to include temperance, the formation of day nurseries and free kindergartens, protective and employment agencies for women, and clubs and homes for working girls; the "home and its needs" to comprehend the solution of the domestic service question, as well as plans to unite the interests and tastes of the different members of the family. Each active member of the league registers under some one branch of work according to her special attraction. The underlying idea of the league is that Catholic women realize that there is a duty devolving on them to help the needy on lines which our religious cannot reach, even were they not already so sadly overworked. Tens of thousands of our ablest

*A mythical king associated with the invention of beer.

**Margaret Gaffney Haughery (1813–82) won the affections of the New Orleans public by her self-sacrifice, abundant charity, and simple, unaffected goodwill. Her statue, unveiled in 1884, carried only this inscription: "Margaret."

Catholic women are working with the W.C.T.U. and other non-Catholic philanthropies, because they find no organization in their own church as a field for their activities. Every Catholic woman who has had much association outside the church is frequently met with the question: Why don't you Catholics take care of your own poor, and not leave so much work for other churches to do for you? The truth is that ours is the church of the poor, and manifold as is the charity work of the religious and the benevolent societies, a vast amount has to go undone because there is no one to attend to it. It seems safe to compute that fully one-half our church members are among the needy, one-tenth of our members are wealthy, and the remaining forty percent are well to do. The occupations of the very wealthy seem so all-engrossing that the care of the needy seems to fall naturally on the well to do, who are happily not so far removed from the poor in condition as to be insensible to their wants. Mankind has repeated the "Our Father" for well-nigh two thousand years, and yet the great body of humanity seems only now waking up to the fact that "*our* Father" implies a common brotherhood: that "no man liveth unto himself alone": that we are our brothers' keepers. Surely then, in the face of these facts, it can only be through misapprehension of terms that the question is asked, "Is there a public sphere for Catholic women?" As well as ask, "Is there a public sphere for the religious?" since who is so public as the man or woman who gives his whole life, with all its powers, for the good of humanity? It cannot be that the estimate of the Catholic woman is so poor that it is supposed that her love of home, her sense of duty and womanly instincts will suffer by her taking counsel with a body of women for a few hours every week as to the best methods of improving the condition of her fellow-women? Catholic women enter into the gaieties and even the follies of society. Many lose more money and time for dress and fashion than would be consumed by works of philanthropy. Yet no alarm seems to be taken as to the danger to womanliness in this sphere!

Almost every subject of practical utility to humanity has been set for discussion during the Chicago congresses. Already many vital questions of morals and progress have been ably considered by experts. Many of those experts have been women, and even some of these women were Catholics. Can anyone doubt that the church and the world have gained by their success? Is not every good thought crystallized into a plan of action—a fresh guidance in well-doing?

However wise or pious a woman may be, she meets with daily problems for which no literature offers solution, but from which the light of other women's experience may clear away the difficulty. The great power of the age is organization, and nowhere is it more needed than among Catholic women, whose consciences and hearts are so keenly alive to evils that individuals find themselves powerless to overcome. The proof that the Catholic Women's League is needed is shown by the daily applications for affiliation, and for an organizer to go to other cities and establish branches.

Academy

Some women found in the Bible the sanction for their reforming efforts, the grounds for their emancipation. Others, however, saw the Bible —at least as presently translated and widely understood —as a major part of the problem. Elizabeth Cady Stanton (1815 – 1902), feminist of great impact, joined with the Quaker preacher Lucretia Mott in organizing the famous 1848 convention for women's rights at Seneca Falls, New York. Later working with Susan B. Anthony, Stanton took women's suffrage as her chief cause. And in the final decade of the nineteenth century, she courted even more controversy by taking the leading role in preparing a new edition of the Holy Scriptures, this one to be known as The Woman's Bible *(in two volumes, 1895, 1898).*

From the inauguration of the movement for woman's emancipation the Bible has been used to hold her in the "divinely ordained sphere," prescribed in the Old and New Testaments.

The canon and civil law; church and state; priests and legislators; all political parties and religious denominations have alike taught that woman was made after man, of man, and for man, an inferior being, subject to man. Creeds, codes, Scriptures and statutes, are all based on this idea. The fashions, forms, ceremonies and customs of society, church ordinances and discipline all grow out of this idea.

Of the old English common law, responsible for woman's civil and political status, Lord Brougham said, "it is a disgrace to the civilization and Christianity of the Nineteenth Century." Of the canon law, which is responsible for woman's status in the church, Charles Kingsley said, "this will never be a good world for women until the last remnant of the canon law is swept from the face of the earth."

The Bible teaches that woman brought sin and death into the world, that she precipitated the fall of the race, that she was arraigned before the judgment seat of Heaven, tried, condemned and sentenced. Marriage for her was to be a condition of bondage, maternity a period of suffering and anguish, and in silence and subjection, she was to play the role of a dependent on man's bounty for all her material wants, and for all the information she might desire on the vital questions of the hour, she was commanded to ask her husband at home. Here is the Bible position of woman briefly summed up.

Those who have the divine insight to translate, transpose and transfigure this mournful object of pity into an exalted, dignified personage, worthy our worship as the mother of the race, are to be congratulated as having a share of the occult mystic power of the eastern Mahatmas.

[Source: E. C. Stanton, *The Woman's Bible,* Part I (New York: European Publishing Co., 1895), pp. 7 – 8, 9, 10.]

The plain English to the ordinary mind admits of no such liberal interpretation. The unvarnished texts speak for themselves. The canon law, church
ordinances and Scriptures, are homogeneous, and all reflect the same spirit
and sentiments.

These familiar texts are quoted by clergymen in their pulpits, by statesmen
in the halls of legislation, by lawyers in the courts, and are echoed by the
press of all civilized nations, and accepted by woman herself as "The Word
of God." So perverted is the religious element in her nature, that with faith
and works she is the chief support of the church and clergy; the very powers
that make her emancipation impossible. When, in the early part of the Nineteenth Century, women began to protest against their civil and political degradation, they were referred to the Bible for an answer. When they protested
against their unequal position in the church, they were referred to the Bible
for an answer. . . .

Listening to the varied opinions of women, I have long thought it would
be interesting and profitable to get them clearly stated in book form. To this
end six years ago I proposed to a committee of women to issue a Woman's
Bible, that we might have women's commentaries on women's position in the

Lucretia Mott (1793–1880), Quaker minister and human rights advocate
(National Portrait Gallery, Smithsonian Institution, Washington, D.C.)

Old and New Testaments. It was agreed on by several leading women in England and America and the work was begun, but from various causes it has been delayed, until now the idea is received with renewed enthusiasm, and a large committee has been formed, and we hope to complete the work within a year.

Those who have undertaken the labor are desirous to have some Hebrew and Greek scholars, versed in Biblical criticism, to gild our pages with their learning. Several distinguished women have been urged to do so, but they are afraid that their high reputation and scholarly attainments might be compromised by taking part in an enterprise that for a time may prove very unpopular. Hence we may not be able to get help from that class.

Others fear that they might compromise their evangelical faith by affiliating with those of more liberal views, who do not regard the Bible as the "Word of God," but like any other book, to be judged by its merits. If the Bible teaches the equality of Woman, why does the church refuse to ordain women to preach the gospel, to fill the offices of deacons and elders, and to administer the Sacraments, or to admit them as delegates to the Synods, General Assemblies and Conferences of the different denominations? They have never yet invited a woman to join one of their Revising Committees, nor tried to mitigate the sentence pronounced on her by changing one count in the indictment served on her in Paradise. . . .

Forty years ago it seemed as ridiculous to timid, time-serving and retrograde folk for women to demand an expurgated edition of the laws, as it now does to demand an expurgated edition of the Liturgies and the Scriptures. Come, come, my conservative friend, wipe the dew off your spectacles, and see that the world is moving. Whatever your views may be as to the importance of the proposed work, your political and social degradation are but an outgrowth of your status in the Bible. When you express your aversion, based on a blind feeling of reverence in which reason has no control, to the revision of the Scriptures, you do but echo Cowper, who, when asked to read Paine's "Rights of Man," exclaimed, "No man shall convince me that I am improperly governed while I *feel* the contrary."

5. THE WEST

Western Indians

Pierre Jean De Smet (1801–1873) and the Sioux

As the still young American nation occupied more and more land east of the Mississippi River, Indians ceased to be a political or military presence in that half of the continent. Farther west, however, Indian tribes continued to maintain some semblance of civil independence and of cultural integrity. Inevitably, therefore, conflicts arose between the Indian minority and the expanding United States government. Especially with the Sioux, "this large and hostile tribe," many violent confrontations took place. As potential peacemaker and as one of the few whites whom they trusted, the Belgian Jesuit Pierre Jean De Smet was repeatedly called upon to intercede. His effectiveness in that role earned this tribute from David S. Stanley, Major General of the United States Army. Writing from the Dakota Territory in 1864, Stanley addressed his letter to John Baptist Purcell, Archbishop of Cincinnati.

In the month of May of the current year the commission succeeded in convoking at Fort Laramie, on the Platte river, a certain number of chiefs belonging to the most formidable and most warlike tribes. The Hunkpapas, however, still refused to enter into any arrangement with the whites, and it is unnecessary to say that no treaty with the Sioux was possible, if this large and hostile tribe was unwilling to concur in it. In this condition of affairs, the Reverend Father De Smet, who has consecrated his life to the service of the true religion and of humanity, offered himself, despite his great age, to endeavor to penetrate to the hostile camps and to use his influence with the chiefs to induce them to appear before the commission at Fort Rice. As the letter of the members of the [Peace] commission will inform you, there is reason to believe that his mission has been wholly successful.

I could give you only an imperfect idea of the privations and dangers of this journey, unless you were acquainted with the great plains and the Indian

[Source: *Life, Letters, and Travels of Father De Smet* (New York: Arno Press, 1969 [1905]), IV, pp. 1584–86, 1587–88.]

character, which is naturally inclined to vengeance. Father De Smet, alone of the entire white race, could penetrate to these cruel savages and return safe and sound. One of the chiefs, in speaking to him while he was in the hostile camp, told him, "if it had been any other man than you, Black-robe, this day would have been his last."

The Reverend Father had with him, as interpreter, Mr. Galpin, who is married to an Indian woman of the Hunkpapa tribe. This lady is a good Catholic and an excellent person, a striking example of what the influence of religion and civilization can accomplish for the welfare of the Indian. On leaving Fort Rice, Father De Smet had to direct his course straight west. The enemy had pitched his camp a little above the mouth of the Yellowstone river, near Powder river. The distance to be traveled, going and coming, was 700 miles. The country is a barren desert. Nothing in the way of vegetation is to be seen save sagebrush, the *artemisia* of the plains. No buffalo are to be found except along the Yellowstone, where they are very numerous.

The Reverend Father is known among the Indians by the name of "Black-robe" and "Big Medicine Man." When he is among them he always wears the cassock and crucifix. He is the only man for whom I have ever seen Indians evince a real affection. They say, in their simple and open language, that he is the only white man who has not a forked tongue; that is, who never lies to them. The reception that they gave him in the hostile camp was enthusiastic and magnificent. They came twenty miles to meet him, and the principal chiefs, riding beside him, conducted him to the camp in great

Nez Perce Woman's Missionary Society (Presbyterian) in Idaho, 1891
(Presbyterian Historical Society)

triumph. This camp comprised more than 500 lodges, which, at the ratio of six persons to the lodge, gave a total of 3,000 Indians. During his visit, which lasted three days, the principal chiefs, Black Moon and Sitting Bull, who had been redoubtable adversaries of the whites for the last four years of the war, watched constantly over the safety of the missionary; they slept beside him at night, lest some Indian might seek to avenge upon his person the death of some kinsman killed by the whites. During the day time, multitudes of children flocked to his lodge, and the mothers brought him their new babies that he might lay his hands on them and bless them.

In the gathering of the Indians the head chiefs promised to put an end to the war. Sitting Bull declared that he had been the most mortal enemy of the whites, and had fought them by every means in his power; but now that the Black-robe had come to utter the words of peace, he renounced warfare and would never again lift his hand against the whites. The chiefs delegated several of their principal warriors, who, in the company with Father De Smet, arrived at Fort Rice on the 30th of June. . . .

But it is time to close this long letter. Whatever may be the result of the treaty which the commission has just concluded with the Sioux, we can never forget nor shall we ever cease to admire, the disinterested devotion of the Reverend Father De Smet, who, at the age of sixty-eight years, did not hesitate, in the midst of the heat of summer, to undertake a long and perilous journey, across the burning plains, destitute of trees and even of grass; having none but corrupted and unwholesome water, constantly exposed to scalping

Pierre Jean De Smet, S. J. (1801–73)
(Library of Congress)

by Indians, and this without seeking either honors or remuneration of any sort; but solely to arrest the shedding of blood and save, if it might be, some lives, and preserve some habitations to these savage children of the desert, to whose spiritual and temporal welfare he has consecrated a long life of labor and solicitude. The head chief of the Yanktonnais, Two Bears, said in his speech: "When we are settled down sowing grain, raising cattle and living in houses, we want Father De Smet to come and live with us, and to bring us other Black-robes to live among us also; we will listen to their words, and the Great Spirit will love us and bless us."

Sheldon Jackson (1834— 1909), John Brady (1848— 1918), and Alaska's natives

Like Father De Smet, the Presbyterian missionary Sheldon Jackson tirelessly crossed and recrossed the Great Plains on behalf of the Indian. As though those trackless miles were not enough, however, Jackson proceeded to the even more remote vastness of Alaska. Another appointee of the Presbyterian Board of Home Missions, John Brady, also journeyed to Alaska, arriving there a few years ahead of Jackson. And like Sheldon Jackson, Brady stayed on to become a public official, serving as Alaska's governor from 1897 to 1906. Because of the labors of men such as Brady and Jackson, the Presbyterians dominated all missionary efforts in Alaska in the final quarter of the nineteenth century. In the excerpt below, Brady writes to Jackson shortly after arriving in Sitka in 1878.

Sitka, Alaska, May, 1878

Rev. Sheldon Jackson, D.D.

Dear Doctor: We arrived here the night of April the 11th. Our first meeting occurred on Sunday in the castle.* The day was charming, for the clouds had vanished, the sun was warm, and the scenery was all that could be asked. Far out beyond the harbor, protected by innumerable green islets, lay the vast Pacific, in a sort of rolling calmness. At another point rose the funnel-topped Edgecumbe, crested with snow. Back of the town, and as far down the coast as the eye can reach, we have all the variety of grand mountain scenery. When these days come all nature seems to be still with solemnity, and one appears to be near the presence-chamber of the Almighty. Alaska scenery has a peculiar effect upon my emotions.

The castle has been stripped of everything, and is in a dilapidated condi-

[Source: Sheldon Jackson, *Alaska, and Missions on the North Pacific Coast* (New York: Dodd, Mead, & Co., 1880), pp. 204— 5, 206— 7, 208.]

*This "castle" was built for Russian nobles in the period when Sitka served as head-quarters for the Russian empire in North America; it still dominated the town at this time.

tion. As we began to sing some of the Moody* and Sankey hymns, the Indians began to steal in and squat themselves on the floor along the wall. Most of them had their faces painted black; some were black and red, and a few had the whole face black with the exception of the right eye, which was surrounded with a coat of red. All but a few of the chiefs were in their bare feet, and wrapped in blankets of various colors.

Sitka Jack is the chief who seems to have the most influence among them, and he is their orator. He and Annahootz, the war chief, were clad in some old suits of the naval officers who have been here. They think a great deal of the buttons, shoulder-pieces and the like. Several wore soldiers' caps. The rest were bareheaded.

The natives along the coast from Cape Fox to Mount St. Elias, speak the same tongue. Mr. Cohen, a Jew who keeps a store here, kindly volunteered to hunt up the old Russian interpreter. This man is about sixty years old. He is a half-breed. The Russian American Fur Company took him, when a boy, and educated him for a priest to the natives; but for some reason he was never ordained to that office. He has always been employed as interpreter. He speaks both languages well, and can read and write the Russian. Mr. George Kastrometinoff turned my English into Russian, and the interpreter turned that into good Indian. The people listened very attentively to all that I had to say. Jack, becoming impatient to speak, broke into a gesticulating speech, telling how bad they were heretofore, fighting and killing one another. Now they were glad that they were going to have a school and a church, and people to teach them. . . .

I explained to them why we wished them to go to school, and the advantages which they would have if they would learn English. I centred everything upon the Bible, and tried to impress upon their minds its value to all men, because it is God speaking to us when we read it. . . .

I hired some Indians, and we all worked hard to put the upper floor of the soldiers' barracks in trim for our school and church services. Mr. Whitford, who bought nearly everything which the soldiers left, sold us twenty benches, a stove, cord of wood, two brooms, and a box of chalk. The Russian priest loaned us a blackboard with half-inch cracks between the boards. These things, together with two tables, make up the list of our furniture. The school opened on Wednesday, April 17th, with fifty present, and after asking God's blessing upon this beginning of a work, which will surely prove to be one of the most interesting in the history of missions. . . .

If our churches had known the facts concerning this people, and the wonderful coast upon which they live, missionaries would have been sent out years ago. The money spent in teaching and Christianizing these people will not be thrown away. "Blessed are they which do hunger and thirst after righteousness: for they shall be filled." This promise will surely be fulfilled

*See below, pp. 286–88.

to these people, for they are hungering and thirsting for more light. It would be a great wrong for the Church to neglect these people longer.

I hope that before the leaves fall we shall be able to organize the Presbytery of Alaska. This will be a great thing for this Territory, which has been so wilfully misrepresented to the public. Such a body can be the source of information concerning the people and the country and its resources which will be trusted by the reading public.

"Western Orthodoxy": Russia in America

Russian Orthodoxy in Alaska

Unlike most denominations in America which moved from East to West, Russian Orthodoxy came first to the West: to Russian America, or Alaska. Under the leadership of Father John Veniaminov, Russian Orthodoxy was planted with sufficient nurture to endure to the present day. Thus, native Alaskans first heard the Christian message not as dispatched from Boston or Philadelphia, but Moscow. In 1840, Father Veniaminov published in his homeland a report on "The Condition of the Orthodox Church in Russian America." "Russian America" dipped all the way down to northern California where in 1812 at Fort Ross (or Colony Ross as the Russians had called it) a trading post had been established. Veniaminov himself had visited the area in 1836 and 1838 and now reports that the settlement is to be abandoned. But of the missionary work there as well as in Alaska, the Russian priest is confident: the light of the Gospels still shines.

Knowing how pleasant it is for a true Christian to hear about the spread of Christianity among people who are still unilluminated by the light of the Gospels, I have decided to set forth the information I collected on the dissemination and strengthening of Christ's Faith in one of the most remote territories of our Society, where through God's pleasure I had the opportunity of spending many years. . . .

Of the number of Mr. Baranov's* many enterprises regarding the spread of Russian possessions in America, he succeeded in founding a settlement and establishing himself in California (38 degrees north latitude). But the local settlement, called *Ross*, has now been ordered to give up everything, and as a result of this all Russians and Aleuts living there will be removed to Sitka.

[Source: *Journal of the Ministry of National Education*, 26, no. 5 (St. Petersburg: Imperatorskaia Nauk, 1840), pp. 17, 24, 41–44. I am grateful to two colleagues for their invaluable assistance: Dr. J. Arch Getty for securing a copy of the document, and Dr. Louis A. Pedrotti for providing the translation.]

*Mr. Baranov was the Russian administrator in Sitka.

Therefore, the Orthodox Church, which has existed for about 30 years in the local region, has to be removed from there to our colonies, along with the removal of the Russians. Its existence here, however, has also not been fruitless. In the course of this time it added to its membership more than 40 persons from the natives, who also, together with the Russians, can be removed to the colonies.

On my last visit to the village of Ross (in 1838) there were 216 Russians, Creoles and Aleuts and 39 baptized Indians, and in all the Russian Church there consisted of 255 members. . . .

We know for sure that Father Macarius finally baptized all the Aleuts of the Unalaska Department, and after this there remained not a single unbaptized person. Like all our Orthodox Preachers, Father Macarius not by sword and fire proposed to them the new Faith, which forbade them their usual enjoyments, i.e., polygamy and intemperance. But in spite of this the Aleuts accepted it gladly and quickly. As proof of this may serve the fact that Macarius spent only one year in the Unalaska Department, and, while traveling around the remote islands and moving from place to place, he had with himself neither sentry nor bodyguards, other than a single Russian male-servant. The same Aleuts whom he had baptized or whom he was to baptize transported him, fed him and protected him, all without the slightest reward or payment. There are several examples of this kind. One might object that the Aleuts quickly accepted the Faith out of fear of the Russians and that they received the advantage of payment of tribute in furs for accepting Baptism. And actually, such reasons are sufficiently capable of inducing savages who have submitted to the authority of powerful strangers to accept the new Faith, especially since through the advantage of tribute in furs, they rid themselves of every influence of the tax-collectors, who are more terrible for the savages than the tribute in furs itself, and since their former Faith no longer satisfied the inner needs of their souls. But these means can only force them to accept the new Faith, and they cannot serve to induce them to become zealous and true fulfillers of the laws of the new Faith. And the Aleuts have remained examples of piety even to this day. If one were to examine more closely the very reasons that might have induced the Aleuts to accept Christianity, then at first glance they will seem to be sham: for the Russians, in all their (formerly) perhaps too immoderate dealings with the Aleuts, never even thought about compelling them to do this. And the payment of tribute in furs was very negligible, and they paid it when and how they wished to; moreover, the advantage of payment of tribute in furs was made to them only for three years. And so the reason for the rapid and true conversion to Christianity of the Aleuts must be sought in their character and the disposition of their souls.

Although the Aleuts willingly and quickly accepted Christianity and prayed to God as they had been taught, still it must be said in truth that up to the time of the permanent residence among them of a Priest they believed in and prayed to *an unknown God*: because Father Macarius, as much because of the

Russian Orthodox cathedral, Sitka, Alaska, c. 1900
(Keystone-Mast Collection, University of California, Riverside)

shortness of time as for the lack of good interpreters, was unable to communicate to them Christian truths, except for general concepts about God, His omnipotence, His grace, etc. In the face of all this the Aleuts remained Christian, or at least right after baptism, they not only completely gave up shamanism and destroyed all the guises and masks that they had used at their festivals and shaman rites but also the songs themselves, which might somehow have reminded them of their former faith, so much so that after I arrived among them I tried (out of my personal curiosity), but I could find nothing like this. But even from among their very superstitions, to which only a man who possessed the living Evangelical faith is alien, very many were completely abandoned, and many lost their force.

But of all the good qualities of the Aleuts nothing so gladdened and delighted my heart as their zeal, or, more accurately, their thirst for hearing the word of God, so that sooner would the indefatigable Preacher himself become tired than they would weaken their heed and zeal for hearing the Word. Let us illustrate this by examples: upon my arrival in some settlement, one and all, completely abandoning all their business and occupations, no matter how important they might be for them, at my first summons would immediately gather to hear my sermons, and one and all with remarkable attentiveness would listen to them, without becoming distracted, without taking their eyes off me, and it may even be said that during this time the tenderest of mothers became as if insensitive to the crying of their children, whom they did not even bring with them, if the children could not understand.

Before there appeared among them anything written and printed in their language, I sometimes had occasion to see one of the Aleuts, not knowing at all a single word in Russian, sitting almost the whole day and reading the Slavic Psaltery of the *Chetyi-Miney* [the Reading Minaea, lives of saints]. And when they saw the books in their own language, i.e., the Catechism that I translated and printed in first edition, even the old men began to become literate in order to read on their own (and therefore there are more than a sixth among them that are able to read).

Possessing such zeal for hearing the Word of God, they are likewise zealous toward its Preacher (but their zeal does not manifest itself in material donations, because they cannot deliver furs to anyone except to the Company, which pays them a certain price). At least I can say this on my own. My visit and my arrival in the settlement would be a true holiday for the Aleuts, an Easter, because only at this time would they be able to hear the Word and partake of the Holy Sacraments. No matter where I arrived and at what time of day or night, if only the news went around that the *father* (Adak) had come, then right away one and all, whoever could manage to walk, would come out to meet me at the very dock (i.e., on the shore of the sea, where the kayaks usually pull up). One and all would greet me with real cordiality and obvious pleasure written on their faces. Often they would bring the sick to me to meet with me and receive my blessing.

Russian Orthodoxy in Western America

Shortly before the middle of the nineteenth century, the United States, by acquiring California and the Oregon Territory, stretched all the way to the Pacific Ocean. Then, in 1867, the fortunate purchase of Alaska enormously expanded the nation's western domain. In all of this new territory, from Sitka to San Francisco, the official church of Russia (a representative of Eastern or "Greek" Orthodoxy) had been the official church for employees

[Source: *Overland Monthly*, 2nd ser., 26, no. 155 (Nov., 1895), 478–79.]

of the Russian American Company as well as for a significant segment of the native population. (The Aleuts, mentioned below, are Eskimo natives of the Aleutian Island chain, and "Oonalashka" is more familiarly known as Unalaska, the easternmost island in that chain.) Russian Orthodoxy continued to be the major religious force in Alaska throughout the nineteenth century, including within its fold about one-sixth of the population.

In 1861 there were in the Russian American colonies seven churches and thirty-five chapels, several of them, including the cathedral, having been built at the cost of the Russian American Company, which also kept them in repair. The cost of maintenance was defrayed by voluntary contributions, and by the profits realized from the sale of candles. At about this time the total capital of the churches amounted to more than 255,000 rubles, and was kept by the treasurer of the Company, interest at five per cent being allowed upon it. The contributions to the Church were made partly in money and partly in furs, the Company allowing the Church from seven to fourteen rubles for the skin of a sea-otter. The Company expended on behalf of the Church nearly 40,000 rubles per annum, and built a residence for the Bishop at a cost of 30,000 rubles.

At the time of the transfer of Russian America to the United States, the Greek Church maintained a considerable establishment, consisting of a Bishop, three priests, two deacons, and numerous acolytes, at Sitka. Then the Bishop made Oonalashka his headquarters, and now San Francisco is his seat, from which place as a center he administers the whole of his vast diocese, apportioning the funds at his disposal according to the needs of the various parishes. . . .

When a community is too poor to maintain a priest or reader, the Bishop, with money supplied to him from Russia, defrays the cost of maintaining a chapel there. Where there is no resident priest, the higher rites of the church, such as baptism, marriage, etc., are performed by a regularly ordained clergyman from Oonalashka, Belkovsky, Sitka, or even from San Francisco, who makes the entire round of the religious establishments in Alaska about once in two years.

Outwardly the Aleuts are intensely pious, greeting you with a prayer, and bidding you farewell with a blessing. Before a meal they always ask the blessing of God; when they enter a neighbor's house, they cross themselves, and in most of their dwellings there is a picture of a patron saint, towards which the members of the household turn on rising in the morning and retiring at night. They will assemble for prayer whenever a priest's services can be obtained; and no matter how long the service may be, they give it their whole attention without manifesting any signs of weariness or impatience. They listen with the greatest interest to the reading of the Bible, and keep all fast-days and other religious observances strictly. In every village there is a church or chapel; the churches being erected and kept in repair,

Russian Orthodox deputation from the Soviet Union worshipping at Fort Ross, California, 1963
(National Council of Churches)

and the chapels supported, by the natives. No other religious denominations have succeeded among the Aleuts except the Greek Church, the ornate services and frequent festivals of which appeal strongly to their taste. They willingly contribute towards the maintenance of a Reader or Deacon, who performs the daily services, and teaches the young people to read, first in the Aleut dialect, and then in Russian.

The best specimen of a Greek church and one of the most interesting structures in the United States is the cathedral at Sitka, whose dome and graceful spirelet are the most striking objects of that town, the peculiar green hue of their roofs catching the tourist's eye ere the steamer has yet touched the wharf. The church is a cruciform wooden building, consisting of a nearly square hall, with a sanctuary to the east, and chapels on its north and south sides. It is well lighted by windows in and below the dome, which is supported by columns of the Byzantine order and has suspended from its center a heavy silver candelabrum. The church also contains eight fine silver candlesticks more than four feet in height. The belfry has a fine peal of bells, the original cost of which was 8,700 rubles in silver. On the altar used to rest a representation in miniature of the Holy Sepulcher wrought in silver and gold, and the communion cup was of gold set with diamonds. But many of the books and vestments which were formerly at Sitka are now in San Francisco, brought by Bishop Vladimir.

"Western" Orient: Asia in Hawaii

As Eastern Orthodoxy reached North American lands before the United States had stretched that far, so Oriental faiths reached the Hawaiian Islands well before the annexation of 1898. Confucian, Buddhist, and Shinto shrines sprang up as Chinese and Japanese emigrants settled there. The first organized missionary activity on the part of Buddhism in Hawaii came with the arrival of Japanese laborers in the late 1880s. Japanese language schools (largely Buddhist) were soon established, temples were built, and in 1900 a Young Men's Buddhist Association was founded. The strongest Buddhist sect in Japan, Jodo-Shinshu, is also the strongest in Hawaii. Under the auspices of the Honpa Hongwanji Mission, this Shin sect established itself as a vigorous missionary religion —teaching salvation by faith, faith in the Amita Buddha. The following excerpt, dealing with this "Buddha of Infinite Life," is taken from the holy scriptures of the Shinshu (literally, "true religion") sect, a group associated with the name of its twelfth-century founder, Shinran Shonin.

In Buddhism the Ways are many, just as there are ways difficult and easy in our earthly life. To travel by land on foot is difficult, while to go by water in a ship is easy. The way of a bodhisattva* can also be like this. Some there are who work hard and diligent, while others attain at once the Unretrogressive State by the expediency of the easy path of faith.

Now I will tell you in detail about the Buddha of Eternal Life. There were [many other Buddhas]. . . . All these Buddhas now live in the Pure Lands** of the ten quarters. They thus all pronounce His name and meditate upon the vow of Amita Buddha, which says: "Should any direct his thought toward me, pronounce my name, and take refuge in me, he will at once attain the *Right Established State,* arriving at the Highest Perfect Knowledge". Therefore we should always meditate on Him. I will now praise Him in a gatha.***

> O Wisdom's Light, Light Infinite!
> Thou standest like a mount of gold.
> Now, bow, my body, mouth, and mind!
> I go to Him. O my hands, fold!

[Source: *The Shinshu Seiten* (Honolulu: The Honpa Hongwanji Mission, 1955), pp. 109– 10.]

*One who practices the Way of Buddhism and seeks to save others.
**Worlds of highest happiness.
***Verse.

His light is gold'n with wondrous hues.
It shineth bright the worlds all o'er.
With each it varieth its hues.
I therefore kneel and Him adore.

As an end cometh to this life
And as awake we in His land,
There virtues countless garb us all.
Hence trust I my self in His hand.

As we trust fully in His power,
The power that doth no limit know,
We at once gain the *State Assured*.
So my thoughts e'er toward Him flow.

Be it life endeth in His land,
Be it pains us again enthrall,
Once born there never see we hell.
That is why I on my knees fall.

6. THE WORLD

World Parliament of Religions, 1893

Hinduism

The 1893 gathering in Chicago was remarkable in many ways: it demonstrated the wide currency of the English language throughout much of the world, it presented the better nature of Oriental religions to a largely Occidental audience, it offered some hope for tolerance in an arena more often filled with blood, and it brought together representatives of America's churches and synagogues who otherwise had no common meeting ground. A most impressive visitor, Swami Vivekananda, made his case for Hinduism with enough persuasive force that this Oriental religion, in the form of the Vedanta Society, remained a presence in America from that time forward.

Three religions stand now in the world which have come down to us from time pre-historic — Hinduism, Zoroastrianism, and Judaism.

They all have received tremendous shocks and all of them prove by their survival their internal strength; but while Judaism failed to absorb Christianity, and was driven out of its place of birth by its all-conquering daughter, and a handful of Parsees, are all that remains to tell the tale of his grand religion, sect after sect have arisen in India and seemed to shake the religion of the Vedas to its very foundation, but like the waters of the seashore in a tremendous earthquake, it receded only for a while, only to return in an all-absorbing flood, a thousand times more vigorous, and when the tumult of the rush was over, they have been all sucked in, absorbed and assimilated in the immense body of another faith.

From the high spiritual flights of Vedantic philosophy, of which the latest discoveries of science seem like the echoes, the agnosticism of the Buddhas, the atheism of the Jains, and the low ideas of idolatry with the multifarious mythology, each and all have a place in the Hindu's religion.

[Source: John H. Barrows, ed., *The World's Parliament of Religions* (Chicago: The Parliament Publishing Co., 1893), I, pp. 968–69, 972.]

Where then, the question arises, where is the common center to which all these widely diverging radii converge; where is the common basis upon which all these seemingly hopeless contradictions rest? And this is the question I shall attempt to answer.

The Hindus have received their religion through their revelation, the Vedas. They hold that the Vedas are without beginning and without end. It may sound ludicrous to this audience, how a book can be without beginning or end. But by the Vedas no books are meant. They mean the accumulated treasury of spiritual law discovered by different persons in different times. Just as the law of gravitation existed before its discovery, and would exist if all humanity forgot it, so with the laws that govern the spiritual world. The moral, ethical and spiritual relation between soul and souls and between individual spirits and the Father of all spirits were there before their discovery and would remain even if we forgot them. . . .

Thus it is that the Vedas proclaim not a dreadful combination of unforgiving laws, not an endless prison of cause and effect, but that at the head of all these laws, in and through every particle of matter and force, stands one through whose command the wind blows, the fire burns, the clouds rain, and death stalks upon the earth. And what is his nature?

He is everywhere the pure and formless one. The Almighty and the All-merciful. "Thou art our father, thou art our mother; thou art our beloved friend; thou art the source of all strength; give us strength. Thou art he that bearest the burdens of the universe: help me bear the little burden of this life." Thus sang the Rishis of the Veda; and how to worship him — through love. "He is to be worshiped as the one beloved," "dearer than everything in this and the next life."

This is the doctrine of love preached in the Vedas, and let us see how it is fully developed and preached by Krishna, whom the Hindus believe to have been God incarnate on earth.

He taught that a man ought to live in this world like a lotus leaf, which grows in water but is never moistened by water — so a man ought to live in this world — his heart to God and his hands to work. It is good to love God for hope of reward in this or the next world, but it is better to love God for love's sake, and the prayer goes: "Lord, I do not want wealth, nor children, nor learning. If it be thy will I will go to a hundred hells, but grant me this, that I may love thee without the hope of reward — unselfishly love for love's sake." One of the disciples of Krishna, the then Emperor of India, was driven from his throne by his enemies, and had to take shelter in a forest in the Himalayas with his queen, and there one day the queen was asking him how it was that he, the most virtuous of men, should suffer so much misery; and Yuohistera answered: "Behold, my queen, the Himalayas, how beautiful they are; I love them. They do not give me anything, but my nature is to love the grand, the beautiful, therefore I love them. Similarly, I love the Lord. He is the source of all beauty, of all sublimity. He is the only object to be loved;

my nature is to love him, and therefore I love. I do not pray for anything; I do not ask for anything. Let him place me wherever he likes. I must love him for love's sake. I cannot trade in love."

Buddhism

One of the world's great missionary religions, Buddhism was scarcely known in the West prior to the nineteenth century — as the excerpt below suggests. And, except for Hawaii, Buddhism was scarcely known in America until the twentieth century. Thus, H. Dharmapala, the representative to the World Parliament from Sri Lanka [Ceylon] (where the more historical or more traditional form of Buddhism prevails), felt obliged to instruct his Chicago audience in the "fundamentals" of the religion as proclaimed by Gautama Buddha in India in the sixth and fifth centuries before the birth of Christ.

History is repeating itself. Twenty-five centuries ago India witnessed an intellectual and religious revolution which culminated in the overthrow of monotheism, priestly selfishness, and the establishment of a synthetic religion, a system of life and thought which was appropriately called *Dhamma* — Philosophical Religion. All that was good was collected from every source and embodied therein, and all that was bad discarded. The grand personality who promulgated the Synthetic Religion is known as BUDDHA. For forty years he lived a life of absolute purity, and taught a system of life and thought, practical, simple, yet philosophical, which makes man — the active, intelligent, compassionate, and unselfish man — to realize the fruits of holiness in this life on this earth. The dream of the visionary, the hope of the theologian, was brought into objective reality. Speculation in the domain of false philosophy and theology ceased, and active altruism reigned supreme.

Five hundred and forty-three years before the birth of Christ, the great being was born in the Royal Lumbini Gardens in the City of Kapilavastu. His mother was Maya, the Queen of Raja Sudohodana of the Solar Race of India. The story of his conception and birth, and the details of his life up to the twenty-ninth year of his age, his great renunciation, his ascetic life, and his enlightenment under the great Bo tree at Buddha Jaya, in Middle India, are embodied in that incomparable epic, *The Light of Asia*, by Sir Edwin Arnold. I recommend that beautiful poem to all who appreciate a life of holiness and purity.

Six centuries before Jesus of Nazareth walked over the plains of Galilee preaching a life of holiness and purity, the Tathagata Buddha, the enlightened

[Source: John H. Barrows, ed., *The World's Parliament of Religions* (Chicago: The Parliament Publishing Co., 1893), I, pp. 863–65.]

Messiah of the World, with his retinue of Arhats, or holy men, traversed the whole peninsula of India with the message of peace and holiness to the sin-burdened world. Heart-stirring were the words he spoke to the first five disciples at the Deer Park, the hermitage of Saints at Benares.

His First Message. —"Open ye your ears, O Bhikshus, deliverance from death is found. I teach you, I preach the Law. If ye walk according to my teaching, ye shall be partakers in a short time of that for which sons of noble families leave their homes, and go to homelessness—the highest end of religious effort: ye shall even in this present life apprehend the truth itself and see it face to face." And then the exalted Buddha spoke thus: "There are two extremes, O Bhikshus, which the truth-seeker ought not to follow: the one a life of sensualism, which is low, ignoble, vulgar, unworthy and unprofitable; the other the pessimistic life of extreme asceticism, which is painful, unworthy and unprofitable. There is a Middle Path, discovered by the Tathagata—the Messiah—a path which opens the eyes and bestows understanding, which leads to peace of mind, to the higher wisdom, to full enlightenment, to eternal peace. This Middle Path, which the Tathagata has discovered, is the noble Eight-fold Path, viz.: Right Knowledge—the perception of the Law of Cause and Effect, Right Thinking, Right Speech, Right Action, Right Profession, Right Exertion, Right Mindfulness, Right Contemplation. This is the Middle Path which the Tathagata has discovered, and it is the path which opens the eyes, bestows understanding, which leads to peace of mind, to the higher wisdom, to perfect enlightenment, to eternal peace."

Continuing his discourse, he said: "Birth is attended with pain, old age is painful, disease is painful, death is painful, association with the unpleasant is painful, separation from the pleasant is painful, the non-satisfaction of one's desires is painful, in short, the coming into existence is painful. This is the Noble Truth of suffering.

"Verily it is that clinging to life which causes the renewal of existence, accompanied by several delights, seeking satisfaction now here, now there—that is to say, the craving for the gratification of the passions, or the craving for a continuity of individual existences, or the craving for annihilation. This is the Noble Truth of the origin of suffering. And the Noble Truth of the cessation of suffering consists in the destruction of passions, the destruction of all desires, the laying aside of, the getting rid of, the being free from, the harboring no longer of this thirst. And the Noble Truth which points the way is the Noble Eight-fold Path." This is the foundation of the Kingdom of Righteousness, and from that center at Benares, this message of peace and love was sent abroad to all humanity: "Go ye, O Bhikshus and wander forth for the gain of the many, in compassion for the world for the good, for the gain, for the welfare of gods and men. Proclaim, O Bhikshus, the doctrine glorious. Preach ye a life of holiness, perfect and pure. Go then through every country, convert those not converted. Go therefore, each one traveling alone filled with compassion. Go, rescue and receive. Proclaim that a blessed

Buddha has appeared in the world, and that he is preaching the Law of Holiness."

Zen Buddhist meditation
(Zen Center of Los Angeles)

Islam

*Like Buddhism and Christianity, Islam is a vigorously missionary religion.
And like Buddhism and Hinduism, Islam was virtually unknown — in its
own terms — to Americans at the end of the nineteenth century. Mohammed
Webb, the Moslem representative to the Parliament, therefore felt it necessary
to sweep away as much misinformation and prejudice as possible. Only then
could he proceed to portray with any hope of success the "Spirit of Islam."
His only regret, as he tells his audience, is that "the subject is so broad that
I can only touch upon it."*

Do you suppose that any active religionist who has studied only his own
system of religion, who knows nothing about any other system, can write
fairly of any other system? It is absolutely impossible. I have read every
history of Mohammed and Islam published in English, and I say to you,
there is not a single one of them, except the work of Ameer Ali, of Calcutta,
which reflects at all in any sense the spirit of Islam. We will take the work
of Washington Irving for example. Washington Irving evidently intended to
be fair and honest; it is apparent in every line that he meant to tell the truth,
but his information came through channels that were muddy, and while he
is appalled at what he considers the vicious character of the prophet, he is
completely surprised at times to find out what a pure and holy man he was.
Now, the first book I ever read in English upon Islam was *The Life of
Mohammed*, by Washington Irving, and the strongest feature of that work to
me was its uncertainty.

In one page he would say Mohammed was a very good, a very pure and
holy man, and it was a shame that he was not a Christian, but his impious
rejection of the Trinity shut him out from salvation and made him an im-
postor. These were not the exact words that Irving used, but they convey
practically his meaning. After saying these things, he goes on to say what a
sensuous, grasping, avaricious tyrant the prophet was, and he closed his work
by saying that the character of the prophet is so enigmatical that he cannot
fathom it. He is uncertain, finally, whether Mohammed was a good man or
a bad man.

Now, to understand the character of Mohammed and his teachings, we
must learn to read between the lines; we must learn to study human nature;
we must carefully analyze the condition of the Arabians at the time Mohammed lived; we must carefully analyze the existing social conditions; we
must understand what woman's position was in the social system; the various
conditions that had possession of the whole Arabian nation. They were not,
however, a nation at that time, but divided into predatory tribes, with all the
vices and weaknesses that man possesses, almost as bad as men in some of the

[Source: John H. Barrows, ed., *The World's Parliament of Religions* (Chicago: The
Parliament Publishing Co., 1893), II, 990–91, 991–92.]

slums of Chicago and New York. Mohammed came among his people intending to purify and elevate them, to make them a better people, and he did so. The history of Mohammedanism we have in English, as I have shown, is inaccurate, untruthful, and full of prejudice. . . .

Now, let us see what the word Islam means. It is the most expressive word in existence for a religion. It means simply and literally resignation to the will of God. It means aspiration to God. The Moslem system is designed to cultivate all that is purest and noblest and grandest in the human character. Some people say Islam is impossible in a high state of civilization. Now, that is the result of ignorance. Look at Spain in the eighth century, when it was the center of all the arts and sciences, when Christian Europe went to Moslem Spain to learn all that there was worth knowing — languages, arts, all the new discoveries were to be found in Moslem Spain and in Moslem Spain alone. There was no civilization in the world as high as that of Moslem Spain.

With this spirit of resignation to the will of God is inculcated the idea of individual responsibility, that every man is responsible not to this man or that man, or the other man, but responsible to God for every thought and act of his life. He must pay for every act that he commits; he is rewarded for every thought he thinks. There is no mediator, there is no priesthood, there is no ministry.

The Moslem brotherhood stands upon a perfect equality, recognizing only the fatherhood of God and the brotherhood of man. The Emir, who leads in prayer, preaches no sermon. He goes to the mosque every day at noon and reads two chapters from the holy Koran. He descends to the floor upon a perfect level with the hundreds, or thousands, of worshipers, and the prayer goes on, he simply leading it. The whole system is calculated to inculcate that idea of perfect brotherhood.

The Uses of Diversity

American Scene

In 1890 the Federal Census for the first time asked questions concerning religious membership in America. (Such questions continued to be asked through 1936.) A Methodist layman and editor, H. K. Carroll (1848 – 1931), was appointed "special commissioner" in charge of the division of churches for the Eleventh Census. Using his data (first published in 1893, revised in 1896), one notes that the religious picture in America is one of ever-multiplying colors. Older family groups such as Lutheran and

[Source: H. K. Carroll, *The Religious Forces of the United States.* . . , rev. ed. (New York: Christian Literature Co., 1896), p. 457 (with corrections).]

Baptist continue to divide; newer American-born groups such as Disciples of Christ and Latter-Day Saints continue to grow. While all religious statistics must be interpreted with caution, the following list of largest denominational families provides a rough sketch of the nation's religious profile near the end of the nineteenth century.

THE FOURTEEN LARGEST DENOMINATIONAL FAMILIES (1895)

	Communicants			*Communicants*
1. Catholic	8,014,911		8. Congregationalist	600,000
2. Methodist	5,452,654		9. Reformed	343,981
3. Baptist	4,068,539		10. United Brethren	262,950
4. Presbyterian	1,458,999		11. Latter-Day Saints	234,000
5. Lutheran	1,390,775		12. Evangelical	145,904
6. Disciples of Christ	923,663		13. Jewish	139,500
7. Episcopalian	626,290		14. Friends	114,711

American Dream

In 1865 Philip Schaff had sounded a note of hope for America and its religious future (see above, p. 11). America was not a spiritual chaos, Schaff had argued then. Now, a generation later (1893) and in the final weeks of his life, Schaff addressed the World Parliament on his —and much of the nation's —recurring dream: "the reunion of Christendom." While the religious diversity evident at the Parliament was fascinating, it was also — at another level —threatening. How could badly divided bickering churches make a meaningful impression upon a spiritually hungry world? A current religious paper, The Independent *(45, Apr. 13, 1893), filled its front page with talk of "Christian Union" and "A Plan for Denominational Consolidation" and "How to Prevent Waste and Reduce Rivalry." And Schaff, in this his last major address, thought the time of recrimination and harsh judgment was over: "Let us forget and forgive, remembering only each other's virtues and merits."*

We welcome to the reunion of Christendom all denominations which have followed the divine Master and have done his work. Let us forget and forgive their many sins and errors, and remember only their virtues and merits. The Greek Church is a glorious church; for in her language have come down to

[Source: John H. Barrows, ed., *The World's Parliament of Religions* (Chicago: The Parliament Publishing Co., 1893), II, pp. 1199– 1201.]

us the oracles of God, the Septuagint, the Gospels and Epistles; hers are the early confessors and martyrs, the Christian fathers, bishops, patriarchs and emperors; hers the immortal writings of Origen, Eusebius, Athanasius and Chrysostom; hers the Ecumenical Councils and the Nicene Creed, which can never die.

American Diversity: La Cienaga, New Mexico
El Rancho de Las Golondrinas (swallows) where since the 1650s a fall harvest festival has honored San Ysidro (St. Isidore the Farmer), whose statue is housed in the small chapel shown here. *(Photo by Peggy Gaustad)*

The Latin Church is a glorious church; she was the *Alma Mater* of the barbarians of Europe; she stimulated and patronized the Renaissance, the printing press and the discovery of a new world; she still stands, like an immovable rock, bearing witness to the fundamental truths and facts of our holy religion, and to the catholicity, unity, unbroken continuity, and independence of the church; and she is as zealous as ever in missionary enterprise and self-denying works of Christian charity.

We hail the Reformation which redeemed us from the yoke of spiritual despotism, and secured us religious liberty — the most precious of all liberties — and made the Bible in every language a book for all classes and conditions of men. The Evangelical Lutheran Church, the first-born daughter of the reformation, is a glorious church: for she set the word of God above the traditions of men, and bore witness to the comforting truth of justification by faith; she struck the keynote to thousands of sweet hymns in praise of the Redeemer; she is boldly and reverently investigating the problems of faith and philosophy, and is constantly making valuable additions to theological lore. The Evangelical Reformed Church is a glorious church: for she carried the reformation from the Alps and lakes of Switzerland "to the end of the West;" she is rich in learning and good works of faith; she keeps pace with all true progress; she grapples with the problems and evils of modern society; and she sends the Gospel to the ends of the earth. The Episcopal Church of England, the most churchly of the reformed family, is a glorious church: for she gave to the English-speaking world the best version of the Holy Scriptures and the best prayer-book; she preserved the order and dignity of the ministry and public worship; she nursed the knowledge and love of antiquity, and enriched the treasury of Christian literature. The Presbyterian Church of Scotland is a glorious church: for she turned a barren country into a garden, and raised a poor and semi-barbarous people to a level with the richest and most intelligent nations; she diffused the knowledge of the Bible and a love of the kirk in the huts of the peasant as well as the palaces of the nobleman; she has always stood up for church order and discipline, for the rights of the laity, and first and last for the crown-rights of King Jesus, which are above all earthly crowns, even that of the proudest monarch in whose dominion the sun never sets. The Congregational Church is a glorious church: for she has taught the principle, and proved the capacity, of congregational independence and self-government based upon a living faith in Christ, without diminishing the effect of voluntary cooperation in the Master's service, and has laid the foundation of New England, with its literary and theological institutions and high social culture. The Baptist Church is a glorious church: for she bore, and still bears, testimony to the primitive mode of baptism, to the purity of the congregation, to the separation of church and state, and the liberty of conscience. The Methodist Church is a glorious church: for she produced the greatest religious revival since the day of Pentecost; she preaches a free and full salvation to all; she is never afraid to fight the devil, and she is hopefully and cheerfully marching on, in both hemispheres, as an army of conquest. The Society of Friends, though one of the smallest tribes in Israel, is a glorious society: for it has borne witness to the inner light which "lighteth every man that cometh into the world"; it has proved the superiority of the Spirit over all forms; it has done noble service in promoting tolerance and liberty, in prison reform, the emancipation of slaves, and other works of Christian philanthropy. The Brotherhood of the Moravians, founded by Count Zinzendorf—a true nobleman of nature and of grace—is a glorious brotherhood: for it is the pioneer of heathen missions and of Christian union among Protestant Churches; it was like an oasis in the desert of German rationalism at home, while its missionaries went forth to the lowest savages in distant lands to bring them to Christ.

Nor should we forget the services of many who are accounted heretics. The Waldenses were witnesses of a pure and simple faith in times of superstition, and have outlived many bloody persecutions to be missionaries among the descendants of their persecutors. The Anabaptists and Socinians, who were so cruelly treated in the sixteenth century by Protestants and Romanists alike, were the first to raise their voice for religious liberty and the voluntary principle in religion. Unitarianism is a serious departure from the trinitarian faith of orthodox Christendom, but it was justified as a protest against tritheism, and against a stiff, narrow and uncharitable orthodoxy. It has brought into prominence the human perfection of Christ's character and illustrated the effect of his example in the noble lives and devotional writings of such men as Channing and Martineau. Universalism may be condemned as a doctrine; but it has a right to protest against a gross materialistic theory of hell with all its Dantesque horrors, and against the once widely spread popular belief that the overwhelming majority of the human race, including countless millions of innocent infants, will forever perish. And, coming down to the latest organization of Christian work, which does not claim to be a church, but which is a help to all churches—the Salvation Army: we hail it, in spite of its strange and abnormal methods, as the most effective revival agency since the days of Wesley and Whitefield; for it descends to the lowest depths of degradation and misery, and brings the light and comfort of the Gospel to the slums of our large cities.

There is room for all these and many other churches and societies in the Kingdom of God, whose height and depth and length and breadth, variety and beauty, surpass human comprehension.

Suggested Reading
(Chapter Seven)

General works treating the difficult period of readjustment after the Civil War include Kenneth Stampp, *The Era of Reconstruction* (1965), and R. W. Patrick,

The Reconstruction of the Nation (1967). On the "religion of the lost cause," see C. R. Wilson, *Baptized in Blood* (1980). For the profoundly affected black population, one may turn to Leon Litwack's prize-winning volume, *Been in the Storm So Long* (1979), especially Chapter Nine, "The Gospel and the Primer." Two other books concentrating on the blacks should be noted: W. E. B. DuBois, *Black Reconstruction* (1935), and Grady McWhiney, *Reconstruction and the Freedman* (1963). The religious dimension is examined broadly in H. Shelton Smith, *In His Image, But . . . Racism in Southern Religion, 1780–1910* (1972), and more narrowly in R. E. Morrow, *Northern Methodism and Reconstruction* (1956). William A. Clebsch has provided a thoughtful analysis of "Christian Interpretations of the Civil War" in *Church History*, 30 (June, 1961). For suggested readings on Horace Bushnell, see Vol. I, p. 526.

The early years of the American Missionary Association, so active after the war, are skillfully unfolded in Bertram Wyatt-Brown, *Lewis Tappan and the Evangelical War Against Slavery* (1969). In addition to the Daniel Payne volume cited in the chapter above, one should also know of his *Recollections of Seventy Years* (1888). The organizational development of black Baptists may be followed in O. D. Pelt and R. L. Smith, *The Story of the National Baptists* (1960), while the heavy missionary involvement is described in E. A. Freeman, *Epoch of Negro Baptists and the Foreign Mission Board* (1953); also see Lewis G. Jordan, *Negro Baptist History, U. S. A.* (1930). On Howard University and other black schools, consult R. O. W. Holmes, *The Evolution of the Negro College* (1934). But for an exhaustive guide to the literature of blacks and religion, one may turn with confidence to E. L. Williams and C. F. Brown, *The Howard University Bibliography of African and Afro-American Religious Studies* (1977).

Nineteenth-century immigration is so much the story of modern America that historians have given the subject considerable attention. General surveys include M. A. Jones, *American Immigration* (1960), and Oscar Handlin, *The Uprooted* (1950). Specifically with respect to Asian immigration, see S. C. Miller, *Unwelcome Immigrant* (1969), and M. R. Konvitz, *Alien and the Asiatic in American Law* (1946). For Roman Catholic immigration, the excellent study of Jay P. Dolan, *The Immigrant Church* (1975), makes the perfect starting point; then, for later years, these titles are relevant: R. J. Linkh, *American Catholicism and European Immigrants, 1900–1924* (1975); K. P. Dyrud et al., *The Other Catholics* (1978); and T. N. Brown, *Irish-American Nationalism* (1964). The Harvard edition of Josiah Strong's *Our Country* (1963), edited by Jergen Herbst, includes a valuable introduction to this influential figure. Esther L. Panitz discussed late nineteenth-century Jewish immigration in the *American Jewish Historical Quarterly* (1963, 1965), while the "denominational" development in Judaism may be followed in these works: David Philipson, *Reform Movement in Judaism* (1931); Moshe Davis, *Emergence of Conservative Judaism* (1963), as well as his long article, "Jewish Religious Life and Institutions in America," in Louis Finkelstein, ed., *The Jews: Their Religion and Culture* (1971).

Volume I of a first-rate documentary history, *Women & Religion in America* (edited by R. R. Ruether and R. S. Keller; 1981), focuses on the nineteenth century. Treating such subjects as revivalism, utopianism, immigrant Catholicism, Jewish women, social reform, and Protestant women, the book helpfully introduces each set of documents. Thirteen topical essays explore the same general subjects, but through the whole sweep of American history, in Janet W. James, ed., *Women in American Religion* (1980). Antoinette Brown Blackwell has received biographical treatment in Laura Kerr's *Lady in the Pulpit* (1951). Frances Willard's life has been often told, most recently in 1944: Mary Earhart, *Frances Willard: From Prayer to Politics*. But also see on Willard and the whole temperance movement in this period Ruth Bordin, *Women and Temperance: The Quest for Power and Liberty, 1873 – 1900* (1981). Alice Toomy's concern for Catholic women and social reform is placed in context in Aaron I. Abell, *American Catholicism and Social Action* (1963). Elizabeth Cady Stanton has provided her own reminiscences: *Eighty Years and More* (1898), while James H. Smylie has written specifically on "The Woman's Bible and the Spiritual Crisis," in *Soundings*, 59 (Fall, 1976). The influence of Lucretia Mott (1793 – 1880) upon these later women can be traced in Dana Greene, ed., *Lucretia Mott: Her Complete Speeches and Sermons* (1980).

In the American West, missionary work with the Indians can be followed in Henry W. Bowden, *American Indians and Christian Missions* (1981), along with the exclusively nineteenth-century story in Francis P. Prucha, *American Indian Policy in Crisis: Christian Reformers and the Indians, 1865 – 1900* (1976). Barbara S. Smith's *Russian Orthodoxy in Alaska* (1981) not only introduces the subject, but locates the relevant archives as well; Kenneth S. Latourette's classic *History of the Expansion of Christianity* provides the broad context in Volume IV (1941). On Sheldon Jackson's work in that vast northern acquisition, see J. A. Lazell, *Alaskan Apostle* (1960). With respect to Buddhism on the American scene, these recent studies should be noted: Emma McCloy Layman, *Buddhism in America* (1976); a 1977 book with the same title by Tetsuden Kashima; and Louise H. Hunter, *Buddhism in Hawaii* (1971). *Hawaii's Religions* (1970) in general are described by John F. Mulholland.

For the religious picture in America toward the end of the nineteenth century, good guidance is offered in Paul A. Carter, *The Spiritual Crisis of the Gilded Age* (1971); in William G. McLoughlin, *The Meaning of Henry Ward Beecher*; and in Larzar Ziff, *American 1890's: Life and Times of a Lost Generation* (1966). Henry W. Bowden's *Church History in the Age of Science* (1971) analyzes the cultural currents in connection with the writing of religious history generally and the contributions of Philip Schaff specifically.

EIGHT:
Religion and
Society Engaged

By the end of the nineteenth century, the nation's "manifest destiny" had been fulfilled—at least in a territorial sense. Covered wagons and handbarrows had pushed their way across mountains, plains, and more mountains to a sparkling Pacific Ocean. Alaska had been purchased (1867), Hawaii annexed (1898), and the Philippines and Puerto Rico ceded to the United States at the conclusion of the Spanish-American War. By the opening of the twentieth century, the nation stood at the threshold of world power. Seventy-six million Americans could proudly survey a land mass far larger than all of Western Europe combined, could confidently flex muscles of both military and industrial might.

LOVE AND JUSTICE

Great growth had its measure of pain, and world power inevitably brought world responsibility. Internal problems pressed hard upon a citizenry weaned on Jefferson's dream of an agricultural republic of virtuous villages and independent farmers. Suddenly—or so it seemed—the thinly populated frontier had given birth to large cities: Chicago's population by 1900 was second only to New York's, while the top ten urban areas included such "frontier" hamlets as St. Louis, Cleveland, San Francisco, and Cincinnati. These and other cities boasted large factories that had produced sharp divisions of class that had, in turn, produced alienation, violence, and despair. It was not merely another case of the popular complaint that "things aren't what they used to be." In fact, things, almost all things, *were* different. Even in agriculture, the independent Jeffersonian farmer would no longer recognize a land now marked by chilled-iron plows and huge steam tractors, by the miles of barbed wire and railroads, by the huge domains now made available for ranching or grazing. The world was being created anew, and not everyone was pleased by what he saw unfolding all around him.

98

The city, for example, seemed less a center of culture and promise than it did a blight upon a heretofore healthy pastoral scene. "The modern city a menace," proclaimed Josiah Strong: disease, dirt, death, crime, and corruption made it so. Within the city, growth in population and corporate wealth outran growth in morality and goodwill. Huge companies acted not as faithful stewards of their economic power but as exploiters interested only in profit—and more power. "Our Christianity has not much vigor," Washington Gladden observed, "if it cannot make men ashamed of such unneighborly conduct." Men and women crowded into tenement housing no longer constituted families, and "lodging houses where people sleep and eat" no longer constituted homes. What happens to the fabric of a nation, John Lancaster Spalding anxiously asked, when family life collapses, when traditional values can no longer be passed on from one generation to the next? Not only did the city make it difficult for its denizens to cling to their own values, the city itself often flaunted prevailing morality and courted corruption on a frighteningly large scale. Churches and synagogues found themselves obliged to do more than encourage and exhort their own flock: they must shield those flocks from wholesale manipulation and abuse by new and unregulated powers. In the streets and slums and labor marts of the modern city, what was one to do? Well, what would Jesus do?, asked a Topeka, Kansas, clergyman in a novel of unprecedented popularity. He along with many others endeavored to turn abstract issues of "social gospel" and "social justice" into religiously guided options of daily life.

Rapid industrial growth posed especially difficult problems, partly because that growth threatened permanently to divide American society into warring classes called "Capital" and "Labor." Could religion prevent such deep division, could it provide some bridges between those so divided, could it at the very least press the claims of "love and justice" upon both the factory owner who had nothing to guide him but gain and upon the laborer who had nothing to sell but his sweat? These questions were not merely theoretical, for in the 1880s and 1890s tensions turned into confrontations, boycotts into general strikes, and demonstrations into bloody riots. Haymarket (1886) and Pullman (1894) stood as symbols of a society under siege. "Man has killed or maimed his fellow-man," Boston's Frederic D. Huntington sadly observed in 1886, only "for lack of knowing who the fellow-man was and what he meant." The time had come to abandon bloodshed and embrace brotherhood—a principle which "includes justice and wisdom along with charity, as in fact love is the fulfilling of the law."

Baltimore's Cardinal Gibbons, finding the prejudices against organized labor to be strong in Protestant America but perhaps even stronger in Catholic Europe, pleaded before the Vatican in 1887 for "the right of the laboring classes to protect themselves." That meant, for Gibbons as for many others besides, the right of laborers to associate and to organize (as the predominantly Catholic Knights of Labor had done in 1869 and as the predominantly non-

Catholic American Federation of Labor had done in 1881). Rochester's Walter Rauschenbusch followed Gibbons's plea with a protest against the dehumanizing of the laborer, against the tendency to turn the worker into a "thing" whose only task was to "produce more things." "It is the function of religion," Rauschenbusch argued, "to teach the individual to value his soul more than his body, and his moral integrity more than his income." With similar sentiments, much of the nation's religious leadership put forth social creeds, called welfare conferences, wrote pastoral letters, and issued commission reports. In various ways, they contended that "machinery and industry exist for man and not man for them."

In the last years of the nineteenth century, and well into the twentieth, some theologians and prophets moved beyond the questions of urbanization and industrialization to probe the very character of society itself. Beyond curing the specific municipal ills and beyond ameliorating the bitterness between capital and labor, religion might hold promise for redeeming, for refashioning, the national fabric as a whole. Christianity is, in fact, a revolutionary religion, Rauschenbusch wrote. Equality was a cornerstone of the American creed, but exactly what did that imply in the economic sphere? "All men, inalienably, always, everywhere," announced New York pastor Edward McGlynn in 1887, "have a common right to all the general bounties of nature. . . ." The mission of the church, added Richard T. Ely, is to bring a "kingdom of righteousness" to the earth, "to redeem all our social relations." And whether by a new devotion to Christian socialism (George Herron) or by a new application of papal moralism (John A. Ryan), "the whole field of human action" falls under religion's sacred canopy.

WAR AND PEACE

Difficult and perplexing as these problems were, neither the nation nor the nation's churches escaped serious distraction from other quarters. Near the end of the nineteenth century, the Spanish-American War raised the issue of American destiny and American morality. Such clergymen as Henry Van Dyke wondered aloud: "Have we set the Cubans free or have we lost our faith in freedom?" The "Philippine Question" concerned not only the balance of Protestant and Catholic additions to the empire, but also the question of the "white man's burden" with respect to the "weaker races" (to use the language of another Protestant clergyman, Thomas Dixon, in his popular and prejudiced 1902 novel, *The Leopard's Spots*). It is one thing to export our creed of human rights, freedom, and opportunity, said Roman Catholic John Spalding; it is quite another to thrust this or any other creed "down unwilling throats at the point of a bayonet."

World War I, of course, involved the country even more profoundly, evoked moral passions even more lastingly. As the nation's first full plunge into world affairs, it proved for some a heady and exhilarating experience, for others a disillusioning and sobering one. Many of the clergy who proudly "presented arms" in 1917 and 1918 pursued world peace earnestly, even frantically, in the decades that followed. A Church Peace Union was formed in 1914, a Washington Disarmament Conference called in 1921, and a Briand-Kellogg Peace Pact signed in 1928 — all this with strong and determinative support from Protestants, Catholics, and Jews. In the 1930s Frank Buchman attracted international attention by proclaiming that the only re-armament which the world needed was a "moral re-armament."

EVANGELIZATION OF THE WORLD

Yet, the contest over who should rule the world was fought on other fronts, with other weapons. If from the perspective of world history, the nineteenth century was (as historian Kenneth Scott Latourette called it) the "great century" of missionary advance, in America's history the twentieth century revealed the most impressive development. Despite World War I, or in some ways because of it, Protestants envisioned an evangelization that would transcend and triumph over all boundaries political and ecclesiastical. The nation's Roman Catholics, themselves regarded for so long as the passive *object* of missions, now assumed the role of active *sponsors*. "The Church in America," as Chicago's Archbishop Quigley announced in 1908, "is at the beginning of a new era in its history . . . prepared to go forth conquering . . . in the cause of Christ." And even those groups sometimes ignored or mocked in the United States ventured to Asia, Africa, or Europe to win victories abroad often denied them at home. Enormous amounts of energy, money, and zeal flowed into "foreign missions" in the early decades of the twentieth century. Was it worth all that effort? Questions concerned not only "cost effectiveness," to use a modern cliché, but more fundamentally the appropriateness of intruding into other cultures, of enticing persons away from their own ancient religious heritages. In some quarters "evangelism" began to be justified as only part of a larger effort, as one noted the "social achievements of missionaries" or the humanitarian goal of improving the quality of life. On what grounds, ultimately, were missions all around the world to be defended or promoted?

NEW STRUCTURES

Meanwhile back home, many churches and synagogues found themselves ill-equipped to minister effectively to a burgeoning population of the vagrant, poor, and despairing. Other institutions, born of the times and specific in their purposes, arose to feed the hungry, rescue the fallen, and provide temporary shelter for those who knew no home. The Salvation Army, an import from England, quickly adapted to American soil, offering as an unshakeable article of faith that "the poor were to be treated with love, and not with suspicion or contempt." Young Men's and Young Women's Christian Associations found their initial reason for being in the great numbers of young people, uprooted from farm and family, thrust into an environment devoid of almost everything except temptation. In New York City alone, where so many of the impoverished immigrants arrived and stayed, the demands upon charity and goodwill multiplied beyond the capacity of traditional institutions to respond. In a society that had not yet heard of medicare, social security, unemployment compensation, or food stamps, it was up to private resources, and largely religious ones, to cope with urgent and expanding needs. About half of the population in New York City was Roman Catholic in 1868, and "it is notorious," a fellow Catholic wrote, that our own people "comprise a great deal more than half the pauper population. Are we doing a fair proportion of the work of taking care of our poor?" Though the answer at that time was "no," the creation of new societies and orders (for example, the Sisters of Charity and Mercy, the Society of St. Vincent de Paul) helped change that answer to "yes."

Confronted by social needs that threatened to overwhelm them, many of the nation's religious leaders began to explore ways of working together. What needed to be done was too much for any to do alone. In 1908, some thirty denominations representing a membership of about eighteen million agreed to create a "Federal Council of the Churches of Christ in America." In the midst of World War I, some sixty-eight dioceses together with many national Catholic organizations formed the National Catholic War Council, a "temporary" structure refashioned in 1919 into the enduring National Catholic Welfare Council. This Council (later "Conference"), like the Federal Council, saw its social responsibilities in the broadest terms, as indeed did the Synagogue Council of America, formed in 1926. All three groups embraced this unity not for its own sake, but for the sake of a society whose only hope seemed to lie in a collective ministry of concern. The question in those days was not so much how religious institutions might merge as it was how churches and synagogues might effectively address themselves to common tasks. Christian unity will come, Charles Macfarland observed, "not so much by abstract process as by concrete experience. . . ."

One memorable instance of concrete experience transpired in this period: the passage of the Eighteenth Amendment in 1917 and its ratification a little over a year later. This Prohibition Amendment (repealed in 1933) represented the climax of a long history of condemnation — in the name of religion — of alcoholic beverages. Tracts had been written, sermons preached, crusades launched, and organizations developed to fight the "liquor traffic" and to rescue or assist liquor's victims. The best known revivalist of this period, Billy Sunday, battled "booze" with every theatrical trick and oratorical flourish at his command. But as with the ecumenical entities noted above, an organized religious force was required to confront and defeat an organized enemy. That force, the Anti-Saloon League, emerged by 1895 as a national organization. Led by Methodists and heavily supported by Baptists, Presbyterians, and others (including significant leaders within Roman Catholicism), the League provided an early and effective example of "single-issue politics": one question and one question only was asked of every politician at every level — "Will you vote dry?" Enough life remained in the Evangelical Empire to launch, if not to sustain, the Noble Experiment of the 1920s.

Through urban growth, industrial strife, world war, and probes toward peace, a nation moved from adolescence to adulthood. Many of religion's resources were marshalled to attend to and assist in that time of maturation, to be engaged in the public problems of the day and not withdrawn, involved and not aloof. There were risks, of course, in being drawn into the messy world of politics and economics, of foreign policy and international relations. Those whose voices follow, however, saw even faith itself as a kind of risk.

1. LOVE AND JUSTICE

Redeeming the City

Josiah Strong (1847–1916)

A native of Illinois and a graduate of Western Reserve in Ohio, Congregationalist Josiah Strong left the Midwest in 1886 to assume leadership of the American Evangelical Alliance. He had come into national prominence the year before with the publication of his first book, Our Country *(see above, p. 46). More than twenty years after that early work, Strong concentrated his attention more narrowly upon the city and its promises and perils.*

The problems of government increase with the increase in population. As cities become more populous, relations whose harmony must be preserved increase in number and complexity. A mistake is further reaching; it has a longer leverage; and as efficient government grows more essential it becomes increasingly difficult. To administer the affairs of a village of 1,000 inhabitants is a simple matter, requiring only ordinary intelligence; the government of a city of 100,000 is much more complicated; while that of a city of 1,000,000 or of 5,000,000 demands expert knowledge, ability, and character of the very highest order.

Our political development in the United States has been along national and state lines rather than municipal. The principles of the state and national governments are well settled and clearly defined, but those of municipal organization and government are confused and uncertain. We are as yet in the experimental stage, and need the insight and genius of the highest statesmanship to solve the new and complex problems of the city, which are the problems of the new civilization. Among them are those created by the industrial revolution which has taken place during the nineteenth century — such as adjusting an aristocratic system of industry to a democratic system of government.

[Source: Josiah Strong, *The Challenge of the City* (New York: Young People's Missionary Movement of the United States and Canada, 1909 [1907]), pp. 44–46.]

If upon these and other municipal problems we should bring to bear the wisdom of the fathers who framed the constitution, not a scrap of it would be wasted. It does not seem to me extravagant to say that higher intellectual qualities are required to solve these problems than to administer successfully the office of the nation's chief executive.

Does any one imagine that we are meeting these high demands? As our cities grow larger are we calling to office larger-minded men, capable of grappling with these profound problems? As a general rule, the larger our cities the worse and more incompetent is their government. We are permitting the most ignorant classes to control them. Only as far as the intelligence of a city is brought to bear upon public affairs, does it practically exist.

Washington Gladden (1836– 1918)

Unlike Strong, Washington Gladden began in the East but spent the last third of his life in the Midwest: namely, Columbus, Ohio. As minister of the First Congregational Church there, Gladden established a reputation in "applied Christianity," to use the title of his first book (published in 1886, one year after Strong's first book). Before his career ended, Gladden had written some thirty-eight books and delivered countless sermons and speeches. His many efforts made him a powerful leader in what came to be called the "Social Gospel." Here, in his autobiographical reflections, he describes his own direct involvement in the municipal government of Columbus, together with the moral or theological lessons to be derived therefrom.

. . . No plan can be devised which will give us good city government, so long as the great majority of our citizens are unwilling to take any responsibility for the government of our cities. It is not the fashion, in America, for men of substance and standing to take any active part in the administration of city affairs. Many of them seem to think it bad form to interest themselves in such matters; more of them feel that they cannot afford the sacrifice of their business interests which such a service would require of them. So long as anything resembling this is true, we shall, of course, have bad government in our cities. We are shirking the primary obligations of our democracy, and we shall get our deserts.

Some sense of these obligations constrained me, in the spring of 1900, to take upon myself a task for which I could claim no special fitness, and which might have been far better performed by some of my neighbors. . . . Without taking counsel with any one, I announced . . . over my own signature, in all the daily papers, that if the people of the Seventh Ward desired to have

[Source: Washington Gladden, *Recollections* (Boston: Houghton Mifflin Co., 1909), pp. 336– 37, 345– 46, 351– 52.]

me serve them the next term in the city council, I would endeavor to do so. This was all that I found it necessary to do. My neighbors took up the matter and elected me; not only did I make no canvass for the place, I scarcely mentioned the matter in conversation to any one.

In April, 1900, I took up the duties of this office, and served in it for two years. . . .

I am not at all sorry that I had a chance to serve the city . . . and that I was able to contribute toward the formation of the public opinion which resulted in the adoption, to this extent, of the principle of municipal ownership. For I am as sure as I can be of anything that the municipal ownership and control of public-service industries is the right policy, —the only policy under which there is any hope of preventing corruption and oppression. As I have already tried to show, the public-service industries are necessarily monopolies; they are monopolies which furnish us with the necessaries of life; and monopolies of that nature must belong to the people. It would be just as rational to give a private corporation the right of levying taxes, as it is to give it the exclusive control of an industry by which the welfare of all the people is affected. No such control as this over the public welfare can rationally be delegated by the people to any private agency. If this does not belong to the rudiments of democracy, it would be hard to think of anything that does.

Congregationalist Washington Gladden (1836–1918) in his study in
Columbus, Ohio
(Library of Congress)

To say that the people cannot be trusted to manage such matters is simply to say that the people cannot govern themselves. Even, therefore, if it could be shown that municipal ownership resulted, for a time, in increasing the cost of the service, that would be no reason why it should not be chosen. If the people thus, by their carelessness and neglect, bring suffering upon themselves, that is just as it should be; they will know that they have brought it upon themselves, and will know how to avoid it. Nothing is safe in a democracy but the method which brings directly home to the people themselves the consequences of their own misdoing. That is the only way in which they can be educated. . . .

I took my leave of the Columbus city council in April, 1902, with a sincere regret. I had no consciousness of having achieved great things; but I had come into close contact with the vital needs of my city, and I had had some part in solving some of its most pressing problems. I laid the burden down because it was not possible for me to bear it any longer. The work of my church was heavy and exacting, it could not be delegated, I must resign either my charge or my office. The results of my experience were a deepened sense of the seriousness of the business of municipal government and a more vivid realization of the lack of knowledge and skill on the part of those who are handling it. This is the crying evil — incompetency. There were not many occasions on which I suspected the presence of corrupting influences in the council; I do not think that money was often used; but the lack of the adequate knowledge and experience for the tasks in hand was often painfully apparent. I believe that this is true of city governments as a rule, — perhaps of state governments also. They are generally in the hands of men who have no fitness to deal with them; and this is mainly because the men who have the necessary equipment for such work almost uniformly refuse to undertake it.

John Lancaster Spalding (1840–1916)

A Kentuckian, John Lancaster Spalding served as bishop of Peoria, Illinois, for over thirty years. But his most significant service to Roman Catholicism in America came in the form of his articulate leadership in many a political or social cause. He spoke well and wrote well, defending his Church when that was necessary but more often goading his Church in directions which he thought it needed to go. The Church, he argued, could not avoid the problems of modernity, not even the problems of the modern industrial and secular state. Here his concern is for the modern family and the unhappy effects which city life seem to have upon it.

[Source: J. L. Spalding, *The Religious Mission of the Irish People and Catholic Colonization* (New York: The Catholic Publication Society, 1880), pp. 87–89.]

Moral degradation accompanies great physical wretchedness; and the low moral state of manufacturing populations affords inexhaustible matter for discussion and consideration. The conditions of life are not favorable to purity, and the grossest sensuality prevails. Where people have no settled home and no local traditions the loss of good name is often looked upon as a mere trifle; and the sense of shame is stifled in the young who from their earliest years have lived in an atmosphere polluted by foul language. In the city old age and childhood are thrust out of sight, and the domestic morals and simple manners, which are above all price, cease to be handed down as sacred heirlooms.

One of the greatest evils which afflicts a manufacturing population is the breaking down of the family life. What family life is possible where there is no continuity, where there are no traditions that descend from father to son? The soul of the family is respect for ancestors, and where there are no traditions this respect dies out and the family becomes an accidental collection of individual existences. A home is essential to the family, and the traditional spirit is transmitted with the home from father to son. With the possession of a fireside the family receives a life of its own, and its permanency and complete identity can be assured only by the hereditary transmission of the home. To take from it the perpetuity of its fireside is to deprive it of a great part of its strength. A house that is occupied but not owned is not a home. A true family ought to be abiding; it ought to endure while the nation exists. It reposes upon love and religion; it is nurtured by traditions of honor and virtue; and the symbol of its continuity and permanence is the home owned and transmitted from generation to generation.

Now, the poor in our great cities and manufacturing towns have no homes. They live in tenements and hired rooms; or if the more fortunate own their cottages they can have little hope of leaving them to their children, who will go to swell the great floating population that is up for universal hire, and which, work failing, sinks lower to join the army of paupers and outcasts who form, to use the modern phrase, the dangerous classes of our great commercial and manufacturing centres. What hope can we have of men or women whose childhood has never been *consecrated* by home-life to pure thoughts and generous deeds, and who too often carry through the world the heavy burden of physical and moral disease planted in the infant heart, in which the whole human being was yet enfolded like the rose within the tender bud? Lodging-houses where people sleep and eat are not homes. Hired rooms which are changed from year to year, and often from month to month, are not homes. The operative's cottage, without yard or garden, without flowers or privacy, is not a home. The house which is empty day after day, because the mother and her little ones are chained to the great machine in the factory mill, is the grave of the family, not its home.

Samuel S. Mayerberg (1892-1964)

As the rabbi of Congregation B'nai Jehudah in Kansas City, Missouri, in the 1930s, Samuel Mayerberg did not have to search hard or far for municipal corruption. One of the nation's most notorious political machines, that of Thomas J. Pendergast, controlled every appointment to political office, every building dependent on city permits, and—according to Mayerberg—"People were actually told what physicians they might use, what lawyers might practice, what merchants might do business." Kansas City had a good charter; the only problem was that no politician paid any attention to it. Forming a Charter League and speaking to any who would listen, Rabbi Mayerberg led a risky crusade against crime, greed, and corruption. He fought many fights, but the hardest one of all, he writes, was "to convince thoroughly nice people, honorable men," that they too should join in the fight.

Pendergast is one of the most interesting personalities I have ever known. He is broken in spirit and in body now. He has suffered the tortures of the damned from his illness, while he has been incarcerated in a Federal prison. The humiliation, as his empire crumbled upon him, has been agonizing. You will not think me maudlin if I tell you sincerely that I feel a deep sympathy for this man who could have been great. He possessed the powers of mind and heart to have served the people nobly. He chose rather to play a ruthless political gamble, and he won huge stakes for a while; but he lost ultimately, as they all must.

He was a saloonkeeper in his early years and inherited his political kingdom from his uncle. Through the years, by his indomitable will and through those tricks known only to politicians, he became the dominant boss within his party. Then a quirk in American history helped him gain complete control of Kansas City. The Prohibition amendment had given rise to "bootlegging," and illicit sale of forbidden liquor had built the racketeering system in the United States, with unscrupulous leaders like Capone in Chicago and John Lazia in Kansas City. I shall have much more to say about this gangster; it will suffice to relate here that he was a minor politician, who controlled, by fear and crime, thousands of voters in the North End. At that time 7,500 votes could swing any election in Kansas City. Lazia threw his political strength to Pendergast; the reasons will become obvious. In the next election, Pendergast, with his machine and the machine's use of fraudulent ballots, elected the Mayor and all the members of the City Council.

As a result the City Manager gleefully announced that the people had given him a mandate to conduct city affairs on a strictly partisan basis. He dismissed every city employee affiliated with the opposition party. Any person

[Source: Samuel S. Mayerberg, *Chronicle of an American Crusader* (New York: Bloch Publishing Co., 1944), pp. 107–8, 109, 110–11, 118–20, 130–31.]

desiring city employment could obtain it only by receiving a card from his precinct captain and having it endorsed by the "big boss" at 1908 Main Street. The card was then taken personally to the City Manager, who unhesitatingly put the man to work. When the city hall was filled to overflowing, the job-seekers were listed in various departments and were assigned no work. . . .

Other political workers were abundantly enriched by contracts given to favorites. Competitive bidding was ignored or became a farce. Gasoline and oil for city purposes were bought entirely through one firm, which had been formed for that purpose. Half interest in it belonged to Pendergast. Top prices were invariably paid. Pendergast rapidly increased his growing fortune through a perfectly legitimate business. He owned the Red-D-Mix Concrete Co., which produced a good cement, mixed and ready for use. No building, public or private, could be erected unless the builder used Pendergast's product. If one dared to defy the "boss" in this respect, he was allowed to excavate the basement and lay cement foundations; then the city inspector would nonchalantly appear upon the scene, chip off a bit of the foundation and regretfully say, "This cement isn't up to specification. You will have to tear it out and use the right material." In desperation the recalcitrant builder would plead for permission to continue. When he had been sufficiently humbled, he would be told that one cement met all requirements; if he used it, no hindrance would disturb him. Thus through political control of the City Manager and his hirelings, Pendergast obtained a complete monopoly of that essential product. . . .

It is difficult for us to imagine how extensively political control gripped our city. It ranged far beyond the limits of municipal activities. It reached out in subtle ways to affect private lives. People were actually told what physicians they might use, what lawyers might practice, what merchants might do business. Personnel men in our factories came under the domination of the machine; and for years they would refuse to employ men unless they had passes from the boss. All city insurance and all surety bonds for contractors working for the city or county had to be negotiated through one insurance broker, a very good man, a close personal friend of the boss. Respectable business men soon found it a matter of safety to have Pendergast or [Henry J.] McElroy identified with them in their concerns; in some instances they received blocks of stock; in others they were paid for serving on executive boards. These are some of the methods by which the tyrants of the machine profited personally. Later, it was proved in Federal court that Pendergast had also been receiving hundreds of thousands of dollars over a period of years from the big and the little gamblers who, in turn, were given complete political protection. . . .

In brief, this is a sketch of the deplorable and menacing conditions which prevailed in my city on the afternoon of May 21, 1932, when I addressed the Government Study Club. I knew beyond the peradventure of a doubt that there was an alliance between our city administration of Kansas City and the underworld.

In that address I contrasted the successful administration of Cincinnati under Colonel Sherrill with that in our own city under McElroy. I showed paragraph by paragraph how the City Manager was violating the letter and spirit of the Charter. Without equivocation I called him the biggest law-breaker in the city. I properly laid the blame upon him for the disastrous conditions existing on the grounds that organized crime cannot exist without the protection of civic authorities. I charged him with manipulation and misuse of public funds. My indictment included all elements of malfeasance and misfeasance in office. I claimed that he had spoken falsely when he annually made a statement, under oath, that the city treasury contained a surplus. It was proved that this so-called surplus was, in reality, only a daily bank balance, which he maintained by juggling public funds. After an hour's exposure of the multifarious iniquities of the administration, I read the charter provisions for the legal punishment of those officials who violated the charter. I demanded that the City Council dismiss the City Manager. In its failure to do so, I challenged the County Prosecutor to exercise his authority under the state law to remove him from office.

The reception given that address amazed me. Those gentlewomen, leaders in the club life of the city, arose and shouted their approval. The same afternoon *The Kansas City Star,* one of America's great newspapers, which had from time to time attacked the machinations of the boss, carried in its home edition a two-column lead on the front page, containing a very full account. The next day editorial comment followed.

That night my telephone rang constantly. Some calls were from friends anxious about my welfare. Some were fearful that the gangsters would speedily bring retaliation upon me. Some exhorted me to drop the matter entirely; it was too dangerous. Other calls brought invitations from luncheon clubs and churches to repeat the address for them. The largest and most powerful organization in the city, the Chamber of Commerce, was silent. Its president was an intimate friend of Pendergast and McElroy. Its attorney was a member of the City Council. Of course I was pleased with the eager and enthusiastic interest displayed by the groups who wanted me to appear. It told me that the community wanted direction and stimulation in a mighty struggle, which they knew must ultimately come. During that week I delivered three or four addresses a day, and wherever I spoke the audiences overflowed the room. The boss only chuckled and McElroy insultingly denied my charges; the Council scoffed. Politicians try to laugh their opponents to shame. Being a preacher, I was an easy target for their jeering.

On May 24th I was cordially invited to lay the case before the Ministerial Alliance of Kansas City. One hundred and twenty-five ministers were present; at the conclusion of the address, after a few questions were asked, a ringing resolution endorsing my stand was passed unanimously. Aid was promised

and many ministers later held meetings in their churches for me. I regret,
however, that only four, Roy O. Chanel, Joseph Myers, Edmund Kulp and
G. Charles Gray, remained with me to the end. . . .

Sufficient evidence had now been compiled to lend significance to the recall
movement I would inaugurate through the Charter League. *The Kansas City
Star* magnificently carried full length items, as we continued to expose the
knavery of our city officials. Without the columns and the editorials of the
Star our best efforts would have been futile.

It is difficult for me to describe succinctly the reactions that came from
two groups, the racketeering politicians and my own congregational membership. The politicians were plainly worried and raised a great clamor over
the self-righteous closing of a few dives and houses of ill fame. To this petty
boasting I replied: "The elimination of a few filthy saloons and brothels will
not satisfy the people of Kansas City. Those are only pimples on the body
politic; only symptoms of the corruption within the body which has existed
for years." As long as our charter group spent its time in harassing the gang
merely by oratory at large and excited public gatherings, especially in churches,
the politicians were not disturbed. They could scoff and sneer and be smug
in the expressed thought, "The preachers will soon grow tired and the noise
will blow over." However, as soon as plans for the Charter League pro-
gressed, the politicians saw clearly that we were translating words and ideals
into action. The racketeers began to fight back in their vicious way. They
tapped my telephones in my Temple study and in the Charter League offices.
They ransacked the files in my study and stole the records from the League
office. They threatened me and they attempted to bribe me. Pendergast,
McElroy and Council members used their vast and powerful influence upon
my highly-respected members to exert all pressure upon me to force me out
of the fight. All through the years until the city was cleansed, one of my
hardest jobs was not fighting the underworld, but in using my energy and
time to convince thoroughly nice people, honorable men, that conscience and
the power of religious conviction drove me unswervingly into the fray and
that, as respectable citizens, they ought to be in it also.

In His Steps (1897)

A large percentage of the millions who read —and passed along —the popular novel, In His Steps: Or, What Would Jesus Do?, *hardly realized that they too were caught up in the social gospel. In another Kansas town (Topeka), a Congregationalist pastor, Charles M. Sheldon (1857–1946), offered in fictional form the pressing dilemmas that modernity imposed. Even small town America at the turn of the century faced questions of labor and capital, immigration and race, city and slum. In the excerpt below, the novelist presents his message in the form of a sermon by the fictional minister, Henry Maxwell, in the fictional town of Raymond.*

Sunday morning the great church was filled to its utmost. Henry Maxwell, coming into the pulpit from that all-night vigil, felt the pressure of a great curiosity on the part of the people. . . .

He had never been what would be called a great preacher. He had not the force or the quality that makes remarkable preachers. But ever since he had promised to do as Jesus would do, he had grown in a certain quality of persuasiveness that had all the essentials of true eloquence. This morning the people felt the complete sincerity and humility of a man who had gone deep into the heart of a great truth.

After telling briefly of some results in his own church in Raymond since the pledge was taken, he went on to ask the question he had been asking since the Settlement meeting. He had taken for his theme the story of the young man who came to Jesus, asking what he must do to obtain eternal life? Jesus had tested him: "Sell all that thou hast and give to the poor and thou shalt have treasure in heaven, and come, follow Me." But the young man was not willing to suffer to that extent. If following Jesus meant suffering in that way, he was not willing. He would like to follow Jesus, but not if he had to give so much.

"Is it true," continued Henry Maxwell, and his fine, thoughtful face glowed with a passion of appeal that stirred the people as they had seldom been stirred, "is it true that the church of to-day, the church that is called after Christ's own name, would refuse to follow Him at the expense of suffering, of physical loss, of temporary gain? The statement was made, at a large gathering in the Settlement last week by a leader of workingmen, that it was hopeless to look to the church for any reform or redemption of society. On what was that statement based? Plainly on the assumption that the church contained, for the most part, men and women who thought more of their own ease and luxury than of the sufferings and needs and sins of humanity. How far was that true? Are the Christians of America ready to have their discipleship tested? How about the men who possess large wealth? Are they

[Source: Charles M. Sheldon, *In His Steps* (Chicago: John C. Winston Co., 1957) [1897, and countless editions thereafter]), pp. 254–57, 259.]

ready to take that wealth and use it as Jesus would? How about the men and women of great talent? Are they ready to consecrate that talent to humanity as Jesus undoubtedly would do?

"Is it not true that the call has come in this age for a new exhibition of discipleship, Christian discipleship? You who live in this great, sinful city must know that better than I do. Is it possible you can go your ways careless or thoughtless of the awful condition of men and women and children who are dying, body and soul, for need of Christian help? Is it not a matter of concern to you personally that the saloon kills its thousands more surely than war? Is it not a matter of personal suffering in some form for you, that thousands of able-bodied, willing men tramp the streets of this city, and all cities, crying for work, and drifting into crime and suicide because they cannot find it? Can you say that this is none of your business? Let each man look after himself! Would it not be true, think you, that if every Christian in America did as Jesus would do, society itself, the business world, yes, the very political system under which our commercial and governmental activity is carried on, would be so changed that human suffering would be reduced to a minimum? . . .

"What would be the result, if in this city every church member should begin to do as Jesus would do? It is not easy to go into details of the result. But we all know that certain things would be impossible that are now practiced by church members. What would Jesus do in the matter of wealth? How would He spend it? What principle would regulate His use of money? Would He be likely to live in great luxury and spend ten times as much on personal adornment and entertainment as He spent to relieve the needs of suffering humanity? How would Jesus be governed in the making of money? Would He take rentals from saloon and other disreputable property, or even from tenement property that was so constructed that the inmates had no such thing as a home and no such possibility as privacy or cleanliness?

"What would Jesus do about the great army of unemployed and desperate who tramp the streets and curse the church, or are indifferent to it, lost in the bitter struggle for the bread that tastes bitter when it is earned, on account of the desperate conflict to get it. Would Jesus care nothing for them? Would He go His way in comparative ease and comfort? Would He say it was none of His business? Would He excuse Himself from all responsibility to remove the causes of such a condition?

"What would Jesus do in the center of a civilization that hurries so fast after money that the very girls employed in great business houses are not paid enough to keep soul and body together without fearful temptations, so great that scores of them fall and are swept over the great, boiling abyss; where the demands of trade sacrifice hundreds of lads in a business that ignores all Christian duties toward them in the way of education and moral training and personal affection? Would Jesus, if He were here today, as a part of our age and commercial industry, feel nothing, do nothing, say nothing, in the face of these facts, which every business man knows? . . .

"Are we ready to make and live a new discipleship? Are we ready to reconsider our definition of a Christian? What is it to be a Christian? It is to imitate Jesus. It is to do as He would do. It is to walk in His steps."

When Henry Maxwell finished his sermon, he paused and looked at the people with a look they never forgot, and at the moment did not understand. Crowded into that fashionable church that day were hundreds of men and women who had for years lived the easy, satisfied life of a nominal Christianity. A great silence fell over the congregation. Through the silence, there came to the consciousness of all the souls there present a knowledge, stranger to them now for years, of a Divine Power. Everyone expected the preacher to call for volunteers who would do as Jesus would do. But Maxwell had been led by the Spirit to deliver his message this time and wait for results to come.

Redeeming the Factory

Frederic Dan Huntington (1819– 1904)

While most of his life was spent in and around Boston, Huntington did serve for thirty-five years as the Episcopal bishop of central New York. Along with his steady theological development, he reflected with increasing clarity upon the obligations and opportunities which the new economic order presented to the Christian. In a denominational journal in 1886, Huntington argued that Christianity must be relevant to the awful clashes between capital and labor —otherwise, it is tragically irrelevant to the most pressing problems of the day. The "labor question" is a religious question, and the church must take its place on the side of the powerless and oppressed.

What is wanted most of all in these social distractions and industrial confusions is that any two parties in opposition should take pains to look at the issue from one another's point of view. This requires some breadth of mind as well as a benevolent regard to the common good; but neither of these, in a land of general education and Christian traditions, is entirely impracticable. It is only necessary to use the faculty of thinking patiently, to quiet anger, to dismiss jealousy, to go out of the petty sphere of immediate occupations, and to examine facts. Let intelligent workmen who work for wages make a candid study of the actual methods, aims, and condition of the masters of the

[Source: F. D. Huntington, "Some Points in the Labor Question," *The Church Review,* 48 (July, 1886), 7– 8, 14– 15.]

particular industry in which they are engaged. Let the employer, on the other hand, give an equally candid hearing to half a dozen of the best operatives in his employ, while both are in good temper and at leisure. Each party will learn a great deal, and very likely be somewhat surprised. If they could break bread together so much the better. Nothing is plainer to observers at a little distance than that the contestants in these recent struggles are fighting in the dark, striking with strokes that hit friends along with foes and are often suicidal, —a pathetic repetition of a thousand tragedies where man has killed or maimed his fellow-man for lack of knowing who the fellow-man was and what he meant. The "classes" are suffering for want of a mutual introduction and mutual interpretation, though they may live close together, serve the same establishment, and really depend upon each other's good will. . . .

More profound and far-reaching yet as a remedy for these barbarous quarrels in a half-civilised civilisation is the principle of human brotherhood. It includes justice and wisdom along with charity, as in fact love is the fulfilling of the law. It will be difficult to find any social disruption not curable by the rule so simply laid down in the New Testament as a precept, "Let no man seek his own but every man another's wealth;" i.e., allowing for the idiom, Let no man seek exclusively his own but every man also another's welfare. Call it Utopianism, call it altruism, call it impracticable theory; it is at any rate Christianity, and it yet remains for objectors to discover a spot where it has been fairly tried without certain effects following, viz., the allaying of discord and malice; the abatement of crime; the increase of thrift, contentment, economy, and every species of virtue; the growth of public prosperity and private liberty. That it would extinguish the natural distinctions in men's gifts and powers, in gain or external fortune, any more than in sex, size, or feature, is nowhere promised. But that it would reduce excessive inequalities, and prevent the evil of violent or unrighteous contrasts, and forestall or heal social shocks, no political economy or experience is in a position to deny. One of the most deplorable results of these rash uprisings of an oppressed or injured class, therefore, is that it discourages the hopes of a true philanthropy, disappoints the best friends that labor and poverty and ignorance have, and chills our sympathies where they ought to go out with the most generous and practical activity. There can be no question on which side in the debate the voice of Christ and the Gospel and the Church is most distinctly heard. Whoever reads the sharp instructions of S. James in the fifth chapter of his Epistle, or the repeated warnings of the other Apostles, or the most tender and yet piercing commands of the Great Master Workman Himself, will be obliged to confess that it is the rich and prosperous, not the less successful and less favored, who are most severely denounced, most in danger of ruin, and most in need of a changed and watchful mind, and of a quickened conscience.

James Cardinal Gibbons (1834– 1921)

Cardinal Gibbons stood as the laborer's stalwart friend in the testy confrontations between workers and owners in America. In the second half of the nineteenth century, the right of workers to organize was sharply questioned, and the dangers of allowing them to organize were repeatedly asserted. Labor unions were seen as radical, perhaps even communistic (the first volume of Marx's Das Kapital *was published in 1867); they were also seen as a threat to private property, and perhaps to Christianity as well. This was the common "wisdom" in many circles, both European and American. In Europe, the Roman Catholic Church had suffered severe reversals of fortune in revolutions that seemed simultaneously prolabor and anti-Church. Thus, it took great courage for Cardinal Gibbons in 1887 to take his case to Europe, indeed to the Vatican itself, there to defend labor's right to form unions. He did more: he defended the right of Catholic workers to form a Catholic union. And should the pope be so ill-advised as to condemn such a union, the Church in America would suffer severe and permanent damage.*

2. That there exist among us, as in all other countries of the world, grave and threatening social evils, public injustices which call for strong resistance and legal remedy, is a fact which no one dares to deny —a fact already acknowledged by the Congress and the President of the United States. Without entering into the sad details of these evils, whose full discussion is not necessary, I will only mention that monopolies, on the part of both individuals and of corporations, have everywhere called forth not only the complaints of our working classes, but also the opposition of our public men and legislators; that the efforts of monopolists, not always without success, to control legislation to their own profit, cause serious apprehensions among the disinterested friends of liberty; that the heartless avarice which, through greed of gain, pitilessly grinds not only the men, but even the women and children in various employments, make it clear to all who love humanity and justice that it is not only the right of the laboring classes to protect themselves, but the duty of the whole people to aid them in finding a remedy against the dangers with which both civilization and social order are menaced by avarice, oppression and corruption.

It would be vain to dispute either the existence of the evils, or the right of legitimate resistance, or the necessity of a remedy. At most a doubt might be raised about the legitimacy of the form of resistance, and of the remedy employed by the Knights of Labor. This, then, is the next point to be examined.

3. It can hardly be doubted that, for the attainment of any public end,

[Source: James Gibbons, *A Retrospect of Fifty Years* (Baltimore: John Murphy, 1916), I, pp. 194– 98.]

association — the organization of all interested — is the most efficacious means —
a means altogether natural and just. This is so evident, and besides so com-
formable to the genius of our country, of our essentially popular social conditions, that it is unnecessary to insist upon it. It is almost the only means to
invite public attention, to give force to the most legitimate resistance, to add
weight to the most just demands.

Now, there already exists an organization which presents innumerable
attractions and advantages, but with which our Catholic workingmen, filially
obedient to the Holy See, refuse to unite themselves; this is the Masonic
Order, which exists everywhere in our country, and which, as Mr. [Terence]
Powderly has expressly pointed out to us, unites employers and employed in
a brotherhood very advantageous to the latter, but which numbers in its ranks
hardly a single Catholic. Nobly renouncing advantages which the Church and
conscience forbid, our workingmen join associations in no way in conflict
with religion, seeking nothing but mutual protection and help, and the legitimate assertion of their rights. Must they here also find themselves threatened with condemnation, hindered from their only means of self-defense?

4. Let us now consider the objections made against this sort of organization.

(a) It is objected that in such organizations, Catholics are mixed with
Protestants, to the peril of their faith. Naturally, yes; they are mixed with
Protestants at their work; for, in a mixed people like ours the separation of
religious creeds in civil affairs is an impossibility. But to suppose that the
faith of our Catholics suffers thereby is not to know the Catholic working
men of America, who are not like the working men of so many European
countries — misguided children, estranged from their Mother, the Church,
and regarding her with suspicion and dread — but intelligent, well-instructed
and devoted Catholics, ready to give their blood, if necessary, as they continually give their hard-earned means, for her support and protection. And,
in fact, it is not here a question of Catholics mixed with Protestants, but
rather that Protestants are admitted to share in the advantages of an association,
many of whose members and officers are Catholics; and, in a country like
ours, their exclusion would be simply impossible.

(b) But it is asked, instead of such an organization, could there not be
confraternities, in which the working men would be united under the direction of the clergy and the influence of religion? I answer frankly that I do not
consider this either possible or necessary in our country. I sincerely admire
the efforts of this sort which are made in countries where the working people
are led astray by the enemies of religion, but, thanks be to God, that is not
our condition. We find that in our country the presence and direct influence
of the clergy would not be advisable where our citizens, without distinction
of religious belief, come together in regard to their industrial interests alone.
Short of that we have abundant means for making our working people faithful
Catholics, and simple good sense advises us not to go to extremes.

(c) Again, it is objected that, in such organizations, Catholics are exposed

James Cardinal Gibbons (1834–1921), Archbishop of Baltimore, Maryland
(Library of Congress)

to the evil influences of the most dangerous associates, even of atheists, communists and anarchists. That is true, but it is one of those trials of faith which our brave American Catholics are accustomed to meet almost daily, and which they know how to face with good sense and firmness. The press of our country tells us, and the president of the Knights has related to us, how these violent, aggressive elements have endeavored to control the association, or to inject poison into its principles; but they also inform us with what determination these machinators have been repulsed and beaten.

The presence among our citizens of those dangerous social elements, which have mostly come from certain countries of Europe, is assuredly for us an occasion of great regret and of vigilant precautions; it is a fact, however, which we have to accept, but which the close union between the Church and her children that exists in our country renders comparatively free from danger. In truth, the only thing from which we would fear serious danger would be a cooling of this relationship between the Church and her children, and I know nothing that would be more likely to occasion it than imprudent condemnations.

Walter Rauschenbusch (1861—1918)

If any Protestant deserves more credit than Washington Gladden for applying Christian principles to social problems, it is clearly Walter Rauschenbusch. Professor at Rochester Seminary in New York from 1897 until his death, this German Baptist gave the social gospel its firmest theological support (in A Theology for the Social Gospel, *1917) and its most untiring leadership. Nothing in the out-of-joint world around him escaped his attention or comment, but industry's monopolistic control and rapacious methods made that segment of modern life a first order of religion's business. To put it simply, "materialism and mammonism" must go.*

The spiritual force of Christianity should be turned against the materialism and mammonism of our industrial and social order.

If a man sacrifices his human dignity and self-respect to increase his income, or stunts his intellectual growth and his human affections to swell his bank account, he is to that extent serving mammon and denying God. Likewise if he uses up and injures the life of his fellow-men to make money for himself, he serves mammon and denies God. But our industrial order does both. It makes property the end, and man the means to produce it.

Man is treated as a *thing* to produce more things. Men are hired as hands and not as men. They are paid only enough to maintain their working capacity and not enough to develop their manhood. When their working force is exhausted, they are flung aside without consideration of their human needs. Jesus asked, "Is not a man more than a sheep?" Our industry says "No." It is careful of its live stock and machinery, and careless of its human working force. It keeps its electrical engines immaculate in burnished cleanliness and lets its human dynamos sicken in dirt. . . .

"Life is more than food and raiment." More, too, than the apparatus which makes food and raiment. What is all the machinery of our industrial organization worth if it does not make human life healthful and happy? But is it doing that? Men are first of all men, folks, members of our human family. To view them first of all as labor force is civilized barbarism. It is the attitude of the exploiter. Yet unconsciously we have all been taught to take that attitude and talk of men as if they were horse-powers or volts. Our commercialism has tainted our sense of fundamental human verities and values. We measure our national prosperity by pig-iron and steel instead of by the welfare of the people. . . .

It is the function of religion to teach the individual to value his soul more than his body, and his moral integrity more than his income. In the same way it is the function of religion to teach society to value human life more than property, and to value property only in so far as it forms the material

[Source: Walter Rauschenbusch, *Christianity and the Social Crisis* (New York: Harper & Row, 1964 [1907]), pp. 369—70, 370—71, 372.]

basis for the higher development of human life. When life and property are in apparent collision, life must take precedence. This is not only Christian but prudent. When commercialism in its headlong greed deteriorates the mass of human life, it defeats its own covetousness by killing the goose that lays the golden egg. Humanity is that goose — in more senses than one. It takes faith in the moral law to believe that this penny-wise craft is really suicidal folly, and to assert that wealth which uses up the people paves the way to beggary. Religious men have been cowed by the prevailing materialism and arrogant selfishness of our business world. They should have the courage of religious faith and assert that "man liveth not by bread alone," but by doing the will of God, and that the life of a nation "consisteth not in the abundance of things" which it produces, but in the way men live justly with one another and humbly with their God.

Pastoral Letter, 1920

The pontificate of Leo XIII (1878 – 1903) demonstrated an awareness of modern social and economic forces not evident in his immediate predecessor, Pius IX. Leo's 1891 encyclical Rerum Novarum, *cited for decades after by all those concerned with the industrial order, encouraged many Catholics to apply Christian tenets broadly to the marketplace. In 1920, the bishops and archbishops of the United States leaned heavily on* Rerum Novarum *as they signalled that the American hierarchy was committed —if somewhat timidly —to an even-handed justice for capital, for labor, and for the entire community.*

"It is the opinion of some," says Pope Leo XIII, "and the error is already very common, that the social question is merely an economic one, whereas in point of fact, it is first of all a moral and religious matter, and for that reason its settlement is to be sought mainly in the moral law and the pronouncements of religion" (Apostolic Letter, *Graves de communi*, January 18, 1901). These words are as pertinent and their teaching as necessary today as they were nineteen years ago. Their meaning, substantially, has been reaffirmed by Pope Benedict XV in his recent statement that "without justice and charity there will be no social progress." The fact that men are striving for what they consider to be their rights, puts their dispute on a moral basis; and wherever justice may lie, whichever of the opposing claims may have the better foundation, it is justice that all demand.

In the prosecution of their respective claims, the parties have, apparently, disregarded the fact that the people as a whole have a prior claim. The great

[Source: John A. Ryan and Joseph Husslein, eds., *The Church and Labor* (New York: Macmillan Co., 1920), pp. 243 – 45.]

number of unnecessary strikes which have occurred within the last few months, is evidence that justice has been widely violated as regards the rights and needs of the public. To assume that the only rights involved in an industrial dispute are those of capital and labor, is a radical error. It leads, practically, to the conclusion that at any time and for an indefinite period, even the most necessary products can be withheld from general use until the controversy is settled. In fact, while it lasts, millions of persons are compelled to suffer hardship for want of goods and sevices which they require for reasonable living. The first step, therefore, toward correcting the evil is to insist that the rights of the community shall prevail, and that no individual claim conflicting with those rights shall be valid. . . .

"The great mistake in regard to the matter now under consideration is to take up with the notion that class is naturally hostile to class, and that the wealthy and the workingmen are intended by nature to live in mutual conflict" (*Rerum Novarum*). On the contrary, as Pope Leo adds, "each needs the other: Capital cannot do without Labor, nor Labor without Capital. Religion is a powerful agency in drawing the rich and the bread-winner together, by reminding each class of its duties to the other and especially of the obligation of justice. Religion teaches the laboring man and the artisan to carry out honestly and fairly all equitable agreements freely arranged, to refrain from injuring person or property, from using violence and creating disorder. It teaches the owner and employer that the laborer is not their bondsman, that in every man they must respect his dignity and worth as a man and as a Christian; that labor is not a thing to be ashamed of, if we listen to right reason and to Christian philosophy, but is an honorable calling, enabling a man to sustain his life in a way upright and creditable; and that it is shameful and inhuman to treat men like chattels, as means for making money, or as machines for grinding out work." The moral value of man and the dignity of human labor are cardinal points in this whole question. Let them be the directive principles in industry, and they will go far toward preventing disputes. By treating the laborer first of all as a man, the employer will make him a better workingman; by respecting his own moral dignity as a man, the laborer will compel the respect of his employer and of the community.

Commission on Social Justice, 1928

Jewish immigrants of the late nineteenth century, like Catholic immigrants of a generation or so earlier, often found themselves at the lower rungs of the economic ladder. In such a vulnerable position, they needed no lessons but their own lives to learn of exploitation, uneven distribution of wealth, class conflict, and an economy seemingly divorced from morality. Speaking on behalf of these and other workers, and speaking most of all on behalf of social justice, the Central Conference of American Rabbis (the organizational arm of Reform Judaism; see above, pp. 54 – 56) drew upon the heritage of ancient Israel to make their case for "applied Judaism."

Deriving our inspiration for social justice from the great teachings of the prophets of Israel and the other great traditions of our faith, and applying these teachings concretely to the economic and social problems of today, we, the Central Conference of American Rabbis, make this declaration of social principles: . . .

II. The Distribution and Responsibilities of Wealth

We regard those tendencies to be unjust which would make the fundamental goal of industry the exploitation of the material world on the basis of unbridled competition and the unlimited and unrestricted accretion of goods in the hands of a few while millions are in want. Inequalities of wealth can find no moral justification in a society where poverty and want, due to exploitation, exist. We sympathize with measures designed to prevent private monopoly. We regard all ownership as a social trust implying the responsibility of administration for the good of all mankind. We maintain that the unrestrained and unlimited exercise of the right of private ownership without regard for social results is morally untenable.

III. Industrial Democracy

In the production and distribution of the material goods of life, the dictatorship of any class, capital or labor, employer or employee, is alike autocracy. The solution of the ills which beset our social order is to be found not in any class conscious struggle but in the triumph of sound humanitarian principles which regard mankind as ONE. No materialistic philosophy, whether it be exploitation for the many or the few, can solve these problems. It is in a finer industrial democracy that we place our hopes. The worker who invests

[Source: Albert Vorspan and Eugene Lipman, *Justice and Judaism: The Work of Social Action* (New York: Union of American Hebrew Congregations, fourth ed., 1959), pp. 255 – 57.]

his life's energies and stakes the welfare of his family in the industry in which he works has inviolable rights along with him who stakes his family's welfare in that industry through the investment of capital.

IV. The Sacredness of the Individual Personality

The mechanization of our present age and the building of large industries employing hundreds and thousands of workers have led to the custom of regarding labor as a mass in which the personality of the individual is lost or is not considered. We who uphold a religious philosophy of life cannot sanction this practice which tends more and more to treat labor as only an instrument. The dignity of the individual soul before God cannot be lost sight of before men. Machinery and industry exist for man and not man for them.

V. The Right of Organization

The same rights of organization which rest with employers rest also with those whom they employ. Modern life has permitted wealth to consolidate itself through organization into corporations. Workers have the same inalienable right to organize according to their own plan for their common good and to bargain collectively with their employers through such honorable means as they may choose.

VI. The Fundamental Rights of Society

Contribution to the common good and not the selfish service of a class is the touchstone of all moral endeavor. A moral order in industry must achieve the betterment of society as a whole above all else. Those who labor, those who lead labor, as well as those who employ labor or invest capital in industry must alike recognize this principle in the exercise of any and all functions, rights and privileges.

Redeeming the Land

Walter Rauschenbusch

One could reform the city or restrain the factory or, on a grander scale, one could think in terms of an entirely new social order. Broad principles, moral or religious principles, might in that event be followed wherever they led. When Rauschenbusch begins the excerpt below by announcing that "Christianity is in its nature revolutionary," it is obvious that to follow his broad principles could upset many. Indeed, the work from which this selection is taken, though written in the 1890s, was not published until 1968. For even if one were to agree that what happened two thousand years ago was a revolution, many would prefer to believe that one Christian revolution was quite enough.

Christianity is in its nature revolutionary. Its revolutionary character is apparent from the spiritual ancestry to which it traces its lineage. Jesus was the successor of the Old Testament prophets. The common people of his day discerned this kinship and whispered that he must be Elijah or Jeremiah or some other of the prophets. (Lk. 9, 19.) Although he denied his identification with them, he himself repeatedly drew the parallel between the work and lot of the prophets and his own. Like the prophets he was rejected in his own country. (Matt. 13, 57.) Like the prophets he was to suffer at the hands of the wicked husbandmen. (Lk. 20, 4–18.) Like all the prophets he must perish at Jerusalem. (Lk. 13, 34–35.) His forerunner he calls a prophet, a second Elijah (Mk. 9, 11–13; Lk. 7, 26); and to his followers he predicts that like the prophets they will be slandered and persecuted (Matt. 5, 10–12), and at last like the prophets meet their death. (Matt. 23, 29–36.)

Now what were these prophets, to whose spirit and purpose Jesus felt so close a kinship, and whose lot he expected to share?

The prophets were the revolutionists of their age. They were dreamers of Utopias. They pictured an ideal state of society in which the poor should be judged with equity and the cry of the oppressed should no longer be heard; a time in which men would beat their idle swords into ploughshares and their spears into pruning hooks, for then the nations would learn war no more. (Isa. 2, 4.) No slight amelioration contented them, nothing but a change so radical that they dared to represent it as a repealing of the ancient and hallowed covenant and the construction of a new one. A proposal to abolish the Constitution of the United States would not seem so revolutionary to us as this proposal must have seemed to the contemporaries of the prophets. . . .

[Source: Walter Rauschenbusch, *The Righteousness of the Kingdom* (New York: Abingdon Press, 1968), pp. 70–72.]

Nor were the prophets mere impractical dreamers and declaimers. They were men of action. They overthrew dynasties. They were popular agitators, tribunes of the people. They rebuked to their faces kings who had robbed the plain man of his wife or tricked him out of his ancestral holding.

These were the men whose successor Christ professed to be. This does not imply that he sanctioned all their actions or proposed to copy all their methods. But it does imply that of all the forces in the national history of Israel the prophets were the most worthy of his approval and most akin to his spirit.

The revolutionary character of Christ's work appears also from the elements in contemporary life to which he allied himself.

The Messianic hope, kindled and fanned by the prophets, was still glowing in the hearts of the people. When John the Baptist lifted up his voice by the Jordan, men were on the alert immediately, querying "whether haply he were the Messiah." (Lk. 3, 15.) The atmosphere of Palestine was surcharged with this electricity. When, in the synagogue at Nazareth, Jesus chose for his text that passage of Isaiah which tells of glad tidings to the poor, of release to the captives, of liberty to the bruised, and of the acceptable year of the Lord, "the eyes of all in the synagogue were fastened upon him." The passage was universally understood to refer to the Messianic era. They were breathlessly eager to hear what attitude he would assume. And what was his attitude? He told them the time had now come: "To-day hath this scripture been fulfilled in your ears." (Lk. 4, 16−21.)

Walter Rauschenbusch (1861–1918)
(Religious News Service)

It is plain that the people counted him as their own. They were waiting to see him raise the standard of revolt and were ready to follow him as their king. (John 6, 14– 15.) And in spite of all apparent disappointments to which he subjected them, they had their eye on him still. When at the very end he entered Jerusalem with something of public state, all their hopes revived and they hailed him as the Messiah coming to claim the Kingdom of his father David. . . .

The contents of the Messianic hope of course varied. With some it was dyed in blood, with others it was irradiated by heaven. But this element was common to all who entertained it: they were weary of present conditions; they were longing for a radically different state of affairs; and they were sure that it would come and were ready to help it on. In other words, the Messianic hope was a revolutionary hope.

Edward McGlynn (1837– 1900)

One way to redeem the land, it could be argued, was to ensure that all the people possessed it and derived equal benefit from it. In that way, the enormous disparity between rich and poor would even out. All land for which men compete would be taxed —rented to the highest bidder —and "a magnificent ever-increasing fund to supply the wants of increasing civilization" would in this way be created. Directly influenced by the economic reformer Henry George (1839–97), Father McGlynn of New York City campaigned so vigorously for land reform (and for Henry George) as to be censured for his socialist views. When he refused to report to Rome for a trial, he was excommunicated in 1887. Five years later, however, with some friends interceding on his behalf, he was restored to the Church and to his clerical position. Being returned to the bosom of the Church implied no change of mind or heart in McGlynn's social views. The earth was first of all the Lord's, but after that it belonged equally "to the human family, to the community, to the people, to all the children of God."

It is not for nothing that He who came to save the souls of men did so much to minister to the relief of their bodily wants. He healed their diseases; He raised their dead; He cured their distempers; He bore their sorrows; He felt compassion for the multitude, lest they should faint by the wayside. He miraculously supplemented the laws of nature and fed them with miraculous loaves and fishes in the wilderness. He did all this, because doing it He knew full well that the bodies of men as well as their souls are the creatures of God, and that their bodies and the capacities of those bodies are but signs and

[Source: Aaron I. Abell, ed., *American Catholic Thought on Social Questions* (New York and Indianapolis: Bobbs-Merrill Co., 1968), pp. 166– 67, 168– 69.]

symbols of the spiritual things within, even as all the vast universe of God is but His garment, is but the sign and symbol and the thin veil that surrounds Him, through the rifts in which we catch on every hand glimpses of God and of heaven. . . .

This is the word of an apostle of Christ: "This is true religion — to visit the widow and the fatherless in their affliction, and to keep one's self unspotted from the world." So it is necessarily a part of true religion to insist on what is essentially the equality of man, regardless of the comparatively trifling differences in their gifts and acquirements. This is the political economy, the teaching and reducing of which to practice are the core and essence of this new crusade. All men, inalienably, always, everywhere, have a common right to all the general bounties of nature; and this is in perfect and beautiful keeping with the other law of labor that every mouth has two hands with which to feed itself, a necessary corollary of which is that these hands must have equal direct or indirect access to the general bounties of nature out of which to make a living. That is the whole of the doctrine of this new crusade in a nutshell, that the land as well as the sunlight, and the air, and the waters, and the fishes, and the mines in the bowels of the earth, all these things that were made by the Creator through the beautiful processes of nature, belong equally to the human family, to the community, to the people, to all the children of God. . . .

How are we going to give back to the poor man what belongs to him? How shall we have that beautiful state of things in which naught shall be ill and all shall be well? Simply by confiscating rent and allowing people nominally to own, if you choose, the whole of Manhattan Island, if it will do them any good to nominally own it; but while they have the distinguished satisfaction of seeming to own it we are going to scoop the meat out of the shell and allow them to have the shell. And how are we going to do that? By simply taxing all this land and all kindred bounties of nature to the full amount of their rental value. If there isn't any rental value then there won't be any tax. If there is any rental value then it will be precisely what that value is. If the rental value goes up, up goes the tax. If the rental value comes down, down comes the tax. If the rental value ceases, then the tax ceases. Don't you see? It is as clear as the nose on your face.

Richard T. Ely (1854– 1943)

Presbyterian become Episcopalian, Ely found his career in academia as an economist first at Johns Hopkins, then at the University of Wisconsin, and finally at Northwestern. His whole career, however, was infused with a moral intensity and religious concern that would not allow the "science" of economics to be driven only by an impersonal market and a mindless laissez-faire. A righteous social order can be achieved, Ely argued; at least, it can be worked at. But to work at it, one must make decisions, and one must have a sense of direction. And Ely found in his religious understanding the motivating force as well as the purpose. "The mission of the Church is to redeem the world. . . ."

I take this as my thesis: Christianity is primarily concerned with this world, and it is the mission of Christianity to bring to pass here a kingdom of righteousness and to rescue from the evil one and redeem all our social relations.

I believe it a common impression that Christianity is concerned primarily with a future state of existence, and to this unfortunate error I trace an alliance between the Church and the powers of this world which found its exemplification in the alleged conversion of Constantine the Great. The mission of the Church is to redeem the world, and to make peace with it only on its unconditional surrender to Christ. Now, a surrender is one thing, an alliance is another. If peace and harmony prevailed between the powers of the world and the Church because the world had become thoroughly Christian, we would have reason for joy, and joy only. Men, angels, and archangels would then lift up their voices in songs of triumph, and the morning stars would join them all in a glorious chorus.

Unhappily, peace has never been made after this fashion. Whenever an agreement has been reached between the Church and the world, the terms have been a division of territory, as it were, and that on this wise: The world has transferred the domain of dogma and the future life to the Church, but has kept for itself the present life. . . .

But let it never be forgotten that Salvation means infinitely more than the proclamation of glittering generalities and the utterance of sweet sentimentalities. Salvation means righteousness, positive righteousness, in all the earth, and its establishment means hard warfare. The "Church militant" is something more than a phrase, or the Church itself is a mockery. Preaching the gospel means going to men with the words, "Thou, thou, art the man." It means a never-ceasing attack on every wrong institution, until the earth becomes a new earth, and all its cities, cities of God.

It is as truly a religious work to pass good laws, as it is to preach sermons;

[Source: Richard T. Ely, *Social Aspects of Christianity* (New York: Thomas Crowell and Co., 1899), pp. 53, 73– 77.]

as holy a work to lead a crusade against filth, vice, and disease in slums of
cities, and to seek the abolition of the disgraceful tenement-houses of American
cities, as it is to send missionaries to the heathen. Even to hoe potatoes and
plant corn ought to be regarded, and must be regarded by true Christians,
as religious acts; and all legislators, magistrates, and governors are as truly
ministers in God's Church as any bishop or archbishop.

I will now mention, without any attempt at scientific classification, some
of the subjects which, it seems to me, ought to be taken up by the Church, —
all of them religious subjects: —

1. Child labor — a growing evil — diminishing in other countries, increasing in this, removing children from home at a tender age, ruining them
morally, dwarfing them physically and mentally.

2. The labor of women under conditions which imperil the family. . . . .

3. Sunday labor, an increasing evil, against which workingmen throughout the length and breadth of the land are crying out bitterly. . . .

4. Playgrounds and other provision for healthful recreation in cities — an
antidote to the saloon and other forms of sin.

5. Removal of children from parents who have ceased to perform the
duties of parents. Homes, real homes, should be found for these.

6. Public corruption, — about which let us have something precise and
definite. The moral iniquity of city councilmen, who accept street-car passes,
of writers for the press, of legislators and judges, who accept railroad passes,
might profitably be treated under this head.

7. Saturday half-holidays, — a great moral reform which has been accomplished in England, where men work but fifty-four hours a week. . . .

8. A juster distribution of wealth. Under this head a refutation of those
ridiculous persons who would have us believe that wage-earners now receive
nine-tenths of all the wealth produced — quackery and jugglery which must
delight Satan.

9. A manly contest against the deadly optimism of the day which aims to
retard improvement and to blind men to actual dangers. After careful thought
and observation, I believe the social consequences of optimism even more
disastrous than those of pessimism, though both are bad enough. Less spread-
eagleism in America, more repentance for national sins, e.g. the most corrupt
city governments to be found in the civilized world.

George D. Herron (1862—1925)

*Like Ely, Herron also labored in academia, but with less conspicuous success.
At his post in Iowa (Grinnell College), Herron even held a chair in "applied
Christianity," the very title indicating the temper of much American religion
determined to engage the social problems. Herron joined the Socialist Party
around the turn of the century and embraced Christian socialism with such
unbending vigor that he alienated many and diminished his influence as
organizer and leader. As a writer, however, he effectively argued against
a "competitive individualism" that lacked both rational order and moral
purpose.*

There is but one deliverance from the rule of the people by property, and
that is the rule of property by the people. If much of what has been considered
private property is to be absorbed in great monopolistic ownership, as seems
to be the inevitable outcome of the competitive struggle, then the people
should become the monopolists. The whole movement of modern industrial
organization has been toward monopoly, and the movement will become more
rapid, comprehensive, and powerful as present social tendencies increase. The
only hope of the people for either industrial or political freedom lies in their
taking lawful possession of the machinery, forces, and production of great
industrial monopolies. Through the instrumentality of the state the people,
constituted in the realized democracy of a social commonwealth, could organize their social economy in justice, that would insure work and bread for
all who would work, as well as make common to all many social benefits now
exclusively enjoyed by the privileged few; and would find some service that
would give a measure of profit and hope to even the weakest. So organized,
the state as the social organ of the people would furnish and compel work
that would be redemptive to many now given over as worthless by our unsocial
order of selfish and competitive individualism. . . .

The Christian collectivist would take away no liberty from the individual
that would not be returned to him a hundred-fold in the liberty which association would give. The Christian economic state would take away the
liberty to oppress and defraud, but give the liberty to work, to have faith,
and to do justice. The real property rights of the people, the preservation of
the home, and the perpetuity of the family, have their future dependence in
the association of rights under the guardianship of the state as the social organ
of a Christian democracy. Such a mutual surrender and investiture of rights,
instead of endangering the individual and the family, would be the freedom
of the individual to develop the highest personal life, and the security of the
family from the invasion of want and oppression. The collection of rights and
interests in the state as the organ of the Christian economy of the people,

[Source: George D. Herron, *The Christian State: A Political Vision of Christ* (New
York: Thomas Y. Crowell and Co., 1895), pp. 102—3, 106—7.]

would remove life from the sphere of chance to that of a moral social certainty, and give opportunity for that free individual development which is the true end of civilization.

John A. Ryan (1869– 1945)

For herculean effort on behalf of Catholic social action, the long and busy career of Monsignor John Ryan is impossible to match. Preparing himself carefully in economic and ethical theory, Ryan published his first book in 1906: A Living Wage. *A decade later, a second book entitled* Distributive Justice *urged fundamental reforms in the national economic structure, while a third book (*Social Reconstruction, *1920) helped give leadership and voice to the wider Catholic community. When President Franklin D. Roosevelt proposed sweeping social reforms in the 1930s, Ryan —who for thirty years had been arguing along similar lines —joined in with enthusiasm. "The Right Reverend New Dealer," as one biographer called him, saw the Church as responsible for "the whole field of human action," all of which is under moral law. And "moral law is the business of the Church."*

The mission of the Church is to teach and help men to save their souls, to make men fit for the Kingdom of Heaven. They save their souls not alone by faith (the Protestant notion) but by works, by conduct. They must not only believe correctly but live righteously. Now righteous living takes in the whole field of human action. It is not confined to those of man's actions which affect merely himself and his God, nor to those which relate to his family. It concerns those actions which have an economic character, such as, theft, fraud, extortion, slothful performance of labor, oppression of the laborer, violence against property, etc., etc. In a word, all free human actions, whether without or within the field of industry, come under the control of the moral law; and the teaching and application of the moral law is the business of the Church. The notion that business actions and business relations are somehow an exempt territory, free from regulation by the moral law, neither morally good nor morally bad, is a heritage partly from the Protestant Reformation, partly from the false liberalism of the early English economists, and partly from the commercialized ethical code which came into practice owing to the failure of the state or any other powerful social authority to apply and enforce the principles of justice in the province of industry. It never has been and never can be the Catholic doctrine.

Having reasserted the Catholic doctrine and reasoning about the authority of the Church over industrial and business relations, let us see whether there

[Source: John A. Ryan, *Declining Liberty and Other Papers* (Freeport, New York: Books for Libraries Press, 1968 [1927]), pp. 181– 83.]

is anything at all that can be said for the viewpoint expressed by our Catholic business man. To answer this question it will be helpful to distinguish between *principles* and *methods*.

The Pope and the Bishops have authority to lay down the moral *principles* which govern industrial relations. Under this head come Pope Leo's declarations concerning the right of labor to a living wage, the duty of labor to perform a fair day's work, the duty of employers to refrain from overburdening their employees, the right of the State to intervene in the affairs of industry whenever there exist no other means of remedying great abuses, and a host of other specific pronouncements. All these are merely applications of general moral principles to particular economic conditions.

It is conceivable that the Pope and the Bishops should go further, and pronounce judgment upon particular *methods* by which the particular moral principles may be or might be made operative. For example, Pope Leo XIII passed judgment upon and against Socialism as a method of effectuating the principles of justice in the industrial order. Incidentally, one is tempted to observe that the condemnation of Socialism, whether by Pope, Bishop, or priest, is never complained of by Catholic business men as an improper interference in matters of business. However, let that pass. The Pope might declare that a minimum wage law would or would not be a morally lawful method of making effective the doctrine of a living wage. As a matter of fact, no Pope has made any declaration on this subject, but such a declaration

Monsignor John A. Ryan (1869–1945) of the National Catholic Welfare Council
(Library of Congress)

would be an entirely proper exercise of the Pope's authority to apply the general principles of morality to particular industrial situations.

There is a further step which may be taken by the authorities of the Church in their dealing with the moral problems of industry. It consists in not merely pronouncing certain concrete methods morally lawful, but in advocating the adoption of such methods. Pope Leo's great encyclical, "On the Condition of Labor," contains a good number of such specific recommendations; for example, concerning the multiplication of property owners by the State; the means by which the State should prevent strikes, the various kinds of associations that ought to be formed by workers and employers, etc., etc. In their "Program of Social Reconstruction" the Bishops who constituted the Administrative Committee of the National Catholic War Council, advocated many specific measures, such as the legal minimum wage, labor participation in management, and so on.

These, then, are the three principal ways in which the authorities of the Church may properly make pronouncements concerning business and industrial relations: by applying the general principles of morality to particular economic practices; by passing judgment upon the morality of particular methods or measures of reform; and by advocating and urging the adoption of certain methods and measures. All the great encyclicals and other declarations of the Popes on the social question exemplify all three of these forms of "intervention."

2. WAR AND PEACE

Empire or Republic: Spanish-American War

For Republic

The Spanish American War, begun in April of 1898 and effectively concluded three months later, was (said John Hay) a "splendid little war." Whether war is ever splendid, this one at least had the merit of brevity. Nonetheless, about five thousand American lives were lost, largely through disease. The war, moreover, gave the United States the aura of world power as it assumed territories and responsibilities in both the Caribbean (notably, Puerto Rico) and the Pacific (notably, the Philippines). Such swift expansionism raised serious questions of national purpose, and even of national morality. Was the nation to remain a republic (think of ancient Rome) or was it to become an empire (think of decadent Rome)? Here John Lancaster Spalding (introduced above, p. 107) argues vigorously in 1899 for America as republic.

EMPIRE OR REPUBLIC

The rise and fall of nations, as of individuals, are determined by moral causes. The convictions of mankind are but feebly influenced by reason. Our ethics, politics, and religion never spring from what is wholly rational. To a greater or less extent we are all victims of passion and prejudice, are swayed by interests that are selfish and motives that are unworthy. The wise and the good therefore subject themselves to ceaseless self-criticism; so does a noble and generous people. The habit of reflection, of considering seriously and dispassionately whatever grave situation is presented, is a mark of maturity; it is an evidence of self-control, of the prevalence of the true self which is constituted by obedience to what is right and good and becoming.

It is to the power of returning upon itself that a people owes its conservative

[Source: J. L. Spalding, *Opportunity and Other Essays and Addresses* (Freeport, New York: Books for Libraries, 1968 [1900]), pp. 213–15.]

strength, its ability, in the midst of whatever events, to hold steadfastly to the principles by which its life is nourished. We are at present in the midst of a crisis, in which lack of thought and deliberation may lead us far from the ideals which as Americans we have most cherished, and expose us to evils of which we scarcely dream. We stand at the parting of the ways. It is not yet too late to turn from the way which leads, through war and conquest, to imperialism, to standing armies, to alliances with foreign powers and finally to the disruption of the Union itself. It is not too late, because it is still possible, probable even, that the American people will reconsider the whole question of the complications in which our victories over Spain have involved us. . . .

. . . We will not believe that the gaining of a few naval battles over a weak and unprepared foe has power to throw us into such enthusiasm or such madness as to turn us permanently from the principles and policies to which we owe our national existence, our life and liberty; or that Destiny, the divinity of fatalists and materialists, can weaken our faith in the God of justice, righteousness and love, who scorns and thrusts far away those who, having the giant's strength, use it to oppress or destroy the weak and ignorant.

We have never looked upon ourselves as predestined to subdue the earth, to compel other nations, with sword and shell, to accept our rule; we have always believed in human rights, in freedom and opportunity, in education and religion, and we have invited all men to come to enjoy these blessings in this half a world which God has given us; but we have never dreamed that they were articles to be exported and thrust down unwilling throats at the point of the bayonet.

For Empire

On the other hand, Lyman Abbott, influential editor of the Christian Union *and later* Outlook *(also introduced above, p. 12), warmly endorsed the "New National Policy." Writing in the* Outlook *in June of 1898, Abbott argued against the traditional policy of isolation and for one of "fraternization": "We believe that the United States must henceforth take its place with the other nations of the world and share with them the responsibility for the world's development." In his* Reminiscences *written long after this brief war, Abbott makes it clear that his opinion had not changed. That war "was a duty and peace would have been a dishonor": the history of the world records no nobler conflict.*

[Source: Lyman Abbott, *Reminiscences* (Boston: Houghton Mifflin Co., 1915), pp. 436–38.]

Three years later, in 1898, another war cloud appeared upon the horizon. For over a century America had seen with increasing disquiet the sufferings of the Cuban people under an intolerable Spanish despotism. Living themselves on the threshold of the twentieth century, they saw their neighbors oppressed under a government which retained the spirit and methods of the seventeenth century. The Spanish-American War has been often attributed to the destruction of the Maine, an American man-of-war, while on a peaceful visit to Havana. In fact, that destruction took place February 15, and war was not declared until April 24, more than two months later. The real occasion of the war was the report of Senator Proctor, of Vermont, on the conditions which he found existing in the island; it aroused in the country a storm of humanitarian indignation which proved irresistible. This time I believed that war was a duty and peace would have been a dishonor. . . .

And I have never ceased from that time to this to commend the action of our Government and our people in the Spanish-American War. I repeat here what I said at one session of the Lake Mohonk Conference: —

> I believe the proudest chapter in our history is that written by the statesmanship of McKinley, the guns of Dewey, and the administration of Taft. There is nothing to repent, nothing to retract; our duty is to go on and complete the work already so well begun. I do not defend or apologize for what we have done in the Philippines. I glory in it. We must give them a government, not for our benefit, but primarily for the benefit of the Filipinos.

I do not think that the history of the world records a nobler war. We captured Cuba and gave it to the Cubans, extending over them a protectorate which guarantees them from foreign aggression and domestic anarchy. We captured Porto Rico and retained it under the protection of our flag, giving back to the Porto Ricans for expenditure in their own island all the taxes collected from them. We captured the Philippines, sent an army of teachers to follow the army of occupation, and have pledged them our word to give them self-government as fast as they are prepared for it. We asked no war indemnity from Spain; on the contrary, we paid her for all the public works which she had constructed in the conquered Philippines. We fought the American Revolution to free ourselves, the Civil War to free a people whom we had helped to enslave, the Spanish-American War to free a people to whom we owed no other duty than that of a big nation to an oppressed neighbor.

"The Philippine Question"

Quite apart from the broad question of national policy was the narrower question of what the Literary Digest *called "The Religious Problem in the Philippines" (Feb. 10, 1900). That problem, bluntly put, was that the islands were Catholic and many Americans still thought of their country as Protestant. What was to be done about a "Catholic" possession being taken over by a "Protestant" nation? Should Protestant missionaries be sent to the Philippines? And if so, which Protestants? Or is it even appropriate to send missionaries to an already Christianized people? Two opposing points of view are presented below: (1) Archbishop John Ireland of Minneapolis makes the case for a "hands off" policy by America's Protestants; (2) Arthur J. Brown, Secretary of the Presbyterian Board of Foreign Missions, argues that the overthrow of the old civil and educational regime suggests that there should similarly be a change in the old religious regime.*

1.

You ask me what I think of cooperation between Catholics and Protestants towards religious reconstruction in our new American possessions. I will speak frankly, and give expression to my convictions as a Catholic and as an American. As a Catholic, I cannot approve of any efforts of Protestants to affect the religious duties of the inhabitants of the islands. Catholics are there in complete control; they have a thorough church organization; the inhabitants are Catholics; some of them may not live up to the teachings of their faith, but they have no idea of abandoning that faith for another. It represents all they have ever known of a higher life. Protestantism will never take the place in their hearts of that faith. To take from them their faith is to throw them into absolute religious indifference. If the inhabitants of those islands were all Protestants, would Protestants ask Catholics to unite with them in the work of Protestant disintegration? Now, as an American I will no less object to efforts to implant Protestantism in those islands. Why? Because I want to see American rule made possible in those islands. Do your Protestant missionaries realize that they are doing the greatest harm to America by making her flag unpopular? Spain has already begun to say to her former subjects: "You have objected to our rule. Very well, what have you in place? You have given up to strangers not only your civil government; they are also taking away your religion." A great mistake was made, in my opinion, by one of our military officers in Porto Rico; he put himself forth as an official leader in establishing the Protestant Church. Now, as an American ruler he had no

[Sources: (1) John Ireland interview, *Outlook*, 62, no. 17 (Aug. 26, 1899), 933–34. (2) A. J. Brown, *The New Era in the Philippines* (New York: Fleming H. Revell Co., 1903), pp. 152–54.]

right, and he was not asked, to prevent the establishment there of a Protestant church; nor was he asked to take part in Catholic worship; but the fact that he was foremost in founding a Protestant church was enough to make the simple Porto Ricans take the new chapel to represent the established church of the United States. It was enough to make them think that America was officially opposed to the Catholic religion. If I were America's enemy to-day, I would say to American Protestants, Hurry on your missionaries to Cuba, Porto Rico, and the Philippines, and have them tell the inhabitants of those islands that their historic faith is wrong and that they ought to become Protestants. This would be the speediest and most effective way to make the inhabitants of those islands discontented and opposed to America.

Cardinal Gibbons (center) with President William McKinley (left) and
Admiral George Dewey, 1899
(Keystone-Mast Collection, University of California, Riverside)

2.

Archbishop Ireland and his sympathizers in the United States, the Roman Catholic bishops and priests in the Philippines, and a considerable number of Americans both at home and abroad, never tire of reminding us that the Filipinos had a form of the Christian religion before the Americans came, and that it is neither expedient nor just to attempt to change it.

I reply that the Filipinos had a form of civil government before the Americans came and also, a form of public education, forms which were as adequate to their needs as was their form of religion. Indeed, all competent testimony is to the effect that the dissatisfaction of the people with their civil governors and their schools was less than their dissatisfaction with their priests. Nevertheless, Americans have deemed it their duty to forcibly over-throw the entire governmental and educational systems, and to replace them with our own radically different ones. The wishes of the people were not considered. The Taft Commission reports: "Many witnesses were examined as to the form of government best adapted to these Islands and satisfactory to the people. All the evidence taken, no matter what the bias of the witness, showed that the masses of the people are ignorant, credulous and childlike, and that under any government the electoral franchise must be much limited, because the large majority will not for a long time be capable of intelligently exercising it."

So Americans have proceeded on the supposition that as the people did not know what was good for them, that good must be imposed by the strong arm of military power and civil law, confident that in time the Filipinos will see that it is for their welfare. Any argument that could be framed for the inadequacy of the former civil and educational systems would, *mutatis mutandis,* apply with equal force to the Roman Catholic *régime.* Indeed, if disinterested writers are to be trusted, the rottenness of the ecclesiastical administration was the source of nearly all the evils from which the Filipinos were suffering.

Protestant missionary methods are not a tenth part as drastic and revolutionary as the American civil and educational methods. Protestants ask no assistance from soldiers or policemen. They do not wish the Filipinos to be taxed to support their work, as they are taxed to maintain the public schools to which the Roman Catholic Church so strongly objects. The Protestant Churches of the United States rely wholly upon moral suasion and the intrinsic power of the truths which they inculcate. They send to the Philippines as missionaries men and women who represent the purest and highest types of American Christian character and culture. They propose to pay all costs out of voluntary contributions. Now we insist that our justification for this effort is as clear as the justification of the Department of Public Instruction, for example, in superseding the educational control of the Roman Catholics, and that our methods are far less apt to alarm and anger the Roman hierarchy and its followers.

Ploughshares or Swords: World War I

"To Love is To Hate"

War divides not only the opposing armies, but also the respective civilian populations. Just as national motivations in the decision to go to war are inevitably mixed, so individuals support or oppose in varying degrees and for varying reasons their country's choice. World War I began for Europe in 1914, for America in 1917. Some religious leaders made every effort to keep the nation out of war, while others saw the nation as the world's enforcer of approved moral ends. Two spokesmen support the war effort: (1) Lyman Abbott once again in his editorial pages of Outlook; *and (2) N. D. Hillis (1858 – 1929), pastor of Henry Ward Beecher's famous church in Brooklyn, who goes further than Abbott in stirring up mankind's darker passions.*

1.

"To Love is To Hate"

Does not Christ command us to love our enemies? Yes. But he nowhere commands us to love God's enemies or those who treat his children with malignant cruelty.

"I hate every false way."

"I hate vain thoughts."

"I hate and abhor lying."

"The fear of Jehovah is to hate evil."

"Let none of you desire evil in your hearts against your neighbor; and love no false thing; for all these things do I hate."

Have these human experiences recorded in the Old Testament been abolished by the New Testament? No; Jesus Christ looked with infinite pity upon men and women who were the victims of vicious parentage, false education, or their own baser natures — who were their own enemies. But his life affords an excellent illustration of such sayings of the ancient prophets as "I, Jehovah, love justice; I hate robbery with iniquity." Literature, ancient and modern, sacred and secular, will be searched in vain to find a more awful expression

[Sources: (1) Lyman Abbott, *Outlook*, 19 (May 15, 1918), 99. (2) N. D. Hillis, *The Blot on the Kaiser's Scutcheon* (New York: Fleming H. Revell Co., 1918), pp. 56– 57, 58– 59.]

of wrath against the deliberate and purposed oppression by man of his fellowmen than is furnished in the invective poured out by Jesus against the Pharisees:

> Woe unto you, scribes and Pharisees, hypocrites! for ye tithe mint and
> anise and cummin, and have left undone the weightier matters of the law,
> justice, and mercy, and faith: but these ye ought to have done, and not to
> have left the other undone. Ye blind guides, that strain out the gnat, and
> swallow the camel.
> Woe unto you, scribes and Pharisees, hypocrites! for ye cleanse the outside
> of the cup and of the platter, but within they are full from extortion and
> excess. Thou blind Pharisee, cleanse first the inside of the cup and of the
> platter, that the outside thereof may become clean also.
> Woe unto you, scribes and Pharisees, hypocrites! for ye are like unto
> whited sepulchers, which outwardly appear beautiful, but inwardly are full
> of dead men's bones, and of all uncleanness. Even so ye also outwardly appear
> righteous unto men, but inwardly ye are full of hypocrisy and iniquity.
> Woe unto you, scribes and Pharisees, hypocrites! for ye build the sepul-
> chers of the prophets, and garnish the tombs of the righteous, and say, If we
> had been in the days of our fathers, we should not have been partakers with
> them in the blood of the prophets. Wherefore ye witness to yourselves, that
> ye are sons of them that slew the prophets. Fill ye up then the measure of
> your fathers. Ye serpents, ye offspring of vipers, how shall ye escape the
> judgment of hell?

I do not hate the Predatory Potsdam Gang because it is my enemy. I do
not hate it for any evil which it has done to me. I hate it for what it has done
to my defenseless neighbor across the sea. I hate it for what it is. I hate it
because it is a robber, a murderer, a destroyer of homes, a pillager of
churches, a violator of women. I do well to hate it. Dr. Fosdick* says, "We
know, when we think of it, that had we been born in Germany, there is not
one chance in a million that we would be doing other than the Germans do."
If I could believe this true, I should be other than I am. If I could believe
that such lust and cruelty were possible in me, being what I am, I should
hate myself with a bitter hatred.

2.

Must German Men Be Exterminated?

A singular revulsion of sentiment as to what must be done with the German
army after the war, is now sweeping over the civilized world. Men who once
were pacifists, men of chivalry and kindness, men whose life has been devoted
to philanthropy and reform, scholars and statesmen, whose very atmosphere
is compassion and magnanimity towards the poor and weak, are now uttering
sentiments that four years ago would have been astounding beyond compare.

*Dr. Harry Emerson Fosdick; see below, pp. 144, 146.

These men feel that there is no longer any room in the world for the German. Society has organized itself against the rattlesnake and the yellow fever. Shepherds have entered into a conspiracy to exterminate the wolves. The Boards of Health are planning to wipe out typhoid, cholera and the Black Plague. Not otherwise, lovers of their fellow man have finally become perfectly hopeless with reference to the German people. They have no more relations to the civilization of 1918 than an orang-outang, a gorilla, a Judas, a hyena, a thumbscrew, a scalping knife in the hands of a savage. These brutes must be cast out of society.

Some of us, hoping against hope, after the reluctant confession of the truth of the German atrocities, have appealed to education. We knew that Tacitus said, nearly two thousand years ago, that "the German treats women with cruelty, tortures his enemies, and associates kindness with weakness." But nineteen centuries of education have not changed the German one whit. The mere catalogue of the crimes committed by German officers and soldiers and set forth in more than twenty volumes of proofs destroys the last vestige of hope for their future. . . .

The sense of hopelessness as to civilizing the German and keeping him as an element in the new society grew out of the breakdown of education and science in changing the German of the time of Tacitus. Plainly the time has come to make full confession of the fact that education can change the size but not the sort. The German in the time of Tacitus was ignorant when he took the children of his enemy and dashed their brains out against the wall; the German of 1914 and 1918 still butchers children, the only difference being that the butchery is now more efficient and better calculated, through scientific cruelty, to stir horror and spread frightfulness. The leopard has not changed its spots. The rattlesnake is larger and has more poison in the sac; the German wolf has increased in size, and where once he tore the throat of two sheep, now he can rend ten lambs in half the time. In utter despair, therefore, statesmen, generals, diplomats, editors are now talking about the duty of simply exterminating the German people.

The Madness of Men

As strong counterpoint to the jingoism of Abbott and Hillis, other clerical voices condemned war, or urged great caution before plunging into war, or exposed the hideous, thoroughly de-romanticized side of war. (1) John Haynes Holmes (1879 – 1964), New York City Unitarian minister of wide impact, in 1915 denounced war "universally and unconditionally." (2) His good friend, Rabbi Stephen Wise (1874 – 1949), also of New York City, wrote to President Woodrow Wilson late in 1915 to express his dismay that the country seemed to be preparing for war. (3) Still another New York voice, that of Harry Emerson Fosdick (1878 – 1969), professor at Union Theological Seminary at this time, was lifted in 1917 against war; those who call it glorious are "mad." All three men, moreover, joined in various peacemaking efforts and organizations.

1.

IS WAR EVER JUSTIFIABLE?

From every point of view — from the standpoint of things spiritual as well as of things material, from the standpoint of the future as well as of the present — war is the antithesis of life. Its one end is to destroy what has been builded up through many years by the sweat and tears of men. Its one aim is to kill the lives which men have conceived in joy, women borne in agony, and both together reared in love. Its one supreme triumph is to turn a busy factory into a pile of wreckage, a fertile field into a desert, a home of joy into an ash-heap of sorrow, a living soul into a rotting carcass. Why, if war could once be carried through to its logical conclusions — if there were not a limit to all strength, and a point of exhaustion for every passion — mankind would long since have annihilated itself and this planet become as tenantless as the silent moon! And yet there are some — yea, there are many! — who are ready to assert that this foul business is sometimes and somewheres justifiable. This I deny without qualification or evasion of any kind. War is never justifiable at any time or under any circumstances. No man is wise enough, no nation is important enough, no human interest is precious enough, to justify the wholesale destruction and murder which constitute the essence of war. Human life is alone sacred. The interests of human life are alone sovereign. War, as we have now seen, is the enemy of life and all its interests. Therefore, in the name of life and for the sake of life, do I declare to you that war must be condemned universally and unconditionally.

[Sources: (1) J. H. Holmes, *A Summons Unto All Men* . . . (New York: Simon and Schuster, 1970), p. 116. (2) Carl H. Voss, ed., *Stephen Wise: Servant of the People* (Philadelphia: Jewish Publication Society of America, 1969), p. 68. (3) H. E. Fosdick, *The Challenge of the Present Crisis* (London: Student Christian Movement, [1917]), pp. 59 – 62.]

2.

November 12, 1915

To The President, The White House, Washington

From time to time during the last two years, it has been my privilege to write to you in order to express my agreement with the things you have said and done. I therefore regard it as my duty to tell you how deeply I deplore the necessity under which you have found yourself of accepting and advocating a preparedness program. . . .

It is occasion for profound regret to some of us . . . that you have seen fit at this time to urge that so-called defensive preparedness, which at other times and in other hands than your own is not unlikely to be used in the interests of aggression. You will pardon my pointing out that your program, moderate though you believe it to be, will not and of necessity cannot satisfy those advocates of military preparedness who will for a time purport to assent to preparedness measures.

I should not, my dear Mr. President, have written in this way nor would I burden you with my thought on this question if I did not feel in conscience bound to dissent in pulpit and on platform from your position. I regret this not only on personal grounds but because I believe that issues of deepest moment are at stake touching which you will not expect even the most revering of friends should remain silent.

Red Cross ambulance in World War I, donated by B'nai B'rith
(B'nai B'rith, Washington, D.C.)

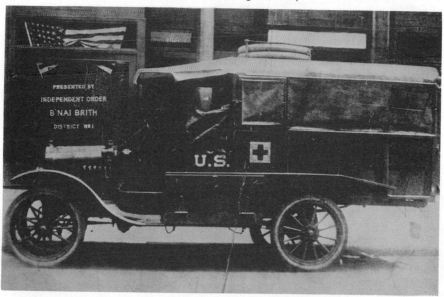

3.

One who knows what really is happening on European battlefields to-day and calls war glorious is morally unsound. Says an eye-witness: "Last night, at an officers' mess there was great laughter at the story of one of our men who had spent his last cartridge in defending an attack. 'Hand me down your spade, Mike,' he said; and as six Germans came one by one round the end of a traverse, he split each man's skull open with a deadly blow." That is war. Says a Young Men's Christian Association secretary: "Many times these fingers have reached through the skulls of wounded men and felt their throbbing brains." That is war. An officer's letter from the front reads:

> "An enemy mine exploded here a few days ago and buried our brigade. Many of the men were killed, but some were not much hurt; so we dug them out and used them over again."

Sons of God and brothers of Jesus Christ —"dug them out and used them over again"! That is war. Said a group of German prisoners, as they bared their gashed forearms, "We were dying with thirst, we had our choice of doing what some men do in such case —drink the blood of an enemy, or else drink our own. We are Christians: so we cut our own arms to get drink." That is war. War is not the gay colour, the rhythmic movement, the thrilling music of the military parade. War is not even killing gallantly as knights once did, matched evenly in armour and in steel and fighting by the rules of chivalry. War now is dropping bombs from aeroplanes and killing women and children in their beds; it is shooting, by telephonic orders, at an unseen place miles away and slaughtering invisible men; it is murdering innocent travellers on merchant ships with torpedoes from unknown submarines; it is launching clouds of poisoned gas and slaying men with their own breath. War means lying days and nights wounded and alone in No-Man's Land; it means men with jaws gone, eyes gone, limbs gone, minds gone; it means countless bodies of boys tossed into the incinerators that follow in the train of every battle; it means prison camps vicious with the inevitable results of enforced idleness; it means untended wounds and gangrene and the long time it takes to die; it means mothers who look for letters they will never see, and wives who wait for voices they will never hear, and children who listen for footsteps that will never come. That is war —"its heroisms are but the glancing sunlight on a sea of blood and tears"—and a man who calls it glorious is mad.

"The Lessons of War"

America's first World War formally ended on November 11, 1918. The time for evaluation then began: what did it achieve? what did it mean? what lessons are to be drawn from it? (1) The nation's Catholic bishops, in addressing themselves to "the lessons of war" in 1919, acknowledged the moral evil inherent in all war. (2) Presbyterian Robert E. Speer (1867 – 1947), missionary executive for over forty years, drew more positive lessons in 1919, seeing the war in essentially moral terms and its idealism as essentially unsullied.

1.

In order that our undertakings may be wisely selected and prudently carried on, we should consider seriously the lessons of the War, the nature of our present situation and the principles which must guide the adjustment of all our relations.

Our estimate of the War begins, naturally, with the obvious facts: with the number of peoples involved, the vastness and effectiveness of their armaments, the outlay in treasure and toil, the destruction of life and the consequent desolation which still lies heavy on the nations of Europe. Besides these visible aspects, we know somewhat of the spiritual suffering — of the sorrow and hopelessness which have stricken the souls of men. And deeper than these, beyond our power of estimation, is the moral evil, the wrong whose magnitude only the Searcher of hearts can determine.

For we may not forget that in all this strife of the peoples, in the loosening of passion and the seeking of hate, sin abounded. Not the rights of man alone but the law of God was openly disregarded. And if we come before Him now in thankfulness, we must come with contrite hearts, in all humility beseeching Him that He continue His mercies toward us, and enable us so to order our human relations that we may atone for our past transgressions and strengthen the bond of peace with a deeper charity for our fellowmen and purer devotion to His service.

2.

I venture to say again, accordingly, what was said at the outset of this chapter, that the war has clarified and confirmed our fundamental religious ideas and revealed the power of their appeal to the present day mind. The war also has unmistakably set in the supreme place those moral and spiritual principles

[Sources: (1) Peter Guilday, ed., *The National Pastorals of the American Hierarchy, 1792 – 1919* (Westminster, Md.: Newman Press, 1954), p. 297. (2) R. E. Speer, *The New Opportunity of the Church* (New York: Macmillan Co., 1919), pp. 48 – 49.]

which constitute the message of the Church. It has revealed the responsiveness of men to the essential ethical ideals of Christianity. Christianity proclaims that moral and spiritual values are absolute and dominant. Much of our modern teaching denied this. The war has affirmed it. It has shown that these values are supreme over personal loss and material interest. Fathers and mothers have given up their only sons to die for a cause. Soldiers have served in the war for pay so small as to be negligible. Thousands of men have served for nothing. More than that, they have made untold sacrifices. In the case of Belgium we have seen a nation give up its material interests utterly and lay the very body of its national existence upon the altar. For four years it was a national soul without a body or a home. The war itself in its essence was a moral not a material struggle and it was moral ideas which prevailed. The very materialism of the struggle was marked by the idealism of self denial. It avowed itself as nothing but the vehicle and weapon of a righteous purpose and a human hope. What is idealism but the belief in the possibility of the best, a confidence in the good faith of all who love liberty and are ready to die for it, the brotherly trust of the democratic principle? We succeeded in the war whenever and wherever this was our spirit and elsewhere and always we failed and will fail. The war says that what Christ said is forever true.

Peace and Disarmament

Church Peace Union

Once the guns of World War I were silent, a great many religious leaders in America expressed their strong reservations about war as a proper instrument of national policy. In the 1920s and 1930s pacifist sentiment spread far beyond the small, traditionally antiwar churches to include a far broader spectrum of American religion. Pacifism was respectable; peace-making was popular. Indeed, a thoroughly establishment figure, Andrew Carnegie (1835–1919), who made his enormous fortune in steel, dedicated a sizable segment of that fortune to the search for peace. Among his many spectacular philanthropies were the Carnegie Endowment for International Peace (1910) and the Church Peace Union (1914). The latter organization, consisting of Protestant, Catholic, and Jewish leaders, became the principal voice of institutional religion on behalf of peace-seeking and peace-making. What follows are Carnegie's welcoming words to those who came to his home in New York City on the afternoon of February 10, 1914, to join in the creation of this Union; his words reveal, among other things, his extra-

[Source: Charles S. Macfarland, *Pioneers for Peace Through Religion* (New York: Fleming H. Revell Co., 1946), pp. 21–23.]

*ordinarily high hope that peace would indeed break out around the world,
enabling the endowment monies then to be used for other purposes.*

In greeting his guests, Mr. Carnegie said: "We meet today under wholly
exceptional conditions, for never in the history of man has such a body
assembled for such a purpose; no less than twelve of the chief religious bodies
of the civilized world being here represented by their prominent official
leaders . . . to cooperate as one body in the holy task of abolishing war."
"Yours," concluded Mr. Carnegie, "is a 'divine mission.' You are making
history."

After the meeting had organized itself as "The Church Peace Union
(Founded by Andrew Carnegie)," Mr. Carnegie resumed:

"Gentlemen of many religious bodies all irrevocably opposed to war and
devoted advocates of peace, we all feel, I believe, that the killing of man by
man in battle is barbaric and negatives our claim to civilization. This crime
we wish to banish from the earth; some progress has already been made in
this direction, but recently men have shed more of their fellows' blood than
for years previously. We need to be aroused to our duty and banish war.

"Certain that the strongest appeal that can be made is to members of the
religious bodies, to you I hereby appeal, hoping that you will feel it to be not
only your duty but your pleasure to undertake the administration of Two
Millions of Dollars in five per cent bonds, the income to be used as in your
judgment will most successfully appeal to the people in the cause of peace
through arbitration of international disputes; that as man in civilized lands
is compelled by law to submit personal disputes to courts of law or through
other channels, this trust shall have fulfilled its mission.

"After the arbitration of international disputes is established and war abolished, as it certainly will be some day, and that sooner than expected, probably
by the Teutonic nations, Germany, Britain and the United States first deciding
to act in unison, other powers joining later, the trustees will divert the rev-
enues of this fund to relieve the deserving poor and afflicted in their distress,
especially those who have struggled long and earnestly against misfortune and
have not themselves to blame for their poverty. Members of the various
churches will naturally know such members well, and can therefore the better
judge; but this does not debar them from going beyond membership when
that is necessary or desirable. As a general rule, it is best to help those who
help themselves, but there are unfortunates from whom this cannot be expected.

"After war is abolished by the leading nations, the trustees by a vote of
two-thirds may decide that a better use for the funds than that named in the
preceding paragraph has been found and are free according to their own
judgment to devote the income to the best advantage for the good of their
fellowmen.

"I am happy in the belief that the civilized world will not, cannot, long
tolerate the killing of man by man as a means of settling its international

disputes, and that civilized men will not, cannot long enter a profession which binds them to go forth and kill their fellowmen as ordered, although they will continue to defend their homes if attacked, as a duty, which also involves the duty of never attacking homes of others."

Mr. Carnegie was gracious and full of humor in the reception of his guests, but impressive in the earnestness with which he gave expression to his faith and hope.

Such was the birth of The Church Peace Union. It was the first occasion on which any substantial funds had been made available for a peace movement by an organized religious body and it was also the first peace society to unite official and representative members of the three major faiths in that capacity. From this time on The Church Peace Union became the hub about which revolved a world-wide movement.

Kirby Page and the Churches

As the sentiment for peace spread ever more widely throughout American society, minister after minister, church after church, lined up to issue a renunciation of war. War was "utterly destructive," entirely "nefarious," hopelessly "archaic," and totally "incompatible with the teaching and example of our Lord Jesus Christ." A Disciples of Christ minister, Kirby Page (1890 – 1957), proved a most effective and vigorous leader in rallying the churches behind the cause for peace. Peace was his passion, a passion manifest in hundreds of lectures and magazine articles (he even edited the important pacifist organ, The World Tomorrow, *from 1926 to 1934) and more than two dozen books whose impact reached far beyond the borders of the United States. In the excerpt below, we hear not only his voice but also, along with it, many voices from the nation's households of faith.*

Should followers of a religion based on reverence for every person and recognition of kinship of all peoples seek justice and security by resorting to planned devastation of extensive territories and organized slaughter of men, women and children indiscriminately? Should they endeavor to starve entire populations and to burn whole cities? Should they deal in falsehood and devote themselves to the engendering of hatred and fury?

If premeditated and deliberate planning to perpetrate the countless atrocities of war is not a flagrant violation of Jesus' way of life, then no method of resisting aggression and tyranny can be contrary to that way. To say that the method of war may be consistent with his teaching and example is to say that he could consistently have joined the zealots and taken up arms against the

[Source: Kirby Page, *Must We Go to War?* (New York: Farrar & Rinehart, 1937), pp. 182 – 86.]

invading Romans. But surely it is indisputable that if he had resorted to the sword against tyranny he would not now be revered as the noblest of all religious leaders. He could not have manifested active goodwill toward the Romans by plunging a dagger to their hearts. He could not have set an example of forgiveness seventy times seven by calling upon his fellow countrymen to massacre the Romans. The way of Jesus and the method of war stand in utter opposition to one another. We can choose the road of atrocity or the way of the cross, but we cannot at the same time travel both highways since they lead in opposite directions. War with its atrocities is irreconcilable with the religion of Jesus and this incontestable truth has been widely proclaimed by numerous religious bodies:

The General Conference of the Methodist Episcopal Church in 1936 said officially: "War as we now know it is utterly destructive. It is the greatest social sin of modern times; a denial of the ideals of Christ, a violation of human personality and a threat to civilization. Therefore, we declare that the Methodist Episcopal Church as an institution does not endorse, support or purpose to participate in war. . . . We therefore petition the government of the United States to grant to members of the Methodist Episcopal Church, who may be conscientious objectors to war, the same exemption from military service as has long been granted to members of the Society of Friends and similar religious organizations."

The College of Bishops of the Methodist Episcopal Church, South, in 1935 issued an official statement on war: "We shall hold in contempt this entire nefarious war business. War as a method of settling international disputes has not one single defensible argument in its behalf. We reiterate what we said a year ago to the General Conference: 'It is archaic, belongs to the jungle period of human development and should be branded as an iniquitous and inhuman procedure. . . . It is an unhallowed thing utterly contrary to the genius of Christianity.' . . . We shall teach our children and youth to despise the unclean thing and to swear eternal loyalty to the ways of peace and to the sacred honor of their brother man."

The General Convention of the Protestant Episcopal Church said: "As stated by the last Lambeth Conference: 'War, as a method of settling international disputes, is incompatible with the teaching and example of our Lord Jesus Christ. We believe that as the Christian conscience has condemned infanticide and slavery and torture, it is now called to condemn war as an outrage on the fatherhood of God and the brotherhood of all mankind.' " In a Pastoral Letter issued by the House of Bishops of the Protestant Episcopal Church the statement is made that "war is murder on a colossal scale. . . . The Christian Church cannot and will not deny loyalty and fealty to its Lord by being partner in any scheme, national or international, that contemplates the wholesale destruction of human life." The Northern Baptist Convention went on record: "War is the supreme social sin, and so long as the war system is maintained there can be no safety for our homes or for our civilization and no realization of the kingdom of heaven on earth." The Synod of the Reformed Presbyterian Church declared: "War is essentially and inherently a supreme violation of the teachings and spirit of Jesus . . . as a method for securing national ends, however just and right, is antichristian."

The International Convention of the Disciples of Christ said: "We believe that war is pagan, futile, and destructive of the spiritual values for which the churches of Christ stand . . . we therefore dissociate ourselves from war and the war system, and hereby serve notice to whom it may concern that we never again expect to bless or sanction war." The Universalist Convention of California resolved: "That the Universalist principles of the Fatherhood of God and the Brotherhood of Man cannot be reconciled with the deliberate taking of life in war. That, since our country has renounced all war, we urge our people to adopt the historical position of the Friends, and take the attitude of conscientious objection to all war. That the faith of the Universalist Church should be recognized by all governmental agencies in the same way as they accept the belief of the Society of Friends."

The General Council of Congregational and Christian Churches thus went on record: "The cleavage between the way of Jesus and the system of war is clear. We of this council are convinced that we must now make this declaration, 'The church is through with war!' We of this council call upon the people of our churches to renounce war and all its works and ways and to refuse to support, sanction or bless it." The 1934 General Assembly of the Presbyterian Church in the U.S.A. "declares anew its break with the entire war system. . . . Christians cannot give their support to war as a method of carrying on international conflict." The Southern Presbyterian Church asserts that "the church should never again bless a war, or be used as an instrument in the promotion of war."

A *Manifesto Against War* was released on Armistice Day, 1934, under the auspices of the Church Peace Union. This forthright declaration was signed by more than 200 outstanding citizens of the United States, *including 60 bishops and 45 college presidents.* Here is a quotation from this pronouncement: "The time has come when organized religion must proclaim that never again shall war be waged under the sanction of the Church. . . . With the ruins of the last war piled high at its feet the Church should solemnly declare herself the implacable enemy of war. . . . We have had in our generation an appalling revelation of the true nature of war. War is not what it was. When science added the airplane, the submarine and poison gas, warfare entered on a new stage. With the advent of poison gas and bacteriological germs it laid aside the last vestige of decency. War has always been bloody and brutal. It is now an atrocity. . . . War is as futile as it is barbarous. . . . There is no victor. All are defeated. . . . Modern war is suicide. The sword is so sharp that a nation can cut not only the throats of its neighbors but its own throat also. Civilization itself is in jeopardy."

The Ohio State Pastors' Conference asserted: "We are convinced that war is un-Christian, futile, and suicidal, and we renounce completly the whole war system. We will never again sanction or participate in any war. We will not use our pulpits or classrooms as recruiting stations. We set ourselves to educate and lead youth in the principles and practice of goodwill, justice, understanding, brotherhood, and peace. We will not give our financial or moral support to any war." The National Study Conference on the Churches and World Peace declared: "War denies the fatherhood of God, scorns the brotherhood of man, mocks the sacredness of human life, is merciless to helpless women and children, uses falsehood, ignores justice, releases the passions, and cultivates hate. War means everything that Jesus did not mean, and means nothing that he did mean. We therefore hold that the Churches should condemn resort to the war-system as sin and should henceforth refuse, as institutions, to sanction it or to be used as agencies in its support." While the Commission on International Justice and Goodwill of the Federal Council of the Churches of Christ in America said bluntly: "The war system of the nations is the outstanding evil of present-day civilization. It is the most ominous antichristian phase of modern life."

Out of 20,870 clergymen who in 1934 replied to a questionnaire, 12,904 said "yes" to this question: "Are you personally prepared to state that it is your present purpose not to sanction any future war or participate as an armed combatant?" While 13,997 answered affirmatively: "Do you believe that the churches of America should now go on record as refusing to sanction or support any future war?"

Frank Buchman and Moral Re-Armament

One of the more intriguing religious developments of the 1920s and 1930s was associated with the name of Frank Buchman (1878–1961). A Lutheran minister and sometime YMCA worker, Buchman was a revivalist — but with a difference. Avoiding the large mass meetings and crowded tents, Buchman preferred the intimate "house parties" where young men and women gathered for prayer, Bible study, and group confession. Because of his unofficial association with Oxford University in the early 1920s, Buchman and his followers took the name of the "Oxford Group Movement." Gradually, however, the energetic and visionary Buchman, growing more interested in world affairs and world peace, took his message to the opinion makers and political leaders of the nations. In 1938 he called for a worldwide spiritual mobilization, a "Moral Re-Armament." Riding the crest of pervading pacifist desires, the movement attracted much attention for a time,

[Sources: (1) H. P. Van Dusen, "The Oxford Group Movement," *Atlantic Monthly,* 154, no. 2 (Aug., 1934), 240–41. (2) Frank Buchman, *Remaking the World* (London: Blandford Press, 1961 [1947]), pp. 45–46, 47–48.]

only to be drowned out by the mighty engines of World War II. (1) The first excerpt, written by Henry P. Van Dusen (1897 – 1975), long-time professor and president of Union Theological Seminary in New York City, offers an evaluation of the Oxford Group as of 1934. (2) In 1938 Frank Buchman issued his call for Moral Re-Armament.

1.

It is always with the utmost hesitancy that I attempt to describe and appraise the Oxford Group Movement. This is not at all because the facts are difficult to ascertain and report. On the contrary, anyone passingly familiar with the history of religion who has watched this Movement's extraordinary advance over the past ten years can readily detail its principal features and its underlying assumptions, and suggest their parallels in earlier phenomena of religion. But the most faithful recountal of the facts must fail lamentably to convey a true impression of the Movement's extraordinary character and power to one who has not felt its temper personally. And any estimate of its significance, however honest, will be finally determined by the presuppositions which the appraiser brings to his inquiry.

The protagonists of the Groups are quite right in their contention that the inquirer may come into an adequate understanding of them in only one way — by intimate acquaintance with their life from within. And they would be further justified in contending that, after such acquaintance, one's final attitude will largely reflect prior value-judgments on such basic issues as these: the inner character of true religion, the needs of the human soul, the state of religion in our day, the malaise of civilization and the possibilities for its cure — and what short-comings may be forgiven in a spiritual strategy of searching criticism and overwhelming vitality. This Movement thrusts itself upon us with a radical and drastic critique of the unchallenged assumptions of most of the readers of these words; not until its critique has been squarely faced is one entitled to give a verdict concerning the Movement.

Thus is suggested the first affirmation about the Oxford Group Movement which I should like to underscore. Any facile and categorical judgment of its importance, whether favorable or unfavorable, is to be dismissed at once as superficial and misleading. Much current comment is either extravagantly laudatory or sharply contemptuous. Neither attitude is sound. The plain truth is that there is probably no spiritual force in the world to-day which is bringing to the lives of hundreds such light and power and freedom and happiness and spiritual certainty — gifts quite beyond the measurement of any human calculus. And there is no contemporary religious movement of similar proportions which, in the judgment of many wise and consecrated persons, is so freighted with danger, self-deception, and even perversion of authentic Christian experience. Just when one has determined to dismiss it from consideration because of its excesses or its perils or its self-righteousness, one is confronted with a concrete instance of the liberation and empowerment of a defeated and despairing soul, like as not someone within one's own acquaintance. Criticism is silenced, gratitude wells spontaneously, one wonders whether even friendly questioning of so magnificent a work can be justified. Just when one is moved to lend cordial support, one meets an example of bumptious impertinence or pitiable pharisaism or tragic mishandling of a human personality so flagrant that the most tolerant sympathy cannot forgive. Doubts return, sympathy shrivels, one questions whether even qualified approval of the Movement can honestly be given. Clearly we are here face to face with something which eludes easy generalization.

In brief, the Oxford Group Movement is the most baffling religious phenomenon of our time. Nor is this a personal opinion only. Many of the foremost leaders of the Church on both sides of the Atlantic have, in personal conversation, voiced their bewilderment. Never have they encountered a movement which so defied final estimate. Never have they felt themselves so puzzled in deciding their own relationship to a vital religious work.

2.

The world's condition cannot but cause disquiet and anxiety. Hostility piles up between nation and nation, labour and capital, class and class. The cost of bitterness and fear mounts daily. Friction and frustration are undermining our homes.

Is there a remedy that will cure the individual and the nation and give the hope of a speedy and satisfactory recovery?

The remedy may lie in a return to those simple home truths that some of us learned at our mother's knee, and which many of us have forgotten and neglected — honesty, purity, unselfishness and love.

The crisis is fundamentally a moral one. The nations must re-arm morally. Moral recovery is essentially the forerunner of economic recovery. Imagine a rising tide of absolute honesty and absolute unselfishness sweeping across every country! What would be the effect? What about taxes? Debts? Savings? A wave of absolute unselfishness throughout the nations would be the end of war.

Moral recovery creates not crisis but confidence and unity in every phase of life. How can we precipitate this moral recovery throughout the nations? We need a power strong enough to change human nature and build bridges between man and man, faction and faction. This starts when everyone admits his own faults instead of spot-lighting the other fellow's.

God alone can change human nature.

The secret lies in that great forgotten truth that when man listens, God speaks; when man obeys, God acts; when men change, nations change. That power active in a minority can be the solvent of a whole country's problems. Leaders changed, a nation's thinking changed, a world at peace with itself. . . .

God has a nation-wide programme that provides inspiration and liberty for all and anticipates all political programmes.

Every employed and unemployed man employed in Moral Re-Armament; this is the greatest programme of national service — putting everybody to work remaking people, homes and businesses. A Swedish steelworker told me: 'Only a spiritual revolution goes far enough to meet the needs of men and industry.'

A Labour leader said: 'I have seen the Labour Movement triumph and felt in the midst of triumph an emptiness. The Oxford Group gave my life new content. I see in its message the only key to the future of the Labour Movement and of industry the world over.'

Only a new spirit in men can bring a new spirit in industry. Industry can be the pioneer of a new order, where national service replaces selfishness, and where industrial planning is based upon the guidance of God. When Labour, Management and Capital become partners under God's guidance, then industry takes its true place in national life.

New men, new homes, new industry, new nations, a new world.

We have not yet tapped the great creative sources in the Mind of God. God has a plan, and the combined moral and spiritual forces of the nation can find that plan.

We can, we must, and we will generate a moral and spiritual force that is powerful enough to remake the world.

3. EVANGELIZATION OF THE WORLD

Protestant Empire Revived

John R. Mott (1865– 1955)

If the United States were indeed becoming more empire than republic, then should not that empire be a Protestant one? It was an old idea (see Vol. I, Chapter Six), but previously the notion had extended only across a continent: now it embraced the whole world. John R. Mott had welcomed the twentieth century with a call in 1900 for The Evangelization of the World in This Generation. *A Methodist layman and an administrative wonder, Mott dreamed grand dreams. But his labor matched his vision, as he worked with students all over the world, creating in 1895 the World's Student Christian Federation. He also worked with churches without respect to political boundaries, becoming one of the forces behind the creation of the World Council of Churches in 1948. Here, in the excerpt below, it is his passion as missionary that is most evident.*

The closing years of the nineteenth century have witnessed in all parts of Protestant Christendom an unprecedented development of missionary life and activity among young men and young women. A remarkable manifestation of this interest in the extension of the Kingdom of Christ has been among students. The Student Volunteer Movement for Foreign Missions, taking its rise at a conference of American and Canadian students in 1886, has spread from land to land, until it has now assumed an organized form in all Protestant countries. It has been transplanted even to the colleges of mission lands, so that today the Christian students of the Occident and the Orient, of the Northern and the Southern Hemispheres, are united in the sublime purpose of enthroning Jesus Christ as King among all nations and races of men. The

[Source: J. R. Mott, *The Evangelization of the World in This Generation* (New York: Student Volunteer Movement for Foreign Missions, 1900), pp. 1– 2, 4– 6.]

reality of their consecration is proved by the fact that during the past decade over two thousand of them, after completing a thorough college or university preparation, have gone out from North America and Europe under the regular missionary societies of the Church to work in non-Christian lands. A still larger number are equipping themselves for similar service abroad.

In several countries, notably in the United States, Canada, Great Britain and Ireland, the members of this Movement have adopted as their watchword, The Evangelization of the World in this Generation. A great number of their fellow-students who, although not volunteers for foreign missions, recognize their equal burden of responsibility for the world's evangelization, have taken the same watchword as a molding influence in their life plans. The idea is taking strong hold, also, on a multitude of other men and women. Eminent leaders of the various branches of the Church of Christ, both in Christian lands and on the mission field, have endorsed the Watchword and have urged the desirability of its adoption by all Christians as expressive of an inspiring ideal as well as of a primary and urgent duty. . . .

What is it to preach the Gospel? The Greek words principally used in the New Testament mean to proclaim as heralds, or to transmit good news. Other words or expressions less frequently used are to talk or converse, to reason or discuss, to testify or bear witness, to teach and to exhort. Examples of all these forms of preaching, or of communicating a knowledge of Christ and His mission to men, are to be found in the practice of the early Church. The qualifications of the worker or speaker, and the circumstances in which he found himself placed, determined the manner of his presentation of the truth as it is in Christ.

So to-day we find the missionaries proclaiming and applying the Gospel in sermons or addresses in mission halls; expounding and discussing the truth in bazaars, inns and street chapels; conversing about Christ as they visit from house to house and as they mingle with the people socially at feasts and public gatherings; teaching the system of Christian doctrine in schools and colleges; circulating the printed Scriptures and other Christian literature; illustrating the Gospel by Christ-like ministry to the body, and by the powerful object lessons of the consistent Christian life and of the well-ordered Christian home; and ever pressing the claims of Christ upon individuals as they are met within the sphere of one's daily calling. In all these and in other ways the Christian worker by voice and by life, by pen and by printed page, in season and out of season, seeks to set forth those facts about Christ which in all lands have been found to be the power of God unto the salvation of every man that believeth.

Robert E. Speer (1867 – 1947)

Having found a moral justification for World War I, Robert Speer proceeded to offer a moral justification for "the missionary enterprise" around the world. Speer, in his capacity as Presbyterian missionary executive, traveled himself to most of those mission fields he supported: China, Japan, India, Southeast Asia, the Near East, and Latin America. Like Mott, he saw denominational division as a great liability in the missionary effort and, again like Mott, Speer labored to transcend those divisions. Speer was especially far-sighted in his advocating that the newly created churches abroad train their own native clergy and not continue as merely "colonial" extensions of American denominations.

I have named just as briefly as I could what seem to me to be five of the great moral justifications for the war, justifications that made legitimate the sacrifices that were poured out, and that laid the obligation of the struggle to the last effort upon every life in our land. But, when we have said this, have we said anything more than just to put into political terms, in connection with the great struggle, the aims and ideals and purposes for which many men have been living all their lives, which have actuated the missionary enterprise, and which underlie it to-day? What does that enterprise exist for? What has it been seeking to do, and in reality doing all the years since it began?

It has been in the world as an instrumentality of peace and international good will. Wherever it has gone, it has erased racial prejudice and bitterness, the great root of international conflict and struggle. It has helped men to understand one another. It has rubbed off the frictions. "Christianity continues to spread among the Karens," said the Administration Report for British Burmah for 1880 – 1881, "to the great advantage of the Commonwealth, and the Christian Karen communities are distinctly more industrious, better educated and more law-abiding than the Burman and Karen villages around them. The Karen race and the British government owe a great debt to the American missionaries who have, under Providence, wrought this change among the Karens of Burmah." . . .

It has been an agency of righteousness. As the years have gone by, it alone has represented in many non-Christian lands the inner moral character of the Western world. By our political agencies and activities we have forced great wrongs upon the non-Christian peoples — commercial exploitation, the liquor traffic, and the slave trade upon Africa and the South Sea Islands, the opium traffic upon China. Against these things the one element of the West that has made protest has been the missionary enterprise. Year after year in those lands it has joined with what wholesome moral sentiment existed among the people in a death struggle against the great iniquities that Western civilization had

[Source: R. E. Speer, *The New Opportunity of the Church* (New York: Macmillan Co., 1919), pp. 94 – 95, 97 – 98, 100 – 1.]

spread over the world. It has been an instrumentality of international righteousness.

It has been and is a great instrumentality of human service. It has scattered tens of thousands of men and women over many lands, teaching school in city and country, in town and village. It has built its hospitals by the thousand. It has sent its medical missionaries to deal every year with millions of sick and diseased peoples in Asia and Africa. It has been the one great, continuing, unselfish agency of unquestioning, loving, human service throughout the world, dealing not with emergency needs of famine and flood and pestilence alone, but, year in and year out, serving all human need and seeking to introduce into human society the creative and healing influences of Christ. "It is they" (the missionaries), says Sir H. H. Johnston, of British Central Africa, "who in many cases have first taught the natives carpentry, joinery, masonry, tailoring, cobbling, engineering, bookkeeping, printing, and European cookery; to say nothing of reading, writing, arithmetic, and a smattering of general knowledge. Almost invariably, it has been to missionaries that the natives of Interior Africa have owed their first acquaintance with a printing press, the turning-lathe, the mangle, the flat-iron, the sawmill, and the brick mold. Industrial teaching is coming more and more in favor, and its immediate results in British Central Africa have been most encouraging. Instead of importing painters, carpenters, store clerks, cooks, telegraphists,

Graduating class of the China Bible School
(Billy Graham Center)

gardeners, natural history collectors from England or India, we are gradually becoming able to obtain them amongst the natives of the country, who are trained in the missionaries' schools, and who having been given simple, wholesome local education, have not had their heads turned, and are not above their station in life." . . .

Foreign missions have been a great agency of human unity and concord. They, at least, have believed and acted upon the belief that all men belong to one family. They have laughed at racial discords and prejudices. They have made themselves unpopular with many representatives of the Western nations who have gone into the non-Christian world, because they have not been willing to foster racial distrust, because they have insisted on bridging the divisions which separated men of different bloods and different nationalities. We are talking now about building the new world after the war. But it would be hopeless if we had not already begun it. We are talking about some form of international organization. It may need to be very simple, with few and primitive functions, but it must come. And it can come only as first, we sustain in men's hearts a faith in its possibility; as second, we devise the instrumentalities necessary to it and make them effective; as third, we build up a spirit that will support it. Across the world for a hundred years the missionary enterprise has been the proclamation that this day must come, and that some such international body of relationships as this, based on right principles, must be set up among the nations of the world.

It would not be hard to go on analyzing further what the missionary enterprise has been doing. It has been doing peacefully, constructively, unselfishly, quietly for a hundred years exactly the things that now, in a great outburst of titanic and necessarily destructive struggle, we were compelled to do by war. I say it again, that one of the most significant things of the day is to see how the great ideals and purposes of the missionary enterprise, that have been the commonplaces of some men's lives, have been gathered up as a great moral discovery and made the legitimate moral aims of the nation in the great conflict in which we have been engaged.

E. Stanley Jones (1884– 1973)

A Methodist missionary who went to India in his early twenties, Jones acquired fame in that capacity as well as in the role of popular lecturer and author. Elected bishop in the Methodist Episcopal Church in 1928, he soon resigned that office in order to return to his missionary labors. In India he wished to reach the high caste, hoping that Christian instruction at that level would filter down to the masses. As his widely translated Christ of the

[Source: E. Stanley Jones, *Christ of the Indian Road* (New York: Abingdon Press, 1925), pp. 193– 94, 195– 96.]

Indian Road makes evident, however, he also thought that Christianity had much to learn from the rich spiritual heritage of India. In the momentous encounter between Christianity and Hinduism, both could be transformed, both could be enriched.

The religious genius of India is the richest in the world, the forms that it has taken have often been the most extravagant, sometimes degrading and cruel. These forms are falling away, or will fall away, but the spirit persists and will be poured through other forms. As that genius pours itself through Christian molds it will enrich the collective expression of Christianity. But in order to do that the Indian must remain Indian. He must stand in the stream of India's culture and life and let the force of that stream go through his soul so that the expression of his Christianity will be essentially Eastern and not Western. This does not mean that Indian Christianity will be denied what is best in Western thought and life, for when firmly planted on its own soil it can then lift its antennae to the heavens and catch the voices of the world. But it must be particular before it can be universal. Only thus will it be creative — a voice, not an echo. . . .

The reason that the Indian Christian has not made any real contribution to Christian theology is because he has been trying, on the whole, to think through Western forms and here he is like a fish out of water. But now that India is awakened and self-conscious and the process of denationalization is probably over, we may expect that genius to work. We must be willing to trust the Indian to make his contribution.

It is no more fair to say that we cannot trust Indian genius to interpret Christianity because of the extravagances of the past than to have said that the Western mind could not be trusted because the Druids in England used to perform human sacrifices in their religion and the Scots practiced cannibalism.

Every nation has its peculiar contribution to make to the interpretation of Christianity. The Son of man is too great to be expressed by any one portion of humanity. Those that differ from us most will probably contribute most to our expression of Christianity. . . .

India too hopes that the world may some day be in need of a new formula. She too has her word ready. It will be spelled "Atma" —*spirit*. That word "Atma" runs like a refrain through everything in India. The followers of the Christ of the Indian Road will show us the real meaning of a *spiritual* life. They will sit lightly to earthly things and abandon themselves to the spirit.

Along with that will come the sense of the unity and harmony running through things. "Don't you think atonement would mean attunement?" said a Hindu to me one day. He felt his life was "like sweet bells jangled out of tune" by sin and evil, and to his mind, craving inward peace and harmony, atonement would bring attunement to the nature of God — music instead of a discord. No wonder peace has been the great thought and craving of India. Anything like losing one's temper is thought to be utterly incompatible with the truly religious life. "I know I haven't salvation yet," said a villager to me one day, "for while I have conquered everything else anger still remains, I haven't got it yet." The followers of the Christ of the Indian Road will be harmonized and peaceful. Meditation to them will be real. Religion will mean quiet realization. God will be the harmonizing bond of all.

Finally the followers of the Christ of the Indian Road will know the meaning of the cross, for India stands for the cost of being religious. Renunciation will be a reality, for India instinctively grasps the meaning of Jesus when he says that the way to realize life is to renounce it — to lose it is to find it. In the footprints of many of his followers as they walk along the Indian Road will be blood stains, for they will be Apostles of the Bleeding Feet. They will know the meaning of being crucified followers of a crucified Lord.

American Catholicism's New Era

Missionary Conference (1908)

Catholics in America —some fifteen million strong by 1908 —had moved from weakness to strength, from dependence to independent vigor. No longer was it necessary to send missionary priests to America: now the American Church was ready to send its own missionaries abroad. In the very year that the Vatican formally removed the Church in the United States from mission status, Catholics held a Missionary Conference in Chicago, November 16 to 18, 1908. (1) Chicago's Archbishop James Edward Quigley (1854 – 1915) opened the conference by calling attention to the "new era" into which the Church in America now entered. (2) Closing the conference, Boston's Archbishop William H. O'Connell (1859 – 1944) declared that "all indications point to our vocation as a great missionary nation."

1.

The reasons and object of this Missionary Congress and its opportuneness at this time are tersely and comprehensively summed up and set forth in the following words which I quote from the call or invitation sent out by the officers of the Catholic Church Extension Society of the U.S.A., under whose auspices the Congress is held:

"To mark the change of the Church in North America from missionary conditions to its full share in the efforts of the Church Universal by striking the note of unselfishness clearly and forcibly.

[Sources: (1) Francis C. Kelley, ed., *The First American Catholic Missionary Conference* (Chicago: J. S. Hyland and Co., 1909), pp. 43 – 44. (2) Ibid., pp. 362 – 65.]

"To crystallize the missionary sentiment now being awakened in the Catholic clergy and people, to the end that all may realize their common duty of preserving and extending the Church of Christ. To study missionary conditions and plan for their improvement.

"To pledge to the Holy Father America's loyal support and active cooperation in the mighty task of restoring all things in Christ."

As expressed in the first of these points, the Church in America, by Pontifical Act, is at the beginning of a new era in its history. It is practically only one hundred years old, yet it has reached its majority. The old order of things is changed and a new order established. It passes from the jurisdiction and tutelage of the great missionary organization known as the Sacred Congregation de Propaganda Fide, and takes its stand among the bright galaxy of fully organized and equipped hierarchical unities of the world-wide Church of God, that encircle and glorify the throne of the Vicar of Christ, the successor of the Prince of the Apostles, Pope Pius X. It has covered the whole land of its birth and growth with its network of provinces and dioceses and parishes; developed its own legislation and customs; taken on a character of its own; become conscious of its own mission and destiny; and full of a strength and courage born of the air and free institutions of the land whence it derives its name, is prepared to go forth conquering and to conquer in the cause of Christ.

This Congress is called at this time to give us occasion to study our duties and responsibilities as a hierarchical unity and national Church in the closer intimacy of government, association and affection, with Himself and the Church Universal, to which we have been advanced by the Sovereign Pontiff. These duties and responsibilities are well expressed in the second and third of the reasons given for the call of this Congress — to crystallize the missionary sentiment now being awakened in the Catholic clergy and people, to the end that all may realize their common duty of preserving and extending the Church of Christ, to study missionary conditions and plan for their improvement, and to pledge to the Holy Father America's loyal support and active cooperation in the work which Pius X has made the special aim of his Pontificate, "restaurare omnia in Christo" — to restore all things in Christ.

2.

The spirit of religion, like virtue, must grow; it cannot stand still or rest in complacency upon its laurels without dealing a deadly blow to the very core of its life and progress. To rest self-satisfied with what has been accomplished is to stagnate, and stagnation is the beginning of death. So vital to the very life of religion is the fostering of the Apostolic spirit of zeal for the spread of Christ's faith that it must be nurtured at the cost of any sacrifice. The luxuries of religion we may well dispense with. Too often they have brought only harm to the Church and have been the enemies within the gates.

Magnificent buildings, splendid ceremonials, superb appurtenances are all good in their place, for the worship of Christ can never be too adequately expressed, even by all that the noblest endeavor and most brilliant genius of man may bring to its expression, but if these things are to breed a selfish content and rob the Catholics of any generation of that primitive Apostolic zeal which inflamed the breasts of their first teachers, then it is far better to dispense with these external embellishments, and in poverty and hardship cultivate the gift which made the first promulgators of the faith of Christ the conquerors of the world.

It is time, then, for the Church in America to be vigilant in preserving the unselfishness and generosity of spirit which animated the pioneer Catholic missionaries who planted on this continent the seed of faith. In no other way may the steadfastness of faith which is distinctive of our people in the United States be fully safeguarded. It is the inexorable law of self-preservation, and failure to comply with it can bring only disaster and ruin.

We may well draw a lesson from the foresight and prudence displayed by the great nations of the world. There comes a time in their history when they must reach out to find an outlet for the national life and activity. They well understand the folly of remaining quiescent and shutting the door of opportunity to the surplus talent of their people. Instinctively and inevitably led on by this feeling of self-preservation, they reach out into other lands and find new fields for the unworked energies of the nation.

They recognize that to keep doing is the law of life, and that the accumulation of unused forces is the precursor to stagnation and death. The Church in the United States must avoid this peril at all costs. It must not rest on what has been already accomplished, but even in the face of sacrifice reach out in spreading the faith of Christ where it is now either unknown or dormant, for the very necessary reason that in this way alone may it conserve intact and undimmed the brightness of the faith which has already done so much for the progress of the Church. To the isolated regions where there are scattered populations of Catholics without the ministrations of the priest the zeal of the more favored must assist actively to bring the blessings of the faith.

In the Philippines, in Porto Rico, and in all our outlying possessions, the Church must go, heralded by the missionaries of the English-speaking race who are now called upon by providential design to perform the work which has long been so nobly done by others. It is the time set by divine providence for this Apostolic undertaking. In the first ages of the Church, when imperial Rome ruled the world and Latin was the universal language, it was the missionaries of the Latin tongue who went forth from Rome, and for centuries spread the faith in the countries of Europe. In a later day, when French was the diplomatic language of the nations, France became the missionary country, and her sons and daughters have given an example of self-sacrifice and devotion in spreading the faith in foreign lands that is worthy of all emulation.

Time inevitably brings changes. Today the language of the whole Orient is English. The language of diplomatic usage has been succeeded by the language of trade, and from Port Said to the furthermost point of Japan the language which the people know best next to their own, and like best, is English. Already Japan is clamoring for English-speaking missionaries, and the field which once yielded such a fruitful harvest to the Apostolic labors of St. Francis Xavier lies ready for cultivation at the hands of English-speaking apostles.

The providential hour of opportunity has struck. We must be up and doing. All indications point to our vocation as a great missionary nation. To be recreant to such a high calling is to abdicate a blessed vantage ground and to undo gradually the good which has already been accomplished in this land by the apostolic zeal of the Church's followers. Our country has already reached out beyond her boundaries and is striving to do a work of extension of American civic ideals for other peoples. Shall it be said that the Church in this land has been outstripped in zeal and energy by the civil power under which we live?

Maryknoll, 1911

If the 1908 conference set the tone, the seminary launched in 1911 set the pace. Under the energetic leadership of two priests, Fathers Thomas F. Price and James A. Walsh, the Catholic Foreign Missionary Society of America came into being with a training center for missionaries located in New York state at Maryknoll. The formal title for this center was the "American Seminary for Foreign Missions," but "Maryknoll" became a kind of shorthand for the Roman Catholic commitment in America to missionary work around the world. By the middle of the twentieth century, that work was particularly conspicuous in Latin America.

On March 25, 1911, Cardinal Gibbons addressed a letter to the archbishops of the United States, outlining the plan of the two founders, urging the need of a foreign mission seminary, and pleading for cooperation in the new venture. His Eminence suggested that the archbishops confer with the bishops of their respective provinces and be ready to take action in the matter at their next meeting, to be held in April. Cardinal Gibbons on this occasion wrote:

"The priests of the United States number more than seventeen thousand, but I am informed there are hardly sixteen on the foreign missions. This fact recalls a warning which the late Cardinal Vaughan gave, in a kindly, brotherly letter to me twenty years ago, urging us American Catholics not to delay

[Source: George C. Powers, *The Maryknoll Movement* (Maryknoll: Catholic Foreign Mission Society of America, 1926), pp. 57, 59, 60–61.]

Maryknoll missionary in Molina, Chile
(Maryknoll Fathers)

participation in foreign missions, LEST OUR OWN FAITH SHOULD SUFFER."

The archbishops, having conferred previously with their suffragans in accordance with the plan of Cardinal Gibbons, met in Washington, April 27,

1911, and voicing the wishes of the entire hierarchy, unanimously passed these resolutions:

"We heartily approve the establishment of an American Seminary for Foreign Missions as outlined in the letter sent by His Eminence Cardinal Gibbons to the Archbishops.

"We warmly commend to the Holy Father the two priests mentioned as organizers of this seminary, and we instruct them to proceed to Rome without delay, for the purpose of securing all necessary authorization and direction from Propaganda for the proposed work." . . .

Events followed rapidly. The two organizers left Boston for Europe on May 30, 1911, and did not return until the late summer. They took advantage of their opportunity to visit foreign mission seminaries and apostolic colleges in England and on the Continent, and made a summary study of methods and rules of these institutions. They arrived in Rome on June 19, and between that date and June 29 had several interviews. . . .

On the feast of Saints Peter and Paul (June 29, 1911), with the kindly help of Doctor Schut of Mill Hill, they were able to present their formal petition for authorization and a detailed outline of their proposed operations, to the Cardinal Prefect. Cardinal Gotti at once formally authorized them to begin their work, to purchase property, and to appeal for students. For the present the founders were to conduct the Society jointly under the bishop in whose diocese they should begin their work; later, when they should be in a position to have a council and hold an election, they were to communicate with Propaganda; in the meantime they were to keep Propaganda informed of their progress. They then received the blessing of the Cardinal Prefect and made arrangements for an audience with the Holy Father, Pius X.

On the following day, they were graciously received by the Successor of Saint Peter and knelt before that saintly Pontiff to receive his blessing for themselves, their project, and its benefactors.

The two priests then went into consultation to decide upon the legal title of the new Society. They agreed on THE CATHOLIC FOREIGN MISSION SOCIETY OF AMERICA: *Catholic,* to distinguish it from all sectarian societies; *Foreign,* lest it be confused with home mission societies; and *of America* because it was the only society of that nature set on foot through the official sanction of the American hierarchy. Then, too, the phrase was necessary to distinguish it from all European societies of a like purpose. This title met with the instant approval of Cardinal Gibbons.

Maryknoll missionary in Kyoto, Japan
(Maryknoll Fathers)

The Disinherited Abroad

Black Baptists, 1903

Missionary efforts were not the monopoly of the wealthy, nor even of the middle class. Those to whom American society had not been generous nonetheless seized the opportunity to take their messages and mission abroad. Black Baptists, growing rapidly in number after the Civil War and organizing themselves into the National Baptist Convention in 1895, saw a certain logic in selecting Africa as an area of missionary endeavor. C. S. Morris, Commissioner for the Foreign Mission Board of the National Bap-

[Source: C. S. Morris, "Africa Waiting," in L. G. Jordan, *Up the Ladder in Foreign Missions* (Nashville: National Baptist Publishing House, 1903), pp. 168–69, 170–71, 173–74.]

tist Convention, in 1899 made a tour of inspection of Africa. Upon his return, he spoke of a much-abused continent: abused by slavery, by liquor, by colonialism. Victim of the world's avarice, Africa now deserved some of its charity: ". . . what a noble atonement we might make in sending missionaries. . . ."

If there is a continent on the face of the earth that needs the Gospel of Jesus Christ more, if possible, than any other, that continent is Africa. It has been more cruelly neglected. Sixty generations of its people have perished in rayless paganism. Africa's darkest millions have not yet begun their forward march out of centuries of midnight darkness. There are regions large as all Europe *packed with fifty million souls* without *one* single missionary. . . .

Africa has been more deeply wronged. Northern Africa gave to Christianity its first Latin Bible, produced Athenasius (who stood against the world contending for the Deity of our Lord), Tertullian, Cyprian, Augustine and Ambrose. At one time there were 500 Bishops in North Africa, but the ruthless invasion of the Vandals put thousands of Christians to the sword and scattered the remainder to the four corners of the earth. Then came the red deluge of Mohammedanism, rolling like a bloody sea over that fair region, completing the work of annihilating the last vestiges of Christianity, and *Africa's doom was sealed.*

Then came slavery, "the heart disease of Africa." Vasco de Gama discovered West Africa about the same time that Columbus discovered America, and Africa was sacrificed for America. Europe and America inaugurated the most *gigantic crime of the Christian era* against her. Unnumbered millions of her children were slain in slave raids, other millions perished in the horrors of the "middle passage;" sometimes 700 would be stowed away on board one ship. Only sixty years ago 250,000 were being exported every year by Christian States. . . .

Then came the civilized rum traffic, *hell's masterpiece of damnation,* that has turned the whole ocean front into one long bar-room, at which *two million frenzied savages drop dead* every year of delirium tremens. Rum is deadly in the temperate regions, it is rank poison in the tropics. . . .

In the eighteenth century Europe stole the African from Africa; in the nineteenth, she is stealing Africa from the African. The unhallowed spirit of civilized greed for aggrandizement at the African's expense is not yet sated. The slave raiding of other days is to give place to the second magnificently unscrupulous conspiracy that is to partition Africa and plunder the African of the bounds of his habitation which God has determined beforehand, and thus deprive two hundred million people of their birthright; to seize upon their property and permanently drain the wealth of Africa and the African's labor into European channels, leaving her like a sucked orange, like a rifled treasure house — her keepers slain, her treasures stolen, the marauders gone.

What an awful many-sided charge the vast cloud of African witnesses will have against the civilized world on the day of judgment. A continent turned into a slave pen, a rum shop, great open running ulcers on either breast. Robbed of her children, rifled of her treasures, fettered in soul, manacled in mind, enslaved in body — *Africa lies prostrate before the rapine and avarice of the world.* . . .

The Church of Christ has been entrusted with the *great commission of the King of Kings.* She has men by the millions and money by the billions. Yet *nineteen centuries have gone over her head and there are whole continents* that have not *heard it.* Some say, "I don't *believe* in foreign missions;" some, "there is plenty to do at *home;*" some, "we have more *now* on hand than we can do." Jesus says, "Go ye into *all* the world, preach the gospel to *every creature,*" and in the Judgment, when the Son of Man shall sit upon the throne of His glory and behold the unreached millions for whom He died, to whom He sent a message of pardon they *never heard,* will He not turn to His recreant disciples whom He entrusted with the message and say, "I made you My stewards and you took My wealth and clothed yourselves in purple and fine linen; you fared sumptuously every day while I was hungry in India, and ye gave Me no bread; thirsty in China, and ye gave Me no drink; sick and in prison in Africa, and ye visited Me not;" "*Inasmuch as ye did it not unto the least of these my brethren, ye did it not unto Me.*" We have not done our duty to Africa, as will be seen by a comparison of what American societies spend in Asia and Africa respectively, but if, in addition to her claim on account of her numbers we should, in the spirit of the repentant Zacheus, restore unto Africa four fold that which we have taken by false accusation, what a noble atonement we might make in sending missionaries for the slaves that were taken and Bibles for the rum which America is dumping on her shores by the million gallons annually. Your money or your life is a terribly true expression of spiritual conditions. Your money is the concrete representative of your love, your gratitude, your obedience. God grant that there may come to all who read this a new vision of the whitening fields, a profounder sense of personal duty and warmer touch of the Saviour's sympathy. God grant that all may do something; that some may give grandly to this grand need, and that none may imitate those servants "who with one consent began to make excuse."

Mormons, 1904

No other religious body in America has made "mission" so central a part of its life, so commonplace a word in its vocabulary. Long before the Church of Jesus Christ of Latter Day Saints had settled in Utah, long before the "Gentile" persecution of Mormons had ceased, the followers of Joseph Smith and Brigham Young had gone abroad to tell of the new revelation and to recruit members for the new church. They thereby set a pattern followed to the present wherein most able-bodied young Mormon males spend a year or two away from home on their "mission." Early in the twentieth century, two Mormon missionaries, writing for their church's paper, tell of the great work abroad: (1) Anthon L. Skanchy on Scandinavia, and (2) Francis M. Lyman on other areas of Europe and beyond.

1.

This mission, to which I have been called, is a rather extensive one — comprising Denmark, Sweden and Norway, with their numerous surrounding islands — and is known as the Scandinavian mission. Denmark is a small, level lowland, very fertile and thickly populated. It consists mainly of islands, and is located between parallels 55 and 57, north latitude, and contains 38,311 square kilometers, with a population of about 2,500,000. Copenhagen, the capital, has 500,000 inhabitants, and it was here that our venerable brother, Apostle Erastus Snow, fifty-five years ago, opened the door of the Gospel to these nations. It appears that, a couple of years before his arrival, the spirit of liberty had been poured out upon the Danish nation, upon the government and upon the royal family to such an extent that a very liberal constitution had been framed, which guaranteed religious liberty for the people in the land — a preparation for the proclamation of the Gospel. Persecutions were, nevertheless, started against our brethren when they came with the Latter-day message, and although no violent measures were taken against them by the authorities, the mob spirit sometimes ran very high. Violence went so far that blood was shed, and a young man who had embraced the Gospel fell an innocent victim to an assassin's dagger, in the city of Aalborg, in Jylland. The earthly remains of that young martyr are now resting in Aalborg cemetery, and loving hands are still keeping his grave trimmed and decorated with flowers. But here, as in other places, it was only a question of time until the Gospel should find its way to the honest among the people, and, as its principles became more and more known, many were convinced of their truth, and received the Gospel message. Charity and liberality are characteristic of the people here, and the Elders, who in those days were mostly called

[Source: (1) *The Latter-Day Saint Millennial Star*, 46 (Feb. 11, 1904), 81–82. (2) Ibid., 46 (Jan. 7, 1904), 1–2.]

from among the native Saints, had but little trouble in finding shelter and subsistence. From that time until the present 46,911 noble souls have embraced the Gospel.

From the year 1850 until the end of 1903, in Denmark alone 24,039 persons have been baptized into the Church, and 16,000 of these have emigrated in charge of the Elders. These emigrants have made themselves prominent as faithful, industrious Latter-day Saints, who have taken an active part in the upbuilding of the stakes of Zion.

Informal portrait of the First Presidency of the Church of Jesus Christ of Latter-day Saints, c. 1904: Joseph Fielding Smith, Anthon H. Lund, John R. Winder
(Keystone-Mast Collection, University of California, Riverside)

2.

At the close of my presidency over the European mission, it is a pleasing task to express to the ministry, the Saints and our friends, the gratitude I feel to the Lord for His abundant blessings and to them for their personal kindness and hearty support. It is also appropriate to state briefly the condition of the mission and something of the work that has been done during the past two and half years. At the last October conference, the Saints will remember, Elder Heber J. Grant of the Council of Twelve Apostles was appointed to preside over this field. The business has all been turned over to him now, and he begins his administration with our love and confidence and most cordial wish that he may be prosperous and happy in his work. I hope he will find the field in a satisfactory condition.

The Elders of the European mission are, almost without exception, full of zeal and the spirit of their work. There are at the present time five hundred and ninety-seven missionaries from Zion, five of whom are sisters. They are laboring mainly in the British Isles, Scandinavia, Germany, Switzerland, and the Netherlands, but are also found in Iceland, Austria and Hungary, Palestine and South Africa. Since the time of my arrival, May 17, 1901, seven hundred and forty missionaries have registered at Liverpool; six hundred and eight have during this time departed for home. We have been called to mourn the death of three of our fellow-laborers. . . .

A cause of far greater concern and grief has been the fall of Elders from honor and virtue. During my presidency there have been seven, who disregarding their holy covenants and all that is worth living for, have yielded to the temptations of the adversary. They have been stripped of every vestige of authority and excommunicated from the Church. There was no alternative course to take with them. It is deplorable when an Elder thus turns from his high calling. The cases have been scattered, each of the large missions having had at least one. It is about one Elder in a hundred that has fallen. Let the anguish which each of them has suffered be a life's warning to the ninety and nine who thus far, by the help of the Lord, have been able to stand.

During the time it has been my privilege to labor here there have been, in the European mission, exclusive of the work done during last December, 5,193,824 tracts and 184,085 books distributed, and 4,018 baptisms performed. Greater efficiency of the Elders has been gained in the mission by doing away with what were known as conference houses. The present system of having not more than two men live together, and their lodgings to be taken with strangers, has brought the Elders into contact with more people and been followed by very satisfactory results.

The field of missionary effort is broadening. In both Austria and Hungary openings have been made and Elders are now laboring. In India Elder John H. Cooper, who has just returned after laboring alone a year and a half, raised up a thriving branch. More Elders will be sent there soon, we hope, to carry on the good work. The mission in South Africa was opened last July by President Warren H. Lyon and three companions. This is an old field which has not been worked for about forty years. The prospects are that the mission will prosper. Personally I have visited Africa, Palestine, Greece, Italy, France, Finland, Russia and Poland, and have dedicated these lands to the preaching of the Gospel, and besought the Lord to open the way for His servants to come in and lead souls to accept His plan of salvation. Since I thus dedicated Africa, the mission has been established in the southern part, and since my visit to Russia Elder Mischa Markow has gone into that land and declared his message. These are small beginnings, but the Lord, if He wills, can make them great.

Persecuted Witnesses, 1934

In Allegheny, Pennsylvania, in 1872, "Christian persons met together . . . to consider the Scriptures relative to the coming of Christ and His Kingdom." Out of this gathering came the group ultimately to be known as "Jehovah's Witnesses." In 1916 Joseph Franklin Rutherford (1869–1942) took over leadership of the rapidly expanding fellowship, guiding it through the difficulties of World War I (the Witnesses declined to serve in the armed forces) and beyond. Noted for their vigorous missionary efforts at home, these "Watch Tower Bible Students" also pressed on with their message north to Canada, south to Latin America, east to Britain and the continent of Europe. Everywhere they met with persecution: from capitalist, communist, fascist, from devout believer, and from callous unbeliever. The excerpt below tells of their difficult days in Hitler's Germany and of their uncompromising protest against any interference in the exercise of their religion.

A convention was arranged to be held at the fair-grounds in Basel, Switzerland, from September 7 to 9, 1934. Brother Rutherford hoped to meet a number of brothers from Germany there, to hear from them firsthand about the actual situation in the country. Under most adverse conditions almost a thousand brothers from Germany were able to attend. They later reported how distressed Brother Rutherford was when he personally heard what the brothers had already been forced to suffer.

On the other hand, he was forced to recognize that even the traveling overseers present were not of one mind as regards the preaching work. He spoke to them about steps to be taken in Germany after the convention. Plans for united action were made.

October 7, 1934, will forever remain something special in the memories

[Source: *1974 Yearbook of Jehovah's Witnesses* (Brooklyn: Watchtower Bible and Tract Society, 1974), pp. 132–33, 136–37.]

of all those who had the privilege of participating in the events of that day. On that day Hitler and his government were confronted by the fearless action of Jehovah's witnesses — in his eyes a ridiculous minority.

Details were spelled out in a letter from Brother Rutherford, a copy of which was to be taken by special messenger to every congregation in Germany. At the same time these messengers were instructed to make preparations for meetings to be held throughout Germany on this particular day. Brother Rutherford's letter said, in part:

"Every group of Jehovah's witnesses in Germany should gather together at a convenient place in the city where they live, on Sunday morning, October 7, 1934, at 9:00 o'clock. This letter should be read to all present. You should join together in prayer to Jehovah asking him through Christ Jesus, our Head and King, for his guidance, protection, deliverance and blessing. Immediately thereafter send a letter to German government officials which text will have been prepared beforehand and will then be available. A few minutes should be spent discussing Matthew 10:16–24, keeping in mind that by doing as this text says, you are 'standing for your lives.' (Esther 8:11) The meeting should then be closed and you should go out to your neighbors giving them a witness about Jehovah's name, about our God and his Kingdom under Christ Jesus.

"Your brothers throughout the world will be thinking of you and will direct a similar prayer to Jehovah at the same time." . . .

In harmony with the action being taken by Jehovah's witnesses throughout Germany, everyone . . . enthusiastically agreed that the following letter should be sent to the government on that day by registered mail:

"To the Officials of the Government:

"The Word of Jehovah God, as set out in the Holy Bible, is the supreme law, and to us it is our sole guide for the reason that we have devoted ourselves to God and are true and sincere followers of Christ Jesus.

"During the past year, and contrary to God's law and in violation of our rights, you have forbidden us as Jehovah's witnesses to meet together to study God's Word and worship and serve him. In his Word he commands us that we shall not forsake the assembling of ourselves together. (Hebrews 10:25) To us Jehovah commands: 'Ye are my witnesses that I am God. Go and tell the people my message.' (Isaiah 43:10, 12; Isaiah 6:9; Matthew 24:14) There is a direct conflict between your law and God's law, and, following the lead of the faithful apostles, 'we ought to obey God rather than men,' and this we will do. (Acts 5:29) Therefore this is to advise you that at any cost we will obey God's commandments, will meet together for the study of his Word, and will worship and serve him as he has commanded. If your government or officers do violence to us because we are obeying God, then our blood will be upon you and you will answer to Almighty God.

"We have no interest in political affairs, but are wholly devoted to God's kingdom under Christ his King. We will do no injury or harm to anyone. We would delight to dwell in peace and do good to all men as we have opportunity, but, since your government and its officers continue in your attempt to force us to disobey the highest law of the universe, we are compelled to now give you notice that we will, by his grace, obey Jehovah God and fully trust Him to deliver us from all oppression and oppressors."

Missions Reevaluated

W. H. P. Faunce (1859–1930)

President of Brown University for thirty years (1899–1929) and leading Baptist spokesman, Faunce in 1914 looked at the burgeoning missionary activity not in terms of the number of converts but in terms of its "social aspects." What impact have missionaries had on culture, on health and welfare, on the civilizing process itself? One should not claim too much for missions, Faunce cautioned; nor, however, should one overlook "the mainspring of human progress."

No one would claim that the Christian missionary enterprise, or even the Christian faith itself, has been the sole source of recent progress in the non-Christian world. The obligation of perfect candor, which rests on every historian, is peculiarly binding on one who deals with the facts or the narratives of religious enterprise. To view all missionary statistics through rose-colored glasses, ignoring the grim obstacles that face all noble effort, and the failures that are common to all good men at home and abroad, is to prepare for a rude awakening and reaction when the full truth is known. To suppress discouraging facts in order to secure continued support, or to ignore contributory causes in order to magnify our own effort, would be both dishonest and suicidal. The Book of Acts, the first missionary journal, is in this respect a marvel of candor. Belonging avowedly to the literature of propaganda, it nevertheless does not hesitate to record the small results of the magnificent address on Mars' Hill, the lamentable dissension of Paul and Barnabas, and the "many adversaries" to be faced at Ephesus.

There is glory enough for the foreign missionary enterprise, even when all other powers have been given their full credit. Traders from Western lands, with no altruistic motive, have often carried the tools of civilization far and wide. Commercial companies are to-day sending thousands of plows

[Source: W. H. P. Faunce, *The Social Aspects of Foreign Missions* (New York: Missionary Education Movement of the United States and Canada, 1914), pp. 101–3.]

into Africa, looms into India, oil into China, sewing-machines into the South Sea Islands, and are constructing railways, canals, and telephone lines throughout the Orient. It was the United States government behind Commodore Perry that compelled the opening of Japan in 1853. It is the British government that by the building of the great dam across the Nile at Assuan, and the introduction of better methods of tilling the soil, is now lifting the Egyptian peasant out of poverty six thousand years old. Applied science, as we have already seen, is reshaping vast regions of the world, both East and West. It is changing ancient modes of life, creating new wants, putting Sheffield cutlery and Lancashire cottons into Bombay and Calcutta, German rifles into Turkey, and American automobiles into Java and Borneo.

But when all this has been admitted, it remains true that the mainspring of human progress has been for nineteen hundred years, and is to-day, the Christian faith. The moral dynamic that transformed our wild forefathers, the Saxons, Celts, and Scandinavians, into civilized nations was not science — then unborn — not politics, literature, or art; it was Christianity.

William E. Hocking (1873 – 1966)

Professor of Philosophy at Harvard (1914 – 43) and Congregational churchman, Hocking led a "Layman's Inquiry" into a century of missionary activity. This probing evaluation inquired into the design and purpose of missions, their scope and effectiveness, their merit and ultimate validity. In the document below, Hocking sees this enterprise as having matured from its earlier evangelical phase to its present humanitarian one — though the two aspects are not to be thought of as mutually exclusive. And while he defends the importance of "a true and well-qualified evangelism," Hocking also urges that the "spirit of Christian service" be distinguished from "the work of conscious and direct evangelization."

When the modern missionary movement came to birth at the end of the eighteenth century its objectives were clear and definite. It was an outflow of the widespread religious awakening which came to Europe and America near the middle of that century. This movement, commonly called the "Evangelical Awakening," put its chief emphasis on individual salvation. Under its stimulus men felt impelled to go to the ends of the earth to save souls and build them into the church. The great personalities who led this movement were primarily evangelists.

But they were more than evangelists. Their enterprise would not so pro-

[Source: W. E. Hocking, *Re-thinking Missions: A Layman's Inquiry after One Hundred Years* (New York: Harper & Brothers, 1932), pp. 60 – 62, 63 – 64, 69 – 70.]

foundly have altered the course of events in the regions where they worked if they had not quickly perceived how much more than preaching was involved in their undertaking. In order to proclaim their own message they were obliged to master languages, translate the Scriptures, and produce literature in those languages. Almost from the beginning of their work in the Orient, there were missionaries who saw that a scheme of education was a necessity, if enlightened leaders and pastors were to be developed. The missionary as a man has always been sensitive to the suffering of others, and as a Christian has accepted a peculiar responsibility for relieving it. Hospitals and other medical service were natural developments. Thus there has been no time in the history of modern missions when the philanthropic objective has not had a place.

But in the course of a hundred years, this place has become a very large one, as thoughtful and forward-looking missionaries have gradually realized what is involved in their enterprise. Starting with the purpose of saving individual souls, they have been drawn on by necessity into efforts to build up the minds, and the bodies, and to improve the social life in which these souls are engaged. The educational and other associated interests have grown until in volume and variety they now outrank the parent activity. There is a visible tendency to regard them as having a value of their own, and as being legitimate functions of Christian missions apart from any explicit evangelization. It is as if "salvation" had begun to take on a new meaning: men are to be saved, not for the next world alone, and not out of human life, but within human life. A thoroughgoing acceptance of this view would mean a new epoch in the conception of the task of mission. . . .

There is a danger that diversifying the scope of effort horizontally may be at the expense of depth. Uplifters and social betterment experts easily fall into the vain supposition that by simply improving the economic basis of life or by cleverly re-shuffling human relationships they can produce the happy world of their hopes. All proposals for cure through philanthropy alone, miss the point of central importance, namely, that there must be *first of all a new kind of person as the unit of society if there is to be a new social order*. Social efforts which ignore this principle have at times brought disillusionment: impressive and stable results are difficult and rare. What count most in the progress of society are simple day by day events, such as may take place in the mind of a youth here and there or in the formation of a new friendship. These tiny rootlet processes in the long run remake civilization. The main contribution of the mission has been not in devising new social programs, but in forming the men who do the devising. Nothing therefore can displace or minimize the importance of a true and well-qualified evangelism. . . .

But there is a special reason for regarding the ministry of deeds as a fit vehicle for a Christian message. For Christianity, in contrast to religions of illusion or of pessimism, regards the condition of the human being in human society as an express object of God's concern. Human history becomes a field in which the divine life and the divine solicitude are manifested. "Inasmuch as ye have done it unto one of the least of these my brethren ye have done it unto me." To regard social service as something more than a humanitarian act of relief, namely, as an act of union with God's will, is thus in a special sense an expression of the kernel of the Christian faith.

We believe, then, that the time has come to set the educational and other philanthropic aspects of mission work free from organized responsibility to the work of conscious and direct evangelization. We must be willing to give largely without any preaching; to cooperate with non-Christian agencies for social improvement; and to foster the initiative of the Orient in defining the ways in which we shall be invited to help.

This means that we must work with *greater faith* in invisible successes. We must count it a gain when without addition to our institutional strength the societies of the East are slowly permeated with the spirit of Christian service. This attitude will be in accord with the *greater patience* implied in the permanent mission program: the universal church is to arrive, but by its own mode of building, and in God's own time.

4. NEW STRUCTURES

Comforting the Afflicted

Salvation Army

Organized in England in 1865, the Salvation Army spread to the United States soon thereafter. This "new structure" seemed peculiarly adapted to the human needs which urbanization and industrialization accentuated or aggravated. (1) In a 1900 description of the Army's work in America, Frederick Booth-Tucker (1853 – 1929; son-in-law of William Booth, the founder) tells of the organization's evolution from personal evangelism to "social salvation." (2) And in an account written one year earlier, Booth-Tucker acknowledges the central role of women in every level of ministry within the Salvation Army.

1.

Social Salvation

As its name signifies, the Salvation army was originally started with the sole aim of reaching the non-church-going masses with the Gospel. Here was the appalling statement made by those who had given the matter years of patient study, that 90% of the working classes in the older civilizations of Europe habitually neglected public worship and had practically cut themselves loose from even the outward profession of religion. It was to remedy this condition of affairs that William and Catherine Booth set to work.

As evangelists they could crowd the largest buildings with the vast crowds who flocked to their meetings. Their converts were numbered by thousands. Yet they could not fail to notice and mourn over the fact that those who came were mostly church-goers and professors of religion. The godless multitudes drifted past their doors. To reach them, other methods must be pursued. Their habits must be studied and they must be followed to their haunts and hiding-places.

[Sources: Frederick Booth-Tucker, *The Social Relief Work of the Salvation Army in the United States* (1900), pp. 6–7, 9–10; and (2), by the same author, *The Salvation Army in the United States* (1899), n. p. —both found in *The Salvation Army in America* (New York: Arno Press, 1972).]

When, however, this had been done, it became daily more and more evident that the evils to be combatted were of a temporal as well as of a spiritual character. Churchlessness was with these classes the natural outcome of homelessness, worklessness and worthlessness. To combat the evil, its causes must be radically dealt with. The task was truly a gigantic one. But General Booth was not the man to shrink from it. Cautiously and experimentally at first, and finally with the confidence that was the natural outcome of repeated success, he grappled with the problem.

In traversing and transforming these melancholy wastes of woe, root principles were discovered and laid down for the guidance of the legion of well-trained workers who had been rapidly enrolled.

The poor were to be treated with love, and not with suspicion or contempt.

They were to be classified, not as the worthy and unworthy, but as those who were willing to work out their own regeneration, and the unwilling.

They were to be encouraged in every possible way to become their own deliverers.

Each institution was to aim at self-support by the labor or payments of its inmates.

Social reform to be complete must include the soul as well as the body. In other words the man himself must be changed and not merely his circumstances.

To save a man for this world should be but a stepping-stone toward saving him for the next. . . .

From the above facts it may be regarded as certain that the "submerged" classes in America, including the criminal, the vicious and the purely pauper elements, number not less than 3,000,000 under favorable sociological circumstances, while the number is liable to increase alarmingly during seasons of commercial depression.

For dealing with this mass of poverty and suffering the Salvation army in the United States has organized the various institutions and agencies described in the following pages. These include:

Shelters for homeless men; shelters for homeless women; homes for clerks and artisans; homes for girls working in stores and offices; homes for children; rescue homes for fallen women; slum posts for slum visitation and meetings; slum day nurseries for infants; cheap food depots and cent-meals; cheap clothing and second-hand stores; salvage brigades for collection of household and office waste; woodyards; employment bureaus; Knights of hope for prison visitation and ex-criminals; winter relief; medical relief, including free hospital and dispensaries; summer outings for the poor; penny ice wagons; Christmas and Thanksgiving dinners; missing friends and inquiry department; farm colonies for the poor.

The complex character of the remedies above indicated has been necessitated by the complex nature of the evil to be dealt with. To the uninitiated eye poverty appears to be one seething cauldron of dirt, rags, hunger, hypocrisy and misery. To the skilled eye of our officers, who devote their lives

Salvation Army coal distribution depot, 1902
(New York Public Library)

to the practical task of combatting the evil, the poor may be divided into classes which are as sharply defined and unmixable as the castes of the Hindoos, or the stratas of geology. To deal successfully with the monster of poverty, each of its hydra heads must be separately handled, with methods peculiar to itself and with a staff of workers who are trained to become experts in their own particular department, whilst the sunshine of love and the tender showers of Gospel grace are made to permeate the mass.

2.

A Sphere for Woman's Work.

In no religious or secular organization is there so free a hand allowed to women as in The Salvation Army, and to this fact is undoubtedly due a large measure of its success. The Hallelujah Lass has from the earliest days of the movement proved herself its Joan of Arc. Into the heart of slumdom she has carried the banner of salvation, and if her bonnet has become an equally familiar sight in the offices of our merchant princes, it is only that she may plead the claims of the poor and champion their cause.

Problems that statesmanship and philanthropy have failed to solve have yielded to the gentle magic of these heroines of slumdom. "If there is a fight we make straight for the centre of it," said one of these girl warriors, who had been born and bred in the lap of luxury and had forsaken a comfortable home and brilliant social prospects in order to minister to the semi-savages of our city jungles. "Even if they are inflamed with drink or are using knives or revolvers, they never touch us. The people would almost tear them to pieces if they did."

"There are only two saloons in Chicago where we are not allowed to visit," said another of these officers, "and we go to them regularly every week. When the proprietor reminds us that he has already forbidden us to come, we answer, 'Yes, sir; but we have come to see whether you have changed your mind yet!'"

Thousands of those who never cross the threshold of a church are to be found night after night in our meetings. Even when they do not profess to be converted, a marked change comes frequently over their lives. The meetings possess for these men a strange fascination, drawing them away from the glittering allurements of the saloons and dives and low music halls.

The personal magnetism of these women, their fearless face-to-face dealing with the wicked and their patient toil in behalf of the suffering poor are not the only secrets of their success. Prayer and faith equip the most timid of them for the platform duties from which they would naturally shrink. "It is so much easier," they say, "to act than to talk." And yet the burning words which fall from their lips, powerful in their simplicity, go straight to the hearts of their hearers and result in wonderful reformations.

As organizers and administrators many of our women officers have proven themselves to be in no sense inferior to the men, and the fact that they are equally eligible for our most responsible offices has helped to draw forth gifts which have only been latent for want of exercise.

The "Y" Movement

The nation's churches and synagogues demonstrated particular concern for the young people removed from familiar and supportive surroundings, deprived of family and friends. Again, England led the way, with a London Young Men's Christian Association (YMCA) being started in 1844. Only after the Civil War, however, did the "Y" movement become a significant force in America. By the time of the nation's next great war in 1917–18, the

[Source: C. Howard Hopkins, *History of the Y.M.C.A. in North America* (New York: Association Press, 1951), pp. 524–25.]

YMCA was in a position to play a major role in providing off-duty rec-
reation and refreshment to servicemen at home and abroad. Also by that
time, all major religious groups in America were sponsoring distinct asso-
ciations for their young people. The YMCA, oldest of these several groups,
started out in close affiliation with evangelical religion and Protestant re-
vivalism. Like the Salvation Army, however, the "Y" moved gradually
from an emphasis on personal Bible-reading and prayer to a concern with
social problems and community welfare. The 1936 statement of "Objectives
and Characteristics," excerpted below, also indicates the developing inter-
racial and interdenominational emphasis.

DISTINCTIVE OBJECTIVES AND CHARACTERISTICS

The Young Men's Christian Association we regard as being in its essential
genius a world-wide fellowship of men and boys, united by a common loyalty
to Jesus, for the purpose of developing Christian personality and building a
Christian society.

1. Developing Christian Personality

The first Young Men's Christian Association was formed by a group of
young men, who worked and lived together, for mutual helpfulness in maintaining Christian standards and growing in Christian experience in the face
of their working and living conditions. What characterized the first Association group has been distinctive of the Y.M.C.A. throughout its development. It provides a medium for mutual helpfulness in Christian living to
boys, young and older men, where they live, attend school, work, or spend
their leisure time. It seeks to enlist boys and men in the Christian life and
to lead them to avail themselves of the opportunities it offers for the development of Christian experience.

To these ends Association work at its best provides:

1. *Groups* around school, vocational, neighborhood, friendship, leisuretime,
   and other social relations which furnish a medium for mutual helpfulness
   to boys and men in their everyday lives.

2. *A group program, leadership* and *methodology* through which boys and men
   — may find opportunity for a group fellowship through which they can
     help one another in personal problems and can reinforce one another's
     ideals and purposes, and in which they may share and discuss experi-
     ence in meeting their life situations.
   — may live coöperatively rather than competitively amid the consequences
     of the competitive struggle so common in our modern world.
   — may be challenged through the study of the Bible and of the writings
     of others in the nineteen centuries of Christian experience to explore
     the meaning of the Christian religion and its applicability to one's own

life, and through prayer and worship use its resources in facing personal problems.

— may have opportunity to enrich their lives in areas of need or interest.

— may obtain counsel from a leader or other competent individuals on their intimate personal problems, thus becoming happier and more skillful in their work, recreation, social and religious life.

3. *Service buildings* providing wholesome living, eating and recreational conditions for young and older men away from home or in the community. These centers are located near neighborhood, work, or school relationships, at railroad junction and lay-over points, important shore-leave ports for the Navy, near Army posts, industrial plants, and in student communities.

4. *Service to individuals* where there is need or strain in their living, school, work, or leisure-time relations. Counsel is made available to boys and men on personal difficulties, putting them in touch with experts where needed, helping them to make satisfactory church, social and other connections in strange communities, aiding them in vocational choice and placement and helping them to find the resources of the Christian religion. Healthful physical exercise, is provided. Courses of study are offered, suited in content and method to individual needs, so that younger and older men may improve their vocational status through proper training, and that individuals may enrich their lives in fields which they have not had previous opportunity to explore.

II. Building a Christian Society

Although the Association started as an agency for personal helpfulness, more recently it has come to recognize the close inter-relation of personal and social problems. Personal problems can be successfully solved only in a society that respects personal values. Further, the Christian gospel implies both the sacredness of individual personality and the necessity of a society based on sacredness of individual personality wherein people live together coöperatively in the spirit of good-will. Consequently the Association work seeks to enlist its functional groups in such group and intergroup programs as to:

1. Stimulate competent, constructive, independent thinking and action both on personal problems and on economic, political, inter-racial, and other issues.

2. Challenge men to explore the meaning of Christian principles and of the gospel and bring them to feel and understand the tension between life as it is and as it would be if the Christian ideals operated more fully in our economic, political, business, inter-racial and national affairs.

3. Encourage groups to re-make on the Christian pattern the life of which they are a part.

4. Encourage coöperation by dissenting groups or minorities within groups with those of like mind in the community to put into effect their varying Christian convictions.

5. Bring about through such activities a fellowship characterized by understanding and friendship, in which boys and men shall work together positively and constructively to transform the contemporary life of which they are a part.

Society of St. Vincent de Paul

Like the YMCA, the Society of St. Vincent de Paul had its origins abroad (France, 1845), but also like the "Y," it had its major impact in the United States after the Civil War. By the end of the century, the society had taken the lead in cooperating with other agencies and charities in order to accomplish as much as possible. So overwhelming were the needs and so overmultiplying the numbers that denominations must work together, must trust each other. That was the argument of Thomas M. Mulry (1855–1916), businessman and guiding hand of the Society in the city of New York.

In 1882, or thereabouts, the charity organization society was started in New York city. The objects of the society were to prevent the indiscriminate giving of relief, to evolve a system that would be acceptable to all, and to bring the various charities closer together.

The organization gave no relief, but acted as a sort of charities exchange, where all information could be obtained, and where people applying for assistance would be investigated and referred to proper relief societies. There was something repugnant to the catholic idea of charity in this new scheme. It seemed like dragging the worthy poor before the public, and there was nothing to appeal to our people in an organization which expended *all* its receipts in salaries and expenses, none going to the poor.

We refused to co-operate with them, but after a few years a better understanding developed itself. It was seen that there was a good side to the work.

After the organization had been in existence a few years, the attention of some of the members of the society of St. Vincent de Paul was called to the large number of catholic children attending the various protestant missions and Sunday schools. Immediately the charity organization society was looked upon as the cause.

[Source: Aaron I. Abell, *American Catholic Thought on Social Questions* (New York and Indianapolis: Bobbs-Merrill Co., 1968), pp. 179–80.]

It happened that the work of investigating the matter was assigned to me. I called upon the committee of the charity organization society. What did I find? A body of ladies and gentlemen earnestly endeavoring to do something to help God's poor, and most anxious for our moral support and co-operation.

There had been some catholic gentlemen's names used, but they had taken no active part. I found letters had been sent to clergymen, to conferences of the society of St. Vincent de Paul, to the various charitable organizations; but in most cases the letter had been thrown into the waste basket, the requests to assist ignored; and yet the people needed care and looking after.

Despairing of obtaining assistance from catholic sources, other people took on themselves the care of helping the families, with the result that, in many cases, the children were weaned from the Church.

We saw at once the field this work opened for us. We saw also the danger of neglecting this great means of doing good. Therefore, several catholic gentlemen became actively connected with the association. We soon made our people familiar with its purposes; we also received a warm welcome from the charity organization society. Our assistance was valued very highly and our advice appreciated.

From this beginning has spread a better feeling, a closer relation between the various charities than we had ever hoped for. It will certainly contribute more than anything else to that Christian unity which our beloved, august, and respected Pontiff so earnestly recommends. Perhaps the grand spectacle of a body of laymen devoting their leisure time, the world over, to visiting and relieving the poor has excited the admiration of our non-catholic friends more than anything else; — no paid agents, no class distinction, no petty social differences, all working gratuitously for God's poor, following the same rule, and practicing the same methods.

I have dwelt somewhat at length on the relations of the society of St. Vincent de Paul with the charity organization society because that society has been the great means of accomplishing this co-operation and of extending all the other charities.

Jewish Welfare Board

The Jewish Welfare Board, an American creation, arose in direct response to the requirements of the nation during World War I. For one thing, the selection of Jewish chaplains for the armed services required a Jewish voice. But, as noted below, "no single agency could be selected as representative of the Jewry in America." Thus the new board met the external need even as it satisfied internal requirements for greater unity in action. In this respect,

[Source: *American Jewish Yearbook*, XX (Philadelphia: Jewish Publication Society of America, 1918), pp. 88–89.]

it resembled the "Y" movement (and there were also Young Men's and Young Women's Hebrew Associations) as well as the Knights of Columbus, also referred to in the following document. (The major Roman Catholic fraternal order, the Knights of Columbus started out as a heavily Irish mutual aid society in New Haven, Connecticut, in 1882. In World War I it served as the chief channel of assistance and support for Roman Catholic servicemen.)

THE JEWISH WELFARE BOARD

By Chester Jacob Teller
Executive Director, Jewish Welfare Board

Primarily the purpose of the Jewish Welfare Board is to help America win the war. Despite the basic American principle of a separate Church and State, or, to be more exact, because of it, the American Government in the first days of the war perceived the necessity of calling upon certain religious welfare agencies to co-operate with it. It sought this co-operation because it recognized the value of morale in warfare, and knew how close was the relationship between morale and modern community ways of life. With a breadth of view and a degree of foresight, perhaps never before equalled by a war administration of any other country, the United States Government set itself to thinking out the war problems not only in terms of ships, guns, munitions, and supplies, but also in health, decency, personal improvement of the men, contentment, esprit. In short, all those elements that go to make up the concept of morale in its broadest implications received the closest study and the most thorough-going application.

A special Commission on Training Camp Activities was created, as a branch of the War Department, charged with the specific duties of making life in the new American camps and in the communities adjoining the camps as normal as conditions of actual war and the problems of an unprecedented national emergency would permit. This commission sought to utilize the potential social resources of the country, and it early brought to bear on the problem the whole strength of the Young Men's Christian Association, with its nation-wide organization, so thoroughly alive to the needs of young men, and so excellently adapted to the nation's new work.

In the same spirit and for the same purposes the War Department . . . invited the large Catholic group in America to participate in the national welfare program, with the result that the Knights of Columbus was nominated by the Catholic Church and accepted by the American Government as the authoritative Catholic agency for war purposes.

The selection of the third agency to represent what might be considered the third largest religious group in America, namely, the Jewish group, was fraught with difficulties. It is a commentary upon Jewish life in America, and particularly upon its work of national organization and management, that with 260 years of history behind it, and with literally thousands of organizations, no single agency could be selected as representative of the Jewry of America. True, one or two of them seemed to have some special claim to such recognition, but by reason of their limited constitution or platform, or for some other reason, they failed to secure the endorsement of the Jews as a whole. The result was a meeting of representatives of some ten or more national Jewish organizations, at which it was decided that each organization present should delegate certain powers to a new agency. This was the beginning of the organization which has since become known as the Jewish Welfare Board, and which has obtained the official recognition of the Government and, indeed, its mandate to contribute on behalf of the Jews of America to the national work of welfare among the nation's uniformed men.

Gathering the Divided

Federal Council and Christian Cooperation

The first quarter of the twentieth century saw a great increase in cooperation across denominational lines, even across religious lines. World War I, as we have seen, provided much of the impetus, but certainly not all. The Federal Council of Churches, for example, had been formed well before the war when, in 1908, thirty denominations joined together "to bring the Christian bodies of America into united service for Christ and the world." Writing more than a decade later, Charles S. Macfarland (General Secretary of the Federal Council from 1911 to 1930) explained that in the "new and complex social order" everything was getting federated and organized except religion. That condition required changing, for "we spoke with voices, but not with a voice."

Our various denominations and sects arose largely from the demand for freedom, and through much suffering we found our freedom. We are now recognizing as denominations, however, that the highest freedom we possess may be the freedom to give up some of our freedom for the sake of the common good. This was the kind of freedom to which Paul referred in his discussion of those denominational differences which had already begun in the Apostolic Church. We are ready to acknowledge, without forgetting perhaps that in our intellectual expression of truth we have been of Apollos or Cephas, that we are all of Christ, and that in allegiance to Him we must maintain or regain unity even in the midst of our diversity. We are following still farther our denominational search for freedom, and are seeking this

[Source: C. S. Macfarland, *The Progress of Church Federation* (New York: Fleming H. Revell Co., 1921), pp. 10–11, 11–12, 14–16.]

highest freedom in our modern movements towards Christian unity. . . .

Meanwhile one of the most startling of modern discoveries is that we have been so sadly and thoughtlessly wasteful. We have wasted our mineral wealth, squandered our forests, and allowed the mighty forces of our streams to run out into an unneeding sea.

Worse still, in the development of industry, and by social neglect, we have wretchedly wasted our human power and, as our new legislation witnesses, we have been criminally prodigal with human life itself. We have poisoned, neglected, maimed, and mangled by our inefficient speeding up, by our twelve-hour days and seven-day weeks. . . .

But these are not an intimation of the worst of our dissipations, and indeed these wastes have been largely because of a deeper and more serious prodigality. We have let the very light within us become darkness, and the saddest of all has been the waste of our moral powers, our finer emotions, and our religious enthusiasms, through sectarian divisions, denominational rivalries, and unrestrained caprice often deluding itself as a religious loyalty. . . .

Meanwhile the development of a new and complex social order about us was getting ready for the call of a persuasive and effective gospel. New foes were arising on every hand. They were all united, and we found ourselves facing federated vice, the federated saloon, federated corruption in political life, federated human exploitation, and then all these together multiplied in one strong federation, the federation of commercialized iniquity. All of these were bound together in a solemn league and covenant, and the reason they so confidently faced a derided Church was because they faced a divided one.

On the one hand were the federations of labor and on the other hand federations of capital, girding themselves for their conflict, waiting the voice which should speak with power and influence, that should quell their human hatreds.

Problems of social justice were looking to us with beseeching voice, and we found ourselves obliged to face them, or, worse still, to shun them, with shame upon our faces and with a bewildered consciousness, because we had no common articulation of a code of spiritual principles or moral laws. Our spiritual authority was not equal to our human sympathy, because it was divided.

On all these things we had a multitude of voices trying to express the same consciousness, but the great world of men did not know it. Why should they know it when we had not found it out ourselves? We spoke with voices, but not with a voice.

Very nearly up to our own day the Church has faced united iniquity while there has been scarcely a city in which it could be said, in any real or serious sense, that its churches moved as one great force. And in many a town and rural village we yet have churches wearying themselves to death in a vain struggle for competitive existence, or suffering from that worst of diseases, to be "sick with their brothers' health."

What wonder that we have lost our civic virtue! Why should we not lose, not only our Sabbath as a day of worship, but also our Sunday as a day of rest? Why are we surprised that we have lost not only temperance laws but also our temperate ways? Why should we be astonished that with the loss of these we have also lost our sons and filled our houses of refuge with our daughters? Why should we wonder that the rich have left us for their unrestrained, unholy pleasure and the poor because we had no united sense of power of social justice to restrain an industry that devoured widows' houses and that bound heavy burdens grievous to be borne, especially when this was sometimes done by those who for a pretense made long prayers? What wonder that, with disintegrated religions which gave no adequate sense of religion, the home should lose its sacredness and the family become the easy prey of easy divorce and of unholy marriage? Still we went on singing: "Like a mighty army moves the Church of God." And when we came to resolve it to its final analysis the only trouble was that we did not sing together.

National Catholicism

World War I did provide the direct stimulus for a more unified social engagement on the part of America's Roman Catholics. In 1917 a general convention in Washington, D.C., led to the creation of a National Catholic War Council to supervise the recruitment and training of military chaplains as well as to oversee other war-related activities. But when the war ended, the new-found unity was not allowed to lapse. A National Catholic Welfare Council (and later Conference) kept the same initials in 1919 but widened its scope to include a broad array of social concerns. The entire American hierarchy, gathered at the Catholic University of America, addressed many issues in their long Pastoral Letter of 1919, but among them was the scope and structure of this revised organization.

In view of the results obtained through the merging of our activities for the time and purpose of war, we determined to maintain, for the ends of peace, the spirit of union and the coordination of our forces. We have accordingly grouped together, under the National Catholic Welfare Council, the various agencies by which the cause of religion is furthered. Each of these, continuing its own special work in its chosen field, will now derive additional support through general cooperation. And all will be brought into closer contact with the Hierarchy, which bears the burden alike of authority and of responsibility for the interests of the Catholic Church.

Under the direction of the Council and, immediately, of the Administrative Committee, several Departments have been established, each with a specific function, as follows:

[Source: Peter Guilday, ed., *The National Pastorals of the American Hierarchy, 1792–1919* (Westminster, Md.: Newman Press, 1954), pp. 296–97.]

The Department of Education, to study the problems and conditions which affect the work and development of our Catholic schools;

The Department of Social Welfare, to coordinate those activities which aim at improving social conditions in accordance with the spirit of the Church;

The Department of Press and Literature, to systematize the work of publication;

The Department of Societies and Lay Activities, to secure a more thoroughly unified action among our Catholic organizations.

For the development and guidance of missionary activity, provision has been made through The American Board of Catholic Missions, which will have in charge both the Home and the Foreign Missions.

The organization of these Departments is now in progress. To complete it, time and earnest cooperation will be required. The task assigned to each is so laborious and yet so promising of results, that we may surely expect, with the Divine assistance and the loyal support of our clergy and people, to promote more effectually the glory of God, the interests of His Church, and the welfare of our country.

Cooperative Judaism

By the end of the first quarter of the twentieth century, the divisions in Judaism described above (see pp. 54 – 60) were familiar across much of the American landscape. Many voices spoke for Judaism in America. Was it possible for Judaism on certain subjects and under certain circumstances to speak with one voice? That hope led to the formation of the Synagogue Council of America on November 9, 1926, in the city of New York. Never as integrative as some of its founders hoped, the Council did nonetheless become the cooperative arm of Judaism in dealing with the Federal Council of Churches as well as the National Catholic Welfare Council. It also played a major role in the National Conference of Christians and Jews, an interfaith agency formed in 1928. A portion of the 1926 Constitution of the Synagogue Council is excerpted below, along with part of a 1931 statement of its progress to that point.

CONSTITUTION AND BY-LAWS OF THE SYNAGOGUE COUNCIL OF AMERICA

Preamble

Whereas, The synagogue is the basic and essential unit of our Jewish life, and whereas it is desirable that the representatives of the synagogues in

[Source: *The Synagogue Council of America: Its Origin and Activities* (New York: n. p., 1931), pp. 2 – 3, 6.]

America meet from time to time in order to take counsel together for the sacred purpose of preserving and fostering Judaism,

Be it resolved, That a Council composed of representatives of national congregational and rabbinical organizations of America be formed, for the purpose of speaking and acting unitedly in furthering such religious interests as the constituent organizations in the council have in common; it being clearly provided that the council interfere in no way with the religious and administrative autonomy of any of the constituent organizations.

Name

The name of the organization shall be "The Synagogue Council of America."

Membership

The organizations constituting this council shall be

> Central Conference of American Rabbis
> Rabbinical Assembly of the United Synagogue of America
> Rabbinical Council of the Union of Orthodox Jewish Congregations of
>   America
> Union of American Hebrew Congregations
> Union of Orthodox Jewish Congregations of America
> United Synagogue of America

and such other similar national organizations as may be admitted from time to time. Each constituent organization shall be entitled to three members in the Synagogue Council as well as to three alternates. The alternates shall have the privilege of attending all meetings of the Council and participating in discussion. In case of the absence or disability of a delegate, an alternate shall be entitled to vote in his stead. . . .

THE SPIRIT OF THE COUNCIL

Whatever doubts existed as to the practical need of the Synagogue Council, or that representatives of different shades of religious doctrine in American Israel could meet in candor and good will for mutual action were soon dissipated. In four years of earnest and thoughtful conference the Synagogue Council of America has vindicated the high expectations of its advocates. More than good will between Jews and Christians is good will between Jews and Jews and an appreciation of their differing viewpoints is necessary and desirable.

Devotion and candor dominate the delegates. The sacred cause of advancing Judaism guides its representatives. The Council is not given over to a compilation of statistics. It is not carried away by the cry of the majority nor by passion for publicity. Essentially a deliberative body, its conclusions are arrived at only through careful and thoughtful study.

The combined membership of the three rabbinical associations in the Council represents 800 rabbis, or sixty-five percent of all the Jewish ministers in the United States. The Union of Orthodox Congregations, the United Synagogue of America, and the Union of American Hebrew Congregations have a joint membership of 800 congregations. Conservatively estimated, this means that the Synagogue Council of America speaks for at least one million Jewish men and women in our country, and is therefore representative of the religious affiliation of the majority of American Jews. If so, religious Israel has found a voice. The Synagogue Council of America must interpret that voice. Why then should it not develop a statesmanship of policy, authority, and direction?

Drying Out the Republic

Billy Sunday (1862– 1935)

Serving as the prototype for Sinclair Lewis's Elmer Gantry, *Billy Sunday dominated the revivalist scene in the early years of the twentieth century. Lacking the professionalism of C. G. Finney (see Vol. I, pp. 336–39) and the quiet assurance of D. L. Moody (see below, pp. 286–88), Sunday compensated with sensationalism and high drama. A former professional baseball player, this preacher sought to be nothing more than "one of the boys": unsophisticated, sometimes coarse, given to oversimplification, and sharing the limits of the culture that spawned him. What follows is a portion of his vigorous attack on "the hell-soaked liquor business"; the excerpt also illustrates something of Billy Sunday's sermon style.*

Listen! Here is an extract from the *Saturday Evening Post* of November 9, 1907, taken from a paper read by a brewer. You will say that a man didn't say it: "It appears from these facts that the success of our business lies in the creation of appetite among the boys. Men who have formed the habit scarcely ever reform, but they, like others, will die, and unless there are recruits made to take their places, our coffers will be empty, and I recommend to you that money spent in the creation of appetite will return in dollars to your tills after the habit is formed."

What is your raw materials, saloons? American boys. Say, I would not

[Source: William T. Ellis, *"Billy" Sunday: The Man and His Message* (Philadelphia: L. T. Myers, 1914), pp. 113, 114– 15.]

give one boy for all the distilleries and saloons this side of hell. And they have to have 2,000,000 boys every generation. And then you tell me you are a man when you will vote for an institution like that. What do you want to do, pay taxes in money or in boys?

I feel like an old fellow in Tennessee who made his living by catching rattlesnakes. He caught one with fourteen rattles and put it in a box with a glass top. One day when he was sawing wood his little five-year old boy, Jim, took the lid off and the rattler wriggled out and struck him in the cheek. He ran to his father and said, "The rattler has bit me." The father ran and chopped the rattler to pieces, and with his jack-knife he cut a chunk from the boy's cheek and then sucked and sucked at the wound to draw out the poison. He looked at little Jim, watched the pupils of his eyes dilate and watched him swell to three times his normal size, watched his lips become parched and cracked, and eyes roll, and little Jim gasped and died.

The father took him in his arms, carried him over by the side of the rattler, got on his knees and said, "O God, I would not give little Jim for all the rattlers that ever crawled over the Blue Ridge mountains."

And I would not give one boy for every dirty dollar you get from the hell-soaked liquor business or from every brewery and distillery this side of hell. . . .

You men have a chance to show your manhood. Then in the name of your pure mother, in the name of your manhood, in the name of your wife and the poor innocent children that climb up on your lap and put their arms around your neck, in the name of all that is good and noble, fight the curse. Shall you men, who hold in your hands the ballot, and in that ballot hold the destiny of womanhood and childhood and manhood, shall you, the sovereign power, refuse to rally in the name of the defenseless men and women and native land? No.

I want every man to say, "God, you can count on me to protect my wife, my home, my mother and my children and the manhood of America."

By the mercy of God, which has given to you the unshaken and unshakable confidence of her you love, I beseech you, make a fight for the women who wait until the saloons spew out their husbands and their sons, and send them home maudlin, brutish, devilish, stinking, blear-eyed, bloated-faced drunkards.

You say you can't prohibit men from drinking. Why, if Jesus Christ were here today some of you would keep on in sin just the same. But the law can be enforced against whisky just the same as it can be enforced against anything else, if you have honest officials to enforce it. Of course it doesn't prohibit. There isn't a law on the books of the state that prohibits. We have laws against murder. Do they prohibit? We have laws against burglary. Do they prohibit? We have laws against arson, rape, but they do not prohibit. Would you introduce a bill to repeal all the laws that do not prohibit? Any law will prohibit to a certain extent if honest officials enforce it. But no law will absolutely prohibit. We can make a law against liquor prohibit as much as any law prohibits.

Anti-Saloon League

Once again effective social action demanded organization. To make the Eighteenth Amendment (1919) a reality, more was required than the passionate denunciations of a Billy Sunday. Political action was called for: organized, deliberate, and as patient and single-minded as the circumstances demanded. The Anti-Saloon League, formed in 1895, worked slowly but steadily toward its goal of a national prohibition against the manufacture and sale of alcoholic beverages. In an article written in 1908, one sees this calm, unwavering purpose. The author, Superintendent of the Oakland District (California) for the League, also explains that the churches were the "natural starting point" and most fertile soil for cultivating members, monies, and energies. Individual reform can go only so far; then, social organization and political action are required.

There are but two methods of accomplishing reforms where the action of others is necessary for success. Either the will of these others must be influenced by persuading them that the change is right, or they must be forced to take certain action because it is best for their own welfare. When a moral reform is started, its method is always that of persuasion, but the time always comes when persuasion has accomplished its purpose, and the cause of reform is abated; or it is seen that the method is useless because it is too slow; or enough people have been convinced by this method to make a use of force hopeful.

As in other reforms, the agitation and effort to curb the vice of drunkenness began by persuasion and with the individual. A hundred years ago, men began signing pledges in order to bolster up a weak will, and then set about organizing societies and persuading others to join and sign pledges. Many confirmed drunkards were reformed, and with a true missionary spirit they began to induce others to follow their example. In the United States, seventy years ago, so great was the work done by these reformed drunkards — mainly by platform lectures — that thousands of men and women were persuaded.

Thirty years later, another great wave of persuasion was started, slightly different because it aimed, not at the drinker himself, but at the man who sold the drink. Moreover, it was the women, for the most part, who never drank at all, who were most active. Their method of persuasion was to appeal to the saloon keeper in a public way, through his religious instincts and his

[Source: W. M. Burke, "The Anti-Saloon League as a Political Force," in *Annals of the American Academy of Political and Social Science*, 33 (Nov., 1908), 27–28, 29–30.]

family affection, by praying and singing hymns in his place of business or
on the sidewalk before it, and by personal solicitation for the sake of his
mother's memory or his wife and children, or because of the injury to his
customers and their families. This method was successful, in many cases, in
persuading the saloon keeper to give up the business, but its greatest success
lay in the fact that out of it grew an organization whose sole purpose it was
to combat drunkenness through persuasion. The Woman's Christian Temperance Union has never seriously attempted anything but to persuade children to shun intoxicants, drinkers to give it up, men in the business to get
out of it, or legislators to legislate against it. In the hands of this organization,
the moral suasion method has been remarkably successful, and the present
attitude of the public is largely due to its incessant propaganda.

The first attempt to substitute compelling force for moral suasion is to be
found in the formation of a political party with a single plank in its platform,
viz., the prohibition of the manufacture and sale of intoxicating liquors. Its
avowed object was to put its own candidates in office, pass the necessary laws
and enforce them. Many of the leaders in this movement believed it to be
hopeless, but expected to gain adherents enough to hold the balance of power.
In some cases, this was accomplished, and the old parties were forced to take
account of the prohibition vote. The best recognition they could force from
either of the old parties was the statement in the platform of the Republican
party, in one national campaign, that "That first concern of all good government is the virtue and sobriety of the people and the purity of the home. The
Republican party cordially sympathizes with all wise and well-directed efforts
for the promotion of temperance and morality." The work of the Prohibition
party has been very largely the same as that of other temperance organizations,
viz., the changing of the attitude of the people toward drunkenness and the
licensing of the liquor traffic.

As a result of all this agitation, and the public sentiment adverse to the
saloon, the trade began to protect itself, entrenching itself behind state laws,
and for this purpose made a very effective political organization. There was
no organized political opposition, and as a result they held the balance of
power between the parties. . . .

The Anti-Saloon League was organized to combat the political organization
of the liquor traffic. It was believed, and the event has largely proven it true,
that in most communities there were more anti-saloon than there were pro-
saloon votes, and if the great mass of anti-saloon votes could be organized,
the power of the saloon in politics would be broken.

The natural starting point was the church, for here was already an organization, which, by ideal and aim, by tradition and leadership, was in direct
and absolute opposition to everything the saloon was doing. It was already
recognized that if the church was right, the saloon was wrong, and that the
church must overcome the saloon or eventually be overcome by it. The great
obstacle had been that the saloon did not go to the church, and it was contrary

Suffragette parade in Washington, D.C., March 3, 1913
(Keystone-Mast Collection, University of California, Riverside)

to church tradition and policy for the church to go where the saloon was, viz., into politics. Church forces finally found the answer to the problem thus presented in an agency more or less organically combined with the church, and in its organization rather indirectly responsible to the church which could go into politics and could in time organize and concentrate the votes of the church men and the independent anti-saloon vote against pro-saloon candidates. The organization of the church was effected by having delegates from the different denominations meet in convention and elect a board of trustees. This board of trustees outline the entire policy for the league. They elect an executive committee which is, in reality, a board of strategy, and also a superintendent who is the leader or general of the forces in the field. He appoints his subordinates or district leaders throughout the state. This is the state organization which does the actual work. The board of trustees meet once a year or oftener, while the executive committee meets at least once a month, and in the heat of a campaign will be found meeting very much oftener.

Suggested Reading
(Chapter Eight)

What is variously known as social justice, social action, or social gospel has received considerable attention in American religious history. Two older treatments still merit careful study: C. H. Hopkins, *The Rise of the Social Gospel in American Protestantism, 1865–1915* (1940), and H. F. May, *Protestant Churches and Industrial America* (1949). A generous sample of the writings of three major figures (Washington Gladden, Richard Ely, and Walter Rauschenbusch) is provided in Robert T. Handy, *The Social Gospel in America, 1870–1920* (1966). And for the period between this century's two world wars, see Robert M. Miller, *American Protestantism and Social Issues, 1919–1939* (1958). Many books also describe the social action of specific denominations. On the Roman Catholic side, the best place to begin is with two books of Aaron I. Abell: *American Catholicism and Social Action: A Search for Social Justice, 1865–1900* (1963), and his edited collection, *American Catholic Thought on Social Questions* (1968). From these one may turn to D. J. O'Brien's *American Catholics and Social Reform* (1968) and to the sprightly biography of John A. Ryan, *Right Reverend New Dealer* (1963), by F. L. Broderick. On the central question of the Church's relations with labor, the best book is H. J. Browne, *The Catholic Church and the Knights of Labor* (1949). A 1952 Yale dissertation, published in 1976, pays much attention to the labor question, but also explicates the relationship between Henry George and Edward McGlynn: J. E. Roohan, *American Catholics and the Social Question, 1865–1900*.

Judaism, especially of the Reform variety, committed itself to a resolution of the problems imposed by city and factory. A popular survey is provided by Albert Vorspan and Eugene J. Lipman, *Justice and Judaism: The Work of Social Action* (rev. ed., 1959), but also see the account of the "unique experiment" at the Stephen Wise Free Synagogue in New York City: S. E. Goldstein, *The Synagogue and Social Welfare* (1955). Vorspan's *Giants of Justice* (1960) helpfully introduces several rabbis conspicuously engaged in trying to ameliorate the problems of society. On municipal reform — or its absence — the anthology by Robert D. Cross, *The Church and the City, 1865–1910* (1967), is most instructive; the monograph by Carroll S. Rosenberg, *Religion and the Rise of the American City* (1971), shows just how intimately enmeshed those two entities were. A more general treatment by Arthur M. Schlesinger, Jr., *The American as Reformer* (1968), gives much credit to the depth of religious motivation in initiating municipal reform. And while the Bible was appealed to by both those proposing and those resisting reform, its wide use in this and other periods of American history is treated in Ernest R. Sandeen, ed., *The Bible and Social Reform* (1982); see especially therein the chapter by W. M. King, "The Biblical Base of the Social Gospel."

How religion meets the challenges of war is never a simple question of resistance or support. Generally one finds some of both, often in the same denomination, sometimes even in the same individual. The Spanish-American War, concluded so quickly, granted little time for attitude to develop or shift, so that sentiments fixed at the beginning remained to the end. The wider frame for this period can be found in Julius W. Pratt, *Expansionists of 1898: Acquisition of Hawaii and the Spanish Islands* (1936). For the two churchmen taking opposing sides in this chapter, see Ira V. Brown on *Lyman Abbott . . .* (1953) and D. F. Sweeney, O. F. M., on *The Life of John Lancaster Spalding . . .* (1965). In World War I, the support (often uncritical) of the clergy for the war is fully revealed in R. H. Abrams, *Preachers Present Arms* (1933), while the resistance during the war or a pacifist stance thereafter is discussed in John K. Nelson, *The Peace Prophets* (1967), and in Charles Chatfield, *For Peace and Justice* (1971). On Kirby Page specifically, see Chatfield's *Kirby Page and the Social Gospel: Pacifist and Socialist Aspects* (1974). The most scholarly study of "Buchmanism" is that by W. H. Clark, *The Oxford Group, Its History and Significance* (1951)—though an insider's account provides a useful complement: Geoffrey Williamson, *Inside Buchmanism* (1954).

For Americans learning about and taking some responsibility for the world, the early twentieth century represented a time of swift advance in missionary effort. Any probe of missions in the modern period should begin with the Olympian perspective provided by Kenneth S. Latourette in his five-volume *Christianity in a Revolutionary Age* (1958–62). This may be followed by C. H. Hopkins's exhaustive biography, *John R. Mott, 1865–1955* (1979), and W. R. Wheeler's life of Robert E. Speer, *A Man Sent from God* (1956). For a "spiritual autobiography" of E. Stanley Jones, see his *Song of Ascents* (1968). Roman Catholic missions from the United States are comprehensively described in *The Mission Apostolate: A Study of the Mission Activity of the Roman Catholic Church . . .* (1942), issued under the auspices of the Society for the Propagation of the Faith, U.S. More modern studies of Maryknoll than that cited in the chapter include R. B. Considine, *The Maryknoll Story* (1950); A. J. Nevins, *The Meaning of Maryknoll* (1954); and Sister Marcelline, *Sisters Carry the Gospel* (1956). Detailed responses to the critique of foreign missions include these volumes: C. H. Patton, *Foreign Missions Under Fire* (1928); C. A. Selden, *Are Missions a Failure?* (1927); and R. E. Speer, *Are Foreign Missions Done For?* (1928). The famous novelist of China, Pearl S. Buck, approached the "Laymen's Mission Report" (quoted above, pp. 178–80) with great skepticism, but concluded by declaring, "I want every American Christian to read this book." Her sentiments were similar to those of Hocking: ". . . above all, let the spread of the spirit of Christ be rather by mode of life than preaching. I am weary unto death with this incessant preaching" (*Christian Century*, 49 [Nov. 23, 1932], 1434–37).

On the new organizations brought into being in order to meet society's new and pressing needs, the bibliographical choices are many. The best recent account of the Salvation Army is that of Sallie Chesham, *Born to Battle: The Salvation Army in America* (1965). Along with C. H. Hopkins's history of the YMCA (cited in the chapter), one should consult Andrew Greeley's book, covering a somewhat later period: *Strangers in the House: Catholic Youth in America* (1961). The Society of St. Vincent de Paul has been more fortunate than most in its historian: D. T. McColgan, *A Century of Charity. . .* , 2 vols. (1951). In addition, many accounts of various Sisters of Charity and Sisters of Mercy detail the work in a single diocese or a single state. Christopher Kauffman's recent study, *Faith and Fraternalism: The History of the Knights of Columbus, 1882–1982* (1982), is a careful examination of this important Catholic men's organization. Beginning in 1890, the *Yearbook* of the Central Conference of American Rabbis offers repeated examples of the commitment of Reform Judaism to social problems.

The first quarter of the twentieth century saw intensified ecumenical activity, not all of it related to World War I. The creation of the Federal Council of Churches and the fortunes of its early years may be discerned in these histories: E. B. Sanford, *Origin and History of the Federal Council . . .* (1916); John Hutchinson, *We Are Not Divided* (1941); and, with a wider sweep, Samuel E. Cavert, *The American Churches in the Ecumenical Movement, 1900–1968* (1968). Even broader cooperation is evident in C. E. Silcox, *Catholics, Jews and Protestants: A Study of the Relationships in the U.S. and Canada* (1934); and E. R. Clinchy, *The Growth of Goodwill* (1953). A first-rate biography of revivalist Sunday is by William G. McLoughlin, *Billy Sunday Was His Real Name* (1955), while the story of the Anti-Saloon League and its times is engagingly described in Andrew Sinclair, *Prohibition: Era of Excess* (1962). From the facile pen of Virginius Dabney has come the biography of a major Methodist prohibitionist: namely, *Dry Messiah: The Life of Bishop [James] Cannon* (1949).

NINE:

Worlds Within and Beyond

Much of American religion remains hidden from public view, operating in quiet privacy or within a subculture to which the wider world is largely oblivious. Still other religious elements do not so much engage the surrounding culture as they stand aloof from or in opposition to that "mainstream." Yet to ignore all of these manifestations of religion in America would be to ignore a very great deal; indeed, it might be to ignore the principal points at which religion bears upon the daily lives of most men and women in the nation.

PRIVATE RELIGION

In a sweeping oversimplification, Alfred North Whitehead once defined religion as what a man does with his solitariness, a definition that nevertheless contains a certain kernel of truth. It is in those lonely emergencies of life, to cite William James, another Harvard philosopher and colleague of Whitehead, that one's creed is tested. Not all such lonely emergencies lend themselves to documentation, of course, but one can observe those places where people turn for inspiration or solace, for guidance in how to live and in how to find meaning in whatever life has offered to them.

For a hundred years or more, one of those places to which vast segments of the American public have turned is the novel and its various fictionalized lives of Jesus. Though the novel is a modern art form (and therefore under some suspicion earlier in many religious circles), it had by the end of the nineteenth century won a place among many of the religiously minded. The novel, it was discovered, could offer instruction in virtue, could demonstrate the calamities awaiting the wicked, and could even convey insight into religious history and doctrine. For the American reading public, that last service was most conspicuously rendered in those imaginative reconstructions of the life of Jesus which, beginning with *Ben-Hur* in 1880, held millions enthralled. Through such novels, one walked the dusty roads of Judea, observed the political-military fortunes of Imperial Rome, marveled at the origins and progress of Christianity. But most of all, one found personal assurance and sustaining inspiration.

However popular such books proved to be, they of course only complemented, never challenged, that perennial best-seller, the Bible. In whatever translation or edition or abridgment, the Bible sold and the Bible was read. In red letter format (the red being used for the words of Jesus), in slim single-book paperbacks (the Gospel of John being the most popular), in pocket-size, India-paper editions (often, the New Testament plus the Book of Psalms), in mammoth pulpit size, in print enlarged for failing eyes, in braille, on records, with study outlines, commentaries, concordances, and an entire industry of "aids" and "helps," the Bible reached every hamlet and into nearly every home. Daily Bible reading, widely encouraged, was often regarded as the mark of the serious and committed believer as opposed to the mere church-attending dilettante.

Along with Bible reading (although by no means limited solely to that context), the most private moments of prayer and meditation took place. To commune with the Divine and perchance to enter into the presence of the Divine may be to approach the very heart of the religious life. Something of the nature of these activities, then, however intimate or however solitary, must be understood. For "the joy of communion with God," as Rufus Jones noted, "is the central function of prayer and it is one of the most impressive facts of life."

In the rhythms of the religious life, some celebrations coincide with such central events as birth, puberty, marriage, death. Other events superimpose an ecclesiastical calendar upon the seasonal rotations of sun, moon, and earth. Thus, for example, we observe a springtime Easter, a harvesttime Rosh Hashana, a winter solstice Christmas. But the most obvious rhythm in America's religious life is the special setting aside of one day in seven: Remember the sabbath day, to keep it holy. How that day should be remembered, and even when, has been severely contested throughout the nation's history. That contest has not been limited to the churches and synagogues, but has time and again crowded the dockets of municipal, state, and federal courts. For millions of Americans, controversy notwithstanding, being religious has had direct implications for what one did, where one went, how one's thoughts were guided on that single special day of the week.

Pulpits served as one obvious and often powerful instrument for the guidance of sabbath thoughts, the voices from some of those pulpits reverberating far beyond the walls of a local sanctuary. While not exclusively a Protestant art form, preaching was more the centerpiece, more the "main event" of Protestant services than of most others. Protestant clergy were commonly addressed as "Preacher" for such was their most obvious—and often their most influential—role. In 1924 the nondenominational *Christian Century* conducted a poll to determine the most effective practitioners of the pulpiteering art: "men of prophetic vision, of pulpit power, whose message seems most vitally to interpret the mind of Christ." From over twenty thousand responses, twenty-five ministers were selected as the country's "pulpit leaders." Four of these are presented individually later in the chapter, but here a few general comments may be in order. The denominations most generously represented among the winners were Presbyterian, Congregational, Methodist, and Baptist. While it is perhaps not surprising that in the 1920s one finds neither blacks nor women in the top twenty-five, it is surprising that such large and national groups as Lutheran and Episcopalian are wholly absent. Whatever the merits and the criteria of choice, it is evident that American pulpits, long before the electronic age, commanded large audiences and influenced many lives.

NEW THOUGHT AND NEW THOUGHTS

In the second half of the nineteenth century a mixture of ideas, visions, and techniques joined in varying ways to win zealous followings and fashion new institutions. Some of the mixture was foreign born. Sweden's Emmanuel Swedenborg (1688– 1771), for example, left a legacy of visionary writings that migrated to America (though he did not), where they influenced a small number profoundly and a large number superficially. Swedenborg's emphasis on health and healing appealed to some, his "spiritualizing" of biblical history and law to others, his optimistic certainties to still others. He emphasized "the eternal lustre of the gospel," wrote Henry James, Sr. (one of those influenced profoundly), "by disclosing its interior or spiritual and philosophical contents. . . ." Another European, Friedrich Mesmer (c. 1734– 1815), Austrian physician and astrologer, stressed the power of the mind to heal and to communicate with the beyond, thereby contributing "mesmerism" (or hypnotism; also, animal magnetism) to the American vocabulary. From the Orient, religious and philosophical concepts, severed from their ancient cultural roots, made their way to the West where they competed with the traditional orthodoxies of Judaism and Christianity. All reality is one, and all reality (including humankind) is divine; evil has no independent existence, and sin leaves no enduring stain. East and West met in America, mixing and mutating in ways that brought further variety onto the national scene.

An International New Thought Alliance, organized in 1915, resolved "to teach the infinitude of the Supreme One, the Divinity of Man and his Infinite possibilities through the creative power of constructive thinking. . . ." The Alliance also dedicated itself to maintaining some semblance of unity among its many proponents and advocates, but that goal proved ever elusive. New Thought had too much rich complexity, too much wide ambiguity, too much ready opportunity for it to be able to keep everything together. And even those specific institutions discussed in the chapter —Christian Science, Unity, Religious Science—struggled within their own subcategories to keep the household of the faithful under a single roof. Those struggles never wholly succeeded.

Private proclaimers, freshly inspired healers, charismatic leaders—all cultivated their own followings. In some instances, however, as with Russell H. Conwell and Norman Vincent Peale (see below), the following was purely personal so that no new church or denomination emerged. What did emerge was the application of a transcendental optimism to the tasks or travails of this world: you *can* find health, happiness, and prosperity; you *can* win!

But connections between the spiritual and the material worlds, between mind and body, were not the preoccupations alone of the New Thought practitioners. The late nineteenth century also saw the development of psychology, psychiatry, and psychoanalysis as the names of other Europeans— Freud (1856–1939), Adler (1870–1937), Jung (1876–1961)—became familiar in more and more households. "Spiritual healing" in this context came to be discussed by the clinically trained physician along with the theologically informed clergyman. And in most of these discussions, the emphasis was not on faith versus medicine, or on the spiritual versus the physical, but on an openness to whatever therapy seemed most appropriate to the case at hand. As Seward Hiltner wrote: "In some situations the surgeon's knife must cut out the offending tissue in order to release the forces of healing; in other cases the personality analysis is the central need; and in still other cases the conscious recognition of the power of these healing influences is most needed." The point is to know the virtues and the limits of each type of therapy, then to discover how the three methods, "applied intelligently, benefit the whole person more than any single one without the others."

SOCIETY OUT OF JOINT

Those who saw maladjustments in largely personal terms found comfort or cure in many options newly available in the twentieth century. Those who saw ills more in the body social than in the body personal also proposed novel options and assorted remedies. Some argued that the time had come to put some limits on democracy in America, at least on that kind of democracy represented by an open, prodigal invitation to all the world's tired, poor, hungry, and what-have-you. For example, should America's Protestants (or was it "Protestant America") continue to be deluged by the flood of Roman Catholic immigration? New England, once the bastion of Puritanism and the Protestant work ethic, was being totally transformed. Writing for the *Forum* in 1889, a Massachusetts headmaster decried that great change from "a homogenous people of common faith and common speech and common love for the commonwealth" to "populations diverse in creed and in tongue, untrained to liberty and a republican form of government, and with no respect for the ashes of the dead from which has sprung our fatherland." And so in 1894 an Immigration Restriction League was formed in New England, even as in Iowa an American Protective Association, anti-Catholic in purpose, had been organized seven years earlier. These voices helped prepare the soil for a revived Ku Klux Klan which in the 1920s became even more explicit about what constituted the true American: namely, native, white, Protestant. It was a good time for shutting down open immigration (accomplished in 1924), a bad time for Catholic Alfred Smith to run for President (defeated in 1928).

On the economic front, questions raised timidly about capitalism in the 1920s boomed boldly in the 1930s as the grim grip of the Great Depression refused to let go. The American economic system was desperately ill: none would deny that. But was it fundamentally incurable? At bottom, could one reconcile the ethics of Jesus with the mindless pursuit of profit? or the motive of love with the drive of greed? or the absolute ideals of faith with the arbitrary operations of the marketplace? These questions, not easy ones at any time, pressed cruelly when all seemed so wrong in the Western economic world, when much seemed so promising in a rising Marxist world. And to these queries that sounded more like anguished cries, what did religion in America have to say? Not much, a young Reinhold Niebuhr feared: "If religion is to contribute anything to the solution of the industrial problem, a more heroic type of religion than flourishes in the average church must be set to the task."

WORLD OUT OF TIME

Whatever the ills of the time, other religious voices were raised to remind Americans of a God above and beyond time, to remind them, in other words, of eternity. Revivalists of this period were the prime reminders: eternity, and how one spends it, is life's central question and most crucial choice. Nothing very complicated about the plan of salvation, Billy Sunday explained. It has only two parts: believe with your heart, and confess with your mouth. The crowds that pressed in to hear Dwight Moody in Brooklyn, Sam Jones in Atlanta, and Sunday in Chicago demonstrated that thousands shared the view that the issue of eternal life transcended all other issues. Earthly troubles, personal woes, social sicknesses — all those must be placed in the perspective of eternity. One can seek health, happiness, and prosperity, but none of these — nor anything else — can a man or woman exchange for his or her soul.

While some messengers stressed the rescue of the soul from a sinful world, others promised the rescue of that sinful world itself: a rescue in the form of the Second Coming of Jesus, the establishment of a New Jerusalem on earth. Millennialism, a familiar theme in American history (see Vol. I, pp. 369–74), in the twentieth century proved its persisting popularity yet again. Jehovah's Witnesses spoke of 1914 as the fateful year, while Aimee Semple McPherson preferred to assert with finality but with less temporal precision: "JESUS IS COMING SOON — GET READY TO MEET HIM." An especially pervasive form of millennialism, that known as dispensationalism, spread through many denominations and dominated the theology of such popular preachers as G. Campbell Morgan and Dwight L. Moody, both treated herein, and of many more besides. A single volume, the *Scofield Reference Bible,* found such wide acceptance as to insure that expectations concerning the imminent end of the world reached from pulpit into pew, from school desk to family hearth.

But if God delayed in descending from heaven to purify and redeem the earth, perhaps individual Christians could, through the aid of the Holy Spirit, reach a heavenly purification and perfection on their own. Methodism's John Wesley had written a "plain account" of Christian perfection in 1739 (revised often through 1777, and reprinted countless times thereafter) which encouraged many to move beyond "the elementary doctrines of Christ" to the maturity of entire sanctification. The holiness movement began in America before the Civil War, but flourished and proliferated abundantly after that conflict. A "National Camp Meeting for the Promotion of Christian Holiness," formed in 1867, gave promotional direction and impetus to the movement. Sired by Methodism, a whole progeny of independent holiness denominations grew up in the late nineteenth and early twentieth centuries. So also the closely related pentecostal movement, which stressed an even more charismatic, spirit-filled service of worship, the most distinctive feature of which was glossolalia, or speaking in tongues. For many, this powerful experience proved beyond doubt the presence of the Holy Spirit and the gift of God's "second blessing," the first having been salvation itself. For others, an even more dramatic evidence of the Spirit's presence and power came in the act of healing. "Once I was blind, but now I see" had proved a powerful testimony many centuries ago; it continued to draw the unbelievers, even as for the believers it sealed and confirmed their faith.

1. PRIVATE RELIGION

Inspirational Reading: Lives of Jesus

The Greatest Story

Fulton Oursler (1893 – 1952), long associated with Reader's Digest, *became a Roman Catholic in the course of the eleven years that he spent writing* The Greatest Story Ever Told *(1949). One generalization about the novels discussed here should be offered: they were all enormously successful in sales. This was certainly true of Oursler's book, which was in no degree limited to or directed toward a specifically Catholic audience. Soon after its publication in 1949,* The Greatest Story *topped the best-seller list, was syndicated in over two hundred newspapers, and was translated into several languages. The episode below tells of Jesus' birth, though, as with all fictionalized versions of such events, it moves far beyond the meagre details offered in the Gospels of Matthew and Luke.*

Now they entered the streets of Bethlehem, and the press of pilgrims was so great that the pair could scarcely move forward; no one would even listen to Joseph when he asked the way to a hotel; one urchin laughed in his face at such a question. Five hostelries they tried but all were filled up. Joseph kept on doggedly; he forced his way through the door of the last tavern and demanded to talk to the host.

"My wife is ill," pleaded Joseph. "Her baby is about to be born."

The innkeeper was a stout and grumpy man with an enormous stomach. He had rolls of fat under his chin, and little dumplings hanging under his eyes, and oily gray curls.

With red hands clasped in front of him, he gaped at these four Nazarenes, and it seemed to Joseph as if all mercy fled from his little eyes. For a moment he said nothing; then he curled fat fingers around his mouth and bawled hoarsely:

[Source: Fulton Oursler, *The Greatest Story Ever Told* (Garden City: Doubleday & Co., 1951 [1949]), pp. 49 – 51.]

"Sarah!"

His wife, just as stout as he was — she might have been himself in women's clothes — came shuffling from the back of the house.

"What you want?" she demanded, hoarse voice a replica of his own.

"Look at this woman."

"Which?"

"The young one, not the old one."

"I see her, yes."

"Is she having her baby now or is this a scheme to get lodgings?"

The greasy wife leaned forward, hardening the creases in her neck.

"This one," she announced, voice even hoarser with fright, "is having the baby now. I know. I have had ten."

"Please," implored Joseph, "for the love of God — —"

"Don't you realize," growled Sarah, "the place is full? All Bethlehem is full. There's not a bed in the town tonight. But she can't have a baby here on the floor. We've got to do something. Gabriel!"

"Hah?" answered the innkeeper obediently.

"There is one warm and comfortable place where we haven't put anybody yet."

"Is there now? Where? Just where?" demanded Gabriel.

"In the stable!"

"The stable!" echoed Joseph miserably, and Anna put her arms around Mary. But the young wife looked gratefully at the innkeeper's wife.

"You are very kind to think of it," she said. "A stable is warm. And it will be like home, because often I slept downstairs with the sheep and the goats." She turned to Joseph. "These people would surely take good care of their animals. And we will be alone there."

She turned quickly back to the old woman.

"You will not rent it to anyone else besides us?" she pleaded.

"No," smiled Sarah slowly, with a reluctant chuckle. "And I will help you. God knows we women have got to help each other."

The stable was in a roomy cave that extended under the whole building of the inn. Joseph held Mary's hand as he led her down twisting stone steps to an earthen floor; in his free hand he held a lantern that threw against the rough walls the magnified shadows of Anna and Joachim and Mary and himself.

"Where are we going to put her down?" cried Anna distractedly.

Heaving and puffing, the stout Sarah came clumping down the stairs behind them, and after her Gabriel, puffing even louder than his wife, both clasping fresh bundles of straw. They laid a bed against the inner wall, which was warmer and not so damp, and they brought linen and a coverlet and a pillow for Mary's head.

Then Gabriel and Sarah had to leave them, for business was brisk upstairs, but both of them paused to give a hoarse: "God be with you tonight!" As their footsteps died away the four at last felt relieved, if only to be alone. Anna helped Mary to undress, and then she went upstairs in search of jars of heated water, while Joseph stood near brooding.

"Why do we have no sign now?" he was asking himself. "Where is the angel? Why doesn't Anna hurry back?"

Anna soon came back with the water. She briskly exiled Joseph and Joachim through a rear door in the stable, bidding them to stay out until they were sent for. It was dark outside, the night air moist and cold.

Meanwhile Anna, with the wisdom of old wives, urged Mary not to lie on the straw but to get up and walk. Mary obeyed. Back and forth in the stable she walked, amid the braying of donkeys and bleating of sheep, her nostrils filled with the sweet, pungent odors of barley and oats and hay. To and fro she walked.

And Joseph was trudging up and down in the dark area behind the stable. Again and again he tightened and then loosened the frayed girdle around his travel-stained robe. He fingered the pouch that held his store of coins and wondered whether he had enough money to see them through. The hours dragged on. Joachim had sat down on his haunches and soon fell asleep. But Joseph walked on like a man in a nightmare, waiting, praying until at last and suddenly he heard the sound — a child's first cry.

In the dimmish light he knelt beside the bed of staw where Mary lay, pale and weak but wide-eyed and with a small, brave smile for him.

"See!" she murmured.

Joseph was on his knees. Mary held out firm hands, lifting up her son, wrapped in Grandmother Anna's swaddling clothes — lifting him up adoringly, the fate of the world reposing in the chalice of her hands.

Even in the first instant of seeing the child Joseph was aware of something extraordinarily different about him. Somehow he knew that this newborn baby, whose face was not red and crinkled but smooth and white, and whose expression was of such potent innocence and affection, had come into the world to get nothing and to give everything.

The Nazarene

A decade earlier Sholem Asch (1880 – 1957), a Polish-born Jew, published his life of Jesus, The Nazarene *(1939). With a thorough Hebrew education in rabbinical schools in Poland, Asch emigrated to the United States in 1914 and became a naturalized citizen six years later. Offering a much more informed commentary on Jewish life and times in the first century of the present era, Asch lifted the genre to a higher level. Though Asch hoped that*

[Source: Sholem Asch, *The Nazarene* (New York: G. P. Putnam's Sons, 1939), pp. 212 – 14.]

his life of Jesus (Yeshua, or simply "Rabbi" in the novel) would have significant impact on the Jewish community, its great and enduring popularity was among the Gentiles. In the excerpt below, the narrator (one of the twelve disciples) relates an episode that, while it resonates with New Testament language, is the imaginative creation of the author.

And we were then twelve disciples who had left our own, wife and child, house and field; we had forsaken all that was ours and we had followed after him. For he persuaded us and we hearkened unto him, and we became his possession, the souls which he had made. And we were in his hand as the clay in the hand of the potter, and he could do with us as he willed, for we believed in his words.

And it came to pass on a certain day that we were on the way with our Rabbi and it was the oncoming of night, and we reached a certain inn and we entered there. And we encountered therein a company of scorners, and the chief among them was a dissolute old man; and they drank beer mixed with honey and they laughed and mocked and spoke much folly. And the slave that served them was a scholar and a man of learning who had been sold into slavery for debt. And it came to pass that when the company of scorners grew merry, they threw what was left of their drinks in the face of him that served them, and they broke the vessels on his head, and the slave stood and endured the shame that they did unto him and answered not a word. And the dissolute old man laughed loudly so that his cheeks became red and the white locks of his beard shook, and he said:

"Tell me thy text, thou son of an ass."

And the learned man that was the slave answered and said: "The days of man are like the grass, he is like the blossom of the field." And when the old man heard these words he smote the slave with his fist and said:

"I have come out with my friends to rejoice and be merry, and thou comest and disturbest our joy. A bad servant art thou."

And when we saw this thing, then Jochanan, of the brothers Zebedee, spoke unto our Rabbi:

"Rabbi, why sufferest thou him to have dominion? Shall I make him silent?"

And our Rabbi answered: "I am not come to destroy a soul, but to build up." And he drew near the old man and said unto him:

"I will give thee such joy as none shall ever disturb, and none shall ever take it from thee."

And the old man answered:

"Thou speakest assuredly of wine. For it is written: 'Wine rejoiceth the heart of man.' "

And the Rabbi answered him and said:

"A joy whereof the end is sadness is not a joy. Come, I will give thee a joy which is like unto a well, which groweth ever stronger and it hath no end."

And the old man asked:

"What is that joy which hath no end?"

And the Rabbi answered him:

"It is the joy which a man hath of his father, the creator of the world. This is the joy that hath no end, and the joy of the kingdom of heaven none shall take from thee, for it is not outside of thee but within thee."

And the old man said:

"That joy is hidden from me, for the path to my father in heaven is cut off by many sins which I have committed in my life."

And the Rabbi said:

"Thou makest thyself great in that thou makest thyself little. The gates are ever open for those that would return."

And the old man said:

"Is there still hope for me? I in no wise knew it."

And he drew near to the slave and fell at his feet and begged forgiveness of him; and our Rabbi said unto us:

"Come and behold: with one word canst thou fling thy brother into the nethermost pit and with one word canst thou bring him under the wings of the glory. Therefore be not deceived by that which your eyes see, but see what is in the heart of a man." And to the servant he said: "When thy brother sinneth against thee, punish him, and when he repenteth, forgive him." And he made peace between them. And he said to the old man:

"Arise, thou art comforted."

And he sat down with them, and drank wine with them, and he changed the company of the scornful into a company of brothers, as it is written: Brothers dwelling together.

The Robe

The crucifixion scene, and specifically the untold, unknown fate of Jesus' robe, provided the plot line for Lloyd C. Douglas (1877–1951), Lutheran clergyman turned full-time novelist. In The Robe, *Douglas consciously followed in the tradition set by Lew Wallace (1827–1905) in the much reprinted, often dramatized,* Ben-Hur: A Tale of the Christ *(1880). Strictly speaking,* The Robe *is not a life of Jesus, but a novelistic reflection on Christ's influence via the garment which he wore at his death. But the whole context of the Near East is so amply provided as to give the reader a sense of immediacy with Jesus and the first followers. In the episode below, the Roman*

[Source: Lloyd C. Douglas, *The Robe* (Boston: Houghton Mifflin Co., 1942), pp. 134–37.]

soldier Marcellus, hero of the story, has fortified himself with alcohol for the unpleasant task of standing guard during Jesus' hours on the cross.

There was not as large a crowd as he had expected to see. There was no disorder, probably because the legionaries were scattered about among the people. It was apparent, from the negligence of the soldiers' posture, as they stood leaning on their lances, that no rioting had occurred or was anticipated.

Demetrius moved closer in and joined the outer rim of spectators. Not many of the well-to-do, who had been conspicuous at the Insula, were present. Most of the civilians were poorly dressed. Many of them were weeping. There were several women, heavily veiled and huddled in little groups, in attitudes of silent, hopeless grief. A large circle had been left unoccupied below the crosses.

Edging his way slowly forward, occasionally rising on tiptoe to search for his master, Demetrius paused beside one of the legionaries who, recognizing him with a brief nod, replied to his low-voiced inquiry. The Commander and several other officers were on the other side of the knoll, at the rear of the crosses, he said.

'I brought him some water,' explained Demetrius, holding up the jug. The soldier showed how many of his teeth were missing.

'That's good,' he said. 'He can wash his hands. They're not drinking water today. The Procurator sent out a wineskin.'

'Is the man dead?' asked Demetrius.

'No — he said something awhile ago.'

'What did he say? Could you hear?'

'Said he was thirsty.'

'Did they give him water?'

'No — they filled a sponge with vinegar that had some sort of balm in it, and raised it to his mouth; but he wouldn't have it. I don't rightly understand what he is up there for — but he's no coward.' The legionary shifted his position, pointed to the darkening sky, remarked that there was going to be a storm, and moved on through the crowd.

Demetrius did not look at the lonely man again. He edged out into the open and made a wide détour around to the other side of the knoll. Marcellus, Paulus, and four or five others were lounging in a small circle on the ground. A leather dice-cup was being shaken negligently, and passed from hand to hand. At first sight of it, Demetrius was hotly indignant. It wasn't like Marcellus to be so brutally unfeeling. A decent man would have to be very drunk indeed to exhibit such callous unconcern in this circumstance.

Now that he was here, Demetrius thought he should inquire whether there was anything he could do for his master. He slowly approached the group of preoccupied officers. After a while, Marcellus glanced up dully and beckoned to him. The others gave him a brief glance and resumed their play.

'Anything you want to tell me?' asked Marcellus, thickly.

'I brought you some water, sir.'

'Very good. Put it down there. I'll have a drink presently.' It was his turn to play. He shook the cup languidly and tossed out the dice.

'Your lucky day!' growled Paulus. 'That finishes me.' He stretched his long arms and laced his fingers behind his head. 'Demetrius,' he said, nodding toward a rumpled brown mantle that lay near the foot of the central cross, 'hand me that coat. I want to look at it.'

Demetrius picked up the garment and gave it to him. Paulus examined it with idle interest.

'Not a bad robe,' he remarked, holding it up at arm's length. 'Woven in the country; dyed with walnut juice. He'll not be needing it any more. I think I'll say it's mine. How about it, Tribune?'

'Why should it be yours?' asked Marcellus, indifferently. 'If it's worth anything, let us toss for it.' He handed Paulus the dice-cup. 'High number wins. It's your turn.'

There was a low mutter of thunder in the north and a savage tongue of flame leaped through the black cloud. Paulus tossed a pair of threes, and stared apprehensively at the sky.

'Not hard to beat,' said Vinitius, who sat next him. He took the cup and poured out a five and a four. The cup made the circle without bettering this cast until it arrived at Marcellus.

'Double six!' he called. 'Demetrius, you take care of the robe.' Paulus handed up the garment.

'Shall I wait here for you, sir?' asked Demetrius.

'No—nothing you can do. Go back to the Insula. Begin packing up. We want to be off to an early start in the morning.' Marcellus looked up at the sky. 'Paulus, go around and see how they are doing. There's going to be a hard storm.' He rose heavily to his feet, and stood swaying. Demetrius wanted to take his arm and steady him, but felt that any solicitude would be resented. His indignation had cooled now. It was evident that Marcellus had been drinking because he couldn't bear to do this shameful work in his right mind. There was a deafening, stunning thunderclap that fairly shook the ground on which they stood. Marcellus put out a hand and steadied himself against the central cross. There was blood on his hand when he regained his balance. He wiped it off on his toga.

A fat man, expensively dressed in a black robe, waddled out of the crowd and confronted Marcellus with surly arrogance.

'Rebuke these people!' he shouted, angrily. 'They are saying that the storm is a judgment on us!'

There was another gigantic crash of thunder.

'Maybe it is!' yelled Marcellus, recklessly.

The fat man waved a menacing fist.

'It is your duty to keep order here!' he shrieked.

'Do you want me to stop the storm?' demanded Marcellus.

'Stop the blasphemy! These people are crying out that this Galilean is the Son of God!'

'Maybe he *is*!' shouted Marcellus. '*You* wouldn't know!' He was fumbling with the hilt of his sword. The fat man backed away, howling that the Procurator should hear of this.

Circling the knoll, Demetrius paused for a final look at the lonely man on the central cross. He had raised his face and was gazing up into the black sky. Suddenly he burst forth with a resonant call, as if crying to a distant friend for aid.

Bible Reading and Daily Meditation

Advice to Catholic Girls

Books that change history are seldom the same books that change or profoundly influence the lives of "ordinary" men and women. In many American homes where few books are to be found, traditionally one of those has been the Bible. In addition, one may find a service book, a missal, a guide to daily devotions. Or, in the case of those who have no books or perhaps do not read, meditations may center upon an icon, an amulet, a rosary, a crucifix. In the popular guide represented here (over thirty editions between 1868 and 1897), Paulist priest George Deshon (1823 – 1903) stressed the importance of good thoughts, good books, and the Good Book.

Books are, next to sermons, next to the living voice of the preacher, the most powerful means to excite us to virtue. Get, then, at least a few books, and read them when you get a chance.

"Oh!" says a good girl, "I wish I could! I have never been taught to read, and am now too old to learn; besides, I have no opportunity for learning; there is no one to teach me, and I haven't the time."

Now, do not be cast down on that account. There is one beautiful book, at least, we can read; and that is the Crucifix. What fountains of knowledge and true wisdom it contains! You can look at it, and think over what it means, from one year's end to another, yet you will never reach the bottom of it.

St. Bonaventure, who wrote so many beautiful things, was asked where he got them all? What books he had learned them out of? "There is my book," said he, pointing to the Crucifix; "all my knowledge, all my thoughts come from that."

Another lovely book you have that you can read, though you never learned

[Source: George Deshon, *Guide for Catholic Young Women*, 31st ed., rev. (New York: Arno Press, 1978 [1897]), pp. 77 – 80, 80 – 82.]

a letter of the alphabet, and that is the Rosary. Millions who could not read a word have read that book every day. Get some one to teach you the meaning of the mysteries, and you will never fail to have the best of books always at hand. There is no need, then, to be cast down because you cannot read; only keep your heart simply directed to God, and he will make up abundantly for all that is lacking. Many of the saints have not been able to read, but they could pray, and think of Christ's sufferings and love for them, wonderfully well.

"But why say a word about those who cannot read, since they cannot read what you say?" That is true; but somebody else may read it to them, or tell them, and then my object will be accomplished, which is to give every one such instruction and consolation as is necessary for them.

If you can read, then it is the Lord's will that you should make use of this gift; for He required us to make good use of all our talents and opportunities. "To whom much is given, of him much will be required" (St. Luke xii. 48). . . .

You need not, however, have a great many books; a few good ones are all-sufficient to furnish food for your souls. Such books can be read over and over without getting tired of them. They will always renew some good impression, and excite in you a strong desire to regulate your life so as to please God better. There is one book far above all others that have ever been written or ever will be — that is, the Holy Bible. This book is different from all other books, because we can put the most entire confidence in all that is written in it. Why? It is God Himself, the Holy Ghost, that has caused it to be written for our benefit. This is what the Scripture itself says: "All Scripture, divinely inspired, is profitable to teach, to reprove, to correct, to instruct in justice, that the man of God may be perfect, furnished unto every good work" (2 Tim. iii. 16).

Especially is this the case with the New Testament, which is better fitted to our times and circumstances, which is for the most part plainer and easier to be understood, and which tells us all that has been done for us by our Saviour and His apostles. . . .

Every part of it is full of holy instruction, and I am not at all afraid that any harm will come to a well-intentioned, pure-minded person, from reading it; on the contrary, such persons will not fail to derive much good from it.

But does not St. Peter say, speaking of the epistles of St. Paul and the other Scriptures, that in them "are many things hard to be understood which the unlearned and the unstable wrest to their own perdition?" (2 Peter iii. 16). Undoubtedly he does, and nothing can be more true. There are even things which seem perfectly plain and easy to understand, that would certainly mislead any but a scholar unless they were explained. Such things were understood well enough at the time they were written, because all the people were accustomed to use words in the sense in which the writers meant to use them. But now that language and manners have changed, these words have

Sharecropper, Butler County, Missouri, 1939
(Library of Congress)

lost the meaning they had at that time, and convey a very different one to us. They must be explained or we shall be misled.

Other things are very deep and difficult in themselves, even to scholars, and it is a real folly to set up one's opinion about them without an explanation.

It is the Church's office to guard and preserve the true sense of the Scripture, as you remember the Scripture itself calls her "the pillar and ground of the truth." The Church, where the meaning of a passage is obscure, or has become changed in the translation from one language to another, has placed notes and explanations to preserve the original meaning. There can be no objection to reading a Catholic Bible, and I find it strongly recommended to the faithful as the best of all books to read.

A Protestant "Book of Hours"

In the Middle Ages, richly illustrated and painstakingly copied manuals of private devotion were called Books of Hours. The most popular Protestant devotional guide of the twentieth century, The Upper Room, *was the inspiration of a southern Methodist minister, Grover C. Emmons. Launched in 1935 (at five cents per copy), this quarterly of "daily devotions for family and individual use" grew in circulation from one hundred thousand to more than three million within a single generation. During that same period of growth,* The Upper Room *had also spread far beyond the borders of the United States. Translated into at least thirty languages, this guide called upon its faithful users to make this covenant: "1) To seek an enrichment of my own spiritual life by observing a period for devotions each day; and, 2) To share Christ with my fellows and endeavor to enlist them in His service." What follows is from the first issue of April, 1935; the pattern of Bible reading, meditation, and prayer was to continue unchanged.*

APRIL 2

"Jesus . . . departed . . . into a desert place apart." Matt. 14:13.

A one-roomed house is fatal to refinement. Where there are no privacies the sweet and holy sentiments of life are inevitably lost. This is true also of spiritual attainments. Religion is born and fostered in the secret place. Much of the drabness and listlessness of present-day Christianity is our neglect of private meditation and prayer. Is this the reason for your uncertainty, and for the lack of joy in your religious experience? Religion without a closet loses its gentle refinements, its glow, its power.

We must not fail to observe how the life of the Lord Jesus moved constantly from great thoughts to great works, from solitude to society, from the closet of prayer to the field of action. The secret place was for Him central and essential. "What was indispensable to the Redeemer must always be indispensable to the redeemed." Therefore, He says to us, "Come ye yourselves apart." "Enter into thy closet, and when thou hast shut the door, pray."

Read Matt. 14

Prayer

"My God, is any hour so sweet,
From blush of morn to evening star,
As that which calls me to Thy feet,
The hour of prayer?" Amen.

—*Charlotte Elliott*

[Source: *The Upper Room* (Nashville, Tenn.: Methodist Episcopal Church, South, 1935), n.p.]

Thought for the Day

The root of the spiritual life is a continuing sense of the presence of God.
Costen J. Harrell.

Synagogue service during World War II (June, 1944), New York City
(Library of Congress)

The Inner Life

Prayer

While some prayers are published and some (the Lord's Prayer, for example) even set to music, prayer is for the most part a private and therefore not readily visible affair. To ignore it, however, would be as inappropriate as it is misleading, for to many prayer is the essence of the religious life. The Quaker historian and Haverford College professor of philosophy, Rufus Jones (1863 – 1948), makes clear in the segment below that prayer is not primarily petition or asking of God, but it is communion with God. It is "practicing the presence of God," to use the title of a medieval classic. As such, prayer is not one of religion's props or extras or frills: it is the root of the matter.

Religion is primarily and at heart the personal meeting of the soul with God and conscious communion with Him. To give up the cultivation of prayer would mean in the long run the loss of the central thing in religion; it would involve the surrender of the priceless jewel of the soul. We might try in its stead to perfect the other aspects of religion. We might make our form of divine service very artistic or very popular; we might speak with the tongues of men and sing with the tongues almost of angels, but if we lose the power to discover and appreciate the real presence of God and if we miss the supreme joy of feeling ourselves environed by the Spirit of the living and present God, we have made a bad exchange and have dropped from a higher to a lower type of religion.

Prayer, no doubt, is a great deal more than this inner act of discovery and appreciation of God, but the joy of communion and intercourse with God is the central feature of prayer and it is one of the most impressive facts of life.

The early Franciscans remained on their knees rapt in ardent contemplation praying with their hearts rather than with their lips. It was a prayer of quiet rather than a specific request. Francis thought of prayer as a time of storing up grace and power through union with God. He called it, in his happy phrase, sharing the life of the angels—a needed preparation for the life of action and service which were to follow it. . . .

One of these deep constructive energies of life is prayer. It is a way of life that is as old as the human race is, and it is as difficult to "explain" as is our joy over love and beauty. It came into power in man's early life and it has persisted through all the stages of it because it has proved to be essential to spiritual health and growth and life-advance. Like all other great springs of

[Source: Rufus Jones, *Pathways to the Reality of God* (New York: Macmillan Co., 1931), pp. 241 – 42, 243.]

life, it has sometimes been turned to cheap ends and brought down to low levels, but on the whole it has been a pretty steady uplifting power in the long story of human progress. The only way we could completely understand it would be to understand the eternal nature of God and man. Then we should no doubt comprehend why He and we seek one another and why we are unsatisfied until we mutually find one another.

Mysticism

In the whole repertoire of religious experience, no term is more badly used than "mysticism." Often treated as a synonym for the strange, occult, mysterious, and irrational, the word loses all significant content. Relying on Rufus Jones once more, we learn that the mystic is disciplined and determined in his or her strenuous search for "that more than ourselves whom we call God." Himself a mystic, Jones was fully aware of the criticism frequently levied against the mystical experience — as against all strictly private experience insofar as it seeks to be a source of knowledge. But the quest is worthy, Jones argues, and the truth possibilities are real.

The mystic, as I hope to show, is not a peculiarly favored mortal who by a lucky chance has received into his life a windfall from some heavenly Breadfruit tree, while he lay dreaming of iridescent rainbows. He is, rather, a person who has cultivated, with more strenuous care and discipline than others have done, the native homing passion of the soul for the Beyond, and has creatively developed the outreach of his nature in the God-direction. The result is that he has occasions when the larger Life with which he feels himself kin seems to surround him and answer back to his soul's quest, as a sensitized magnetic needle, if it were conscious, might feel itself enveloped by the currents that sweep back upon it from the electrical storehouse of the sun. . . .

When we raise the question of the objectivity of these experiences there is no easy answer. The proof of objectivity in any field, even in that of sense perception, has been the intellectual task of all the centuries, and after all the coöperative labor it is difficult to produce an argument that is bound to convince the doubter who questions whether the external world *is* the way it appears. Fortunately our common sense solves the problem for most of us. That and our practical nature carry us forward without waiting for the slow proofs.

In the world of values the case is somewhat different. There is present here a private, personal aspect which does not attach, to anything like the same degree, to objects of sense perception. My appreciation of music or of

[Source: Rufus Jones, *New Studies in Mystical Experience* (New York: Macmillan Co., 1928), pp. 15–16, 18–20, 22–24.]

poetry has a subjective color all its own. No one else would feel quite at home in my inner aesthetic world. Nor can we without much adaptation pass on to others our judgments of right and wrong or our consciousness of duty. And yet the noblest minds have always refused to admit that beauty or obligation are out and out, through and through, subjective. These experiences in some sense have their ground in the eternal nature of things, and they conform, in inner law and substance, to some overarching reality beyond us but not alien to our finite minds. It seems evident that moral practice slowly builds up a richer, deeper inner life within us and reveals a cumulative power of moral advance which indicates that something in the deepest nature of the universe *backs* a person who is making his life an organ of ethical goodness.

There is the same kind of objective evidence in the highest forms of mystical experience. There is, to begin with, a majestic *conviction of objectivity*. The mystic is sure that he has found what he has been seeking — as sure as the climber is that he has reached his peak. The sight itself is convincing. It has all the certainty that objects of sense have to the normal man. But it must be admitted that the usual verifications of our sense facts are wanting. The mystic cannot describe his object in the categories of common speech, nor can he get the corroborative testimony of other spectators. He has seen what he has seen, and in its first-hand quality of acquaintance it forever remains just his incommunicable experience. That seems, no doubt, a damaging admission and, for some, ends the debate. . . .

Important as the mystical element is, it would be a grave mistake to *reduce* religion to the bare basis of uninterpreted experience. We cannot have knowledge in any field without a body of observed facts, but knowledge does not consist of mere observations or experiments or empirical occurrences. It consists rather of systematic interpretation of observations and experiments and facts of experience. They are lifted up and seen in the light of the laws and principles which they exhibit.

So, too, religion in its full meaning is vastly more than flashes of insight, intuitions of a Beyond, invasions of an environing Life, convictions of a Light that never was on sea or land. Religion builds on these deep-lying intimations of the soul and would be poor without them, but there is immensely more to say before the whole truth is uttered. Religion draws upon the whole nature and all the resources of man's complete life. It is essentially bound up with all the processes of the intellect and with all the deeper issues of the will as well as with these first-hand intimations of the soul's vision. The present-day revolt from doctrine is in many ways superficial. There can be no great religion without the interpretation of life, of the universe, of experience, of mind, of God. What we ought to revolt from is traditional dogma. We ought to challenge the elaborate logical constructions of bygone metaphysics, and base our interpretations on the sure ground of *vital religious experience* and on the unescapable implications of our minds as they coöperate with a universe which reveals rationality from outermost husk to innermost

Buddhist inner life: prayer and meditation in the lotus position
(Zen Center of Los Angeles)

core. In insisting on *experience* I am not unmindful of the more yet that must go with experience. It is no lazy mysticism that we want, no vain hope that God will give all the treasures of the Spirit "to His beloved in sleep." I have no word of encouragement to offer those persons who expect the palaces of the soul to be built and furnished by magically rubbing an Aladdin's lamp, or by saying over some "blessed word" like Mesopotamia, or some phrase from "the *patois* of Canaan." The religious life is of all things strenuous business. It calls for heroic adventure. But one of the essential aspects of religion now and always is the experiment, made in the soul's inner laboratory, of the personal discovery of that more than ourselves whom we call God.

Contemplation

For some pursuers of the holy grail, contemplation is not a few moments of quiet reflection but an entire way of life. Among the many orders of the Roman Catholic Church, for example, some are described as "contemplative" to distinguish them from orders whose primary mission is teaching or nursing or missions or some other specialized activity. No twentieth-century American monastic attracted more attention than Thomas Merton (1915–68), a member of the Reformed Cistercians of the Strict Observance, or Trappists. Merton's popular autobiography, Seven Storey Mountain *(1948), told of his decision to enter the monastic order that required (in addition to the traditional vows of poverty, chastity, and obedience) the vow of silence. In a later book, Merton tells of his call to contemplation and of the necessity to remember that contemplation is never the end in itself: God and his glory is the end.*

March 10 [1947]

Yesterday I read a couple of chapters of the *Cloud of Unknowing.* Every time I pick up a book in that tradition, especially Saint John of the Cross, I feel like the three wise men when they came out of Jerusalem and out of the hands of Herod, and once more saw their star. They rejoiced with great joy. They were once more delivered from questions and uncertainties, and could see their road straight ahead. In this case it is not even a question of seeing a road. It is simpler than that. For as soon as you stop traveling you have arrived.

I can remember other passages of other books that have hit me with the same impact. They bear witness to moments when I knew, right down to the very depths of my being, that I had found the thing that God wanted for me. I remember, for instance, Saint Teresa's* chapter on the real unimportance of involuntary distractions in the prayer of quiet, in *The Way of Perfec-*

[Source: Thomas Merton, *Sign of Jonas* (New York: Harcourt, Brace and Co., 1953), pp. 28–30.]
*See Volume I, pp. 24–26.

tion. Then, four years ago, in the novitiate, I discovered all that section of *The Living Flame of Love,* in the third Stanza, where Saint John of the Cross talks about the "deep caverns" and about prayer. More recently there was a chapter in *Le Paradis Blanc,* about the interior life. The chapter is called *"Un Chartreux Parle."* But it applies just as well to us. In a different mode, I have been deeply impressed by Duns Scotus's distinction on beatitude, the 49th, in the IVth book of the *Oxoniense,* and by all Saint Bonaventure has to say about desire, especially in the *Itinerarium.* These things have gone deep into me and have shaped my life and my prayer. They have not only arrested my attention, they have transformed my soul. And yet I think that they have only been the last step in processes that grace was working secretly before. They have made me realize what had been going on inside me without my having been quite aware of it. For I read much the same things before I came to Gethsemani,* and they did not transform me at all. In fact I was barely able to grasp what they were all about. . . .

March 11

My intention is to give myself entirely and without compromise to whatever work God wants to perform in me and through me. But this gift is not something absolutely blind and without definition. It is already defined by the fact that God has given me a *contemplative* vocation. By so doing He has signified a certain path, a certain goal to be mine. That is what I am to keep in view, because that is His will. It means renouncing the business, ambitions, honors and pleasures and other activities of the world. It means only a minimum of concern with temporal things. Nevertheless, I have promised to do whatever a Superior may legitimately ask of me. That may, under certain circumstances, involve the sacrifice of contemplation. But it seems to me this sacrifice can only be a temporary thing. It can not mean the sacrifice of the whole contemplative vocation as such.

However, the important thing is not to live for contemplation but to live for God. That is obvious, because, after all, that is the contemplative vocation. That is why it is best to take religious obedience quite literally. As soon as obedience is tempered with conditions, the mind becomes unfit for contemplation. It falls into division because it has to choose between its own solicitudes and the will of the Superior. It has reserved to itself a whole useless field of interior activity (that of judging all the commands that come to it) and this will inevitably interfere with contemplation. If activity becomes too intense — there is no reason why you should not ask your Superiors to have a little pity on you.

March 12 Feast of Saint Gregory the Great
What I wrote yesterday is ambiguous because it assumes that the Rule of Saint Benedict is ordered to a life of pure contemplation. As a matter of fact,

*Our Lady of Gethsemani Abbey, near Bardstown, Kentucky.

it is not. The Fathers would perhaps have said that the Benedictine life was active, in so far as it involved labor, asceticism, active glorification of God in the office, and even a certain amount of teaching and preaching, at least within the monastic community.

Nevertheless, work in the fields helps contemplation. Yesterday we were out in the middle bottom, spreading manure all over the gray mud of the cornfields. I was so happy I almost laughed out loud. It was such a relief to get away from a typewriter.

One Day in Seven

"Remember the Sabbath Day"

Those standing in the Judeo-Christian tradition (where in fact the vast majority of religious Americans do stand) give special attention to the rituals of religion on one day of every week. For Orthodox Jews (and Seventh-Day Baptists, Seventh-Day Adventists, Worldwide Church of God, and others), that day is the sabbath, the seventh day of the week, honored in accordance with ancient command. Hannah G. Solomon (1858–1942), Chicagoan and founder of the National Council of Jewish Women in 1893, had the difficult task of relating her organization to a Jewish constituency of varying opinions and convictions. That variety was evident in the way that the sabbath was being kept — or not being kept. "Bring the Sabbath back into our homes," she urged, for the home is "the true center of lofty inspiration and hallowing customs."

[Council of Jewish Women]

If we followed the advice of all, we would be at one and the same time orthodox, conservative, radical. We refrain altogether from attempting to settle questions of theology. The most serious step we took was to pass resolutions. The effects of these we will learn at our next convention. The one that probably interests you the most was the one relative to the observance of a rest day, championed as was the day we observe by a member of this congregation. The opinions upon the question were various. We must acknowledge that Jews have no one rest day. Some worship on Friday evening, some on Saturday, some on Sunday. The sentiments connected with those days also vary. To the large majority at the convention, the Sabbath of the early home, with hallowed memories of childhood, was too sacred to be uprooted. They were teraphim of the fathers. Sentiment and feeling are never out of date, and we must hesitate to put down that resolution as an outbreak

[Source: Hannah G. Solomon, *A Sheaf of Leaves* (Chicago: privately printed, 1911), pp. 79–81.]

of hysteria. Hysterical women are out of fashion, anyway. Anyone interested
in that specimen must go to the antiquity shops. He will find her lolling on
a sofa of a hundred years ago. We are too healthy now for that. The new rest
day fails to bring to many the message of the old. We know that the hour
passed in this house has been a prop to modern Judaism. It is capable of
supplying the spiritual need of any human being. But if the hour is passed
with longing thoughts for the hours to follow, it is no improvement upon
the Saturday morning when the men who come to say Kadish cannot wait for
the benediction in order to get their mail.

If we look at it squarely, we have grown satisfied with half a Sabbath.
Saturday afternoon is now a legal holiday, and we may see the services transferred to the afternoon. We must admit that we, like the rest, are satisfied
with half a day. Our Sunday afternoons are not passed in accordance with the
spirit of the old Sabbath. I am too strong a believer in clubs to say one word
against them. I consider the social club one of the finest institutions of our
day, one of the most potent agencies for fostering fellowship and good feeling.
But a community which is able, as is this one, to give a practical lesson to
the world upon the Sunday sabbath, should do something better in those
beautiful places than turn them into gambling houses upon that day. I shall
not say one word against gambling. I used to do that when I was young — I
mean, very young. The only way to counteract vice is to make it powerless.
This lies first in proper education, in giving other resources to boys. Every
good actor and artist who comes to this city, which so liberally patronizes art,
should devote some of his time to the amusement of the poorer class. We
know it is not the poor alone who gamble and visit cheap amusements; but
they are the only ones who can have nothing better. Our social clubs could
do much toward introducing other methods of enjoyment on the rest day.

The Sunday service is one of the twentieth century reforms. Its associations
are but forming. As yet we should have too much conscience to offer, to
anyone who has the true sentiment for the old Sabbath and the religious spirit
that comes with the day, such a half-day as a substitute. We must above all
keep the heart warm. We cannot force, we must allow and encourage
growth. . . .

We must bring the Sabbath back into our homes — the true center of lofty
inspiration and hallowing customs. We must instruct our children in religion,
however little we may seem to impress them at the time. In spite of the
natural cynicism of youth, time comes in the life of everyone when religion
affords a prop and a consolation. Without hope and faith were the world
bleak indeed at times. We may not comprehend Deity, yet religion brings
trust and a consciousness of the Divine that we cannot well afford to lose.

"Now will you be good?" *New York Herald,* March 15, 1908
(Library of Congress)

"And on the First Day of the Week . . ."

The early Christian church gradually shifted its day of worship from the seventh day to the first, the shift being in part a memorial to the Resurrection. Such a shift was not without controversy, and controversies regarding Sunday—Sunday sports, Sunday mails, Sunday shopping, and the like—have continued to the present. Even among earnest Christians, many disagreements arose concerning the proper observance of the "Lord's Day." In the 1920s a Canadian Methodist, Charles H. Huestis (1863–1953), wrote a book on the development of Sunday as opposed to the sabbath, combining both history and homily in his presentation. Like Hannah G. Solomon, Huestis argued that Sunday was "pre-eminently a day for the Home."

The church has a duty to perform in guiding the minds and conduct of its people in the proper observance of Sunday. The time has come for the church to work out some definite program of Sunday observance in this modern

[Source: Charles H. Huestis, *Sunday in the Making* (New York: Abingdon Press, 1929), pp. 245–47.]

world, so that the minds of the people may be clear upon the question. In making the following suggestions for such a program, I shall follow, as I have throughout the latter part of this study, the great word of Jesus. If the Sabbath was made for man — and Sunday also — then it was made for his threefold nature — body, mind, spirit.

Body. Sunday should be a day of recreation. The thought of freedom and joy is associated with the Sabbath idea from earliest times, and any attempts to make it a day of gloom, however well intentioned, have not been a success. Hence recreation must have its place in Sunday observance, especially for children whose natural expression is in play. It need not be said that Sunday recreation should be in harmony with the character of the day as one of rest and spiritual uplift, so that one may go back to his work on Monday not only with renewed corporeal vigor, but also with a deeper sense of the presence of God in the world and in his own life.

Mind. Sunday should be a day of thought and meditation. No man can "live on twenty-four hours a day" — really live, not simply exist — who does not give some attention to the serious side of life and the cultivation of his mind. Sunday affords additional leisure for this occupation, and the man who does not devote a part of the day to reading and thinking about matters outside his daily life and occupation, becomes a mere slave to routine, and the ability to think quickly declines.

Spirit. Sunday is a day of worship. No man is spending Sunday well, or doing his duty to himself, his family or his community, who does not go to church on Sunday. "I go to church on Sunday," said Mr. Gladstone, "because I love religion, and I go to church on Sunday because I love England." I need not add that Sunday is pre-eminently a day for the *Home,* and family life, a day when we have leisure to follow the beautiful injunction of Froebel: "Come, let us live with our children."

Popular Preaching

G. Campbell Morgan (1863 – 1945)

When Theodore Roosevelt described the White House as a "bully pulpit," he was speaking in the days before radio and television when a good many of the nation's pulpits were, in fact, "bully": that is, excellent or splendid. Pulpit and press were twin instruments of communication and persuasion, with congregations often finding their opinions sharpened or shaped by what they heard on Sunday mornings. G. Campbell Morgan, an Englishman and

[Source: G. C. Morgan, *God's Methods with Man* (New York: Fleming H. Revell Co., 1898), pp. 26 – 27.]

Congregationalist, traveled widely in this country lecturing on Bible subjects. He also for a time held pastoral responsibilities in New York City and Philadelphia. In the brief excerpt below, Morgan reviews biblical history "from Creation to Christ" in order to draw some "evident lessons."

The evident lessons of our study are two—first, *human failure*; second, *Divine progress*. Look where you will in human history, you find failure. The Fall and the Flood, Corruption and the Cross. Every time humanity is put upon a new footing it fails. Has God failed? Not once; everything has been preparatory and progressive. Let us retrace our steps. The Cross and all that it means was prepared for throughout Judaic history. This one nation of Israel learned, through battle and smoke, murmuring and forgiveness, captivity and deliverance, the great truth that there is but one God. Monotheism is the lesson which humanity has learned through Israelitish history. From the time when Israel came back out of Babylon, she never again set up idols. When that truth was enshrined for the world in the chosen nation, then the one God became flesh. God was preparing through the wonderful history of their times for the Incarnation. What of the failure that preceded the Flood? Sin worked itself out to the utmost head of corruption. God allowed it to have its own free working, and then He swept it away, and started man upon the next stage of history, having behind him that terrific example of what sin is when it is left to its own course. I am bold to say that human corruption, so far as its actual effects upon men's lives are concerned, has never reached the awful depths of degradation which prevailed before the flood, when the sons of men were holding intercourse with evil spirits.

Thus we have sin manifested and the one God seen; while the Incarnate Word takes that sin upon Himself, that the world may ever know, from that point onward, the meaning of sin as well as the meaning of God and His Divine government.

George W. Truett (1867– 1944)

An intense and effective speaker, George W. Truett was long identified with all things Baptist in the state of Texas. For nearly half a century he occupied the pulpit of the First Baptist Church in Dallas, exercising wide influence throughout the South and, in his capacity as president of the Baptist World Alliance from 1934 to 1939, throughout much of the world. "Soul winning" was what he preached, and what he practiced. In this sample of his sermon style, one sees an explicit and unapologetic evangelism which indeed characterized the Southern Baptist Convention of which Truett was a vital part.

[Source: George W. Truett, *A Quest for Souls* (Dallas: Texas Baptist Book Store, 1917), pp. 57–58.]

A Quest for Souls.

Text: "And he brought him to Jesus." — John 1:42.

The bringing of a soul to Jesus is the highest achievement possible to a human life. Some one asked Lyman Beecher,* probably the greatest of all the Beechers, this question: "Mr. Beecher, you know a great many things. What do you count the greatest thing that a human being can be or do?" And without any hesitation the famous pulpiteer replied: "The greatest thing is, not that one shall be a scientist, important as that is; nor that one shall be a statesman, vastly important as that is; nor even that one shall be a theologian, immeasurably important as that is; but the greatest thing of all," he said, "is for one human being to bring another to Christ Jesus the Savior."

Surely, he spoke wisely and well. The supreme ambition for every church and for every individual Christian should be to bring somebody to Christ. The supreme method for bringing people to Christ is indicated here in the story of Andrew, who brought his brother Simon to Jesus. The supreme method for winning the world to Christ is the personal method, the bringing of people to Christ one by one. That is Christ's plan. When you turn to the Holy Scriptures, they are as clear as light, that God expects every friend He has to go out and see if he cannot win other friends to the same great side and service of Jesus.

"Ye shall be witnesses unto me," said Jesus, "both in Jerusalem, and in all Judea, and in Samaria, and unto the uttermost parts of the earth." The early church went out and in one short generation shook the Roman empire to its very foundation. It was a pagan, selfish, sodden, rotten empire, and yet in one short generation, that early church had shaken that Roman empire from center to circumference, and kindled a gospel light in every part of the vast domain. And they did it by the personal method. The men and the women and the children who loved Christ, went out everywhere, and talked for Christ, in the hearing of those who knew Him not, and the hearers became interested, and followed on, and found out for themselves the saving truth that there is in Christ's gospel. Every Christian, no matter how humble, can win somebody else to Christ. You would not challenge that, would you? Let me say it again. Every Christian, however humble, can win somebody to Christ.

*See Vol. I, pp. 317 – 18.

Francis J. McConnell (1871–1953)

Bishop of the Methodist Episcopal Church and from 1909 to 1912 president of De Pauw University, Francis McConnell was a prolific author as well as an effective spokesmen from the pulpit. He was in particular demand by college audiences, and the following "chapel address" is an example of his art as well as a hint as to his theology. A social activist, McConnell none-theless saw the responsible individual as the only foundation for any program of social improvement.

Zebedee

"And they left their father Zebedee in the boat with the hired servants." — Mark 1. 20.

The passage tells us that at the call of Jesus James and John left their father Zebedee, a fisherman, with his hired servants and followed the new Master. Because Zebedee remained in his boat he has suffered some rather severe treatment from homiletic interpretation. He has been painted as the stay-at-home who did not heed the call of Jesus. A brilliant preacher of the last generation had a notable sermon from the text which tells us that the mother of Zebedee's sons came with her sons upon one occasion to honor Jesus. The preacher entitled his sermon "Where was Zebedee?" And Zebedee was duly cudgeled for his lack of interest in religion.

On the occasion to which the brilliant pulpiteer referred it seems to me rather to the credit of Zebedee that he was not present. The motive that brought the mother of Zebedee's sons, with her sons, to Jesus was not wholly to honor Jesus but to seek the chief places in the Kingdom for James and John. It will be recalled that Jesus had to use some harsh words on that occasion. Probably the mother and the sons were in the after-years heartily ashamed of their request.

Another famous preacher has made it appear that this call to the men in the boat was a call to repentance and salvation and that Zebedee missed his chance. This explanation is hardly convincing. Jesus was not just then on an evangelistic tour. He was seeking men for membership in that group of disciples which was to be with him and learn of his teaching and his ways. It does not seem from the narrative that Jesus called Zebedee to discipleship.

These preachers just mentioned are typical of the point of view from which many have approached Zebedee. I have known of revival appeals in which the deadness of Zebedee's heart has been dwelt upon with various expositions as to what had hardened his heart. He was too old, and had let too many appeals pass ever to be stirred again, an explanation which is, of course, sheer

[Source: Francis J. McConnell, *The Just Weight and Other Chapel Addresses* (New York: Abingdon Press, 1925), pp. 151–54, 155–56.]

imagination. Or he was too much interested in fish. I once heard a young preacher shrewdly suspect that Zebedee was a capitalist, and had the capitalistic lack of interest in spiritual adventure.

Why not take the narrative just as it stands? Jesus called James and John, and they left Zebedee and followed Jesus. There is no hint that Zebedee was not a well-meaning man of good will, a hard-working fisherman, attending to his own business and taking things almost as they came, after the manner of fishermen. It was rather remarkable that he did not utter any word of remonstrance when his sons so summarily left him. There is this much of point in the hint that he was a capitalist—he had a boat and some nets. Those were tools. He hired and fired servants. That made him an employer of labor. All of which gives us a clue to his industry and sensible management, but none of which conveys a hint of any sort of dishonesty and exploitation.

Zebedee seems to me to stand out as the type of man who is an honorable stay-at-home, the man who keeps the ordinary work of the world going while the selected and called younger men fit themselves for special forms of service to God and man and move forth to make the world better. There is not much place for Zebedee personally in the field of such service itself. He is a little too old. It is no reflection on him that he does not at first glance recognize the Christ in this or that new movement. The trained disciples in the day of Jesus were themselves slow in recognizing the Christ in Jesus, or at least in recognizing the implications of Messiahship. Zebedee's age, however, prevents his making the readjustments necessary for active carrying out into apostleship the truth which he recognizes. It is best for him to stay where he is. . . .

An interesting and fruitful question concerning any forward social movement is, "Who pays?" War has had to meet the question, "Who pays?" and the question is deadly for the militarist. So with the constructive movements. All of these cost something, and somebody has to pay. Now, it may seem farfetched to ask of the school of the disciples, "Who paid?" but the question is pertinent. Zebedee paid. He paid in the fact that his sons left him and he allowed them to go, apparently without demur. He had to work harder because James and John were away with Jesus, or he had to hire more servants. The cost fell on Zebedee. He was not likely to be called on to suffer martyrdom, but he had to pay nevertheless. That he pays ungrudgingly is a mighty item to be put down to his credit. We see and hear James and John. We are charmed by their eloquence and zeal. Let us not forget Zebedee, who gave them their chance. He never writes any Gospels or Epistles but his signature is eloquent at the bottom of a check. The bright, ardent, young apostle starts out from the college amid the plaudits of those who expect him to turn the world upside down. If he ever does thus revolutionize the world, it will be because Zebedee, back among the boats and the nets and the fish, supplied him the leverage.

Does this seem fanciful? James and John, it appears, had some of this world's goods. They were not directly earning anything. Where did the contribution they made toward the upkeep of the little group come from? Where, but from Zebedee's nets? Zebedee knew that James and John were with Jesus. He did not understand what Jesus was trying to do. All he knew was that his sons believed in Jesus, that Jesus seemed to him to be in the right path, and that good for Israel might come out of it all. So he kept at his nets and helped feed the villages while the Master got his chance, occasionally sending fish and money to James and John. Let us not forget Zebedee who helped pay to teach the disciples.

Henry S. Coffin (1877 – 1954)

The youngest of the four ministers presented here, Henry Sloane Coffin had the advantage of an excellent education at Yale, in Edinburgh, and then in Marburg, Germany. Such heavy academic training made it highly probable that Coffin would have a career as seminary professor or even president — both of which he became at Union Theological Seminary in New York City. But Coffin was also a Presbyterian preacher (Madison Avenue Presbyterian Church) of major influence, and it is in that capacity that we read his explication of the "new life" in Christ.

THE NEW LIFE—INDIVIDUAL AND SOCIAL

The health department of a modern city is charged with a double duty: it has to care for cases of disease, and it has to suggest and enforce laws to keep the city sanitary. The former task—the treament of sickness—is much more widely recognized as the proper function of the medical profession; the latter—the prevention of the causes of illness—is a newer, but a more far-reaching, undertaking. When Pasteur was carrying on his investigations into the origins of certain diseases, most of the leading physicians and surgeons made light of his work: "How should this chemist, who cannot treat the simplest case of sickness nor perform the most trifling operation, have anything to contribute to medical science?" But Pasteur's discovery of the part played by bacilli not only altered profoundly the work of physicians and surgeons, but opened up the larger task of preventive medicine.

The Gospel of Christ, in its endeavor to make and keep men whole, faces a similarly double labor. It has its ministry of rescue and healing for sinning men and women; it has its plan of spiritual health for society. It comes to every man with its offer of rebirth into newness of life: "If any man be in Christ, he is a new creature." It comes to society with its offer of a regenesis,

[Source: H. S. Coffin, *Some Christian Convictions* (New Haven: Yale University Press, 1915), pp. 160 – 61.]

a paradise of love on earth. The life of God enters our world by two paths —
personally, through individuals whom it recreates, and by whom it remakes
society; socially, through a new communal order which reshapes the men and
women who live under it. The New Testament speaks of both entrances of
the Spirit of God into human life: it pictures "*one* born from above," and
"the holy *city* coming down from God out of heaven." The two processes
supplement each other. Consecrated man and wife make their home Christian;
a Christian home renders the conversion of its children unnecessary; they
know themselves children of God as soon as they know themselves anything
at all. Saved souls save society, and a saved society saves souls.

2. NEW THOUGHT AND NEW THOUGHTS

Theosophy and New Thought

H. P. Blavatsky (1831–91)

A native of Russia, Madame Blavatsky came to America in 1873, though "settled" in America would not be the proper expression. For a restlessness of mind, body, and spirit characterized all of her adult life. As Robert Ellwood wrote, ". . . always a wanderer, [she was] a colorful misfit in whatever society she found herself." Together with Henry S. Olcott (1832–1907), she founded the Theosophical Society in 1875. This organizational structure permitted expression of her deep interest in psychic phenomena, in the ancient wisdom of India, in the comparative study of the world's religions, and in universal brotherhood. She wrote voluminously, notably Isis Unveiled *(in two volumes, 1877) and* The Secret Doctrine *(in three volumes, 1888–97). In a dialogue between the "Enquirer" and the "Theosophist," the document below tells of the Society's broad purpose.*

ENQ. What are the objects of the Theosophical Society?

THEO. They are three, and have been so from the beginning. (1) To form the nucleus of a Universal Brotherhood of Humanity without distinction of race, colour, or creed. (2) To promote the study of the world's religion and sciences, and to vindicate the importance of old Asiatic literature, namely, of the Brahmanical, Buddhist, and Zoroastrian philosophies. (3) To investigate the hidden mysteries of Nature under every aspect possible, and the psychic and spiritual powers latent in man especially. These are, broadly stated, the three chief objects of the Theosophical Society.

ENQ. Can you give me some more detailed information upon these?

[Source: H. P. Blavatsky, *The Key to Theosophy: An Abridgement* (ed. by Joy Mills) (Wheaton, Ill.: Theosophical Publishing House, 1972 [1889]), pp. 24–27.]

THEO. We may divide each of the three objects into as many explanatory clauses as may be found necessary.

ENQ. Then let us begin with the first. What means would you resort to, in order to promote such a feeling of brotherhood among races that are known to be of the most diversified religions, customs, beliefs, and modes of thought?

THEO. Allow me to add that which you seem unwilling to express. Of course we know that every nation is divided, not merely against all other nations, but even against itself. Hence your wonder, and the reason why our first object appears to you a Utopia. Is it not so?

ENQ. Well, yes; but what have you to say against it?

THEO. Nothing against the fact; but much about the necessity of removing the causes which make Universal Brotherhood a Utopia at present.

ENQ. What are, in your view, these causes?

THEO. First and foremost, the natural selfishness of human nature. All the unselfishness of the altruistic teachings of Jesus has become merely a theoretical subject for pulpit oratory; while the precepts of practical selfishness, against which Christ so vainly preached, have become in-grained into the innermost life of the Western nations. "An eye for an eye and a tooth for a tooth" has come to be the first maxim of your law. Now, I state openly and fearlessly that the perversity of this doctrine and of so many others *Theosophy alone* can eradicate.

ENQ. How?

THEO. Simply by demonstrating on logical, philosophical, metaphysical, and even scientific grounds that: (*a*) All men have spiritually and phys-ically the same origin, which is the fundamental teaching of Theosophy. (*b*) As mankind is essentially of one and the same essence, and that essence is one — infinite, uncreate, and eternal, whether we call it God or Nature — nothing, therefore, can affect one nation or one man with-out affecting all other nations and all other men.

ENQ. But this is not the teaching of Christ, but rather a pantheistic notion.

THEO. That is where your mistake lies. It is purely *Christian*.

ENQ. Where are your proofs for such a statement?

THEO. They are ready at hand. Christ is alleged to have said: "Love each other" and "Love your enemies"; for "if ye love them (only) which love you, what reward (or merit) have ye? Do not even the *publicans* the same? And if you salute your brethren only, what do ye more than others? Do not even publicans so?" These are Christ's words. But *Gen-esis*, ix, 25, says "Cursed be Canaan; a servant of servants shall he be upon his brethren." And, therefore, Biblical people prefer the law of Moses to Christ's law of love. They base upon the Old Testament, which panders to all their passions, their laws of conquest, annexation, and tyranny over races which they call *inferior*. What crimes have been committed on the strength of this infernal (if taken in its dead letter) passage in Genesis, history alone gives us an idea, however inadequate.

ENQ. I have heard you say that the identity of our physical origin is proved by science, that of our spiritual origin by Wisdom-Religion. Yet we do not find Darwinists exhibiting great fraternal affection.

THEO. This is what shows the deficiency of the materialistic systems, and proves that we Theosophists are in the right. The identity of our physical origin makes no appeal to our higher and deeper feelings. Matter, deprived of its soul and spirit, or its divine essence, cannot speak to the human heart. But the identity of the soul and spirit, of real, immortal man, as Theosophy teaches us, once proven and deep-rooted in our hearts, would lead us far on the road of real charity and brotherly goodwill.

ENQ. But how does Theosophy explain the common origin of man?

THEO. By teaching that the *root* of all nature, objective and subjective, and everything else in the universe, visible and invisible, *is, was,* and *ever will be* one absolute essence, from which all starts, and into which everything returns.

ENQ. What do the statutes of your Society advise its members to do besides this? On the physical plane, I mean?

THEO. In order to awaken brotherly feeling among nations we have to assist in the international exchange of useful arts and products, by advice, information, and cooperation with all worthy individuals and associations. What is also needed is to impress men with the idea that, if the root of mankind is *one,* then there must also be one truth which finds expression in all the various religions.

ENQ. This refers to the common origin of religions, and you may be right there. But how does it apply to practical brotherhood on the physical plane?

THEO. First, because that which is true on the metaphysical plane must be also true on the physical. Secondly, because there is no more fertile source of hatred and strife than religious differences. When one party or another thinks himself the sole possessor of absolute truth, it becomes only natural that he should think his neighbour absolutely in the clutches of Error or the Devil. But once get a man to see that none of them has the *whole* truth, but that they are mutually complementary, that the complete truth can be found only in the combined views of all, after that which is false in each of them has been sifted out — then true brotherhood in religion will be established.

Warren Felt Evans (1817 – 89)

Starting out as a Methodist minister, Evans grew increasingly interested in the power of the mind over the body and in the intimate connection between the physical and the spiritual worlds. Cured himself through the ministrations of Phineas P. Quimby (1802 – 66), that fascinating clockmaker, hypnotist, and mental healer of antebellum America, and influenced as well by the writings of Emmanuel Swedenborg (see above, p. 205), Evans became one of the founders of New Thought. Though a specific organization did not emerge until the 1890s, Evans's books in the 1870s and 1880s enunciated many of New Thought's characteristic themes: the overriding significance of spiritual reality, the unity of all religions, the harmony between science and religion, and the ability of the individual to harness the Divine Nature in order to effect all manner of change —including the change from sickness to health. All of these themes are evident in the excerpt below.

Christ and Disease; or, The Power of the Spiritual Life Over the Body.

The highest form of existence is that of a true religious life, which, in its essence, is a harmonious union of goodness and truth, love and wisdom, benevolence and faith, in the character and activity of the individual. Where intellect and love are harmoniously united and blended, and act in perfect concordance, the resulting product is spiritual power. The omnipotence of God is the union of infinite wisdom and infinite love, or the knowing how to do what His goodness inclines Him to do. He who is, in this respect, an image of God, partakes of His spiritual almightiness. When a true philosophy is taken into the mount of transfiguration, and transformed into a divinely human religion, its face shines from the radiance of a higher sun, and possesses a power over ourselves and others that it could not otherwise have. When philosophy and religion are combined into a harmonious unity, each adds power and influence to the other. All religion should be made scientific, and all science religious. There is no inharmony between them when both are properly understood. The attempt to demonstrate the perfect agreement and concordance of the two, which is being made by many at the present time, is a laudable one, and promotive of the best interests of the race, though to accomplish this the current religious creeds must part company with some of their irrational dogmas, and science give up many of its unproved assumptions. But this will be no loss to either, as it is only eliminating an element of weakness from each. . . .

The founders of the great religions of the world were men in whom the intellect and the religious nature were blended more or less harmoniously. This is what gives their systems of doctrine such an almost unyielding grasp

[Source: W. F. Evans, *The Divine Law of Cure* (Boston: H. H. Carter & Co., 1886), pp. 119–20, 120–23.]

upon the minds of men, and such influence over so great masses of the world's population. Such men were Confucius, Buddha, Zoroaster, and we may add Mohammed. In all these examples which we have given of spiritual power there is some common principle. Can we discover what it is? It is that they were men of strong intellect, and were profoundly religious men. They were religious, not superficially, not in momentary and transient moods, but all through their being. Their religious fervor transported them into the third heavens, but also carried the intellect with it into a Divine realm of life and thought. Hence their thoughts, when given to others in their writings, have a Divine warmth and spiritual vitality in them, and are not mere cold and logical intellectual conceptions, like moonbeams reflected from polar ice. The religious nature exalted the intellect to a Divine realm of thought, where they became inspired, and recipient of the living Word, the indwelling Logos, of which they became in a true sense the incarnations. In all such men, in a mitigated sense, the Word is made flesh and dwells among us. It is impossible to be spiritual in our intellectual conceptions without being religious. To reach the higher degrees of inspiration, or quickened intuition, without a fervor of religious feeling is as impossible as to fly without wings.

The highest example in human history of the perfect union of the intellect with the religious nature, and the resultant spiritual power, is seen in Jesus the Christ. In him there was the most intimate blending of the purely human and the truly Divine, so that in his personality where the human nature ended and the Divinity commenced no one can perceive. The boundary line between the Godhead and manhood is not clearly drawn. There is in him a deification of humanity and a humanization of God, and somehow in him God comes very near to the souls of men. In him we witness the spectacle of a human nature and soul filled with God, —with all the fullness of God. But he expected, and expressed the wish, that all his disciples in every age should be, in this respect, a copy of the Master, —that they should be one with God as he and the Father were one. (John xvii: 20—23.) As the highest representation of God in human history, there is in his life, as unfolded in the Gospels, a revelation of the thoughts and feelings of God. No man can be actuated by a Divine influence and afflatus without in some way, and to some extent, manifesting the feelings of the Deity. But Paul affirms that God gave the Spirit to the Christ without measure, and the Divine love was the motive power of all his activity. He spent a large fraction of his public life in the cure of "all manner of sickness and disease" among the people. His activity seemed naturally to take that beneficent direction. So far as the Christ-principle is in us, we shall have power to do the same. The drift and current of our inner life will exhibit itself as a spontaneous impulse to do good to the souls and bodies of men. Jesus seemed to have a divinely clear conception of the spiritual origin of disease, and of the efficacy of spiritual remedies in its cure. He did not look upon sickness of the flesh as the real disease, but as the effect of an *a priori* spiritual malady; and when this antecedent cause ceases to operate, the morbid effect comes to an end. As Jesus the Christ was perpetually moved by a Divine influence and impulse in his career as the great Physician, it shows that in God there is a perpetual *conatus,* an irrepressible endeavor, an unchangeable willingness to heal our diseases of mind and body. In all our struggles against every morbid condition, within and without, we can, with unerring certainty, count upon God and his omnipotent love as our unfailing ally in the battle with evil and suffering. If God be for us, what can prevail against us? Here is the standing-ground of an assured and unyielding faith in Him for the cure of our own sicknesses and those of others through us. If I have any understanding of the system of the Christ in the cure of disease, he found the cause of it in some prior disturbance of the spiritual principle in man, and he applied his healing power to the mental root of the malady. All his *mighty works* had a redemptive aim, that is, they were designed primarily to deliver men from spiritual evil. Matter was viewed by him as an unsubstantial *appearance,* and mind was the only reality. Through the restored and redeemed soul he healed the body of its diseases, both functional and organic. To illustrate his Divine method of cure, and to make it an available, practical system, will be the aim of all I have to say in the subsequent chapters of this volume.

Ralph Waldo Trine (1866–1958)

If Evans planted the seeds of New Thought, R. W. Trine harvested that crop and broadcast more seeds. Trine's conviction that all that men and women needed was to get "in tune with the Infinite" struck responsive chords from coast to coast. He knew What All the World's A-Seeking, *to use the title of his first book (1896) —or so it seemed, as the products of his pen sold in the millions of copies. Not only health was in one's grasp, but success, power, and prosperity as well. "Hold to this thought, never allow it to weaken. . . ."*

Recognize, working in and through you, the same Infinite Power that creates and governs all things in the universe, the same Infinite Power that governs the endless systems of worlds in space. Send out your thought—thought is a force, and it has occult power of unknown proportions when rightly used and wisely directed—send out your thought that the right situation or the right work will come to you at the right time, in the right way, and that you will recognize it when it comes. Hold to this thought, never allow it to weaken, hold to it, and continually water it with firm expectation. You in this way put your advertisement into a psychical, a spiritual newspaper, a paper

[Source: R. W. Trine, *In Tune with the Infinite* (Indianapolis: Bobbs-Merrill, 1970 [1908]), pp. 137, 138–39.]

that has not a limited circulation, but one that will make its way not only to the utmost bounds of the earth, but of the very universe itself. It is an advertisement, moreover, which, if rightly placed on your part, will be far more effective than any advertisement you could possibly put into any printed sheet, no matter what claims are made in regard to its being "the great advertising medium." In the degree that you come into this realization and live in harmony with the higher laws and forces, in that degree will you be able to do this effectively. . . .

This is the law of prosperity: When apparent adversity comes, be not cast down by it, but make the best of it, and always look forward for better things, for conditions more prosperous. To hold yourself in this attitude of mind is to set into operation subtle, silent and irresistible forces that sooner or later will actualize in material form that which is today merely an idea. But ideas have occult power, and ideas, when rightly planted and rightly tended, are the seeds that actualize material conditions.

Never give a moment to complaint, but utilize the time that would otherwise be spent in this way in looking forward and actualizing the conditions you desire. Suggest prosperity to your self. See yourself in a prosperous condition. Affirm that you will before long be in a prosperous condition. Affirm it calmly and quietly but strongly and confidently. Believe it, believe it absolutely. Expect it — keep it continually watered with expectation. You thus make yourself a magnet to attract the things that you desire. Don't be afraid to suggest, to affirm these things, for by so doing you put forth an ideal which will begin to clothe itself in material form. In this way you are utilizing agents among the most subtle and powerful in the universe. If you are particularly desirous for anything that you feel it is good and right for you to have, something that will broaden your life or that will increase your usefulness to others, simply hold the thought that at the right time, in the right way and through the right instrumentality there will come to you or there will open up for you the way whereby you can attain what you desire.

Institutions of New Thought

Christian Science

The very name suggesting the harmony between religion and science of which W. F. Evans wrote, this highly visible, highly successful institution gained its first charter from the state of Massachusetts in 1879. The founder, Mary Baker Eddy (1821–1910), had like Evans come into contact with Phineas Quimby and had —again like Evans —herself experienced a mental or spir-

[Source: Mary B. G. Eddy, *Miscellaneous Writings, 1883–1896*, 3rd ed. (Boston: Joseph Armstrong, 1897), pp. 98–99, 100–2.]

*itual cure of physical infirmity. In 1875, Mrs. Eddy published the basic
text, the sacred text, of her theology:* Science and Health with Key to the
Scriptures. *The book and the church (Boston's "Mother Church") had won
an impressive following by the time of Mrs. Eddy's death in 1910. What
follows is a portion of her address to adherents gathered in Chicago in 1888.*

SCIENCE AND THE SENSES.

*Substance of my address at the National Convention in Chicago,
June 13, 1888.*

The National Christian Scientist Association has brought us together to minister and to be ministered unto; to mutually aid one another in finding ways and means for helping the whole human family; to quicken and extend the interest already felt in a higher mode of medicine; to watch with eager joy the individual growth of Christian Scientists, and the progress of our common cause in Chicago, —the miracle of the Occident. We come to strengthen and perpetuate our organizations and institutions; and to find strength in union, — strength to build up, through God's right hand, that pure and undefiled religion whose Science demonstrates God and the perfectibility of man. This purpose is immense, and it must begin with individual growth, a "consummation devoutly to be wished." The lives of all reformers attest the authenticity of their mission, and call the world to acknowledge its divine Principle. Truly is it written: —

> "Thou must be true thyself, if thou the Truth would'st teach;
> Thy heart must overflow, if thou another's heart would'st reach."

Science is absolute and final. It is revolutionary in its very nature; for it upsets all that is not upright. It annuls false evidence, and saith to the five material senses, "Having eyes ye see not, and ears ye hear not; neither can you understand." To weave one thread of Science through the looms of time, is a miracle in itself. The risk is stupendous. It cost Galileo, what? This awful price: the temporary loss of his self-respect. His fear overcame his loyalty; the courage of his convictions fell before it. Fear is the weapon in the hands of tyrants.

Men and women of the nineteenth century, are you called to voice a higher order of Science? Then obey this call. Go, if you must, to the dungeon or the scaffold, but take not back the words of Truth. How many are there ready to suffer for a righteous cause, to stand a long siege, take the front rank, face the foe, and be in the battle every day? . . .

Past, present, future, will show the word and Spirit of Truth —healing the sick and reclaiming the sinner —so long as there remains a claim of error for Truth to deny or to destroy. Love's labors are not lost. The five personal senses, that grasp neither the meaning nor the magnitude of self-abnegation, may lose sight thereof; but Science voices unselfish love, unfolds infinite Good, leads on irresistible forces, and will finally show the fruits of Love. Human reason is inaccurate; and the scope of the senses is inadequate to grasp the word of Truth, and teach the eternal.

Science speaks when the senses are silent, and then the evermore of Truth is triumphant. The spiritual monitor understood is coincidence of the divine with the human, the acme of Christian Science. Pure humanity, friendship, home, the interchange of love, bring to earth a foretaste of Heaven. They unite terrestrial and celestial joys, and crown them with blessings infinite.

The Christian Scientist loves man more because he loves God most. He understands this Principle, — Love. Who is sufficient for these things? Who remembers that patience, forgiveness, abiding faith, and affection, are the symptoms by which our Father indicates the different stages of man's recovery from sin and his entrance into Science? Who knows how the feeble lips are

Christian Science sanitarium in San Francisco, c. 1935
(Keystone-Mast Collection, University of California, Riverside)

made eloquent, how hearts are inspired, how healing becomes spontaneous, and how the divine Mind is understood and demonstrated? He alone knows these wonders who is departing from the thraldom of the senses and accepting spiritual Truth, — that which blesses its adoption by the refinement of joy and the dismissal of sorrow.

Christian Science and the senses are at war. It is a revolutionary struggle. We already have had two in this nation; and they began and ended in a contest for the true idea, for human liberty and rights. Now cometh a third struggle; for the freedom of health, holiness, and the attainment of Heaven.

The scientific sense of Being which establishes harmony, enters into no compromise with finiteness and feebleness. It undermines the foundations of mortality, of physical law, breaks their chains, and sets the captive free, opening the doors for them that are bound.

He who turns to the body for evidence, bases his conclusions on mortality, on imperfection; but Science saith to man, "God hath all power."

The Science of Omnipotence demonstrates but one power, and this power is good, not evil, not matter, — but Mind. This virtually destroys matter and evil, including sin and disease.

If God is all, and God is good, it follows that all must be good; and no other power, law, or intelligence can exist. On this proof rest premise and conclusion in Science, and the facts that disprove the evidence of the senses.

God is individual Mind. This one Mind and His individuality comprise the elements of all forms and individualities, and prophesy the nature and stature of Christ, the ideal man.

A corporeal God, as often defined by lexicographers and scholastic theologians, is only an infinite finite being, an unlimited man, — a theory to me inconceivable. If the unlimited and immortal Mind could originate in a limited body, and eventually return to those limits, it would be forever limited.

In this limited and lower sense God is not personal. His infinity precludes the possibility of corporeal personality. His being is individual, but not physical.

God is like Himself, and like nothing else. He is universal and primitive. His character admits of no degrees of comparison. God is not part, but the whole. In His individuality I recognize the loving, divine Father, Mother God. Infinite personality must be incorporeal.

God's ways are not ours. His pity is expressed in modes above the human. His chastisements are the manifestations of Love. The sympathy of His eternal Mind is fully expressed in Divine Science, which blots out all our iniquities and heals all our diseases. Human pity often brings pain.

Science supports harmony, denies suffering, and destroys it with the sympathy of Truth. Whatever seems material, seems thus only to the material senses, and is but the subjective state of mortal and material thought.

Science has inaugurated the irrepressible conflict between sense and Soul.

Mortal thought wars with this sense as one that beateth the air, but Science outmasters it, and ends the warfare. This proves daily that "one with God is a majority."

Unity School of Christianity

While Christian Science managed to build and maintain a substantial organization, it did not escape factionalism and schism. Some persons (for example, Emma C. Hopkins and Ursula Gestefeld) were dismissed from the parent church for expressing divergent views and attracting personal followings. The Fillmores, Charles (1854–1948) and Myrtle (1845–1931), came under the influence of these excommunicants, even as they too had already been influenced by Phineas Quimby and W. F. Evans. Beginning a publishing program in 1889, the Fillmores (husband and wife) in 1903 applied for incorporation of the "Unity School of Practical Christianity." With headquarters in Kansas City, Missouri, the Unity School at first saw its mission as working within the established churches. Gradually, however, Unity developed its own professional ministry, its widely scattered centers, and its standards of orthodoxy. Another New Thought movement had become a church. In the excerpt below, Charles Fillmore informs his readers that they can be either an Adam or a Christ: "The choice lies with you."

Let us repeat that the body of man is the visible record of his thoughts. It is the identification of the individual's interpretation of man, and each individual shows in his body just what his views of man are. The body is the corporeal record of the mind of its owner, and there is no limit to its infinite differentiation. The individual may become any type of being that he elects to be. Man selects the mental model and the body images it. So the body is the image and likeness of the individual's idea of man. We may embody any conception of life or being that we can conceive. The body is the exact reproduction of the thoughts of its occupant. As a man thinks in his mind, so is his body.

You can be an Adam if you choose, or you may be a Christ, or any other type of being that you see fit to idealize. The choice lies with you. The body merely executes the mandates of the mind. The mind dictates the model according to which the body shall manifest. Therefore, "as he thinketh within himself [in his vital nature], so is he." Each is just what he believes he is.

It is safe to say that nine hundred and ninety-nine people out of every thousand believe that the resurrection of the body has something specifically to do with the getting of a new body after death; so we find more than ninety-nine percent of the world waiting for death to get something new in the way

[Source: Charles Fillmore, *Unity*, June, 1947, pp. 3–6.]

of a body. This belief is not based on the principles of Truth, for there is no ready-made-body factory in the universe, and none will get the body that thus he expects. Waiting for death in order to get a new body is the folly of ignorance. The thing to do is to improve the body that we now have; it can be done, and it must be done by those who would follow Jesus in the regeneration.

The "resurrection" of the body has nothing whatever to do with death, except that we may resurrect ourselves from every dead condition into which sense ignorance has plunged us. To be resurrected means *to get out of the place that you are in* and to get into another place. Resurrection is a rising into new vigor, new prosperity; a restoration to some higher state. It is absurd to suppose that it applies only to the resuscitation of a dead body.

Paul hints at a time when the body will be changed, and he says that it is when "Death is swallowed up in victory." Here are Paul's words: "When this corruptible shall put on incorruption, and this mortal shall have put on immortality . . . Death is swallowed up in victory."

This transformation is worked out by the individual himself, and is not the result of physical death, but rather of the death or annihilation of the erroneous ideas that ignorance has stored in the cells of the body. It is first a mental resurrection, followed by a body demonstration.

It is the privilege of the individual to express any type of body that he sees fit to idealize. Man may become a Christ in mind and in body by incorporating into his every thought the ideas given to the world by Jesus.

"But we all, with unveiled face beholding as in a mirror the glory of the Lord, are transformed into the same image from glory to glory, even as from the Lord the Spirit."

Creative Mind has imaged in the soul of every one a picture of the perfect-man body. The imaging process of creative Mind may well be illustrated by the picture that light makes on the photographic plate, which must be "developed" before it becomes visible. Or man's invisible body may be compared to the blue prints of a building that the architect delivers to the builder. Man is a builder of flesh and blood. Jesus was a carpenter. Also He was indeed the Master Mason. He restored "the temple of Jehovah," the Lord's body, in Jerusalem, in His mind and heart.

When we call ourselves fleshly, mortal, finite, we manifest bodily upon a fleshly, mortal and finite plane. We sow to the flesh, and of the flesh reap corruption. The time has arrived for the whole human family to repudiate the estimate of man as corrupt and instead to think of him as he was designed by creative Mind. "This corruptible must put on incorruption, and this mortal must put on immortality," says Paul.

We must stop calling our bodies flesh and blood, but see them as they are in Spirit-Mind—pure and incorruptible. This realization of man's perfect body will arrest decay, disintegration, and death.

We must rise above material thoughts into spiritual realization, and live, move, and have our being in a divine reality. When our views of man are elevated to spiritual understanding, we shall begin the expression of bodily perfection. Our thoughts must first be perfect before we can expect to manifest perfection in body. The issues of life are within man; the body is merely the record of the state of mind of the individual.

Church of Religious Science

Christian Science began in New England, Unity in the Midwest, and the Church of Religious Science in the Far West. New Thought had spread across the nation. Ernest S. Holmes (1887 – 1960), though born in Maine, settled in Los Angeles where he organized a New Thought group and in 1927 launched a popular New Thought magazine, Science of Mind. *His book of the same title, published the previous year (and much revised and reprinted thereafter), stood as the charter document of this twentieth-century church. Like those before him, Holmes saw the secret of life as lying in a right relationship with Divine Being. Rightly related, the believer possessed the key that could unlock all of the inexhaustible powers of the universe.*

How to Heal

In our work, we treat man, not as a physical body, neither do we treat the disease as belonging to him, *the reason being that if we do, we cannot subsequently free him from it.* We do not think of the disease as being connected with him or a part of him. The practitioner seeks to realize man as *perfect*, not needing to be healed of anything. This is nothing less than the realization of the Presence and the Power of God, or Spirit, as Man's Life, as the only life there is, as complete and perfect in him right now.

First recognize your own perfection, then build up the same recognition for your patient. You are then ready to directly attack the *thought* that binds him, *recognizing that your word destroys it, and stating that it does.* You may then take into account and specifically mention everything that needs to be changed, every so-called broken law or false thought. Then finish your treatment with a realization of peace, remaining for a few moments in silent recognition *that your work is done, complete and perfect.*

The work must not be thought of as hard. When we know that there is but One Mind, we shall realize that this work could not be difficult or laborious. *Mental treatment is a direct statement of belief into Mind, coupled with a realization that the work is already an accomplished fact.* The spiritual man needs no healing, health is an omnipresent reality, and when the ob-

[Source: E. S. Holmes, *The Science of Mind* (New York: Dodd, Mead & Co., 1959 [1926]), pp. 202 – 5.]

structions that hinder healing are removed, *it will be found that health was there all the time.* So in your work, do not feel that you must heal anyone. Your only responsibility is to uncover the Truth.

Never say: "Here is a patient whom I must heal," for if you think of him from this viewpoint, how are you going to heal him? If you mentally see a sick man, he will remain mentally sick. *We cannot heal successfully while we recognize sickness as a reality to the Spirit.* In spiritual healing by this method, no one believes in disease, it has no action nor reaction, it has neither cause nor effect, it has no law to support it and no one through whom it can operate. There is no one to talk with about it, and no one to believe in it. While we maintain that disease is primarily a thing of thought, we do not deny the actuality of its experience nor the suffering it causes, instead we seek to heal it, and we co-operate with all, no matter what method they are using to relieve distress.

You have nothing to do with the patient's thought as a personality, for as your own thought clears, he will be helped. First eliminate doubt and fear from your own thought; realize that your patient is a Divine Being, and that your word is the law unto the thing unto which it is spoken. This is what gave Jesus His power: "For He taught them as one having authority, and not as the scribes."

Healing is Clear Thinking

Scientific mental healing is the result of clear thinking and logical reasoning, which presents itself to consciousness and is acted upon by Mind. It is a systematic process of reasoning, which unearths the mental cause or idea underlying disease, and presents the Truth about man's being.

For instance, say to yourself: "God is all there is. There is only One Life." When you are treating, if there is any slight point which is not clear, do not continue with the treatment. Stop at once, go back to your analysis of Ultimate Reality, and build your whole argument upon It, in order to get a clear consciousness.

Repeat: "God is All. There is but One Power, Intelligence and Consciousness in the Universe, but One Presence. This One Presence cannot change. There is nothing for It to change into but Itself. It is Changeless, *and It is my life now, It is in me now."* Claim that no form of race-suggestion, belief in limitation, subjective idea of limitation, thought of karma, fatalism, theology or hell, horoscope, or any other false belief, has power. Accept none of them. If you have ever believed in them, if you have ever believed that the stars govern you, or that your environment governs you, or that your opportunities govern you, recognize this as an hypnotic condition into which you have fallen, and deny every one of them until there is no longer anything in you that believes in them.

This is a good way to clear your consciousness. We can readily see what it does: it induces a clear concept of Reality, which must reproduce Itself. This process of clear thinking, if carried out every day, will heal.

When you are giving a treatment, you are *thinking*. You are meeting, opposing, neutralizing, erasing and obliterating suppression, fear, doubt, failure, morbid emotion and sense of loss — whatever the trouble may be. Every time your thought hits fairly and squarely, it erases just as definitely as one would erase a chalk line. Such is the mystery of the appearance and the disappearance of thought.

Right thought, constantly poured into consciousness, will eventually purify it. Discord might be likened to a bottle of impure water; healing might be likened to the process of dropping pure water into the bottle, a drop at a time, until the whole is clean and pure. Someone might ask why the bottle could not be turned upside down and at once drain out all the impurities. Sometimes this happens but not often. Meanwhile, a drop at a time will finally eliminate the impurities and produce a healing.

In treating, go beyond the disease and supply a spiritual consciousness. A treatment is not complete without a great realization of Life and Love, of God and Perfection, of Truth and Wisdom, of Power and Reality. Sense the Divine Presence in and through the patient at all times.

Peace and Prosperity

Acres of Diamonds (1890)

While much of New Thought concentrated on the healing of disease, all understood that the power of the universe could be applied to any good purpose. (The Fillmores thought of Unity as merely applied or practical Christianity.) Russell H. Conwell (1843 – 1925), not a member of any New Thought organization but a Baptist minister in Philadelphia, nonetheless shared the view that life's problems were largely internal, life's potential essentially unlimited. His most famous sermon by far, Acres of Diamonds, *delivered over and over again, printed over and over again, made the point that so many wanted to hear — over and over again: you ought to be rich, you can be rich, it is your duty to be rich.*

Now then, I say again that the opportunity to get rich, to attain unto great wealth, is here in Philadelphia now, within the reach of almost every man and woman who hears me speak tonight, and I mean just what I say. I have not come to this platform even under these circumstances to recite something

[Source: R. H. Conwell, *Acres of Diamonds* (New York: Harper & Brothers, 1915 [1890]), pp. 17 – 18, 20.]

to you. I have come to tell you what in God's sight I believe to be the truth, and if the years of life have been of any value to me in the attainment of common sense, I know I am right; that the men and women sitting here, who found it difficult perhaps to buy a ticket to this lecture or gathering to-night, have within their reach "acres of diamonds," opportunities to get largely wealthy. There never was a place on earth more adapted than the city of Philadelphia to-day, and never in the history of the world did a poor man without capital have such an opportunity to get rich quickly and honestly as he has now in our city. I say it is the truth, and I want you to accept it as such; for if you think I have come to simply recite something, then I would better not be here. I have no time to waste in any such talk, but to say the things I believe, and unless some of you get richer for what I am saying to-night my time is wasted.

I say that you ought to get rich, and it is your duty to get rich. How many of my pious brethren say to me, "Do you, a Christian minister, spend your time going up and down the country advising young people to get rich, to get money?" "Yes, of course I do." They say, "Isn't that awful! Why don't you preach the gospel instead of preaching about man's making money?" "Because to make money honestly is to preach the gospel." That is the reason. The men who get rich may be the most honest men you find in the community. . . .

For a man to have money, even in large sums, is not an inconsistent thing. We preach against covetousness, and you know we do, in the pulpit, and oftentimes preach against it so long and use the terms about "filthy lucre" so extremely that Christians get the idea that when we stand in the pulpit we believe it is wicked for any man to have money — until the collection-basket goes around, and then we almost swear at the people because they don't give more money. Oh, the inconsistency of such doctrines as that!

Money is power, and you ought to be reasonably ambitious to have it. You ought because you can do more good with it than you could without it. Money printed your Bible, money builds your churches, money sends your mission-aries, and money pays your preachers, and you would not have many of them, either, if you did not pay them. I am always willing that my church should raise my salary, because the church that pays the largest salary always raises it the easiest. You never knew an exception to it in your life. The man who gets the largest salary can do the most good with the power that is furnished to him. Of course he can if his spirit be right to use it for what it is given to him.

I say, then, you ought to have money. If you can honestly attain unto riches in Philadelphia, it is your Christian and godly duty to do so.

You Can Win (1938)

Far more famous for his later book on The Power of Positive Thinking
*(1952), Norman Vincent Peale (b. 1898) announced those themes in the
1930s that many longed to hear. Religion is not so much obligation as it is
opportunity; life is not so much frustration as it is conquest; the universe is
not so much beyond as it is within. Like Conwell, Peale was not a member
of New Thought; he was in fact a Methodist minister who became a Dutch
Reformed pastor in New York City. And again like Conwell, Peale proved
to be enormously popular. In the case of both men, their spectacular success
brought professional and financial reward enabling both to underwrite educational and religious enterprises.*

Thus your religion, which may now consist largely of the framework of
belief, tradition and ceremonial, and from which you derive not a little
comfort and help, can be — and this is the greatest truth you will ever encounter — a force and power to completely revolutionize your life. From it
you can draw a power beyond anything you have ever experienced, a power
sufficient to overcome any weakness, carry any burden, conquer any sin.
Through a surrendered faith in Christ and a daily intimate living in spirit
with him you can win over adversaries which formerly seemed too great for
the human spirit to bear.

Call the roll of all those things which can defeat a man — suffering and
pain, sorrow, disappointment, hardship, frustration, sin. There they stand,
challenging, menacing, all but invincible. Who can hope to overcome them?
But if one is armed with a strange and wonderful secret, these giants are at
his mercy. This secret is not some cure-all, nicely wrapped in cellophane,
which you can purchase in a store. It is not an achievement for which you
may valiantly struggle. It cannot be purchased, nor can it be won by effort.
It is a gift freely offered to you. All you need do is to take it by an act of
faith and begin to live on it. Why go on being a victim of fear, anxiety,
trouble, and weakness, with vigor of mind and spirit and body being steadily
drained off? Great new power and strength can be yours.

Turn to the Bible. In the Bible you read a statement by a man who long
ago discovered the truth. He said, "I can do all things through Christ who
giveth me the strength." You can learn to say the same thing. That secret can
be yours if you want it. You can win. I mean that because I know it is true.
It is immaterial what your difficulty is. If it is the worst difficulty in the
world, it does not invalidate the fact that you can win if you will adopt this
plan of living. There is nothing magical about the Bible, but the secret I am
talking about is to be found within its pages. Why sit there defeated when
you have at your very elbow a book that can make a new person of you?

[Source: N. V. Peale, *You Can Win* (New York: Abingdon Cokesbury Press, 1938),
pp. 21 – 23.]

When you open it, the most human people come walking out of its pages and sit down with you or me and say: "Listen, I have a secret and I want to share it with you. If you take Christ into your life and put your life in his hands, you too can win over anything." "I can do all things through Christ," says the Bible.

I realize that many people do not understand religion in this vital way. They think of religion as something that has to do with what they regard as stale and musty churches and dull services of worship. But that isn't religion at all. Religion deals with an electric power or force which is all about us, just as sound waves are in the air. When you come into your living room, for instance, your radio is silent and lifeless. You turn a dial. You tune your radio to the sound waves that are filling the air and immediately these sounds are brought into your room and you take into your consciousness that with which the air is filled but which the moment before were meaningless to you because you had not tuned in. All about us in the universe is this value called the power of God, but we are impervious to it. It means nothing to us. We are closed to it. We go on day by day living in our own feeble human strength, which is drawn from inside ourselves and which soon runs dry. Accordingly, we are worried; we are nervous; we are defeated time and time again; we have no sense of conquest at all. Religion means that you get tired of living like that. You become aware of a power in the world that you do not possess. What, then, do you do? You tune in. You bring your spirit into harmony with the Spirit of God. That's very simply done too. You say with the faith of a little child, "Lord, I bring my human spirit to you and I ask you to fill me with your power." Then the miracle happens. As the strains of an orchestra fill the room when a radio is tuned in, so the marvelous melody of God comes into your life.

Psychology and Religion

Emmanuel Movement

Apart from the congeries of ideas gathered under the heading of New Thought, the new science of psychology, even more of psychoanalysis and psychiatry, made its impact upon religion in America. Elwood Worcester (1862 – 1940), Episcopal clergyman in Boston and among the earliest to relate psychology to the pastoral ministry, launched the Emmanuel Movement in 1906. The aim of the movement, as an early associate wrote, was "to unite in friendly alliance a simple New Testament Christianity as modern Biblical scholarship

[Source: Elwood Worcester et al., *Religion and Medicine: The Moral Control of Nervous Disorders* (New York: Moffat Yard and Co., 1908), pp. 2 – 5.]

corroborates it and the proved conclusions of modern medicine, and more especially of modern psychological medicine, in the interests of suffering humanity" (Samuel McComb, Independent, May 21, 1908, p. 1122). In the words of Elwood Worcester below, one also sees an openness to multiple approaches in the curing of human hurts.

As we are attempting to establish no new dogma, and as our motives are entirely disinterested, our single desire is to give each patient the best opportunity of life and health which our means allow. We believe in the power of the mind over the body, and we believe also in medicine, in good habits, and in a wholesome, well-regulated life. In the treatment of functional nervous disorders we make free use of moral and psychical agencies, but we do not believe in overtaxing these valuable aids by expecting the mind to attain results which can be effected more easily through physical instrumentalities. Accordingly we have gladly availed ourselves of the services of the skilled medical and surgical specialists who have offered to co-operate with us, and we believe that our freedom in this respect and the combination of good psychical and physical methods have had much to do with our success. If a bad headache is caused by eye-strain, or a generally enfeebled condition is obviously the result of a digestive disturbance, a pair of glasses or a belt is frequently far more effective than suggestion. Most religious workers in this field have made the mistake of supposing that God can cure in only one way and that the employment of physical means indicates a lack of faith. This is absurd. God cures by many means. He uses the sunlight, healing and nourishing substances, water and air. The knitting of a broken bone, or the furrowing out of new blood courses in a diseased limb, is just as truly His work as the restoration of a wounded spirit. There is no peculiar piety involved in the use of suggestion. We have seen the consumptive nursed back to life, by rest, fresh air, abundant food and kindness, and we have seen more spectacular recovery from other diseases through confident expectation and the spoken word, but we have never felt that the one was necessarily more the act of God than the other. The fact remains that consumption can be cured in no other way, and that those who take a different view of the subject do not cure consumptives; they kill them by robbing them of their last chance of life; the same is true of other diseases.

For this reason we have confined our practice to that large group of maladies which are known to-day as functional nervous disorders. Although a sound psychical and moral method is a valuable adjunct in every branch of medicine, yet viewed as an independent remedial agent the legitimate sphere of psychotherapy is strictly limited. It is in the field of the functional neuroses that all its real victories have been won. Here again our conception of our mission differs decidedly from that of our predecessors. In answer to their taunt: "If you believe in God's power to cure disease, how dare you place any limit to that power?" we are content to reply: "We believe God has power to cure all disease, but we do not believe God cures all disease by the same means." At all events an authentic instance of recovery from organic disease through psychical means is what we are waiting for. While we do not believe that any man knows all that is to be known on this subject, or that we are in a position to affirm dogmatically what the mind can or cannot accomplish, yet we are surely safe in accepting as to this the overwhelming weight of scientific opinion, and in confining our practice to a field in which it is known to be efficacious. By so doing we avoid the one valid objection which has ever been urged against psychotherapeutics, namely, its employment in diseases which obviously require physical interference, with the result that many patients have died through sheer neglect.

Apart from this, it is in the domain of functional nervous disorders that such service as we are able to render is most needed, not merely because this branch of medicine is least developed in America and adequate treatment is difficult to obtain, especially by the poor, but because disorders of this nature are peculiarly associated with the moral life. An attack of typhoid fever may spring from no moral cause and it may have no perceptible influence upon character, but neurasthenia, hysteria, psychasthenia, hypochondria, alcoholism, etc., are afflictions of the personality. They spring from moral causes and they produce moral effects. In this domain the beneficent action of drugs and medicines is extremely limited, and the personality of the physician is everything. Other agencies such as electricity, baths, etc., probably owe much of their value to their suggestional effect, and so long as the training of our physicians is strictly material, such patients will continue to be their despair, for the reason that moral maladies require moral treatment.

Physicians of the Soul

In colonial America, it was not uncommon for the local minister to serve also as the town doctor (the "angelic conjunction," as Cotton Mather called it). The nineteenth century's dedication to professionalism changed all that. In the important work of Anton T. Boisen (1876–1965), however, steps were taken to close the gap between physician and clergyman. Boisen, the founder of clinical pastoral education, helped establish a whole new field with its own extensive literature and collection of learned journals (for example, Journal of Religion and Health, Journal of Pastoral Counseling, Journal of Pastoral Care, *and* Pastoral Psychology). *In 1936, Boisen called for doctors and ministers to understand each other better, approach each other*

[Source: A. T. Boisen, *The Exploration of the Inner World: A Study of Mental Disorder and Religious Experience* (New York: Harper & Brothers, 1936), pp. 238–39, 242–43, 247–48.]

more closely. In writing of "spiritual healing," Boisen had much to say about what a later generation would call "holistic medicine."

In venturing to use the term "spiritual healing" I am probably laying myself open to criticism. Only a few weeks ago I was taken severely to task for using the term "cure of souls." A professor of religious education thought it most unfortunate that I should cling to such an outworn and misleading word as "soul," while a psychiatrist friend suggested that it would be much wiser if I should avoid the use of words like "cure," to which the medical profession laid an exclusive claim. I am afraid the present title will be open to the same objections.

Now I have no desire to become involved in any controversy over the use of words and I should be happy to substitute another phrase if I could find it. I am concerned only to follow out the logical consequences of our findings as regards the distinctive task of the clergyman and the conditions essential to its accomplishment. We have found that mental illness of the functional type has to do with the philosophy of life and usually with the sense of personal failure. We have arrived at the conclusion that acute upheavals are really attempts at reorganization which are closely related to those eruptive solutions of inner conflicts so familiar to the religious worker under the name of "conversion experiences." We have furthermore concluded that in mental illness there are operative those profound and delicate laws of the spiritual life with which theology deals. If our findings are correct it follows that the religious worker, as his major problem, is dealing with precisely those same inner adjustments and conflicts which come within the province of the psychiatrist. It is of course true that he is dealing with these difficulties in their incipient rather than in their terminal stages. But that only makes his task the more important. If only he have understanding, there is no one who has it in his power to do more effective preventive work than the minister who in his professional capacity goes in and out among his people, visiting them in their homes, talking with them individually about their personal problems, and preaching from his pulpit on that which has to do with the end and meaning of life. For the same reason, if he have not understanding, he may be worse than ineffective. He may do actual harm. But the fact remains that so long as the church is in existence and so long as it retains any influence whatsoever, the minister will be engaged in the same general task as the psychiatrist. Regardless of the name we use, for better or for worse, he will be doing psychotherapeutic work. It would seem advisable that this fact should be recognized and that he should be enabled to do his rightful part toward the achievement of mental health among those whom he serves.

I count it, therefore, as not the least important of my obligations as a student of the advanced disorders of the personality that I should do my part toward acquainting ministers generally with the insights derived from dealing with serious mental illness. In endeavoring to perform this task before groups of ministers I have not infrequently encountered among them a certain impatience. They want to be told at once what to do. They want rules of procedure which they can apply and they are apt to be restive under the attempt to discover the meaning of the different forms of mental illness. . . .

Probably there is no more important lesson for the average minister or teacher than this art of listening, for not uncommonly he likes to do the talking himself. From the good psychiatrist he should learn the need of beginning with the other fellow, of listening without condemning, of trying to understand his language, particularly that symbolic language which is intended to be understood only by those who have eyes to see and ears to hear. And seeing back of symptom and symbol to the real needs and the unspoken longings, the man of understanding will be little concerned about creed or formula but will concern himself with the task of leading the sufferer in terms of his own formulations to discover for himself that solution of his problem which is socially acceptable and constructive.

While it is necessary to bear in mind the primary importance of the imponderable and elusive personal factors, we should not fail to recognize that there are different psychotherapeutic techniques, each with its particular point of view and its particular uses.

The methods which in the past have generally been employed by the church belong in the "faith healing" group. This form of psychotherapy is characterized by the fact that it relies chiefly upon suggestion. It takes the patient as he is, making little or no attempt to discover the roots of his difficulty, and directs his attention to comforting and constructive thoughts through prayer, friendly advice and devotional books. It would do the church serious injustice not to recognize that considerable good sense has been brought to bear by individual workers and that rather generally a great deal of stress has been placed on facing the facts and squaring accounts and correcting misunderstandings. But there has never been any systematic attempt at treatment on the basis of diagnosis, while in such forms as Christian Science suggestion is even carried to the point of denying the reality of evil and pain and asserting the absolute omnipotence of Mind and Love and Truth.

A somewhat different form of faith healing is that which some years ago received much publicity through M. Coué and his little formula about "getting better and better." Still another is that which makes use of hypnosis. With the patient in the hypnotic condition the practitioner makes constructive suggestions. Of recent years the use of deep hypnosis has been limited. The tendency among those who use hypnosis at all is merely to give suggestions to the patient while the latter is in relaxed condition or under light hypnosis. It is also used for exploratory purposes in order to discover hidden causes of trouble. The disfavor with which hypnosis is now regarded is due to the view that results secured with its help, while often striking, are not permanent. They are suggestions imposed from without and may even tend to weaken the patient's will. ·

The results secured at religious revivals in the years gone by have undoubtedly been due largely to the influence of suggestion; so also the cures effected at such shrines as Lourdes and Ste. Anne de Beaupré. . . .

. . . We find a striking contrast between the training of the medical man and that of the clergyman. The medical man is trained to deal at first hand with living human nature. He knows particularly the dangers and diseases to which flesh is heir, and if he be a psychiatrist, he knows the vagaries of the human spirit. He has not, however, as an essential part of his training, been introduced to human nature at its best. In the case of the clergyman the primary stress is laid upon character and purpose and he is introduced in his training to the noblest experiences of the race and to its most important insights. As yet however it is not an essential part of his training that he should be introduced under guidance to the raw material of life or that he should learn to recognize and understand experiences that are morbid or pathological.

Now I have no brief for either profession. I have had almost as much difficulty with the one as with the other. I can only say that from the standpoint of the mentally ill, in whose behalf I speak, I scarcely know which is worse, to have to depend upon a clergyman who has never come to close grips with the realities of human nature, or to be at the mercy of a physician who has no understanding of the spiritual needs and aspirations and of the nobler potentialities of mankind. I am merely convinced that our present system of training experts in the maladies of the personality is in need of improvement.

What Spiritual Healing Is

The integration between what medicine had to offer and what religion had to offer grew closer in the 1930s and 1940s, especially where levels of education and competence were on a par. Seward Hiltner (b. 1909), graduate of the University of Chicago Divinity School, worked with the Federal Council of Churches, taught at Chicago, and concluded an active career at Princeton Theological Seminary. In his many journal articles and books, Hiltner won broad acceptance for the potentially productive interaction among surgeon, psychiatrist, and minister.

*W*hat Spiritual Healing Is. One theological assumption has been suggested in previous sections but it remains to be stated directly. It would seem so obviously true as to require no proof. This is that any distinction made between "religious healing" or "spiritual healing" and other healing is only a practical difference so far as method is concerned. That is, healing influences

[Source: Seward Hiltner, *Religion and Health* (New York: Macmillan Co., 1943), pp. 100–2.]

which are permitted to operate through the method of prayer, for example, are not necessarily more "religious" or more "spiritual" than those set in motion by the surgeon's knife or the psychiatrist's analysis. For all healing comes from the *vis medicatrix naturae*, or the *vis medicatrix Dei*, the healing power of nature or of God, depending upon whether we are making an empirical or a religious statement. It is legitimate to make a practical distinction between the surgeon's knife, on the one hand, and prayer, on the other, and even to call the beneficent influence of one "spiritual healing," so long as it is recognized that one is not basically more "spiritual" or "religious" than the other. For both may be looked on in the broader sense as channels of the *vis medicatrix Dei*, which is another way of saying that the healing influences are ready to operate if the conditions are set up to permit them to work. In some situations the surgeon's knife must cut out offending tissue in order to release the forces of healing; in other cases the personality analysis is the central need; and in still other cases the conscious recognition of the power of these healing influences is most needed. In the majority of cases, something of all three may be helpful. We know more about when the surgeon's knife (or drug, or a new diet) is needed than we know about the others. We know more about when personality analysis is needed than we do about when prayer is needed; but we are learning new things about both. And we find increasingly that the three, applied intelligently, benefit the whole person more than any single one without the others.

Perhaps the central matter in what we distinguish practically as "spiritual healing" relates to consciousness in a special sense, to the degree of awareness of the beneficent influences which are ready to operate in a healing direction if they can be released — that is, it relates to affirmation of things which can really be affirmed on the basis of all sound religious experience and which do not conflict with the findings of science. It involves something which has not usually been recognized by those interested in "spiritual healing," a special relation between conscious awareness and the unconscious driving forces of human life. Real spiritual healing is not symptomatic. It does not deal with making affirmations about how wonderful God is to look after us as he does . . . when at the same time these affirmations are used as a cloak shrouding recognition of basic problems (and sins) within us which remain unexamined. Real spiritual healing brings forgiveness for guilt about things concerning which one ought to feel guilty, after the real guiltiness has been recognized. It brings personality reorganization after the powerful elements of disorganization have been investigated. It brings peace after the causes of "internal warfare" have been subjected to scrutiny and have been accepted as "emotional facts." It brings love after one's capacities for hostility have been seen and diagnosed. It brings security after one's anxieties have been understood and faced.

This does not mean that the process is mainly an intellectual one; for it is not. The kind of analysis which we might give of the situation, with some verbal precision required on account of the need to communicate what we mean, is not the basic factor in the situation. It makes comparatively little difference whether the person is capable of carrying out conscious and deliberate analysis of the type we have been doing; but it makes a great difference whether the "conscious" acceptance of one's "unconscious self" is basically honest emotionally, or whether it is merely an intellectual smoke-screen. Generally, intellectual knowledge of what happens in such processes should help, provided it is sound knowledge. But possession of the knowledge does not necessarily bring the forces into operation. The psychiatrists make a similar point in their reference to the difference between "intellectual" and "emotional" insight. All of these phrases are inadequate to explain the reality, but they do offer suggestions.

3. SOCIETY OUT OF JOINT

Unsafe for Democracy

American Protective Association and Immigration

When nativism erupted again in the 1880s and 1890s, its focus tended to be on the largely unrestricted immigration into America. Up until the Civil War, immigration was generally thought of as a "good thing" —new blood, fresh hands, eager settlers. At this period, however, many were having second thoughts, those thoughts prompted not so much by the size of this later immigration as by its character. So many of the "new" immigrants tended, for example, not to be Protestants. In 1887 at Clinton, Iowa, Henry Francis Bowers (1837–1911) founded the American Protective Association (APA), the leading anti-Catholic organization of the closing years of the nineteenth century. Son of a German Lutheran father and an Anglo Methodist mother, Bowers pledged his followers to a "true Americanism," those code words being further explained as demanding that citizenship be denied to all who are subject to "any ecclesiastical power not created and controlled by American citizens. . . ." (1) Disciples of Christ minister, lecturer, and author John L. Brandt (1860–1946) in 1895 published a vigorously anti-Catholic work which carried the "imprimatur" of the APA's second president, W. J. H. Traynor. (2) An Immigration Restriction League was formed in 1894, and in 1924 a National Origins Act was passed that attempted to turn the clock back to the earlier pattern of immigration.

1.

The United States is Rome's favorite missionary field. The extent of our territory, the fertility of our soil, and the freedom of our institutions, offer such strong inducements that our country has been flooded with hordes of foreigners, many of whom are uneducated Roman Catholics, and who, from

[Sources: (1) John L. Brandt, *America or Rome, Christ or the Pope* (Toledo, Ohio: The Loyal Pub. Co., 1895), pp. 4, 5–8. (2) R. L. Garis, *Immigration Restriction* (New York: Macmillan Co., 1927), pp. 203–4, 212–13.]

infancy, have yielded implicit obedience to the Pope. The Jesuits have been expelled from nearly every country in Europe, and they are now turning their eyes to the western hemisphere, and are exerting might and main to take possession of the United States, as the following bold declarations will testify.

At the Centenary Celebration of the Catholic Church in the United States, Archbishop Ireland declared: "The great work, which in God's providence the Catholics in the United States are called to do within the coming century, is, to make America Catholic, and to solve for the Church Universal the all-absorbing problem with which the age confronts her."

At the Baltimore Catholic Congress, Henry F. Brownson, LL.D., said: "The American system is also anti-Protestant, and must either reject Protestantism, or be overthrown by it." . . .

Says Pope Leo XIII., in his encyclical of January 29, 1895: "The church would bring forth more abundant fruits, if, in addition to liberty, she enjoyed the favor of the laws and the patronage of public authority."

In these bold declarations and avowed intentions, Rome is either right or wrong. As Cardinal Manning has put it: "The Catholic Church is either the masterpiece of Satan, or the kingdom of the Son of God." Or to use the words of Cardinal Newman: "Either the Church of Rome is the house of God, or the house of Satan; there is no middle ground between them." If the Church of Rome is the Church of God, we ought to know it. If the Pope is infallible, we ought to know it. If Rome's presence in our country and the objects she has determined to accomplish are for the highest good, the sooner we are convinced of this, the better. On the other hand, if the Church of Rome is the house of Satan, if the Pope is the Antichrist, if her doctrines are the commandments of men, if she is the enemy of our liberties, then our people ought to know it. It is the purpose of this book to assist in settling these questions, and to furnish knowledge that will awaken sympathy and prepare for wise action. I have quoted, at great length, from Rome's highest authorities on the various subjects discussed; for out of her own mouth she must stand condemned or acquitted, and from her own history she must stand approved or disapproved.

There are those who may not see the need of another book upon this subject; I would ask such to reserve their judgment until they have carefully studied the question; until they have read the encyclicals, decrees, catechisms, theologies, and authoritative utterances of this hierarchy; until they have read an account of some of Rome's dogmas, practices and intrigues as depicted by those who have made the subject a lifelong study. Our country is a paradise for Rome. She has, without being disputed, introduced into our beautiful and fair land, many dogmas, founded upon pretended visions and fabulous tales, more fit for pagan darkness than for evangelical light; she has burdened millions of our people with masses, auricular confessions, priestly celibacy, and fears of purgatory; she has attacked our public schools; she has denounced our Bible; she has favored the union of church and state; she has thrust her hand into our treasury; she has monopolized the funds donated to the religious bodies for Indian education; she controls our telegraphic system; she censures and subsidizes the public press; she manipulates many of our political conventions; she rules many of our large cities; she has put eighty men, out of every hundred, at work in the public department at Washington; she has put officers in charge of our army and navy; she has put judges upon the bench; she has muzzled the mouths of many of our ablest statesmen, editors and ministers; she has plotted to destroy our Government; she has made her subjects swear allegiance to a foreign power, and Archbishop Ireland says: "She has the power to speak; she has an organization by which her laws may be enforced. . . . She is the sole living and enduring Christian authority."

These things being true, is it not time to watch this cunning enemy? Is it not time to arouse sleepy Protestants? Is it not time to call a halt? Have we not had enough bloodshed, Tammany rings, anarchism and Jesuitism? The preservation of American liberties is no small consideration, for without these liberties, an American is without a home.

At the very outset I desire to state that there are many good Catholic men and women identified with the Roman Catholic Church, but there is a broad line of distinction between the unsuspecting confidence of the laity and the deliberate scheming of the Roman Catholic priesthood. There is, also, credit due to Rome for the preservation of some learning during the dark ages of the world's history; but the claim that she has done some good, does not prevent us from seeing the evils that have followed in her footsteps.

In this discussion, we have no denunciation to hurl against any individual. We shall discuss Romanism as it is. We shall discuss it as a system. We shall discuss its doctrines, principles, spirit and practices.

2.

At the present time European immigration to the United States may be divided into two groups, the "old" and the "new." The "old" immigration has extended from the beginning of our colonial and national history to the present time and has been and still is derived chiefly from Great Britain and Ireland, Germany, Holland, and the Scandinavian countries. Since practically all the immigrants to 1890 belonged to this "old" immigration, they were predominantly Anglo-Saxon-Germanic in blood and Protestant in religion — of the same stock as that which originally settled the United States, wrote our Constitution and established our democratic institutions. The English, Dutch, Swedes, Germans, and even the Scotch-Irish, who constituted practically the entire immigration prior to 1890, were less than two thousand years ago one Germanic race in the forests surrounding the North Sea. Thus, being similar in blood and in political ideals, social training and economic background, this "old" immigration has merged with the native stock fairly easily and rapidly. Assimilation has always been only a matter of time and this has been aided by the economic, social and political conditions of the country. Even though those already here objected at times to others coming in, yet once in they have soon become Americans, so assimilated as to be indistinguishable from the natives; for this old immigration has consisted almost wholly of families who have come to this country with the full intention of making it their home and of becoming American citizens. It was this immigration that aided so much in the development of agriculture in the great Central West and in the construction of our incomparable transportation system. Furthermore, in comparison with the recent "new" immigration, it has always been small in volume, while the abundance of free land in the past, our need of pioneers and the willingness of these "old" type immigrants to go into the West and settle on the land, prevented the rise of many serious problems.

In the period centering about the year 1880, and in particular in the decade 1880-1890, there was a distinct shift in the immigration movement. Whereas before 1890 most of our immigrants were Anglo-Saxons and Teutons from Northern Europe, since 1890 and prior to the quota legislation in 1924 the great majority were members of the Mediterranean and Slavic races from Southern, Eastern and Southeastern Europe. The great bulk of this "new" immigration has its sources in Russia, Poland, Austria, Hungary, Greece, Turkey, Italy, and the Balkan countries. It is this "new" immigration which constitutes *the* immigration problem of *today*. . . .

Prior to the World War [I] the race map of this [Austro-Hungarian] Empire showed the most complicated social mosaic of all modern nations and as far as present day immigration is concerned the same situation exists despite the break up of the empire. Prior to the war there existed a juxtaposition of hostile races and a fixity of language held together only by the outside pressure of the powerful neighboring nations. This conflict of races aggravated the conditions which caused millions to emigrate. Not only were there five grand divisions of the human family—the German, the Slav, the Magyar, the Latin, and the Jew—within what was formerly Austria-Hungary, but these had to be sub-divided to really understand the situation. In the northern mountainous and hilly sections were the Slavic peoples, the Czechs, or Bohemians, with their closely related Moravians, and the Slavic Slovaks, Poles, and Ruthenians (Russniaks); while in the southern hills and along the Adriatic were other Slavs, the Croatians, Servians, Dalmatians, and Slovenians. Between these divisions were the two dominant races, the Magyars and the Germans. To the southwest was the Italian element and in the east were the Latinized Slavs, the Rumanians. In general the Slavs were the conquered peoples, being dominated by the Germans and Magyars. The northern Slavs were subject to Austria and Hungary. The Ruthenians suffered a double subjection, being serfs of their fellow Slavs, the Poles, whom they hate. The Southern Slavs and Rumanians were subject to Hungary. In general it may be said that the Slavic immigrant furnishes a most difficult problem in assimilation due to the fact that his past, his customs and his inherited traditions make change slow.

"With all of this confusing medley of races, with its diversity of Greek and Roman Catholicism and Judaism, with its history of race oppression and hatred, with its almost universal serfdom and low standards of living, it is not surprising that in America the different races should group and settle together and often break out into factions and feuds wherever thrown together among us."

For, from such a conglomeration of races it is impossible that political and social entanglements and difficulties should not arise. Coming in millions it has been impossible to even begin to assimilate and Americanize them. Practically the entire immigration has been that of peasants. As in other countries of low standards, the number of births in this section of Europe is large in proportion to the inhabitants. Thus poverty, ignorance, inequality and helplessness all play their part in producing a very high birthrate. The result has been the emigration to America of many whose low standards of living, whose ignorance and racial hatreds have made it impossible for us under present conditions to assimilate and have marked them, in the minds of those who favor immigration restriction, along with the Italians and Russians, as undesirable immigrants.

The Klan's Americanism

While the APA worried chiefly about Roman Catholics, the Ku Klux Klan (KKK) worried about Catholics, Jews, blacks, and anyone else who did not measure up to the Klan's definition of American: native, white, Protestant. And like the APA, the Klan took its stance on behalf of an Americanism which "can only be achieved if the pioneer stock is kept pure." The prominence of Klan activity in the 1920s is evident by the space which the prestigious North American Review *gave to it. (1) The first selection by Hiram Wesley Evans, "Imperial Wizard and Emperor, Knights of the Ku Klux Klan," sets forth that organization's firm convictions. (2) A succeeding issue of the* Review *carried responses from Catholic, Jew, and black. The Jewish rejoinder by Rabbi Joseph Silverman of Temple Emanu-El of New York City is excerpted below.*

1.

The fundamentals of our thought are convictions, not mere opinions. We are pleased that modern research is finding scientific backing for these con-

[Sources: (1) *North American Review*, 223 (March, April, May, 1926), 52 – 53, 53 – 55. (2) Ibid. (June, July, August, 1926), 286 – 88.]

victions. We do not need them ourselves; we know that we are right in the same sense that a good Christian knows that he has been saved and that Christ lives — a thing which the intellectual can never understand. These convictions are no more to be argued about than is our love for our children; we are merely willing to state them for the enlightenment and conversion of others.

There are three of these great racial instincts, vital elements in both the historic and the present attempts to build an America which shall fulfill the aspirations and justify the heroism of the men who made the nation. These are the instincts of loyalty to the white race, to the traditions of America, and to the spirit of Protestantism, which has been an essential part of Americanism ever since the days of Roanoke and Plymouth Rock. They are condensed into the Klan slogan: "Native, white, Protestant supremacy."

First in the Klansman's mind is patriotism — America for Americans. He believes religiously that a betrayal of Americanism or the American race is treason to the most sacred of trusts, a trust from his fathers and a trust from God. He believes, too, that Americanism can only be achieved if the pioneer stock is kept pure. There is more than race pride in this. Mongrelization has been proven bad. It is only between closely related stocks of the same race that interbreeding has improved men; the kind of interbreeding that went on in the early days of America between English, Dutch, German, Huguenot, Irish and Scotch.

Racial integrity is a very definite thing to the Klansman. It means even more than good citizenship, for a man may be in all ways a good citizen and yet a poor American, unless he has racial understanding of Americanism, and instinctive loyalty to it. It is in no way a reflection on any man to say that he is un-American; it is merely a statement that he is not one of us. It is often not even wise to try to make an American of the best of aliens. What he is may be spoiled without his becoming American. The races and stocks of men are as distinct as breeds of animals, and every boy knows that if one tries to train a bulldog to herd sheep, he has in the end neither a good bulldog nor a good collie. . . .

The second word in the Klansman's trilogy is "white". The white race must be supreme, not only in America but in the world. This is equally undebatable, except on the ground that the races might live together, each with full regard for the rights and interests of others, and that those rights and interests would never conflict. Such an idea, of course, is absurd; the colored races today, such as Japan, are clamoring not for equality but for their supremacy. The whole history of the world, on its broader lines, has been one of race conflicts, wars, subjugation or extinction. This is not pretty, and certainly disagrees with the maudlin theories of cosmopolitanism, but it is truth. The world has been so made that each race must fight for its life, must conquer, accept slavery or die. The Klansman believes that the whites will not become slaves, and he does not intend to die before his time.

Moreover, the future of progress and civilization depends on the continued supremacy of the white race. The forward movement of the world for centuries has come entirely from it. Other races each had its chance and either failed or stuck fast, while white civilization shows no sign of having reached its limit. Until the whites falter, or some colored civilization has a miracle of awakening, there is not a single colored stock that can claim even equality with the white; much less supremacy.

Ku Klux Klan parade in St. Petersburg, Florida, c. 1926
(Keystone-Mast Collection, University of California, Riverside)

The third of the Klan principles is that Protestantism must be supreme; that Rome shall not rule America. The Klansman believes this not merely because he is a Protestant, nor even because the Colonies that are now our nation were settled for the purpose of wresting America from the control of Rome and establishing a land of free conscience. He believes it also because Protestantism is an essential part of Americanism; without it America could never have been created and without it she cannot go forward. Roman rule would kill it.

Protestantism contains more than religion. It is the expression in religion of the same spirit of independence, self-reliance and freedom which are the highest achievements of the Nordic race. It sprang into being automatically at the time of the great "upsurgence" of strength in the Nordic peoples that opened the spurt of civilization in the fifteenth century It has been a distinctly Nordic religion, and it has been through this religion that the Nordics have found strength to take leadership of all whites and the supremacy of the earth. Its destruction is the deepest purpose of all other peoples, as that would mean the end of Nordic rule.

It is the only religion that permits the unhampered individual development and the unhampered conscience and action which were necessary in the settling of America. Our pioneers were all Protestants, except for an occasional Irishman — Protestants by nature if not by religion — for though French and Spanish dared and explored and showed great heroism, they made little of the land their own. America was Protestant from birth.

She must remain Protestant, if the Nordic stock is to finish its destiny. We of the old stock Americans could not work — and the work is mostly ours to do, if the record of the past proves anything — if we became priest-ridden, if we had to submit our consciences and limit our activities and suppress our thoughts at the command of any man, much less of a man sitting upon Seven Hills thousands of miles away. This we will not permit. Rome shall not rule us. Protestantism must be supreme.

2.

The head and front of the offending on the part of this underground conspiracy are directed, not only against Negroes, but also against Catholics, Jews and aliens, the fixed policy of the organization being based on the "Know Nothing" principle of "America for Americans only", with the modification that America shall be restricted to a citizenry of white Protestants. The Klan also maintains that all other people in America shall only be tolerated, shall be deprived of the right of suffrage and of holding office, and that all further immigration shall be entirely cut off.

On the Klan's efforts for further restricting immigration, or cutting it off altogether, I shall here offer no extended criticism. Immigration comes under the political and economical policies of a country, and its regulation is subject to fluctuating internal conditions. Restriction of immigration, even when justified, may sometimes work injustice to certain classes of foreigners who seek entrance into our shores. The immigration phase of the Klan's policy is, however, to be censured because it is not coupled with a national political or economic policy, but is part of the Klan's general scheme for placing this country under the control of white Protestants. We resent the reasons and the motives for the Klan's restrictive measures because they are not associated with the best interests of the Nation.

It is not difficult to infer that the programme of the Ku Klux Klan includes religious propaganda for the purpose of repressing and oppressing members of the Catholic and Jewish faiths. Indications have already been given in no uncertain terms by local sections that the plan is to Christianize America, to Christianize the public schools, to elect only white Protestants to office — that is, to enforce everywhere the teachings and the practices of the Protestant Church and to place the Government under the control of that branch of Christianity.

This is, in truth, an ambitious programme, and it is well that the country is aware thereof, for to be forewarned, in this respect, is certainly to be forearmed. The Klan had deserved condemnation and punishment for its political and other secret machinations against the Negro, for instigating racial prejudice; and now that it has entered upon a religious crusade against Jews and Catholics, and against the Constitution of the Nation, it has invited additional execration and progressive punishment even up to its total extinction.

It passeth all understanding how American citizens, and especially such as profess to be followers of Christianity, can undertake to carry out any programme that savors of the Spanish Inquisition and the Massacre of the Innocents. We are constantly inveighing against the terrible crimes committed in the name of religion in the Dark Ages, and we speak deprecatingly of those times as the "Dark Ages." But what shall we say of the Klan's ways, that we see are dark, in this so-called enlightened age, and in this noble and free America, that we love and cherish!

What justification is there for this twentieth century religious persecution on American soil? Is the Klan afraid that America may become Romanized? There is more danger (if it is a danger) that America may become Evangelized. Or is the Klan perhaps afraid that America may become Judaized? I have no such fears, or even hopes. Or is the Klan fearful that Catholics, Jews, Negroes, free thinkers and nondescript naturalized citizens may combine to control elections and perhaps place a Catholic, a Jew, a Negro or a free thinker in the Presidential chair? Why does the Klan harrow up such hallucinations? Is it not better to trust the good sense of the American people to do, under any given circumstances, what is best for the country? And let the Klansmen remember that after all, Catholic, Jewish, Negro and atheistic or non-religious citizens are also true Americans — as genuine Americans as the Klansmen claim to be. The American Constitution does not discriminate against the religious or non-religious citizen. It is opposed to a religious test for public office; it is based on the principle of separation of State from Church. The Government, to be sure, is courteous to religion and grants to all sects equal protection — and it behooves religion to be courteous to the Government and it is the duty of all sects to obey and preserve intact the principles and articles of the federal law. The Klan, by injecting into the political life of these States a religious issue, convicts itself thereby of being un-American in principle and act. *The Ku Kluxers violate Americanism in order to enforce their stamp of Americanism.*

Moreover, by what warrant does the Klan assume that white Protestants would make the best Americans? Is Protestantism a better religion than Catholicism? Are they not, both, part of Christianity? Do they not both believe in the same Messiah and in the same Bible? And is not a Protestant or Catholic of the Negro race, if he is sincere, equally as acceptable to God as a Protestant or Catholic of the white race? Or does the Klan wish us to believe that God also draws the color line, and is also prejudiced either against one sect or another of the Christian Church? For my part, I believe that the Klansmen have involved themselves in a hypocritical attitude and dilemma from which it will be impossible to extricate themselves, unless they destroy their unworthy Order.

I am tempted also to defend the Jew against the discrimination to which he is subjected by the Klan on the score of his religion, but I refrain, when I remember that Christianity paid Judaism the greatest compliment that was ever paid to any race or religion when it claimed that God had selected a Son of Israel to be the Messiah to the heathen world two thousand years ago in order to convert it to a better faith, a higher culture and a nobler civilization. We Jews still have the same religion that Jesus originally professed, and it seems to us nothing short of folly for any devotees of Jesus to declare that only self-elected white Protestant Christians are fit to be Americans, and that Jews, from whom Jesus sprang, should be barred from American life. *Verily, the Ku Kluxers violate religion in order to enforce their own type of religion.*

Rum and Rome

In 1928 nativism had a specific target: a Roman Catholic had for the first time in American history won the nomination of a major political party and was now running for the presidency of the United States. That he was no special friend of the Prohibition Amendment (see above, p. 197) only aggravated Protestant anxieties and steeled their resolve to keep this Catholic out of the White House. (1) In September of 1928 the Methodists of Ohio,

[Sources: (1) *New York Times*, Sept. 8, 1928, pp. 1, 3. (2) Alfred E. Smith, *Campaign Addresses* . . . (Washington, D. C.: Democratic National Committee, 1929), pp. 52–53, 56–58.]

meeting in their newly formed conference, heard Mabel Walker Willebrandt
plead for the defeat of Alfred E. Smith and for the election of Herbert C.
Hoover. (2) In that same fall, candidate Smith, on the campaign trail in
Oklahoma City, responded to the Klan, to Mrs. Willebrandt, and to all
who would divide American voters along religious lines.

1.

Special to The New York Times

SPRINGFIELD, Ohio, Sept. 7 [1928]

The newly formed Ohio conference of the Methodist Episcopal Church
today unanimously adopted a resolution endorsing the candidacy of Herbert
Hoover, Republican nominee for the Presidency. The conference went on
record as being unalterably opposed to the election of Governor Smith. The
conferring ministers insisted that the action was taken solely on the prohibition
issue.

The action of the conference this afternoon divided interest with an address
in the evening by Mrs. Mabel Walker Willebrandt, Assistant Attorney General
of the United States. Mrs. Willebrandt described Governor Smith's
candidacy as a result of an alliance between Tammany Hall and wealthy anti-
prohibitionists.

She charged that since the repeal of the New York State Mullan-Gage act,
in Governor Smith's second term, dry enforcement had completely broken
down in the State. New York City, she said, was one of the worst wet spots
in the country. She alleged that liquor was pouring over the Canadian border
into New York, and called on the Methodists to support Mr. Hoover. . . .

Following a reference to the fact that all but two States ratified the 18th
Amendment, Mrs. Willebrandt said that there remained in the nation many
"willful sections" in which the local sentiment was largely against prohibition.

"The worst of these spots," she continued, "was in New York City. The
Empire State as a whole achieved the 'will to unselfishness' which ratification
of the 18th Amendment typifies. But Manhattan is ruled by Tammany, an
organization that for underworld connections and political efficiency is matched
no place else in America.

Anti-Prohibitionists Scored.

"Scattered over the United States were members of the intelligentsia who
organized the Association Against the Prohibition Amendment. They worked
along more or less futilely through 1921, 1922 and 1923. In 1924, at the
Democratic convention in Madison Square Garden, Tammany tried to capture
the Democratic Party.

"Tammany didn't then realize that it could not sweep that party off its feet by typical Tammany methods. Screaming whistles and brass bands failed to win Southern leaders. Tammany's candidate was the man who had just abandoned the policy of cooperation between State and National Government, provided for in the concurrent clause of the Eighteenth Amendment.

"He was the one Governor in all the American States who, notwithstanding his oath to support the Constitution of the United States, pulled down one of the forty-six pillars the people had erected for its support. New York had ratified the amendment. That ratification was a pledge to concurrent effort. But the audacious Governor was unconvinced by such reasoning. Tammany wanted the least possible prohibition. Tammany had reared him; gave him his power. Tammany's desires were his convictions.

"Triple Alliance" Is Alleged.

"Certain leaders in the Association Against the Prohibition Amendment saw the importance of securing as spokesman of their cause so powerful a leader as the Governor of New York.

"Thus the wealthy groups of anti-prohibitionists and Tammany, symbol of predatory politics, and Governor Smith were found in early alliance.

"They have prepared well for this critical hour. Newspapers in rural and Southern communities were bought by New York money and have switched from a long-settled dry policy to preaching the doctrine of 'It can't be enforced.' At the same time there have been insinuated into strategic positions in dry enforcement men who were members of the Association Against the Prohibition Amendment. They have left office proclaiming from the lecture platform and through the press one general chorus that 'prohibition can never be enforced.' . . .

Defense of Amendment Urged.

"Anti-prohibitionists have never won against united drys. It is clever strategy, therefore, to divide their forces. That is what is attempted in making prohibition a party issue. . . . You did not make it a political issue. Your adroit Tammany foe has done so. You can do nothing else but follow wherever defense of the Eighteenth Amendment leads.

"It is not abandoning your non-partisan policy of not discussing politics or letting your organization be torn by political dissensions to take a stand against the Democratic nominee and for the Republican national ticket this year. In fact, there is no choice. The Republican Party platform and both its candidates are, by declaration and record, committed to the principle and the enforcement of prohibition. . . .

"It is reasonable to assume that the Governor's oath promising to 'support the Constitution of the United States' binds him to assist in the letter and spirit of enforcement of the Federal Constitution, but New York since, through

Governor Smith's leadership the enforcement act of the State was repealed, has become the centre, not only of lawlessness and disregard for the Constitution of the United States and Free and open distribution of liquor, but it has also become the centre of the dissemination of the false doctrine that the law can't be enforced.

"That statement could be received with more conviction if it emanated from a State where Federal Government and State had joined hands and worked valiantly to do the job. In New York State there are between 2,000 and 3,000 State police; there are more than 16,000 city police; there are 113 Supreme Court State Judges and sixty-two County Prosecutors.

Says Bootlegging Has Risen.

"All of these agencies might be enlisted to reduce the crime and lawlessness that is alleged to flow from disregard of the prohibition law, but they are now and have been inactive as to prohibition since New York repealed its enforcement act.

"As a consequence bootlegging has vastly increased; liquor running over the Canadian border has multiplied, blind-pigs that used to operate secretly and with some degree of shame operate openly with bars and brass rails; hundreds of night clubs in Manhattan are just a new form of the old-fashioned saloons that Tammany used to protect. These night clubs have open bars, and yet they can exist only so long as they get licenses from the City Administration.

"Of course the law is not being enforced in New York; it is being evaded and nullified; a few hundred Federal agents and thirteen Federal Judges with four United States Attorneys cannot alone cope successfully with so much lawlessness.

"There are 2,000 pastors here. You have in your churches more than 600,000 members of the Methodist Church in Ohio alone. That is enough to swing the election. The 600,000 have friends in other States. Write to them. Every day and every ounce of your energy are needed to rouse the friends of prohibition to register and vote.

"The Eighteenth Amendment is new in politics. You did not put it there. The Republican Party did not put it there.

"Neither did the rank and file of the loyal constitutional Democrats. Neither did the National Democratic Convention put it there. It was put there by its enemies; and Governor Smith by a formal act as ruthless as was ever recorded in American politics became their leader. You have a chance to prove by electing Herbert Hoover that obedience to law can be secured and that America does not retreat before organized crime."

2.

I can think of no greater disaster to this country than to have the voters of it divide upon religious lines. It is contrary to the spirit, not only of the

Declaration of Independence, but of the Constitution itself. During all of our national life we have prided ourselves throughout the world on the declaration of the fundamental American truth that all men are created equal.

Our forefathers, in their wisdom, seeing the danger to the country of a division on religious issues, wrote into the Constitution of the United States in no uncertain words the declaration that no religious test shall ever be applied for public office, and it is a sad thing in 1928, in view of the countless billions of dollars that we have poured into the cause of public education, to see some American citizens proclaiming themselves 100 per cent. American, and in the document that makes that proclamation suggesting that I be defeated for the presidency because of my religious belief.

The Grand Dragon of the Realm of Arkansas, writing to a citizen of that State, urges my defeat because I am a Catholic, and in the letter suggests to the man, who happened to be a delegate to the Democratic convention, that by voting against me he was upholding American ideals and institutions as established by our forefathers.

The Grand Dragon that thus advised a delegate to the national convention to vote against me because of my religion is a member of an order known as the Ku Klux Klan, who have the effrontery to refer to themselves as 100 per cent. Americans,

Yet totally ignorant of the history and tradition of this country and its institutions and, in the name of Americanism, they breathe into the hearts and souls of their members hatred of millions of their fellow countrymen because of their religious belief.

Nothing could be so out of line with the spirit of America. Nothing could be so foreign to the teachings of Jefferson. Nothing could be so contradictory of our whole history. Nothing could be so false to the teachings of our Divine Lord Himself. The world knows no greater mockery than the use of the blazing cross, the cross upon which Christ died, as a symbol to install into the hearts of men a hatred of their brethren, while Christ preached and died for the love and brotherhood of man. . . .

Giving them [the Republicans] the benefit of all reasonable doubt, they at least remain silent on the exhibition that Mrs. Willebrandt made of herself before the Ohio Conference of the Methodist Episcopal Church when she said:

"There are two thousand pastors here. You have in your church more than 600,000 members of the Methodist Church in Ohio alone. That is enough to swing the election. The 600,000 have friends in other states. Write to them."

This is an extract from a speech made by her in favor of a resolution offered to the effect that the conference go on record as being unalterably opposed to the election of Governor Smith and to endorse the candidacy of Herbert Hoover, the Republican candidate.

Mrs. Willebrandt holds a place of prominence in the Republican administration in Washington; she is an Assistant Attorney-General of the United States. By silence, after such a speech, the only inference one can draw is that the administration approves such political tactics. Mrs. Willebrandt is not an irresponsible person. She was Chairman of the Committee on Credentials in the Republican National Convention at Kansas City.

What would the effect be upon these same people if a prominent official of the government of the State of New York under me suggested to a gathering of the pastors of my church that they do for me what Mrs. Willebrandt suggests be done for Hoover?

It needs no words of mine to impress that upon your minds. It is dishonest campaigning. It is un-American. It is out of line with the whole tradition and history of this government. And, to my way of thinking, is in itself sufficient to hold us up to the scorn of the thinking people of other nations.

One of the things, if not the meanest thing, in the campaign is a circular pretending to place someone of my faith in the position of seeking votes for me because of my Catholicism. Like everything of its kind, of course, it is unsigned, and it would be impossible to trace its authorship. It reached me through a member of the Masonic order who, in turn, received it in the mail. It is false in its every line. It was designed on its very face to injure me with members of churches other than my own.

I here emphatically declare that I do not wish any member of my faith in any part of the United States to vote for me on any religious grounds. I want them to vote for me only when in their hearts and consciences they become convinced that my election will promote the best interests of our country.

By the same token, I cannot refrain from saying that any person who votes against me simply because of my religion is not, to my way of thinking, a good citizen.

Let me remind the Democrats of this country that we belong to the party of that Thomas Jefferson whose proudest boast was that he was the author of the Virginia statute for religious freedom. Let me remind the citizens of every political faith that that statute of religious freedom has become a part of the sacred heritage of our land.

The constitutional guaranty that there should be no religious test for public office is not a mere form of words. It represents the most vital principle that ever was given any people.

I attack those who seek to undermine it, not only because I am a good Christian, but because I am a good American and a product of America and of American institutions. Everything I am, and everything I hope to be, I owe to those institutions.

Unsure of Capitalism

Economic Disaster

The stockmarket crash of 1929, followed by the Great Depression of the 1930s, stamped both the nation and its citizenry with such disaster as to leave the national pysche permanently marked. In those years, the nation was on trial, capitalism was on trial, traditional religion was on trial. (1) Writing even before the awful truth was known, Harry F. Ward (1873 – 1966), Methodist minister and seminary professor turned social radical, saw an irreconcilable conflict between the ethic of Jesus and the economic system of America. (2) In the depth of the depression, Charles E. Coughlin (1891 – 1979), Roman Catholic priest and radio preacher turned populist (and later turned anti-Semite), formed a National Union for Social Justice. Coughlin's Union would radically alter the economic structure of the nation, "nationalizing those public necessities which by their very nature are too important to be held in the control of private individuals."

1.

It is the vision of ends that Western life lacks. It has no sense of direction. It is all motion — at unequaled speed — but what is its goal? It is atomic, chaotic — not yet corporate. Why do its millions work and fight and breed and die? Do even their leaders know? For what shall man live? For all, says Communism. For each, says Individualism. For both, says the ethic of Jesus. Having in the course of its development rescued the individual from both the early communal society of the East and the aristocratic society of the West that he may find himself in a voluntary brotherhood, this religious morality is not to be deceived by the suicidal separatism of individualistic democracy nor the equally fatal subordination which dogmatic Communism imposes upon personality. If there is one thing that the ethic of Jesus can help an inevitably collectivist world to remember, it is the creative function of the individual. If there is anything it can help those who have been nurtured in the individualistic tradition to appreciate, it is that personality is social in its origin and nature, needing the Great Society for its fulfillment.

The obligation involved in this relationship has been expressed in the motto, "Each for all and all for each." To choose to live for all in the search for justice and fellowship with the consciousness that they are the eternal

[Sources: (1) H. F. Ward, *Our Economic Morality and the Ethic of Jesus* (New York: Macmillan Co., 1929), pp. 318 – 20, 321, 322 – 23. (2) C. E. Coughlin, *A Series of Lectures on Social Justice, 1935 – 1936* (Royal Oak, Mich.: Radio League of the Little Flower, 1936), pp. 7, 9 – 11.]

values, to achieve solidarity by self-surrender in activity toward the common good and so to find the self—this is the realization of life according to the word of the Nazarene. Whatever theology may make of this view of life—and the Communists have certainly made it into a powerful enough God—it is the necessity of life if human society is to continue. To make the future, man must have some idea of what he would make. To be the creator he must have the creator's vision. What task is more divine than to make and remake human nature, and whatever our ultimate relation to the cosmos, whatever the extent to which we draw on the Eternal Spirit, this is our responsibility. . . .

The final clash between our current economic morality and the ethic of Jesus is over the nature of man. The capitalist economy rests on the hypothesis that man is a creature who prefers material comforts to moral values, who would rather have an increase in goods than in the quality of existence. The only future it can offer man is one in which he will get more conveniences but less freedom, justice, and fellowship, believing that thus he will be content. The ethic of Jesus rejects this estimate of human nature; insists moreover that the very making of it is the negation of personality, whose essence lies in the making of choices and whose development consists in preferring moral satisfactions to material, the ultimate to the immediate, the eternal to the temporal. . . .

Because the central issue in the conflict between our current economic morality and the ethic of Jesus is this difference of judgment concerning the capacities of man, the struggle between them is a matter of life and death for both religion and civilization. "Ye cannot serve God and Mammon!" Either religion proves itself able to bring to the acquisitive society redemption from the making and selling of things, and release from the struggle of greed for power, or it blindly leads this blind age into the twilight that has fallen upon all other civilizations. Therefore if the salvation which an ethical religion has to offer industrial society is to be available in time, the present duty of those to whom the development of this type of religion has been committed is to help this generation to see clearly the nature of the choice which a money-making economy puts before modern man.

2.

. . . Let us turn our attention to the specific program of the National Union for Social Justice. It has been called to my attention that loose-lipped whisperers of various breeds, together with certain mad-cap newspaper columnists, have written the obituary notice of our organization.

Much to the chagrin of these literary crystal-gazers, the National Union will prove to be a most dynamic corpse. There will be no let down. Principles, not men; justice, not partisanship; courage, not cowardice—these motivating forces will not be surrendered, nor shall I stoop either to compromise or betray the members of the National Union. . . .

The two major political parties which already exist, and to which the vast bulk of American citizens already belong, long since have been seized by powerful groups of manipulators. The American Liberty League, the United States Chamber of Commerce, the American Bankers Association, the Manufacturers Association, the oil industries and many other groups so jockeyed your Representative into position that, oftentimes, he became nothing more than the Washington secretary of plutocratic overlords.

Oftentimes there was as little distinction between a Democratic and a Republican member of Congress as there was between two worms gnawing on the one apple. Exploitation of the inarticulate people continued until wealth was concentrated in the hands of a few. The Constitution of the United States was degraded while Congress after Congress supported the private coinage and fixation of money. Consistently they permitted profits to pile up prodigiously for the owners of industry in a machine age when the laborer was being paid less and when his toil was wanted less. Consistently they forced the farmers of the nation, at least since 1920, to operate at a loss. Instead of supplying the country with honest American credit, Congress has flooded it with bankers' credit. Instead of regulating our national credit based on our national wealth, Congress has cooperated with the privately owned Federal Reserve bankers, permitting them to create credit out of nothing while the same Congress expects us and future generations to repay these bankers with currency money that does not exist.

Beyond all doubt, the old economic system of ragged, rugged individualism was nurtured at the twin breasts of successive Republican and Democratic Administrations — the right breast exuding the sour milk of plutocracy and the left breast the skimmed milk of socialistic remedies. The anemic body of our citizenry, nurtured upon such a fatal diet, witnessed the whitening of the bones of justice, experienced the weakening of the flesh of morality, while the tuberculosis of want spread in the midst of plenty. This individualism was clothed by the unclean, ragged garments of putrid politics, among whose folds there were bred the germs of radicalism.

Want in the midst of plenty! Millions of acres of fertile fields beckoning to the millions of idle to come and drink at their breasts! Thousands of factories with cunning machines anxious to produce clothing and conveniences for the mass of our citizens! Stately pine and hemlock and sturdy oak, willing to surrender their timbers for fuel and shelter! Yet, because of some fiat, because of some strange enchantment, because of some diabolical greed in the minds and hearts of a small group of unchristian men, there was echoed down the centuries the sacrilegious philosophy of Cain, denying that men are their brothers' keepers!

Our scientists knew how to harness a Niagara! Dare they intimate to us, in this year of grace, that they do not know how to harness an unnecessary poverty? Our Congressmen knew how to marshal the forces of our nation to fight a commercial war which they called "making the world safe for democracy." Dare you tell me that they know not how to marshal the wealth and the intelligence of the nation to fight our domestic enemies of greed and exploitation?

The National Union is hopeful enough to conquer these domestic enemies. . . .

Christian Love

Of all the solutions proposed for curing America's terrible economic ills, none seemed more improbable than Christian love and none more unlikely a warrior in that struggle than Dorothy Day (1897 – 1980). Converted to Roman Catholicism in 1927, this pacifist, impoverished social radical had no trump cards to play, occupied no important position, held no impressive title. Yet, she inspired thousands through her writing, her simplicity, her single-minded dedication to Christian love. In 1933 she founded the Catholic Worker, *a monthly periodical designed to be the Christian answer to the Marxist* Daily Worker. *Both papers described a society scandalously out of joint, but the solutions proffered were worlds apart. In her autobiography,* The Long Loneliness, *Day wrote (1) of publication and poverty; then (2) of community and love.*

1.

We started publishing *The Catholic Worker* at 436 East Fifteenth Street (now at 39 Spring Street) in May, 1933, with a first issue of 2,500 copies. Within three or four months the circulation bounded to 25,000, and it was cheaper to bring it out as an eight-page tabloid on newsprint rather than the smaller-sized edition on better paper we had started with. By the end of the year we had a circulation of 100,000 and by 1936 it was 150,000. It was certainly a mushroom growth. It was not only that some parishes subscribed for the paper all over the country in bundles of 500 or more. Zealous young people took the paper out in the streets and sold it, and when they could not sell it even at one cent a copy, they gave free copies and left them in streetcar, bus, barber shop and dentist's and doctor's office. We got letters from all parts of the country from people who said they had picked up the paper on trains, in rooming houses. . . .

One of the reasons for the rapid growth was that many young men were coming out of college to face the prospect of no job. If they had started to read *The Catholic Worker* in college, they were ready to spend time as volunteers when they came out. Others were interested in writing, and houses

[Sources: (1) Dorothy Day, *The Long Loneliness* (New York: Harper & Brothers, 1952), pp. 207, 212 – 13. (2) Ibid., pp. 317 – 18.]

in Buffalo, Chicago, Baltimore, Seattle, St. Louis and Philadelphia, to name but a few cities, published their own papers and sold them with the New York *Catholic Worker*. A *Catholic Worker* was started in Australia and one in England. . . .

Voluntary poverty means a good deal of discomfort in these houses of ours. Many of the houses throughout the country are without central heating and have to be warmed by stoves in winter. There are back-yard toilets for some

Fritz Eichenberg woodcut of a Catholic Worker Movement House of Hospitality
(*from Peter Maurin,* The Green Revolution)

even now. The first Philadelphia house had to use water drawn from one
spigot at the end of an alley, which served half a dozen other houses. It was
lit with oil lamps. It was cold and damp and so unbelievably poverty-stricken
that little children coming to see who were the young people meeting there
exclaimed that this could not be a *Catholic* place; it was too poor. We must
be Communists. They were well acquainted with the Communist point of
view since they were Puerto Rican and Spanish and Mexican and this was at
the beginning of the Spanish Civil War.

How hard a thing it is to hear such criticisms made. Voluntary poverty
was only found among the Communists; the Negro and white man on the
masthead of our paper suggested communism; the very word "worker" made
people distrust us at first. We were not taking the position of the great mass
of Catholics, who were quite content with the present in this world. They
were quite willing to give to the poor, but they did not feel called upon to
work for the things of this life for others which they themselves esteemed so
lightly. Our insistence on worker-ownership, on the right of private property,
on the need to de-proletarize the worker, all points which had been emphasized by the popes in their social encyclicals, made many Catholics think we
were Communists in disguise, wolves in sheep's clothing.

2.

The most significant thing about *The Catholic Worker* is poverty, some say.

The most significant thing is community, others say. We are not alone any
more.

But the final word is love. At times it has been, in the words of Father
Zossima,* a harsh and dreadful thing, and our very faith in love has been
tried through fire.

We cannot love God unless we love each other, and to love we must know
each other. We know Him in the breaking of bread, and we know each other
in the breaking of bread, and we are not alone any more. Heaven is a banquet
and life is a banquet, too, even with a crust, where there is companionship.

We have all known the long loneliness and we have learned that the only
solution is love and that love comes with community.

It all happened while we sat there talking, and it is still going on.

*In Dostoyevsky's *Brothers Karamazov*

Political Realism

The most widely read American theologian of the 1930s was Reinhold Nie-
buhr (1892 – 1971), member of the Evangelical and Reformed church
(which later merged into a new United Church of Christ). After graduating
from Yale Divinity School in 1914, Niebuhr assumed a pastorate in the
nation's industrial center, Detroit, Michigan. There the young minister found
his sentimental liberalism inadequate to cope with or speak to brutal economic
realities all around him. Attracted to Marxism, he became a severe critic
of capitalism. Then disillusioned with Marxism, he came to criticize its easy
dogmatisms as well. Rejecting what he saw as naiveté on the part of com-
munists, capitalists, and sentimental moralists, Reinhold Niebuhr advanced
to a position of Christian and political realism. (1) In his autobiographical
work, Leaves from the Notebook of a Tamed Cynic, *one can follow some*
of this painful progression in 1925 and 1926. (2) In 1934, Niebuhr set
forth the "political realism of Christian orthodoxy."

1.

But why not be specific? Why doesn't the church offer specific suggestions
for the application of a Christian ethic to the difficulties of our day? If that
suggestion is made, the answer is that such a policy would breed contention.
It certainly would. No moral project can be presented and no adventure made
without resistance from the traditionalist and debate among experimentalists.
But besides being more effective, such a course would be more interesting
than this constant bathing in sentimentalities. If the church could only achieve
schisms on ethical issues! They would represent life and reality. Its present
schisms are not immoral as such. They are immoral only in the sense that
they perpetuate issues which have no relevancy in our day.

When I sit through a church conference I begin to see a little more clearly
why religion is on the whole so impotent ethically, why the achievements of
the church are so meager compared to its moral pretensions. Sermon after
sermon, speech after speech is based upon the assumption that the people of
the church are committed to the ethical ideals of Jesus and that they are the
sole or at least chief agents of redemptive energy in society.

It is very difficult to persuade people who are committed to a general ideal
to consider the meaning of that ideal in specific situations. It is even more
difficult to prompt them to consider specific ends of social and individual
conduct and to evaluate them in the light of experience.

The church conference begins and ends by attempting to arouse an emotion
of the ideal, usually in terms of personal loyalty to the person of Jesus, but

[Sources: (1) Reinhold Niebuhr, *Leaves from the Notebook of a Tamed Cynic* (Chicago:
Willett, Clark, and Colby, 1929), pp. 74 – 75, 79, 112 – 13. (2) Reinhold Niebuhr, *Re-*
flections on the End of an Era (New York: Charles Scribner's Sons, 1934), pp. 215 – 17.]

very little is done to attach the emotion to specific tasks and projects. Is the industrial life of our day unethical? Are nations imperialistic? Is the family disintegrating? Are young people losing their sense of values? If so, we are told over and over again that nothing will help but "a new baptism of the spirit," a "new revival of religion," a "great awakening of the religious consciousness." . . .

The morality of the church is anachronistic. Will it ever develop a moral insight and courage sufficient to cope with the real problems of modern society? If it does it will require generations of effort and not a few martyr-doms. We ministers maintain our pride and self-respect and our sense of importance only through a vast and inclusive ignorance. If we knew the world in which we live a little better we would perish in shame or be overcome by a sense of futility. . . .

The churches of America are on the whole thoroughly committed to the interests and prejudices of the middle classes. I think it is a bit of unwarranted optimism to expect them to make any serious contribution to the reorgani-zation of society. I still have hopes that they will become sufficiently intelligent and heroic to develop some qualifying considerations in the great industrial struggle, but I can no longer envisage them as really determining factors in the struggle. Neither am I able for this reason to regard them as totally useless, as some of the critics do.

The ethical reconstruction of modern industrial society is, to be sure, a very important problem, but it is not the only concern of mankind. The spiritual amenities and moral decencies which the churches help to develop and preserve in the private lives of individuals are worth something for their own sake. Yet it must be obvious that if anyone is chosen by talent and destiny to put his life into the industrial struggle, the church is hardly his best vehicle.

The church is like the Red Cross service in war time. It keeps life from degenerating into a consistent inhumanity, but it does not materially alter the fact of the struggle itself. The Red Cross neither wins the war nor abolishes it. Since the struggle between those who have and those who have not is a never-ending one, society will always be, in a sense, a battleground. It is therefore of some importance that human loveliness be preserved outside of the battle lines. But those who are engaged in this task ought to realize that the brutalities of the conflict may easily negate the most painstaking human-izing efforts behind the lines, and that these efforts may become a method for evading the dangers and risks of the battlefield.

If religion is to contribute anything to the solution of the industrial prob-lem, a more heroic type of religion than flourishes in the average church must be set to the task. I don't believe that the men who are driven by that kind of religion need to dissociate themselves from the churches, but they must bind themselves together in more effective association than they now possess.

2.

According to the absolute ideal, man was intended to live in perfect love and complete equality with his fellowmen. But his fall into sin made this impossible and created a situation in which the evil lusts of men needed to be checked by the coercion of governments, the restrictions of property and even the inequalities of slavery. The problems of economics and politics were to be regulated by the requirements of "natural law" rather than the absolute ideal of love, a conception which Christianity borrowed from Stoicism. The requirements of the natural law were, broadly speaking, the demands of *justice* (though never equalitarian justice) and they were assumed to have been written into all human hearts by God. In as far as they were not voluntarily obeyed (and the prevalence of sin would make infractions inevitable) they were to be enforced by governments. Government had, in fact, been expressly instituted by God for this purpose. Here the orthodox church from the earliest day to the present has leaned heavily on the words of Paul. "There is no power but of God; the powers that be are ordained of God."

If one were to reconstruct this general philosophy of politics in non-mythological terms it might be put in the following words: The highest moral ideal for human life, the ideal of love can neither be renounced nor completely realized. Its imperative and convincing reality proves that human life has its source and its goal above and beyond the frustrations and hindrances of the world of nature in which man lives. In this world the inordinate egoism of individuals and groups constantly threatens life with self-destruction through anarchy. Since obedience to the absolute demands of love is impossible to natural man he must be restrained by an ideal less rigorous but nevertheless effective in preventing the strong from devouring the weak and from living in the anarchy of constant conflict. The law of justice is such an ideal. It is the moral ideal in a more negative form than the ideal of love. It demands not that the interests of the neighbor be affirmed but that interests of the self be restricted so that they will not infringe upon those of the neighbor. Furthermore it sanctions the coercive force of governments to restrain those who will not voluntarily abide by the rule of rational justice.

4. WORLD OUT OF TIME

Revivalism

Dwight L. Moody (1837 – 99)

"As early as 7 o'clock the streets of Brooklyn presented the unwonted spectacle of long streams of well-dressed men and women hurriedly moving in the direction of the Rink. All the cars from the New-York ferries, as well as from East and South Brooklyn and other outlying points, were crowded to their utmost capacity. The building was filled to its utmost capacity both morning and afternoon. . . ." So the New York Times *(Oct. 25, 1875) began its front-page story of the electric revival in which the polar attractions were Dwight L. Moody, preacher, and Ira D. Sankey (1840 – 1908), song leader. And this meeting was typical of the excitement generated wherever Moody and Sankey went. Fresh from a successful two-year revival in Great Britain, the team returned to an America ready to give them every bit as much extravagant praise as the British had. What follows is the account by a New York journalist (William H. Coleman) of the supercharged atmosphere of a Moody meeting.*

Imagine yourself on the platform of the Madison Avenue Hall at 7.15 P.M., five minutes before the opening of the doors. Platform and near gallery are already well filled by the choir, Christian workers and their escorts, and special-ticket holders; the floor of the house is unoccupied, save by knots of ushers with their wands, no one being allowed to sit there until the doors are opened. In the railed inclosure, just back of the speaker's place, is a telegraph operator, usually a lady. Near by sits the chief superintendent, with aids at hand to transmit orders. At the other end of the hall sit another superintendent and operator. These control the lighting and heating and the seating of the audience.

"Ting! ting! ting!" goes a distant bell ten times — attention! "Ting! ting!"

[Source: William R. Moody, *The Life of Dwight L. Moody* (New York: Fleming H. Revell Co., 1900), pp. 278 – 80, 280 – 81.]

again, and the outer and inner doors slip back at three points, and three streams of people pour into the hall. The foremost enters at a run that would become disorder did not the usher check it, divide the stream, direct it into the front and middle seats, and when a section is filled bar the way with his wand. In ten minutes five thousand persons are seated. The galleries fill more slowly, and when all parts are full the doors are closed, and no one is allowed to stand in the aisles or along the gallery front save a few blue-coated policemen, whose services seem rarely called for.

The half-hour before meeting time passes quickly. One studies the vast throng before him with unceasing interest. The bright light of the many reflectors falls full upon the faces of all sorts and conditions of men — to say nothing of women and children. A more mixed multitude it would be hard to find. At the four o'clock meetings women are the leading element, next to old people, some of them so feeble as almost to be carried to their seats. But at night all classes and ages are present. There is a quiet stir everywhere, but no noise or levity. At 7.45 Mr. Thatcher leads the choir in singing, and shows great skill in managing both choir and congregation in combined and separate parts and in producing tender and powerful effects. One reason is, he has capital music to do it with. The 'Moody and Sankey Hymn-book' is the best for congregational use ever printed. Its words are full of the Gospel, its tunes express the thoughts they are allied to, and are so simple and yet positive in character that any one can sing them after once hearing them. When this vast congregation sings, "Safe in the arms of Jesus" or "I hear Thy welcome voice," one gets a new idea of the power of sacred song.

Eight o'clock, and Mr. Moody is at his post. It is a pleasant night, and though every seat is filled there is a large crowd outside. . . .

How he preaches has already been described. The evening sermon is usually of a bolder offhand character than that of the afternoon, which is intended more specially for Christians. He makes a marked distinction between preaching the Gospel and teaching Christians. His afternoon sermon on the Holy Spirit seemed meant for himself as well as for others, and at the close his voice trembled with emotion as he said: "I want more of this power. Pray for me, that I may be so filled with the Holy Spirit when coming on this platform that men may feel I come with a message from God." The quiet of the audience during Moody's preaching and Sankey's singing is remarkable. Even the rough young fellows who crowd the gallery passages make no sound. At the close Mr. Moody announces a men's meeting in the other hall, a boys' meeting in one of the smaller rooms, and the usual work in the inquiry meeting. Those attending these meetings are requested to go to them while the last hymn is being sung.

The Hippodrome work is a vast business enterprise, organized and conducted by business men, who have put money into it on business principles, for the purpose of saving men. But through all the machinery vibrates the power without which it would be useless — the power of the Holy Ghost. Of

Moody and Sankey revival meeting in Brooklyn
(Billy Graham Center)

course it is successful. Men are being saved day and night, and a moral influence is felt round about the building itself. Two Sundays ago the police returns of that precinct showed no arrests — a thing before unknown — and a recent statement says that in spite of increased destitution among the poor this winter there has been no increase of crime.

Christians have been warmed, "limbered up," and taught to work as they have never worked before; taught how to study their Bibles and how to use them for the good of others; how to reach men simply, naturally, and successfully; how to live consistently and whole-heartedly themselves. The easygoing church life of multitudes has been sharply rebuked by these laborious evangelists. Worshipping in the rude-walled Hippodrome, sitting on wooden chairs, led in song by a man with a melodeon, and preached to by a man without a pulpit, they have learned that costly churches, stained windows, soft cushions, great organs, and quartette choirs are not necessary to the worship of God, and tend to drive away the poor, leaving the rich to enjoy their luxuries alone.

Sam Jones (1847 – 1906)

For Moody, for Jones, and for revivalists generally, every message was a single message: "Believe on the Lord Jesus Christ and thou shalt be saved." In whatever form, drawn from whatever text, the single concern was salvation. Sometimes called the "Moody of the South," Sam Jones started out as a lawyer in Georgia (1868 – 72), then became a Methodist circuit rider (1872 – 80), and spent the last several years of his life as an urban evangelist throughout the South —and well beyond that region. For an understanding of the excerpt below, no sophisticated theological education is required, no program of preparation is demanded. He that has ears to hear, let him hear. Even more crucial, let him choose life and not death.

HOW TO BE SAVED.

"What must I do to be saved? And they said, Believe on the Lord Jesus Christ, and thou shalt be saved and thy house." —Acts XVI, 30, 31.

This is the language of the Philippian jailer to St. Paul, and Paul's answer. As a minister of the Gospel of Jesus Christ, I have no right to advise a man to do any thing that he may not die doing and die saved. I might advise a man to join the Church — I know that is helpful and good advice, and I wish every man was a member of the Church of Jesus Christ, and was living up to the precepts of his blessed religion; and yet I see how a man may join the Church, and live in the Church and die in the Church, and yet be lost at last. And that's the saddest reflection of a human soul — gone from the heights of profession down to the depths of damnation. I might advise a man to read good books, and I wish there were no bad books in the universe. I am sorry that a bad book was ever published. I am sorry that any bad book ever had an entrance into your home, brother. I am sorry that one of your children, or one of you, ever sat down and worse than threw away your time reading bad books. I wish there were only good books, and that men would read them, and when I advise a man to read good books I am giving him good advice; but I see how men may go from the best libraries of earth down to hell at last. I might advise a man to be baptized in the name of the Trinity, and, brethren, this is a rite commanded of God; yet a man who has been baptized may go down to hell, unsaved at last.

I might advise a man to take the sacrament of the Lord's-supper. This is one of the sacraments of the Church of God, and I am sorry for any man who lies down to die with the consciousness, "These hands have never handled the cup of my Lord, and have never tasted of the bread which is emblematic of the broken body of the Son of God." Yet I see how a man may take

[Source: *Sam Jones' Own Book: A Series of Sermons* (Cincinnati: Cranston & Stowe, 1886), pp. 131 – 33.]

communion regularly, may partake of the sacrament once a month, and die and be lost at last.

I might advise a man to keep good company, and I wish all men were good, so that there would be no bad company, for nothing can be more injurious than bad company, and nothing more helpful than good company; and yet I see how it is possible for a man to keep good company all his life and die unsaved. These things are all good. I would not, I say, underestimate a single one of these efficient means to take us to God; but there is only one sufficiency, and that is faith in the Lord Jesus Christ. And he who has this faith with works of love, and purifies his heart and overcomes the world shall be among that blood-washed number that shall shout and shine forever in heaven.

"What must I do to be saved?" The question is given, the question is answered, and I have often thought how good God is to us. He asks us questions and there on the pages of that book six thousand years old, some of them four thousand, some two thousand years, are the answers. But now here's a trembling, ruined man who cries out, "What must I do to be saved?" And the answer in the twinkling of an eye comes ringing down through his soul: "Believe on the Lord Jesus Christ and thou shalt be saved." Thank God for an answer as quick as heaven can give it to all who ask in sincerity and truth what they must do to be saved.

We might stop profitably to-night on the question itself, "What must I do to be saved?" Now, this term, "saved," "salvation," is not a song; it is not a sentiment; it is not a tear; it is not a shout; it is not feeling happy; but in its broadest, highest sense it means simply this — deliverance from sin; deliverance from all that God despises.

Billy Sunday (1862 – 1935)

Sunday, already introduced above (see p. 195) in connection with prohibition, spent far more of his time on that same fundamental concern of the revivalist: salvation, and how to achieve it. The flamboyant, acrobatic Billy Sunday received much criticism from clergy and press, but he gave as good as he got. "If God could convert the preachers," he said, "the world would be saved. Most of them are a lot of evolutionary hot-air merchants." Seminaries, in Sunday's opinion, were a kind of cold storage facility where young ministers were kept "until they get cold enough to practice preaching." And with real insight, he described himself as the "half-way house between the brown-stone church and the Salvation Army."

[Source: William T. Ellis, *"Billy" Sunday: The Man and the Message* (Philadelphia: L. T. Meyers, 1914), pp. 148–49. Quotations above are taken from pp. 200–1.]

What does converted mean? It means completely changed. Converted is not synonymous with reformed. Reforms are from without—conversion from within. Conversion is a complete surrender to Jesus. It's a willingness to do what he wants you to do. Unless you have made a complete surrender and are doing his will it will avail you nothing if you've reformed a thousand times and have your name on fifty church records.

Believe on the Lord Jesus Christ, in your heart and confess him with your mouth and you will be saved. God is good. The plan of salvation is presented to you in two parts. Believe in your heart and confess with your mouth. Many of you here probably do believe. Why don't you confess? Now own up. The truth is that you have a yellow streak. Own up, business men, and business women, and all of you others. Isn't it so? Haven't you got a little saffron? Brave old Elijah ran like a scared deer when he heard old Jezebel had said she would have his head, and he beat it. And he ran to Beersheba and lay down under a juniper tree and cried to the Lord to let him die. The Lord answered his prayer, but not in the way he expected. If he had let him die he would have died with nothing but the wind moaning through the trees as his funeral dirge. But the Lord had something better for Elijah. He had a chariot of fire and it swooped down and carried him into glory without his ever seeing death.

So he says he has something better for you—salvation if he can get you to see it. You've kept your church membership locked up. You've smiled at a smutty story. When God and the Church were scoffed at you never peeped, and when asked to stand up here you've sneaked out the back way and beat it. You're afraid and God despises a coward—a mutt. You cannot be converted by thinking so and sitting still.

Maybe you're a drunkard, an adulterer, a prostitute, a liar; won't admit you are lost; are proud. Maybe you're even proud you're not proud, and Jesus has a time of it.

Jesus said: "Come to me," not to the Church; to me, not to a creed; to me, not to a preacher; to me, not to an evangelist; to me, not to a priest; to me, not to a pope; "Come to me and I will give you rest." Faith in Jesus Christ saves you, not faith in the Church.

You can join church, pay your share of the preacher's salary, attend the services, teach Sunday school, return thanks and do everything that would apparently stamp you as a Christian—even pray—but you won't ever be a Christian until you do what God tells you to do.

That's the road, and that's the only one mapped out for you and for me. God treats all alike. He doesn't furnish one plan for the banker and another for the janitor who sweeps out the bank. He has the same plan for one that he has for another. It's the law—you may not approve of it, but that doesn't make any difference.

Millennialism

Jehovah's Witnesses

The Pennsylvania sect founded by Charles Taze Russell in 1872 began as a Bible study group, that study having a special focus: the coming of Christ and his kingdom. Like other groups in America eagerly awaiting the "restitution of all things," the temptation to name a specific date grew irresistible. The time? For the early Witnesses, the year 1914 was "the farthest limit of the rule of imperfect men." At that time God would rule, and the "Kingdom of Jehovah's Anointed" would begin. Thus, the slogan was repeatedly proclaimed in the early years of the twentieth century: "Millions now living shall never die." From Witness literature, the "Bible evidence" for that proclamation is presented below.

In this chapter we present the Bible evidence proving that the full end of the times of the Gentiles, *i. e.*, the full end of their lease of dominion, will be reached in A.D. 1914; and that that date will be the farthest limit of the rule of imperfect men. And be it observed, that if this is shown to be a fact firmly established by the Scriptures, it will prove: —

Firstly, That at that date the Kingdom of God, for which our Lord taught us to pray, saying, "Thy Kingdom come," will obtain full, universal control, and that it will then be "set up," or firmly established, in the earth, on the ruins of present institutions.

Secondly, It will prove that he whose right it is thus to take the dominion will then be present as earth's new Ruler; and not only so, but it will also prove that he will be present for a considerable period before that date; because the overthrow of these Gentile governments is directly caused by his dashing them to pieces as a potter's vessel (Psa. 2:9; Rev. 2:27), and establishing in their stead his own righteous government.

Thirdly, It will prove that some time before the end of A.D. 1914 the last member of the divinely recognized Church of Christ, the "royal priesthood," "the body of Christ," will be glorified with the Head; because every member is to reign with Christ, being a joint-heir with him of the Kingdom, and it cannot be fully "set up" without every member.

Fourthly, It will prove that from that time forward Jerusalem shall no longer be trodden down of the Gentiles, but shall arise from the dust of divine disfavor, to honor; because the "Times of the Gentiles" will be fulfilled or completed.

Fifthly, It will prove that by that date, or sooner, Israel's blindness will

[Source: *Studies in Scripture*, series II, "The Time is at Hand" (Brooklyn: Watch Tower, Bible and Tract Society, 1910 [1889]), pp. 76–79.]

begin to be turned away; because their "blindness in part" was to continue only "*until* the fulness of the Gentiles be come in" (Rom. 11:25), or, in other words, until the full number from among the Gentiles, who are to be members of the body or bride of Christ, would be fully selected.

Sixthly, It will prove that the great "time of trouble such as never was since there was a nation," will reach its culmination in a world-wide reign of anarchy; and then men will learn to be still, and to know that Jehovah is God and that he will be exalted in the earth. (Psa. 46:10) . . .

Seventhly, It will prove that *before that date* God's Kingdom, organized in power, will be in the earth and then smite and crush the Gentile image (Dan. 2:34) — and fully consume the power of these kings. Its own power and dominion will be established as fast as by its varied influences and agencies it crushes and scatters the "powers that be" — civil and ecclesiastical — iron and clay. . . .

The beginning of these Gentile Times is clearly located by the Scriptures. Hence, if they furnish us the length *also* of the fixed period, or lease of Gentile dominion, we can know positively just when it will terminate. The Bible does furnish this fixed period, which must be fulfilled; but it was furnished in such a way that it could not be understood when written, nor until the lapse of time and the events of history had shed their light upon it; and even then, only by those who were watching and who were not overcharged by the cares of the world.

The Bible evidence is clear and strong that the "Time of the Gentiles" is a period of 2520 years, from the year B.C. 606 to and including A.D. 1914. This lease of universal dominion to Gentile governments, as we have already seen, began with Nebuchadnezzar — not when his reign began, but when the typical kingdom of the Lord passed away, and the dominion of the whole world was left in the hands of the Gentiles. The date for the beginning of the Gentile Times is, therefore, definitely marked as at the time of the removal of the crown of God's typical kingdom, from Zedekiah, their last king.

Foursquare Gospel

Aimee Semple McPherson (1890 – 1944) reached the height of her fame as minister-revivalist in Los Angeles (Angelus Temple) during the final twenty years of her turbulent life. Jesus' ministry, she taught, is a fourfold one: as savior, baptizer, healer, and returning king of kings. A gospel which is faithful to all of these roles is a foursquare gospel. With her own denomination (officially, the International Church of the Foursquare Gospel), her own building, and her own keen sense for the dramatic and newsworthy, Mc-

[Source: Aimee Semple McPherson, *This is That: Personal Experiences, Sermons, and Writings* (Los Angeles: Bridal Call Publishing House, 1919), pp. 653 – 54, 655.]

Pherson was a religious phenomenon. In the excerpt below, it is that fourth aspect of Jesus' work — a returning king of kings who would rule over a New Jerusalem — that attention is being called to. Mrs. McPherson presents her millennialism not in terms of dates and times, but in a very personalized "vision and prophecy."

There came a great voice from Heaven as of a trumpet, crying: JESUS IS COMING SOON — GET READY TO MEET HIM.

My soul longed to see His face. My heart had been cleansed by His blood, and the Spirit had entered the tabernacle. I cried out:

"Yea, Lord," and ran to meet Him.

"Get ready! Get ready!" cried the great voice, again and again. "Get ready! Get ready!!" yet echoed over the hills and through the valleys. "*Get* ready!"

"O! Lord, Lord!" I cried, "Wherefore sayest thou unto me, 'Get ready?' Have I not left all for thee? Didst Thou not wash me in Thy blood? Wherein shall I get ready?"

He held an open Bible before my face and it shone as a mirror. Then showed He me myself, dark and tanned, and uncomely.

"O Lord," I wept, "have thy way. Get Thou me ready, I pray."

Then I lifted up my eyes and beheld a man, tall of stature, clothed in raiment of light, that shone as the sun. A sharp sword gleamed in His hand. I beheld His brightness, and saw His armour gleaming upon Him. He advanced and drew near me. He towered above me. His beauty was of such brightness my eyes could not gaze upon Him. Then I saw my own imperfections, my blemishes, my failures. I withered under His gaze, and was ashamed in His presence. I wept for my foolish blindness, that had boasted of readiness.

Who can dwell in His brightness without showing a blemish?

"O, Lord," I cried, "I am a failure. I am all blackness. I am undone." Then He spake: "Wilt thou let me have My way? Wilt thou let Me make thee ready, no matter what the cost?"

"O Lord," I cried, " I am utterly unworthy, but have your way." . . .

Then I looked and behold! a New creation, as of a beautiful woman. I beheld her coming from the West, and walking towards the East. She approached. I beheld her white raiment, dazzling as the snow in the sunshine. Her movements were gracious and tender. Her voice was mellow and full of sweet fragrance. I smelled the fragrance of her garments, as sweet lillies grown in the valleys, and as the rose of Sharon. Her eyes beheld no guile, but they were tender as a dove's eyes. Her lips were pure, and dropped as the honey-comb. No foolishness, no criticism marred their sweetness. No fleshly words, her ears were kept for IIis alone, her Lover, her Bridegroom, her King.

As she drew nigh, I gazed with amazement into her face, and saw that it was myself. I heard the voice of the Master speaking unto me, saying: "This is My beloved. How far you have fallen short of the standard of my perfections!"

Dispensationalism

In America that view of the world's history and destiny known as "dispensationalism" was most effectively promoted by Cyrus I. Scofield (1843–1921). Converted to Christianity when he was in his late thirties, Scofield turned from a career in law to one in biblical study and instruction. He lectured widely, trained teachers, offered popular correspondence courses in Bible study, and more. Most of all, he prepared what became known as the Scofield Reference Bible, *a work of enormous and enduring impact. First appearing in 1909, this Bible enjoyed a second edition in 1917, and in 1967 Oxford University Press published the* New Scofield Reference Bible. *Notes and outlines in all these Bibles highlight that particular view of the past, present, and future which divides all time into seven periods or "dispensations." The mysteries of biblical prophecy are unlocked, and the exact nature of the events during the "last times" is unfolded. Here, in compact form from one of his popular lecture series, are Scofield's views on "The Seven Dispensations."*

The Scriptures divide time, by which is meant the entire period from the creation of Adam to the "new heaven and a new earth" of Rev. 21: 1, into seven unequal periods, called, usually, "dispensations" (Eph. 3: 2), although these periods are also called "ages" (Eph. 2: 7) and "days" — as, "day of the Lord," etc.

These periods are marked off in Scripture by some change in God's method of dealing with mankind, or a portion of mankind, in respect of the two questions of sin and of man's responsibility. Each of the Dispensations may be regarded as a new test of the natural man, and each ends in judgment — marking his utter failure.

Five of these Dispensations, or periods of time, have been fulfilled; we are living in the sixth, probably toward its close, and have before us the seventh, and last — the millennium.

1. MAN INNOCENT. — This dispensation extends from the creation of Adam, Gen. 2: 7, to the Expulsion. Adam, created innocent, and ignorant of good and evil, was placed in the garden of Eden with his wife, Eve, and put under responsibility to abstain from the fruit of the tree of the knowledge of good and evil. The Dispensation of Innocence resulted in the first and, in its far-reaching effects, the most disastrous of the failures of the natural man,

[Source: C. I. Scofield, *Rightly Dividing the Word of Truth (2 Timothy 2:15),* 2nd ed. (Philadelphia: Philadelphia School of the Bible, 1923), pp. 20–25.]

and was closed by judgment — "So He drove out the man." See Gen. 1: 26; Gen. 2: 16, 17; Gen. 3: 6; Gen. 3: 22-24.

2. MAN UNDER CONSCIENCE. — By the Fall Adam and Eve acquired, and transmitted to the race, the knowledge of good and evil. This gave conscience a basis for right moral judgment, and hence the race came under this measure of responsibility — to do good and eschew evil. The result of the Dispensation of Conscience was that "all flesh had corrupted his way on the earth;" that "the wickedness of man was great in the earth, and that every imagination of the thoughts of his heart was only evil continually;" and God closed the second testing of the natural man with judgment — the Flood. See Gen. 3: 7, 22; Gen. 6: 5, 11, 12; Gen. 7: 11, 12, 23.

3. MAN IN AUTHORITY OVER THE EARTH. — Out of the fearful judgment of the Flood God saved eight persons to whom, after the waters were assuaged, He gave the purified earth with ample power to govern it. This, Noah and his descendants were responsible to do. The Dispensation of Human Government resulted, upon the plain of Shinar, in the impious attempt to become independent of God and closed in judgment — the Confusion of Tongues. See Gen. 9: 1, 2; Gen. 11: 1-4; Gen. 11: 5-8.

4. MAN UNDER PROMISE. — Out of the dispersed descendants of the builders of Babel God now calls one man, Abram, with whom He enters into covenant. Some of the promises to Abram and his descendants were purely gracious and unconditional. These either have been, or will yet be, literally fulfilled. Other promises were conditional upon the faithfulness and obedience of the Israelites. Every one of these conditions was violated, and the Dispensation of Promise resulted in the utter failure of Israel, and closed in the judgment of the Egyptian Bondage.

The book of Genesis, which opens with the sublime words, "In the beginning God created," closes with, "in a coffin in Egypt." [See] Gen. 12: 1-3; Gen. 13: 14-17; Gen. 15: 5; 26: 3; 28: 12, 13; Ex. 1: 13, 14.

5. MAN UNDER LAW. — Again the grace of God came to the help of helpless man and redeemed the chosen people out of the hand of the oppressor. In the Wilderness of Sinai He proposed to them the Covenant of Law. Instead of humbly pleading for a continued relation of grace, they presumptuously answered: "All that the Lord hath spoken we will do." The history of Israel in the Wilderness and in the Land is one long record of flagrant, persistent violation of the Law, and at last, after multiplied warnings, God closed the testing of man by law in judgment, and first Israel, and then Judah, were driven out of the Land into a dispersion which still continues. A feeble remnant returned under Ezra and Nehemiah, of which, in due time, Christ came: "Born of a woman — made under the law." Him both Jews and Gentiles conspired to crucify. See Exodus 19: 1-8; 2 Kings 17: 1-18; Romans 10: 5;

2 Kings 25: 1-11; Gal. 3: 10; Acts 2: 22, 23; Romans 3: 19, 20; Acts 7: 51, 52.

6. MAN UNDER GRACE. — The sacrificial death of the Lord Jesus Christ introduced the dispensation of pure grace — which means undeserved favor, or God GIVING righteousness, instead of God REQUIRING righteousness, as under Law.

Salvation, perfect and eternal, is now freely offered to Jew and Gentile upon the one condition of faith.

Jesus answered and said unto them, This is the work of God, that ye BELIEVE on him whom he hath sent. John 6: 29.

Verily, verily, I say unto you, He that BELIEVETH on me HATH everlasting life. John 6: 47.

Verily, verily, I say unto you, He that heareth my word, and BELIEVETH him that sent me, HATH eternal life, *and cometh not into judgment,* but hath passed out of death into life. John 5: 24. R. V. [Revised Version]

My sheep hear my voice, and I know them, and they follow me: and I give unto them eternal life; and *they shall never perish.* John 10: 27, 28.

For by grace have ye been saved through faith; and that not of yourselves: *it is* the gift of God: not of works, that no man should glory. Eph. 2: 8, 9. R. V.

The predicted result of this testing of man under grace is, judgment upon an unbelieving world and an apostate Church. [See] Rev. 3: 15, 16; Luke 17: 26-30; Luke 18: 8; 2 Thess. 2: 7-12.

The first event in the closing of this dispensation will be the descent of the Lord from Heaven, when sleeping saints will be raised and, together with believers then living, caught up "to meet the Lord in the air: and so shall we ever be with the Lord." 1 Thess. 4: 16, 17.

Then follows the brief period called "the great tribulation." [See] Matt. 24: 21, 22; Dan. 12: 1; Zeph. 1: 15-18; Jer. 30: 5-7.

After this occurs the personal return of the Lord to the earth in power and great glory, and the judgments which introduce the seventh, and last dispensation. [See] Matt. 24: 29, 30; Matt. 25: 31-46.

7. MAN UNDER THE PERSONAL REIGN OF CHRIST. — After the purifying judgments which attended the personal return of Christ to the Earth, He will reign over restored Israel and over the earth for one thousand years. This is the period commonly called the Millennium. The seat of His power will be Jerusalem, and the saints, including the saved of the Dispensation of Grace, viz., the Church, will be associated with Him in His glory. See Acts 15: 14-17; Rev. 19: 11-21; Isa. 2: 1-4; Rev. 20: 1-6; Isa. 11: entire.

But when Satan is "loosed a little season" he finds the natural heart as prone to evil as ever, and easily gathers the nations to battle against the Lord and His saints, and this last dispensation closes, like all the others, in judgment. The "great white throne" is set, the wicked dead are raised and finally judged, and then come the "new heaven and a new earth" — eternity begun. [See] Rev. 20: 3, 7-15; Rev. 21 and 22.

Holiness and Pentecostalism

Doctrine

The father of Methodism, John Wesley (1703 – 91), stimulated profound interest in "Christian perfection" among his followers both in Britain and in America. Some so stimulated went on to create new denominations and associations, greatly adding to this nation's religious variety. The "holiness" movement stressed the process that goes on after salvation. As noted above, the revivalist theme was often salvation and nothing more; for the believer in Christian perfection, however, there was more, much more. Beyond justification lay sanctification, and beyond the new birth lay a life-long process of maturing, of growing in God's grace. But when did one become holy — and how? The notion of perfection was easy to ridicule, difficult to define how it might apply to obviously imperfect human beings. In 1898, Methodist De Witt Clinton Huntington (1830 – 1912), native of Vermont, pastor and presiding elder and professor, undertook to state clearly what sin was and was not, what holiness was and was not. What follows cannot be described as the holiness position, for there were several, but only as one sustained effort to be both helpful and precise.

We shall now attempt to show that Christian holiness, on the human side, belongs to the voluntary states of the mind, that it consists in an abiding state of the will. In submitting a definition, we will say that Christian holiness is *a state of unreserved consecration of the being to God, secured through the constant revelation of Christ to the soul of the believer by the Holy Spirit*. It is distinguished from an *act of consecration* by the feature of *continuousness*. It includes *living* consecration, uninterrupted faith in Christ as a present and sufficient Savior from sin, and a continuous presence and incoming of the Holy Spirit in the soul of the Christian. It is abiding in Christ. It is such a Divinely-strengthened state of the soul, that the will stands in a "supreme preference for God." It is that state in which the will constantly chooses the will of God as the law of its entire activity. In a word, it is voluntary and continuous obedience to all the known will of God, a state in which the believer *does not commit sin*.

On the Divine side it is not so much what the Holy Spirit does in the

[Source: D. W. C. Huntington, *Sin and Holiness, Or What It is to Be Holy* (Cincinnati: Curts & Jennings, 1898), pp. 152 – 54, 156 – 58.]

believer at any given moment, as what he does and what he is at each and every moment. It is his pervading presence, revealing Christ to the soul as all-sufficient for its utmost exigency, and thus strengthening us to abide in unbroken acceptance of the will of God. It is Christ conquering *in* us as he conquered *for* us. It is that state in which, by the power of God through faith, the Christian believer is *kept from committing sin.* In support of this view of Christian holiness we offer the following remarks:

Holiness is the exact opposite of sin. We have endeavored to show that sin is all and always voluntary transgression of law. If this be so, it follows that holiness is voluntary and entire obedience to the known will of God. If, on the other hand, there are two kinds of sin, there must be two kinds of holiness. But if sin is disobedience to the known will of God, then holiness is entire obedience to the apprehended will of God. "All sin has its seat in the will. The appetites and passions and intellectual aspirations are not sins. They belong to the original furnishings of the soul. Sin is volitional indulgence in contravention of law." Holiness, then, is salvation from indulgence in contravention of law, and, by consequence, obedience to known law. . . .

This view of Christian holiness recognizes and necessarily implies the very

Storefront Holiness church on Virginia's eastern shore (Exmore)
(Photo by author)

distinctions in Christian experience and character which are taught in the Bible. The fact has already been noticed that the twofold classification of believers into somewhat distinct bodies, distinguished by the specific fact of the existence or non-existence in them of "inbred sin," does not appear in the Scriptures. But the Bible does recognize the fact that some Christian believers are weak and wavering, that they have need to be "confirmed," to be "established, strengthened, settled." They are exhorted to "grow up into him [Christ] in all things," to "go on unto perfection," to be "made perfect," to be "holy." They are encouraged to expect a realization of a state of entire sanctification, in which they may be preserved blameless; that is, in which they will commit no known sin. The converts of the New Testament stand before us essentially like those of our own day, ardent and sincere, but not in a state of constant, unbroken obedience to God. They committed more or less sin. The differences in Christian experience recognized in such passages are the differences between a weak and wavering state, in which sin is sometimes committed, and a state in which the high Christian privilege is realized of being saved and kept from all sin.

It is true that believers are exhorted to "holiness," to "sanctification," and are encouraged to expect that they shall be "sanctified wholly;" but this in no way proves that the holiness and sanctification here enjoined and promised consist in the destruction or removal of an "inbeing of sin." There is nothing in the passages alluded to in reference to a "second blessing" of "inbred sin" destruction in distinction from a previous or partial one of "inbred sin" subjugation. It would seem impossible so to construe their meaning by any whose minds were not preoccupied by the thought.

Experience

Pentecostalism, taking its name from that first Pentecost described in the Book of Acts (2:1 – 5), arose in close association with the holiness movement. Once more, dozens of new denominations emerged on the American scene. One may think of Pentecostalism as the more radical wing of the holiness movement: more extravagant and uninhibited services of worship, more adventurism in theology (for example, the "Jesus only" faction, a kind of right-wing unitarianism), far more emphasis upon healing. Indeed, so radical did Pentecostalism seem in the eyes of some holiness churches that the latter took steps to separate themselves or at least distinguish themselves from the former. Pentecostals found the validity of their theology in their experience, especially the experiences of healing and of speaking in tongues. For some, glossolalia or speaking in tongues was not merely a sign of God's "second

[Source: *History and Formative Years of the Church of God in Christ* (Memphis: Church of God in Christ Publishing House, 1969), pp. 37 – 39.]

blessing" —it was the *sign. The largest black Pentecostal group, the Church of God in Christ (founded in 1895 by C. H. Mason [1866–1961]), includes in its official history this explanation of and justification for speaking in tongues.*

And these signs shall follow those that believe: In my name shall they cast out devils; they shall speak with new tongues. Our Lord Jesus did not say that some of those that believe should speak with new tongues, but those that believe shall speak with new tongues. This promise is to those that believe; it is not to the unbeliever. When did this great work begin? On the day of Pentecost (Acts 2:1-5). And when the day of Pentecost was fully come, they were all with one accord in one place. Suddenly there came a sound from heaven, as of rushing, mighty wind, and it filled all the house where they were sitting and there appeared unto them cloven tongues like as of fire, and it sat upon each of them; and they were all filled with the Holy Ghost and began to speak with new tongues as the spirit gave them utterance.

This promise is to all that believe. Acts 2:38-39. They spake with tongues at Cesarea, when the Holy Ghost fell upon them which heard the word. Acts 10:44-45.

Believers that went with Peter knew that these Gentiles had received the Holy Ghost when they heard them speak with tongues and magnify God. Acts 10:45-46. The Church at Ephesus spake with tongues when they received the Holy Ghost. Acts 19:6. When we are baptized with the Holy Ghost the glory of the son will be revealed to us as never before. He will glorify Christ. He will show us the things of Christ. John 16:14.

Did God intend the speaking in tongues to be in the Church? And God hath set some in the Church, First Apostles; secondly, prophets; thirdly, teachers. After that, miracles; then gifts of healing—and helps, governments, diversities of tongues. 1 Cor. 12:28. For he that speaketh in an unknown tongue, speaketh not to men, but unto God, for no man understandeth him; howbeit in the spirit he speaketh mysteries. 1 Cor. 14:2. No man understands him, but the spirit is speaking the mysteries of God, through us. Is it wrong for one to pray in tongues? No, for if I prayed in an unknown tongue, my spirit prayeth but my understanding in unfruitful. 1 Cor. 14:14. Should we let the spirit pray in us if we do not know what he is saying? Yes, what is it then, I will pray with the spirit and with the understanding also. 1 Cor. 14:15. We do not understand what to pray for as we ought to. Rom. 8:26. Likewise the spirit also helpeth our infirmities, for we know not what we should pray for as we ought; but the spirit itself maketh intercession for us with groanings which can't be uttered. How many ways can the spirit speaking in tongues in us edify the Church? We see four ways. 1 Cor. 14:6. First way, by revelations; second, by knowledge; third, by prophesying; fourth, by doctrinal teaching. What more can we say, wherefore tongues are a sign not to them that believe, but to them that believe not; but prophesying serveth not for them that believe not, but for them which believe. 1 Cor. 14:22. Should we forbid to speak with tongues? No. Wherefore, brethren, covet to prophesy and forbid not to speak with tongues. 1 Cor. 14:39.

Are we helped in any way to speak in tongues? Yes. He that speaketh in an unknown tongue edifieth himself. 1 Cor. 14:4. Would the Holy Ghost have all to speak with tongues? Yes. I would that ye all speak with tongues, but rather that ye prophesy; for greater is he which prophesieth than he that speaketh with tongues except he interpret, that the church may receive edifying, and when he that speaketh with tongues cannot interpret. But if he can interpret he is great or greater, for he may speak in the mysteries of God (1 Cor. 14:2), and he can speak unto men to edification and exhortation and comfort (verse 3). You can see in verse 6 that we may prophesy in tongues and he may speak a revelation with tongues and he may speak the word of knowledge with tongues, teach doctrines with tongues. May the Lord open the eyes of all His people to this great mystery. Paul was one of the greatest of the apostles, and he spoke with tongues more than all. 1 Cor. 14:18. Oh, how the Holy Ghost doth reveal Christ to us when we are baptized with Him, and we do speak with tongues as He gives utterance; He will make

Speaking in tongues (St. Columba Roman Catholic Church in Hopewell, New Jersey, 1973)
(Religious News Service)

us know that we are in Christ and Christ in us; and in the Father and the Father in Christ. John 14:20.

What a sweet unity. Christ is all. What a sweet rest. Christ is all. God speaks Himself in tongues in us. Isa. 28:11; for with stammering lips and other tongue will He speak to His people, to rest. This is the refreshing, yet they would not hear. Rest and refreshing from the Lord when He, the Holy Ghost, is speaking in us with tongues; still the people will not hear. Speaking in tongues is the wonderful work of God. All that did not have this work in them on that day were amazed and in doubt about the wonderful work of God, and so it is today with all that have not this blessed work going on in them — they cannot understand it; they will say everything about it. Sinners, converted ones and sanctified ones and all wonder and will wonder when they hear or see this movement of the Holy Ghost going on in the saints of God. If the Holy Ghost does not speak in them, they can't understand His speaking the wonderful works of God in other tongues. Oh, dear ones, the word of every promise of God must enter into us before we can understand the wonderful works of the promise in others. The word giveth light and understanding that all may be baptized with this one baptism of the Holy Ghost. He will show us then Christ is coming soon again to the earth. Prepare to meet your God in His glory.

ELDER C. H. MASON.

Cure of Souls

As noted above, the Pentecostal service featured not only speaking in tongues but often even more dramatically the cure of physical and spiritual ills. Healing in these instances comes not through the steady application of a religious science, nor through the careful interaction of psychiatry and theology, but through the sudden and powerful manifestation of the presence of the Holy Spirit in the moment of cure. The most nationally visible healer of the twentieth century, Oral Roberts, was born in Pontotoc County, Oklahoma, in 1918. Originally a member of the Pentecostal Holiness Church, Roberts in 1968 moved into that Methodism out of which so many of the newer churches had come. But his nationally televised healing services continued, even as his nationally prominent university in Tulsa continued to evolve from a "University of Evangelism" into a general liberal arts institution. In the selection below, Roberts describes himself both as healer and as one healed.

Jesus is not here today with the seamless robe, nor Paul with his blessed cloths, nor Peter with his shadow that brought healing, nor the elders of the

[Source: Oral Roberts, *If You Need HEALING Do These Things*, rev. ed. (Tulsa: Healing Waters, Inc., 1954), pp. 35–38.]

church with their anointing oil, but God has not left Himself without human instrumentalities to deliver this generation. I have heard His voice: first that I was to be healed, next, that I was to bring healing to the sick and demon-possessed, and that His healing power would be felt in my right hand for all who would believe. It is happening just as the Lord said. I seldom feel anything in my left hand, but through my right hand I feel the healing virtue of the Son of God. Thousands have witnessed this power as it surged through every fiber of their being. God uses this human agency as a point of contact. The time is set when I lay my right hand upon the captive and adjure the afflictions to come out of him in the name of the Master, Jesus Christ of Nazareth. I feel the pressure of the disease rising to meet my right hand, but then as God's healing virtue surges into the person, this pressure is relieved and deliverance is wrought: The deaf ears are opened, the cancers wither and die and pass from the body, demons come out and humanity is set free through faith in God. This gift in my humble life is for the deliverance of my generation and not for my personal gratification. Any gift from God is to be used only for the deliverance of others.

But a gift of healing is not the only means of healing or point of contact for your faith. There is the anointing oil which God's minister anoints you with in Jesus' Name for the purpose of praying the prayer of faith for your healing, using the anointing oil as a point of contact. The moment it is applied turn your faith loose. This was my point of contact when I was healed in 1935 in a big healing revival in Ada, Oklahoma where Rev. George W. Muncie prayed the prayer of faith for my deliverance. As I was being brought to the meeting on a mattress in the back seat of a car, after being bed-fast five months with tuberculosis in both lungs, I was led to use the anointing oil and laying on of hands as a point of contact. Down deep in my heart I was believing in God for deliverance and I told the Lord that when Brother Muncie anointed me and laid his hands on my head that then, and then alone, would I believe the work was done. The healing line was long. Midnight came and I was still waiting. I was suffering but I did not become discouraged nor angry with having to be the last one prayed for. Trembling with antic-ipation, I was waiting for him to anoint and touch me with his hands, through which God was performing miracles. At last my time had come.

They helped me to my feet. I watched every move they made; above all, I was watching for his hands to be laid on my head. Then the anointing oil touched my forehead. His hands were upon me and at that instant I turned my faith loose; the deepest desires and emotions of my hungry spirit pushed outward toward God. I believed God! I found myself thanking Him for deliverance. Every ache and pain disappeared. The glory rushed into my soul. I was tingling from head to toe with new life. And, then, for several minutes I was lost in the sheer ecstacy of divine deliverance. I opened my eyes to the surroundings a little later, astonished to realize that I was leaping and shouting and running on the long platform. I was healed! Faith had wrought it!

Oh, suffering friend, turn your faith loose. Hang it on some Bible means of deliverance and let go of it. Hold nothing back. Pour all your pent-up faith-emotions into the act of believing God for your deliverance.

Suggested Reading (Chapter Nine)

One avenue which opens into that often dimly lit world of private religion, the inspirational "best sellers," can be readily followed through the many editions or reprintings of these works. Scholarly studies of such are less easy to come by, but two books deserve notice: Louis Schneider and S. M. Dornbush, *Popular Religion: Inspirational Books in America* (1958); and Allene S. Phy, ed., *The Bible and Popular Culture in America* (1983), especially the editor's own chapter on "Retelling the Greatest Story Ever Told: Jesus in Popular Fiction." In addition to the lives of Jesus excerpted in the chapter itself, one may wish to read the businessman's biography, Bruce Barton, *The Man Nobody Knows* (1925); or, the journalist's you-were-there biographies, Jim Bishop, *The Day Christ Died* (1957) and *The Day Christ was Born* (1960). The literature of private devotion and Bible reading is largely "in house": that is, most denominations publish their own approved guides, manuals, condensations, and "aids to devotion." No single scholarly monograph has attempted to analyze the extent or character of this pervasive enterprise and, given the enormity of the task, none may ever do so. (Biblical scholarship, on the other hand, which has many scholarly monographs devoted to it, is treated in Chapter Ten.)

On mysticism and prayer, the literature is large. Abraham Heschel, himself a Jewish mystic, provided an excellent discussion of "The Mystical Element in Judaism" in Louis Finkelstein, ed., *The Jews: Their Religion and Culture* (1971). The sometimes forbidding subject of mysticism is made less so in Evelyn Underhill's charming essay, *Practical Mysticism: A Little Book for Normal People* (1914). Hal Bridges in his *American Mysticism from William James to Zen* (1970) includes Heschel along with Rufus Jones and Thomas Merton in this important monograph. For full-length treatments of Jones, see David Hinshaw, *Rufus Jones: Master Quaker* (1951); and Elizabeth G. Vining, *Friend of Life: The Biography of Rufus M. Jones* (1958). Merton's own *Contemplative Prayer* (1969) should be read along with J. J. Higgins, *Merton's Theology of Prayer* (1971) and D. Q. McInerny, *Thomas Merton: The Man and His Work* (1974). More general treatments of prayer include J. B. Coburn, *Prayer and Personal Religion* (1957); Christian Duquoc, *The Prayer Life* (1972); and Louis Jacobs, *Hasidic Prayer* (1973). The centrality of worship, and therefore of the day of the week specifically set aside for such, is the subject of Horton Davies, *Christian Worship: Its Making and Meaning* (1957), of W. R. Bonniwell, *Interpreting the Sunday Mass* (1949), and of Louis Finkelstein (in the volume cited above), "The Jewish Religion: Its Beliefs and Practices." Hannah G. Solomon's life-long involvement with Judaism and with Jewish women may be followed in her autobiography, *Fabric of My Life* (1946). The art of preaching in America continues apace, as is evident in such compilations as the *Pulpit Digest*, beginning in 1936, and the *American Pulpit Series*, which started in 1945.

To wend one's way through the intricate labyrinth of New Thought, one is grateful for expert guides. Three such may be cited: Charles S. Braden, *Spirits in Rebellion: Rise and Development of New Thought* (1963); B. F. Campbell, *Ancient Wisdom Revived: A History of the Theosophical Movement* (1980); and J. Stillson Judah, *The History and Philosophy of the Metaphysical Movements in America* (1967). While Robert S. Ellwood's *Alternative Altars: Unconventional and Eastern Spirituality in America* (1979) is not limited to New Thought, it does place that movement very skillfully in the context of other "unconventional" religion in America. An insider's account which endeavors to do the same for Mary Baker Eddy's institution is that of Robert Peel, *Christian Science: Its Encounter with American Culture* (1958). On Unity's founder, see Hugh D'Andrade, *Charles Fillmore, Herald of the New Age* (1974). The most scholarly treatment for the tradition out of which Russell Conwell and Norman Vincent Peale speak is Donald B. Meyer, *The Positive Thinkers: a Study of the American Quest for Health, Wealth and Personal Power from Mary Baker Eddy to Norman Vincert Peale* (1965). Of the abundant literature on the new relationship between psychology and religion, a few examples must suffice: Samuel Klausner, *Psychiatry and Religion* (1964); John B. Cobb, Jr., *Theology and Pastoral Care* (1977); and the excellent sweep provided by Nathan G. Hale in his *Freud and the Americans* (1971). Some concerns over this continuing relationship between psychology and religion have been expressed by O. H. Mowrer in *The Crisis in Psychiatry and Religion* (1961) and by Karl Menninger in *Whatever Became of Sin?* (1973).

The fear of and resistance to new immigration and to "foreignness" generally is effectively presented in John Higham, *Strangers in the Land: Patterns of American Nativism, 1860 – 1925* (1955). Donald L. Kinzer, in his *Episode in Anti-Catholicism: The American Protective Assocation* (1964), gives that nativist group its first monographic treatment, apart from a "sketch" by an early opponent, H. J. Desmond. The APA as well as the Klan receive major attention in Thomas J. Curran, *Xenophobia and Immigration, 1820 – 1930* (1975), although the Klan is more fully treated in D. M. Chalmers, *Hooded Americanism: The History of the Ku Klux Klan* (1965), and in K. T. Jackson, *The Ku Klux Klan in the City 1915 – 1930* (1967). A national political initiation of sorts, when *A Catholic Runs for President* (1956), is a story well told by E. A. Moore of Alfred Smith's campaign of 1928. The economic ills of the 1930s, together with passionate remedies offered by some, can be followed in Alan Brinkley's *Voices of Protest: Huey Long, Father Coughlin, and the Great Depression* (1982). Equally new and equally impressive is William D. Miller's biography of *Dorothy Day* (1982). And on Niebuhr the most useful introduction remains the weighty anthology edited by C. W. Kegley and R. W. Bretall, *Reinhold Niebuhr: His Religious, Social and Political Thought* (1956), while the most recent biography is the well-received *Reinhold Niebuhr* by Richard W. Fox (1985).

The best account of recent revivalism, giving full attention to all three revivalists excerpted in this chapter (Moody, Jones, and Sunday), is William G. McLoughlin, *Modern Revivalism: Charles Grandison Finney to Billy Graham* (1959). McLoughlin's own biography of Sunday remains the definitive one: *Billy Sunday Was His Real Name* (1955), while James F. Findlay, Jr., has written the authoritative *Dwight L. Moody: American Evangelist, 1837–1890* (1969). The most recent treatment of Jehovah's Witnesses is by an insider turned apostate and also turned professional writer — Barbara G. Harrison, *Visions of Glory: A History and a Memory of Jehovah's Witnesses* (1978). William McLoughlin's sketch of Aimee Semple McPherson (in *Notable American Women*, 3 vols., 1971) is thorough and reliable. *Dispensationalism in America: Its Rise and Development* (1958), by C. Norman Kraus, manages to compress in a few pages a wealth of information — biographical, theological, bibliographical. On millennialism in American history generally, see E. L. Tuveson, *Redeemer Nation: The Idea of America's Millennial Role* (1968). The Holiness and Pentecostal movements, thanks in part to a recent surge of interest in charismatic phenomena, have been examined intensively. See, for example, Vinson Synan, *The Holiness-Pentecostal Movement* (1971); Steve Durasoff, *Bright Wind of the Spirit: Pentecostalism Today* (1972), a volume which gives much attention to Oral Roberts; and D. E. Harrell, Jr., *All Things Are Possible: The Healing and Charismatic Revivals in Modern America* (1975) as well as his biography *Oral Roberts: An American Life* (1985). John T. McNeill in his *History of the Cure of Souls* (1951) places the entire encounter between religion and health in an inclusive, supportive historical context, while on the American scene the same is done authoritatively by E. Brooks Holifield in his *History of Pastoral Care in America: From Salvation to Self-Realization* (1983).

TEN:

Religion and the Life of the Mind

In the realm of ideas, the Western World bubbled and boiled over in the late nineteenth and early twentieth centuries. Whole new disciplines were born: anthropology, sociology, psychology, and more. History turned scientific, and biology interpreted history. Literary critics crossed the line separating the secular from the sacred, while philosophy — so long religion's partner and ally — began to chart its separate course. Modernity had arrived, and the bumptious new guest faced a mixed welcome.

PHILOSOPHY AND RELIGION

The Enlightenment had struck a hard blow against abstract speculation, metaphysical musing, and pompous system-building. In early nineteenth-century America, Scottish Realism or Common Sense (both names sounding reassuringly unmetaphysical) continued to exercise its influence through eastern colleges and prevailing textbooks. A few Hegelian idealists in St. Louis argued that at least one great system remained as an option. But these philosophical possibilities were clearly derivative, imported from afar, not a product of the native soil.

Not until the pragmatic school arose did America begin to make its own contribution to the field, even though pragmatism, as one critic observed, was not so much a philosophy as it was a method of doing without one. But it was a method, and a method of considerable import for religion. Abstract theological system-building tended to give way to creeds clearly based upon experience, upon observable consequences — here and now — of religious belief. Metaphysics yielded to ethics, as the question "Does God exist?" was replaced by the query, "What do you believe about God?"

Yet pragmatism did not drive away all idealism. Josiah Royce, for example, represented that "genteel tradition" effectively as he pursued his life-long interest in religion. The "process philosophy" of Alfred North Whitehead had religious implications as Whitehead himself noted, but in the generation following his death in 1947 a whole school of process theologians emerged. George Santayana, though he created no school, sharply rebuked those acculturated liberals, those mystical modernists, who consciously or otherwise abandoned the historic faith. "The modernist wishes to reconcile the church and the world," Santayana noted. "Therein he forgets what Christianity came into the world to announce and why its message was believed."

SCIENCE AND RELIGION

Once upon a time — the time being the Middle Ages — scientists were churchmen and theology was the queen of science. By the middle of the nineteenth century, if not well before, that state of affairs had surely passed. The scientists and the theologians, both contending for the minds of humankind, both claiming special avenues to or certain guarantees of truth, drew themselves up on opposing sides. Scientists saw their methods as possessing a genuine, not a pretended, infallibility, while theologians saw their precincts as being intentionally invaded, their prerogatives rudely challenged. Both sides indulged in some deliberate caricature, some sharp ridicule, some false hope that the enemy would soon fade away.

Between the opposing armies, a few brave souls ventured forth onto a no-man's-land to see if that ground could by any chance become a common ground. A few souls — from both sides — actually endeavored to look at the issues dividing them from the other camp's point of view. It is probably true that in the long "history of the warfare between science and theology" (to use the title of a famous nineteenth-century work by Andrew D. White), theology had to give more ground than science. But that of course was only because theology had laid claim to so vast a domain. Whenever science went so far as to assert its own omniscience or to see itself as the supplanter of religion, then that ground too had to be surrendered.

In describing the opposition between the cultural forces, the word "battle" is not a synonym for quiet scholarly debate. In the nineteenth century, academic questions in religion only rarely remained merely "academic." And this was conspicuously true in the case of evolution, the doctrine that upended theologians — as White wrote — like a plow pushing its way into an ant hill. Evolution was not some abstract and far-away theory about the cosmic pull of gravity or the strange orbits of planetary motion: it was about life — everyone's life. Evolution said things, or implied things, about design and purpose, value and meaning, ancestry and destiny. It could not be ignored, and it was not ignored. And for a brief period in the summer of 1925, the "greatest show on earth" was not a circus tent run by Barnum & Bailey but a county courthouse in Dayton, Tennessee.

LITERATURE AND RELIGION: THE BIBLE

The metaphor of battle is least metaphorical in the many clashes concerning the Bible. In those instances, metaphor became reality as the bitterest passions were aroused, institutions torn apart, and careers ruined. Words like "inspiration," "infallibility," "plenary," and "inerrancy" competed against other words like "heresy," "atheism," "modernism," and "betrayal." Modern biblical scholarship, or to use a common and more commonly offensive term, "higher criticism" was in one sense only a special category of the science-versus-religion confrontation, but at the same time it was a category all unto itself. For now the "scientific" study of the Bible — empirical, verifiable, wholly without presuppositions or devotional predispositions — threatened to weaken and undermine, perhaps even to destroy, that foundation on which most of Western religion rested.

This challenge hit Protestantism hardest. For out of the Reformation had come a Protestant rejection of tradition in favor of an elevation of scripture. It was then commonly assumed, first, that the two could be completely separated, and, second, that scripture constituted a source, an authority of unshakable integrity. In the nineteenth century, both assumptions came under repeated attack. It was tradition that, by the fourth century of the Christian era, had determined the bounds of scripture. And it was scripture that within its own canon mirrored that development called tradition. Nothing in this world sprang forth full blown, fixed, unchanged and unchanging; all evolved, all developed. Even inspiration, even dogma, had a history. While Protestantism suffered most in seeking or resisting accommodation to this bitterly barbed edge of modernity, neither Catholicism nor Judaism escaped the persisting, nagging force of a "criticism" directed against that which had heretofore been immune to all criticism.

The results of this sharply focused fight are incalculable, for the battle goes on. But quite early one witnessed bruising confrontation and sweeping condemnation. One also witnessed, however, a rebirth of biblical investigation, translation, and interpretation. New societies were born, new commentaries provided, new archaeological expeditions undertaken, and a new intensity in searching the scriptures displayed on both sides. For liberals and conservatives alike, the question of what one did with and said about the Bible was insistent, adamant, and impossible to shake.

MODERNISM/FUNDAMENTALISM

Partaking of all the elements noted above (and of more, besides), the struggle between modernists and fundamentalists cannot be understood as a simple, single issue. At any one moment, the debate may have centered on one proposition or a specific article of faith, but behind each verbal dispute lay a universe of attitudes, approaches, methods, motives, sentiments, and predilections. Opponents rarely understood each other, hardly heard each other. Roman Catholicism faced the problems first in Europe, where so much that came to be tagged "modernism" first arose. Indeed, a good deal of what the Church officially condemned in 1907 could be located much more readily in Europe than in the United States. An earlier encyclical censuring "Americanism" was, despite the terminology, also aimed at ominous tendencies to be resisted in Europe no less than in America. Yet, parties or factions or wings clearly did exist within the Roman Catholic community in this country. The liberalizing influences, evident for example in the group agitating for a Catholic University of America (realized in 1888), found no support in the papal strictures about biblical investigation, public education, private religious feeling, error and its rights, and modern civilization in general. Indeed, the papal condemnation of 1907 was so sweeping, its administrative enforcement so efficient, that Catholic scholarship was stunted in its development for an entire generation or more.

In Protestantism, authority was decentralized, if not invisible. Consequently, all who wished spoke freely, published profusely, and contended against the opposing side unceasingly. Between the extremes of modernism and fundamentalism, a preponderant majority of Protestants hoped that the middle ground they thought they stood on really existed. This majority did not wish to turn its back upon modern philosophy, nor upon the evident blessings of modern science, nor upon the colleges which they had attended or their forefathers had founded. At the same time, however, they had no intention of turning their backs upon the "faith once delivered to the saints," nor upon those scriptures whose very words were woven into the fabric of their daily lives. So all they could do was live with tension and uncertainty, remembering that "all things work together for good to them that love God, to them who are called according to his purpose" (Romans 8:28).

Judaism, in its "denominational" separation into Reform, Conservative, and Orthodox, responded with at least that much variety to the several messages of modernity. Only in Reform, for example, did biblical criticism early find a home. At Hebrew Union College (Cincinnati, Ohio), Jewish scholars joined with Gentiles in exploring the merits of both textual and "higher" criticism. Conservative Judaism urged caution in any hasty abandonment of Mosaic laws, criticizing those too eager to prove themselves cosmopolitan citizens of a sophisticated and scientific world. Orthodoxy, which to some seemed only a vestige of medieval Judaism and therefore destined soon to wither away, preserved a fully observant community of believers, maintaining a strong "fence" around the Law (Torah), rejoicing in being God's covenanted and chosen people. For this status, as for one's own soul, one would not exchange a trendy and tawdry world.

THEOLOGICAL AFTERMATH

An old hymn concludes with the refrain, "And when the battle's over, we shall wear a crown, in the New Jerusalem." Whether or not the battle between modernism and fundamentalism was over in the 1940s and 1950s, none wore unchallenged crowns and none knew exactly where the New Jerusalem was to be found. Both sides were busy adjusting and regrouping, and both sides had been much distracted by depression and war. In the midst of great uncertainty and intellectual confusion, with the future cloudy and a bit scary, the path of wisdom turned toward the past.

The time of "neo's" had arrived: neo-Orthodox, neo-Thomist, neo-Fundamentalist. Whether attention fastened upon the sixteenth century, the thirteenth, or the first, the past appeared to hold more theological gold suitable for mining than did any vague claims staked in the future. Of course, a "neo" is never a precise replication of a "paleo." Such duplication is, to be sure, impossible; it is, moreover, undesirable—even to those whose theme song is "Give Me that Old Time Religion." The contemporary world poses problems and demands solutions for which no previous age provides the precise pattern. So whether the backward glance was toward the theology of the reformers, or the "high" scholasticism of Thomas Aquinas, or the charismatic assurance of the apostles, the theology that resulted belonged to the twentieth century—and to no other.

1. PHILOSOPHY AND RELIGION

William James (1842 – 1910)

Around the turn of the century, no one did more to make philosophy palatable (if not actually tasty) to the average American than William James. Nor in his frequent attention to religion has anyone proved more durable, this being true of many essays as well as the major monograph, The Varieties of Religious Experience, *first published in 1902. James, along with his less lionized contemporary, Charles S. Peirce (1839 – 1914), helped bring into being that characteristically American school of philosophy known as pragmatism. According to this view, the truth of a proposition lies in its predictability, its effect upon future possible experience. And in the view of William James, this gave great significance to religious attitudes and beliefs. For, as James explained in an essay first published in 1897, faith is full of meaning for it is full of productivity and predictive quality. Faith shapes destinies; it has momentous consequences. And if this be true, it is ridiculous — "trebly asinine" — for philosophers to ignore it or dismiss it.*

Now, there is one element of our active nature which the Christian religion has emphatically recognized, but which philosophers as a rule have with great insincerity tried to huddle out of sight in their pretension to found systems of absolute certainty. I mean the element of faith. Faith means belief in something concerning which doubt is still theoretically possible; and as the test of belief is willingness to act, one may say that faith is the readiness to act in a cause the prosperous issue of which is not certified to us in advance. It is in fact the same moral quality which we call courage in practical affairs; and there will be a very widespread tendency in men of vigorous nature to enjoy a certain amount of uncertainty in their philosophic creed, just as risk lends a zest to worldly activity. Absolutely certified philosophies seeking the *inconcussum** are fruits of mental natures in which the passion for identity

[Source: William James, *Essays on Faith and Morals* (New York: Longmans, Green and Co., 1949 [this essay, 1897]), pp. 90 – 92, 93 – 97.]
*constant, unshakable

313

(which we saw to be but one factor of the rational appetite) plays an abnormally exclusive part. In the average man, on the contrary, the power to trust, to risk a little beyond the literal evidence, is an essential function. Any mode of conceiving the universe which makes an appeal to this generous power, and makes the man seem as if he were individually helping to create the actuality of the truth whose metaphysical reality he is willing to assume, will be sure to be responded to by large numbers.

The necessity of faith as an ingredient in our mental attitude is strongly insisted on by the scientific philosophers of the present day; but by a singularly arbitrary caprice they say that it is only legitimate when used in the interests of one particular proposition, — the proposition, namely, that the course of nature is uniform. That nature will follow to-morrow the same laws that she follows to-day is, they all admit, a truth which no man can *know*; but in the interests of cognition as well as of action we must postulate or assume it. . . .

With regard to all other possible truths, however, a number of our most influential contemporaries think that an attitude of faith is not only illogical but shameful. Faith in a religious dogma for which there is no outward proof, but which we are tempted to postulate for our emotional interests, just as we postulate the uniformity of nature for our intellectual interests, is branded by Professor [Thomas] Huxley as "the lowest depth of immorality." Citations of this kind from leaders of the modern *Aufklärung* might be multiplied almost indefinitely. Take Professor [W. K.] Clifford's article on the 'Ethics of Belief.' He calls it 'guilt' and 'sin' to believe even the truth without 'scientific evidence.' But what is the use of being a genius, unless *with the same scientific evidence* as other men, one can reach more truth than they? . . .

The coil is about us, struggle as we may. The only escape from faith is mental nullity. What we enjoy most in a Huxley or a Clifford is not the professor with his learning, but the human personality ready to go in for what it feels to be right, in spite of all appearances. The concrete man has but one interest — to be right. That for him is the art of all arts, and all means are fair which help him to it. Naked he is flung into the world, and between him and nature there are no rules of civilized warfare. The rules of the scientific game, burdens of proof, presumptions, *experimenta crucis*, complete inductions, and the like, are only binding on those who enter that game. As a matter of fact we all more or less do enter it, because it helps us to our end. But if the means presume to frustrate the end and call us cheats for being right in advance of their slow aid, by guesswork or by hook or crook, what shall we say of them? Were all of Clifford's works, except the Ethics of Belief, forgotten, he might well figure in future treatises on psychology in place of the somewhat threadbare instance of the miser who has been led by the association of ideas to prefer his gold to all the goods he might buy therewith.

In short, if I am born with such a superior general reaction to evidence that I can guess right and act accordingly, and gain all that comes of right action, while my less gifted neighbor (paralyzed by his scruples and waiting for more evidence which he dares not anticipate, much as he longs to) still stands shivering on the brink, by what law shall I be forbidden to reap the advantages of my superior native sensitiveness? Of course I yield to my belief in such a case as this or distrust it, alike at my peril, just as I do in any of the great practical decisions of life. If my inborn faculties are good, I am a prophet; if poor, I am a failure: nature spews me out of her mouth, and there is an end to me. In the total game of life we stake our persons all the while; and if in its theoretic part our persons will help us to a conclusion, surely we should also stake them here, however inarticulate they may be.

But in being myself so very articulate in proving what to all readers with a sense for reality will seem of platitude, am I not wasting words? We cannot live or think at all without some degree of faith. Faith is synonymous with working hypothesis. The only difference is that while some hypotheses can be refuted in five minutes, others may defy ages. A chemist who conjectures that a certain wall-paper contains arsenic, and has faith enough to lead him to take the trouble to put some of it into a hydrogen bottle, finds out by the results of his action whether he was right or wrong. But theories like that of Darwin, or that of the kinetic constitution of matter, may exhaust the labors of generations in their corroboration, each tester of their truth proceeding in this simple way, — that he acts as if it were true, and expects the result to disappoint him if his assumption is false. The longer disappointment is delayed, the stronger grows his faith in his theory.

Now, in such questions as God, immortality, absolute morality, and free-will, no non-papal believer at the present day pretends his faith to be of an essentially different complexion; he can always doubt his creed. But his intimate persuasion is that the odds in its favor are strong enough to warrant him in acting all along on the assumption of its truth. His corroboration or repudiation by the nature of things may be deferred until the day of judgment. The uttermost he now means is something like this: "I *expect* then to triumph with tenfold glory; but if it should turn out, as indeed it may, that I have spent my days in a fool's paradise, why, better have been the dupe of *such* a dreamland than the cunning reader of a world like that which then beyond all doubt unmasks itself to view." . . .

Now, I wish to show what to my knowledge has never been clearly pointed out, that belief (as measured by action) not only does and must continually outstrip scientific evidence, but that there is a certain class of truths of whose reality belief is a factor as well as a confessor; and that as regards this class of truths faith is not only licit and pertinent, but essential and indispensable. The truths cannot become true till our faith has made them so.

Suppose, for example, that I am climbing in the Alps, and have had the ill-luck to work myself into a position from which the only escape is by a terrible leap. Being without similar experience, I have no evidence of my ability to perform it successfully; but hope and confidence in myself make me sure I shall not miss my aim, and nerve my feet to execute what without those subjective emotions would perhaps have been impossible. But suppose that, on the contrary, the emotions of fear and mistrust preponderate; or suppose that, having just read the Ethics of Belief, I feel it would be sinful to act upon an assumption unverified by previous experience, — why, then I shall hesitate so long that at last, exhausted and trembling, and launching myself in a moment of despair, I miss my foothold and roll into the abyss. In this case (and it is one of an immense class) the part of wisdom clearly is to believe what one desires; for the belief is one of the indispensable preliminary conditions of the realization of its object. *There are then cases where faith creates its own verification.* Believe, and you shall be right, for you shall save yourself; doubt, and you shall again be right, for you shall perish. The only difference is that to believe is greatly to your advantage.

The future movements of the stars or the facts of past history are determined now once for all, whether I like them or not. They are given irrespective of my wishes, and in all that concerns truths like these subjective preference should have no part; it can only obscure the judgment. But in every fact into which there enters an element of personal contribution on my part, as soon as this personal contribution demands a certain degree of subjective energy which, in its turn, calls for a certain amount of faith in the result, — so that, after all, the future fact is conditioned by my present faith in it, — how trebly asinine would it be for me to deny myself the use of the subjective method, the method of belief based on desire!

Josiah Royce (1885 – 1916)

A native of California but, like James, associated principally with Harvard University in his mature years, Royce was a philosophical idealist, the last great representative of a disappearing breed. Royce was also the last major philosopher on the American scene to mix philosophy with theology so easily, so unselfconsciously. He could take a biblical text (in this instance Romans 7), give exegesis like a preacher and explication like a philosopher. His first major work, The Religious Aspect of Philosophy *(1885), augured a life-long interest in religion, for it was religion (he later noted) that drove him to philosophy. Almost thirty years later, he concentrated on "The Problem of Christianity," developing the three "essential ideas" of that religion: the Beloved Community, the individual's moral responsibility, and atonement. The excerpt below concerns the second of these ideas, that moral burden which, as George Santayana said, "spoiled the pantheistic serenity" of Royce's system. But it was that moral burden which also gave human life its unique dignity and its special purpose.*

[Source: Josiah Royce, *The Problem of Christianity* (with a new introduction by John E. Smith) (Chicago: University of Chicago Press, 1968 [1913]), pp. 99–100, 102–4.]

"All things excellent," says Spinoza, "are as difficult as they are rare;" and Spinoza's word here repeats a lesson that nearly all of the world's religious and moral teachers agree in emphasizing. Whether such a guide speaks simply of "excellence," or uses the distinctively religious phraseology and tells us about the way to "salvation," he is sure, if he is wise, to recognize, and on occasion to say, that whoever is to win the highest goal must first learn to bear a heavy burden. It also belongs to the common lore of the sages to teach that this burden is much more due to the defects of our human nature than to the hostility of fortune. "We ourselves make our time short for our task": such comments are as trite as they are well founded in the facts of life.

But among the essential ideas of Christianity, there is one which goes beyond this common doctrine of the serious-minded guides of humanity. For this idea defines the moral burden, to which the individual who seeks salvation is subject, in so grave a fashion that many lovers of mankind, and, in particular, many modern minds, have been led to declare that so much of Christian doctrine, at least in the forms in which it is usually stated, is an unreasonable and untrue feature of the faith. This idea I stated at the close of our first lecture, side by side with the two other ideas of Christianity which I propose, in these lectures, to discuss. The idea of the Church, — of the universal community, — which was our topic in the second lecture, is expressed by the assertion that there is a real and divinely significant spiritual community to which all must belong who are to win the true goal of life. The idea of the moral burden of the individual is expressed by maintaining that (as I ventured to state this idea in my own words): "The individual human being is by nature subject to some overwhelming moral burden from which, if unaided, he cannot escape. Both because of what has technically been called original sin, and because of the sins that he himself has committed, the individual is doomed to a spiritual ruin from which only a divine intervention can save him."

This doctrine constitutes the second of the three Christian ideas that I propose to discuss. I must take it up in the present lecture. . . . Let us turn, then, to our new topic. The moralists, as we have already pointed out, are generally agreed that whoever is to win the highest things must indeed learn to bear a heavy moral burden. But the Christian idea now in question adds to the common lore of the moralists the sad word: "*The individual cannot bear this burden.* His tainted nature forbids; his guilt weighs him down. If by salvation one means a winning of the true goal of life, the individual, unaided, cannot be saved. And the help that he needs for bearing his burden must come from some source entirely above his own level, — from a source which is, in some genuine sense, divine."

The most familiar brief statement of the present idea is that of Paul in the passage in the seventh chapter of the epistle to the Romans, which culminates in this cry: "O wretched man that I am!" What the Apostle, in the context of this passage, expounds as his interpretation both of his own religious experience and of human nature in general, has been much more fully stated in the form of well-known doctrines, and has formed the subject-matter for ages of Christian controversy.

In working out his own theory of the facts which he reports, Paul was led to certain often cited statements about the significance and the effect of Adam's legendary transgression. And, as a consequence of these words and of a few other Pauline passages, technical problems regarding original sin, predestination, and related topics have come to occupy so large a place in the history of theology, that, to many minds, Paul's own report of personal experience, and his statements about plain facts of human nature, have been lost to sight (so far as concerns the idea of the moral burden of the individual) in a maze of controversial complications. To numerous modern minds the whole idea of the moral burden of the individual seems, therefore, to be an invention of theologians, and to possess little or no religious importance.

Yet I believe that such a view is profoundly mistaken. The idea of the moral burden of the individual is, as we shall see, not without its inherent complications, and not without its relation to very difficult problems, both ethical and metaphysical. Yet, of the three essential ideas of Christianity which constitute our list, it is, relatively speaking, the simplest, and the one which can be most easily interpreted to the enlightened common sense of the modern man. Its most familiar difficulties are due rather to the accidents of controversy than to the nature of the subject.

The fate which has beset those who have dealt with the technical efforts to express this idea is partly explicable by the general history of religion; but is also partly due to varying personal factors, such as those which determined Paul's own training. This fate may be summed up by saying that, regarding just this matter of the moral burden of the individual, those who, by virtue of their genius or of their experience, have most known what they meant, have least succeeded in making clear to others what they know.

Paul, for instance, grasped the essential meaning of the moral burden of the individual with a perfectly straightforward veracity of understanding. What he saw, as to this matter, he saw with tragic clearness, and upon the basis of a type of experience that, in our own day, we can verify, as we shall soon see, much more widely than was possible for him. But when he put his doctrine into words, both his Rabbinical lore, and his habits of interpreting tradition, troubled his speech; and the passages which embody his theory of the sinfulness of man remain as difficult and as remote from his facts, as his report of these facts of life themselves is eloquent and true.

Similar has been the fortune of nearly all subsequent theology regarding the technical treatment of this topic. Yet growing human experience, through all the Christian ages, has kept the topic near to life; and today it is in closer touch with life than ever. The idea of the moral burden of the individual seems, to many cheerful minds, austere; but, if it is grave and stern, it is grave with the gravity of life, and stern only as the call of life, to any awakened mind, ought to be stern. If the traditional technicalities have obscured it, they have not been able to affect its deeper meaning or its practical significance. Rightly interpreted, it forms, I think, not only an essential feature of Christianity, but an indispensable part of every religious and moral view of life which considers man's business justly, and does so with a reasonable regard for the larger connections of our obligations and of our powers.

Alfred North Whitehead (1861 – 1947)

Also at Harvard (from 1924 to 1936), Whitehead brought to the problems of philosophy and religion a background strikingly different from that of James or Royce. A native of England and son of a Church of England clergyman, Whitehead began his academic contributions in the field of mathematics, his first major work being A Treatise on Universal Algebra *(1898). Between 1910 and 1913 Whitehead joined with Bertrand Russell in writing the epoch-making* Principia Mathematica, *thereby establishing his reputation as one of the world's front-rank thinkers. Soon thereafter he turned his attention to persisting problems of metaphysics and cosmology. While at Harvard, he published his major work in this area,* Process and Reality, *the final chapter of which is entitled (with grand simplicity) "God and the World." God is Process rather than static Being; God is Love rather than established Ruler; God moves by persuasion rather than by coercion, which is why —Whitehead explained —the mills of the gods grind so slowly. Great ideas, including great religious ideas, need time to work their way — say a thousand or two thousand years —"nerving the race in its slow ascent"* (Adventures of Ideas, *chap. 2, section V).*

So long as the temporal world is conceived as a self-sufficient completion of the creative act, explicable by its derivation from an ultimate principle which is at once eminently real and the unmoved mover, from this conclusion there is no escape: the best that we can say of the turmoil is, 'For so he giveth his beloved — sleep.' This is the message of religions of the Buddhistic type, and in some sense it is true. In this final discussion we have to ask, whether metaphysical principles impose the belief that it is the whole truth. The complexity of the world must be reflected in the answer. It is childish to enter upon thought with the simple-minded question, What is the world made of? The task of reason is to fathom the deeper depths of the many-sidedness of things. We must not expect simple answers to far-reaching questions. However far our gaze penetrates, there are always heights beyond which block our vision.

[Source: Alfred North Whitehead, *Process and Reality: An Essay in Cosmology* (New York: Harper & Brothers, 1957 [1929]), pp. 519–21.]

The notion of God as the 'unmoved mover' is derived from Aristotle, at least so far as Western thought is concerned. The notion of God as 'eminently real' is a favourite doctrine of Christian theology. The combination of the two into the doctrine of an aboriginal, eminently real, transcendent creator, at whose fiat the world came into being, and whose imposed will it obeys, is the fallacy which has infused tragedy into the histories of Christianity and of Mahometanism.

When the Western world accepted Christianity, Caesar conquered; and the received text of Western theology was edited by his lawyers. The code of Justinian and the theology of Justinian are two volumes expressing one movement of the human spirit. The brief Galilean vision of humility flickered throughout the ages, uncertainly. In the official formulation of the religion it has assumed the trivial form of the mere attribution to the Jews that they cherished a misconception about their Messiah. But the deeper idolatry, of the fashioning of God in the image of the Egyptian, Persian, and Roman imperial rulers, was retained. The Church gave unto God the attributes which belonged exclusively to Caesar.

In the great formative period of theistic philosophy, which ended with the rise of Mahometanism, after a continuance coeval with civilization, three strains of thought emerge which, amid many variations in detail, respectively fashion God in the image of an imperial ruler, God in the image of a personification of moral energy, God in the image of an ultimate philosophical principle. Hume's *Dialogues* criticize unanswerably these modes of explaining the system of the world.

The three schools of thought can be associated respectively with the divine Caesars, the Hebrew prophets, and Aristotle. But Aristotle was antedated by Indian, and Buddhistic, thought; the Hebrew prophets can be paralleled in traces of earlier thought; Mahometanism and the divine Caesars merely represent the most natural, obvious, theistic idolatrous symbolism, at all epochs and places.

The history of theistic philosophy exhibits various stages of combination of these three diverse ways of entertaining the problem. There is, however, in the Galilean origin of Christianity yet another suggestion which does not fit very well with any of the three main strands of thought. It does not emphasize the ruling Caesar, or the ruthless moralist, or the unmoved mover. It dwells upon the tender elements in the world, which slowly and in quietness operate by love; and it finds purpose in the present immediacy of a kingdom not of this world. Love neither rules, nor is it unmoved; also it is a little oblivious as to morals. It does not look to the future; for it finds its own reward in the immediate present.

Apart from any reference to existing religions as they are, or as they ought to be, we must investigate dispassionately what the metaphysical principles, here developed, require on these points, as to the nature of God. There is nothing here in the nature of proof. There is merely the confrontation of the theoretic system with a certain rendering of the facts. But the unsystematized report upon the facts is itself highly controversial, and the system is confessedly inadequate. The deductions from it in this particular sphere of thought cannot be looked upon as more than suggestions as to how the problem is transformed in the light of that system. What follows is merely an attempt to add another speaker to that masterpiece, Hume's *Dialogues Concerning Natural Religion*. Any cogency of argument entirely depends upon elucidation of somewhat exceptional elements in our conscious experience — those elements which may roughly be classed together as religious and moral intuitions.

John Dewey (1859 – 1952)

Like each of the philosophers already treated, Dewey believed that philosophy must relate directly to life, must deal with the problems of men and women; not of philosophers alone. "While saints are engaged in introspection, burly sinners run the world." Dewey was determined to end that deplorable state of affairs by offering a Reconstruction in Philosophy *(1920) that would produce a reconstruction in society. He came closer than most. Unlike the three philosophers above, however, Dewey's interest in religion was more peripheral than central. Art, logic, politics, science, education — these all gripped him far more. In 1934, however, as the nation's best known and most influential philosopher, John Dewey (professor at Columbia University) was invited to Yale to deliver the Terry lectures which, according to their founder, should treat of "a broadened and purified religion." The resulting book,* A Common Faith, *demonstrated little confidence in historic religions and none in revelation. One may have faith, but faith in and a dedication to the "one method for ascertaining fact and truth — that conveyed by the word 'scientific' in its most general and generous sense. . . ."*

The obvious and simple facts of the case are that some views about the origin and constitution of the world and man, some views about the course of human history and personages and incidents in that history, have become so interwoven with religion as to be identified with it. On the other hand, the growth of knowledge and of its methods and tests has been such as to make acceptance of these beliefs increasingly onerous and even impossible for large numbers of cultivated men and women. With such persons, the result is that the more these ideas are used as the basis and justification of a religion, the more dubious that religion becomes.

Protestant denominations have largely abandoned the idea that particular ecclesiastic sources can authoritatively determine cosmic, historic and theo-

[Source: John Dewey, *A Common Faith* (New Haven: Yale University Press, 1934), pp. 30–33.]

logical beliefs. The more liberal among them have at least mitigated the older belief that individual hardness and corruption of heart are the causes of intellectual rejection of the intellectual apparatus of the Christian religion. But these denominations have also, with exceptions numerically insignificant, retained a certain indispensable minimum of intellectual content. They ascribe peculiar religious force to certain literary documents and certain historic personages. Even when they have greatly reduced the bulk of intellectual content to be accepted, they have insisted at least upon theism and the immortality of the individual.

It is no part of my intention to rehearse in any detail the weighty facts that collectively go by the name of the conflict of science and religion — a conflict that is not done away with by calling it a conflict of science with theology, as long as even a minimum of intellectual assent is prescribed as essential. The impact of astronomy not merely upon the older cosmogony of religion but upon elements of creeds dealing with historic events — witness the idea of ascent into heaven — is familiar. Geological discoveries have displaced creation myths which once bulked large. Biology has revolutionized conceptions of soul and mind which once occupied a central place in religious beliefs and ideas, and this science has made a profound impression upon ideas of sin, redemption, and immortality. Anthropology, history and literary criticism have furnished a radically different version of the historic events and personages upon which Christian religions have built. Psychology is already opening to us natural explanations of phenomena so extraordinary that once their supernatural origin was, so to say, the natural explanation.

The significant bearing for my purpose of all this is that new methods of inquiry and reflection have become for the educated man today the final arbiter of all questions of fact, existence, and intellectual assent. Nothing less than a revolution in the "seat of intellectual authority" has taken place. This revolution, rather than any particular aspect of its impact upon this and that religious belief, is the central thing. In this revolution, every defeat is a stimulus to renewed inquiry; every victory won is the open door to more discoveries, and every discovery is a new seed planted in the soil of intelligence, from which grow fresh plants with new fruits. The mind of man is being habituated to a new method and ideal: There is but one sure road of access to truth — the road of patient, cooperative inquiry operating by means of observation, experiment, record and controlled reflection.

The scope of the change is well illustrated by the fact that whenever a particular outpost is surrendered it is usually met by the remark from a liberal theologian that the particular doctrine or supposed historic or literary tenet surrendered was never, after all, an intrinsic part of religious belief, and that without it the true nature of religion stands out more clearly than before. Equally significant is the growing gulf between fundamentalists and liberals in the churches. What is not realized — although perhaps it is more definitely seen by fundamentalists than by liberals — is that the issue does not concern this and that piecemeal *item* of belief, but centers in the question of the method by which any and every item of intellectual belief is to be arrived at and justified.

The positive lesson is that religious qualities and values if they are real at all are not bound up with any single item of intellectual assent, not even that of the existence of the God of theism; and that, under existing conditions, the religious function in experience can be emancipated only through surrender of the whole notion of special truths that are religious by their own nature, together with the idea of peculiar avenues of access to such truths. For were we to admit that there is but one method for ascertaining fact and truth — that conveyed by the word "scientific" in its most general and generous sense — no discovery in any branch of knowledge and inquiry could then disturb the faith that is religious. I should describe this faith as the unification of the self through allegiance to inclusive ideal ends, which imagination presents to us and to which the human will responds as worthy of controlling our desires and choices.

George Santayana (1863 – 1952)

Santayana has already been quoted above (p. 316); indeed, it is difficult to resist quoting Santayana. He wrote widely and well: poetry, fiction, reminiscence, philosophy. Born in Spain, growing up in Boston, lecturing at Oxford, the Sorbonne, and Harvard, and dying in a convent hospital in Rome, Santayana was the true cosomopolitan. In his twenty years or more at Harvard (mostly from 1889 to 1912), Santayana shrewdly observed and later pointedly wrote about Character and Opinion in the United States *(1920). In "A Brief History of My Opinions," written in 1930, he noted: ". . . I have always set myself down officially as a Catholic: but this is a matter of sympathy and allegiance, not of philosophy." The sympathy which was real tended to grow stronger as Santayana grew older. But even in earlier years, he defended Catholicism against the modern tendency to subject it either to a cold impersonal rationalism or to a purely private mysticism. Here he anticipates some of the discussion to be found later in this chapter.*

Modernism is the infiltration into minds that begin by being Catholic and wish to remain so of two contemporary influences: one the rationalistic study of the Bible and of church history, the other modern philosophy, especially

[Source: George Santayana, *Winds of Doctrine* (London: J. M. Dent & Sons, 1913), pp. 40 – 43, 56 – 57.]

in its mystical and idealistic forms. The sensitiveness of the modernists to these two influences is creditable to them as men, however perturbing it may be to them as Catholics; for what makes them adopt the views of rationalistic historians is simply the fact that those views seem, in substance, convincingly true; and what makes them wander into transcendental speculations is the warmth of their souls, needing to express their faith anew, and to follow their inmost inspiration, wherever it may lead them. A scrupulous honesty in admitting the probable facts of history, and a fresh up-welling of mystical experience, these are the motives, creditable to any spiritual man, that have made modernists of so many. But these excellent things appear in the modernists under rather unfortunate circumstances. For the modernists to begin with are Catholics, and usually priests; they are pledged to a fixed creed, touching matters both of history and of philosophy; and it would be a marvel if rationalistic criticism of the Bible and rationalistic church history confirmed that creed on its historical side, or if irresponsible personal speculations, in the manner of Ritschl* or of M. Bergson,** confirmed its metaphysics.

I am far from wishing to suggest that an orthodox Christian cannot be scrupulously honest in admitting the probable facts, or cannot have a fresh spiritual experience, or frame an original philosophy. But what we think probable hangs on our standard of probability and of evidence; the spiritual experiences that come to us are according to our disposition and affections; and any new philosophy we frame will be an answer to the particular problems that beset us, and an expression of the solutions we hope for. Now this standard of probability, this disposition, and these problems and hopes may be those of a Christian or they may not. The true Christian, for instance, will begin by regarding miracles as probable; he will either believe he has experienced them in his own person, or hope for them earnestly; nothing will seem to him more natural, more in consonance with the actual texture of life, than that they should have occurred abundantly and continuously in the past. When he finds the record of one he will not inquire, like the rationalist, how that false record could have been concocted; but rather he will ask how the rationalist, in spite of so many witnesses to the contrary, has acquired his fixed assurance of the universality of the commonplace. An answer perhaps could be offered of which the rationalist need not be ashamed. We might say that faith in the universality of the commonplace (in its origin, no doubt, simply an imaginative presumption) is justified by our systematic mastery of matter in the arts. The rejection of miracles *a priori* expresses a conviction that the laws by which we can always control or predict the movement of matter govern that movement universally; and evidently, if the material

---

*Albrecht Ritschl (1822– 89), German Protestant theologian who emphasized the inner life of Christ as the basis for theology.
**Henri Bergson (1859– 1941), French philosopher who also stressed the inner life and the direct insights of conscience.

course of history is fixed mechanically, the mental and moral course of it is thereby fixed on the same plan; for a mind not expressed somehow in matter cannot be revealed to the historian. This may be good philosophy, but we could not think so if we were good Christians. We should then expect to move matter by prayer. Rationalistic history and criticism are therefore based, as Pius X. most accurately observed in his Encyclical on modernism, on rationalistic philosophy; and we might add that rationalistic philosophy is based on practical art, and that practical art, by which we help ourselves, like Prometheus, and make instruments of what religion worships, when this art is carried beyond the narrowest bounds, is the essence of pride and irreligion. Miners, machinists, and artisans are irreligious by trade. Religion is the love of life in the consciousness of impotence.

Similarly, the spontaneous insight of Christians and their new philosophies will express a Christian disposition. The chief problems in them will be sin and redemption; the conclusion will be some fresh intuition of divine love and heavenly beatitude. It would be no sign of originality in a Christian to begin discoursing on love like Ovid or on heaven like Mohammed, or stop discoursing on them at all; it would be a sign of apostasy.

Now the modernists' criterion of probability in history or of worthiness in philosophy is not the Christian criterion. It is that of their contemporaries outside the church, who are rationalists in history and egotists or voluntarists in philosophy. The biblical criticism and mystical speculations of the modernists call for no special remark; they are such as any studious or spiritual person, with no inherited religion, might compose in our day. But what is remarkable and well-nigh incredible is that even for a moment they should have supposed this non-Christian criterion in history and this non-Christian direction in metaphysics compatible with adherence to the Catholic church. That seems to presuppose, in men who in fact are particularly thoughtful and learned, an inexplicable ignorance of history, of theology, and of the world. . . .

Now religious experience, as I have said, may take other forms than the Christian, and within Christianity it may take other forms than the Catholic; but the Catholic form is as good as any intrinsically for the devotee himself, and it has immense advantages over its probable rivals in charm, in comprehensiveness, in maturity, in internal rationality, in external adaptability; so much so that a strong anti-clerical government, like the French, cannot safely leave the church to be overwhelmed by the forces of science, good sense, ridicule, frivolity, and avarice (all strong forces in France), but must use violence as well to do it. In the English church, too, it is not those who accept the deluge, the resurrection, and the sacraments only as symbols that are the vital party, but those who accept them literally; for only these have anything to say to the poor, or to the rich, that can refresh them. In a frank supernaturalism, in a tight clericalism, not in a pleasant secularisation, lies the sole hope of the church. Its sole dignity also lies there. It will not convert

the world; it never did and it never could. It will remain a voice crying in
the wilderness; but it will believe what it cries, and there will be some to
listen to it in the future, as there have been many in the past. As to modernism,
it is suicide. It is the last of those concessions to the spirit of the world which
half-believers and double-minded prophets have always been found making;
but it is a mortal concession. It concedes everything; for it concedes that
everything in Christianity, as Christians hold it, is an illusion.

2. SCIENCE AND RELIGION

Confrontation

John W. Draper (1811– 82)

The "conflict" or "warfare" between science and religion should not be thought of as a battle by only one side: theologians fighting and sniping away while scientists, hidden away in their monastic laboratories, kept a steady course in their pursuit of Truth. Scientists fought battles too. In the late nineteenth and well into the twentieth century, many scientists were convinced that religion was on its way out and that it ought to be on its way out. Like magic and superstition, religion was a stage of civilization now outmoded, now outgrown. John W. Draper, son of a Methodist minister, received his medical degree from the University of Pennsylvania in 1836, soon thereafter joining the science faculty at New York University where he made notable contributions in chemistry, photography, telegraphy, and physiology. But he is represented here as scientist turned historian, a historian who is delighted to report that the "ecclesiastical spirit no longer inspires the policy of the world."

Whoever has had an opportunity of becoming acquainted with the mental condition of the intelligent classes in Europe and America, must have perceived that there is a great and rapidly-increasing departure from the public religious faith, and that, while among the more frank this divergence is not concealed, there is a far more extensive and far more dangerous secession, private and unacknowledged.

So wide-spread and so powerful is this secession, that it can neither be treated with contempt nor with punishment. It cannot be extinguished by derision, by vituperation, or by force. The time is rapidly approaching when it will give rise to serious political results.

Ecclesiastical spirit no longer inspires the policy of the world. Military

[Source: John W. Draper, *History of the Conflict of Religion and Science* (New York: D. Appleton & Co., 1889), pp. v– viii.]

fervor in behalf of faith has disappeared. Its only souvenirs are the marble effigies of crusading knights, reposing in the silent crypts of churches on their tombs.

That a crisis is impending is shown by the attitude of the great powers toward the papacy. The papacy represents the ideas and aspirations of two-thirds of the population of Europe. It insists on a political supremacy in accordance with its claims to a divine origin and mission, and a restoration of the medieval order of things, loudly declaring that it will accept no rec-onciliation with modern civilization.

The antagonism we thus witness between Religion and Science is the con-tinuation of a struggle that commenced when Christianity began to attain political power. A divine revelation must necessarily be intolerant of contra-diction; it must repudiate all improvement in itself, and view with disdain that arising from the progressive intellectual development of man. But our opinions on every subject are continually liable to modification, from the irresistible advance of human knowledge.

Can we exaggerate the importance of a contention in which every thought-ful person must take part whether he will or not? In a matter so solemn as that of religion, all men, whose temporal interests are not involved in existing institutions, earnestly desire to find the truth. They seek information as to the subjects in dispute, and as to the conduct of the disputants.

The history of Science is not a mere record of isolated discoveries; it is a narrative of the conflict of two contending powers, the expansive force of the human intellect on one side, and the compression arising from traditionary faith and human interests on the other.

No one has hitherto treated the subject from this point of view. Yet from this point it presents itself to us as a living issue — in fact, as the most important of all living issues.

A few years ago, it was the politic and therefore the proper course to abstain from all allusion to this controversy, and to keep it as far as possible in the background. The tranquillity of society depends so much on the stability of its religious convictions, that no one can be justified in wantonly disturbing them. But faith is in its nature unchangeable, stationary; Science is in its nature progressive; and eventually a divergence between them, impossible to conceal, must take place. It then becomes the duty of those whose lives have made them familiar with both modes of thought, to present modestly, but firmly, their views; to compare the antagonistic pretensions calmly, impar-tially, philosophically. History shows that, if this be not done, social misfor-tunes, disastrous and enduring, will ensue. When the old mythological religion of Europe broke down under the weight of its own inconsistencies, neither the Roman emperors nor the philosophers of those times did any thing ade-quate for the guidance of public opinion. They left religious affairs to take their chance, and accordingly those affairs fell into the hands of ignorant and infuriated ecclesiastics, parasites, eunuchs, and slaves.

The intellectual night which settled on Europe, in consequence of that great neglect of duty, is passing away; we live in the daybreak of better things. Society is anxiously expecting light, to see in what direction it is drifting. It plainly discerns that the track along which the voyage of civilization has thus far been made, has been left; and that a new departure, on an unknown sea, has been taken.

John Wesley Powell (1834– 1902)

Powell as geologist is best known for his explorations of the Colorado River. In those and other western travels, he studied the American Indian, defended the natural environment, and reflected on the course of human development — especially as this development related to science and religion. Like Draper, Powell saw the old domination of men's minds by religion as an earlier phase of civilization now happily passing away. We have moved from savagery through barbarism to what Powell calls "monarchacy." From there, with the aid of science, we can enter into a new age of democratic enlightenment. And in the bright future, it will be science, not religion, that gives hope; science, not religion, that offers the "pure water of truth" in place of the "hashish of mystery." In this excerpt, he describes that evolution from barbarism to "monarchacy."

The [physical theism] of barbarism is transformed into [psychological theism], and the deities have psychic attributes, though to a large extent the names of the deities remain the same. Thus there is a god of war and a god of love, a god of agriculture and a god of commerce, a god of hunting and a god of fishing, and in like manner the chief psychic attributes of mankind and the vocation which they follow are all represented by deities in the pantheon. At first the gods constitute a tribe, then they inhabit a city which is above on some mountain like Olympus or in the sky. As time goes on the constitution of the tribe of deities is changed, and the supreme deity is exalted more and more until a qualified monotheism is established.

Worship changes and terpsichorean ceremonies are gradually abandoned, sacrifices are continued, but modified and ameliorated, becoming symbolic. Ceremony is refined and becomes a vast system of symbolism, so that worship becomes highly poetical. Gradually a new element is added to religion, and at last becomes its chief characteristic. Gods who were supposed to be pleased with dancing and then pleased with oblations are now supposed to be best pleased with opinions, and to be worshipped in spirit and in truth through creeds that work their effects in the hearts of men impelling them to righteous conduct. Religion is fiducial, and men are held to be pious who acknowledge

[Source: John Wesley Powell, *The Monist*, 8 (1898), 199–200, 203–4.]

God in all their ways. Another change comes, for men pray less for present blessings and more for blessings in the future world.

The crime of crimes in savagery is witchcraft, in which it is supposed that the gods are induced to do evil to men. This crime lasts on through barbarism and is punished with still greater rigor; it still continues in the third stage and those who practice it are condemned to death. In barbarism the crime of blasphemy is developed, consisting in the omission of rites or in acts of disrespect. This also appears in the third stage. In monarchacy yet a new crime is developed, for creed now becomes essential and the heretic receives more horrible punishment than the witch or the blasphemer.

During the stage of monarchacy six great religions were developed: Judaism, Confucianism, Hindooism, Buddhism, Islamism, and Christianity. In all these religions the priests are propagandists and desire to make their doctrines universal. The great majority of the peoples of the globe are worshippers in one or another of these systems, but there are a few followers of Zoroaster and of Lau-tsze, a few barbarians, and a few savages. Idolatry has never been a religion, but in all the three stages idols are found as insignia of shrines. . . .

The schools were devoted to philosophy and disputation. But little by little the disciplines of science, when they could no longer be ignored, were introduced into the seats of learning. The leaven worked a transformation, so that the schools became agencies of research and instruction in science as well as in philosophy. Gradually philosophy itself came to be known as metaphysics by the accident of a word. At last schools, individuals, and finally governments were enlisted in the work of research, and metaphysics has been relegated to a discipline for one of the years or even one of the scholastic terms in the life of the student. The public schools, colleges, and universities are now engaged mainly in the teaching of science. At last a fourth factor or potent mental agency in civilization has been developed, so that now industry, militancy, religion, and science are the four supreme agencies of change, and the new agency subordinates them all.

It is important to note here the metamorphosis wrought on religion by science, which comes to purify but not to slay. Not as the ages go by, not as the centuries lapse, but as decades fly, a change is wrought in the human conception of the attributes of deity. The pleasure of worship is becoming the contemplation of perfection, the form of worship the agency of instruction, the cause of worship the love of humanity, the purpose of worship the purification of conduct. This is the ideal state to which religion is tending, and it must be understood in order properly to appreciate the characteristics of the existing religions. In the primitive world religions were many, because tribes were many and languages many, names many, and totems many; but they were all on one plan, to secure one purpose, namely, that of pleasure, and to give pleasure to the gods. They were still many in barbarism, though not so many, but all designed to obtain welfare and to give welfare to ancestors. Then religions became few and sought to yield tribute of praise and allegiance to gods, and to gain bliss hereafter with incidental prosperity now. Much of ceremonial worship remains yet in this the first period of the new stage in the evolution of religion. Much of theoretic and practical sacrifice remains; much of creed remains, but more of scientific truth. As this last agency approaches perfection religion advances, for science has no conflict with it but only with metaphysics.

From time to time during the stage of monarchacy prophets arose who became great teachers. Seeing that true ceremony is only impressive symbolism, that true sacrifice is only immolation of unwise desire, and that true creed is only expression of opinion, and being profoundly convinced that true religion is righteous deed, they sought to convert men to better ways and taught a religion of ethics. Some of these great teachers for a time were successful, but by reason of ignorance and sin disciples continually relapsed into ceremony, sacrifice, and creed as true religion and forgot religion itself. But when Moses and Confucius and Buddha and Mahomet and Jesus could teach the world through the magical speech of books, great teachers multiplied and ethical religions gained ground. In democracy one of the great historic religions prevails, and has attained to Catholicity in that stage; though it has many subdivisions, the teaching of Jesus ever more and more in the spirit of the Sermon on the Mount is becoming the religion of the people. Though this religion is represented by diverse ceremonies and by differing theories of sacrifice, it is unified in practical ethics, but not in theoretical ethics. As the years pass, insistence on ceremony, insistence on sacrifice, and insistence on creed grows less and less, while instruction in ethics grows more and more. Ethical religion, though now often vaguely taught, will triumph in Catholicity.

T. DeWitt Talmage (1832–1902)

An almost exact contemporary of Powell's, the popular Calvinist preacher saw science more as menace than as salvation. A graduate of the University of the City of New York and of New Brunswick Seminary in New Jersey, Talmage achieved his great fame in Brooklyn's Free Tabernacle, "free" in the sense that no pew rents were charged, but also free in the sense that Talmage stood above denominational discipline. This pulpit orator inspired thousands with his "Talmagic," and his collected sermons fill twenty volumes. The notion of evolution, if that was the best science could do, did not speak well for science. It was a notion "atheistic and absurd," a "stenchful and

[Source: T. DeWitt Talmage, "The Missing Link," in *Live Coals* (New York: Wilbur B. Ketcham, 1885), pp. 271–75.]

damnable doctrine." Any true Christian would be foolish to trade that de-
grading dogma for the ennobling teaching found in the Bible.

Evolution is one great mystery. It hatches out fifty mysteries, and the fifty hatch out a thousand, and the thousand hatch out a million. Why, my brother, not admit the one great mystery of God, and have that settle all the other mysteries? I can more easily appreciate the fact that God, by one stroke of His omnipotence could make man, than I could realize how, out of five millions of ages, He could have evolved one, putting on a little here and a little there. It would have been just as great a miracle for God to have turned an orang-outang into a man as to make a man out and out — the one job just as big as the other.

It seems to me we had better let God have a little place in our world somewhere. It seems to me if we cannot have Him make all creatures, we had better have Him make two or three. There ought to be some place where He could stay without interfering with the evolutionists. "No," says Darwin, and so for years he is trying to raise fan-tailed pigeons, and to turn these fan-tail pigeons into some other kind of pigeon, or to have them go into something that is not a pigeon — turning them into quail, or barnyard fowl, or brown thresher. But pigeon it is. And others have tried with the ox and the dog and the horse, but they stayed in their species. If they attempt to cross over it is a hybrid, and a hybrid is always sterile and goes into extinction. There has been only one successful attempt to pass over from speechless animal to the articulation of man, and that was the attempt which Baalam witnessed in the beast that he rode; but an angel of the Lord, with drawn sword, soon stopped that long-eared evolutionist.

But, says some one, "If we can not have God make a man let us have Him make a horse." "Oh, no!" says Huxley, in his great lectures in New York several years ago. No, he does not want any God around the premises. God did not make the horse. The horse came of the pliohippus, and the pliohippus came from the protohippus, and the protohippus came from the mio-hippus, and the mio-hippus came from the meshohippus, and the meshohippus came from the orohippus, and so away back, all the living creatures, we trace it in a line, until we get to the moneron, and no evidence of divine intermeddling with the creation until you get to the moneron, and that, Huxley says, is of so low a form of life that the probability is it just made itself, or was the result of spontaneous generation. What a narrow escape from the necessity of having a God.

As near as I can tell, these evolutionists seem to think that God at the start had not made up His mind as to exactly what He would make, and having made up his mind partially, He has been changing it all through the ages. I believe God made the world as He wanted to have it, and that the happiness of all the species will depend upon their staying in the species where they were created.

But, my friends, evolution is not only infidel and atheistic and absurd; it is *brutalizing in its tendencies*. If there is anything in the world that will make a man bestial in his habits it is the idea that he was descended from the beast. Why, according to the idea of these evolutionists, we are only a superior kind of cattle, a sort of Alderney among other herds. To be sure, we browse on better pasture, and we have better stall and better accommodations, but then we are only Southdowns among the great flocks of sheep. Born of a beast, to die like a beast; for the evolutionists have no idea of a future world. They say the mind is only a superior part of the body. They say our thoughts are only molecular formation. They say when the body dies, the whole nature dies. The slab of the sepulchre is not a milestone on a journey upward, but a wall shutting us into eternal nothingness. We all die alike — the cow, the

E. J. Pace cartoon, 1920s
(Billy Graham Center)

ANOTHER PIED PIPER

horse, the sheep, the man, the reptile. Annihilation is the heaven of the evolutionist.

From such a stenchful and damnable doctrine turn away. Compare that idea of your origin — an idea filled with the chatter of apes, and the hiss of serpents, and the croak of frogs — to an idea in one or two stanzas which I shall read to you from an old book of more than Demosthenic, or Homeric, or Dantesque power: "What is man, that thou art mindful of him? and the son of man, that thou visitest him? Thou hast made him a little lower than the angels, and hast crowned him with glory and honor. Thou madest him to have dominion over the works of thy hand; thou hast put all things under his feet. All sheep and oxen, yea, and the beasts of the field; the fowl of the air, and the fish of the sea, and whatsoever passeth through the paths of the seas. Oh, Lord, our Lord, how excellent is Thy name in all the earth."

How do you like that origin? The lion the monarch of the field, the eagle the monarch of the air, behemoth the monarch of the deep, but man monarch of all. Ah! my friends, I have to say to you that I am not so anxious to know what was my origin as to know what will be my destiny. I do not care so much where I came from as where I am going to. I am not so interested in who was my ancestry ten million years ago as I am to know where I will be ten million years from now. I am not so much interested in the preface to my cradle as I am interested in the appendix to my grave. I do not care so much about protoplasm as I do about eternasm. The "was" is overwhelmed with the "to be." And here comes in the evolution I believe in: not natural evolution, but gracious and divine and heavenly evolution — evolution out of sin into holiness, out of grief into gladness, out of mortality into immortality, out of earth into heaven! That is the evolution I believe in.

James Cardinal Gibbons (1834– 1921)

Introduced above (see p. 117), Baltimore's Cardinal Gibbons took a somewhat higher ground in his assessment of the "conflict" between science and religion. There is no conflict, he argued, nor can there be, for God is the Author of all Truth. Sometimes the teachings of the Church are improperly understood, and sometimes the claims of science are irresponsible and false. But Thomas Huxley and John Draper are both wrong, Gibbons declared, and the tendency of their writings is pernicious. Science must be humble and not profane. It remains the responsibility of the Catholic Church, furthermore, to rebuke and reprove when science advocates "some crude theory" or "some hypothesis" at variance with "the Divine Oracle of which she is the custodian." Then the Church must cry out, "Thus far . . . and no farther!"

[Source: James Cardinal Gibbons, Our Christian Heritage (Baltimore: John Murphy & Co., 1889), pp. 301–4, 309–10, 319–20.]

It cannot be denied that there dwells in many sincere minds a lurking suspicion, amounting in some persons almost to a painful conviction, that antagonism exists between certain dogmas of revelation and the results of scientific investigation. Mr. Huxley, Dr. Draper, and other acknowledged leaders of modern thought, have done their utmost to confirm these sinister impressions and to widen the breach between the teachers of religion and those of physical science. They will tell you that the study of nature leads us away from God and ultimately results in the denial of His existence. They maintain that there is and must be an irrepressible conflict between these two great branches of knowledge; that they cannot coexist; and that, in the long run, theology must surrender to her younger and more progressive rival.

They affect to believe that the champions of Christianity, conscious of the unequal conflict, view with alarm the rapid strides of the natural sciences, and do all in their power to discourage the study of them altogether. You will be told, dear reader, by this modern school of thought, that the more you are attached to the teachings of Christian faith, the more will your judgment be warped — your intellect stunted, and the more you will be retarded in the investigation of scientific truth. They will try to persuade you that, in exploring the regions of science, you will be in constant danger of falling foul of some ecclesiastical ukase warning you away from the poisoned tree of knowledge, just as our primitive parents were forbidden to eat the fruit of a certain tree in Paradise. They will tell you that your path is likely to be intercepted by some Pope's bull, which may metaphorically gore you to death. They will, in a word, contend that, to enjoy full freedom in searching the secrets of the physical world, you must emancipate yourself from the intellectual restraints imposed on you by the Christian religion.

Such are the statements deliberately made in our times against Christian revelation. But though they are uttered by bearded men, we call them childish declamations. We call them also ungrateful assertions, since they are spoken by men who are indebted to Christianity for the very discoveries they have made. Many a Christian Moses has wandered for years through the wilderness of investigation, and died almost in sight of the promised land of scientific discovery. And his successors, guided by the path that he had opened, and who might otherwise have died unknown after vain wanderings, entered the coveted territory and enjoyed its fruits. . . .

The truth is, that how much soever scientists and theologians may quarrel among themselves, there will never be any collision, but the most perfect harmony will ever exist between science and religion, as we shall endeavor to demonstrate in the following pages.

There are, indeed, and there ever will remain, truths of religion difficult to be reconciled with facts of science. If the ideas of time and space and the relation of soul to body are beyond our comprehension, we cannot be expected with our unaided reason to explain away the apparent incongruities that we find between the unseen and the visible kingdom of the universe. But difficulties do not necessarily involve doubts, still less denials. If we hold the two ends of a chain, we know that the connection is complete, though some of the links may be concealed from us.

Science and Religion, like Martha and Mary, are sisters, because they are daughters of the same Father. They are both ministering to the same Lord, though in a different way. Science, like Martha, is busy about material things; Religion, like Mary, is kneeling at the feet of her Lord.

The Christian religion teaches nothing but what has been revealed by Almighty God, or what is necessarily derived from revelation. God is truth. All truth comes from Him. He is the Author of all scientific truth, as He is the Author of all revealed truth. "The God who dictated the Bible," as Archbishop Ryan has happily said, "is the God who wrote the illuminated manuscript of the skies." You might as well expect that one ray of the sun would dim the light of another, as that any truth of revelation can be opposed to any truth of science. No truth of natural science can ever be opposed to any truth of revelation; nor can any truth of the natural order be at variance with any truth of the supernatural order. Truth differs from truth only as star differs from star, — each gives out the same pure light that reaches our vision across the expanse of the firmament. . . .

Now, since reason and revelation aid each other in leading us to God, the Author of both, it is manifest that the Catholic Church, so far from being opposed to the cultivation of reason, encourages and fosters science of every kind. The more secrets science will elicit from nature's bosom, the more the Church will rejoice; because she knows that no new revelation of nature will ever utter the words: "There is no God!" Rather will they whisper to the eager investigator, "He made us, and not we ourselves."

Each new discovery of science is a trophy with which religion loves to adorn her altars. She hails every fresh invention as another voice adding its harmonious notes to that grand choir which is ever singing the praises of the God of nature.

At no period of the Church's history did she wield greater authority than from the twelfth to the sixteenth century. She exercised not only spiritual, but also temporal power; and she had great influence with the princes of Christendom. Now, this is the very period of the rise and development of the universities in Europe. During these four centuries, nineteen universities were opened in France, thirteen in Italy, six in Great Britain and Ireland, two in Spain and one in Belgium. At no time did the human intellect revel in greater freedom. No question of speculative science escaped the inquisitive search of men of thought. Successful explorations were made in every field of science and art. The weapons of heathendom were employed in fighting the battles of truth. . . .

The position of the Catholic Church in reference to modern scientists may be thus briefly summarized: The Church fosters and encourages every department of science. But just because she is the friend of true science she is opposed to all false pretensions of science. There is as much difference between true and false science as there is between authority and despotism, liberty and license. When she hears a man advancing some crude theory at variance with the received doctrines of revelation, — with the existence of God, for example, or His superintending providence or His wisdom or His sanctity; when she hears him advocating some hypothesis opposed to the unity of the human species, to the spirituality and the immortality of the soul, to the future destiny of man, and to those other great doctrines that involve at once the dignity and moral responsibility of the human race, she knows that his assumptions must be false, because she knows that God's revelation must be true. She stands between such a man and the Divine Oracle of which she is the custodian; and when she sees him raise his profane hands and attempt to touch the temple of faith, she cries out, "Thus far shalt thou go and no farther!"

Mediation

Joseph Le Conte (1823 – 1901)

From a Georgia family of Huguenot heritage, Joseph Le Conte moved from the University of South Carolina to the University of California at Berkeley as professor of geology. In both states, it had been Le Conte's custom to offer lectures to a "Bible-class of young men," assuring them that modern science — of which he was a practitioner —constituted no threat to Christianity —in which he was a devout believer. To be sure, science and religion have occasionally collided, and the apparent discrepancies between the two are numerous. But Christianity returns from each battle stronger or purer than before. The true scientist, moreover, must see that faith is neither unsettled nor destroyed, but built upon foundations "more solid, enduring, and rational."

My Christian Friends: In all my lectures thus far I have tried to show a general accordance between the teachings of Scripture and the teachings of Nature. I have tried to show that the truths revealed in the one are also revealed in the other. But some one will say, perhaps many have already said: "Is there not a radical discordance between these two books in many passages? Does not skepticism draw its weapons principally from the armory of Nature? If some departments of science and some departments of Nature seem to be in general accordance with Scripture, are there not other departments, especially geology, in which there seems to be a fatal discordance?" It is indeed true, I frankly confess it, that, according to traditional interpretation of Scrip-

[Source: Joseph Le Conte, *Religion and Science: A Series of Sunday Lectures* . . . (New York: D. Appleton & Co., 1874), pp. 227 – 30, 231 – 33.]

ture, there are many particular passages which seem to be in discordance with the teachings of Nature. But let me ask you, shall not the general spirit of the two books outweigh what seems to be the literal interpretation of some passages? Shall not the accordance of the two books, in those grand spiritual truths which form the basis of religion, overbalance apparent minor discrepancies in matters which are of little spiritual significance? Nevertheless, lest some persons should be distressed in mind by these apparent discrepancies in particular passages, I have determined, in this lecture and the next, to take up this subject. It seemed to me appropriate that, in connection with, and introductory to, the subject of man, which will occupy the remainder of these lectures — man the crown of Nature, and the culminating point of the whole *history of creation* — I should say something concerning the supposed *discrepancies in this history*, as recorded in the two books.

Throughout the whole history of Christianity, from the earliest times until now, there have been from time to time collisions between religious faith and the prevailing systems of philosophy. We find it first in St. Paul preaching the unknown God to the scoffing philosophers of ancient Athens; we find it again in the metaphysical discussions of the schoolmen of the middle ages; we find it again, and more severe, in the conflict between faith and the acute metaphysical philosophy of Hume; and last of all, and most serious of all, in the conflict now going on with the material philosophy of the present day. The enemy has incessantly shifted the field of conflict from one ground to another. First it is in the field of metaphysics, then in the field of science. In the field of science, again, it is first in the department of astronomy, then in the department of geology and natural history. Wherever the intellectual activity is greatest, there we find the field of contest.

The general result of these collisions has ever been the same. In every case Christianity has risen from the contest stronger and purer, and in this day, I believe, stronger and purer than ever before. How different, in this respect, is it from all other forms of faith! These simply succumb unresistingly before advancing knowledge — like shadows, or spectres, they simply disappear before the light of science. Christianity, on the contrary, loves the light, seeks the light, lives in the light; it loves the truth, seeks the truth, lives in the truth; its Divine founder was both light and truth. Is this the nature of spectres and shadows? Is it not rather the nature of a permanent living reality? The last conflict has been longest and most deadly. It is still going on. But those who have studied the history of such conflicts cannot doubt the final result.

What, then, are the subjects of conflict? What are the points of discrepancy between the two books? We will very briefly mention the most important.

The Scriptures, according to traditional interpretation, seem to teach — 1. That the age of this earth, and of the whole cosmos, is about six thousand years or earth-revolutions. 2. That creation took place by successive instantaneous acts in the course of six natural days or earth-rotations. (Let me here draw your attention parenthetically to the enormous improbability, not to say absurdity, that the steps of evolution of the infinite cosmos should be determined by the rotations of this our little earth!) 3. By traditional interpretation, it seems to teach that death reigned from Adam until now.

On the other hand, Nature seems very plainly to teach the inconceivable antiquity of the earth and of the cosmos. Again, it seems to teach that creation took place, not by instantaneous acts occupying in all six natural days, but was a gradual process of becoming — each successive condition of the universe having come out of the previous condition by a gradual process of evolution according to law. In the third place, it seems to teach that death has reigned from the beginning of organic creation until now; that death and life are correlative; life cannot exist without its counterpart death, and therefore they are coextensive, and that during an inconceivable lapse of time. You see the discrepancy. . . .

My object, therefore, is rather to adjust, if possible, the *general relations of science and theology*. I wish to show that these two have the same general end and object, viz., the seeking of Divine truth; I wish to change, if possible, their angry conflict into generous emulation.

The science of astronomy is so old, its truths so long and well established, and the changes of interpretation of Scripture necessitated by the discovery of these truths have been now so long accepted, that any attempt to adjust the claims of astronomy with those of theology would be considered unnecessary. We even look back with wonder at the disturbance of religious faith produced by these truths when first established. But with geology the case is quite different. Geology is born of the present century. The generation is not yet gone which saw, and perhaps despised, its helpless infancy. It has advanced with such prodigious strides, it has opened such immense and unexpected fields of intellectual vision, its truths are of so startling a character, and have followed each other in such quick succession, that the popular mind is wholly unprepared to adjust their relations with faith; religious faith has not yet been able to incorporate these truths and to assimilate them to itself, as it eventually must and will do. Thus every step in the advance of the science of geology has tended to sap, and finally to overthrow, our faith in certain dogmas concerning the antiquity of the earth and the introduction of death, dogmas which we have learned at our mothers' knee, and taken in with our mothers' milk; dogmas which, therefore, have been loved and reverenced as Divine truth. These objects of our love and reverence, these our household gods, these images of Divine truth (for have they not been proved to be images made by ourselves?), these images of Deity have been rudely torn from the sanctuary of our hearts, and by some inconsiderate iconoclasts in science have been even trampled upon and defaced. In an agony we are ready to cry out, in the words of Micah to the plundering Danites, "Ye have taken away our gods: what have we more?"

Now, my Christian friends, I do believe that we cannot do a man a greater and a more irreparable injury than to unsettle in any way his religious faith. Faith is the very fountain of all noble activity. Without faith of some kind nothing worthy was ever accomplished, either for this life or the life to come. The faith may be lower or higher. It may be only faith in *self*, it may be faith in our *destiny*, it may be faith in *humanity*, it may be faith in a loving heavenly Father; but without faith of some kind there never was and never will be a noble or successful life. Life is noble in proportion to the nobleness of faith; it is successful in proportion to the fixedness of faith. There is no form of religious faith, however gross, no, not even idolatry or superstition, but is better than no faith at all. Superstition may be spiritual deformity, but unbelief is spiritual death. The light of science is indeed a glorious light — a light absolutely necessary for the perfect growth of the human spirit and its development into forms of perfect beauty and strength, a light absolutely necessary to the tree of humanity, in order that it should bear flower and fruit worthy of its divine origin; but, unless this light be assisted by the dews and showers of heaven received only through faith, it only scorches and withers and blasts; where we look for luxuriant verdure and abundant harvest, we find only blackened trunks and naked, outstretched limbs — noble trunks, it may be, "majestic even in ruin," but yet only dead.

I believe, therefore, it is the duty of every scientific man, who is also a lover of his fellow-men, to attempt to restore again the faith which he himself, perhaps, has helped to destroy; to wrest again, if possible, from the hands of infidelity, the weapons which perhaps he himself has furnished; to build again the foundations of faith upon a more solid, enduring, and rational basis.

James McCosh (1811 – 94)

A native of Scotland and a Presbyterian clergyman, McCosh came to America in 1868 to assume the presidency of Princeton. A philosopher of considerable reputation even before beginning his career in this country, McCosh put that reputation on the line by becoming the first prominent clergyman in the United States strongly to support the theory of evolution. Much of the controversy had bubbled over in the 1870s, and McCosh quickly entered the fray. Later, when things had quieted down somewhat, he published The Religious Aspect of Evolution *in 1888. In the preface to the "enlarged and improved edition" issued two years later, he wrote: "I am pleased to discover that intelligent Christians are coming round gradually to the views which I have had the courage to publish."*

In my first published work, "The Method of Divine Government," I sought to unfold the plan by which God governs the world, and I found it to be in

[Source: James McCosh, *The Religious Aspect of Evolution* (New York: Charles Scribner's Sons, 1890), pp. vii – x.]

an orderly manner — that is, by law. As having pursued this line of research, I was prepared to believe that there might be the like method in the organic kingdoms, and to listen to Darwin when he showed that there was a regular instrumentality in the descent of plants and animals. I noticed that he and others, such as Lewes, Huxley, and Spencer, who took the same view, were not swayed by any religious considerations, and that religious people generally were strongly prepossessed against the new doctrine. But I saw, at the same time, that Darwin was a most careful observer, that he published many important facts, that there was great truth in the theory, and that there was nothing atheistic in it if properly understood — that is, in the acknowledged tenet of the government of organic nature by means and according to law.

I felt it to be my only course not to reject the truth because it was proclaimed by some who turned it to an irreligious use, but to accept it wherever it might lead, and to turn it to a better use. I let it be known that while I thought there was truth, I believed there was error in the common expositions of evolution, and that the work of the coming age must be to separate the truth from the error, when it would be found, I was sure, that this, like every other part of God's work, would illustrate his existence and his wisdom.

When I was called from the Old World to the office which I now hold as president of an important college, I had to consider — I remember seriously pondering the question in the vessel which brought me to this country — whether I should at once avow my convictions or keep them in abeyance because of the prejudices of religious men, and lest I might unsettle the faith of the students committed to my care. I decided to pursue the open and honest course, as being sure that it would be the best in the end. I was not a week in Princeton till I let it be known to the upper classes of the college that I was in favor of evolution properly limited and explained; and I have proclaimed my views in lectures and papers in a number of cities and before various associations, literary and religious. I have been gratified to find that none of the churches has assailed me, and this has convinced me that their doubts about evolution have proceeded mainly from the bad use to which the doctrine has been turned. I am pleased to discover that intelligent Christians are coming round gradually to the views which I have had the courage to publish.

I have all along had a sensitive apprehension that the undiscriminating denunciation of evolution from so many pulpits, periodicals, and seminaries might drive some of our thoughtful young men to infidelity, as they clearly saw development everywhere in nature, and were at the same time told by their advisers that they could not believe in evolution and yet be Christians. I am gratified beyond measure to find that I am thanked by my pupils, some of whom have reached the highest position as naturalists, because in showing them evolution in the works of God, I showed them that this was not inconsistent with religion, and thus enabled them to follow science and yet retain their faith in the Bible.

Henry Ward Beecher (1813 – 87)

Following McCosh's early lead, the influential pastor of Plymouth Congre-gational Church in Brooklyn carried the message of reconciliation from academia to laity. Beecher, son of Lyman Beecher (see Vol. I, pp. 317 – 18, 322 – 27) and brother of Harriet Beecher Stowe (see Vol. I, pp. 403 – 7), alluded to those family connections when he took up the controverted cause of evolution. ". . . With every hereditary necessity upon me," he declared, he would surely not espouse evolution if he thought it meant the "funeral" of that religion to which he and his family had given so much. An effective orator and — like Talmage — moving beyond the authority of the denomina-tions, Beecher two years before his death preached a series of sermons on "evolution and religion," contending that the history of Christianity is itself evidence of "that Providence that inspires growth upon growth." The sermon excerpted below, "Evolution and the Church," was preached in the Plymouth pulpit on July 5, 1885.

Do you suppose that now, after fifty years in the Christian ministry, I could attend the funeral of religion cheerfully and joyfully, with every hereditary necessity on me, with the whole education of my youth, with all my associ-ations, all the endearments of my past life in my memory, and with vivid and living sympathy with men; do you suppose that I could stand here to advocate any truth that would destroy the substance, or in any degree mate-rially injure even the forms, of religion? I would die sooner! Do you suppose from my nature and my whole example, I could go into the course of sermons that I have preached, and into the course of sermons that, God willing, I will preach yet, for any other reason than that I believe that the new view is to give to religion a power, and a scope, and a character such as has never yet been taken and known in the world at large? Better men than some have been, I suppose, will never be born; better lives than certain single lives will never appear over the horizon of time; but that which I look for is the change of the human race. I am not thinking of men, but of mankind. I am not in sympathy alone with the Church, but with the whole human family. And my longing, as it has been for years, is for such teaching and such philosophies as shall lead the whole human race to a higher and a nobler condition.

Suppose, then, that Evolution should practically approve itself to be true and should be carried out as a basis of thought and teaching concerning the ways of God in his universe, will it materially affect the Church? And if so, will it be favorable or unfavorable? I say, it will, favorably. That it is going to surround the Church with alleged truths that must need be considered, you know and I know. No great development can be made in these modern times of universal intelligence and democratic liberty, and not be felt everywhere

[Source: H. W. Beecher, *Evolution and Religion* (Boston: Pilgrim Press, [1885]), pp. 127 – 28, 136 – 37, 142 – 43.]

by all men. The attempt to repress investigation, to keep out of the hands of our sons and daughters the books of the day, written by great men, full of honest and inspiring thought, expressed in lucid and attractive style, is not only wrong but impracticable. You cannot keep these books out of their hands, and it is bad to have them read by stealth. Open-faced, clear-eyed, frank, the young should be encouraged to investigate the truth; and when investigation has been permitted and has gone on, we should not allow ourselves to be terrified. . . .

But then is there anything in Evolution that would desire to destroy the Church? Is not this influence in the Church itself one of the signs of the diversified unfolding of God's plans on the earth going to show the truth-fulness of that philosophy of God's methods which modern philosophers have named Evolution, one of the results of that Providence that inspires growth upon growth, and growth upon growth? Nay more, —and this is the point, — I firmly believe that the acceptance of this doctrine, which seems to me inevitable, is to be one of God's most effective instruments in intensifying and hastening the progress of these and similar blessed changes. In short, *Evolution will affect the Church,* but for its greater health and power among men.

Then, next, is there any danger that the Pulpit and preaching will be injuriously affected by the progress of Evolution? One would think, from the vehemence and zeal with which the pulpit sometimes preaches against Evolution, that it was afraid itself of being extinguished. That it will in some respects be changed and bettered, I cannot doubt; but the function itself is divine, and it is necessary to the human race. It walks with the progress of God in the whole evolutionary scheme. . . .

Enough of this—for let who will look upon every part of organized Christianity as it exists now, and he will see the changes that are taking place. But they will be gradual. That is right. They will help man. They will give men's minds time to accommodate themselves to changing views. Simply to hold views of fundamental moral principles is one thing; holding these views of moral principles organized into physical institution is another thing. Men of Babylonish genius are still crying to the young and thoughtful, "Search for the old paths." Yes, those as old as God! It is the old paths of man's making that may well be relocated. To search for the old paths is against the practice of the modern engineer, who seeks to lay out the road on a straight line. The old paths used to run round and round, up and down, through swamps and quagmires, and over almost impassable hills; yet when at last the best path is struck straight through between the two great cities, the croakers say, "Search for the old paths." That which is true of physics is truer yet of morality and religion. Theology and the Church are undergoing a process of evolution, towards perfection, changing upwards and for the better. Those elements that are changing the other way are gradually approaching dissolution, for destruction and evolution are twins. They work together. In

Lyman Abbott (1835–1922) in 1905, author of *The Theology of an Evolutionist*
(Keystone-Mast Collection, University of California, Riverside)

the history of God's creation, things that are not good, or that are too weak to live, perish right alongside of things that are stronger and better adapted. Deterioration and destruction are part and parcel of the great process of evolution going on all the time. The presumption of Evolution is adverse to the claims of authority both in the Church and in the State. You know what the history of civil liberty has been. Nothing has been accounted to be so dangerous and so disastrous to man as the liberty of the individual. At every stage of unfolding from the beginning down to the commonwealth of America, all philosophers almost, and all potentates, have resisted this wild fanaticism of democracy. It is not safe, they say, to trust men by themselves; and the danger of trusting men by themselves in commonwealths has been the theme of ages. Alongside that has been the cry of churches with aristocratic ministries and ponderous governments — the cry of "Authority;" it will not do to let men think for themselves. It will not do to leave men in democratic Christian conditions in regard to what they believe. You must have ordained men and ordained customs, and ordinances fixed of God. The same liturgy of folly that ran through the civil progress of the world has been running also through the ecclesiastical and the theological. In both one and the other, experiment will show that under the great canopy of God's providence men, as they grow in intelligence, are safer the more you give them liberty. Their dissuasions and dissensions and such elements are preparatory to a new co-adhesion. Pruning makes more fruit, not less, in every vine and in every fruit-tree; and so it is in the Church.

John Augustine Zahm (1851 – 1921)

In 1896 a Holy Cross priest and professor of physics at Notre Dame offered his reconciliation of Darwinian investigation and Roman Catholic instruction. Like McCosh, Zahm did not see evolution as a threat to the Christian faith nor an attack upon the Bible. We must remember that much being said about evolution is still hypothetical, he noted, but even supposing it all were to be established as incontrovertible fact, still "Catholic Dogma would remain absolutely intact and unchanged." Evolution for the agnostic or atheist means one thing, but for the "theistic evolutionist" everything "is a part of a grand unity betokening an omnipotent Creator." Within two years of its publication, Zahm's work was placed on the Index of Prohibited Books and withdrawn from further circulation.

Suppose, then, that a demonstrative proof of the theory of Evolution should eventually be given, a proof such as would satisfy the most exacting and the most skeptical, it is evident, from what has already been stated, that Catholic Dogma would remain absolutely intact and unchanged. Individual theorists would be obliged to accommodate their views to the facts of nature, but the doctrines of the Church would not be affected in the slightest. The hypothesis of St. Augustine and St. Thomas Aquinas would then become a thesis, and all reasonable and consistent men would yield ready, unconditional and un-equivocal assent.

And suppose, further, that in the course of time science shall demon-strate — a most highly improbable event — the animal origin of man as to his body. There need, even then, be no anxiety so far as the truths of faith are concerned. Proving that the body of the common ancestor of humanity is descended from some higher form of ape, or from some extinct anthropo-pithecus, would not necessarily contravene either the declarations of Genesis, or the principles regarding derivative creation which found acceptance with the greatest of the Church's Fathers and Doctors.

Mr. Gladstone, in the work just quoted from,* expresses the same idea

[Source: J. A. Zahm, *Evolution and Dogma* (Chicago: D. H. McBride & Co., 1896), pp. 428 – 30, 435 – 38.]

*William E. Gladstone, introduction to G. C. Lorimer, ed., *The People's Bible History* . . . (1895).

with characteristic force and lucidity. "If," he says, "while Genesis asserts a separate creation of man, science should eventually prove that man sprang, by a countless multitude of indefinitely small variations, from a lower, and even from the lowest ancestry, the statement of the great chapter would still remain undisturbed. For every one of those variations, however minute, is absolutely separate, in the points wherein it varies, from what followed and also from what preceded it; is in fact and in effect a distinct or separate creation. And the fact that the variation is so small that, taken singly, our use may not be to reckon it, is nothing whatever to the purpose. For it is the finiteness of our faculties which shuts us off by a barrier downward, beyond a certain limit, from the small, as it shuts us off by a barrier upward from the great; whereas for Him whose faculties are infinite, the small and the great are, like the light and the darkness, 'both alike,' and if man came up by innumerable stages from a low origin to the image of God, it is God only who can say, as He has said in other cases, which of those stages may be worthy to be noted with the distinctive name of creation, and at what point of the ascent man could first be justly said to exhibit the image of God."

But the derivation of man from the ape, we are told, degrades man. Not at all. It would be truer to say that such derivation ennobles the ape. Sentiment aside, it is quite unimportant to the Christian "whether he is to trace back his pedigree directly or indirectly to the dust." St. Francis of Assisi, as we learn from his life, "called the birds his brothers." Whether he was correct, either theologically or zoölogically, he was plainly free from that fear of being mistaken for an ape which haunts so many in these modern times. Perfectly sure that he, himself, was a spiritual being, he thought it at least possible that birds might be spiritual beings, likewise incarnate like himself in mortal flesh; and saw no degradation to the dignity of human nature in claiming kindred lovingly with creatures so beautiful, so wonderful, who, as he fancied, "praised God in the forest, even as angels did in heaven." . . .

And as Evolution ennobles our conceptions of God and of man, so also does it permit us to detect new beauties, and discover new lessons, in a world that, according to the agnostic and monistic views, is so dark and hopeless. To the one who says there is no God, "the immeasurable universe," in the language of Jean Paul, "has become but a cold mass of iron, which hides an eternity without form and void."

To the theistic evolutionist, however, all is instinct with invitations to a higher life and a happier existence in the future; all is vocal with hymns of praise and benediction. Everything is a part of a grand unity betokening an omnipotent Creator. All is foresight, purpose, wisdom. We have the entire history of the world and of all systems of worlds, "gathered, as it were, into one original, creative act, from which the infinite variety of the universe has come, and more is coming yet." And God's hand is seen in the least as in the greatest. His power and goodness are disclosed in the beauteous crystalline form of the snow-flake, in the delicate texture, fragrance and color of the rose, in the marvelous pencilings of the butterfly's wing, in the gladsome and melodious notes of the lark and the thrush, in the tiniest morning dew-drop with all its gorgeous prismatic hues and wondrous hidden mysteries. All are pregnant with truths of the highest order, and calculated to inspire courage, and to strengthen our hope in faith's promise of a blissful immortality. . . .

Science and Evolution tell us of the transcendence and immanence of the First Cause, of the Cause of causes, the Author of all the order and beauty in the world, but it is revelation which furnishes us with the strongest evidence of the relations between the natural and supernatural orders, and brings out in the boldest relief the absolute dependence of the creature on its Maker. It is faith which teaches us how God "binds all together into Himself;" how He quickens and sustains "each thing separately, and all as collected in one."

I can, indeed, no better express the ideas which Evolution so beautifully shadows forth, nor can I more happily conclude this long discussion than by appropriating the words used long ago by that noble champion of the faith, St. Athanasius. "As the musician," says the great Alexandrine Doctor, in his "Oratio Contra Gentiles," "having tuned his lyre, and harmonized together the high with the low notes, and the middle notes with the extremes, makes the resulting music one; so the Wisdom of God, grasping the universe like a lyre, blending the things of air with those of earth, and the things of heaven with those of air, binding together the whole and the parts, and ordering all by His counsel and His will, makes the world itself and its appointed order one in fair and harmonious perfection; yet He, Himself, moving all things, remains unmoved with the Father."

Litigation: The Scopes Trial

The most famous, if not necessarily the most significant, controversy between science and religion did not come until 1925. By then most minds in the scholarly community had already been made up, the courses of most universities and seminaries already charted. But "Scopes" was the main event in the public arena. A young biology teacher in Dayton, Tennessee, John Thomas Scopes (1900–70), taught evolution in opposition to a state law. Or at least he was so charged, for the precise thrust of the state law was one of the points at issue (as is evident below). One reason for the trial's fame was the reputation of the major figures involved: Clarence S. Darrow (1857–1938), outstanding Chicago trial lawyer for the defense; Kirtley F. Mather (1888–1978), Harvard geologist and expert witness for the defence (also the author a few years later of Science in Search of God, *1928); but above all others, William Jennings Bryan (1860–1925), thrice pres-*

[Source: Leslie Allen, ed., *Bryan and Darrow at Dayton* (New York: A. Lee & Co., 1925), (1) pp. 16–19; (2) pp. 64–66; (3) pp. 112–14; (4) pp. 195–96.]

idential candidate and the prosecution's tireless voice. Bryan's final summa-
tion was never delivered because both sides had agreed to conclude the sweltering
proceedings on July 21, 1925. Five days later Bryan died, and two days
after that his widow released the remarks that he would have given if the
trial had reached its final drama. Without further introduction, four docu-
ments follow: (1) Darrow early in the trial; (2) Bryan in response; (3)
Mather as Bible student and scientist; and (4) Bryan's never-delivered
summation. All of this comes from a reporter's transcription of the events of
which a nation waited eagerly to hear.

1.

Clarence Darrow

"There is not a single line of any constitution that can withstand bigotry and
ignorance when it seeks to destroy the rights of the individual; and bigotry
and ignorance are ever active. Here we find today as brazen and as bold an
attempt to destroy learning as was ever made in the Middle Ages, and the
only difference is we have not provided that they shall be burned at the stake.
But there is time for that, your Honor. We have to approach these things
gradually.

"Now let us see what we claim with reference to this law. If this proceeding, both in form and substance, can prevail in this court, then, your Honor,
any law, no matter how foolish, wicked, ambiguous, or ancient, can come
back to Tennessee. All the guarantees go for nothing. All of the past has gone
to waste, been forgotten, if this can succeed.

"I am going to begin with some of the simpler reasons why it is absolutely
absurd to think that this statute, indictment, or any part of the proceedings
in this case are legal; and I think the sooner we get rid of it in Tennessee the
better for the people of Tennessee, and the better for the pursuit of knowledge
in the world; so let me begin at the beginning.

"The first point we made in this suit is that it is unconstitutional on account
of divergence and the difference between the statute and the caption and
because it contains more than one subject.

"Every Constitution with which I am familiar has substantially this same
proposition, that the caption and the law must correspond.

"Lots of things are put through the Legislature in the night time. Everybody does not read all of the statutes, even members of the Legislature — I
have been a member of the Legislature myself, and I know how it is. They
may vote for them without reading them, but the substance of the act is put
in the caption, so it may be seen and read, and nothing may be in the act that
is not contained in the caption. There is not any question about it, and only
one subject shall be legislated on at once. Of course, the caption may be
broader than the act. They may make a caption and the act may fall far short

of it, but the substance of the act must be in the caption, and there can be no variance.

"Now let us see what they have done. There is not much dispute about the English language, I take it. Here is the caption:

" 'Public Act, Chapter 37, 1925, an act prohibiting the teaching of the evolution theory in all the universities, normals, and all the public schools of Tennessee which are supported in whole or in part by the public school funds of the State, and to prescribe penalties for the violation thereof.'

"Now what is it — an act to prohibit the teaching of the evolution theory in Tennessee? Is this the act? Is this statute to prevent the teaching of the evolution theory? There is not a word said in the statute about evolution. There is not a word said in the statute about preventing the teaching of the theory of evolution — not a word.

"This caption says what follows is an act forbidding the teaching of evolution, and the Catholic could have gone home without any thought that his faith was about to be attacked. The Protestant could have gone home without any thought that his religion could be attacked. The intelligent, scholarly Christians, who by the millions in the United States find no inconsistency between evolution and religion, could have gone home without any fear that a narrow, ignorant, bigoted shrew of religion could have destroyed their religious freedom and their right to think and act and speak; and the nation and the State could have laid down peacefully to sleep that night without the slightest fear that religious hatred and bigotry were to be turned loose in a great State.

"Any question about that? Anything in this caption whatever about religion, or anything about measuring science and knowledge and learning by the Book of Genesis, written when everybody thought the world was flat? Nothing.

"They went to bed in peace, probably, and they woke up to find this, which has not the slightest reference to it; which does not refer to evolution in any way; which is, as claimed, a religious statute.

"That is what they found and here is what it is:

" 'Be it enacted by the General Assembly of the State of Tennessee, that it shall be unlawful for any teacher in any of the universities, normals, and all other public schools in the State, which are supported in whole or in part by the public school funds of the State, to teach' — what, teach evolution? Oh, no. — 'To teach the theory that denies the story of the divine creation of man as taught in the Bible, and to teach instead that man has descended from a lower order of animals.'

"That is what was foisted on the people of this State, under a caption which never meant it, and could give no hint of it; that it should be a crime in the State of Tennessee to teach any theory, — not evolution, but any theory of the origin of man, except that contained in the divine account as recorded in the Bible.

"But the State of Tennessee, under an honest and fair interpretation of the Constitution, has no more right to teach the Bible as the Divine Book than that the Koran is one, or the Book of Mormon, or the Book of Confucius, or the Buddha, or the Essays of Emerson, or any one of the 10,000 books to which human souls have gone for consolation and aid in their troubles."

2.

William Jennings Bryan

"Our position is that the statute is sufficient. The statute defines exactly what the people of Tennessee decided and intended and did declare unlawful, and it needs no interpretation.

"The caption speaks of the evolutionary theory, and the statute specifically states that teachers are forbidden to teach in the schools supported by taxation in this State any theory of creation of man that denies the Divine record of man's creation as found in the Bible, and that there might be no difference of opinion — there might be no ambiguity — that there might be no such confusion of thought as our learned friends attempt to inject into it. The Legislature was careful to define what is meant by the first of the statute.

"It says 'to teach that man is a descendant of any lower form of life.' If that had not been there, if the first sentence had been the only sentence in the statute, then these gentlemen might come and ask to define what that meant or to explain whether the thing that was taught was contrary to the language of the statute in the first sentence. But the second sentence removes all doubt, as has been stated by my colleague.

"The second sentence points out specifically what is meant, and that is the teaching that man is the descendant of any lower form of life; and if the defendant taught that, as we have proved by the textbook that he used and as we have proved by the students that went to hear him, if he taught that man is a descendant of any lower form of life, he violated the statute, and more than that, we have his own confession that he knew he was violating the statute."

After summarizing the evidence, Mr. Bryan continued:

"We do not need any expert to tell us what the law means. An expert cannot be permitted to come in here and try to defeat the enforcement of a law by testifying that it isn't a bad law, and it isn't — I mean a bad doctrine — no matter how these people phrase that doctrine, no matter how they eulogize it. This is not the place to try to prove that the law ought never to have been passed. The place to prove that was at the Legislature.

"If these people were so anxious to keep the State of Tennessee from disgracing itself, if they were so afraid that by this action taken by the Legislature, the State would put itself before the people of the nation as ignorant people and bigoted people — if they had half the affection for Tennessee that you would think they had as they come here to testify — they would have come at a time when their testimony would have been valuable, and not at this time to ask you to refuse to enforce a law because they did not think the law ought to have been passed.

"And if the people of Tennessee were to go into a state, into New York, the one from which this impulse comes to resist this law, or go into any state . . . and try to convince the people that a law they had passed ought not to be enforced (just because the people who went there didn't think it ought to have been passed), don't you think it would be resented as an impertinence? . . .

"The people of this State passed this law. The people of this State knew what they were doing when they passed the law, and they knew the dangers of the doctrine that they did not want it taught to their children. And, my friends, it isn't proper to bring experts in here to try to defeat the purpose of the people of this State by trying to show that this thing that they denounce and outlaw is a beautiful thing that everybody ought to believe in. . . .

"These people want to come here with experts to make your Honor believe that the law should never have been passed, and because in their opinion it ought not to have been passed, it ought not to be enforced. It isn't a place for expert testimony. We have sufficient proof in the book. Doesn't the book state the very thing that is objected to and outlawed in this State? Who has a copy of that book?"

JUDGE RAULSTON — Do you mean the Bible?

MR. BRYAN — No, sir, the biology. [Laughter]

A VOICE — Here it is, Hunter's Biology.

MR. BRYAN — "No, not the Bible. You see, in this State they cannot teach the Bible. They can only teach things that declare it to be a lie, according to the learned counsel. These people in the State, Christian people, have tied their hands by their Constitution. They say we all believe in the Bible, for it is the overwhelming belief in the State, but we will not teach that Bible, which we believe — even to our children, through teachers that we pay with our money.

"No, no, it isn't the teaching of the Bible, and we are not asking it.

"The question is, Can a minority in this State come in and compel a teacher to teach that the Bible is not true and make the parents of these children pay the expenses of the teacher to tell their children what these people believe is false and dangerous?

"Has it come to a time when the minority can take charge of a state like Tennessee and compel the majority to pay their teachers while they take religion out of the heart of the children of the parents who pay the teachers?"

3.

Kirtley F. Mather

Dr. Mather's statement was introduced as coming from a student of the Bible, lecturer to Bible students at the Boston University School of Religious

Education, member of the Baptist Church at Newton Center, Mass., and teacher of the Mather Class in its Bible school. Professor Mather said that evolution was "not a power, not a force," but "a process, a method." God was "a power, a force"; He necessarily uses processes and methods in displaying His Power and exerting force.

Not one of the facts of evolution "contradicts any teaching of Jesus Christ known to me," his statement read. "None could, for His teachings deal with moral law and spiritual realities. Natural science deals with physical laws and material results. When men are offered their choice between science, with its confident and unanimous acceptance of the evolutionary principle on the one hand, and religion, with its necessary appeal to things unseen and unproven on the other, they are more likely to abandon religion than to abandon science.

"If such a choice is forced upon us the churches will lose many of their best educated young people, the very ones upon whom they must depend for leadership in the coming years.

"Fortunately such a choice is absolutely unnecessary. To say that one must choose between evolution and Christianity is exactly like telling the child as he starts for school that he must choose between spelling and arithmetic. Thorough knowledge of each is essential to success — both individual and racial — in life.

"Good religion is founded on facts, even as the evolutionary principle. A true religion faces the facts fearlessly, regardless of where or how the facts may be found. The theories of evolution commonly accepted in the scientific world do not deny any reasonable interpretations of the story of Divine creation as recorded in the Bible. Rather they affirm that story and give it larger and more profound meaning.

"This, of course, depends upon what the meaning and interpretation of the stories are to each individual. I have been a Bible student all of my life, and ever since my college days I have been intensely interested in the relations between science and the Bible.

"It is obvious to any careful and intelligent reader of the Book of Genesis that some interpretation of its account must be made by each individual. Very evidently, it is not intended to be a scientific statement of the order and method of creation.

"In the first chapter of Genesis we are told that man was made after the plants and the other animals had been formed, and that man and woman were both created on the same day.

"In the second chapter of Genesis we read that man was formed from the dust of the ground before plants and other animals were made; that trees grew until fruit was upon them; that all the animals passed in review before man to be named, and then, after these events, woman was made.

"There is obvious lack of harmony between these two Biblical accounts of creation so far as details of process and order of events are concerned. They are, however, in perfect accord in presenting the spiritual truth that God is the author and the administrator of the universe, and that is the sort of truth we find in the Bible.

"It is a textbook of religion, not a textbook of biology or astronomy or geology. Moreover, it is just exactly the Biblical spiritual truth concerning God which rings clearly and unmistakably through every theory of theistic evolution. With it, modern science is in perfect accord.

"There are a number of reasons why sincere and honest Christians have recently come to distrust evolution. . . . Too many people who loudly proclaim their allegiance to the Book, know very little about what it really contains.

"The Bible does not state that the world was made about 6,000 years ago. The date 4004 B.C., set opposite Genesis 1:1 in many versions of the Bible, was placed there by Archbishop Usher only a few centuries ago. It is a man's interpretation of the Bible; it is in the footnotes added recently; it is not a part of the book itself.

"Concerning the length of earth history and of human history, the Bible is absolutely silent. Science may conclude that the earth is 100,000,000 or 100,000,000,000 years old; the conclusion does not affect the Bible in the slightest degree. Or, if one is worried over the progressive appearance of land, plants, animals, and man on the successive six days of a 'Creation Week,' there is a well-known Biblical support for the scientists' contention that eons rather than hours elapsed while these things were taking place.

" 'A day in the sight of the Lord is as a thousand years, and a thousand years as a day.'

"Taking the Bible itself as an authority dissipates many of the difficulties which threaten to make a gulf between religion and science."

4.

Bryan

"Let us, then, hear the conclusion of the whole matter. Science is a magnificent material force, but it is not a teacher of morals. It can perfect machinery, but it adds no moral restraints to protect society from the misuse of the machine. It can also build gigantic intellectual ships, but it constructs no moral rudders for the control of storm-tossed human vessels. It not only fails to supply the spiritual element needed, but some of its unproven hypotheses rob the ship of its compass and thus endanger its cargo.

"In war, science has proven itself an evil genius; it has made war more terrible than it ever was before. Man used to be content to slaughter his fellowmen on a single plane — the earth's surface. Science has taught him to go down into the water and shoot up from below, and to go up into the clouds and shoot down from above, thus making the battlefield three times as bloody as it was before; but science does not teach brotherly love.

Mr. and Mrs. William Jennings Bryan, two decades before Scopes trial
(Keystone-Mast Collection, University of California, Riverside)

"Science has made war so hellish that civilization was about to commit suicide; and now we are told that newly discovered instruments of destruction will make the cruelties of the late war seem trivial in comparison with the cruelties of wars that may come in the future.

"If civilization is to be saved from the wreckage threatened by intelligence not consecrated by love, it must be saved by the moral code of the meek and lowly Nazarene. His teachings, and His teachings alone can solve the problems that vex the heart and perplex the world.

"The world needs a saviour more than it ever did before, and there is only one name under heaven given among men whereby we must be saved. It is this name that evolution degrades, for, carried to its logical conclusion, it robs Christ of the glory of a Virgin birth, of the majesty of His deity and mission, and of the triumph of His resurrection. It also disputes the doctrine of the atonement.

"This case is no longer local; the defendant ceases to play an important part. The case has assumed the proportions of a battle royal between unbelief that attempts to speak through so-called science and the defenders of the Christian faith, speaking through the legislators of Tennessee.

"It is again a choice between God and Baal; it is also a renewal of the issue in Pilate's court.

"In that historic trial — the greatest in history — force, impersonated by Pilate, occupied the throne. Behind it was the Roman Government, mistress of the world, and behind the Roman Government were the legions of Rome. Before Pilate stood Christ, the Apostle of love. Force triumphed; they nailed him to the tree and those who stood around mocked and jeered and said, 'He is dead.' But from that day the power of Caesar waned and the power of Christ increased. In a few centuries the Roman Government was gone and its legions forgotten; while the crucified and risen Lord has become the greatest fact in history and the growing figure of all time.

"Again force and love meet face to face, and the question, 'What shall I do with Jesus?' must be answered. A bloody, brutal doctrine — evolution — demands, as the rabble did 1900 years ago, that He be crucified. That cannot be the answer of this jury, representing a Christian State and sworn to uphold the laws of Tennessee.

"Your answer will be heard throughout the world; it is eagerly awaited by a praying multitude. If the law is nullified, there will be rejoicing wherever God is repudiated, the Saviour scoffed at, and the Bible ridiculed. Every unbeliever of every kind and degree will be happy.

"If, on the other hand, the law is upheld* and the religion of the school children protected, millions of Christians will call you blessed and, with hearts full of gratitude to God, will sing again that grand old song of triumph:

> *Faith of our Fathers, living still,*
> *In spite of dungeon, fire and sword;*
> *O, how our hearts beat high with joy,*
> *Whene'er we hear that glorious word!*
> *Faith of our fathers — holy faith;*
> *We will be true to thee till death!*

---

*Scopes was found guilty and fined $100; the conviction, however, was overturned on a technicality by the Tennessee Supreme Court.

3. LITERATURE AND RELIGION: THE BIBLE

Text and Context

"Bibles within the Bible"

In the sixteenth-century Reformation, Protestants had discounted tradition in order to magnify scripture. Scripture was the only foundation of faith and practice; scripture was sufficient in and of itself — sola scriptura. *But in the nineteenth century that single and firm foundation began to weaken, or at least came to be looked at in a different way. Private universities such as Harvard and Yale, not under strict denominational control by this time, took the lead in both textual and "higher" criticism. Harvard's Ezra Abbot (1819 – 94), for example, in his capacity as professor of New Testament criticism forged ahead in textual analysis, with the American Revised Version of the Bible (1901) standing as his monument. Yale's Benjamin W. Bacon (1860 – 1932) moved a generation later from efforts to arrive at the best text to those "higher" questions of authorship, editing, revision, and layers of development and understanding within any given text. In the document below, Bacon explores the several sources that lie behind or within the book of Genesis, thereby — as his title page says — "illustrating the presence of Bibles within the Bible."*

The attention of the reading public of America has been called frequently of late to the claims of the science of Higher Criticism, a study all-important to a correct understanding of the Scriptures; and in particular to that theory of the science which maintains the origin of the Pentateuch from a compilation of older documents. They have been assured of the practically unanimous acceptance of this theory abroad, and have been themselves witnesses of the divided opinions of scholars at home. Considering the importance of the subject, the enormous mass of accumulated evidence pro and con, the con-

[Source: B. W. Bacon, *The Genesis of Genesis* (Hartford: Student Publishing Co., 1893), pp. vii – viii, ix – x, xii – xiii.]

flicting claims of scholars as to the resulting benefit or injury to accrue to Christian faith from the acceptance of the theory, it should be apparent to all, as a primary axiom, that the reading public are entitled to judge for themselves.

As to the method of presenting the facts to the public, two propositions are easily established.

I. The public require, not controversial argument, but explanation.

The method of the controversialist, which ever side be championed, rarely gains more than a partisan applause guaranteed in advance, and the converts to be made among those "convinced against their will." It assumes that the public has already made up its mind, or else to judge for the public. The assumption is either false or impertinent. A public accustomed to exercise the right of private judgment demands, in the case of so important and widely supported a theory, a plain statement of the case, an explanation of the general principles involved, of the nature, rather than the details, of the argument, and as simple a presentation of methods and results as possible. It wants "the documents in the case."

II. It is not necessary that the presentation of the case should be made from a standpoint of hostility to the new theory, nor even from one of indifference.

The public wishes to do justice to the new theory. Until it has had opportunity to obtain a general conspectus thereof it occupies the standpoint of traditional opinion. It has not time to give to the minutiae of controversial discussion, but desires to be informed in general outline of the method pursued by the critics and the results propounded. Such an explanation can only be given by one familiar with the critical argument and at least in some degree in sympathy with the theory. The position of such an expositor differs however from that of the advocate and special pleader, in that he undertakes to explain and not to argue. He does not pretend to have no opinion, but refrains from obtruding his opinion upon the reader, preferring to state the most general facts and grounds of critical procedure in an unbiassed way, and leave the reader to draw his own conclusions.

In accordance with the general proposition first laid down, the present work is addressed not merely to scholars and technical investigators, but to the general public. The author believes that critics and biblical scholars will find contributions of value to the science of documentary analysis within its pages; but argument in support of these original investigations has been relegated to technical reviews, and even notes which require the use of Hebrew text have been inserted in a special appendix. . . .

In recent years, thanks largely to the efforts of Profs. W. R. Harper of Chicago and C. A. Briggs of Union Seminary, the claims of Semitic literature to a position in the curriculum of study for every person of liberal education are coming to be felt. The literary and scientific study of the development of the Hebrew and Hellenistic religious consciousness as exhibited in their literature — the Bible — is beginning to be recognized as something not to be left merely to the pulpit orator and the Sunday-school teacher, but to be eagerly welcomed into the domain of school, college and university training. With the recognition has come a perception of the transcendent interest of these studies and a growing demand from beyond the academic walls for admission to at least a gleaner's share in these new fields of scientific investigation.

The author desires to meet this demand, and to present to all classes of Bible students, in churches, Sunday-schools, academies and other institutions of learning, as well as to the general public, that which might be expected to be gained from a course of lectures on the Documentary Theory of the Pentateuch, if delivered on one of the recently endowed university foundations for instruction in Biblical Literature. . . . To the reader who may approach these pages in the endeavor to find a deeper, clearer meaning in the ancient book than hitherto, he would express the sincere and sanguine hope that new light upon the unknown history of this long revered and cherished literature may prove it ever more and more clearly a "word of God," fragments providentially preserved of religious thought from that people whose history is the history of the development of the religious consciousness. If "given unto the fathers in the prophets by divers portions and in divers manners," it was no less "given of God," because the gift extended over many centuries, "line upon line and precept upon precept." It is no less divine if the fruit of generations of consecrated human hearts and consciences, rather than the utterance of a single individual.

What is true of the individual investigator is in a still higher degree true of any science, the science of criticism included. "We can do nothing against the truth, but for the truth." If reassurance is needed in regard to the effect of presenting to the public these claims of the higher criticism, I prefer to give it in the words of others rather than my own. Says Prof. Briggs of Union Seminary: "The higher criticism has rent the crust with which rabbinical tradition and Christian scholasticism have encased the Old Testament, overlaying the poetic and prophetic elements with the legal and the ritual. Younger biblical scholars have caught glimpses of the beauty and glory of biblical literature. The Old Testament is studied as never before in the Christian Church. It is beginning to exert its charming influence upon ministers and people. Christian theology and Christian life will be ere long enriched by it. God's blessing is in it to those who have the Christian wisdom to recognize, and the grace to receive and employ it."

In the firm confidence that a general acquaintance with the discoveries claimed to have been made by the higher criticism in the Pentateuch can only conduce to the lasting benefit of His cause, who said, "Thy word is Truth," this volume is respectfully submitted to the Christian public.

BENJAMIN WISNER BACON.

Parsonage, Oswego, N. Y., October, 1891.

Origins of the New Testament

Not only did scholars raise questions about the specific books in the Bible, they also asked why these books and not others were designated as "sacred." What was the process by which the New Testament, for example, came to consist of twenty-seven particular writings from the first century or so of Christian history? Did other Christian writings exist at that time? Who made the decision about this collection, and when, and by what criteria? Edward C. Moore (1857–1943), Harvard professor of theology, wrote in 1904 of this "evolution of a simple literature into an authoritative Canon." And like Bacon, Moore hoped to communicate his views to a wider public. We simply carry on the spirit of the Reformation, Moore explained, being true to its passion for truth and understanding as we trace the gradual development evident in all things.

We have spoken thus far in these lectures of the origin and growth of that collection of the literature of early Christianity which we know under the name of the New Testament. We need now to stand apart a little from this movement, to set it in what appears to be its true light. The remarkable development which we have endeavored to trace, the evolution of a simple literature into an authoritative Canon, is then first really understood when it is seen in the light of parallel developments which took place in the same age. It has been said that all the great intellectual and spiritual phenomena of a given era may safely be assumed to be but the manifestations of a common impulse, which pervades and possesses the minds of the men of that era. But there are two main comparisons which in this and in the following lecture we shall need to institute. We shall discern that that movement with which we have thus far been dealing is only a part of a far greater movement. Not less illuminating than the discovery that the New Testament has a history such as that which we have tried to sketch, is the recognition that even that history is but the evidence of tendencies and the product of causes which had at least two other issues that are hardly less wonderful than the one which we have named. Nothing in the life of the race is isolated, just as nothing in our own personal experience stands apart and out of relation to all other things. . . .

We cannot heartily adhere to the historic evolution of Scripture, without holding to the evolution of church government, and of doctrine and ritual as well. Or, rather, inasmuch as we, in common with most men since the Reformation, do hold to the evolution of church government, from the simplest and most natural beginnings in the time of the Apostles to the great structure and colossal organization which in the Middle Ages overshadowed all the world; and since, if we ever thought of it, we do hold to the growth of the great historic forms of worship, we cannot therefore consistently do

[Source: E. C. Moore, *The New Testament in the Christian Church* (New York: Macmillan Co., 1904), pp. 213–14, 215–18.]

otherwise than hold to the historic development of Scripture and of dogma as well. We do but bring to bear to-day upon the Scripture the same criticism which the Reformers employed so justly and effectively upon the tradition of the church four hundred years ago. We do but vindicate ourselves the children of their spirit. And surely a far nobler and more vital conception of the church has come through the criticism which in the Reformation was applied to the traditional theory of the church.

This is true as to dogma. The confessions, whatever be their names, to which men give their assent, have tended to become to the Protestant church exactly what the tradition is to the Roman church. It has been made in the Protestant polemic a standing reproach to the Roman Catholic church that it rests upon the Scripture and upon the tradition. It has been deemed the fame of the Protestant churches that they rest upon the Scripture alone. But this contention can scarcely be maintained. In the name of creeds and confessions, from the Apostles' Creed down to the confessions of our own time, the attempt has been made to fix an authoritative interpretation of Scripture, and to praise or to blame men as they accord or disagree with that interpretation. But assuredly this is only traditionalism over again. Indeed, one may say that the Roman tradition has this advantage, that it receives its utterance, in the concrete case, from living men. Confessionalism tends to confer the power of the authoritative interpretation of Scripture only upon men who are dead. We have passed through a period of abuse of doctrine, and of the assumption upon the part of some that we can get on without doctrine. But this is merely reaction against an unhistoric notion of the nature of doctrine. Doctrine is nothing but the adjustment of men's thoughts concerning religion to their thoughts concerning all other things. That adjustment is a perennially necessary task. The attempt to hold our thoughts concerning religion out of all relation to our other thoughts is the sure road by which men, according to temperament, arrive at one of two conditions. They end either in having thoughts without any religion or else in having religion without thoughts. Either condition is deplorable. These are signs that we are on the eve of a noble reconstruction of Christian doctrine. That reconstruction is made possible by the clear historic sense which we have gained as to what doctrine is.

So is it also as to Scripture. It was not unnatural that the men of four hundred years ago should set up against the authority of an infallible church an authority of Scripture which they soon came to apprehend in an almost equally external way. Those men could not have done differently. Their theory of Scripture had a certain historic inevitableness and a great historic right. But they did not perceive that the light of history, and that right reasoning upon history which they so successfully applied to the prevailing theory of the authority of the church, would one day have its way with the idea of an external authority of Scripture as well. It ought to be repeated, to the honor of the first generation of the Reformers, that they began thus to reason upon the problem. There is something pathetic in the defection of the later generations of Protestants from this true example of the Reformers. The authority of Scripture, when thought of as something external and not subject to rational review, has come near to being as great a tyranny and source of darkness as was ever the authority of the church. But, as we have seen, the most vital and potent conception of Scripture has been regained for us, the most reverent and worshipful acknowledgment of the authority of Scripture has been again made possible for us, exactly through the historic sense of what the Christian Scripture really is.

"A Jewish Interpretation"

Within Judaism, and especially within the Reform branch, scholars also wrestled with the implications of both the lower (textual) and higher (contextual) criticism. At Hebrew Union College in Cincinnati, the intellectual stronghold of Reform, Julian Morgenstern (1881–1976), professor of Bible and Semitic languages —and later the college's president, presented "a Jewish interpretation" of the Book of Genesis. The scholarship for Hebrew scriptures as well as for the New Testament had been largely if not exclusively a Gentile enterprise. Morgenstern argued that the Pentateuch, the first Five Books of Moses, could "be correctly understood only when interpreted from a positive Jewish standpoint." This perspective Morgenstern endeavored to provide as early as 1919 in his own commentary on the Book of Genesis. The excerpt below is taken from the preface to the second edition of this book "designed primarily for use by Jewish religious school teachers."

The book aims to be precisely what its title indicates, a Jewish interpretation of Genesis. We have had countless books on Genesis by Jewish authors. But, with rare exceptions, they have sought only to recount the stories of Genesis literally, without penetrating adequately to the fundamental Jewish spiritual truth beneath, and without consideration of the many significant discoveries and teachings of modern Biblical science with regard to Genesis. They have confounded Biblical myths, legends and traditions with what they have mistakenly called Biblical history. Thereby they have, on the one hand, only too frequently worked mischievous confusion and misunderstanding in the minds of those whom they sought to instruct, and, on the other hand, they have missed almost entirely the golden opportunity to impart the really basic truths of Judaism to the most receptive minds.

We have also had numerous scientific interpretations of Genesis, almost all by non-Jewish scholars. Their work has been almost entirely analytic in character. They have picked Genesis, and the entire Old Testament in fact, to

[Source: Julian Morgenstern, *The Book of Genesis: A Jewish Interpretation*, rev. ed. (New York: Schocken Books, 1965 [1919]), pp. 7–9.]

pieces. They have resolved it into its component sources, and have determined with quite reliable accuracy when and under what conditions these were written. They have also determined when, how and by whom these originally independent sources were gradually combined, until at last our present Old Testament came into being.

But singularly enough, they have failed in considerable measure to determine the ends for which these sources were combined and the thoughts and aims which animated the editors. They have, apparently, tacitly assumed that this was an inevitable and largely incidental and purposeless process. Therefore they have failed to realize and to stress that the Old Testament, and particularly the Torah, the Five Books of Moses, is entirely a Jewish work, written by Jewish authors and edited by Jewish thinkers, the product of Jewish religious genius and a unit of Jewish religious thought and doctrine, and that it must be animated throughout by some deeply Jewish purpose, and can, in the final analysis, be correctly understood only when interpreted from a positive Jewish standpoint. Consequently, while science has taught us much about the Old Testament, new, unsuspected, and significant truths, it has failed almost entirely to catch its real Jewish purpose, spirit and flavor. For this reason the usual scientific, analytic interpretation of the Old Testament is inadequate and fails to achieve its ultimate and positive potentials.

The present work aims to be a popular scientific interpretation of Genesis, but an interpretation which is not merely analytic, and therefore largely negative and destructive, but which is also, and more pronouncedly, synthetic, constructive and Jewish. It accepts the established and irrefutable teachings of science with regard to Genesis, and seeks constantly to determine what is the fundamental Jewish thought and teaching of the various stories and groups of stories, for the sake of which their Jewish authors and editors cast them into their present form. It operates on the principle that the Old Testament is a Jewish work throughout, and that it can be understood correctly and authoritatively only when interpreted from the standpoint of its Jewish teachings. It proceeds with deep love and reverence for Judaism and its teachings and practices and for Jewish tradition and history. But it is animated by equal love and reverence for the future of Judaism and for the evolution and expansion which its beliefs and teachings must inevitably undergo in the constant and steady progress of human thought and knowledge and in the irresistible compulsion to adapt and apply these teachings and principles to the needs and standards of modern existence, in order that Judaism may continue to be, what it has always been, a true religion of life, by which men may not only die resignedly but, even more, may live nobly, bravely and usefully.

In this spirit and for this purpose and with this eager hope this book is offered once again, in this second edition, to the public, to a new, a larger and, religiously, a broader and more composite public. May this hope be richly fulfilled.

"The New Approach"

Introduced above (p. 144), Harry Emerson Fosdick —unlike Bacon, Moore, or Morgenstern —was not primarily a biblical scholar or student of the early church. He was a pastor and preacher caught up in the turmoil of modern philosophy, science, and biblical criticism. But Fosdick did resemble the three men named above in his desire to communicate the results of modern speculations and investigations to a broader public, to let Americans at large know what was going on and to assist them in their accommodation to or assimilation of all this new knowledge. And in this role, Fosdick was enormously successful, his Modern Use of the Bible *(1924) being often reprinted and widely read.*

The results of the modern study of Scripture can be grouped under two heads, and to one of these we now turn our attention. For the first time in the history of the church, we of this generation are able to arrange the writings of the Bible in approximately chronological order. That statement, like other summaries of human knowledge such as that the earth is round, can be swiftly and simply made, but its involved meanings reach far and deep. The total consequence of all the work of the Higher Criticism is that at last we are able to see the Bible a good deal as a geologist sees the strata of the earth; we can tell when and in what order the deposits were laid down whose accumulated results constitute our Scriptures. Was there ever such an unfortunate label put upon an entirely legitimate procedure as the name "Higher Criticism"? Were one to search the dictionary for two words suggestive of superciliousness, condescension, and destructiveness, one could hardly find any to surpass these. Yet the Higher Criticism simply asks about the books of the Bible: who wrote them, when and why they were written, and to whom. Every efficient Sunday School teacher, according to his own ability, has always been a Higher Critic. This process, however, armed with our modern instruments of literary, historical, and archeological research, pushed with unremitting zeal and tireless labor, after following many false trails and landing in many cul-de-sacs, has gotten a result, at least in its outlines, well assured. . . .

From the purely scientific point of view this is an absorbingly interesting matter, but even more from the standpoint of practical results its importance is difficult to exaggerate. It means that we can trace the great ideas of Scripture in their development from their simple and elementary forms, when they first appear in the earliest writings, until they come to their full maturity in the latest books. Indeed, the general soundness of the critical results is tested by this fact that as one moves up from the earlier writings toward the later he can observe the development of any idea he chooses to select, such as God,

[Source: H. E. Fosdick, *The Modern Use of the Bible* (New York: Association Press, 1926), pp. 6–8, 11–12, 28–31.]

man, duty, sin, worship. Plainly we are dealing with ideas that enlarge their scope, deepen their meaning, are played upon by changing circumstance and maturing thought, so that from its lowliest beginning in the earliest writings of the Hebrews any religious or ethical idea of the Bible can now be traced, traveling an often uneven but ascending roadway to its climax in the teaching of Jesus.

That this involves a new approach to the Bible is plain. To be sure, our fathers were not blind to the fact that the New Testament overtops, fulfils, and in part supersedes the Old. They had the Sermon on the Mount and the opening verses of the Epistle to the Hebrews to assure them of that. But our fathers never possessed such concrete and detailed illustration of that idea as we have now. . . .

E. J. Pace cartoon, 1920s
(Billy Graham Center)

Fortunately for us, spiritual efficiency in the use of the Bible is not entirely dependent upon correctness of exegesis. These older interpreters who used the Book in ways now impossible for us did not on that account fail to find there the sustenance and inspiration which we may miss if we trust too much to our keener instruments and too little to spiritual insight. Just as men raised life-sustaining crops from the earth's soil long before they analyzed the earth's strata, so they got from Scripture the bread of life even if the chronological arrangement of the documents was yet undreamed. Nevertheless, it is of obvious importance that a new approach to the Bible has been forced upon us. No longer can we think of the Book as on a level, no longer read its maturer messages back into its earlier sources. We know now that every idea in the Bible started from primitive and childlike origins and, with however many setbacks and delays, grew in scope and height toward the culmination in Christ's Gospel. We know now that the Bible is the record of an amazing spiritual development. . . .

This leads us to our final statement about the consequences of the new approach to the Bible. It restores to us the whole Book. It gives to us a comprehensive, inclusive view of the Scriptures and enables us to see them, not piecemeal, but as a whole. Those of us who accept the modern knowledge of the Bible as assured and endeavor to put it to good use are continually being accused of tearing the Book to pieces, of cutting out this or that, and of leaving a mere tattered patchwork of what was once a glorious unity. The fact is precisely the opposite. The new approach to the Bible once more integrates the Scriptures, saves us from our piecemeal treatment of them, and restores to us the whole book seen as a unified development from early and simple beginnings to a great conclusion.

One who has mastered the new approach is at home in any part of the Bible and can use all of it. He opens its pages at any point and knows where he is. He knows the road by which the thought that he finds there has traveled. He knows the contribution that there is being made to the enlarging revelation. He knows where next the road will turn and climb, and he knows where it all comes out in the Gospel. Once more, in a new way, he has regained what once our fathers had and what recently the church has lost: ability to see the Bible in its entirety and to use it as a whole.

For no part of it is without its usefulness. People to-day are living in all the stages of development which its records represent. Its earliest, crudest sins and shames, views of God, and ideals of man are all among us. As one travels through the Book there is no place on the road where one does not meet some problems which modern folk are facing, some points of view which they ought to get or ought to outgrow, some faiths which they ought to achieve or ought to improve upon. So long as a man knows the whole road and judges every step of it by the spirit of Christ, who is its climax, he can use it all.

This is the finest consequence of the new approach to the Bible: it gives us the whole Book back again.

If some one protests that it spoils the idea of inspiration, I ask why. We used to think that God created the world by fiat on the instant, and then, learning that the world evolves, many were tempted to cry out that God did not create it at all. We now know that changing one's idea of a process does not in itself alter one's philosophy of origins. So we used to think of inspiration as a procedure which produced a book guaranteed in all its parts against error, and containing from beginning to end a unanimous system of truth. No well-instructed mind, I think, can hold that now. Our idea of the nature of the process has changed. What has actually happened is the production of a Book which from lowly beginnings to great conclusions records the development of truth about God and his will, beyond all comparison the richest in spiritual issue that the world has known. Personally, I think that the Spirit of God was behind that process and in it. I do not believe that man ever found God when God was not seeking to be found. The under side of the process is man's discovery; the upper side is God's revelation. Our ideas of the method of inspiration have changed; verbal dictation, inerrant manuscripts, uniformity of doctrine between 1000 B.C. and 70 A.D. —all such ideas have become incredible in the face of the facts. But one who earnestly believes in the divine Spirit will be led by the new approach to the Bible to repeat with freshened meaning and deepened content the opening words of the Epistle to the Hebrews:

> "God, having of old time spoken unto the fathers in the prophets by divers portions and in divers manners, hath at the end of these days spoken unto us in his Son."

Reactions and Results

Protestant Trials

So much to adjust to, and it came so fast. Denominational officers and institutions confronted controversy that would not go away and could not be quietly contained. (1) An early trial of the spirit —not a formal proceeding —involved Crawford Howell Toy (1836–1919) when he was on the faculty of Southern Baptist Seminary, recently moved to Louisville, Kentucky. Having studied abroad in Berlin, Toy had absorbed the latest techniques and conclusions of biblical scholarship. When he returned to the seminary

[Sources: (1) George Shriver, ed., *American Religious Heretics* (Nashville: Abingdon Press, 1966), pp. 79–81, 82–84. (2) C. A. Briggs, *The Defence of Professor Briggs before the Presbytery of New York* (New York: Charles Scribner's Sons, 1893), pp. 84–85, 88–90.]

in 1869, his introduction of some of this into the classroom (though "some things I have not thought expedient to state in my classes") led to growing uneasiness in a financially insecure institution. After much uneasiness on both sides, Toy wrote the letter below much more in sorrow than in anger. He taught thereafter at Harvard for nearly thirty years. (2) A trial in the fullest sense was the lot of Charles A. Briggs (1841–1912; mentioned by B. W. Bacon above). Associated with Union Theological Seminary in New York City for virtually all of his adult life, this leading Old Testament scholar was tried before the Presbyterians' judicial body in New York. He was charged with many deviations from orthodoxy, among them his questioning of the "inerrancy of Holy Scripture." A portion of Briggs's defense on this point is given below. Adjudged guilty, Briggs was suspended from the Presbyterian ministry, casting his lot in 1899 with the Episcopalians. His association with Union, however, continued uninterrupted until the end of his life.

1.

To the Board of Trustees of the Southern Baptist Theological Seminary.

Dear Brethren: — It having lately become apparent to me that my views of Inspiration differ considerably from those of the body of my brethren, I ask leave to lay my opinions on that subject before you, and submit them to your judgment.

At the outset I may say that I fully accept the first article of the Fundamental Principles of the Seminary; "the Scriptures of the Old and New Testament were given by inspiration of God, and are the only sufficient, certain and authoritative rule of all saving knowledge and obedience," and that I have always taught and do now teach in accordance with, and not contrary to it.

It is in the details of the subject that my divergence from the prevailing views in the denomination occurs. This divergence has gradually increased in connection with my studies, from year to year, till it has become perceptible to myself and others.

In looking for light on Inspiration, my resort has been, and is, to the Scriptures themselves alone, and I rest myself wholly on their testimony. It seems to me that while they declare the fact of Divine Inspiration, they say nothing of the manner of its action. We are told that men spake from God, borne along by the Holy Ghost, and that all Scripture is given by Inspiration of God, and is profitable for doctrine, for reproof, for correction, for instruction in righteousness, that the man of God may be complete, thoroughly furnished for every good work. The object of the Scriptures is here said to be an ethical, spiritual one. They were given man for his guidance and edification in religion, as our Lord also says: "Sanctify them in the truth; Thy word is truth."

As nothing is said of the mode of operation of the Divine Spirit, of the manner in which the divine saving truth is impressed on the mind, of the relation of the divine influence to the ordinary workings of the human intellect, we must, as to these points, consult the books of the Bible themselves and examine the facts. Against facts, no theory can stand, and I prefer, therefore, to have no theory, but submit myself to the guidance of the actual words of Holy Scripture.

As the result of my examination, I believe that the Bible is wholly divine and wholly human; the Scripture is the truth of God communicated by Him to the human soul, appropriated by it and then given out with free, human energy, as the sincere, real conviction of the soul. To undertake to say what must be the outward forms of God's revelation of himself to man, seems to me presumptuous. If rationalism be the decision of religious questions by human reason, then it appears to me to be rationalistic to say that a Divine revelation must conform to certain outward conditions; to insist, for example, that it must be written in a certain style, or that it *must* teach certain things in geography, or astronomy, or similar matters.

I hold all *a priori* reasoning here to be out of place, and all theories based on it to be worthless. Such procedure seems to me to be out of keeping with the simple, reverent spirit appropriate to him who comes to search into the truth of God. For this reason I am forced to discard the theories of some pious men as Fichte and Wordsworth, who have proceeded in this *a priori* way, and to keep myself to the facts given in the Bible itself.

These facts make on me the impression that the Scripture writers are men who have received messages from God and utter them under purely free, human conditions. The inspired man speaks his own language, not another man's, and writes under the conditions of his own age, not under those of some other age. His personality, his individuality, has the freest play, all under the control of the guiding Divine Spirit. . . .

In one word, I regard the Old Testament as the record of the whole circle of the experiences of Israel, the people whom God chose to be the depository of His truth, all whose life He so guided as to bring out of it lessons of instruction which He then caused to be written down for preservation. The nation lived out its life in a free, human way, yet under divine guidance, and its Prophets, Priests and Psalmist recorded the spiritual, religious history under the condition of their times. The divine truth is presented in a framework of relatively unessential things, as Christ in his Parables introduced accessories merely for the purpose of bringing out a principle, so that the Parable of the Ten Virgins, for example, may properly be said to be the framework or vehicle of religious truth. As a whole the Parable may in a sense be called a religious teaching, but speaking more precisely we should say that a part of it is such teaching, or that the teaching is contained in it.

What I have said of the outward form of the Old Testament applies, as I think, to the outward form of the New Testament. I will not lightly see a historical or other inaccuracy in the Gospels or the Acts, but if I find such, they do not for me affect the divine teachings of these books. The centre of the New Testament is Christ himself, salvation is in Him, and a historical error cannot affect the fact of His existence and His teachings. The Apostles wrote out of their personal convictions of the reality of the truth of Christ. If Paul makes a slip of memory, . . . that cannot affect his spiritual relation to Christ and to the Father, nor detract from his power as an inspired man. If his numerical statements do not always agree with those of the Old Testament, (as in Gal. iii. 17, compared with Exodus xiii. 40), that seems to me a matter of no consequence.

If the New Testament writers sometimes quote the Old Testament in the Greek Version, which does not correctly render the Hebrew, (as in Heb. x:5, quoted from Psa. xl:6.) that does not affect the main thought or the religious teaching. And it may be that in some cases my principles of exegesis lead me to a different interpretation of an Old Testament passage from that which I find given by some New Testament writer, as in Psa. xl:6, above mentioned; this again I look on as an incidental thing, of which the true religious teaching is independent. I should add that in the majority of cases I hold that the New Testament quotations correctly represent the sense of the Old Testament, and there is always a true spiritual feeling controlling them. I think that Peter's discourse, in Acts ii, gives the true spiritual sense of the passage in Joel, and so, many references of Old Testament passages to Christ throughout the New Testament. It ought also to be noticed that the ancient ideas of quotations were different from ours: ancient writers cite in a general way from memory for illustration, and permit themselves without remark such alterations as a modern writer would think it necessary to call attention to. This is to be regarded as a difference of habit arising from a difference of the times. The freeness of quotation in the Scripture writers does not, for example, affect their general honesty and truthfulness, nor their spiritual train of thought, nor their spiritual authority. It is only a human condition of the divine truth they utter. In these men the Spirit of God dwelt, and out of their writings comes a divine power. Recognizing in them a divine element, I cannot reject it because of what seems to me outward or non-spiritual limitation. I do not condition divine action, but accept it in the form in which I find it.

As to criticism (question of date and authorship) and exegesis, these stand by themselves, and have nothing to do with Inspiration. The prophecy in Isa. xl — lxvi. is not less inspired if it be assigned to the period of the Babylonian Exile, and the "Servant of Jehovah" be regarded as referring primarily to Israel. These are questions of interpretation and historical research, in which, as it seems to me, the largest liberty must be allowed. If some of the Psalms should be put in the Maccabean period (B.C. 160), this is no reason for doubting their inspiration; God could as easily act on men in the year B.C. 160 as B.C. 400 or B.C. 700.

It is proper to add that the above statement of my views of Inspiration is the fullest that I have ever expressed. Some things I have not thought it expedient to state to my classes in the Seminary. At the same time I regard these views as helpful for Bible study. If at first they seem strange, I am convinced that they will appear more natural with further strict study of the text.

I beg leave to repeat that I am guided wholly by what seems to me the correct interpretation of the Scriptures themselves. If an error in my interpretation is pointed out, I shall straightway give it up. I cannot accept *a priori* reasoning, but I stake everything on the words of the Bible, and this course I believe to be for the furtherance of the truth of God.

And now, in conclusion, I wish to say distinctly and strongly that I consider the view above given to be not only lawful for me to teach as Professor in the Seminary, but one that will bring aid and firm standing-ground to many a perplexed mind and establish the truth of God on a firm foundation.

But that I may relieve the Board of all embarrassment in the matter, I tender my resignation as Professor in the Southern Baptist Theological Seminary.

Respectfully submitted,

May, 1879   C. H. Toy

2.

"The Presbyterian Church in the United States of America charges the Rev. Charles A. Briggs, D.D., being a Minister of the said Church and a member of the Presbytery of New York, with teaching that errors may have existed in the original text of the Holy Scripture, as it came from its authors, which is contrary to the essential doctrine taught in the Holy Scriptures and in the Standards of the said Church, that the Holy Scripture is the Word of God written, immediately inspired, and the rule of faith and practice." . . .

(1) The Charge alleges three offences. It alleges that the doctrine taught by me is contrary to these three essential doctrines — (*a*) that Holy Scripture is the Word of God written; (*b*) that Holy Scripture is immediately inspired; and (*c*) that Holy Scripture is the rule of faith and practice.

(2) It is alleged that I teach "that errors may have existed in the original text of the Holy Scripture, as it came from its authors." This statement of my doctrine I can admit as fairly accurate. But when we look at the specification, notice that it consists of a long extract from the Inaugural Address. You should bear in mind that the only proper use of this extract is to prove the doctrine attributed to me in the Charge, which doctrine I admit. You have no right to use it to impute to me any other objectionable doctrine. You have no right to vote me guilty on the ground of any other objection to my words than that stated in the Charge. This is all the more important in view of the irrelevant passages of Scripture cited to sustain the Charge, which may be interpreted by you in a sense different from the true sense. You have no right to vote me guilty on the basis of these passages. You can consider nothing

but my doctrine as stated in the Charge and determine whether that is contrary or not contrary to the essential doctrines named in the Charge.

(3) The only question which need concern us, therefore, is whether my doctrine is contrary to any one, or any two, or all three of the essential doctrines of the Confession stated in the Charge. Doubtless the prosecution think that there is contradiction here; and it may be that a majority of this Presbytery think so. . . .

I agree to the doctrines (1) that "Holy Scripture is the Word of God written;" (2) "immediately inspired;" and (3) "the rule of faith and practice."

Do these statements necessarily involve the doctrine that there are no errors in Holy Scripture? (*a*) The doctrine that "the Holy Scriptures are the rule of faith and practice" clearly does not involve that "the Holy Scriptures are the rule in matters other than faith and practice." If I find fallibility in Holy Scripture in matters of faith and practice, I am inconsistent with the Confession. But in the Inaugural, I expressly disclaimed such fallibility. . . .

The only errors I have found or ever recognized in Holy Scripture have been beyond the range of faith and practice, and therefore they do not impair the infallibility of Holy Scripture as a rule of faith and practice.

But it is claimed that if I recognize errors in matters beyond the range of faith and practice, I excite suspicion as to the infallibility of Holy Scripture within the range of faith and practice. You are entitled to that opinion for yourselves, but you have no right to force your opinion upon me. The Confession does not say "rule of all things," but "the rule of faith and practice." You must judge by the Confession, not by your fears, or your impressions, or by the conclusions you have made. But is it true that fallibility in the Bible in matters beyond the scope of the divine revelation impairs the infallibility in matters within the scope of divine revelation? We claim that it does not. The sacred writings were not composed in heaven by the Holy Spirit, they were not sent down from heaven by angel hands, they were not committed to the care of perfect men, they were not kept by a succession of perfect priests from that moment until the present time. If these had been the facts in the case, we might have had a Bible infallible in every particular. But none of these things are true. God gave His Holy Word to men in an entirely different way. He used the human reason and all the faculties of imperfect human nature. He used the voice and hands of imperfect men. He allowed the sacred writings to be edited and re-edited, arranged and re-arranged and rearranged again by imperfect scribes. It is improbable that such imperfect instrumentalities should attain perfect results. It was improbable that fallible men should produce a series of writings infallible in every respect. It was sufficient that divine inspiration and the guidance of the Holy Spirit should make their writings an infallible rule of faith and practice, and that the divine energy should push the human and the fallible into the external forms, into the unessential and unnecessary matters, into the human setting of the divine ideals. As the river of life flowing forth from the throne of

God, according to Ezekiel's Vision, entering into the Dead Sea quickens its waters and fills them with new life, so that "everything shall live whithersoever the river cometh" . . . "But the miry places thereof and the marshes thereof shall not be healed" (Ez. xlvii. 9– 11); so may it be with that divine influence which we call inspiration, when it flows into a man. It quickens and enriches his whole nature, his experience, his utterance, his expressions, with truth and life divine, and yet leaves some human infirmities unhealed in order that the revelation may be essentially divine and infallible and yet bear traces of the human and fallible into the midst of which it came.

Catholic Concerns

Catholic biblical scholarship had not advanced far enough in America by the end of the nineteenth century to alarm the Vatican. But in Europe, Alfred F. Loisy (1857 – 1940) had aroused much anxiety and calls for caution. In 1893 Pope Leo XIII issued Providentissimus Deus, *a statement designed to discourage the newer critical methods being applied to biblical study. "There has arisen, to the great detriment of religion," the pope wrote, "an inept method, dignified by the name of 'higher criticism,' which pretends to judge the origin, integrity, and authority of each book from internal indications alone." The authority of the Church, mother and teacher, was being by-passed in the name of science. Six years later in an encyclical dealing with "Americanism," the papacy rejected the notion that "the Church ought to adapt herself somewhat to our advanced civilization, and, relaxing her ancient vigor, show some indulgence to modern popular theories and methods." Then in 1907 Pope Pius X in a long letter (*Pascendi Dominici Gregis*) condemned the Modernists without equivocation, the Church having already earlier that year listed some sixty-five "Errors of the Modernists." Many of those "errors," as is evident below, pertained to the proper approach to and understanding of "the Sacred Books." (Loisy was excommunicated in 1908.)*

With truly lamentable results, our age, casting aside all restraint in its search for the ultimate causes of things, frequently pursues novelites so ardently that it rejects the legacy of the human race. Thus it falls into very serious errors, which are even more serious when they concern sacred authority, the interpretation of Sacred Scripture, and the principal mysteries of Faith. The fact that many Catholic writers also go beyond the limits determined by the Fathers and the Church herself is extremely regrettable. In the name of higher knowl-

[Source: *Lamentibili Sane,* July 3, 1907 (Washington: National Catholic Welfare Conference, 1963), pp. 45– 47.]

edge and historical research (they say), they are looking for that progress of dogmas which is, in reality, nothing but the corruption of dogmas.

These errors are being daily spread among the faithful. Lest they captivate the faithful's minds and corrupt the purity of their faith, His Holiness, Pius X, by Divine Providence, Pope, has decided that the chief errors should be noted and condemned by the Office of this Holy Roman and Universal Inquisition.

Therefore, after a very diligent investigation and consultation with the Reverend Consultors, the Most Eminent and Reverend Lord Cardinals, the General Inquisitors in matters of faith and morals have judged the following propositions to be condemned and proscribed. In fact, by this general decree, they are condemned and proscribed.

✝   ✝   ✠   ✠   ✠

1. The ecclesiastical law which prescribes that books concerning the Divine Scriptures are subject to previous examination does not apply to critical scholars and students of scientific exegesis of the Old and New Testament.

2. The Church's interpretation of the Sacred Books is by no means to be rejected; nevertheless, it is subject to the more accurate judgment and correction of the exegetes.

3. From the ecclesiastical judgments and censures passed against free and more scientific exegesis, one can conclude that the Faith the Church proposes contradicts history and that Catholic teaching cannot really be reconciled with the true origins of the Christian religion.

4. Even by dogmatic definitions the Church's magisterium cannot determine the genuine sense of the Sacred Scriptures.

5. Since the deposit of Faith contains only revealed truths, the Church has no right to pass judgment on the assertions of the human sciences.

6. The "Church learning" and the "Church teaching" collaborate in such a way in defining truths that it only remains for the "Church teaching" to sanction the opinions of the "Church learning."

7. In proscribing errors, the Church cannot demand any internal assent from the faithful by which the judgments she issues are to be embraced.

8. They are free from all blame who treat lightly the condemnations passed by the Sacred Congregation of the Index or by the Roman Congregations.

9. They display excessive simplicity or ignorance who believe that God is really the author of the Sacred Scriptures.

10. The inspiration of the books of the Old Testament consists in this: The Israelite writers handed down religious doctrines under a peculiar aspect which was either little or not at all known to the Gentiles.

11. Divine inspiration does not extend to all of Sacred Scriptures so that it renders its parts, each and every one, free from every error.

12. If he wishes to apply himself usefully to Biblical studies, the exegete

must first put aside all preconceived opinions about the supernatural origin of Sacred Scripture and interpret it the same as any other merely human document.

13. The Evangelists themselves, as well as the Christians of the second and third generation, artificially arranged the evangelical parables. In such a way they explained the scanty fruit of the preaching of Christ among the Jews.

14. In many narrations the Evangelists recorded, not so much things that are true, as things which, even though false, they judged to be more profitable for their readers.

15. Until the time the canon was defined and constituted, the Gospels were increased by additions and corrections. Therefore there remained in them only a faint and uncertain trace of the doctrine of Christ.

16. The narrations of John are not properly history, but a mystical contemplation of the Gospel. The discourses contained in his Gospel are theological meditations, lacking historical truth concerning the mystery of salvation.

17. The fourth Gospel exaggerated miracles not only in order that the extraordinary might stand out but also in order that it might become more suitable for showing forth the work and glory of the Word Incarnate.

18. John claims for himself the quality of witness concerning Christ. In reality, however, he is only a distinguished witness of the Christian life, or of the life of Christ in the Church at the close of the first century.

19. Heterodox exegetes have expressed the true sense of the Scriptures more faithfully than Catholic exegetes.

Biblical Societies and Studies

In 1880 in the home of Philip Schaff (see Vol. I, pp. 517–18, and above, p. 10) in New York City, the Society of Biblical Literature came into being, with its own journal appearing two years later. A dozen years after the Society's founding, its president (J. H. Thayer) recommended the establishment of "an American School of Oriental Studies in Palestine," now the American School for Oriental Research. The great energies expended in the new biblical scholarship around this time may be suggested by noting a few titles: Strong, Exhaustive Concordance of the Bible *(1894); Smith,* Historical Geography of the Holy Land *(1894); Cheyne and Black,* Encyclopedia Biblica *(1899) in four volumes; and Hastings,* Dictionary of the Bible *(1908) in five volumes. And the list is by no means exhaustive. (1) An ambitious biblical commentary, the International Critical Commen-*

[Sources: (1) S. R. Driver, *A Critical and Exegetical Commentary on Deuteronomy* (Edinburgh: T. & T. Clark, 1895), pp. xi–xiii. (2) *Divino Afflante Spiritu*, 1943 (Washington: National Catholic Welfare Conference, n. d.), pp. 14–15, 17, 18–19, 22.]

*tary, also began publication in this period, its earliest volumes appearing in
1895. This work, an Anglo-American effort, was under the general editorship of S. R. Driver of Oxford, Alfred Plummer of Durham, and the
aforementioned Charles A. Briggs of Union. The excerpt below is from the
preface to Driver's own commentary on the Book of Deuteronomy. (2) The
"Catholic concerns" noted above delayed the full participation of America's
Roman Catholic scholars in this renaissance of biblical study. In 1938,
however, the Catholic Biblical Association was founded, with the* Catholic
Biblical Quarterly *emerging the following year. When in 1943 Pope Pius
XII issued an encyclical giving his encouragement and blessing to such scholarly undertakings, biblical study in the Catholic community was placed on
solid footing. A portion of that 1943 statement is given below.*

1.

The aim of the present volume (in accordance with the plan of the series,
of which it forms part) is to supply the English reader with a Commentary
which, so far as the writer's powers permit it, may be abreast of the best
scholarship and knowledge of the day. Deuteronomy is one of the most
attractive, as it is also one of the most important, books of the Old Testament;
and a Commentary which may render even approximate justice to its many-
sided contents has for long been a desideratum in English theological literature. Certainly the Hebrew text (except in parts of c. 32. 33) is not, as a
rule, difficult; nevertheless, even this has frequently afforded me the opportunity of illustrating delicacies of Hebrew usage, which might escape the
attention of some readers. On the other hand, the contents of Deuteronomy
call for much explanation and discussion: they raise many difficult and controverted questions; and they afford frequent scope for interesting and sometimes far-reaching inquiry. Deuteronomy stands out conspicuously in the
literature of the Old Testament: it has important relations, literary, theological, and historical, with other parts of the Old Testament; it possesses itself a
profound moral and spiritual significance; it is an epoch-making expression
of the life and feeling of the prophetic nation. I have done my best to give
due prominence to these and similar characteristic features; and by pointing
out both the spiritual and other factors which Deuteronomy presupposes, and
the spiritual and other influences which either originated with it, or received
from it a fresh impulse, to define the position which it occupies in the national
and religious history of Israel. Deuteronomy, moreover, by many of the
observances which it enjoins, bears witness to the fact that Israel's civilization,
though permeated by a different spirit from that of other ancient nations, was
nevertheless reared upon the same material basis; and much light may often
be thrown, both upon the institutions and customs to which it alludes, and
upon the manner in which they are treated by the Hebrew legislator, from
the archaeological researches of recent years. Nor is this all. The study of

Deuteronomy carries the reader into the very heart of the critical problems which arise in connexion with the Old Testament. At almost every step, especially in the central, legislative part (c. 12–26), the question of the relation of Deuteronomy to other parts of the Pentateuch forces itself upon the student's attention. In dealing with the passages where this is the case, I have stated the facts as clearly and completely as was possible within the limits of space at my disposal, adding, where necessary, references to authorities who treat them at greater length. As a work of the Mosaic age, Deuteronomy, I must own, though intelligible, *if it stood perfectly alone,* —*i.e.* if the history of Israel had been other than it was, —does not seem to me to be intelligible, when viewed in the light shed upon it by other parts of the Old Testament: a study of it in that light reveals too many features which are inconsistent with such a supposition. The entire secret of its composition, and the full nature of the sources of which its author availed himself, we cannot hope to discover; but enough is clear to show that, however regretfully we may abandon it, the traditional view of its origin and authorship cannot be maintained. The adoption of this verdict of criticism implies no detraction either from the inspired authority of Deuteronomy, or from its ethical and religious value. Deuteronomy marks a stage in the Divine education of the chosen people: but the methods of God's spiritual providence are analogous to those of His natural providence: the revelation of Himself to man was accomplished not once for all, but through many diverse channels (Heb. I), and by a gradual historical process; and the stage in that process to which Deuteronomy belongs is not the age of Moses, but a later age. Deuteronomy gathers up the spiritual lessons and experiences not of a single lifetime, but of many generations of God-inspired men. It is a nobly-conceived endeavour to stir the conscience of the individual Israelite, and to infuse Israel's whole national life with new spiritual and moral energy. And in virtue of the wonderful combination of the national with the universal, which characterizes the higher teaching of the Old Testament, it fulfils a yet wider mission: it speaks in accents which all can still understand; it appeals to motives and principles, which can never lose their validity and truth, so long as human nature remains what it is: it is the bearer of a message to all time.

2.

23. Being thoroughly prepared by the knowledge of the ancient languages and by the aids afforded by the art of criticism, let the Catholic exegete undertake the task, of all those imposed on him the greatest, that namely of discovering and expounding the genuine meaning of the Sacred Books. In the performance of this task let the interpreters bear in mind that their foremost and greatest endeavor should be to discern and define clearly that sense of the biblical words which is called literal. Aided by the context and by comparison with similar passages, let them therefore by means of their

knowledge of languages search out with all diligence the literal meaning of the words; all these helps indeed are wont to be pressed into service in the explanation also of profane writers, so that the mind of the author may be made abundantly clear.

24. The commentators of the Sacred Letters, mindful of the fact that where there is question of a divinely inspired text, the care and interpretation of which have been confided to the Church by God Himself, should no less diligently take into account the explanations and declarations of the teaching authority of the Church, as likewise the interpretation given by the Holy Fathers, and even "the analogy of faith" as Leo XIII most wisely observed in the Encyclical Letter *Providentissimus Deus*. With special zeal should they apply themselves, not only to expounding exclusively these matters which belong to the historical, archeological, philological and other auxiliary sciences — as, to Our regret, is done in certain commentaries, — but, having duly referred to these, in so far as they may aid the exegesis, they should set forth in particular the theological doctrine in faith and morals of the individual books or texts so that their exposition may not only aid the professors of theology in their explanations and proofs of the dogmas of faith, but may also be of assistance to priests in their presentation of Christian doctrine to the people, and in fine may help all the faithful to lead a life that is holy and worthy of a Christian. . . .

31. Moreover we may rightly and deservedly hope that our times also can contribute something towards the deeper and more accurate interpretation of Sacred Scripture. For not a few things, especially in matters pertaining to history, were scarcely at all or not fully explained by the commentators of past ages, since they lacked almost all the information, which was needed for their clearer exposition. How difficult for the Fathers themselves, and indeed well nigh unintelligible, were certain passages is shown, among other things, by the oft-repeated efforts of many of them to explain the first chapters of Genesis; likewise by the reiterated attempts of St. Jerome so to translate the Psalms that the literal sense, that, namely, which is expressed by the words themselves, might be clearly revealed.

32. There are, in fine, other books or texts, which contain difficulties brought to light only in quite recent times, since a more profound knowledge of antiquity has given rise to new questions, on the basis of which the point at issue may be more appropriately examined. Quite wrongly therefore do some pretend, not rightly understanding the conditions of biblical study, that nothing remains to be added by the Catholic exegete of our time to what Christian antiquity has produced; since, on the contrary, these our times have brought to light so many things, which call for a fresh investigation and a new examination, and which stimulate not a little the practical zeal of the present-day interpreter.

35. What is the literal sense of a passage is not always as obvious in the speeches and writings of the ancient authors of the East, as it is in the works

of the writers of our own time. For what they wished to express is not to be determined by the rules of grammar and philology alone, nor solely by the context; the interpreter must, as it were, go back wholly in spirit to those remote centuries of the East and with the aid of history, archaeology, ethnology and other sciences, accurately determine what modes of writing, so to speak, the authors of that ancient period would be likely to use, and in fact did use.

36. For the ancient peoples of the East, in order to express their ideas, did not always employ those forms or kinds of speech, which we use today; but rather those used by the men of their times and countries. What those exactly were the commentator cannot determine as it were in advance, but only after a careful examination of the ancient literature of the East. The investigation, carried out, on this point, during the past forty or fifty years with greater care and diligence than ever before, has more clearly shown what forms of expression were used in those far off times, whether in poetic description or in the formulation of laws and rules of life or in recording the facts and events of history. The same inquiry has also clearly shown the special preeminence of the people of Israel among all the other ancient nations of the East in their mode of compiling history, both by reason of its antiquity and by reason of the faithful record of the events; qualities which may well be attributed to the gift of divine inspiration and to the peculiar religious purpose of biblical history.

37. Nevertheless no one, who has a correct idea of biblical inspiration, will be surprised to find, even in the Sacred Writers, as in other ancient authors, certain fixed ways of expounding and narrating, certain definite idioms, especially of a kind peculiar to the Semitic tongues, so-called approximations, and certain hyperbolical modes of expression, nay, at times, even paradoxical, which help to impress the ideas more deeply on the mind. For of the modes of expression which, among ancient peoples, and especially those of the East, human language used to express its thought, none is excluded from the Sacred Books, provided the way of speaking adopted in no wise contradicts the holiness and truth of God. . . .

46. But this state of things is no reason why the Catholic commentator, inspired by an active and ardent love of his subject and sincerely devoted to Holy Mother Church, should in any way be deterred from grappling again and again with these difficult problems, hitherto unsolved, not only that he may refute the objections of the adversaries, but also may attempt to find a satisfactory solution, which will be in full accord with the doctrine of the Church, in particular with the traditional teaching regarding the inerrancy of Sacred Scripture, and which will at the same time satisfy the indubitable conclusions of profane sciences.

47. Let all the other sons of the Church bear in mind that the efforts of these resolute laborers in the vineyard of the Lord should be judged not only with equity and justice, but also with the greatest charity; all moreover should

abhor that intemperate zeal which imagines that whatever is new should for that very reason be opposed or suspected. Let them bear in mind above all that in the rules and laws promulgated by the Church there is question of doctrine regarding faith and morals; and that in the immense matter contained in the Sacred Books — legislative, historical, sapiential and prophetical — there are but few texts whose sense has been defined by the authority of the Church, nor are those more numerous about which the teaching of the Holy Fathers is unanimous. There remain therefore many things, and of the greatest importance, in the discussion and exposition of which the skill and genius of Catholic commentators may and ought to be freely exercised, so that each may contribute his part to the advantage of all, to the continued progress of the sacred doctrine and to the defense and honor of the Church.

Biblical Translations

The King James Version (KJV) of the English Bible, first published in 1611, occupies a unique niche in all of English literature. By common agreement and long usage, it has become the English Bible: "the noblest monument of English prose." By the latter decades of the nineteenth century, however, with the discovery of many ancient manuscripts unknown in 1611 and with the explosion in biblical scholarship, the need for a new translation was widely recognized. In 1870 the Church of England authorized a new translation, the result eleven years later being the English Revised Version. An American counterpart, with many differing readings, was published in 1901: the American Standard Version (ASV). The latter was clearly a scholarly advance over the KJV, but not necessarily a stylistic or liturgical improvement; consequently, the ASV never gained wide acceptance by the churches or the Bible-reading public. As the matter of further revisions was debated in succeeding decades, it was clear that the problems were two: first, weaning the English-speaking people away from the KJV; and second, providing a fresh translation that was as satisfying to the worshipper as to the scholar. (1) Edgar J. Goodspeed (1871–1962) of the University of Chicago offers below a good-humored account of the great American resistance to any tinkering around with the KJV. Goodspeed encountered this resistance in preparing his own New Testament: An American Translation, *published in 1923. (2) When the long-awaited Revised Standard Version (RSV) appeared (the New Testament in 1946, and the full Bible in 1952), the public outcry was shrill. In some areas of the country, RSV Bibles were tossed in bonfires, while elsewhere RSV translators were condemned to other kinds of*

[Sources: (1) E. J. Goodspeed, *As I Remember* (New York: Harper & Brothers, 1953), pp. 155–56, 166–69. (2) W. A. Irwin, in *An Introduction to the Revised Standard Version of the Old Testament* (New York: Thomas Nelson & Sons, 1952), pp. 12–14.]

fires. Yet the RSV —unlike the ASV —did endure, steadily growing in its
popularity and its acceptance, not only among Protestants, but among Cath-
olics and Jews as well. In the excerpt below, written to help "introduce" the
RSV to a skeptical if not hostile audience, William A. Irwin (1884 – 1967),
also of the University of Chicago, explained something of the methods of the
translators working to produce a Bible for the modern age.

1.

Many other men have translated the New Testament into English and published it, but I don't believe any of them has found the experience such an
exciting and bewildering romance as I did. And yet I found my way to the
task and performed it without the slightest expectation of any such result.

It may seem ungracious to revive a controversy thirty years old, when the
international verdict has gone so sweepingly in one's favor, and yet it has
such instructive and amusing aspects that one cannot pass it over. For it was
in the year 1923 that I performed the horrendous deed of publishing an
American translation of the New Testament. This simple act, obscurely done,
in my own field of specialization, on the basis of many years of close study,
with no expectation of any publicity at all, and quietly published at the
University of Chicago Press, called forth from the public press a nation-
wide, indeed world-wide and vehement protest, though now [1953], when
Jews, Catholics, and Protestants, yes and the Jehovah's Witnesses also are
engaged upon modern speech translations or revisions of the Old Testament,
or the New Testament, or the Old and New Testament and the Apocrypha,
hardly an editor dares lift up his voice against these dreadful undertakings. . . .

The *Examiner* had sent out a reporter, Bruce Grant, for an interview and
I gave him a long one, talking steadily for nearly two hours. He did not take
a note but seemed to be listening closely. I read his interview the next morning
with grave apprehensions but it was admirable. He got my points and presented them clearly and fairly in what I believe is called a six-column spread.
This was about the way the papers handled the matter, the news columns
generally fairly and informedly. The excitement was provided by the editorials.

On Thursday I parted with the last section of the final proof, and in the
afternoon I was interviewed for an hour by Duncan Clark, for *Success*
magazine.

Friday the 24th began early, for at 7:45 the United Press was on the wire.
Somehow or other it had become possessed of a galley proof of the eleventh
chapter of Luke, with its somewhat abbreviated form of the Lord's Prayer,
and the U.P. man, one H. E. Caylor, mistakenly supposing that that was
where the Lord's Prayer came from, leaped to the conclusion that I had
shortened the Lord's Prayer. Now if there is one thing the English-speaking
world will not tolerate, it is shortening the Lord's Prayer, and the U.P.
proceeded to make the most of it.

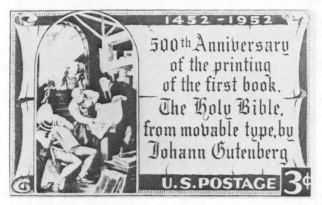

1452 – 1952

500th Anniversary
of the printing
of the first book,
The Holy Bible,
from movable type, by
Johann Gutenberg

U.S. POSTAGE 3¢

Stamp celebrating the five hundredth anniversary of the Gutenberg Bible, coinciding with publication of the Revised Standard Version of the Bible in 1952. *(Religious News Service)*

In Philadelphia the *Bulletin* recorded the unanimous disapproval of the clergy. In Boston it so aroused the old Boston *Transcript* that it devoted two editorials to excoriating me for abbreviating the Lord's Prayer, and the long shadow of this altogether groundless accusation reached even to Capetown, South Africa, where further editorial disapproval was evinced. Of course, it is actually from the Sermon on the Mount in Matthew that all churches derive the Lord's Prayer, as well as the Beatitudes and the Golden Rule, of all of which Luke has variant forms. Certainly the charge made against me can be made just as truly against every serious New Testament translation or revision from Alexander Campbell in 1826 down to the Catholic revision of 1941, the *Revised Standard Version* of 1946, and the Jehovah's Witnesses New Testament of 1951. Not one has transferred Matthew's Lord's Prayer to Luke; that is, as the U.P. puts it, they have all shortened the Lord's Prayer!

The fact was, nothing could have been more mistaken than to say I had tampered with the text. I had taught textual criticism for twenty years, and had the utmost confidence in its results. No translator had been more rigorously faithful to them, to the very last, minutest detail. I had deciphered, collated and published half a dozen Greek manuscripts of the gospels. The United Press was attacking the book on the point on which it was strongest, in fact unassailable, by any truthful means.

That Friday afternoon Underwood sent its photographer around to take my picture, and at 10:30 Friday night the *Tribune* telephoned for my translation of the Beatitudes to print side by side with those of King James next morning. . . .

Monday morning I was awakened from a troubled sleep by a friend calling, "Have you seen the *Tribune?*" It was Ernest Wilkins, afterward President of Oberlin College, who thus introduced me to the *Tribune*'s tribute, entitled "Monkeying with the Bible." The *Tribune* spoke up strongly for the

King James version. "Tampering with it," it declared, "is chipping a cathedral." It regarded the King James version as a seamless coat, a perfect version. I was reminded that the King James version, the first issue of the first edition of which I have before me, underwent a lamentable amount of chipping after the appearance of Samuel Johnson's dictionary in 1755, to which of course it had to be conformed. The current forms of it, as we all know, go back without exception to Professor Benjamin Blayney's revision of 1769. These alterations have so far as I know never been counted, but it is safe to say they are not less than eighty thousand, and they may reach a hundred thousand. But as I hastened to inform the *Tribune,* this was all done a hundred years before my birth so that it is unreasonable to hold me responsible for any part of it. Worse, yet, the Apocrypha, the whole transept of the *Tribune's* noble cathedral, has long since disappeared from the King James version, and the *Tribune* has never missed it!

2.

The present work . . . is primarily a revision. Its official title declares this: it is the Revised Standard Version, that is, a revision of the American Standard

Catholic University of America professor, Monsignor Patrick Skehan, studies notes for the New American Bible, 1970. *(Baptist Joint Committee on Public Affairs)*

Version of 1901, which had its ultimate inception in the official action of the Church of England in 1870 that authorized a revision of the King James Version. Through its entire activity the committee for the Revised Standard Version has been conscious of its role as reviser. The American Standard Version was its basic English text, and from it deviations were permitted only by majority vote, subject to final ratification by a two-thirds vote.

A task of revision entails all the problems and difficulties of translation, and in addition, one that is peculiarly its own: what degree of change from the basic text is permissible? It is a question of peculiar urgency when the revision concerns the Bible, for its very words quickly endear themselves to the devout student, so that any alteration, however slight, can well appear almost a desecration.

But further, any process of translation is in a sense an effort at the impossible. Languages differ; they are projections of the personalities of those for whom the speech learned in childhood is as intimate and personal as their native air. From these, the translators are separated by insuperable psychological barriers. The best that can be hoped is an approximation to the thought of the original, but its finer points, its overtones, its allusions, the feeling and atmosphere of its words lie beyond any process of translation. This is especially true when the task is that of rendering classics of an ancient language, such as the Old Testament includes, into a modern tongue of far remote genius and relationships. All speech develops its peculiar expressions that vary from mere slang across a diverse terrain to proverbial sayings at the other end. Colloquialisms soon pass, either into standard speech, or into desuetude as derelicts of a once pulsing reality; then life moves on and forgets their occasion and significance. One who works long and seriously with the Hebrew Old Testament grows steadily more conscious that much of its allusive and delicate meaning has been for ever lost; the words are known — generally — but their significance in particular combinations allures, but evades, the student.

However this may be, the responsibility of the translator is clear. Representing the best extant understanding of the language with which he deals, he is charged to tell as accurately as he can in his own language precisely what the original says. This is of an importance to bear some emphasis. The Bible translator assumes a strict responsibility to say in English just what the Biblical writers said in Hebrew, or in Aramaic, or in Greek, as the case may have been. In response to early publicity about the launching of the Revised Standard project, letters came in to one or another of the committee pointing out their opportunity to deal a blow to certain anti-social views which unfortunately base themselves on this or that Bible passage — the committee should change the offending passage! The only answer that could be given was that the committee did not intend, nor had it any authority, to change the Bible. The purpose was to give a more accurate rendering of what it said, even in

these passages. Correction of wrong uses of the Bible, important as this may
be, lay entirely outside its responsibility.

Yet this is not all. The danger here is of a subtle sort. A recent speaker
has told of a project to issue "a theologically conservative translation of the
Bible." Doubtless this is an appealing undertaking in the eyes of many. But
the fact must be stressed that there is no place for theology in Bible translation,
whether conservative or radical or whatever else. A "theological translation"
is not a translation at all, but merely a dogmatic perversion of the Bible.
Linguistic science knows no theology; those of most contradictory views can
meet on common ground devoid of polemic, agreed that Hebrew words mean
such and such, and their inflection and syntactical relations imply this or that.
These facts establish an agreed translation. Then, and then only, may the
exegete and dogmatist busy himself with theological deductions from the
thoughts of the Biblical writers. The Bible translator is not an expositor;
however pronounced his views about Biblical doctrines, he has no right whatever to intrude his opinions into the translation, or to permit his dogmatic
convictions to qualify or shape its wording. His one responsibility, and it is
absolute, is to render the Biblical meaning as accurately and effectively as is
possible into appropriate English.

4. MODERNISM/FUNDAMEN-
TALISM

Roman Catholicism

Battle of the Bishops

On the American scene the tensions within Catholicism are dramatically revealed in the antagonism between John Ireland (1838–1918), Archbishop of St. Paul, Minnesota, from 1888 to 1918, and Bernard J. McQuaid (1823–1909), Bishop of Rochester, New York, from 1868 to 1909. Ireland and McQuaid, temperamentally different and philosophically opposed, contested for the mind of America's Catholics and for the ear of the Vatican. Ireland was politically progressive, interested in urban reform, in "Americanizing" the Catholic church, in democratic reform and public education, in better relations with all races and religions. McQuaid, politically conservative and a strict disciplinarian, opposed the liberalizing tendencies within his Church, resisted the founding of Catholic University of America, and vigorously supported the parochial school system as the only means of assuring a faithful constituency for generations to come. (1) Ireland's sentiments are revealed in a preface that he wrote in 1891 for a biography of Isaac Hecker (see Vol. I, pp. 445–51). (2) In angry remarks delivered in the Rochester Cathedral in 1894, McQuaid denounces Ireland publicly not only for being wrong on nearly everything but also for being wrong in McQuaid's own territory.

1.

Father Hecker was the typical American priest; his were the gifts of mind and heart that go to do great work for God and for souls in America at the present time. Those qualities, assuredly, were not lacking in him which are

[Sources: (1) John Ireland in Walter Elliott, *The Life of Father Hecker* (New York: Columbus Press, 1891), pp. ix–xiii. (2) F. J. Zwierlein, *The Life and Letters of Bishop McQuaid* (Rome & Louvain, no pub., 1927), III, pp. 207–8, 210.]

the necessary elements of character of the good priest and the great man in any time and place. Those are the subsoil of priestly culture, and with the absence of them no one will succeed in America any more than elsewhere. But suffice they do not. There must be added, over and above, the practical intelligence and the pliability of will to understand one's surroundings, the ground upon which he is to deploy his forces, and to adapt himself to circumstances and opportunities as Providence appoints. I do not expect that my words, as I am here writing, will receive universal approval, and I am not at all sure that their expression would have been countenanced by the priest whose memory brings them to my lips. I write as I think, and the responsibility must be all my own. It is as clear to me as noon-day light that countries and peoples have each their peculiar needs and aspirations as they have their peculiar environments, and that, if we would enter into souls and control them, we must deal with them according to their conditions. The ideal line of conduct for the priest in Assyria will be out of all measure in Mexico or Minnesota, and I doubt not that one doing fairly well in Minnesota would by similar methods set things sadly astray in Leinster or Bavaria. The Saviour prescribed timeliness in pastoral caring. The master of a house, He said, "bringeth forth out of his treasury new things and old," as there is demand for one kind or the other. The apostles of nations, from Paul before the Areopagus to Patrick upon the summit of Tara, followed no different principle.

The circumstances of Catholics have been peculiar in the United States, and we have unavoidably suffered on this account. Catholics in largest numbers were Europeans, and so were their priests, many of whom —by no means all—remained in heart and mind and mode of action as alien to America as if they had never been removed from the Shannon, the Loire, or the Rhine. No one need remind me that immigration has brought us inestimable blessings, or that without it the Church in America would be of small stature. The remembrance of a precious fact is not put aside, if I recall an accidental evil attaching to it. Priests foreign in disposition and work were not fitted to make favorable impressions upon the non-Catholic American population, and the American-born children of Catholic immigrants were likely to escape their action. And, lest I be misunderstood, I assert all this is as true of priests coming from Ireland as from any other foreign country. Even priests of American ancestry, ministering to immigrants, not unfrequently fell into the lines of those around them, and did but little to make the Church in America throb with American life. Not so Isaac Thomas Hecker. Whether consciously or unconsciously I do not know, and it matters not, he looked on America as the fairest conquest for divine truth, and he girded himself with arms shaped and tempered to the American pattern. I think that it may be said that the American current, so plain for the last quarter of a century in the flow of Catholic affairs, is, largely at least, to be traced back to Father Hecker and his early co-workers. It used to be said of them in reproach that they were the "Yankee" Catholic Church; the reproach was their praise.

Father Hecker understood and loved the country and its institutions. He saw nothing in them to be deprecated or changed; he had no longing for the fleshpots and bread-stuffs of empires and monarchies. His favorite topic in book and lecture was, that the Constitution of the United States requires, as its necessary basis, the truths of Catholic teaching regarding man's natural state, as opposed to the errors of Luther and Calvin. The republic, he taught, presupposes the Church's doctrine, and the Church ought to love a polity which is the offspring of her own spirit. . . .

He laid stress on the natural and social virtues. The American people hold these in highest esteem. They are the virtues that are most apparent, and are seemingly the most needed for the building up and the preservation of an earthly commonwealth. Truthfulness, honesty in business dealings, loyalty to law and social order, temperance, respect for the rights of others, and the like virtues are prescribed by reason before the voice of revelation is heard, and the absence of specifically supernatural virtues has led the non-Catholic to place paramount importance upon them. It will be a difficult task to persuade the American that a church which will not enforce those primary virtues can enforce others which she herself declares to be higher and more arduous, and as he has implicit confidence in the destiny of his country to produce a high order of social existence, his first test of a religion will be its

Archbishop John Ireland (1839–1918) of St. Paul, Minnesota
(Library of Congress)

powers in this direction. This is according to Catholic teaching. Christ came not to destroy, but to perfect what was in man, and the graces and truths of revelation lead most securely to the elevation of the life that is, no less than to the gaining of the life to come. It is a fact, however, that in other times and other countries the Church has been impeded in her social work, and certain things or customs of those times and countries, transplanted upon American soil and allowed to grow here under a Catholic name, will do her no honor among Americans. The human mind, among the best of us, inclines to narrow limitations, and certain Catholics, aware of the comparatively greater importance of the supernatural, partially overlook the natural. . . .

On a line with his principles, as I have so far delineated them, Father Hecker believed that if he would succeed in his work for souls, he should use in it all the natural energy that God had given him, and he acted up to his belief. I once heard a good old priest, who said his beads well and made a desert around his pulpit by miserable preaching, criticise Father Hecker, who, he imagined, put too much reliance in man, and not enough in God. Father Hecker's piety, his assiduity in prayer, his personal habits of self-denial, repel the aspersion that he failed in reliance upon God. But my old priest — and he has in the church to-day, both in America and Europe, tens of thousands of counterparts — was more than half willing to see in all out-puttings of human energy a lack of confidence in God. We sometimes rely far more upon God than God desires us to do, and there are occasions when a novena is the refuge of laziness or cowardice. God has endowed us with natural talents, and not one of them shall be, with His permission, enshrouded in a napkin. He will not work a miracle, or supply grace, to make up for our deficiencies. We must work as if all depended on us, and pray as if all depended on God.

2.

You are well aware that, since I came to Rochester as bishop, I have most sedulously refrained from taking sides in politics, because I did not wish to throw the weight of my official position into the scales of either party, or to drag my episcopal robes in the mire of political partisanship. In my forty-seven years of priesthood, I have never put myself under obligation to any party, or to any official of national, state, or municipal government. No applicant for office has ever been helped by my personal solicitation, or by the signing of an application for office to the party in power. In other words, the sacredness of my office has never been a matter of barter in the mart of the political office-seeker. In this city of Rochester, I have been more frequently classed as a Republican than as a Democrat. No one has ever had warrant to put me in either class, and for twenty-seven years I have never cast a vote, out of anxiety not to put it in any man's power to say that I had voted for one party or the other. While it may have been a duty to exercise the privilege of a citizen and vote, I have felt that a more sacred duty devolved on me of preserving unsullied the high and holy office of bishop by keeping clear of entanglements with any political party. It has been traditional in the Church of the United States for Bishops to hold aloof from politics. This tradition has been handed down to us by Bishops, whose greatness was real, and not mere newspaper greatness, pandering to the sensational popularity of the day. Although often accused, by our enemies, of actively participating in political plottings and partisanship, we have been able, until of late, to deny and repel the false accusation.

Having said this much by way of preface, I will now advert to the late scandal, which caused these remarks. Every Catholic, having respect for his bishops and priests and the honor and good name of his Church, must have been pained and mortified when he learned, during the late political campaign, that one of our bishops, the Archbishop of St. Paul [John Ireland], cast to one side the traditions of the past and entered the political arena like any layman. The newspapers were careful to keep the public daily informed of his arrival in New York weeks before the election, of his appearance on the platform of ratification meetings, surrounded by the leaders of the Republican party, of his views of political questions, strongly expressed through interviews carefully prepared for the press, and of his mingling in a crowd of excited politicians and partisans on the night of election.

I contend that this coming to New York of the Archbishop of St. Paul, to take part in a political contest, was undignified, disgraceful to his episcopal office, and a scandal in the eyes of all right-minded Catholics of both parties. It was, furthermore, a piece of meddlesome interference on his part, to come from his State to another to break down all discipline among our priests and to justify the charge of those inimical to us, that priests are partisans and use their office and opportunities for political work. If Archbishop Ireland had made himself as conspicuous in favor of the Democratic party, he would be just as blameworthy in my estimation. If his conduct in the last political campaign were not censured and condemned, it would not be possible for me to restrain the priests of this diocese from imitating his example and descending from the pulpit to the political platform and marshalling their parishioners up to the polls on the day of election. Not one of them but has an equal right, with his Grace of St. Paul, to turn electioneering agent for one party or another and absent himself from his parish, as the Archbishop absented himself from his diocese. It is no excuse to say that the Archbishop was working in the interest of good government. Every other clerical aspirant to political distinction would say the same. New York is abundantly able to take care of itself, without extraneous help, as the last election showed. And if the newspapers report correctly, the legislature of Minnesota is itself sadly in need of purification, and his Grace might have found full scope for his political scheming and skill right at home, if politician he would be. . . .

These remarks will suffice for the present. If no other remedy can be found, then recourse to Rome will teach prelates that they would do well to stay at home and give their undivided attention to the field assigned them. I have made these remarks, because I want it understood that it is the policy of the Catholic Church in this country that her bishops and priests should take no active part in political campaigns and contests; that what bishops can do in political matters with impunity priests also can do; that neither have any right to become tools or agents of any party; that, when they do so, they descend from their high dignity, lay themselves open to censure and bitter remarks from those whom they oppose, remarks which recoil upon the sacred office they hold, and expose themselves and office to the vituperation so common in electioneering times.

I also wish it to be understood that this meddling in the political affairs of another state by Archbishop Ireland is altogether exceptional, — as he is the only bishop who thus interfered with others, that this scandal deserved rebuke as public as the offense committed. I sincerely hope that the Church will be spared its repetition.

Rome Speaks — and Is Spoken To

(1) The encyclical condemning modernism noted above, Pascendi Dominici Gregis, *was issued by Pope Pius X in September of 1907. While modernism was never a "school" nor quite so systematic as the encyclical suggests, the pope made clear what was objectionable in the new philosophy, history, psychology, science, and biblical study. Only a small portion of the text is excerpted below. (2) The major representatives of modernism were more often European than American (though Bishop Ireland had some fear that the encyclical was aimed at him too), but in 1910 a strong American reply to the pope appeared. Published anonymously but written by W. L. Sullivan (1872 – 1935), priest and Paulist father until leaving the Church in 1909, the reply took the form of a series of "letters of his Holiness." Sullivan spoke without gentleness or restraint — or effect.*

1.

The Modernist Personality.

5. To proceed in an orderly manner in this somewhat abstruse subject, it must first of all be noted that the Modernist sustains and includes within himself a manifold personality; he is a philosopher, a believer, a theologian, an historian, a critic, an apologist, a reformer. These roles must be clearly

[Sources: (1) *Pascendi Dominici Gregis* (Washington: National Catholic Welfare Conference, 1963), pp. 3, 8–9, 18–19, 20–21. (2) *Letters to His Holiness Pope Pius X,* by a Modernist (Chicago: Open Court Publishing Co., 1910), pp. 186–88.]

distinguished one from another by all who would accurately understand their system and thoroughly grasp the principles and the outcome of their doctrines.

Agnosticism.

6. We begin, then, with the philosopher. Modernists place the foundation of religious philosophy in that doctrine which is commonly called *Agnosticism*. According to this teaching human reason is confined entirely within the field of *phenomena*, that is to say, to things that appear, and in the manner in which they appear: it has neither the right nor the power to overstep these limits. Hence it is incapable of lifting itself up to God, and of recognizing His existence, even by means of visible things. From this it is inferred that God can never be the direct object of science, and that, as regards history, He must not be considered as an historical subject. Given these premises, everyone will at once perceive what becomes of *Natural Theology*, of the *motives of credibility*, of *external revelation*. The Modernists simply sweep them entirely aside; they include them in *Intellectualism*, which they denounce as a system which is ridiculous and long since defunct. . . .

Evolution of dogma.

13. Dogma is not only able, but ought to evolve and to be changed. This is strongly affirmed by the Modernists, and clearly flows from their principles. For among the chief points of their teaching is the following, which they deduce from the principle of *vital immanence*, namely, that *religious formulas*, if they are to be really *religious* and not merely intellectual speculations, ought to be living and to live the life of the *religious sense*. This is not to be understood to mean that these formulas, especially if merely imaginative, were to be invented for the religious sense. Their origin matters nothing, any more than their number or quality. What is necessary is that the *religious sense* — with some modification when needful — should vitally assimilate them. In other words, it is necessary that the *primitive formula* be accepted and sanctioned by the heart; and similarly the subsequent work from which are brought forth the *secondary formulas* must proceed under the guidance of the heart. Hence it comes that these formulas, in order to be living, should be, and should remain, adapted to the faith and to him who believes. Wherefore, if for any reason this adaptation should cease to exist, they lose their first meaning and accordingly need to be changed. In view of the fact that the character and lot of dogmatic formulas are so unstable, it is no wonder that Modernists should regard them so lightly and in such open disrespect, and have no consideration or praise for anything but the religious sense and for the religious life. In this way, with consummate audacity, they criticise the Church, as having strayed from the true path by failing to distinguish between the religious and moral sense of formulas and their surface meaning, and by

clinging vainly and tenaciously to meaningless formulas, while religion itself is allowed to go to ruin. "Blind" they are, and "leaders of the blind" puffed up with the proud name of science, they have reached that pitch of folly at which they pervert the eternal concept of truth and the true meaning of religion. . . .

The Modernist as believer.

14. Thus far, Venerable Brethren, We have considered the Modernist as a philosopher. Now if We proceed to consider him as a believer, and seek to know how the believer, according to Modernism, is marked off from the philosopher, it must be observed that, although the philosopher recognises the *reality of the divine* as the object of faith, still this *reality* is not to be found by him but in the heart of the believer, as an object of feeling and affirmation, and therefore confined within the sphere of phenomena; but the question as to whether in itself it exists outside that feeling and affirmation is one which the philosopher passes over and neglects. For the Modernist believer, on the contrary, it is an established and certain fact that the reality of the divine does really exist in itself and quite independently of the person who believes in it. If you ask on what foundation this assertion of the believer rests, he answers: In the personal *experience* of the individual. On this head the Modernists differ from the Rationalists only to fall into the views of the Protestants and pseudo-mystics. . . .

The evolution of doctrine.

26. To conclude this whole question of faith and its various branches, we have still to consider, Venerable Brethren, what the Modernists have to say about the development of the one and the other. First of all they lay down the general principle that in a living religion everything is subject to change, and must in fact be changed. In this way they pass to what is practically their principal doctrine, namely, *evolution*. To the laws of evolution everything is subject under penalty of death—dogma, Church, worship, the Books we revere as sacred, even faith itself. The enunciation of this principle will not be a matter of surprise to anyone who bears in mind what the Modernists have had to say about each of these subjects. Having laid down this law of evolution, the Modernists themselves teach us how it operates. And first, with regard to faith. The primitive form of faith, they tell us, was rudimentary and common to all men alike, for it had its origin in human nature and human life. Vital evolution brought with it progress, not by the accretion of new and purely adventitious forms from without, but by an increasing per-fusion of the religious sense into the conscience. The progress was of two kinds: *negative,* by the elimination of all extraneous elements, such, for ex-ample, as those derived from the family or nationality; and *positive,* by that

intellectual and moral refining of man, by means of which the idea of the divine became fuller and clearer, while the *religious sense* became more acute. . . .

The Modernist complex.

With all this in mind, one understands how it is that the Modernists express astonishment when they are reprimanded or punished. What is imputed to them as a fault they regard as a sacred duty. They understand the needs of consciences better than anyone else, since they come into closer touch with them than does the ecclesiastical authority. Nay, they embody them, so to speak, in themselves. Hence, for them to speak and to write publicly is a bounden duty. Let authority rebuke them if it pleases —they have their own conscience on their side and an intimate experience which tells them with certainty that what they deserve is not blame but praise. Then they reflect that, after all, there is no progress without a battle and no battle without its victims; and victims they are willing to be like the prophets and Christ Himself. They have no bitterness in their hearts against the authority which uses them roughly, for after all they readily admit that it is only doing its duty as authority. Their sole grief is that it remains deaf to their warnings, for in this way it impedes the progress of souls, but the hour will most surely come when further delay will be impossible, for if the laws of evolution may be checked for a while they cannot be finally evaded. And thus they go their way, reprimands and condemnations notwithstanding, masking an incredible audacity under a mock semblance of humility. While they make a pretence of bowing their heads, their minds and hands are more boldly intent than ever on carrying out their purposes. And this policy they follow willingly and wittingly, both because it is part of their system that authority is to be stimulated but not dethroned, and because it is necessary for them to remain within the ranks of the Church in order that they may gradually transform the collective conscience. And in saying this, they fail to perceive that they are avowing that the collective conscience is not with them, and that they have no right to claim to be its interpreters.

2.

Your Holiness:

I have now finished the first and greater part of my task, which is to set forth frankly the reasons for that antipathy to Rome which has been for three centuries so striking a feature in the religious life of the most progressive and enlightened nations of the world. I have tried to show, what I think must be obvious to every man of sound sense, that this antipathy does not rest on blind bigotry or unreasonable malice, but is based upon the notorious past history and the perfectly evident present policy of the Roman See. The Papal and Italian autocracy is considered by the world to be in theoretical and practical hostility to the main principles of modern civilization — to freedom of conscience, democracy, respect for individual personality, and liberty of intellect. How it is that peoples who were once in union with Rome have arrived at so momentous a change of conviction, the foregoing letters, I think, will help toward explaining.

Holy Father, if you have any desire to emerge out of the darkness of inexcusable sophistication which surrounds you, and look honestly at reality, these letters, or any other similar expression of candid criticism, may help you in no small degree. If you wish to make Catholicism respectable, and avert from it the ruin and death which now appear inevitable, is it possible for you not to see that no other means will avail to this end than the spiritualizing, and let us not shrink from the word, the modernizing of the Church? If the Catholic religion is to continue holding to persecution in principle, to the present doctrine of church and state, to Italian absolutism, to the prevailing attitude toward indulgences and other superstitions, and to its war of extermination upon critical scholars, then may we as well begin to write its epitaph; then may those honest students who, in the teeth of despair have been faintly hoping for some spiritualizing change, as well go forth into exile, and seek peace in a strange land, since peace and even honor are becoming impossible in what they loved as home.

That the changes which spirituality and scholarship demand from Roman Catholicism are profound and even perilous, there can be no denying. The perplexity indeed is awful. To remain as of old means certain death; to obey the summons of Reform may mean distress and scandal to many, and great injury to some. But surely we cannot lessen the gravity of the situation by not thinking of it. Think of it we must in prudence; provide for it we must in conscience. The adaptations called for need not after all, be the work of a day. Only let the Roman Church begin to show even common courtesy to our civilization, and in this, small as it is, we shall recognize the beginning of a better day, a sign of life in the midst of death. Let Catholics be allowed to hold that freedom of conscience is an inalienable right of man. Let some Pope speak out a brave word of execration upon the Inquisition. Let there be liberty for Catholic professors to teach that union of Church and State is not demanded by the Christian religion as an ideal. Let indulgences and all other heathenism be abolished. Let a representative government, autonomous local synods, and home-rule generally, supersede the present Italian and Papal despotism. Let scholars hold the modernist views as to the nature of dogma and the function of authority. Above all — and this is the one condition which will prevent these concessions from resulting in any great measure of harm — let the whole endeavor of the Church and hierarchy be to promote the Christ-ideal on earth.

Protestantism

Christianity and Liberalism

It is easy to caricature fundamentalism as the religion of the illiterate and untrained. J. Gresham Machen (1881–1937) effectively refutes that stereotype. Graduate of Johns Hopkins University and Princeton Seminary, further educated in Germany, and for over twenty years engaged as professor of New Testament at Princeton, Machen ultimately broke with his own Presbyterian church over the growing divergence between their respective theological positions. While Machen did not flaunt the label of "fundamentalism," he wrote that if it were necessary for him to choose between only two alternatives, namely, liberalism and fundamentalism, he would without hesitation choose the latter. Fundamentalism had to do with Christianity, while liberalism —in Machen's view—was something quite separate and distinct.

What is the relation between Christianity and modern culture; may Christianity be maintained in a scientific age?

It is this problem which modern liberalism attempts to solve. Admitting that scientific objections may arise against the particularities of the Christian religion —against the Christian doctrines of the person of Christ, and of redemption through His death and resurrection —the liberal theologian seeks to rescue certain of the general principles of religion, of which these particularities are thought to be mere temporary symbols, and these general principles he regards as constituting "the essence of Christianity."

It may well be questioned, however, whether this method of defence will really prove to be efficacious; for after the apologist has abandoned his outer defences to the enemy and withdrawn into some inner citadel, he will probably discover that the enemy pursues him even there. Modern materialism, especially in the realm of psychology, is not content with occupying the lower quarters of the Christian city, but pushes its way into all the higher reaches of life; it is just as much opposed to the philosophical idealism of the liberal preacher as to the Biblical doctrines that the liberal preacher has abandoned in the interests of peace. Mere concessiveness, therefore, will never succeed in avoiding the intellectual conflict. In the intellectual battle of the present day there can be no "peace without victory"; one side or the other must win.

As a matter of fact, however, it may appear that the figure which has just been used is altogether misleading; it may appear that what the liberal theo-

[Source: J. G. Machen, *Christianity and Liberalism* (New York: Macmillan Co., 1923), pp. 6–8, 15–16.]

logian has retained after abandoning to the enemy one Christian doctrine after another is not Christianity at all, but a religion which is so entirely different from Christianity as to belong in a distinct category. It may appear further that the fears of the modern man as to Christianity were entirely ungrounded, and that in abandoning the embattled walls of the city of God he has fled in needless panic into the open plains of a vague natural religion only to fall an easy victim to the enemy who ever lies in ambush there.

Two lines of criticism, then, are possible with respect to the liberal attempt at reconciling science and Christianity. Modern liberalism may be criticized (1) on the ground that it is un-Christian and (2) on the ground that it is unscientific. We shall concern ourselves here chiefly with the former line of criticism; we shall be interested in showing that despite the liberal use of traditional phraseology modern liberalism not only is a different religion from Christianity but belongs in a totally different class of religions. But in showing that the liberal attempt at rescuing Christianity is false we are not showing that there is no way of rescuing Christianity at all; on the contrary, it may appear incidentally, even in the present little book, that it is not the Christianity of the New Testament which is in conflict with science, but the supposed Christianity of the modern liberal Church, and that the real city of God, and that city alone, has defences which are capable of warding off the assaults of modern unbelief. However, our immediate concern is with the other side of the problem; our principal concern just now is to show that the liberal attempt at reconciling Christianity with modern science has really relinquished everything distinctive of Christianity, so that what remains is in essentials only that same indefinite type of religious aspiration which was in the world before Christianity came upon the scene. In trying to remove from Christianity everything that could possibly be objected to in the name of science, in trying to bribe off the enemy by those concessions which the enemy most desires, the apologist has really abandoned what he started out to defend. Here as in many other departments of life it appears that the things that are sometimes thought to be hardest to defend are also the things that are most worth defending.

In maintaining that liberalism in the modern Church represents a return to an un-Christian and sub-Christian form of the religious life, we are particularly anxious not to be misunderstood. "Un-Christian" in such a connection is sometimes taken as a term of opprobrium. We do not mean it at all as such. Socrates was not a Christian, neither was Goethe; yet we share to the full the respect with which their names are regarded. They tower immeasurably above the common run of men; if he that is least in the Kingdom of Heaven is greater than they, he is certainly greater not by any inherent superiority, but by virtue of an undeserved privilege which ought to make him humble rather than contemptuous.

Such considerations, however, should not be allowed to obscure the vital importance of the question at issue. If a condition could be conceived in which all the preaching of the Church should be controlled by the liberalism which in many quarters has already become preponderant, then, we believe, Christianity would at last have perished from the earth and the gospel would have sounded forth for the last time. If so, it follows that the inquiry with which we are now concerned is immeasurably the most important of all those with which the Church has to deal. Vastly more important than all questions with regard to methods of preaching is the root question as to what it is that shall be preached. . . .

. . . The condition of mankind is such that one may well ask what it is that made the men of past generations so great and the men of the present generation so small. In the midst of all the material achievements of modern life, one may well ask the question whether in gaining the whole world we have not lost our own soul. Are we forever condemned to live the sordid life of utilitarianism? Or is there some lost secret which if rediscovered will restore to mankind something of the glories of the past?

Such a secret the writer of this little book would discover in the Christian religion. But the Christian religion which is meant is certainly not the religion of the modern liberal Church, but a message of divine grace, almost forgotten now, as it was in the middle ages, but destined to burst forth once more in God's good time, in a new Reformation, and bring light and freedom to mankind. What that message is can be made clear, as is the case with all definition, only by way of exclusion, by way of contrast. In setting forth the current liberalism, now almost dominant in the Church, over against Christianity, we are animated, therefore, by no merely negative or polemic purpose; on the contrary, by showing what Christianity is not we hope to be able to show what Christianity is, in order that men may be led to turn from the weak and beggarly elements and have recourse again to the grace of God.

The Faith of Modernism

Shailer Mathews (1863 – 1941), professor of Historical and Comparative Theology at Chicago and dean of the Divinity School from 1908 to 1933, did not shy away from the term "modernism" — an epithet even more frightening than "liberalism." Believing that one must accept development in all things, even religious doctrines, and further affirming that the scientific method was the best avenue to truth, Mathews saw modernism not as negative and destructive, but as a positive religious force. A lifelong Baptist, the Chicago professor remained committed to the churches and to their important role in modern life.

[Source: Shailer Mathews, *The Faith of Modernism* (New York: Macmillan Co., 1924), pp. 22 – 23, 179 – 82.]

What then is Modernism? A heresy? An infidelity? A denial of truth? A new religion? So its ecclesiastical opponents have called it. But it is none of these. To describe it is like describing that science which has made our modern intellectual world so creative. It is not a denomination or a theology. *It is the use of the methods of modern science to find, state and use the permanent and central values of inherited orthodoxy in meeting the needs of a modern world.* The needs themselves point the way to formulas. Modernists endeavor to reach beliefs and their application in the same way that chemists or historians reach and apply their conclusions. They do not vote in convention and do not enforce beliefs by discipline. Modernism has no Confession. Its theological affirmations are the formulation of results of investigation both of human needs and the Christian religion. The Dogmatist starts with doctrines, the Modernist with the religion that gave rise to doctrines. The Dogmatist relies on conformity through group authority; the Modernist, upon inductive method and action in accord with group loyalty. . . .

While by its very nature the Modernist movement will never have a creed or authoritative confession, it does have its beliefs. And these beliefs are those attitudes and convictions which gave rise to the Christian religion and have determined the development of the century long Christian movement. No formula can altogether express the depths of a man's religious faith or hope to express the general beliefs of a movement in which individuals share. Every man will shape his own credo. But since he is loyal to the on-going Christian community with its dominant convictions, a Modernist in his own words and with his own patterns can make affirmations which will not be unlike the following:

> I believe in God, immanent in the forces and processes of nature, revealed in Jesus Christ and human history as Love.
> I believe in Jesus Christ, who by his teaching, life, death and resurrection, revealed God as Savior.
> I believe in the Holy Spirit, the God of love experienced in human life.
> I believe in the Bible, when interpreted historically, as the product and the trustworthy record of the progressive revelation of God through a developing religious experience.
> I believe that humanity without God is incapable of full moral life and liable to suffering because of its sin and weakness.
> I believe in prayer as a means of gaining help from God in every need and in every intelligent effort to establish and give justice in human relations.
> I believe in freely forgiving those who trespass against me, and in good will rather than acquisitiveness, coercion, and war as the divinely established law of human relations.
> I believe in the need and the reality of God's forgiveness of sins, that is, the transformation of human lives by fellowship with God from subjection to outgrown goods to the practice of the love exemplified in Jesus Christ.
> I believe in the practicability of the teaching of Jesus in social life.
> I believe in the continuance of individual personality beyond death; and

that the future life will be one of growth and joy in proportion to its fellowship with God and its moral likeness to Jesus Christ.

I believe in the church as the community of those who in different conditions and ages loyally further the religion of Jesus Christ.

I believe that all things work together for good to those who love God and in their lives express the sacrificial good will of Jesus Christ.

I believe in the ultimate triumph of love and justice because I believe in the God revealed in Jesus Christ.

Such affirmations are more than the acceptance of biblical records, ancient facts or the successive doctrinal patterns of the Christian church. They are the substance of a faith that will move mountains. Under their control no man can deliberately seek to injure his neighbor or distrust his God. They are moral motive and direction for social action.

To trust God who is good will is to find a cure for the cynical doubt born of war and its aftermath.

To be loyal to the sinless Son of Man is to gain new confidence in the possibility of transforming human nature and society from selfishness to brotherliness.

To discover in the death of Jesus that God himself shares in sacrifice for the good of others is to gain confidence in the struggle for the rights of others.

To know that the God of law and love has made good will the only source of permanent happiness is to possess a standard of moral judgment.

To follow Jesus in international affairs is to end war.

To find God in natural law and evolution is an assurance that love is as final as any other cosmic expression of the divine will.

To embody the spirit of Jesus Christ in all action is to enjoy the peace which can come only to those who are at one with the cosmic God.

To experience the regenerating power of God is to have new hope for the ultimate completion of the human personality through death as well as life.

The final test of such generic Christianity is the ability of the Christian movement to meet human needs. And of this we have no doubt. Whoever does the will of God will know that the gospel of and about Jesus Christ is not the dream of a noble though impracticable victim of circumstance, but the revelation of the good will of the God of nature, the Father of our spirits, the Savior of His world. And through that knowledge he will gain the fruit of the Spirit — love, joy, peace, long-suffering, kindness, goodness, faithfulness, meekness, self-control.

Judaism

Reform Platforms

(1) In 1885 Reform Jews gathered in Pittsburgh and adopted a set of principles which has come to be known as the "Pittsburgh Platform." A "Declaration of Independence," Rabbi Isaac Mayer Wise had called it, and indeed it did set Reform on a path apart from traditional or Orthodox Judaism. This 1885 platform accepted biblical criticism, spoke of "the Bible reflecting the primitive ideas of its own age," and stated regarding the laws of Moses: we "reject all such as are not adapted to the views and habits of modern civilization." Modernity was whole-heartedly embraced. (One should also note the anti-Zionist stance at this time; the large question of Zionism will be taken up in Chapter 11.) (2) About a half-century later, in Columbus, Ohio, Reform Jews adopted another set of principles which placed a somewhat higher value on tradition and heritage. While still holding to the developmental view of the Bible, the framers of the 1937 statement emphasized that the Mosaic Law or Torah "remains the dynamic source of the life of Israel." And "such customs, symbols and ceremonies as possess inspirational value" are to be cherished, not forsaken.

1.   (1885)

In view of the wide divergence of opinion and of the conflicting ideas prevailing in Judaism today, we, as representatives of Reform Judaism in America, in continuation of the work begun at Philadelphia in 1869, unite upon the following principles:

First — We recognize in every religion an attempt to grasp the Infinite One, and in every mode, source or book of revelation held sacred in any religious system the consciousness of the indwelling of God in man. We hold that Judaism presents the highest conception of the God-idea as taught in our holy Scriptures and developed and spiritualized by the Jewish teachers in accordance with the moral and philosophical progress of their respective ages. We maintain that Judaism preserved and defended amid continual struggles and trials and under enforced isolation this God-idea as the central religious truth for the human race.

Second — We recognize in the Bible the record of the consecration of the Jewish people to its mission as priest of the One God, and value it as the

[Sources: (1) Central Conference of American Rabbis *Yearbook,* vol. 45 (New York: CCAR, 1935), pp. 198–200. (2) W. Gunther Plaut, *The Growth of Reform Judaism* (New York: World Union for Progressive Judaism, 1965), pp. 96–99.]

most potent instrument of religious and moral instruction. We hold that the modern discoveries of scientific researches in the domains of nature and history are not antagonistic to the doctrines of Judaism, the Bible reflecting the primitive ideas of its own age and at times clothing its conception of divine providence and justice dealing with man in miraculous narratives.

Third—We recognize in the Mosaic legislation a system of training the Jewish people for its mission during its national life in Palestine, and today we accept as binding only the moral laws and maintain only such ceremonies as elevate and sanctify our lives, but reject all such as are not adapted to the views and habits of modern civilization.

Fourth—We hold that all such Mosaic and Rabbinical laws as regulate diet, priestly purity and dress originated in ages and under the influence of ideas altogether foreign to our present mental and spiritual state. They fail to impress the modern Jew with a spirit of priestly holiness; their observance in our day is apt rather to obstruct than to further modern spiritual elevation.

Fifth—We recognize in the modern era of universal culture of heart and intellect the approach of the realization of Israel's great Messianic hope for the establishment of the Kingdom of truth, justice and peace among all men. We consider ourselves no longer a nation but a religious community, and therefore expect neither a return to Palestine, nor a sacrificial worship under the administration of the sons of Aaron, nor the restoration of any of the laws concerning the Jewish state.

Sixth—We recognize in Judaism a progressive religion, ever striving to be in accord with the postulates of reason. We are convinced of the utmost necessity of preserving the historical identity with our great past. Christianity and Islam, being daughter religions of Judaism, we appreciate their mission to aid in the spreading of monotheistic and moral truth. We acknowledge that the spirit of broad humanity of our age is our ally in the fulfilment of our mission, and therefore we extend the hand of fellowship to all who co-operate with us in the establishment of the reign of truth and righteousness among men.

Seventh—We reassert the doctrine of Judaism, that the soul of man is immortal, grounding this belief on the divine nature of the human spirit, which forever finds bliss in righteousness and misery in wickedness. We reject as ideas not rooted in Judaism the belief both in bodily resurrection and in Gehenna and Eden (hell and paradise), as abodes for everlasting punishment or reward.

Eighth—In full accordance with the spirit of Mosaic legislation which strives to regulate the relation between rich and poor, we deem it our duty to participate in the great task of modern times, to solve on the basis of justice and righteousness the problems presented by the contrasts and evils of the present organization of society.

2.

GUIDING PRINCIPLES OF REFORM JUDAISM (1937)

In view of the changes that have taken place in the modern world and the consequent need of stating anew the teachings of Reform Judaism, the Central Conference of American Rabbis makes the following declaration of principles. It presents them not as a fixed creed but as a guide for the progressive elements of Jewry.

A. Judaism and Its Foundations

1. *Nature of Judaism.* Judaism is the historical religious experience of the Jewish people. Though growing out of Jewish life, its message is universal, aiming at the union and perfection of mankind under the sovereignty of God. Reform Judaism recognizes the principle of progressive development in religion and consciously applies this principle to spiritual as well as to cultural and social life.

Judaism welcomes all truth, whether written in the pages of scripture or deciphered from the records of nature. The new discoveries of science, while replacing the older scientific views underlying our sacred literature, do not conflict with the essential spirit of religion as manifested in the consecration of man's will, heart and mind to the service of God and of humanity.

2. *God.* The heart of Judaism and its chief contribution to religion is the doctrine of the One, living God, who rules the world through law and love. In Him all existence has its creative source and mankind its ideal of conduct. Through transcending time and space, He is the indwelling Presence of the world. We worship Him as the Lord of the universe and as our merciful Father.

3. *Man.* Judaism affirms that man is created in the Divine image. His spirit is immortal. He is an active co-worker with God. As a child of God, he is endowed with moral freedom and is charged with the responsibility of overcoming evil and striving after ideal ends.

4. *Torah.* God reveals Himself not only in the majesty, beauty and orderliness of nature, but also in the vision and moral striving of the human spirit. Revelation is a continuous process, confined to no one group and to no one age. Yet the people of Israel, through its prophets and sages, achieved unique insight in the realm of religious truth. The Torah, both written and oral, enshrines Israel's ever-growing consciousness of God and of the moral law. It preserves the historical precedents, sanctions and norms of Jewish life, and seeks to mould it in the patterns of goodness and of holiness. Being products of historical processes, certain of its laws have lost their binding force with the passing of the conditions that called them forth. But as a depository of

permanent spiritual ideals, the Torah remains the dynamic source of the life of Israel. Each age has the obligation to adapt the teachings of the Torah to its basic needs in consonance with the genius of Judaism.

5. *Israel*. Judaism is the soul of which Israel is the body. Living in all parts of the world, Israel has been held together by the ties of a common history, and above all, by the heritage of faith. Though we recognize in the group loyalty of Jews who have become estranged from our religious tradition, a bond which still unites them with us, we maintain that it is by its religion and for its religion that the Jewish people has lived. The non-Jew who accepts our faith is welcomed as a full member of the Jewish community.

In all lands where our people live, they assume and seek to share loyally the full duties and responsibilities of citizenship and to create seats of Jewish knowledge and religion. In the rehabilitation of Palestine, the land hallowed by memories and hopes, we behold the promise of renewed life for many of our brethren. We affirm the obligation of all Jewry to aid in its upbuilding as a Jewish homeland by endeavoring to make it not only a haven of refuge for the oppressed but also a center of Jewish culture and spiritual life.

Throughout the ages it has been Israel's mission to witness to the Divine in the face of every form of paganism and materialism. We regard it as our historic task to cooperate with all men in the establishment of the kingdom of God, of universal brotherhood, justice, truth and peace on earth. This is our Messianic goal.

B. Ethics

6. *Ethics and Religion*. In Judaism religion and morality blend into an indissoluble unity. Seeking God means to strive after holiness, righteousness and goodness. The love of God is incomplete without the love of one's fellowmen. Judaism emphasizes the kinship of the human race, the sanctity and worth of human life and personality and the right of the individual to freedom and to the pursuit of his chosen vocation. Justice to all, irrespective of race, sect or class is the inalienable right and the inescapable obligation of all. The state and organized government exist in order to further these ends.

7. *Social Justice*. Judaism seeks the attainment of a just society by the application of its teachings to the economic order, to industry and commerce, and to national and international affairs. It aims at the elimination of man-made misery and suffering, of poverty and degradation, of tyranny and slavery, of social inequality and prejudice, of ill-will and strife. It advocates the promotion of harmonious relations between warring classes on the basis of equity and justice, and the creation of conditions under which human personality may flourish. It pleads for the safeguarding of childhood against exploitation. It champions the cause of all who work and of their right to an adequate standard of living, as prior to the rights of property. Judaism emphasizes the

duty of charity, and strives for a social order which will protect men against the material disabilities of old age, sickness and unemployment.

8. *Peace.* Judaism, from the days of the prophets, has proclaimed to mankind the ideal of universal peace. The spiritual and physical disarmament of all nations has been one of its essential teachings. It abhors all violence and relies upon moral education, love and sympathy to secure human progress. It regards justice as the foundation of the well-being of nations and the condition of enduring peace. It urges organized international action for disarmament, collective security and world peace.

C. Religious Practice

9. *The Religious Life.* Jewish life is marked by consecration to these ideals of Judaism. It calls for faithful participation in the life of the Jewish community as it finds expression in home, synagog and school and in all other agencies that enrich Jewish life and promote its welfare.

The Home has been and must continue to be a stronghold of Jewish life, hallowed by the spirit of love and reverence, by moral discipline and religious observance and worship.

The Synagog is the oldest and most democratic institution in Jewish life. It is the prime communal agency by which Judaism is fostered and preserved. It links the Jews of each community and unites them with all Israel.

The perpetuation of Judaism as a living force depends upon religious knowledge and upon the Education of each new generation in our rich cultural and spiritual heritage.

Prayer is the voice of religion, the language of faith and aspiration. It directs man's heart and mind Godward, voices the needs and hopes of the community, and reaches out after goals which invest life with supreme value. To deepen the spiritual life of our people, we must cultivate the traditional habit of communion with God through prayer in both home and synagog.

Judaism as a way of life requires in addition to its moral and spiritual demands, the preservation of the Sabbath, festivals and Holy Days, the retention and development of such customs, symbols and ceremonies as possess inspirational value, the cultivation of distinctive forms of religious art and music and the use of Hebrew, together with the vernacular, in our worship and instruction.

These timeless aims and ideals of our faith we present anew to a confused and troubled world. We call upon our fellow Jews to rededicate themselves to them, and, in harmony with all men, hopefully and courageously to continue Israel's eternal quest after God and His kingdom.

Conservative Approaches

The major rabbinical training center for Conservative Judaism, the Jewish Theological Seminary of America (New York City), was presided over from 1901 to 1915 by the able scholar, Solomon Schechter (1850–1915). (1) Schechter found "higher criticism" to be ill-informed, damaging in its effect, and possibly anti-Semitic in its intent. "Our great claim to the gratitude of mankind," Schechter declared, "is that we gave to the world the word of God, the Bible." And it is just this great gift "which the Higher anti-Semitism is seeking to destroy, denying all our claims for the past, and leaving us without hope for the future." (2) A half century later, the Jewish Theological Seminary undertook the publication of a series of volumes on "The Heritage of Biblical Israel." Now, higher criticism is accepted and the fundamentalists and literalists are being set aside. Nahum Sarna (b. 1923), professor of biblical studies at Brandeis University since 1967, but formerly on the faculty of the Jewish Theological Seminary, wrote Understanding Genesis. *This book, Sarna noted, is "based on the belief that the study of the Book of Books must constitute a mature intellectual challenge, an exposure to the expanding universe of scientific biblical scholarship." Those who continue to reject or ignore that "expanding universe" (and Orthodox Judaism manifests no great interest therein), taking refuge in "tradition," really rely on medieval authority that is now superseded by the "modern sciences of literary and textual criticism."*

1.

Now, the first thing that we have to recover is the Bible. There is a story of a Catholic saint who was beheaded by his pagan persecutors, but, like a good saint, he took his head under his arm and walked off. You smile, and think it perhaps too much of a miracle, but a Judaism without a Bible is even a greater miracle. It would mean a headless Judaism, for, gentlemen, Judaism is not merely an ethical society placed under the auspices of Abraham, Isaac, Jacob, Moses and Aaron. . . .

Judaism is a revealed religion, with sacred writings revealing the history of the past, making positive demands on the present and holding out solemn promises for the future. And these sacred writings are the Bible, and they ought to be the possession of every Jew, interpreted and commented on in the

[Sources: (1) Solomon Schechter, *Seminary Addresses and Other Papers* (Cincinnati: Ark Publishing Co., 1915), pp. 3–5, 6–7, 37–38. (2) Nahum Sarna, *Understanding Genesis* (New York: Jewish Theological Seminary of America, 1966), pp. xx–xxiii.]

Jewish spirit. I am in no way antagonistic to all that is modern. I confess that my sympathies for Wellhausen are not very strong and that I have a tolerable antipathy against "painted Bibles" and mutilated Scriptures.* But I know that the demands of science are inexorable. . . . But the question may be asked whether it is really all science that is claimed as such. My studies within the past years, which centered largely around the Bible, have convinced me that there is much in the higher criticism, which is at best theology of a kind, not philology and history.

But apart from this question there is another consideration. An old friend of mine once said to me, "Even if you are able to translate a Psalm, you understand only the Psalm but not the Psalmist." Now I put it to you, whether in a school where a man like Duhm, one of the oracles of higher criticism, can declare that the Psalms are all mere rancorous party pamphlets, the Psalmist is understood or not.

Another instance is the attempt by a majority of higher critics to eliminate the personal element from the Psalms—I mean the *ich* question. You will agree with me, I think, that our grandmothers and grandfathers, who did read the Psalms and had a good cry over them, understood them better than all the professors. I am not pleading here for an orthodox commentary to the Bible, but there is a Jewish liberalism and a Christian liberalism and even from the point of view of liberalism let a commentary be written in the spirit of a Jewish and not a Christian liberalism. Remember that the Bible was not discovered by Cheyne** and Wellhausen. We worked over it thousands of years before the Occidentals could read a Hebrew sentence correctly. . . .

Perhaps you will allow me to conclude with a passage from the Zohar*** which I have often used before, and possibly many others before me, but it bears repetition. The story runs that a certain Rabbi once sailed in a ship. When the ship came upon the high seas, a storm arose and wrecked the vessel. Down it went; but the Rabbi was a saint, and, of course, a miracle happened. The vessel came out at the other side of the globe, and he found men engaged in prayer; but he did not understand them. It is supposed by the commentaries, which are still to be written, that the cause of his inability to understand them was that they did not pray in Hebrew. But even worse would it be if the religious literature of the Jews should not be accessible to all the Jews. And here in New York, where the West and the East meet in such close proximity, it is especially necessary if we are all to remain brothers

---

*Julius Wellhausen (1844–1918) was an early biblical critic out of German Protestantism. The reference to painted and mutilated Bibles is to the printing of early Old Testament materials in such a way as to indicate the several sources or "documents" that lay behind the final product.

**T. K. Cheyne (1841–1915), contemporary of Wellhausen, introduced much of German scholarship into England.

***The central book of the medieval cabala (or kabbala) literature of Judaism.

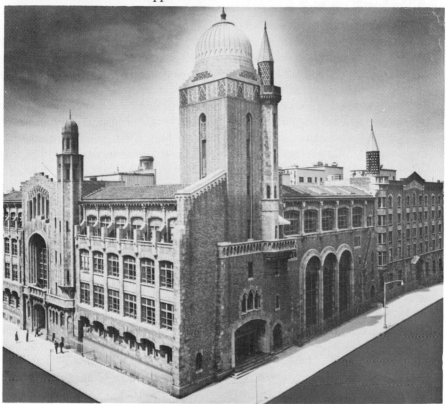

Main building of Orthodox Judaism's Yeshiva University, founded in 1928
(Yeshiva University)

on earth, as we hope to be in heaven, that our religious literature should be based on and developed from that Sacred Book and Sacred Language which have always been the means of communion between Israel and Israel, and between Israel and his God.

Some time ago I saw in one of the numerous sheets of this country a reference to the Hammurabi Code, concluding with the words, "this means a blow to Orthodoxy." I hold no brief for Orthodoxy in this country or elsewhere. But, may I ask: Is there any wing in Judaism which is prepared to confirm the reproach of Carlyle, who, in one of his anti-Semitic fits, exclaimed, "The Jews are always dealing in old clothes; spiritual or material." We are here between ourselves, so we may frankly make the confession that we did not invent the art of printing; we did not discover America, in spite of Kayserling; we did not inaugurate the French Revolution, in spite of some one else; we were not the first to utilize the power of steam or electricity, in spite of any future Kayserling. Our great claim to the gratitude of mankind is that we gave to the world the word of God, the Bible. We have stormed heaven to snatch down this heavenly gift. . . , we threw ourselves into the

breach and covered it with our bodies against every attack; we allowed ourselves to be slain by hundreds and thousands rather than become unfaithful
to it; and we bore witness to its truth and watched over its purity in the face
of a hostile world. The Bible is our sole *raison d'être,* and it is just this which
the Higher anti-Semitism is seeking to destroy, denying all our claims for
the past, and leaving us without hope for the future.

Can any section among us afford to concede to this professorial and imperial
anti-Semitism and confess "for a truth we and our ancestors have sinned;" we
have lived on false pretenses and were the worst shams in the world? Forget
not that we live in an historical age in which everybody must show his
credentials from the past. The Bible is our patent of nobility granted to us
by the Almighty God, and if we disown the Bible, leaving it to the tender
mercies of a Wellhausen, Stade and Duhm, and other beautiful souls working
away at diminishing the "nimbus of the Chosen People," the world will
disown us. There is no room in it for spiritual parvenus. But this intellectual
persecution can only be fought by intellectual weapons and unless we make
an effort to recover our Bible and to think out our theology for ourselves,
we are irrevocably lost from both worlds. A mere protest in the pulpit or a
vigorous editorial in a paper, or an amateur essay in a monthly, or even a
special monograph will not help us. We have to create a really living, great
literature, and do the same for the subjects of theology and the Bible that
Europe has done for Jewish history and philology.

2.

. . . The crux of the matter is that in the eyes of modern, secularized
man, the Bible has very largely lost its sanctity and relevance.

It would not be profitable to trace here in any detail the rather complex
pattern of events that has produced this unprecedented situation. It was probably an inevitable outgrowth of various intellectual movements which had
long been gathering momentum and which converged in the nineteenth century. Already in 1670, Benedict Spinoza, in his *Theologico-Political Treatise,*
had conceived of biblical studies as a science, and had formulated a methodology involving the use of rationalism and historical criticism. For this
alone, and for his revolutionary conclusions, he must be regarded as the true
founder of the modern scientific approach to the Bible. But he was not the
primary inspiration for further studies in this direction. The new cosmology
that had been gaining ground for three centuries and the later evolutionary
theories were bound to lead to a questioning of the Genesis narrative. Moreover, the scope of the evolutionary thesis was sure to be broadened beyond
the realms of geology and biology, so that it is not surprising that attempts
were made to explain thereby the religious, cultural and social history of

Interior of traditionalist synagogue in Colchester, Connecticut, 1940
(Library of Congress)

Israel. The revolt against intellectual and ecclesiastical authority that marked the rise of humanism, and the new concept of history that underplayed the supernatural and made the decisions of men predominant, could not but affect the approach to the theocentricity of the biblical narrative. But above all, biblical scholarship was touched decisively by the development and application of critical, historical and analytical methods used in the identification and isolation of literary sources and the determination of their dating. No longer could the Pentateuch be regarded as a unitary work, divinely dictated, word for word, to Moses. It became one of the finalities of scholarship that the narrative portions of the Pentateuch were thoroughly unreliable for any attempted reconstruction of the times about which they purported to relate. The devastating effect of all this upon faith, when faith was exclusively identified with a literalist approach to Scripture, is abundantly obvious. No wonder that the Bible became desanctified in the eyes of so many educated men.

Unfortunately, the response of the fundamentalists to the challenge of scientism served only to exacerbate the situation. They mistakenly regarded all critical biblical studies as a challenge to faith. There remained no room for the play of individual conscience; the validity of genuine intellectual doubt was refused recognition. By insisting dogmatically upon interpretations and doctrines that flagrantly contradicted the facts, the fundamentalist did not realize the self-exposure of an obvious insecurity that was more a reflection upon his own religious position than a judgment upon biblical scholarship. For it declared, in effect, that spiritual relevance can be maintained only at the expense of the intellect and the stifling of conscience.

The deadly effects of this approach can be easily measured by discussing the Bible with university students. It becomes immediately apparent that the literature of ancient Israel is not treated with the same seriousness and respect as that of ancient Greece. The childish image of the Scriptures, imparted at an early age, is well-nigh ineradicable. For this reason, the teaching of the Bible in the religious schools has, more often than not, become a self-defeating exercise in futility. Any intelligent child who studies mathematical logic in school, and most children now do, cannot but note the contrast in intellectual challenge between this and his biblical studies. He must, willy-nilly, conclude that the latter is inferior, an attitude hardly calculated to instil or encourage a feeling for the sanctity and relevance of Scripture. Why the elementary pedagogical absurdity of present-day Bible teaching in the religious schools is not obvious to those in control of curriculum and teacher training, is an utter mystery.

Of course, the fundamentalists frequently take refuge from modern scholarship by appealing to "tradition," by which they mean medieval authority. The illegitimacy of this position as an argument of faith is, however, easily demonstrable. The medieval scholars made the most of all the limited tools at their disposal. But they did not have access, naturally, to the modern sciences of literary and textual criticism and to the disciplines of sociology, anthropology, linguistics and comparative religion. We simply do not know how they would have reacted had all this material been available to them. To assume a blind disregard of evidence on their part is as unwarranted as it is unfair. Be this as it may, it is clear, at any rate, that "pietism," no less than its "scientific" opposition, bears a goodly measure of responsibility for the alienation of modern man from the sacred Scriptures.

This book, the first of a projected series, is designed to make the Bible of Israel intelligible, relevant and, hopefully, inspiring to a sophisticated generation, possessed of intellectual curiosity and ethical sensitivity. It recognizes the fact that the twentieth century has transformed our categories of thought and has provided us with new criteria for critical judgment. It is based on the belief that the study of the Book of Books must constitute a mature intellectual challenge, an exposure to the expanding universe of scientific biblical scholarship. It is predicated upon the profound conviction, born of personal experience, that the findings of modern biblical studies, in all their scholarly ramifications, provide the means to a keener understanding of the Hebrew Scriptures and may prove to be the key to a deeper appreciation of their religious message. Far from presenting a threat to faith, a challenge to the intellect may reinforce faith and purify it.

5. THEOLOGICAL AFTERMATH

Neo-Orthodoxy

H. Richard Niebuhr (1894 – 1962)

The problem, Walter Rauschenbusch had written in 1917, was to see that men and women no longer had "to believe with all their hearts what they could not possibly understand with all their heads." A generation later, however, the problem was whether anything remained to be believed with all one's heart. The time for theological reconstruction or return had come. And in once more turning toward the transcendent, moving beyond the "modern" and the natural to the timeless and the supernatural, none rendered more valiant service than Richard Niebuhr and his brother, Reinhold (introduced above, p. 283). A native of Missouri and reared in the German Evangelical tradition, Richard Niebuhr spent his professional life chiefly at Yale University. In the course of his own theological maturing, he discovered new value in old ideas, notably in those of Jonathan Edwards (see Vol. I, pp. 214 – 20), even as he assisted his students and a wide reading public to appreciate and apprehend anew the insights of basic Christian doctrines. His Kingdom of God in America *(1937) recognized liberalism's deficiencies, orthodoxy's resilient and enduring strengths. In 1941, he addressed the subject of revelation, but not in the stale terms of battles over this text or that, this emendation or that. We must see revelation, Niebuhr argued, not as a part of apologetics, not as a record of things past, but as an encounter in the present with the ever-living, ever-revealing God.*

What is the meaning of revelation? The question has been raised many times in the history of the Christian church. But its reappearance in contemporary theological discussion puzzles many men who are accustomed to associate the word revelation with ancient quarrels and their fruitless issue. They remember particularly the turgid debate about miracles, prophecy, revelation and reason in which Deists and Supernaturalists engaged at the beginning of the eighteenth century. The defense of revelation at that time seemed to mean social and intellectual conservatism; what was at stake in the quarrel was the

[Source: H. Richard Niebuhr, *The Meaning of Revelation* (New York: Macmillan Co., 1941), pp. 1 – 4, 38 – 42.]

right of the church, clergy, and traditional authority in general to exercise their ancient guardianship over society; the appeal to revelation seemed simply a defensive device. The cause of reason on the other hand was espoused by the rebellious and fresh powers of democratic, mercantile civilization which used it for the attainment of other victories than those of reason. And whatever the fortunes of the contending parties in that conflict were, reason and revelation were sadly damaged. At its close, as at the end of every war, victor and victim were almost indistinguishable. Scepticism, clothed in the episcopal vestments Butler gave it, or in the more worldly armor Hume supplied, was left in possession of the intellectual field. . . .

With Wesley, Whitefield, Edwards and their associates, Christianity abandoned the defense of revelation as well as the attack on reason; it turned rather to its proper work of preaching the gospel, of exorcising the demons which inhabit human hearts and of guiding souls to fellowship with a holy spirit. Problems of relationship between reason and faith, theology and philosophy, natural and religious experience arose occasionally, of course, but for a while it seemed that a Platonic justice had been established in which each part of the Christian soul and each institution in Christian society minded its own business and made its contribution to the whole without lapsing again into imperialistic adventures. As for "revelation," the word was used sparingly, however much Scriptures and Christian history were employed in the preaching of the gospel.

When we recall that quarrel and its consequences we are tempted to turn away with some distaste from a revival of the revelation idea. Does not the re-establishment of a theology of revelation mean the renewal of a fruitless warfare between faith and reason? Is it not the sign of a retreat to old entrenchments in which only those veterans of a lost cause, the fundamentalists, are interested? To speak of revelation now seems to imply a reversal of the enlightenment in religious thought which began when Schleiermacher asked and answered his rhetorical question to the cultured despisers of faith: "Do you say that you cannot away with miracles, revelation, inspiration? You are right; the time for fairy tales is past." Such a reversal appears to be as impossible as it is undesirable. The work of a hundred and fifty years in theology cannot be ignored; the methods and the fruits of Biblical and historical criticism as well as of natural and social science cannot be so eliminated from men's minds as to allow them to recover the same attitude toward Scriptures which their seventeenth-century forbears had. We may admire the simplicity and directness with which these answered the question about the meaning of revelation by pointing to the Scriptures and may be ready to concede that there was a wisdom in this simplicity which is lacking in our complicated and analytical scholarship. Nevertheless it is evident that we cannot achieve their innocence of vision by wishing for it. . . .

The justification of the Christian, or of the church, or of religion, or of the gospel, or of revelation seems forever necessary in the face of the attacks which are made upon these from the outside and in view of the doubts that arise within. Fear of defeat and loss turn men away from single-minded devotion to their ends in order that they may defend themselves and their means of attaining their ends. We not only employ methods for the discovery of truths but somehow feel it necessary to show, otherwise than by the fruits of our work, that these methods are the best. We not only desire to live in Christian faith but we endeavor to recommend ourselves by means of it and to justify it as superior to all other faiths. Such defense may be innocuous when it is strictly subordinated to the main task of living toward our ends, but put into the first place it becomes more destructive of religion, Christianity and the soul than any foe's attack can possibly be.

   A theology of revelation which begins with the historic faith of the Christian community is no less tempted to self-justification and so to abandonment of its starting point than any other theology. It may seek to make a virtue out of its necessity and to recommend itself as not only inescapable but as superior in results to all other methods. It may direct attention away from the God visible to the community of faith and seek to defend that community, its faith and its theology. The idea of revelation itself may be employed, not for the greater glory of God, but as a weapon for the defense and aggrandizement of the church or even of the individual theologian. A recent book on the subject of revelation states that "the question of revelation is at the very root of the claim of the Christian religion to universal empire over the souls of men." Such an apologetic statement contains an evident inherent self-contradiction; for revelation and the "claim of the Christian religion to universal empire over the souls of men" are absolute incompatibles. The faith of Christian revelation is directed toward a God who reveals himself as the only universal sovereign and as the one who judges all men — but particularly those directed to him in faith — to be sinners wholly unworthy of sovereignty. To substitute the sovereignty of Christian religion for the sovereignty of the God of Christian faith, though it be done by means of the revelation idea, is to fall into a new type of idolatry, to abandon the standpoint of Christian faith and revelation which are directed toward the God of Jesus Christ and to take the standpoint of a faith directed toward religion or revelation. A revelation that can be used to undergird the claim of Christian faith to universal empire over the souls of men must be something else than the revelation of the God of that Jesus Christ who in faith emptied himself, made himself of no reputation and refused to claim the kingly crown.

   The inherent self-contradiction in all such self-defensive uses of the revelation idea indicates that every effort to deal with the subject must be resolutely confessional. As we begin with revelation only because we are forced to do so by our limited standpoint in history and faith so we can proceed only by stating in simple, confessional form what has happened to us in our community, how we came to believe, how we reason about things and what we see from our point of view.

Other considerations also warn against the apologetic use of revelation and make necessary the adoption of a confessional method. Whenever the revelation idea is used to justify the church's claims to superior knowledge or some other excellence, revelation is necessarily identified with something that the church can possess. Such possessed revelation must be a static thing and under the human control of the Christian community — a book, a creed, or a set of doctrines. It cannot be revelation in act whereby the church itself is convicted of its poverty, its sin and misery before God. Furthermore, it cannot be the revelation of a living God; for the God of a revelation that can be possessed must be a God of the past, a God of the dead who communicated his truths to men in another time but who to all effects and purposes has now retired from the world, leaving the administration of his interests to some custodian of revelation — a church, a priesthood, or a school of theology.

Paul Tillich (1886–1965)

Neither the Niebuhrs nor Tillich fit neatly under narrow labels nor sit politely behind the desks of some particular "school." But Tillich, like the Niebuhrs, turned squarely toward the supernatural and engaged heroically with the ancient doctrines of the Christian religion. Refugee from Hitler's Germany, Tillich — through the good offices of Reinhold Niebuhr — came to America in 1933 to start a new career at Union Theological Seminary in New York City. Tillich made theology respectable again, one measure of his impact being the cover story in Time *magazine (March 16, 1959) on Tillich and his theology for a new age. His influences moved well beyond the confines of Protestantism as artists, philosophers, historians, pyschotherapists, and others not confessionally identified as Protestants found themselves speaking "god talk." In mid-twentieth-century America, this was a surprising thing to be doing. Even more surprising was the attempt at such a time and in such a fragmented world to do "systematic theology." But in 1951 Tillich undertook just such a task, bringing that labor to completion (in three volumes) a dozen years later. The excerpt below, taken from the introduction to the first volume, describes the task of theology in the current "situation."*

Theology, as a function of the Christian church, must serve the needs of the church. A theological system is supposed to satisfy two basic needs: the statement of the truth of the Christian message and the interpretation of this truth for every new generation. Theology moves back and forth between two poles, the eternal truth of its foundation and the temporal situation in which the eternal truth must be received. Not many theological systems have been able

[Source: Paul Tillich, *Systematic Theology*, Vol. I (Chicago: University of Chicago Press, 1951), pp. 3–4, 11–12, 15–16.]

to balance these two demands perfectly. Most of them either sacrifice elements of the truth or are not able to speak to the situation. Some of them combine both shortcomings. Afraid of missing the eternal truth, they identify it with some previous theological work, with traditional concepts and solutions, and try to impose these on a new, different situation. They confuse eternal truth with a temporal expression of this truth. This is evident in European theological orthodoxy, which in America is known as fundamentalism. When fundamentalism is combined with an antitheological bias, as it is, for instance, in its biblicistic-evangelical form, the theological truth of yesterday is defended as an unchangeable message against the theological truth of today and tomorrow. Fundamentalism fails to make contact with the present situation, not because it speaks from beyond every situation, but because it speaks from a situation of the past. It elevates something finite and transitory to infinite and eternal validity. In this respect fundamentalism has demonic traits. It destroys the humble honesty of the search for truth, it splits the conscience of its thoughtful adherents, and it makes them fanatical because they are forced to suppress elements of truth of which they are dimly aware.

Fundamentalists in America and orthodox theologians in Europe can point to the fact that their theology is eagerly received and held by many people just because of the historical or biographical situation in which men find themselves today. The fact is obvious, but the interpretation is wrong. "Situation," as one pole of all theological work, does not refer to the psychological or sociological state in which individuals or groups live. It refers to the scientific and artistic, the economic, political, and ethical forms in which they express their interpretation of existence. The "situation" to which theology must speak relevantly is not the situation of the individual as individual and not the situation of the group as group. Theology is neither preaching nor counseling; therefore, the success of a theology when it is applied to preaching or to the care of souls is not necessarily a criterion of its truth. The fact that fundamentalist ideas are eagerly grasped in a period of personal or communal disintegration does not prove their theological validity, just as the success of a liberal theology in periods of personal or communal integration is no certification of its truth. The "situation" theology must consider is the creative interpretation of existence, an interpretation which is carried on in every period of history under all kinds of psychological and sociological conditions. . . .

We have used the term "ultimate concern" without explanation. Ultimate concern is the abstract translation of the great commandment: "The Lord, our God, the Lord is one; and you shall love the Lord your God with all you heart, and with all your soul and with all your mind, and with all your strength." The religious concern is ultimate; it excludes all other concerns from ultimate significance; it makes them preliminary. The ultimate concern is unconditional, independent of any conditions of character, desire, or circumstance. The unconditional concern is total: no part of ourselves or of our

Paul Tillich (1886–1965)
(Religious News Service)

world is excluded from it; there is no "place" to flee from it. The total concern is infinite: no moment of relaxation and rest is possible in the face of a religious concern which is ultimate, unconditional, total, and infinite.

The word "concern" points to the "existential" character of religious experience. We cannot speak adequately of the "object of religion" without simultaneously removing its character as an object. That which is ultimate gives itself only to the attitude of ultimate concern. It is the correlate of an unconditional concern but not a "highest thing" called "the absolute" or "the unconditioned," about which we could argue in detached objectivity. It is the object of total surrender, demanding also the surrender of our subjectivity while we look at it. It is a matter of infinite passion and interest (Kierkegaard), making us its object whenever we try to make it our object. For this reason we have avoided terms like "*the* ultimate," "*the* unconditioned," "*the* universal," "*the* infinite," and have spoken of ultimate, unconditional, total, infinite concern. Of course, in every concern there is *something* about which one is concerned; but this something should not appear as a separated object which could be known and handled without concern. This, then, is the first formal criterion of theology: *The object of theology is what concerns us ultimately.*

Only those propositions are theological which deal with their object in so far as it can become a matter of ultimate concern for us.

The negative meaning of this proposition is obvious. Theology should never leave the situation of ultimate concern and try to play a role within the arena of preliminary concerns. Theology cannot and should not give judgments about the aesthetic value of an artistic creation, about the scientific value of a physical theory or a historical conjecture, about the best methods of medical healing or social reconstruction, about the solution of political or international conflicts. The theologian *as* theologian is no expert in any matters of preliminary concern. And, conversely, those who are experts in these matters should not *as such* claim to be experts in theology. The first formal principle of theology, guarding the boundary line between ultimate concern and preliminary concerns, protects theology as well as the cultural realms on the other side of the line. . . .

If taken in the broadest sense of the word, theology, the *logos* or the reasoning about *theos* (God and divine things), is as old as religion. Thinking pervades all the spiritual activities of man. Man would not be spiritual without words, thoughts, concepts. This is especially true in religion, the all-embracing function of man's spiritual life. It was a misunderstanding of Schleiermacher's definition of religion ("the feeling of absolute dependence") and a symptom of religious weakness when successors of Schleiermacher located religion in the realm of feeling as one psychological function among others. The banishment of religion into the nonrational corner of subjective emotions in order to have the realms of thought and action free from religious interference was an easy way of escaping the conflicts between religious tradition and modern thought. But this was a death sentence against religion, and religion did not and could not accept it.

Every myth contains a theological thought which can be, and often has been, made explicit. Priestly harmonizations of different myths sometimes disclose profound theological insights. Mystical speculations, as in Vedanta Hinduism, unite meditative elevation with theological penetration. Metaphysical speculations, as in classical Greek philosophy, unite rational analysis with theological vision. Ethical, legal, and ritual interpretations of the divine law create another form of theology on the soil of prophetic monotheism. All this is "theo-logy," *logos* of *theos*, a rational interpretation of the religious substance of rites, symbols, and myths.

Christian theology is no exception. It does the same thing, but it does it in a way which implies the claim that it is *the* theology. The basis of this claim is the Christian doctrine that the Logos became flesh, that the principle of the divine self-revelation has become manifest in the event "Jesus as the Christ." If this message is true, Christian theology has received a foundation which transcends the foundation of any other theology and which itself cannot be transcended. Christian theology has received something which is absolutely concrete and absolutely universal at the same time. No myth, no mystical vision, no metaphysical principle, no sacred law, has the concreteness of a personal life. In comparison with a personal life everything else is relatively abstract. And none of these relatively abstract foundations of theology has the universality of the Logos, which itself is the principle of universality. In comparison with the Logos everything else is relatively particular. Christian theology is *the* theology in so far as it is based on the tension between the absolutely concrete and the absolutely universal.

Neo-Thomism

The French Philosophers

The herculean theological achievement of Thomas Aquinas (c. 1225 – 74; "Saint" Thomas by 1323) represents the high point of medieval scholasticism, even as it constitutes the masterful synthesizing of Hebrew and Greek, of Christian doctrine and "worldly" thought. By the twentieth century, however, given all of the new knowledge and new methods which had come to the fore, "Thomism" —it could be argued—was thoroughly obsolete and archaic, hopelessly "unmodern." Yet, like traditional orthodoxy among Protestants, the thought of Thomas Aquinas enjoyed a great revival of interest in a very modern world. The two principal popularizers (in the best sense) of Thomism in America were not Americans but "imports": Jacques Maritain (1882 – 1973) and Etienne Gilson (1884 – 1978). Both were French and both were laymen, not clergymen. (1) Maritain in 1941 described the scope and significance of "the Thomist renaissance." (2) Gilson, in an autobiographical work published in 1962, discussed what it meant to be a Thomist.

1.

The historical importance of the Thomist renaissance comes from the fact that it constitutes a vast movement of thought affecting the life itself of the Church and the efforts of lay Christian workers, and from the fact that it consists of something rare in intellectual work, namely, a durable and progressive collaboration founded upon common principles and a living tradition. . . .

The tendencies that the Thomist revival represent are at once philosophical and theological. Accordingly, as Dom Chapman remarked with penetration, if one wishes to compare Thomism with modern thought, which has assumed all the divine and human problems of our destiny, one must compare modern

[Sources: (1) Jacques Maritain in *Religion and the Modern World* (Philadelphia: University of Pennsylvania Press, 1941), pp. 10, 11 – 13. (2) Etienne Gilson, *The Philosopher and Theology* (New York: Random House, 1962), pp. 201 – 4.]

philosophy not merely with Thomist philosophy, which is strictly limited to
problems accessible to reason, but with the ensemble of Thomist philosophy
and Thomist theology.

Thomism states as an absolute principle the unconditional affirmation of
faith in the divine order, and it also affirms in the human order the unshakable
intrinsic value of nature and reason, for every creature of God is good, as St.
Paul said. Thomist thought appears from the very first as an effort to distinguish and to unite or rather to distinguish in order to unite.

Thomism can be characterized as an integralist and progressive Christian
position. If we seek our conceptual weapons in the arsenal of Aristotle and
Thomas Aquinas, it is not in order to return to ancient Greece or to the
Middle Ages. We think that it is a sort of blasphemy against the Providence
of God in history to want to go back to a past age, and we hold that there is
an organic increase both in the Church and in the world. Hence the task of
the Christian is, we believe, to save those "truths gone mad," as Chesterton
said, which four centuries of Anthropocentric Humanism have disfigured,
and to reconcile them with the truths of higher origin misunderstood by this
Humanism, and to return them to Him who is Truth and to whose voice
faith listens.

The Humanism of Thomas Aquinas is an Integral Humanism; I mean a
Humanism which neglects nothing present in man. Such Humanism knows
that man is made of nothing and that everything that comes from nothing
tends of itself towards nothing; and it also knows that man is the image of
God and that within man there is more than man; it knows that man is
inhabited by a God who not only gives him life and activity but who gives
him His Very Self and wishes him to have as final fruition the three Divine
Persons.

It is a Humanism of the redemptive Incarnation — a Gospel-minded Humanism. I think that St. Thomas Aquinas is the apostle of modern times
because these times have loved intelligence and have abused it and can be
truly cured by it alone; and because Thomas Aquinas is the saint of the
intellect; he reduces all things to the light of the Word, that Light which is
at once — and this Karl Barth does not see — the Light that illuminates the
reason of all men coming into this world and the Light that illuminates
supernaturally all men reborn by faith. All the philosophy and all the theology
of St. Thomas are constructed in the illumination of the word received by
Moses: "I am Who Am."

The philosophy of St. Thomas is a philosophy not of essences but of
existence; it lives from the natural intuitions of sensory experience and of the
intelligence. His theology lives from faith; it is a theology of the incompre-
hensible Pure Act *to be* which subsists by itself and does not exist in the same
way as anything exists, and whose inmost life we cannot know except by its
own Word. Accordingly, it can be said that Thomist thought is above all an
existential one, although it is existential in a different manner from that of

the various philosophies which have adopted this term. And it must be also said that it is a personalist thought, according as the philosophic realism of St. Thomas implies at every moment the act of the entire human person, body and soul, confronted with being to penetrate; and according as the theological Transcendentalism of St. Thomas is a perpetual dialogue between Christ speaking through the Church and Scripture, and reason listening and seeking.

The synthetic character of Thomistic thought has been often emphasized, and rightly so. It tends to make for unity in man and to prepare him for that peace which surpasses all understanding, in joining or reconciling in him grace and nature, faith and reason, theology and philosophy, the supernatural virtues and the natural virtues, the spiritual order and the temporal order, the speculative order and the practical one, mystical contemplation and knowledge merely human, fidelity to eternal data and understanding of time. But this view would be incomplete if we did not add that such a reconciliation has nothing to do with the more or less easy arrangements of bookish reason; it demands repeatedly surmounting conflicts repeatedly arising; it demands of man a tension and an extension which are possible only in the agony of the Cross. For the words of St. Paul are valid also in the order of things of the spirit: "Without shedding of blood there is no redemption." The reconciliation we spoke of is a false reconciliation if it is not a redemption; and it cannot be accomplished without mysterious suffering, the focus of which is the spirit itself.

2.

How does one become a Thomist? At what moment? This is not easy to say. For some reason or other a philosopher begins to read Saint Thomas. If he happens to be allergic to that way of thinking, he drops the book and never picks it up again. But if there exists between him and Saint Thomas some spiritual affinity, he will read and reread it. He will then talk about Thomism, write about it, with no other intention than to help others to dispel their ignorance as he slowly dispels his, but many will want something else. They will want to know, not what Saint Thomas Aquinas thinks, but whether you are a Thomist. The only honest answer to give is that, before proclaiming yourself a Thomist, you ought first to try to find out what the Saint actually thought. To do so is a long undertaking and it is an insult to the Saint's memory to proclaim oneself his disciple without knowing exactly what he said. Such scruples are foreign to the noisiest among his followers. What they want you to do is to say that you are a Thomist. They want you to join the Thomist party. Knowing what some of them call Thomism, and that they do not even suspect there is a problem in knowing what it is, the proposition *I am a Thomist* hardly makes sense. Unfortunately, the contrary proposition has a very definite sense. It would seem that many accept being called Thomists because of their deep reluctance to say that they are not.

He who enters upon this road must be ready for some surprises. The first one is that from this moment on he will be treated by the "Thomists" according to their customary ways, which are not always gentle. Should he be French, he can expect to become the object of particular attentions on the part of integrists whose theological fanaticism is matched by the intolerance so common among Frenchmen. The only Thomist in contemporary France whose thought was lofty, bold, and creative, capable of meeting the most urgent problems and, so to speak, to stand ever ready before all emergencies, was rewarded for his zeal by the incessant, active, and venomous hostility of unhappy creatures who have little else to put in the service of God than their hatred of their neighbors.* True enough, greatness as such is unbearable in their eyes. The disciple is not above the master. Every victim of their injustice will remember that Saint Thomas himself suffered from it.

Another possible surprise for the man who "turns Thomist" is that for the rationalist, that is for the "true philosopher," he will have ceased to exist. This is easily understood. Confronted with the prodigious inflation of books, philosophical journals and conventions prevalent in all civilized countries, it becomes necessary for readers to choose. Now the Thomist is a man who makes it a point to think in philosophy what another man already thought in the thirteenth century. What an excellent pretext to get rid of him! From then on he will find himself honorably classified as belonging among the modern survivors of the "Thomistic school." More simply still, he will find himself labeled a "Neoscholastic," a man neither to be read nor discussed. . . .

The professed Thomist, then, should not be surprised at the solitude that will surround him. If his own country does not want him, Christendom is vast enough and some countries are generous enough to offer him the public he cannot find at home. Such things have happened. If the synagogue of the "laicists" excludes him, he still will have the opportunity, no doubt without enthusiasm, to turn to the Gentiles. The main thing is that, in a great mind that is also a great heart, such isolation never breeds bitterness. Let his generosity be an example to us. A man may have to live in isolation from his own country and his own time, but he should not let his country and time become foreign to him. On the contrary, the only legitimate reason to call oneself a Thomist is that one feels happy to be one and is anxious to share this happiness with those who are receptive to it.

A man becomes aware of being a Thomist on the day he realizes that from then on he will no longer be able to live without the company of Saint Thomas Aquinas. He feels in the *Summa Theologiae* as a fish in the sea; away from it he feels out of his element, and cannot wait to go back to it. More deeply, this is what gives the Thomist the joyous feeling that he is free. Essentially a Thomist is a free mind. His freedom does not consist in having neither

---

*The allusion here is to Maritain who, encountering much hostility in his native France, left for North America.

master nor God but rather in having no master other than God. And indeed God is for man the only bulwark against the tyrannies of other men. God alone delivers from fears and timidities a mind that otherwise would die of starvation in the midst of plenty. Left to itself, it will be unable to choose and will therefore die either from starvation or from indigestion. The happiness of the Thomist is the joy he experiences in feeling free to welcome all truth from whichever side it may come. The perfect expression of this liberty of the Christian man is that of Saint Augustine: *Dilige et quod vis fac: Love and do what you will.* In exactly the same spirit and the same deep sense, but in no other, the disciple of Saint Thomas can likewise say: *Believe, and think what you will.* Like charity, faith is a liberator. Incidentally, this is a reason why the Christian should willingly accept being considered as a rather unusual specimen by non-Christian thinkers.

An American Perspective

The remarkable popularity of Gilson and Maritain in the American Catholic community is helpfully commented on below. America itself really had no "central" Catholic theologian to put forward, though some were on the horizon. Thus, these two Europeans filled a void even as they gave "American Catholics the assurance of continuity with the past that they need. . . ." Walter J. Ong (b. 1912), long-time member of the faculty of English of St. Louis University and sometime member of the Society of Jesus, explains that the French philosophers met "some deep-felt emotional need."

The first half of the twentieth century will doubtless go down in history as the age when American Catholics were specializing in symbols of frontier or borderline operations. Their idols (the word is hardly too strong) include not only figures such as Chesterton, Waugh, Greene, Mrs. Clare Boothe Luce, and numbers of converted Communists and other converts who have appeared in England and the United States to testify to the religio-intellectual charge at the borderline between the Church and her surroundings, as well as similar figures in France . . . but most especially two Europeans who have been first borrowed and more recently simply annexed by the English-speaking Catholics of North America, MM. Gilson and Maritain.

There can be little doubt that Professor Gilson has been sponsored by American Catholics not only out of admiration for his superb scholarship, but also out of some deep-felt emotional need. American Catholics commonly think of M. Gilson simply as a Thomist, but the author of *Thomism* himself has credited much of his interest in philosophy and inspiration to Bergson;

[Source: Walter J. Ong, S. J., *Frontiers in American Catholicism* (New York: Macmillan Co., 1957), pp. 113–14.]

and Bergson's sense of history, of a present which is and has always been the frontier where the past moves into the future, is undoubtedly one of the things which gave M. Gilson his appeal to the contemporary American Catholic mind. For this mind, Gilson helps symbolically to endow even the reputed static qualities of the Middle Ages, and with them the similar qualities imputed (mistakenly) by Americans to Europe in general, with the sense of movement in history so congenial to the American sensibility.

As a symbol, M. Gilson affects the American Catholic mind apparently well below the threshold of consciousness, for he himself appears much more explicitly aware of the necessity of establishing a dialogue between the Faith and America and more inclined explicitly to view his own work as contributing to this dialogue than are his own American backers. So far as I have observed, American Catholics seem quite unaware that the title of M. Gilson's Harvard lectures in honor of their fellow American William James which they so widely read, *The Unity of Philosophical Experience*, is a take-off and commentary on the title of an earlier series of Gifford Lectures by William James himself, *The Varieties of Religious Experience*. It is fascinating to note that in this exchange of views — at a distance of some years — it is James whose sense of history was not very compelling and who studies the various manifestations of drives common to all, or many individuals, focusing on an anhistorical diversity, whereas Gilson focuses on the unity evinced within movement or history, and thus gives comfort to the American Catholic unconscious in its own orientation toward movement.

The other favorite symbol of borderline activity, Professor Maritain, has been sponsored even more than Professor Gilson in the United States, where he is now more eminent than in his own country. Emerging from the same European-medieval context as Gilson, and thus giving American Catholics the assurance of continuity with the past that they need, Maritain puts the American Catholic ethos in contact less with the movement of history than with something else in its surroundings: the post-Newtonian scientific developments of a generation or two ago. It may fairly be said that he predigested these developments for American Catholic consumption. On the whole, his work in this field has been more widely attended to in America than his own more valuable work on Church-state relationships, which has had to compete with the parallel work of an American Jesuit, Father John Courtney Murray.*

*On Murray, see below, p. 475.

Neo-Fundamentalism: Evangelical Responsibility

"The recovery of interest in special divine revelation is," wrote Carl F. H. Henry (b. 1912) in 1957, "one of the gracious providences of our century." So saying in Christianity Today, *a conservative journal of which Henry became the first editor, he called for a return to biblical theology and a rejection of that natural theology so dear to modernism. But the new fundamentalism, or "evangelical theology" to use Henry's term, is not a mere replication of the older fundamentalism. In the earlier time, genuine Christian living was so often interpreted as "personal abstinence from dubious social externals." Now, one moves toward "comprehending the whole of the moral law in fuller exposition of love for God and neighbor. . . ." The time, for negativism and narrow legalism is over; the time for "positive preaching" and the "social application of Christian theology" is at hand.*

The way theology defines the relation of revelation and reason will color its comprehension of Christianity and culture, Christianity and science, Christianity and philosophy, no less than the exposition of Christian doctrine and apologetics. If divine revelation stands in essential contrast to human reason, or if it impinges only dialectically upon the human mind, so that divine revelation cannot be grasped in concepts and words, then a Christian philosophy is a vain hope. It is part of the glory of evangelical theology that it rises above the modern contrast between God-truth and world-truth which divides human reason and precludes the intellectual integration of experience.

The recovery of interest in special divine revelation is one of the gracious providences of our century. It comes significantly at a time when the world must contend with the tactical initiatives of Communism and of irreligion. Protestant modernism deflected Western Christianity's theological interest from biblical revelation to natural theology.

This retrograde idealistic philosophy only briefly resisted a further decline to humanism. Evangelicals once reveled in the divine oracles; the modernists now asked whether God exists. Modernism's surrender of biblical revelation finally enmeshed American Christianity in the loss of the self-revealed God; in the noncommunist world, as well as the communist, naturalism surged to ascendancy. Now that special revelation is once again recognized as integral to Hebrew-Christian redemptive religion, it becomes a duty of evangelical theology to conserve this gain, and to shield it from speculative misunderstanding.

A higher spirit to quicken and to fulfill the theological fortunes of this

[Source: Carl F. H. Henry, in *Christianity Today*, July 8, 1957, p. 18; July 22, 1957, pp. 23 – 24.]

century will require more than the displacement of modernism, more than the revision of neo-orthodoxy, more than the revival of fundamentalism. Recovery of apostolic perspective and dedication of the evangelical movement to biblical realities are foundational to this hope.

Exalt Biblical Theology

Evangelical theology has nothing to fear, and much to gain, from aligning itself earnestly with the current plea for a return to biblical theology. To measure this moving front of creative theology sympathetically, to understand its concern and courage and to name its weaknesses without depreciating its strength will best preserve relevant theological interaction with the contemporary debate.

The evangelical movement must make its very own the passionate concern for the reality of special divine revelation, for a theology of the Word of God, for attentive hearing of the witness of the Bible, for a return to biblical theology.

Positive Preaching

Rededication to positive and triumphant preaching is the evangelical pulpit's great need. The note of Christ's lordship over this dark century, of the victory of Christianity, has been obscured. If it be evangelical, preaching must enforce the living communication of the changeless realities of divine redemption. The minister whose pulpit does not become the life-giving center of his community fails in his major mission. Perspective on Christianity's current gains and final triumph will avoid a myopic and melancholy discipleship. The Christian pulpit must present the invisible and exalted Head of the body of Christ; linked to him this earthly colony of heaven moves to inevitable vindication and glory. The perplexing problems of our perverse social orders find their hopeful solution only in this regenerative union. Out of its spiritual power must spring the incentives to creative cultural contributions.

Enlarge Christian Living

The evangelical fellowship needs a fresh and pervading conception of the Christian life. Too long fundamentalists have swiftly referred the question, "What distinguishes Christian living?" to personal abstinence from dubious social externals. The Christian conscience, of course, will always need to justify outward behavior, in home, in vocation and in leisure. But Christian ethics probes deeper. It bares the invisible zone of personality where lurk pride, covetousness and hatred.

Unfortunately, fundamentalism minimized the exemplary Jesus in the sphere of personal ethics. The theme of Christ's oneness with God was developed so exclusively in terms of his deity that the import of his dependence upon God for all human nature was lost. . . .

Another way in which evangelicals need to move beyond the fundamentalist ethic is in comprehending the whole of the moral law in fuller exposition of love for God and neighbor, and in the larger experience of the Holy Spirit in New Testament terms of ethical virtue. Often quite legalistically, and with an absoluteness beyond New Testament authority, fundamentalism's doctrine of surrender, of rededication, has merely proscripted worldly practices, from which the believer was discouraged. Unemphasized, however, are the fruit of the Spirit and those many virtues which differentiate dedicated living in terms of biblical Christianity.

Social Concern

We need a new concern for the individual in the entirety of his Christian experience. He is a member of all life's communities, of faith, of the family, of labor, of the state, of culture. Christianity is by no means the social gospel of modernism, but is nonetheless vibrant with social implications as a religion of redemptive transformation. To express and continue the vitality of the gospel message, marriage and the home, labor and economics, politics and the state, culture and the arts, in fact, every sphere of life, must evidence the lordship of Christ. . . .

Approach to Science

Evangelical confidence in the ontological significance of reason makes possible a positive, courageous approach to science. For more than a century and a half modern philosophy has regrettably minimized the role of reason. Kant disjoined it from the spiritual world. Darwin naturalized and constricted it within the physical world. Dewey allowed it only a pragmatic or an instrumental role. These speculations took a heavy toll in Christian circles. A segment of evangelical Christianity nonetheless maintained its insistence upon the Logos as integral to the Godhead, the universe as a rational-purposive order, and man's finite reason as related to the image of God.

Yet for more than a generation the evangelical attitude in scientific matters has been largely defensive. Evolutionary thought is met only obliquely. American fundamentalism often neglected scrutinizing its own position in the light of recent historical and scientific research. It even failed to buttress its convictions with rigorous theological supports.

Yet modernism, despite its eager pursuit of such revision, achieved no true correlation of Christianity and science. While modernism adjusted Christianity swiftly to the prevailing climate of technical conviction, its scientific respect was gained by a costly neglect of Christianity's import to science.

Today a new mood pervades the scientific sphere. That mood may not fully validate the evangelical view of nature, but it does at least deflate the presuppositions on which the older liberalism built its bias against the miraculous. The evangelical movement is now given a strategic opportunity to transcend its hesitant attitude toward scientific endeavor, and to stress the realities of a rational, purposive universe that coheres in the Logos as the agent in creation, preservation, redemption, sanctification and judgment.

Suggested Reading (Chapter Ten)

The Spirit of American Philosophy (1963), to use the title of John E. Smith's beautifully clear survey, may prove elusive, but it certainly cannot be defined without attention to the five figures whom Smith treats: Peirce, James, Royce, Dewey, and Whitehead. Precisely the same five are discussed by Robert J. Roth, S. J., in a book to which he gives the title *American Religious Philosophy* (1967). The addition of the word "religious" does suggest that the "spirit" of American philosophy, at least as represented by this quintet, is to a considerable degree a religious one. Santayana, passed over in the two titles above, is rescued from neglect in Morton White's *Science and Sentiment in America: Philosophical Thought from Jonathan Edwards to John Dewey* (1972); White provides his own documentary history in *Documents in the History of American Philosophy*, also published in 1972. William A. Clebsch in his sweep of *American Religious Thought* (1973) likewise begins with Edwards, concluding with insightful attention to William James. One is introduced to some members of the theological "school" built upon Whiteheadian foundations in Delwin Brown et al., eds., *Process Philosophy and Christian Thought* (1971).

The many encounters between science and religion, more often unfriendly than not, continue to fascinate and to be responsible for a large literature. The long struggle in Christian history is reviewed in D. C. Lindberg and R. L. Numbers, *God and Nature: Historical Essays on the Encounter between Christianity and Science* (1986). E. A. White confines his survey to the United States: *Science and Religion in American Thought* (1952). Cross-cultural perspectives within Protestantism are offered in detail in J. R. Moore's impressive book, *The Post-Darwinian Controversies* (1979), which looks at both Britain and America during the thirty-year period from 1870 to 1900. A Roman Catholic survey, not limited to the United States, *Science and Religion* (1962), has been translated from the French of Paul Chauchard. Individuals discussed in the chapter above have often been the subject of full monographic investigation. Valuable examples of such include the following: Donald Fleming, *John William Draper and the Religion of Science* (1950); W. C. Darrah, *Powell of the Colorado* (1951); Lester Stephens, *Joseph Le Conte: Gentle Prophet of Evolution* (1982); William G. McLoughlin, *The Meaning of Henry Ward Beecher* (1970); and Lawrence W. Levine's biography of William Jennings Bryan, appropriately entitled *Defender of the Faith* (1965).

The best approach to early American contributions to the "scientific" study of the Bible is through the history of divinity schools and seminaries associated with major universities. Two outstanding examples of such histories are George H. Williams, ed., *The Harvard Divinity School* (1954); and Roland H. Bainton, *Yale and the Ministry* (1957). How the old heresy of C. A. Briggs became the new orthodoxy of contemporary Protestants is demonstrated in Jack B. Rogers and Donald E. McKim, *The Authority and Interpretation of The Bible* (1979). Two important Society of Biblical Literature volumes deserve notice: Ernest Sanders's history of the Society, *Searching the Scriptures* (1982); and Eugene Tucker and Douglas Knight, eds., *Humanizing America's Iconic Book* (1982), a collection of major addresses given at the centennial celebration in Dallas, Texas. A 1958 survey of *Biblical Criticism*, written by Jean Steinmann and designed for the Roman Catholic community, concludes with a chapter entitled "The Triumph of Historical Exegesis." Criticism, the author notes, only rids "the reader of the false ideas *he thought he found* in the Bible." "Nothing is affected by criticism except misconceptions. . . ." Not until 1981 did religious Jewry issue a biblical commentary that incorporated recent scholarship. *The Torah: A Modern Commentary* (W. Gunther Plaut et al.) appeared under the auspices of Reform Judaism, but the commentary is expected to appeal to some Conservative synagogues as well.

The context necessary for understanding Roman Catholic modernism in this country is carefully put forward by Robert D. Cross in *The Emergence of Liberal Catholicism in America* (1958) and by Thomas T. McAvoy, C. S. C., in *The Americanist Heresy in Roman Catholicism, 1895–1900* (1957, 1963). John Ratté in *Three Modernists* (1967) treats at length two European exemplars, Alfred Loisy and George Tyrrell, but also the combative career of America's lonely William L. Sullivan. For Protestantism, the context may be found in two particularly fine books faithful to the complexity of their respective subjects: William R. Hutchison, *The Modernist Impulse in American Protestantism* (1976); and George M. Marsden, *Fundamentalism and American Culture* (1980). See also Ernest R. Sandeen, *The Roots of Fundamentalism* (1970), along with *The Fundamentals* themselves, first published in four volumes in 1917 and reprinted in 1972. Harry Emerson Fosdick's engaging autobiography, *The Living of These Days* (1956), offers a view of the confrontations through the eyes of an active participant. Judaism's varying responses to modernity may be followed in these works: Samuel Belkin, *Essays in Traditional Jewish Thought* (1956); Solomon Poll, *The Hasidic Community of Williamsburg* (1962); Mordecai Waxman, ed., *Tradition and Change: the Development of Conservative Judaism* (1958); and David Philipson, *The Reform Movement in Judaism* (rev. ed., 1967).

Neo–Orthodoxy and associated emphases in Protestant theology are treated in Arnold Nash, ed., *Protestant Thought in the Twentieth Century* (1951) and in Daniel Day Williams, *What Present Day Theologians are Thinking* (1952; rev., 1967). On Richard Niebuhr, see L. A. Hoedemaker, *The Theology of H. Richard Niebuhr* (1970); the best access to Paul Tillich is through the anthology edited by C. W. Kegley and R. W. Bretall, *The Theology of Paul Tillich* (1952). For Neo-Thomism, besides the many writings of Maritain and Gilson themselves, one may turn to the influential Chicago educator, Mortimer J. Adler, who provided his quite positive appraisal in *Saint Thomas and the Gentiles* (1938). At about the same time, the Dominican Fathers of the Province of St. Joseph launched "A Speculative Quarterly

Review" devoted entirely to the thought of Thomas Aquinas and called simply *The Thomist* (1939–   ). Much attention has been given to the "new evangelicals," some of whom follow the lead of Carl F. H. Henry while others do not. The most carefully analytical studies of conservative moderns include the following: Donald W. Dayton, *Discovering an Evangelical Heritage* (1976); David F. Wells and John Woodbridge, eds., *The Evangelicals* (1975); Donald G. Bloesch, *The Evangelical Renaissance* (1973); and Richard Quebedeaux, *The Worldly Evangelicals* (1978). For a conservative analysis of what "went wrong" in the first half of the twentieth century, see Carl F. H. Henry's succinct *Fifty Years of Protestant Theology* (1950); this may then be supplemented by his more constructive effort, *Christian Faith and Modern Theology* (1964).

ELEVEN:
Consensus and Conflict

In the decades following World War II, the relationship between religion in America and its surrounding culture was an uneasy one. On the one hand, a postwar "revival" of religion suggested a scene that was upbeat and positive. On the other hand, theology grew less assured and less constructive while a statistical profile of mainline denominations suggested that, by the end of the 1960s, all was not well. So too, from one perspective, the postwar years brought a flood of ecumenical activity, enough so that one might even characterize this period as the "era of good will." Yet, from another perspective, the country and its churches were deeply divided over civil rights, over communist and anticommunist crusades, over moral obligations to the culturally and economically deprived, and over moral integrity — or the conspicuous absence thereof — in the nation's highest offices. The signals were mixed, as religion now and then functioned as the agent of consensus, now and then as the occasion of conflict.

THE WORLD AND ITS WARS

As in all of the nation's other wars before and since, World War II had its religious dissenters — those who for cause of conscience could not bear arms or agree to slay the enemy. Yet, unlike many of America's other wars, this one created no widespread dissent, resulted in no sharp social division. No "loyalists" to purge or force into exile as in the American Revolution, no antiimperialists to suppress or denounce as in the Mexican or in the later Spanish-American War, and of course no horrible clash between brother and brother as in the Civil War. Aside from the disgraceful treatment of the Japanese Americans, World War II was a national effort: reviving the economy, unifying the nation internally, and elevating the United States to the highest peak of world influence and power. Nevertheless, for all its glory and unconditional victories over Germany, Italy, and Japan, this World War left two haunting legacies. Hiroshima revealed the enormity of mankind's new power to destroy; the Holocaust revealed the enormity of mankind's old power

431

to hate. Both legacies were of such a scale as to defy comparisons, and both demanded new efforts to "justify the ways of God to man."

One of the by-products of World War II and the Allied victory was the creation of the state of Israel in 1948. Sentiment for such a Jewish homeland did not originate, of course, in the 1940s. For generations before, those favoring such a state *somewhere* (and at times, anywhere) — the Zionists — had appealed to Jews around the world and to consciences in all the world for help in bringing such a homeland into being. The Zionist movement, European in origin, found wide though not universal support in America. After the founding of Israel, however, and even more after the 1967 Six Day War, anti-Zionism in America was reduced to a whisper. Vindication had at last come for the Hungarian Theodor Herzl, Zionism's passionate and persuasive nineteenth-century voice.

If Israel's brief war in 1967 was a conspicuous success, America's long war of the 1960s and 1970s was a tragic failure: tragic on the battlefield, and tragic at home. Never since the Civil War had the nation found itself so bitterly divided, so much at cross purposes with its own vision of what "America" as symbol had meant since 1776. One of the reasons for swelling criticism was simply the Vietnam War's interminable course. It turned out to be the country's longest war, from 1964 to 1975, and surely its least satisfying one. What were the vital interests of the United States in far-off Indochina? What were our purposes: politically, economically, militarily, morally? The whole encounter, moreover, had a kind of David and Goliath aspect, with this nation seen as the heavy-handed, bullying giant. "The picture of the world's greatest superpower killing or seriously injuring 1,000 noncombatants a week, while trying to pound a tiny backward nation into submission," wrote Secretary of Defense Robert S. McNamara to President Lyndon B. Johnson on May 19, 1967, "is not a pretty one." And the picture turned even uglier as the costs mounted in both dollars and lives, as the cries and acts of dissent grew more desperate. By war's end, 57,000 Americans had died and untold thousands of Vietnamese. The living were left shaken, sobered, morally confused. In 1963 Pope John XXIII dared all humankind to dream with his precedent-shattering encyclical, *Peace on Earth,* addressed "to the clergy and faithful of the whole world and to all men of good will." This bold and thoughtful letter raised hopes high as it made the subject of peace a high priority for press, for government, for synagogue and church. A decade later, the dreams inspired by *Peace on Earth* lay in ruin.

THE NATION AND ITS CHURCHES

On the domestic religious front, the second half of the twentieth century began with the reorganizing of the old (1908) Federal Council of Churches into a strengthened and more visible National Council of Churches (1950). The World Council of Churches, founded two years earlier in Amsterdam, selected the United States for its second great gathering: at Evanston, Illinois, in 1954. In 1956, the fortnightly magazine, *Christianity Today,* began publication, giving a more cohesive and unifying voice to large segments of conservative Christianity in America. Then in 1960 Presbyterian Eugene Carson Blake and Episcopal James Albert Pike stimulated the formation of the Consultation on Church Union, a wide-ranging "Proposal Toward the Reunion of Christ's Church." In the decade that followed, Episcopalians and Presbyterians, Congregationalists and Methodists (both black and white denominations), Disciples of Christ, and others probed into the nature of the church and its ministry, the sacraments and liturgy, the creeds and theology in search of that firm foundation on which all could build together.

Of course, against this chorus of ecumenical goodwill, other voices were raised. Presbyterian Carl McIntire organized the American Council of Christian Churches and the International Council of Christian Churches not so much to give evidence of further ecumenicity as to protest vigorously against it. McIntire was anti-Catholic, anti-Orthodox, anti-Billy Graham, anti-Revised Standard Version of the Bible, and anti-Brotherhood Week (sponsored by the National Conference of Christians and Jews) which he characterized as a "gross perversion of scriptural teaching." The Lutherans, who had sailed rather majestically through the troubled waters of modernism and fundamentalism earlier in the century, found themselves thrown against the rocks in the 1970s. At that time the Lutheran Church–Missouri Synod fired faculty, expelled students, and drove away churches—all on grounds repeatedly marched over in America's religious history. Only the timing was occasion for surprise. (In the 1980s, on the other hand, Lutheranism's remaining great churches, the American Lutheran Church and the Lutheran Church in America, took momentous steps toward full union. And while Presbyterians—north and south—also voted to merge, the Episcopal Church, so often above schism, suffered departures in the 1960s and 1970s over revision of the prayer book and the ordination of women.)

By any accounting, the top religious story, worldwide, of the early sixties concerned the convening of the most important church council since the sixteenth century. Vatican II (1962–65) met not in secret but in open daylight, as an entranced world listened on radio, watched on television, and read the countless pamphlets, articles, columns of newsprint, and books which poured forth like an avalanche. Pope John's "revolution," as it has been called without exaggeration, was the heroic if tardy struggle of the Roman Catholic Church to come to terms with the modern world, such a "settlement" having been emphatically rejected by Pope Pius IX (*Syllabus of Errors,* 1864), by Vatican I (Dogma of Papal Infallibility, 1870), and by Pius X (*Pascendi Dominici Gregis,* 1907). Decades after the fourth and final session of Vatican II (concluded ceremonially with a mass in St. Peter's Square in Rome, December 8, 1965), Roman Catholics in America—and elsewhere around the world—still busily worked at the far-reaching implications of this Council.

In 1955 Jewish sociologist-theologian Will Herberg published a popular treatment of religion in America; he called it *Protestant, Catholic, Jew* and spoke of these affiliations as America's three ways of being religious. But there was then, and is now, a fourth way of major significance: Eastern Orthodoxy. The Orthodox in America, chiefly gathered into Greek and Russian communions, had a membership of well over two million in 1960, roughly equivalent to the number of religiously observant Jews at that time. Yet, these Americans have been scarcely visible, except for an occasional "fourth" prayer at presidential inaugurations (who *is* that bearded man?). The reason for this near invisibility has nothing to do with that church's numbers, nothing to do with its long history, and certainly nothing to do with the nature of its worship and pageantry. Anyone who has attended an Eastern Orthodox service where every one of his or her senses was stimulated if not overwhelmed would have real difficulty imagining how such a church could escape wide public notice. The answer to the mystery lies in ethnicity and unbending tradition. Ethnic enclaves are nothing new to American religion: the colonial period is full of such small groups huddled together for survival, while in the nineteenth century Lutheranism provides the best example of those who found their togetherness more in terms of language, ethnicity, and national origin than in terms of theological tradition or creedal loyalty. In the twentieth century, Eastern Orthodoxy affords the best example. Language, ethnicity, and national ties are clung to, while steps toward Americanization or acculturation are taken only tentatively. Joined with this ethnic environment is the firm dedication to tradition, to — if you will — "Orthodoxy." The Eastern Orthodox churches have undergone no Reformation, no Enlightenment, no direct challenge by the familiar forces of modernism and fundamentalism, no Vatican II (though observers did attend that Council and have participated in various ways in the National and World Council of Churches). As a result of all this, it becomes deplorably easy, unjustifiably easy, to write of "religion in America" with little or no attention to this ancient, colorful, sometime powerful force in world Christendom.

SOCIETY AND ITS CONFLICTS

The "age of ecumenicity" apart, the 1950s and 1960s were difficult times for synagogue and church, for politician and president. The World War II alliance with the Soviet Union, an alliance of convenience for some and a pact with the devil for others, did not long survive the postwar negotiating and global positioning by England, France, the Soviet Union, and the United States. As the Cold War cast its pall, the whole world seemed divided between communist (despotic and atheistic) and noncommunist (free and godly) halves. In the 1950s the Americans' pledge of allegiance to the flag was amended to include the phrase "under God," as if to emphasize that the Cold War was also to some degree a Holy War. The passions aroused on all sides were equal to such a crusade. In the days of Senator Joseph McCarthy's greatest power, from around 1948 to around 1954 (he died in 1957), mainline churches, and especially Protestant churches, found themselves thrown on the defensive, shielding themselves from being attacked as dupes, cowards, or traitors. For the historic Protestant churches of America, it was a position of striking anomaly: surprising in its novelty and unnerving in its severity. Like measles or whooping cough, this epidemic also passed, but it left a religious establishment weakened and unwell.

Remarkably, however, near the close of the "McCarthy era," the United States Supreme Court (under the leadership of Chief Justice Earl Warren) unanimously decided that separate education (for blacks and for whites) did not constitute equal education. Then, under the even more remarkable leadership of Martin Luther King, Jr., the late 1950s and the 1960s saw Protestant, Catholic, Jew—and Orthodox—caught up in and effectively contributing to the civil rights movement. The rhetoric was moving, the dedication widespread, the resistance (including, of course, religious resistance) deep-seated and often bloody. It would be a mistake, to be sure, to regard that struggle as now over, or to delude oneself into thinking that some permanent peace had been agreed upon. But advances were made (notably in the presidential years of Lyndon B. Johnson, 1963–69), as the nation inched closer to the ideal proclaimed long ago of all men's equal creation.

In 1960, the Democratic party put forward its nomination for the presidency of the United States: John F. Kennedy, then a U. S. senator, formerly a U. S. representative, a veteran of World War II, a graduate of Harvard, and a native of the colonial state of Massachusetts. To some segments of the voting public, however, the only fact about him that really mattered was that he was a Roman Catholic. In 1928, the Democrats had nominated Alfred E. Smith (see above, pp. 271–72), and while his Catholicism was not the only issue, it was a highly inflammatory one. Would 1960 be a repeat of 1928? It was not, as everyone knows, but "the religious issue" occupied a disproportionate amount of time and space in press, pulpit, and presidential coverage. A kind of maturing, it could be argued, had taken place between 1928 and 1960, a maturing also evident in the effort that followed Kennedy's assassination in 1963 to extend the benefits of an affluent society to all its citizens. The argument for maturity became harder to make in the early 1970s, however, as a vice president resigned for the first time in American history amid charges of bribery and corruption; and then, as a president resigned for the first time in American history amid charges of lying, covering up a crime, and attempting to create an imperial presidency. The Great Society had so soon become the Betrayed Society.

REVIVALISM AND RETREAT

In three hundred or so years of American history, it would be difficult to find a more "American" phenomenon or one more potent with possibility than the religious revival. Over and over, revivalism has been dismissed as only a feeble survivor of an earlier and simpler time: weak, wobbly, and barely able to thump some crude pulpit in some obscure church. Over and over, this caricature has proved to be utterly false. The person most responsible for revivalism's enduring vitality in the decades after World War II is Billy Graham. Since 1949 at least, Graham has captured national and international headlines; he has been interviewed, acclaimed, excoriated, and written off as a mere flash in the pan. The flash has been a long time fading. Being in the limelight for so long almost guarantees a kind of arrested development, a refusal to do anything but echo the sure formulas of success. Graham has defied this pattern, however, as he has over many years become more socially sensitive, more politically wary, and more theologically self-critical. So with Graham, and quite apart from Graham, religion revived in the 1950s, some of the larger churches beginning to falter by the end of the 1960s.

Theology also faltered, as the most popular religious books could hardly be distinguished from the best-selling self-help books. New Thought (see above, pp. 237–38) proved highly marketable thought, but now emerging from the bosoms of the older ecclesiastical traditions. Then for a time in the 1960s it became fashionable to speak of the "death of God" or to argue for a "religious humanism" that could preserve all the old values with few of the old verities. No wonder, then, that religious statistics that had arched ever upward took a surprising, discomforting downward turn. In many of the mainline denominations, if there was any growth at all, it did not even match the modest increase in national population. In other instances, the decline was absolute. So, a line portraying a centuries-old trend of enlarging member- ship — from, say, less than 20 percent in the colonial period to over 60 percent in the 1960s — leveled out or slid slightly toward the bottom of the graph. In 1970, according to the Gallup Poll, only 14 percent of the sampled population were prepared to agree that religion in this country was "increasing its influence." Tables, graphs, charts, and polls did not reveal a bullish market in religion; nor did the older schools of theology, monasteries, convents, and the ranks of young recruits for ministry and mission.

1. THE WORLD AND ITS WARS
Legacy of World War II

Hiroshima

The world was introduced into the atomic age neither gradually nor gently. That abrupt introduction came on August 6, 1945. Nearly one hundred thousand people were killed almost instantly, another hundred thousand fatally injured, a whole city left in rubble, and a whole world left in anxious dread and moral confusion. "America's Atomic Atrocity," a leading Protestant journal editorialized (Christian Century, August 29, 1945), this after a second bomb had been dropped on Nagasaki, obliterating that urban center as well. The task of reconciliation, the editor noted, falls to the churches who must restore "the spiritual basis of community between the Christian church and the Japanese people." In the document below, Richard M. Fagley (b. 1910), a member of the Federal Council of Churches' Commission on a Just and Durable Peace, also insisted that "we cannot escape this crisis by secularist means."

If there was any doubt that beneath the crisis of the Second World War lay a more profound crisis of man, the explosions in New Mexico, Hiroshima and Nagasaki should have shattered the illusion. The fact that the illusion widely persists reveals the depth of our present, and possibly final, crisis.

Through the sacrifices of young men and scientific discovery, our secularized society survived the crisis of Hitler's pagan conspiracy. The faith of modern man in his own self-sufficiency unfortunately also survived, weakened perhaps but not broken. Consequently, the end of one crisis becomes, with the discovery of atomic power, the beginning of a far greater crisis. From this crisis there is no escape by the ways familiar to secularism or worldliness. The inexorable "either-or" of the atomic bomb, upon which hangs the fate of life on this planet, leaves the pride of man no means by which to save itself. The only alternative to Armageddon is repentance and regeneration.

One tragic reflection of the present crisis is the picture, conjured up by some of our writers, of vast power and plenty made possible by atomic energy.

[Source: R. M. Fagley, "The Atomic Bomb and the Crisis of Man," *Christianity and Crisis*, Oct. 1, 1945, p. 5.]

The Promised Land of freedom from want lies just ahead. Man has made the power of the sun his servant, and freed himself for luxury and leisure. How distorted is our vision to see so easily the vista of mechanical progress in this Atomic Age, and to fail to see clearly the greed, pride and fear in ourselves which have now brought us to the doorstep of doom! Of course, atomic energy can lift the burden of poverty from the backs of countless millions and give all mankind the material basis for creative living. What should be equally obvious is that only if man has a new spirit within him can he pass over into this Promised Land. The Atomic Age is otherwise almost certain to be extremely short and extremely brutish!

Equally revealing is the naive faith of many in the ability of science to control the threat of atomic bombs by creating effective counter-weapons. The end of a scientific race between the development of anti-bombs and the

Refugees at Ibinokuchi, near Nagasaki, Japan, on August 10, 1945
(© by Hiroshima City and Nagasaki City)

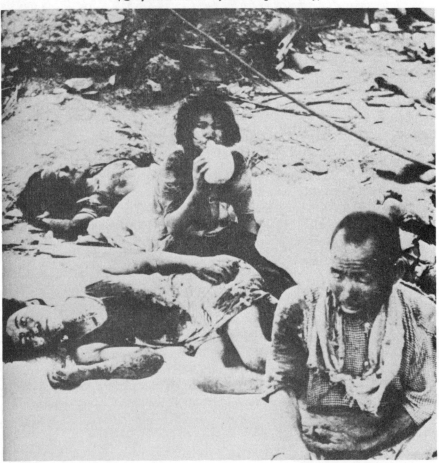

development of bigger, faster bombs is not hard to see. It is the end of man on this earth. Not machines but man with God's help can control the power God has permitted man to discover.

Again, there is the common illusion that fear can protect mankind from atomic war. Fear, it is true, may help — if it leads men to seek, with a contrite heart, the protection and guidance of God. But fear by itself offers a shortcut to catastrophe. The fear of destruction from atomic bombs in the present world of competing states would insure and hasten sudden, ruthless attacks with atomic bombs. Total aggression would become the strategy for survival. As Norman Cousins writes: "If history teaches us anything, it is that the possibility of war increases in direct proportion to the effectiveness of the instruments of war."

Of a piece with the above patterns of thought is the notion that the present crisis might be exorcised, if only the inventors would destroy their infernal machine, or if they would discontinue the manufacture of bombs, while the nations signed a pledge not to use them. For better or worse, however, the clock of history does not run backwards. Nor can its cosmic hands be stayed by Kellogg-Briand pacts. Atomic power is here to stay for the remainder of human history. And unless man can control himself as well as atomic power according to the moral law, both will no doubt terminate within a comparatively few years.

The argument for world government as a way to control the perils and potentialities of atomic energy is logical in detail. But its fundamental premise, that changes in political institutions by themselves would assure human survival, is false like the rest of the secularist arguments. No form of government is foolproof. No system of international control can provide a final answer. Political institutions can be corrupted. Controls can break down.

This does not mean that the form of institution or the differences among types of political controls are unimportant. Far from it. Yet twist and turn as we may, we cannot escape from this crisis by secularist means. We are driven inexorably from one false solution to another, unless and until we seek a more profound, religious solution. A deeper faith in God and therefore in man as a child of God and a more sacrificial effort to make brotherhood a guiding principle of society, alone offer real hope that atomic rockets can be kept under control, and the new energy be put to the service of human needs. Unless men everywhere are moved to confess their own inadequacy, and seek to follow God's will rather than their own, no other strategy can save mankind.

The fate of the world, therefore, in a literal sense, depends upon the ability of the moral and religious forces, and above all, of the Christian churches, to call men effectively to repentance, worship, and service. The conversion of man, who, as Cousins puts it, "has exalted change in everything but himself," has suddenly become a life-and-death issue, not merely for individuals, but for the race. Beyond all other groups, our churches are confronted with the ultimatum of the atomic bomb, for they alone can provide a significant answer.

Holocaust

*If the enormity of Hiroshima was almost instantaneously evident, the horror
of the Holocaust came only by degrees. Even that way, it proved impossible
to absorb: millions of Jews, along with hundreds of thousands of others,
systematically imprisoned, degraded, experimented with, tortured, gassed,
buried. The camp at Auschwitz came to symbolize the depravity of this
event, an event unique in "the whole history of human depravity." And
Auschwitz became for many a kind of moral and theological line of demar-
cation. After Auschwitz, one could never reflect in quite the same way
concerning the nature of God or man, and concerning the meaning of human
history. Emil L. Fackenheim (b. 1916), rabbi and professor of philosophy
at the University of Toronto, writes below of "The Commanding Voice of
Auschwitz."*

My mind and spirit are still numbed. I have, however, acquired one religious certainty as great as any in this religiously uncertain age. Søren Kierkegaard once perceived his "knight of faith" as forever obliged to retrace
Abraham's road to Mount Moriah, the place where he was to sacrifice Isaac.
The Jewish believer and theological thinker today — as well as a century or
a millennium hence — is obliged to retrace, again and again, the *via dolorosa*
that led one-third of his people to the human sacrifice in the Nazi gas chambers. He is forbidden the cheap and often sacrilegious evasions that tempt
him on every side: the "progressive" ideology that asserts that memory is
unnecessary, that Auschwitz was an accidental "relapse into tribalism" (an
insult to any tribe ever in existence); the "psychiatric" ideology that holds that
memory is masochism even as Auschwitz itself was sadism, thus safely belit-
tling both; the "liberal-universalist" ideology that asserts that memory is actually immoral, that because Jews must care about Vietnam, the Black ghetto,
and Arab refugees, they are obliged to forget the greatest catastrophe suffered
by their own people.

   That last-named ideology is especially insidious, for good Jews are tempted
by it. When I first called Auschwitz unique my assertion was at once taken
to mean that a dead Jewish child at Auschwitz is a greater tragedy than a dead
German child at Dresden. That was a misunderstanding possible only because
of an antisemitism (conscious or unconscious) that distinguishes "universal-
istic" Jews concerned with others to the point of consenting to group suicide,
and "particularistic" Jews who deserve this nasty epithet if they show any
concern whatever for the fate of their own people. This ideology, I say,
tempts many: witness the countless Jews today who risk much in behalf of
Vietnam or the Black ghetto but will not utter a word against Polish or Soviet
antisemitism. Hatred of Jews on the part of others has always produced self-
hating Jews — never more so than when disguised as a moral ideology.

   [Source: E. L. Fackenheim, *The Jewish Return into History* (New York: Schocken
Books, 1978), pp. 44 – 47.]

I call Auschwitz unique because it *is* unique. As my wife, Rose, put it in a letter to a minister, Auschwitz was

> overwhelming in its scope, shattering in its fury, inexplicable in its demonism. Unlike Hiroshima, it was no miscalculation of a government at war. It was minutely planned and executed over a twelve-year period, with the compliance of thousands of citizens, to the deafening silence of the world. Unlike slaughtered Russian villages, these were no chance victims of the fury of war. They were carefully chosen, named, listed, tabulated, and stamped. The Nazis went to incredible lengths to find even a single missing Jew. It did not help but hindered the war effort. For while antisemitism was in the beginning politically advantageous to the Nazis the actual crime of genocide had often to be carefully hidden from their own people. Troop trains were diverted from the Russian front in order to transport Jews to Auschwitz. Unique in all human history, the Holocaust was evil for evil's sake.

The woman who wrote those words is a Christian. I doubt whether I or any other Jew could have been so relentless as she was in her evaluation.

No wonder the mind seeks refuge in comparisons — some shallow, some obscene, all false — between Auschwitz and Hiroshima, or Vietnam, or the Black ghetto, or even the American campus. Indeed, the very words "Holocaust" and "six million" are evasive abstractions, empty universal substitutes

Desecrated synagogue in Munich, Germany
(Archives, City of Munich)

for the countless particulars each of which is an inexhaustible mystery of sin and suffering. . . .

Let me take just one of those particulars. In issuing "work permits" that were designed to separate "useless" Jews to be murdered at once from "useful" ones to be kept useful by diabolically contrived false hopes and murdered later, the Nazis customarily issued two such permits to an able-bodied Jewish man. One was untransferable, to be kept for himself; the other was to be given at his own discretion to his able-bodied mother, father, wife, or one child. The Nazis would not make the choice, even though to do so would have produced a more efficient labor force. Jewish sons, husbands, or fathers themselves were forced to decide who among their loved ones was — for the time being — to live, who to die at once.

I search the whole history of human depravity for comparisons. In vain. I would reject the comparisons cited above even if they compared the comparable: let each human evil be understood in its own terms. What makes the comparisons utterly odious is that in effect if not intention they abuse Auschwitz, deny that it ever happened, rob its victims even of memory. There is a qualitative distinction between evils — even gigantic ones — perpetuated for such "rational" ends as gain, victory, real or imagined self-interest, and evils perpetrated for evil's sake.

Moreover, there can be a difference even among evils for evil's sake. Theologians call these "the demonic," and I myself once found escape in this theological abstraction. I find it no more. In the history of demonic evil (which, incidentally, in this age of uncritical theological celebrations, someone should write) conceivably there are examples comparable to the Nazi custom of issuing the two work permits. But until such examples are found my religious life and theological thought must lack the comfort of comparisons as I retrace the *via dolorosa* that leads to Auschwitz, trying at the desperate utmost to match the solitude, the despair, the utter abandonment of every one of my brethren who walked that road. And I shall always fail.

Zionism and the State of Israel

"Let Sovereignty Be Granted"

The history of Zionism in the modern world as well as its place in power politics must begin with Theodor Herzl (1860–1904), native of Budapest, student of law, of German language and culture, and a journalist. The infamous 1894 trial of Alfred Dreyfus, a French army officer, proved the persisting force of anti-Semitism and turned Herzl into a passionate Zionist.

[Source: Arthur Hertzberg, ed., *The Zionist Idea* (Westport, Conn.: Greenwood Press, 1959 [this document 1896]), pp. 215–16, 220–21, 222–23.]

> *He wrote* The Jewish State *(excerpted below) in 1896, launched the Zionist newspaper,* Die Welt, *in 1897, and gathered Jews together in World Congresses to educate them concerning the absolute necessity for Jews to be granted sovereignty "over a portion of the globe adequate to meet our rightful national requirements." Then, Herzl added, "we will attend to the rest."*

No one can deny the gravity of the Jewish situation. Wherever they live in appreciable number, Jews are persecuted in greater or lesser measure. Their equality before the law, granted by statute, has become practically a dead letter. They are debarred from filling even moderately high offices in the army, or in any public or private institutions. And attempts are being made to thrust them out of business also: "Don't buy from Jews!"

Attacks in parliaments, in assemblies, in the press, in the pulpit, in the street, on journeys — for example, their exclusion from certain hotels — even in places of recreation are increasing from day to day. The forms of persecutions vary according to country and social circle. In Russia, special taxes are levied on Jewish villages; in Romania, a few persons are put to death; in Germany, they get a good beating occasionally; in Austria, anti-Semites exercise their terrorism over all public life; in Algeria, there are traveling agitators; in Paris, the Jews are shut out of the so-called best social circles and excluded from clubs. The varieties of anti-Jewish expression are innumerable. But this is not the occasion to attempt the sorry catalogue of Jewish hardships. We shall not dwell on particular cases, however painful.

I do not aim to arouse sympathy on our behalf. All that is nonsense, as futile as it is dishonorable. I shall content myself with putting the following questions to the Jews: Is it not true that, in countries where we live in appreciable numbers, the position of Jewish lawyers, doctors, technicians, teachers, and employees of every description becomes daily more intolerable? Is it not true that the Jewish middle classes are seriously threatened? Is it not true that the passions of the mob are incited against our wealthy? Is it not true that our poor endure greater suffering than any other proletariat? I think that this pressure is everywhere present. In our upper economic classes it causes discomfort, in our middle classes utter despair.

The fact of the matter is, everything tends to one and the same conclusion, which is expressed in the classic Berlin cry: "*Juden 'raus!*" ("Out with the Jews!").

I shall now put the question in the briefest possible form: Shouldn't we "get out" at once, and if so, whither?

Or, may we remain, and if so, how long?

Let us first settle the point of remaining. Can we hope for better days, can we possess our souls in patience, can we wait in pious resignation till the princes and peoples of this earth are more mercifully disposed toward us? I say that we cannot hope for the current to shift. And why not? Even if we were as near to the hearts of princes as are their other subjects, they could not protect us. They would only incur popular hatred by showing us too much favor. And this "too much" implies less than is claimed as a right by any ordinary citizen or ethnic group. The nations in whose midst Jews live are all covertly or openly anti-Semitic.

The common people have not, and indeed cannot have, any comprehension of history. They do not know that the sins of the Middle Ages are now being visited on the nations of Europe. We are what the ghetto made us. We have without a doubt attained pre-eminence in finance because medieval conditions drove us to it. The same process is now being repeated. We are again being forced into money-lending — now named stock exchange — by being kept out of other occupations. But once on the stock exchange, we are again objects of contempt. At the same time we continue to produce an abundance of mediocre intellectuals who find no outlet, and this endangers our social position as much as does our increasing wealth. Educated Jews without means are now rapidly becoming socialists. Hence we are certain to suffer acutely in the struggle between the classes, because we stand in the most exposed position in both the capitalist and the socialist camps. . . .

The Plan

The whole plan is essentially quite simple, as it must necessarily be if it is to be comprehensible to all.

Let sovereignty be granted us over a portion of the globe adequate to meet our rightful national requirements; we will attend to the rest.

To create a new State is neither ridiculous nor impossible. Haven't we witnessed the process in our own day, among nations which were not largely middle class as we are, but poorer, less educated, and consequently weaker than ourselves? The governments of all countries scourged by anti-Semitism will be keenly interested in obtaining sovereignty for us.

The plan, simple in design but complicated in execution, will be executed by two agencies: the Society of Jews and the Jewish Company.

The scientific plan and political policies which the Society of Jews will establish will be carried out by the Jewish Company.

The Jewish Company will be the liquidating agent for the business interests of departing Jews, and will organize trade and commerce in the new country.

We must not visualize the exodus of the Jews as a sudden one. It will be gradual, proceeding over a period of decades. The poorest will go first and cultivate the soil. They will construct roads, bridges, railways, and telegraph installations, regulate rivers, and provide themselves with homesteads, all according to predetermined plans. Their labor will create trade, trade will create markets, and markets will attract new settlers — for every man will go voluntarily, at his own expense and his own risk. The labor invested in the soil will enhance its value. The Jews will soon perceive that a new and permanent frontier has been opened up for that spirit of enterprise which has heretofore brought them only hatred and obloquy. . . .

Palestine or Argentina?

Is Palestine or Argentina preferable? The Society will take whatever it is given and whatever Jewish public opinion favors. The Society will determine both these points.

Argentina is one of the most fertile countries in the world, extends over a vast area, is sparsely populated, and has a temperate climate. It would be in its own highest interest for the Republic of Argentina to cede us a portion of its territory. The present *infiltration* of Jews has certainly produced some discontent, and it would be necessary to enlighten the Republic on the intrinsic difference of the new *immigration* of Jews.

Palestine is our unforgettable historic homeland. The very name would be a marvelously effective rallying cry. If His Majesty the Sultan were to give us Palestine, we could in return undertake the complete management of the finances of Turkey. We should there form a part of a wall of defense for Europe in Asia, an outpost of civilization against barbarism. We should as a neutral state remain in contact with all Europe, which would have to guarantee our existence. The holy places of Christendom could be placed under some form of international exterritoriality. We should form a guard of honor about these holy places, answering for the fulfillment of this duty with our existence. The guard of honor would be the great symbol of the solution of the Jewish question after what were for us eighteen centuries of affliction.

"Zionism in America"

For more than half a century, the spiritual descendants of Herzl agitated, cajoled, bargained, and prayed until at last in 1948 the state of Israel came into being. It was an occasion of incalculable significance for Jews throughout the whole world, of course, but Jews in America had a special role: "to marshal political and financial support" that would not only help bring such a state into being but also would insure its stability and safety in the years ahead. Writing in the year of America's own bicentennial in 1976 (with Israel not yet a full generation old), Rabbi Arthur Hertzberg (b. 1921), author, lecturer, and member of the World Zionist Organization, wrote of the way in which "America is different." In that Diaspora (that is, in that

[Source: Arthur Hertzberg, *Being Jewish in America: The Modern Experience* (New York: Schocken Books, 1979), pp. 220–24.]

land far away from the Holy Land), the "overarching religion of American Jews" is a "pride and glory in American Jewry's sharing in Israel. . . ."

Zionism is supposed to make Jews realize how uncomfortable they are in the Diaspora and how such living has too little dignity. In the United States, Zionism has acted to the contrary — to make Jews more comfortable in the Diaspora and a greater force within the society at large. Rhetoric obscures this truth, for do not American Zionists and even non-Zionists march through the streets of Jerusalem proclaiming their assent to the "centrality of Israel," which is the very core of Zionism's Jerusalem platform? The truth is that those from Kansas, California, and even New York who assert this mean not that they condemn their *galut* [exile] but that the involvement in Israel gives content and verve to lives they intend to continue to live in the American Diaspora.

It is therefore relatively easy to conceive of a celebration by Israelis of the bicentenary year of the United States of America. This is not more difficult than the Canadian celebration of that event. America's neighbor to the north has a complex relationship to the powerful giant to the south, on which it is overdependent but from which it nonetheless maintains substantial distance. Comparably, as I sometimes imagine, the true emotional border of Israel is not on the Mediterranean but immediately off the coast of the United States.

To define an attitude toward the American bicentennial is, however, much more difficult when "Jewish issues" are involved. Can one praise the United States as the home of a unique freedom and influence for Jews, whose power there is a critical factor in the very building of Israel, without raising the troubling question: Is this American Diaspora therefore unthinkable as an abode for Jews?

From its very beginnings American Zionism has answered this question by insisting that "America is different." Here the Zionist task was to marshal political and financial support. A small elite continued to emigrate to Zion, but the great Zionist crisis in America was not a quarrel between Zionists and others over the question: Is America a fit habitation for Jews? That ideological quarrel was fought in Russia, in Poland, and even in Germany, but never in the United States. Here the Zionists fought within the Jewish community for half a century before they succeeded in making support of the Jewish homeland the almost universally shared central purpose of American Jewish life. More crucial and more difficult still was the concurrent struggle to establish in America the right of Zionists to battle for their political aims.

Politically, the most damaging charge ever hurled against any group in America was that of being a hyphenated American, or, as it was later put, of being guilty of "dual loyalty." This charge silenced the German-Americans in World War I and it acted to keep all other ethnic groups, including the

Irish, from having a particular foreign policy of their own for any significant length of time.

The only group in America which withstood the charge, both within its own community and in the politics of the larger society, was the Zionists. American Zionists were crucial to making an end of the "melting pot" image of America in the name of a minority commitment of their own. . . . Only Zionism has translated itself into a second and third generation. The one commitment that is universally shared in American Jewry is to make sure that the foreign policy of the United States does not turn against Israel. At this bicentenary moment all other major special-interest groups are defined in America by their domestic programs: labor, blacks, ethnics in the big cities, and even big business, except, in part, for big oil. The only special-interest group which is defined by its foreign policy is the Jews.

The great success of Zionism is to have made this acceptable on the American scene. This has represented a profound change in America's conception of itself, and it has consequences in other realms. The insistence of blacks in America for "affirmative action," that is, for acts of special reparation in this generation for three centuries of injustice done to them by slavery, fell on ears which had been hearing for decades the Zionist claim that the Jewish people was entitled to an act in this century of unique reparation for twenty centuries of exile by having its homeland returned to it. All other kinds of dissent from the American consensus, such as the movement against the Vietnam War, became possible in a society which no longer equated, as it had at the beginning of the twentieth century, patriotism with conformity. To reverse the argument, in the America of 1976 a Jewish community deeply devoted to Israel is no longer outrageously unique. This represents a fundamental change in American life from the self-definition of this society at the beginning of the twentieth century.

Within American Jewry, Zionism has also successfully conquered the community's inner life so that the labors that it commands have become American Jewry's "religion."

It is simply not true that excommunication no longer exists in modern Judaism. On the contrary, it has reappeared in new forms. One can, indeed, no longer be excommunicated in modern America for not believing in God, for living totally outside the tradition, or even for marrying out. Indeed, none of these formerly excommunicable offenses debar one today from occupying high offices in positions of Jewish leadership — but that does not mean that all is permitted. On the contrary, the case of the American Council for Judaism, the well-known anti-Zionist body, is instructive. It has been effectively debarred from any participation in Jewish life on any issue, even, for example, a matter as uncontroversial and as universally acceptable as the American Jewish struggle for the rights of Soviet Jews. . . .

The overarching religion of American Jews is therefore not Orthodox, Conservative, or Reform; it is not Hebrew or the national culture. It is pride and glory in American Jewry's sharing in Israel—and it is therefore disappointed in rebbes who do not perform miracles on order, who are sometimes fallible on Yom Kippur when a war breaks out, even as mortal men, and whose courts are not as perfect as dreams would have them.

Most important of all, I think, is a cliché which is even more deeply true than it seems to be. Zionism and Israel have, indeed, provided American Jews with great dignity in the eyes of the American majority. Even in today's less glorious times than those which followed June 1967, Israel remains in America the symbol of achievement against odds and of the kind of pioneering creativity that Americans respect.

"Fighting for Israel"

The Six Day War of 1967 galvanized the opinion of American Jewry behind the state of Israel as no single event has done, before or since. Israel, whose very survival was threatened, had defended itself successfully, dramatically, even gloriously. From that point on, to be a Jew meant to be committed to Israel. This, at least, is the argument of Nathan Glazer (b. 1923), sociologist, professor, and author of the popular survey American Judaism *(1957; revised, 1972, mainly to take into account the 1967 war and its impact on American Jews). Like Hertzberg, Glazer also suggests that "Israel has become* the *Jewish religion for American Jews," but —unlike Hertzberg —he is less sanguine about the future in that regard.*

Israel has become the pre-eminent issue in American Jewish life, to a degree that could not have been envisaged in 1948, or 1957, or 1966. Newspapers, the mass media generally, political candidates (especially presidential candidates) are aware of how important Israel is to American Jews. What is not often realized is how relatively new is the absolute predominance of Israel in American Jewish concerns.

In the early postwar period, the Jewish community of Israel amounted to only six percent of the Jewish people. Within individual Jewish communities, including that of the United States, Zionism had been a minority movement. Jewish organizations fought over how much of the money raised for Jewish causes should go to Israel and how much to other claimants. Jews in other countries who were in distress (particularly those who emerged from the concentration camps of Europe and the Jews of Arab lands) had a strong claim to Jewish charitable funds. Domestic needs—synagogues, temples, schools, hospitals, social service agencies—also rated high among Jewish priorities.

The exclusive and overwhelming concern of American Jews with Israel dates from the Six Day War of 1967, when it appeared at first that Israel

[Source: Nathan Glazer, "Jewish Loyalties," *Wilson Quarterly*, 5 (1981), 137–38.]

might be defeated and its Jewish inhabitants massacred. American Jews discovered then that Israel meant much more to them than they realized. Everything possible was done to save Israel. Political pressure was mobilized, large sums of money were raised in a surprisingly short time, and thousands of U.S. volunteers left to fight. If in the past it was possible for some Jews to separate their commitment to Judaism from their commitment to Israel, after 1967 this was no longer possible.

Israel has become *the* Jewish religion for American Jews. To those who think in terms of Christianity — and perhaps to some Jews, too — that may sound blasphemous or heretical. How can anything of this world be absolutized to the point where it becomes the central theme of religion, while "other-worldly" themes are put aside? That, I would argue, is a rather non-Jewish way of looking at religion.

The Jewish religion has always been linked to a single people. Among the great religions, it is perhaps unique in this respect. Judaism is inconceivable without Jews, the actual and living people. Christianity is quite conceivable without the adherence of any particular ethnic group, as is Islam. After the Holocaust, this apparently archaic feature of the Jewish religion became very modern again. The most creative Jewish theologian on the North American continent, Emil Fackenheim, emphasizes in his theology the centrality of the *physical* survival of the Jewish people — particularly in the aftermath of a diabolical effort, which enjoyed considerable success, to destroy them.

One can thus make an argument out of Jewish theology and history that the Jewish commitment to Israel has something of a religious character. The problem is that Israel is a state, as well as the Zion whose restoration God promised to the Jews. And therein hangs a potential difficulty that Jews have only recently become aware of — one that can only become more serious with time, it appears to me. The difficulty is the potential conflict between loyalty to the United States and loyalty to Israel.

Peace and War: Vietnam

While pacifism, especially pacifism based on clear religious conviction, has a long history in this nation, never before Vietnam had pacifism engaged so many or become so powerful a countervailing force in the corridors of power. The longer the war continued, the louder the voice of protest became. It was indeed for the whole nation a "crisis of conscience" as Protestant, Jew, and Catholic declared in 1967 (Robert M. Brown, Abraham J. Heschel, and

[Sources: (1) *Pacem in Terris*, April 11, 1963 (Washington, D. C.: National Catholic Welfare Conference, n. d.), pp. 34, 35–36, 37, 40. (2) United Presbyterian Church, *Vietnam: The Christian, the Gospel, the Church* (Philadelphia: General Assembly of the United Presbyterian Church, U. S. A., 1967), pp. 132, 133–34. (3) A. J. Heschel, in *Vietnam: Crisis of Conscience* (New York: Association Press, 1967), pp. 52–53, 55–56.]

Michael Novak, Vietnam: Crisis of Conscience*). In that same year the United Presbyterian Church voiced its conviction that "There is no moral issue more urgently confronting our Church and nation than the war in Vietnam." And four years before either of these, Pope John XXIII (papacy, 1958 – 63) had raised hopes not alone of Catholics but of millions besides that "Peace on Earth"* (Pacem in Terris) *might somehow be within the reach of men and women of goodwill. Three excerpts of longer documents follow: (1) Pope John's* Pacem in Terris; *(2) the United Presbyterian's "Declaration of Conscience"; and (3) a segment of the statement by Rabbi Abraham Heschel (1907 – 73) entitled "Military Victory — A Moral Defeat."*

1.

143. An act of the highest importance performed by the United Nations Organization was the Universal Declaration of Human Rights, approved in the General Assembly of December 10, 1948. In the preamble of that Declaration, the recognition and respect of those rights and respective liberties is proclaimed as a goal to be achieved by all peoples and all countries.

144. We are fully aware that some objections and reservations were raised regarding certain points in the Declaration, and rightly so. There is no doubt, however, that the document represents an important step on the path towards the juridical-political organization of all the peoples of the world. For in it, in most solemn form, the dignity of a human person is acknowledged to all human beings; and as a consequence there is proclaimed, as a fundamental right, the right of every man freely to investigate the truth and to follow the norms of moral good and justice, and also the right to a life worthy of man's dignity, while other rights connected with those mentioned are likewise proclaimed.

145. It is therefore our ardent desire that the United Nations Organization — in its structure and in its means — may become ever more equal to the magnitude and nobility of its tasks, and may the time come as quickly as possible when every human being will find therein an effective safeguard for the rights which derive directly from his dignity as a person, and which are therefore universal, inviolable and inalienable rights. This is all the more to be hoped for since all human beings, as they take an ever more active part in the public life of their own country, are showing an increasing interest in the affairs of all peoples, and are becoming more consciously aware that they are living members of the whole human family. . . .

151. It is no less clear that today, in traditionally Christian nations, secular institutions, although demonstrating a high degree of scientific and technical perfection, and efficiency in achieving their respective ends, not infrequently are but slightly affected by Christian motivation or inspiration.

152. It is beyond question that in the creation of those institutions many

contributed and continue to contribute who were believed to be and who consider themselves Christians; and without doubt, in part at least, they were and are. How does one explain this? It is Our opinion that the explanation is to be found in an inconsistency in their minds between religious belief and their action in the temporal sphere. It is necessary, therefore, that their interior unity be re-established, and that in their temporal activity faith should be present as a beacon to give light, and charity as a force to give life. . . .

157. The doctrinal principles outlined in this document derive from both nature itself and the natural law. In putting these principles into practice it frequently happens that Catholics in many ways cooperate either with Christians separated from this Apostolic See, or with men of no Christian faith whatever, but who are endowed with reason and adorned with a natural uprightness of conduct. *In such relations let the faithful be careful to be always consistent in their actions, so that they may never come to any compromise in matters of religion and morals. At the same time, however, let them be, and show themselves to be, animated by a spirit of understanding and detachment, and disposed to work loyally in the pursuit of objectives which are of their nature good, or conducive to good.* . . .

167. As the humble and unworthy Vicar of Him Whom the Prophet announced as the *Prince of Peace*, We have the duty to expend all Our energies in an effort to protect and strengthen this gift. However, Peace will be but an empty-sounding word unless it is founded on the order which this present document has outlined in confident hope: an order founded on truth, built according to justice, vivified and integrated by charity, and put into practice in freedom.

2.

There is no moral issue more urgently confronting our Church and nation than the war in Vietnam. The hour is late; the Church dare not remain silent. We must declare our conscience.

We share widely-held feelings of sadness that steps were taken in the past which have involved our nation in its present difficulty. Although each step was taken with hope it would be the last, their cumulative result has brought us to an agonizing dilemma. On the one hand, we cannot responsibly withdraw our military forces unilaterally from Vietnam. On the other hand, further escalation seems to us to raise the spectre of World War III and the possibility of a nuclear holocaust.

A. We recognize that our leaders desire an end to the war, and believe that their motives for pursuing the war are those of honorable men. We must nevertheless declare our deep misgivings at the policy of military escalation (further steps being taken during the week of this General Assembly) which leads the world daily closer to the danger of wider war. Acts of escalation tend to commit us to further acts of escalation and may lessen the possibility of settlement by negotiation. . . .

C. We call upon members of every religious faith and communion, and upon all men of good will everywhere, to make common cause with us in an effort to bring about an end to the war. As we do so:

1. *We must continue to affirm the morality of dissent.* Increasing numbers of citizens, including some in high office, are equating dissent with disloyalty.

The enemy can always misunderstand the meaning of dissent. We, however, must affirm unequivocally that the right of dissent is the life-blood of democracy. We also affirm unequivocally that the first mandate under which the Church lives is the mandate, "You shall have no other Gods before me." (Ex. 20:3.) We acknowledge that, "The church which identifies the sovereignty of any one nation or any one way of life with the cause of God denies the Lordship of Christ and betrays its calling." (Confession of 1967.)

We remind ourselves and other citizens addressing themselves to public questions that we must speak in an informed way, and must avoid impugning the loyalty or integrity of those with whom we disagree. We call for candor on the part of policymakers, and the abandonment of cliches and slogans, in order that there may be a frank facing of the extent and limitations of our national interest in Vietnam and Southeast Asia.

2. *We must continue to affirm the morality of restraint.* We recognize that our military actions have been conducted with a high degree of restraint in comparison to the military power we possess. Nevertheless, we are dismayed that as the war gathers momentum this restraint shows signs of erosion. Our people seem willing to accept as normal today what was unthinkable yesterday. We recoil from rash proposals to use nuclear weapons, or to invade the North. We deplore the increasing willingness at home to justify inhumane acts because the enemy also commits them. We mourn the fact that although we had hoped to be in Vietnam to liberate its people, our use of modern weapons is increasingly destructive both to that people and to their country.

3. *We must break new moral ground in courage and in ecumenical action.* Let men of all faiths pray that our nation will have the moral courage to undertake these steps of redirection.

We support the concern over Vietnam already expressed by many Jewish groups, by Protestant and Orthodox bodies such as the World Council of Churches and the National Council of Churches, and join in the plea of Pope Paul VI that "men must come together and get down to sincere negotiations. Things must be settled now, even at the cost of some loss or inconvenience, for later they may have to be settled at the cost of immense harm and enormous slaughter that cannot even be imagined now."

4. *We must declare our conscience at whatever cost.* We recognize that if our military escalation is not reversed, the time may come when those who dissent because they seek peace will be placed under even greater pressure, and that the possibility of significant influence by the Church on public policy will have dissappeared. Should that time come, we urge our corporate Church and our individual church members still to exercise the voice of conscience,

so that faithful witness may be rendered to God's reconciliation in Jesus Christ, which is the only ground of peace.

3.

It is weird to wake up one morning and find that we have been placed in an insane asylum. It is even more weird to wake up and find that we have been involved in slaughter and destruction without knowing it.

What is being done by our government is done in our name. Our labor, our wealth, our civic power, our tacit consent are invested in the production and use of the napalm, the bombs, and the mines that explode and bring carnage and ruin to Vietnam.

The thought that I live a life of peace and nonviolence turns out to be an illusion. I have been decent in tiny matters on a tiny scale, but have become vicious on a large scale. In my own eyes my existence appears to be upright, but in the eyes of my victims my very being is a nightmare.

A sense of moral integrity, the equation of America with the pursuit of justice and peace, has long been part of our self-understanding. Indeed, for generations the image of America has been associated with the defense of human rights and the hope for world peace. And now history is sneering at us.

A ghastly darkness has set in over our souls. Will there be an end to dismay, an end to agony?

Silent protest in Iowa City, Iowa, 1972

The encounter of man and God is an encounter within the world. We meet within a situation of shared suffering, of shared reponsibility.

This is implied in believing in One God in whose eyes there is no dichotomy of here and there, of me and them. They and I are one; here is there, and there is here. What goes on over there happens even here. Oceans divide us, God's presence unites us, and God is present wherever man is afflicted, and all of humanity is embroiled in every agony wherever it may be.

Though not a native of Vietnam, ignorant of its language and traditions, I am involved in the plight of the Vietnamese. To be human means not to be immune to other people's suffering. People in Vietnam, North and South, have suffered, and all of us are hurt.

Unprepared, perplexed, uninformed, ill-advised, our nation finds herself in a spiritual inferno. Where do we stand? Where do we go from here? For a long time we suppressed anxiety, evaded responsibility. Yet the rivers of tears and blood may turn into a flood of guilt, which no excuse will stem.

The blood we shed in Vietnam makes a mockery of all our proclamations, dedications, celebrations. We have been moving from obscurity to confusion, from ignorance to obfuscation. Many are unaware, some acquiesce, most of us detest this unfathomable war, but are unable to envisage a way of getting out of this maze. Millions of Americans who cannot close their minds to the suffering and sorrow are stricken with anguish, and form a large fellowship living in a state of consternation.

We are killing the Vietnamese because we are suspicious of the Chinese. The aim is to kill the elusive Vietcong, yet to come upon one soldier, it is necessary to put an end to a whole village, to the lives of civilians, men, women, and children.

Is it not true that Communists are fellow human beings first, antagonists second? Politically, the concept of the enemy is becoming obsolete; yesterday's enemy is today's ally. The state of cold war between the United States and Soviet Russia has given place to a quest of friendly understanding.

The absurdity of this war is tacitly admitted by almost everyone. Our presence in Vietnam has become a national nightmare, our actions are forced, we dislike what we do; we do what we hate to do. Is this a way to bring democracy to Vietnam: more explosives, more devastation, more human beings crippled, orphaned, killed? Is it not clear that military victory in Vietnam would be a tragic moral defeat? That military triumph would be a human disaster? . . .

What is it that may save us, that may unite men all over the world? The abhorrence of atrocity, the refusal of the conscience to accommodate to the arrogance of military power. Indeed, it is the power of the human conscience which has in the last twenty years inhibited the use of thermonuclear weapons. Yet the power of the conscience is tenuous and exceedingly vulnerable. Its status is undergoing profound upheaveals. We are challenged too frequently, too radically to be able to react adequately.

However, the surrender of conscience destroys first the equilibrium of human existence and then existence itself. In the past, war was regarded as an instrument of politics. Today politics is in the process of becoming an instrument of military technology. How long can total war be avoided?

Militarism is whoredom, voluptuous and vicious, first disliked and then relished. To paraphrase the prophet's words "For the spirit of harlotry is within them, and they know not the Lord" (Hosea 5:4): "Samson with his strong body, had a weak head, or he would not have laid it in a harlot's lap."

2. THE NATION AND ITS CHURCHES

The Ecumenical Age

National Council and World Council

(1) The Federal Council of Churches (see above, p. 190), after nearly one-half century of ecumenical activity, merged with several interdenominational boards in 1950 to form the National Council of Churches of Christ in the U. S. A. Twenty-nine denominations participated in this original structuring, but more would be added. By 1960 the Council, with a membership of about forty million, had reached beyond the limits of Protestantism to include many of the churches within Eastern Orthodoxy. Roman Catholic churches were not affiliated, but dialogue —especially in the 1960s —between Protestants and Catholics, also between Orthodox and Catholics, markedly increased. What follows below is a portion of the National Council's message "To the People of the Nation" on the occasion of the 1950 founding. (2) While the World Council of Churches came into being in 1948 with its First Assembly in Amsterdam, most Americans became conscious of the new organization in 1954 when it held its Second Assembly in the United States, at Evanston, Illinois. A large meeting (the World Council represented more than 150 denominations, again including Eastern Orthodoxy but excluding Roman Catholicism except as observers), the Evanston gathering dramatized the dawning of what did indeed appear to be a new ecumenical age. "The Message" from the Evanston Assembly is presented below.

1.

This Council has been constituted by twenty-nine Churches for the glory of God and the well-being of humanity. It manifests our oneness in Jesus Christ

[Sources: (1) National Council, *Christian Faith in Action: Commemorative Volume . . .* (New York: National Council, 1951), pp. 150, 151– 52, 152– 53. (2) "The Message" of the World Council, Second Assembly, August 31, 1954, in *Christian Century*, Sept. 22, 1954, pp. 1123– 24.]

as divine Lord and Saviour; his is the mandate we obey and his the power upon which we rely. It is designed to be an instrument of the Holy Spirit for such ministries of evangelism, education, and relief as are better achieved through Christian cooperation than by the labors of separated groups. It coordinates and continues the work of eight interdenominational agencies ministering in as many fields of Christian usefulness. . . .

The Council has nothing to fear from the times, though it has much to desire of them. Being the servant of One who holds in His hand all the nations, and the isles, as a very little thing, it is free from the apprehensions of those who, taking counsel of men alone, forget that no age is isolated from God's ageless purpose. We call our fellow citizens to Christian faith: this will defend them from groundless social dreads and lift them to concerns worthy and productive.

The Council stands as a guardian of democratic freedom. The revolutionary truth that men are created free follows from the revelation of God in Jesus Christ, and no person who knows that God as Father has given him all the rights of sonship is likely to remain content under a government which deprives him of basic human rights and fundamental freedoms. The nation may expect in the National Council a sturdy ally of the forces of liberty.

The Council stands for liberty with the richest content. It stands for the freedom of men to be as the Lord God meant them to be. It stands for Christian freedom — including the freedom to pursue happiness and with justice and sympathy to create conditions of happiness for others. It therefore stands against the misuse of freedom. The nation may expect from the National Council, in the name of One who suffered death upon a cross, an unrelenting, open-eyed hostility, as studious as it is deeply passionate, to all of man's inhumanity to man.

The Council opposes materialism as an end in itself. It is the foe of every political system that is nourished on materialism, and of every way of living that follows from it. From that smug idealism which is a form of selfishness, the Council prays to be protected; but danger on this hand does not lessen the necessity it feels to fight a constant fight against all kinds of secular materialism which demolish the slowly built edifice of Christian morality and fair dealing.

Through the Council the churches, as they are dedicated to the doing of God's will, must increasingly become a source of spiritual power to the nation. The American Churches, of which the Council is one of the visible symbols, are in their true estate the soul of the nation. When those Churches take their true course, they draw their standards not from the world around but from the guiding mind of Christ. The Church is not the religious phase of the civilization in which it finds itself; it is the living center out of which lasting civilizations take life and form. In this sense the Council will be an organ through which the will of God may become effective as an animating, creative and unifying force within our national society.

The Council gives thanks to God for all those forces which make for

Official emblem adopted by the National Council of Churches in 1955
(National Council of Churches)

harmony in our society. When, for example, science employs its ingenuity to knit the world together in bonds of communication, when business and industry make a like contribution through the life-bringing mutuality of commerce, when the arts depict the beauty and the tragedy of our existence which draw us into unity with one another, when the many professions and occupations recognize themselves as callings to human usefulness, then the Council salutes and supports them. By word and deed and in the name of Christ who gave his life for all mankind it affirms the brotherhood of men and seeks by every rightful means to arrest those forces of division which rend the nation along racial lines and stay its growth toward unity. . . .

We of the National Council of the Churches of Christ in the U.S.A. begin our work in humility as we see the magnitude of the task ahead. We are not unconscious of our own short-comings. Knowing that men too often dream in marble and then build with straw, we whose very human lives are not separate from sin and ignorance can make no boast of past or future excellence.

But this we have done: by God's grace we have forged an implement for cooperation such as America has never seen before. Into it have been poured the thoughts of wise and noble men and women, the prayers and consecration of the faithful, and the longing of all the participating Churches to serve the spiritual needs of all the people. The Council is our Churches in their highest common effort for mankind.

Our hope is in Jesus Christ. In Him we see the solution of the world's ills, for as human hearts are drawn near to him, they are drawn near in sympathy and understanding to each other. The Council itself is a demonstration of his power to unite his followers in joyous cooperation. Let nation and nation, race and race, class and class unite their aims in his broad purposes for man, and out of that unitedness there will arise new strength like that of which we ourselves already feel the first sure intimations.

In this hope we commend you, our fellow citizens, to God's mercy, grace and peace.

2.

To all our fellow Christians, and to our fellow men everywhere, we send greetings in the name of Jesus Christ. We affirm our faith in Jesus Christ as the hope of the world, and desire to share that faith with all men. May God forgive us that by our sin we have often hidden this hope from the world.

In the ferment of our time there are both hopes and fears. It is indeed good to hope for freedom, justice and peace, and it is God's will that we should have these things. But he has made us for a higher end. He has made us for himself, that we might know and love him, worship and serve him. Nothing other than God can ever satisfy the heart of man. Forgetting this, man becomes his own enemy. He seeks justice but creates oppression. He wants peace but drifts toward war. His very mastery of nature threatens him with ruin. Whether he acknowledges it or not, he stands under the judgment of God and in the shadow of death.

Here where we stand, Jesus Christ stood with us. He came to us, true God and true Man, to seek and to save. Though we were the enemies of God, Christ died for us. We crucified him, but God raised him from the dead. He is risen. He has overcome the powers of sin and death. A new life has begun. And in his risen and ascended power he has sent forth into the world a new community, bound together by his Spirit, sharing his divine life, and commissioned to make him known throughout the world. He will come again as Judge and King to bring all things to their consummation. Then we shall see him as he is and know as we are known. Together with the whole creation we wait for this with eager hope, knowing that God is faithful and that even now he holds all things in his hand.

This is the hope of God's people in every age, and we commend it afresh today to all who will listen. To accept it is to turn from our ways to God's way. It is to live as forgiven sinners, as children growing in his love. It is to have our citizenship in that Kingdom which all man's sin is impotent to destroy, that realm of love and joy and peace which lies about all men, though unseen. It is to enter with Christ into the suffering and despair of men, sharing with them the great secret of that Kingdom which they do not suspect. It is to know that whatever men may do, Jesus reigns and shall reign.

With this assurance we can face the powers of evil and the threat of death

Meeting of World Council of Churches in Evanston, Illinois, in 1954
(National Council of Churches)

with a good courage. Delivered from fear we are made free to love. For beyond the judgment of men and the judgment of history lies the judgment of the King who died for all men, and who will judge us at the last according to what we have done to the least of his brethren. Thus our Christian hope directs us toward our neighbor. It constrains us to pray daily, "Thy will be done on earth as it is in heaven," and to act as we pray in every area of life. It begets a life of believing prayer and expectant action, looking to Jesus and pressing forward to the day of his return in glory. . . .

The forces that separate men from one another are strong. At our meeting here we have missed the presence of Chinese churches which were with us at Amsterdam. There are other lands and churches unrepresented in our council, and we long ardently for their fellowship. But we are thankful that, separated as we are by the deepest political divisions of our time, here at Evanston we are united in Christ. And we rejoice also that, in the bond of prayer and a common hope, we maintain communion with our Christian brethren everywhere. . . .

Consultation on Church Union

The National Council and the World Council represent Christian cooperation and programs of mutual assistance. Neither directly promotes church union or sees this as its primary function. The Consultation on Church Union (more simply, COCU), on the other hand, emerged in the 1960s as the most ambitious effort in modern America to bring about actual union. Proposed initially by the stated clerk of the Presbyterian Church, U. S. A., Eugene Carson Blake, in Bishop James Pike's Episcopal Cathedral in San Francisco in 1960, the discussions continued thereafter, often with great excitement and sometimes amid growing discouragement. The Consultation, if successful along the lines originally conceived, would result in a single church uniting all major Protestant bodies except Baptists and Lutherans. The annual gatherings of participating denominations (and the precise complement has varied from year to year) have taught the churches much about themselves as well as much about their Christian colleagues. The document below is the "Closing Statement" from the third annual Consultation, this one gathered in Princeton, New Jersey. The statement itself was adopted on April 16, 1964.

We are met once again to explore the establishment of a united church. We intend to stay together. We intend to go forward together. We have seen a vision of what the Christian community in every place should be.

Looking back over the two years since we started to work together, the members of the Consultation on Church Union register their satisfaction at the progress so far made.

In Washington in 1962 we organized ourselves for work and there we were reminded of the reasons for the serious exploration of the establishment of a united church in North America, truly catholic, truly reformed, and truly evangelical. The motivations are as strong now as then. The structure of the Consultation has weathered storms and has been taught by experiences favorable and unfavorable.

At Oberlin last year we reached a surprising and welcome consensus on how decision should be reached in a united church on questions of both belief and practice ("Scripture, Tradition, and the Guardians of Tradition," *Digest of the Proceedings* Volumes I & II, p. 44).

Here at Princeton we have faced three of the most difficult theological and ecclesiastical questions which have divided our churches in the past. We have made progress towards finding the answers required in order to establish a united church which would comprehend the rich variety of our several traditions.

[Source: COCU, *The Reports of the Four Meetings* (Cincinnati: Forward Movement Publications, n. d.), pp. 54–55.]

The three statements which we have here approved on "One Ministry," "One Baptism," and "One Table" reveal a consensus which, while not fully comprehensive nor final is, nevertheless, an encouraging basis for the work that lies before us.

Believing that the establishment of one ordained ministry, recognized by us all, is critical to our union effort, we have authorized the executive committee to plan the work for this year so that we can be led to the consideration of proposals which will contain the shape and functions of the ordered ministry of the united church as well as a way or ways by which it might be established.

That difficulties, setbacks, and disappointments will come in the future, as they have already, we realize full well. Yet in obedience to Jesus Christ, and claiming his promise of the presence of the Holy Spirit, we pledge ourselves to press on for a union to the glory of God the Father.

The Denominations: Lutherans

In the 1970s and 1980s some of America's Lutherans stepped boldly into the ecumenical age, while others with equal firmness of stride walked away from it. In 1982 two major Lutheran bodies, the Lutheran Church of America and the American Lutheran Church, voted to enter into a full and complete merger. Together with a smaller third group (to be noted again shortly), these participants in ecumenicity will constitute by the end of the 1980s Lutheranism's largest denomination, with a membership of five to six million. Lutheranism's second largest church at that point will be the Lutheran Church —Missouri Synod, with a membership of two to three million. And it is the Missouri Synod which in the 1970s stepped away from broader cooperation, even within the Lutheran family itself. All this occurred in the context of what one religious journalist called "the Great Lutheran Civil War." Tension within this Synod led to the firing of Concordia Seminary's president and many of its faculty, to the "exile" of many of its students, and to the separation of two hundred or more congregations from the parent church. (That schism resulted in the Association of Evangelical Lutheran Churches, in effect a new denomination of about 100,000 members who voted overwhelmingly to join the 1982 merger mentioned above.) The issue or issues that precipitated the unhappy schism are discussed below by the two "generals" in this civil war: (1) Jacob A. O. Preus, then president of the Lutheran Church —Missouri Synod; and (2), John Tietjen, then president of Concordia Seminary in St. Louis. Not surprisingly, the two accounts do not themselves agree on the fundamental causes for the schism.

[Sources: (1) J. A. O. Preus, in *Christianity Today*, Oct. 25, 1974, pp. 11, 12, 14. (2) John Tietjen, in *Christianity Today*, Apr. 11, 1975, pp. 8–9, 9–10.]

1.

*(Questions were put by the journal, with the answers provided by
J. A. O. Preus.)*

Question. What is the main theological issue in the Lutheran
Church— Missouri Synod?

Answer. The authority of the Bible.

Q. Is there more to the difficulties than theology?

A. When people are involved in arguments on any subject, political issues
and personality conflicts develop, but these are a result of the main problem.
The moderates by their constant discussion of personalities, distortion of the
facts, and emphasis on personalities and politics are obfuscating the doctrinal
issue.

Q. Who are the "moderates"?

A. The moderates are made up largely of clergy, and primarily of younger
graduates of Concordia Seminary in St. Louis who hold to, or are sympathetic
or permissive toward, the use of the historical-critical method of biblical
interpretation. . . .

Q. What has caused the slide from orthodoxy?

A. I think the basic cause of Missouri's departure from its former position
is ecumenicity. We moved from isolation to closer relationships with other
church bodies. And our men picked up other ideas at non-Missouri graduate
schools.

Q. How can this be prevented in other seminaries?

A. We need to establish a recognized orthodox graduate school of theology.

Q. How many students are left?

A. About 200 enrolled for the fall term at Concordia Seminary in St.
Louis.

Q. How about professors?

A. At present the faculty is made up of eighteen men. . . .

Q. What really happened last spring? Could you give us your own version
of the big showdown?

A. The events of last winter and spring go back a long way in history.
Both of my predecessors in office, Dr. Behnken and Dr. Harms, attempted
over a very long period of time and with great efforts to try to stem the tide
of liberalism which was arising at Concordia Seminary. They were not successful. I inaugurated the Fact Finding Committee as a way of trying to get
a fair evaluation of what the situation actually was. The Synod convention in
1971 upheld my efforts and, when I gave a report to the church of what the
situation was, I think the overwhelming majority of the church supported the
doctrinal position of our Synod and took the position that they did not want
theological liberalism and the use of the historical-critical method in the
Synod. They spoke very loudly concerning this matter at the New Orleans
convention. The liberal element of the Synod, under the leadership of the St.

Louis faculty majority at that time, took very strong exception to the actions of New Orleans, with massive protests at the convention, protests following the convention, and the organization of ELIM (Evangelical Lutherans in Mission), which has been recently cautioned by the Board of Directors of the Synod as being a church within the church. All kinds of political actions also took place.

Then in January of 1974 the Board of Control, after very careful study of all aspects of the matter, suspended Dr. John Tietjen, the president of Concordia Seminary, on charges of false doctrine and malfeasance in office. This was followed the next day by a "moratorium" of the students and then the following day by a moratorium of the faculty. After many efforts by me, by the Board of Directors of the Synod, and by the Board of Control to bring about a resumption of normal academic activities on the campus, the Board of Control on February 17, after giving the faculty full information and warning of its intentions (to which there was no reply), dismissed the faculty on the grounds of breach of contract.

This resulted, shortly thereafter, in the creation of Seminex, the term being a shortened form of "seminary in exile." Seminex made use of a consortium arrangement with Eden Seminary of the United Church of Christ and the St. Louis University Theological School, which is under the direction of Jesuits. Thus accreditation of a kind and a place for meeting were assured.

The faculty were finally asked to vacate their homes because housing was a part of their salary and they were no longer in the employ of the Lutheran Church—Missouri Synod. The students of Seminex were permitted to live in their synodically owned homes and also had the use of the gymnasium, dining room, and library of Concordia Seminary.

Finally, in June, Seminex was incorporated under the laws of the State of Missouri with seven professors serving as the members of the Board of Directors. It started as a closed corporation: no parish pastors, no lay people, and no students on the Board of Directors of the institution. About 385 students eventually joined Seminex. . . .

Q. Has there been an infringement upon academic liberty at Concordia Seminary in St. Louis?

A. We don't tell our professors whether to vote Republican or Democratic. We didn't tell them how to stand on the Viet Nam war, and we don't tell them how to stand on civil liberties or the Equal Rights Amendment, but when we get to things taught in the Bible, we are talking about something else. To demand adherence to Scripture in the context of a Bible seminary is not to defy academic freedom.

Q. How does this battle affect Canadian and European Lutherans? Will it cause problems for the mission department?

A. I have been in many of our foreign mission fields very recently. Efforts have been made to inject our American problems into some of our sister churches, and I think this is immoral. While the relation between the Mission

Board and some of our missionaries is not cordial at the moment, partly because of the seminary matter, I do not believe that very much of a problem will be caused in our overseas sister churches, unless Americans do so deliberately.

Q. What is the constitutional situation with regard to elevating your doctrinal statement to the Book of Concord?

A. At the Milwaukee convention we passed resolution 524, stating that the Synod has a right to speak on doctrinal issues and pass resolutions that become the official positions of the church. Now the so-called Preus statement was not an attempt to say anything except what the Missouri Synod was teaching in all its congregations. I received 10,000 letters, 90 per cent favorable. Hundreds of congregations passed resolutions endorsing it. But the critics are noisy. The resolution says that any documents agreeing with Scripture could be accepted as statements of the church. The whole thing is political because my name is associated with it and because it represented the conservative victory in New Orleans.

Q. Who drafted the statement?

A. Dr. Ralph Bohlmann of our Commission on Theology, now the acting president of Concordia Seminary, St. Louis, was very helpful in the production of it. The vice-presidents of the Synod also gave many helpful suggestions.

Q. Would you say that the statement was not in any disagreement with either of the Lutheran confessions?

A. It mentioned some things that the Lutheran confession doesn't. For example, it had a great deal to say in a systematic way about the doctrine of Scripture, biblical authority, and inerrancy, things that weren't issues at the time the confession was formulated.

Q. Isn't it true that the LCMS has always believed in the infallibility of the Bible?

A. Definitely.

Q. If you had it to do all over again, what would you have done differently since 1969?

A. I think I probably would have talked less. Diplomatically, I should have kept a little lower profile. My reports to the church would have been the same, though.

2.

Question. What is the main theological issue in the Lutheran Church—Missouri Synod? *Answer.* The authority of the Bible." So readers of CHRISTIANITY TODAY were informed in an interview with Missouri Synod president Dr. J. A. O. Preus published in the October 25, 1974, issue.

The answer is a smokescreen. The authority of the Bible is not at issue in the Missouri Synod. I personally have been very much at the center of the controversy and have been removed from office presumably because of my position on doctrine. I fully accept the authority of the Bible. I am totally committed to the Bible as the inspired and infallible Word of God. As a pastor of the church I have no other message than what the Bible teaches.

Smokescreens serve a purpose. Focus the concern of people on the issue of the Bible's authority and you divert their attention from what is really going on. Say the answer often enough and people believe it. The result is that many people inside and outside the Missouri Synod are convinced that the dispute is between "Bible believers" and "Bible doubters." They have been hoodwinked by the smokescreen.

The issue of biblical authority has been manufactured and manipulated in the interest of power politics. Everybody knows that the Missouri Synod man in the pew wants to uphold the truth of the Bible and the Bible's authority in the church's life. His valid concern has been manipulated through the manufacture of the issue of biblical authority to enable a particular party wtihin the Synod to gain control of the Synod's institutions in order to remold the Synod's life according to their own ideological and theological standards.

Look at what has happened. First, unspecified rumors of false doctrine in high places were circulated to frighten enough of the rank and file to replace key Synod officials with party candidates, including a new president of the Synod. Then after a prejudiced investigation of the Synod's major seminary the new president himself issued a report accusing unnamed professors of teaching false doctrine, specified as undermining the authority of the Bible, over the objections of the professors that their position had been misrepresented and distorted. Then by majority vote of a Synod convention (New Orleans in 1973), contrary to the Synod's own procedures for due process, the teaching of nearly all professors at Concordia Seminary was condemned as "false doctrine not to be tolerated in the church of God" in the face of protests from official representatives of the seminary that no one held or taught the teachings for which they were being condemned. As president of the seminary I was ousted from office for "holding and defending, allowing and fostering false doctrine" without even being told what the false doctrine is. Those who protested what was happening in the church were immediately called "insurgents" and "rebels against the Word of God." Those who disagreed with the actions of the Synod administration were labeled "Bible doubters."

Did anyone notice what happened in the meantime? Every key power center in the institution fell under the control of the party making the accusation that the authority of the Bible was being subverted. "They Are Taking Your Bible Away" has proved to be an effective political slogan.

You have to look behind the smokescreen to discover the real issues in the Missouri Synod controversy. There *are* genuine issues, and they increase in number with each passing month. In fact, the very soul of the Synod is at stake.

In my estimation the chief issue is confessional. It is about what it means to be a Lutheran church. The classic Lutheran answer to the question is given in the Lutheran confessional writings. Those writings set forth the platform on which Lutherans stand together in one church. The platform consists of the Scriptures as the only rule and norm for all teaching and practice and the creeds and confessions contained in the Book of Concord of 1580 as a correct statement and exposition of what the Scriptures teach. Lutheran congregations and pastors and teachers make a voluntary commitment to that platform and agree to be bound by it in their life together in the church.

But the 1973 convention of the Missouri Synod changed the platform. By majority vote it adopted a new doctrinal statement issued by the president of the Synod and declared it binding on all the members of the Synod. Since the convention the doctrinal statement has served as a confessional writing through its use as a criterion of eligibility for pastors and teachers. Although doctrinal statements can be useful instruments in the church's life, imposing them on the Synod strikes at the heart of what it means to be a Lutheran church. Because of our voluntary commitment to Scriptures and confessions, we Lutherans know what we believe. Imposing binding statements has exactly the opposite effect of assuring conformity to the truth of Scripture. You can't be sure what is going to be imposed on you next. . . .

Isn't the Bible an issue at all in the Missouri Synod controversy? Not the authority of the Bible! Interpreting the Bible is an issue. There is disagreement over what is legitimate and what is illegitimate in biblical interpretation. The role of tradition in biblical interpretation is an issue. Strange to tell, a church body that calls itself after the name of Martin Luther is telling its members that the results of their Bible study must conform to the *tradition* of Bible interpretation sanctioned by the Synod in its past century and a quarter.

Everyone in the Synod accepts the authority of the Bible. At best there is an issue over whether the authority of the Bible can be separated from its gospel content. By its profession the Missouri Synod is a Lutheran church. By that profession it acknowledges that it shares the understanding of biblical authority presented in the Lutheran confessional writings. Those writings clearly affirm the Bible to be the Word of God. They consciously understand the term in accord with what the Bible itself means by "Word of God." As the Lutheran confessional writings clearly affirm, the Word of God is the message of God's judgment and of his promise. Everything in the Bible is either a word of law that condemns or a word of promise that saves. In its proper sense the Word of God is good news about God in action to save. Preeminently the Word of God is Jesus Christ himself.

Without Christ the Bible's authority is reduced to a judging and condemning law. But as Martin Luther wrote, the Bible is the cradle of Christ.

Through it we are brought to him. He gives it its authority. Because of him we know it is the Word of God written by human authors under the inspiration of the Holy Spirit for the purpose of giving the wisdom that leads to salvation through faith in Christ Jesus. At issue in the present controversy is whether the Missouri Synod is going to stay true to that Lutheran insight.

Vatican II

"Pope John's 'Revolution' "

The lovable and unpredictable Pope John XXIII indicated that he planned to open a few windows at the Vatican and let in some fresh air. To many, the momentous gathering in Rome known as Vatican Council II (1962–65) blew more like a gale. Liturgy was modified, authority distributed, ecumenical overtures extended, the modern world more embraced than shunned — all this and much more. It was a Council whose implications would require working out for the remainder of the century, and no doubt well beyond. Something of the high drama and high hope in this epochal gathering is conveyed in the following account of the opening session; it is written by "Xavier Rynne," pseudonym for a well-informed, delightfully literate insider.

To anyone who had the good fortune to be standing in front of the bronze doors leading into the papal palace, on the side of St. Peter's Square, at eight o'clock on the morning of Thursday, October 11, 1962, there was suddenly revealed a dazzling spectacle. At that moment, two papal gendarmes, resplendent in parade uniform of white trousers and black topboots, coats, and busbies, slowly swung the great doors open, exposing to a portion of the crowd row upon row of bishops, clad in flowing white damask copes and mitres, descending Bernini's majestic *scala regia* from the papal apartments. As brilliant television floodlights were switched on along the stairway, the intense light brought to mind Henry Vaughan's lines:

> I saw Eternity the other night,
> Like a great ring of pure and endless light.

In rows of sixes, an apparently inexhaustible phalanx of prelates filed out of the Vatican palace, swung to their right across St. Peter's Square, then wheeled right again, to mount the ramplike steps leading into the basilica. Every now and then, this white mass was dotted with the black cassock, full beard, and round headdress of an oriental bishop, and here and there with the bulbous

[Source: X. Rynne, *Letters from Vatican City* (Garden City, N.Y.: Doubleday & Co., 1963), pp. 73–77.]

gold crown and crossed pectoral reliquaries of a bishop of the Byzantine rite. Toward the end came the scarlet ranks of the Sacred College of Cardinals. Finally, the pope appeared, carried, in deference to the wishes of his entourage, on the *sedia gestatoria,* and looking rather timid, perhaps even frightened — as he always does when first mounting this oriental contraption — but gradually warming to the mild acclamation of the overawed crowd, and gently smiling and quietly weeping as he was carried undulantly forward, blessing the onlookers. At the entrance to the Council hall in the basilica, the procession halted while the pope dismounted and walked the length of the nave to the Confession of St. Peter.

Before the high altar the pope had ordered the substitution of a simpler, more informal style of throne for the unwieldy, pretentious "doctoral" throne, with a red damask backdrop and canopy, that the organizers of the Council had devised. The significance of this was soon made clear by the pope's opening speech, which stressed the Council's pastoral, or ministering, role over the dogmatic, or condemnatory, approach. After the traditional hymn "Veni Creator Spiritus," a solemn mass of the Holy Spirit was celebrated, in which the Epistle and the Gospel were chanted in both Greek and Latin, to signify the unity of both parts of the Church, East and West. The celebrant was the elderly but vigorous Cardinal Tisserant, bearded dean of the College of Cardinals. A touch of Byzantine court ceremonial followed the mass, as the cardinals mounted the steps of the papal throne one by one, with their scarlet mantles trailing behind them, to make their obeisance to the See of Peter. After the bishops' solemn profession of faith in unison, recitation of the litany of the Saints, and more prayers from the Greek rite, Pope John began to deliver his sermon.

In clear and resonant tones that could be distinctly heard throughout the basilica, the pope, after a few introductory remarks, said that he was tired of listening to the prophets of doom among his advisers. "Though burning with zeal," he said, these men "are not endowed with very much sense of discretion or measure." They maintain that "our era, in comparions with past eras, is getting worse, and they behave as though they had learned nothing from history, which is nevertheless the great teacher of life." They were, he said, under the illusion that "at the time of the former Councils, everything was a triumph for the Christian idea and way of life and for proper religious liberty," and he added, "We feel that we must disagree with these prophets of doom, who are always forecasting disaster, as though the end of the world were at hand," and continually warning him, "in the course of our pastoral office," that the modern world is "full of prevarication and ruin." . . .

The pope then proceeded to outline, serenely and optimistically, what he expected of the Council and why he had summoned it. "Divine Providence," he said, "is leading us to a new order of human relations." It was imperative for the Church "to bring herself up to date where required," in order to spread her message "to all men throughout the world." While the Church must "never depart from the sacred patrimony of truth received from the Fathers," she must "ever look to the present, to new conditions and new forms of life introduced into the modern world, which have opened new avenues to the Catholic apostolate."

Then came the phrases, so pregnant with meaning, that either alarmed or gratified his listeners, depending on their theological outlook. The pope said that he had not called the Council to discuss "one article or another of the fundamental doctrine of the Church . . . which is presumed to be well known and familiar to all; for this, a Council was not necessary." Thus were ruled out the hopes of those who had expected the Council to proclaim some new

A first meeting between a Roman Catholic pope (John XXIII) and a former president of the Southern Baptist Convention (Brooks Hays, right), in 1961 *(Religious News Service)*

dogma, isolated from the rest of Christian doctrine, in the manner of the previous Ecumenical Council here, in 1869—70, which concentrated on the dogma of papal infallibility. No, said the pope; "the world expects a step forward toward doctrinal penetration and a formation of consciences." This must be "in conformity with authentic doctrine," of course, but it "should be studied and expounded through the methods of research and through the literary forms of modern thought." In other words, doctrine was to be made more intelligible to contemporaries in the light of scholarship in biblical, theological, philosophical, and historical disciplines.

He next touched on a subject that is almost taboo in traditionalist Catholic theological circles, saying, "The substance of the ancient doctrine of the *depositum fidei* is one thing; the way in which it is expressed is another." That is, Catholic doctrine remains the same in substance, but the formulations of it vary and are not to be regarded as unalterable ends in themselves. The task of the Council, he told the assembled prelates, was to find the best formulas for our time, without being too hidebound or showing a too slavish respect for those of a previous age. He further emphasized the pastoral, rather than the doctrinal, note by declaring, "Nowadays, the bride of Christ [the Church] prefers to make use of the medicine of mercy rather than that of severity. She considers that she meets the needs of the present day by demonstrating the validity of her teaching rather than by condemnation." This was an unmistakable disavowal of the inquisitorial and condemnatory approach of the Holy Office. Finally, the pope turned his attention to the problem of Christian unity. "The entire Christian family has not yet fully attained the visible unity in truth" desired by Christ, he said, and the Catholic Church "therefore considers it her duty to work actively so that there may be fulfilled the great mystery of that unity." He said that the key to "the brotherly unity of all" — embracing not only Christians but "those who follow non-Christian religions" — is "the fullness of charity," or love. Thus Pope John put his seal on the methods and goals of Catholic participation in the ecumenical, or worldwide, movement for reunion.

This inaugural address to the Council, carefully worded and balanced, and delivering a bold message of renewal and reform, marked the end of the closed mentality that has characterized not a few Catholic bishops and theologians since the sixteenth century. Whether this message reached all the prelates to whom it was addressed, or will be heeded by all it did reach, is another matter; one does not cease being a prophet of doom overnight. But the Council as a whole received the pope's message gladly.

Liturgical Renewal

The most conspicuous single alteration for which Vatican II was responsible, changing some of the externals of the mass, reached into every Roman Catholic parish and pew. This reform also provoked the sharpest reaction by those who saw the abandonment of Latin and the adoption of innovations as a surrender to mere novelty and fad. Others, exhilarated by the new openness, went too far too fast so that, some years after the Council, the Vatican found it necessary to emphasize the continued separation between priest and laity, between sacred and secular. And in between the opposers and the runaways, the vast majority of Roman Catholics endeavored to understand just what it all meant. Here, the Trappist Thomas Merton (see above, p. 225) with some humor and much good sense hints at both problems and possibilities.

What is meant by liturgical renewal, and what are some of the problems involved? We, the ordinary clergy and laity, the commoners in the "people of God" need to understand this well, because the main job of renewal is ours. Liturgical reform merely from the top down, renewal by juridical *fiat* alone, is not really likely to work. Yet this is apparently the way many are expecting it to "happen."

Those who are passionately dedicated to the liturgical movement may perhaps be attaching too much importance to the fact that certain desirable changes have been, will be, or at any rate always *can* be legislated. But, as we are aware from the civil rights conflict, the mere opening of new ways by law does not mean that one can always travel them in fact. Hence those who are not so enthusiastic about liturgical renewal are perhaps consoling themselves with stoical reflections on the unwillingness and incapacity of most priests and laypeople to make the required changes in such a way as to effect a real and basic renewal of worship.

Changes are certainly being made. There can be no question that now, after nearly a year of the "new Mass," the changes are pointing in the right direction. Obviously the reform has only begun. The "new Mass," as it now stands, seems to represent certain practical compromises that were needed in order that a certain amount of vernacular might be allowed. But it certainly does seem illogical to switch from English to Latin just for the Prayer and then go back to English for the Epistle; or to say "The Lord be with you" now in English and now in Latin. The logic of Liturgical renewal certainly requires that the entire Mass be said in the language of the people, and this must eventually come. . . .

The best thing about the "new Mass" is the real opening up of opportunities for participation. With the altar now facing the people, there is obviously more sense of communication on both sides, and much less danger of the old

[Source: Thomas Merton, *Seasons of Celebration* (New York: Farrar, Straus, & Giroux, 1965), pp. 231–37.]

wool-gathering distractedness which always threatens the man who is merely absorbed in his own routine thoughts and imaginings. Communication being consciously established and maintained, priest and people can more easily become aware that they are together *celebrating* the mystery of our Redemption in the Eucharistic Sacrifice and the Lord's Supper. . . .

Obviously all is not yet perfect. Those who imagined that it was enough to have the texts translated into the vernacular were perhaps unprepared for the problems that might still remain. Our Bible readings are now in English. But what English! A text is being used that was prepared for private reading and study, and its attempts at bright colloquialism do not stand up well under the exigencies of public and solemn celebration. A certain sacred and timeless seriousness is required in our vernacular liturgical texts, or they will rapidly become unbearably trite.

Complaints are made about the hymn singing, and doubtless it is not always up to the standard of Gregorian. But at least it is something that everyone can do. How many parishes were there, before the Council, where *all* the congregation knew how to sing the common of the Mass in Gregorian?

There remains very much to be done. We are in a period of transition. Neither misplaced enthusiasms nor resentful non-participation will help the Church now. We must go forward in a spirit of sober and reasonable experimentation, and this means facing the hazards of trial and error. No matter what changes are made, if they are only new gestures performed in the old spirit, they will not constitute a liturgical renewal. It is not the old forms that must go so much as the old spirit. So let us take a quick look at the "old spirit," fully aware that it does not belong only to the past. It is still very much with us, even with some of those who favor progressive ideas. . . .

What difference does it make if the priest says the whole canon out loud if it still means something like this: "I am the priest, you are the laity, and this is a strictly business deal. You have your place and I have mine. I am here to confect valid sacraments for you to receive and you are there because if you were not there I would not be here confecting sacraments. Besides everyone knows that unless I exercise my special office as the only one who can validly make Our Lord sacramentally present, you won't even have a religion. Indeed you will be, for all intents, and purposes, godless. As to who you are or what you think about all this, I couldn't care less. So let's get the whole thing over with so that I can go mind my business and you yours." . . .

According to this outlook, what matters is not that the ceremonies have meaning, or that the sacraments eloquently speak the grace which they signify, or that the order and comeliness of worship should help to manifest the splendor of God's love and of His presence in the midst of His people. All that matters is that the sacraments be valid, the formulas correct, and the gestures rubrically exact. Worship is mechanically efficient, the worshipper gets grace with a minimum of trouble, and all goes smoothly!

This mentality is responsible for a deadly atmosphere of officialism in cult,

In reaction to Vatican II, the Catholic Traditionalist Movement maintained an all-Latin mass in Westbury, New York.
(Religious News Service)

a pervasive and deadening influence which one is expected to counteract by interior and subjective worship, governed entirely by one's own individual tastes and needs and which, in the last analysis, is one's own responsibility and nobody else's business.

Let me say at once that this private realm of sincerity and personal awareness is not to be scoffed at. Where worship is cold, formal, official and empty of personal communication, what other refuge is left for the worshipper? I am not too sure I think it is a good thing to make him feel guilty about it, unless you have something better to offer here and now, in the concrete and not just on paper or in your own head.

What is required above all is a new spirit of *openness*, in which the priest is open to his people, and they are open to him and one another. This means that the words of the liturgy should be spoken by a person, to persons, and not just uttered abstractly in a sacred void.

It is true, and this is sometimes forgotten, that the words of the Liturgy are sacred and the people are gathered in a "sacred space." "The Lord be with you" is something else again than "Hello gang!" So the whole idea of "renewal" means something else than saying the formulas of prayer in a familiar language and with the intonations of colloquial and rotarian togetherness. It means discovering a *new* sense of sacred space, of community, of oneness in the Spirit, as a result of a communication on a deep level with which we have long ceased to be familiar: it means learning to experience the mystery of oneness in grace. This demands a community presence and awareness that is distinct from our ordinary assemblies: a presence to one another in Christ. A presence also in celebration. It means therefore a sense of mystery. One cannot possibly experience this liturgical presence and oneness if one is not open to the reality of the Spirit in and through all who have been brought together in the worshipping assembly. Yet this sense is not mystical and esoteric. It is based on our natural human affinities for one another as beings with the same needs, the same joys, the same hopes, fears and loves, who have been brought together by the merciful love of Christ. The words, songs, ceremonies, signs, movements of worship are all designed, by their very nature, to open the mind and heart of the participant to this experience of oneness in Christ. But this sacramental consciousness depends first of all on human sympathy, relatedness and on some degree of mutual understanding. Hence the obligation to be at peace with all before going to worship.

Religious Liberty

By general agreement the most "American" of the sixteen documents issued by Vatican II was its final one, the Declaration on Religious Liberty. Also by general agreement its author, advocate, and ever-watchful shepherd was John Courtney Murray (1904 – 67), Jesuit theologian and professor at Woodstock Seminary in Maryland. As Murray himself noted regarding the Declaration: "It was, of course, the most controversial document of the whole Council, largely because it raised with sharp emphasis . . . the issue of the development of doctrine. The notion of development, not the notion of religious freedom, was the real sticking-point for many of those who opposed the Declaration even to the end." And development there had emphatically been: from a Church privileged, powerful, and often intolerant to an institution now saying that its only civil right was to enjoy a "full measure of freedom." As Murray commented, the Declaration on Religious Liberty is "the Church's final farewell to the sacred society."

Declaration on Religious Freedom: On the Right of the Person and of Communities to Social and Civil Freedom in Matters Religious

1. A sense of the dignity of the human person has been impressing itself more and more deeply on the consciousness of contemporary man. And the demand is increasingly made that men should act on their own judgment, enjoying and making use of a responsible freedom, not driven by coercion but motivated by a sense of duty. The demand is also made that constitutional limits should be set to the powers of government, in order that there may be no encroachment on the rightful freedom of the person and of associations.

This demand for freedom in human society chiefly regards the quest for

[Source: *Declaration on Religious Freedom,* Dec. 7, 1965 (Washington, D. C.: National Catholic Welfare Conference, n. d.), pp. 1– 5, 11– 12.]

the values proper to the human spirit. It regards, in the first place, the free exercise of religion in society.

This Vatican Synod takes careful note of these desires in the minds of men. It proposes to declare them to be greatly in accord with truth and justice. To this end, it searches into the sacred tradition and doctrine of the Church — the treasury out of which the Church continually brings forth new things that are in harmony with the things that are old.

First, this sacred Synod professes its belief that God himself has made known to mankind the way in which men are to serve Him, and thus be saved in Christ and come to blessedness. We believe that this one true religion subsists in the catholic and apostolic Church, to which the Lord Jesus committed the duty of spreading it abroad among all men. Thus He spoke to the apostles: "Go, therefore, and make disciples of all nations, baptizing them in the name of the Father, and of the Son, and of the Holy Spirit, teaching them to observe all that I have commanded you" (Mt. 28:19–20). On their part, all men are bound to seek the truth, especially in what concerns God and His Church, and to embrace the truth they come to know, and to hold fast to it.

This sacred Synod likewise professes its belief that it is upon the human conscience that these obligations fall and exert their binding force. The truth cannot impose itself except by virtue of its own truth, as it makes its entrance into the mind at once quietly and with power. Religious freedom, in turn, which men demand as necessary to fulfill their duty to worship God, has to do with immunity from coercion in civil society. Therefore, it leaves untouched traditional Catholic doctrine on the moral duty of men and societies toward the true religion and toward the one Church of Christ.

Over and above all this, in taking up the matter of religious freedom this sacred Synod intends to develop the doctrine of recent Popes on the inviolable rights of the human person and on the constitutional order of society.

2. This Vatican Synod declares that the human person has a right to religious freedom. This freedom means that all men are to be immune from coercion on the part of individuals or of social groups and of any human power, in such wise that in matters religious no one is to be forced to act in a manner contrary to his own beliefs. Nor is anyone to be restrained from acting in accordance with his own beliefs, whether privately or publicly, whether alone or in association with others, within due limits.

The Synod further declares that the right to religious freedom has its foundation in the very dignity of the human person, as this dignity is known through the revealed Word of God and by reason itself. This right of the human person to religious freedom is to be recognized in the constitutional law whereby society is governed. Thus it is to become a civil right.

It is in accordance with their dignity as persons — that is, beings endowed with reason and free will and therefore privileged to bear personal responsibility — that all men should be at once impelled by nature and also bound by a moral obligation to seek the truth, especially religious truth. They are also bound to adhere to the truth, once it is known, and to order their whole lives in accord with the demands of truth.

However, men cannot discharge these obligations in a manner in keeping with their own nature unless they enjoy immunity from external coercion as well as psychological freedom. Therefore, the right to religious freedom has its foundation, not in the subjective disposition of the person, but in his very nature. In consequence, the right to this immunity continues to exist even in those who do not live up to their obligation of seeking the truth and adhering to it. Nor is the exercise of this right to be impeded, provided that the just requirements of public order are observed.

3. Further light is shed on the subject if one considers that the highest norm of human life is the divine law—eternal, objective, and universal— whereby God orders, directs, and governs the entire universe and all the ways of the human community, by a plan conceived in wisdom and love. Man has been made by God to participate in this law, with the result that,

John Courtney Murray, S. J. (1904-67), guiding hand behind Declaration on Religious Liberty proclaimed by Vatican II
(Woodstock College)

under the gentle disposition of divine Providence, he can come to perceive ever increasingly the unchanging truth. Hence every man has the duty, and therefore the right, to seek the truth in matters religious, in order that he may with prudence form for himself right and true judgments of conscience, with the use of all suitable means.

Truth, however, is to be sought after in a manner proper to the dignity of the human person and his social nature. The inquiry is to be free, carried on with the aid of teaching or instruction, communication, and dialogue. In the course of these, men explain to one another the truth they have discovered, or think they have discovered, in order thus to assist one another in the quest for truth. Moreover, as the truth is discovered, it is by a personal assent that men are to adhere to it.

On his part, man perceives and acknowledges the imperatives of the divine law through the mediation of conscience. In all his activity a man is bound to follow his conscience faithfully, in order that he may come to God, for whom he was created. It follows that he is not to be forced to act in a manner contrary to his conscience. Nor, on the other hand, is he to be restrained from acting in accordance with his conscience, especially in matters religious.

For, of its very nature, the exercise of religion consists before all else in those internal, voluntary, and free acts whereby man sets the course of his life directly toward God. No merely human power can either command or prohibit acts of this kind.

However, the social nature of man itself requires that he should give external expression to his internal acts of religion; that he should participate with others in matters religious; that he should profess his religion in community. Injury, therefore, is done to the human person and to the very order established by God for human life, if the free exercise of religion is denied in society when the just requirements of public order do not so require.

There is a further consideration. The religious acts whereby men, in private and in public and out of a sense of personal conviction, direct their lives to God transcend by their very nature the order of terrestrial and temporal affairs. Government, therefore, ought indeed to take account of the religious life ot the people and show it favor, since the function of government is to make provision for the common welfare. However, it would clearly transgress the limits set to its power were it to presume to direct or inhibit acts that are religious. . . .

12. The Church therefore is being faithful to the truth of the gospel, and is following the way of Christ and the apostles when she recognizes, and gives support to, the principle of religious freedom as befitting the dignity of man and as being in accord with divine revelation. Throughout the ages, the Church has kept safe and handed on the doctrine received from the Master and from the apostles. In the life of the People of God as it has made its pilgrim way through the vicissitudes of human history, there have at times appeared ways of acting which were less in accord with the spirit of the gospel

and even opposed to it. Nevertheless, the doctrine of the Church that no one is to be coerced into faith has always stood firm.

Thus the leaven of the gospel has long been about its quiet work in the minds of men. To it is due in great measure the fact that in the course of time men have come more widely to recognize their dignity as persons, and the conviction has grown stronger that in religious matters the person in society is to be kept free from all manner of human coercion.

Ecumenism

Vatican II was itself an ecumenical event, as non-Catholic observers in large numbers were welcomed guests. The publication of the sixteen documents was likewise ecumenical, as Protestant and Catholic publishers jointly issued the Documents of Vatican Council II, a publication which included non-Catholic responses and commentaries to each of the decrees. Beyond all this, however, was the work of the Council itself in softening the centuries-old culpability of the Jews for the crucifixion of Christ, in opening new lines of communication with Protestants and the Orthodox, and in condemning all "discrimination against men or harassment of them because of their race, color, condition of life, or religion." As the Jesuit editor of this aforementioned volume said of the Decree on Ecumenism, the most remarkable fact about it is that it is there at all. And, W. M. Abbott added, "the focus is more on a 'pilgrim' Church moving toward Christ than on a movement of 'return' to the Roman Catholic Church." In a speech given in 1965 as the deliberations and debates of Vatican II were drawing to a close, editor Abbott summarized the work done by the Council but with emphasis on the work remaining to be done in ecumenical relations by —say —1990.

The Decree on Ecumenism signals every one of us to ecumenical work. Ecumenism, therefore, is not simply a matter one may take or leave; it is to be a central concern for all Catholics, according to their abilities. It will take time to achieve the massive scale of involvement, but the traditionally obedient Catholic people of the United States can be counted on to move in that direction. Some Catholic groups have already moved, on a national scale, and they are already sensitive to criticism. An article in AMERICA recently suggested that the National Council of Catholic Women was not carrying out some of its projects ecumenically enough. There was an immediate and indignant reply.

The Decree on Ecumenism states: "But their primary duty is to make a careful and honest appraisal of whatever needs to be renewed and done in the

[Source: W. M. Abbott, S. J., "The Ecumenical Movement in America: 1990," *Catholic Mind*, Oct., 1965, pp. 26–28.]

Catholic household itself, in order that its life may bear witness more clearly and faithfully to the teachings and institutions which have been handed down from Christ through the Apostles." The decree doesn't say this is the work of bishops only, or priests, or theologians. It says it is the work of "Catholics," and many Catholics have started on this work with zest.

The Decree on Ecumenism stipulates that "the manner and order in which Catholic belief is expressed should in no way become an obstacle to dialogue with our brethren." The decree follows its own advice and avoids such terms as heretic, schismatic, non-Catholic. It does not even use the word Protestant but constantly uses Pope John's expression "separated brethren" and "our brethren." This pattern of courtesy has already spread widely and will continue to commend itself.

The Decree on Ecumenism has brought to an end that polemical approach that used to characterize so much of Catholicism. The Decree orders that seminarians should master a theology that has been worked out in the ecumenical way "and not polemically." As a result, the formation of the laity and of religious will be sure to develop ecumenically, for, as the Decree observes, "it is the formation which priests receive upon which so largely depends the necessary instruction and spiritual formation of the faithful and of religious." With such a development, the ecumenical environment will be secure.

The ecumenical spirit is not merely one of "glossing things over." The Decree on Ecumenism stresses that ecumenical dialogue must present doctrine "in its entirety," and that nothing is so foreign to the spirit of ecumenism as "a false irenicism which harms the purity of Catholic doctrine and obscures its assured genuine meaning." American Catholics are well enough educated to appreciate the whole view that the decree takes. The ecumenical movement in this country is thus assured of good health and sound structure. Projects of research will from time to time produce results that will, at least temporarily, amaze and disturb "comfortable" minds, but in general the educational work of the bishops and religious orders will not have been in vain.

In spite of some prophets of doom, it can be said that the grass-roots ecumenical movement should be the biggest and best injection of vitality that the individual churches have had since they were founded. The necessity to engage in dialogue — to explain one's faith to another — will force many people to learn their faith as they never have before. . . .

The Decree on Ecumenism humbly begs pardon of God "and of our separated brethren" for sins of Catholics in the past against them. The Declaration on Non-Christians, now ready for the final vote at the next session of the Council, admits there has been hatred and persecution of the Jews by Catholics and deplores it. In the years ahead there will be more and more frank discussion of this sad history. Our textbooks will have more of it, and our press will have more of it. The faults of churchmen and laity will be faced. Those who found it hard to take criticism of Catholic education will find it hard to take this future dialogue, too. But it must all come out in the dialogue. If it doesn't, the Jews especially will regard our dialogue with them as a fraud, and we shall not reach them. . . .

American Catholics, like most American people, are doers, not just hearers, readers, talkers. They will not be satisfied with an annual ecumenical breakfast or supper. In the Decree on Ecumenism they have a mandate for much more. They are already looking for common study-club work, regular neighborhood dialogue sessions, and common witness, especially in social work. They are consoled to learn from the Decree on Ecumenism what they had often suspected was true: they can learn a great deal from, and can be inspired in many cases by, their separated brethren. They have been excited by the prospect of a common Bible. They know, as the Decree on Ecumenism says, that "in the dialogue itself, the Sacred Word is a precious instrument in the mighty hand of God for attaining to that unity which the Saviour holds out to all men."

It is risky to attempt to express the divine plans in a timetable, but it seems safe enough to say that by 1990 our Catholic people will be much closer to Holy Scripture —and, thanks to the vernacular, so will our priests. Without Bible study, the ecumenical movement will not go very far. But Bible study is much more than just begun among our people. We shall have a common Bible long before 1990. In the publication, last June, of a Catholic edition of the Revised Standard Version (imprimatur of Archbishop Gray, of Edinburgh; introduction by Cardinal Meyer of Chicago) we have a common Bible for all practical purposes as far as the New Testament is concerned (the Old Testament should come in another year). In the years ahead we can and will work out a common biblical theology. The common Bible will give the ecumenical movement a great psychological boost. With a common biblical theology we shall be on the verge of the Christian union we seek.

Eastern Orthodoxy and American Culture

Ethnicity and Religion

In America's religious history, ethnicity has often determined patterns of settlement, ecclesiastical ties, seating at worship, and the language of theology. Much of this ethnic stamp had worn away by the middle of the twentieth century, but not among the Eastern Orthodox who were, by and large, recent arrivals. For these new Americans, ethnicity continued to determine social

[Sources: Demetrios J. Constantelos, ed., *Encyclicals and Documents of the Greek Orthodox Archdiocese of North and South America* (Thessalonika: Patriarchal Institute for Patristic Studies, 1976), (1) pp. 1173–74; (2) p. 1181.]

fellowship, marital choice, burial ground, and which foreign newspaper to read. The Greek Orthodox, for example, were still Greek even while they were Americans, with one eye turned toward their adopted land and the other cast toward "home." Two documents from Prelate Archbishop Iakovos (he was elevated to that office in 1959) show this ambivalence, as the Greek Orthodox Archdiocese of North and South America (with about two million members) stays very much Greek in the first document, and struggles to be very much American in the second.

1.

October 15, 1964

My dearly beloved in the Lord,

A quarter of a century has now elapsed since that historic day of October 28, 1940, when the heroic Greek people, instead of bowing to the barbarity of invasion, determinedly opposed force, as they had often done in the past, and gained a victory of the greatest moral stature, to the glory of themselves and the entire civilized world.

That historic day, since known as the day of "OXI", when Greece said "No!" to the invader, shines forth resplendent from year to year with new radiance, and illumines the venerable but too often forgotten biblical truth that "not by bread alone can man live".

The abundance of bread and material comforts, and the reality or promise there of, tend to choke within and around us the meaning and intent of the concepts of freedom and justice, and the protection of the weak of this earth by the strong.

Our present age, which is undoubtedly an era of great conquests in the fields of science and technology and space, is also a period of a pernicious degeneration of man, who has strayed from this faith in God and from the spiritual and ethical values which enriched and beautified even the most difficult and distressing times of years gone by.

We cannot help coming to such grievous conclusions, even unwillingly, when we see the unjustified apathy that has become the policy of even the most liberty-loving nations towards the decade-long struggle for self-determination by the Greeks of Cyprus, and towards the pressures and humiliations likewise endured, most recently during the past decade, by the Greeks of Turkey.

In view of all this, the 1964 observance of the unparalleled resistance of the Greek people, which was crowned by the "No!" they answered to force, and by the "Yes!" history will record to their courage, should be celebrated with a total awakening of our consciences and hearts. This is especially necessary today, when compromise is imposed upon as the best solution to the weightiest of problems, as is the issue of whether or not justice will prevail.

Greek Orthodox Church in Belmont, California (winner of architectural award
in 1963)
(National Council of Churches)

2.

Statement by His Eminence Archbishop Iakovos, Primate of the Greek
Orthodox Church of North and South America, on the occasion of the Me-
morial Service for Rev. James Reed [sic]* in Selma, Alabama on Monday,
March 16, 1965:

I came to this Memorial Service because I believe this is an appropriate
occasion not only to dedicate myself as well as our Greek Orthodox Com-
municants to the noble cause for which our friend, the Reverend James Reed
gave his life; but also in order to show our willingness to continue this fight
against prejudice, bias and persecution.

In this God-given cause, I feel sure that I have the full and understanding
support of our Greek Orthodox faithful of America. For our Greek Orthodox

*Actually, James J. Reeb who was attacked in Selma, Alabama on March 10, 1965,
a few hours after his participation in a protest march led by Martin Luther King, Jr. A
graduate of Princeton Theological Seminary, a Presbyterian then Unitarian minister, Reeb
died in a Birmingham hospital on March 12, at the age of thirty-eight. Both President
Lyndon Johnson and Vice President Hubert Humphrey expressed the nation's deep regret
to Reeb's widow and four children then living in Boston.

Church and our people fully understand from our heritage and our tradition such sacrificial involvements. Our Church has never hesitated to fight, when it felt it must, for the rights of mankind; and many of our Churchmen have been in the forefront of these battles time and time again.

The great poet John Milton said in the closing lines of *Samson Agonistes*:

> All is best, though oft we doubt,
> What the invisible dispose of highest wisdom brings about.

I would like to believe that these words have deep relevance to the meaning of the tragic and violent death of the Rev. James Reed. The ways of God are not always revealed to us, but certainly His choice of this dedicated minister to be the victim of racial hatred and the hero of this struggle to gain unalienable constitutional rights for those American brethren of ours who are denied them, and to die, so to speak, on this battlefield for human dignity and equality, was not accidental or haphazard.

Let us seek out in this tragedy a divine lesson for all of us. The Rev. Reed felt he could not be outside the arena of this bitter struggle — and we too must feel that we cannot. Let his martyrdom be an inspiration and a reminder to us that there are times when we must risk everything, including life itself, for those basic American ideals of Freedom, Justice and Equality, without which this land cannot survive.

Our hope and prayer, then, is that we may be given strength to let God know by our acts and deeds, and not only by our words, that like the late Rev. James Reed, we too are the espousers and the fighters in a struggle for which we must be prepared to risk our all.

Elusive Unity

The other ecumenical difficulty besetting Orthodoxy is division within. There is in America no single "Orthodox Church." The two largest ethnic-national groups are Russian and Greek, but in addition to these there are Albanian, Bulgarian, Rumanian, Serbian, Syrian, and Ukrainian groups. Even the single bloc of Russian Orthodoxy has been further plagued by the awkwardness of a Patriarch of Moscow who is under the eye (at least) of a very un-Orthodox government. The largest of three Russian groups in the United States, the Orthodox Church in America, with about one million members, is no longer under Moscow's authority. And its recent Metropolitan, Ireney (1970 – 81), pressed toward the ecumenical goal of "One Orthodox Church" for all America. Orthodoxy, Metropolitan Ireney and his bishops contended, can never really develop in this country until the several autonomous churches

[Source: Constance J. Tarasu, ed., *Orthodox America 1794 – 1976* (Syosset, N. Y.: Orthodox Church in America, 1975), p. 277.]

overcome their "many trials, divisions, and canonical disturbances" to become one. The following call for unity was issued in 1970.

MESSAGE TO ALL ORTHODOX CHRISTIANS IN AMERICA

In the Name of the Father and of the Son and of the Holy Spirit. Amen.

We the Bishops, clergy and laity of the Orthodox Church in America, united in Our Lord and Saviour Jesus Christ at our All-American Church Council, address this message to all our brothers in the Orthodox Faith in America.

The grace and the mercy of God be with you.. Time has come for us to fulfill Christ's prayer, "that all may be one . . . that the world may believe that Thou has sent me" (John 17:21). Our witness to the truth of our Orthodox Faith on this continent, where we Orthodox are a minority, lies in our perfect and total unity. How can the world accept and believe our claim to be the One, Holy, Catholic and Apostolic Church, of having kept in its fulness the Orthodox faith, if we ourselves are divided? We have the same Faith, the same Tradition, the same hope, the same mission. We should then constitute one Church, visibly, organically, fully. Such is the requirement of our Orthodox Faith and we know that always and everywhere the Orthodox Church has existed and exists as one Church. There can, therefore, be no excuse for our jurisdictional divisions, alienation from one another, and parochialism. The removal of such divisions and the organic unity of all-Orthodox in America is the goal of our Church and we invite you to become a part of the unity.

But we also know and fully acknowledge that we have come from different backgrounds and have been nourished by various traditions within the same and unique Orthodox Tradition. We firmly believe that this variety constitutes the richness of American Orthodoxy and that whatever is true, noble, inspiring and Christian in our various customs and practices ought to be fully preserved and, if possible, shared. Therefore, although we insist that the One Orthodox Church here must be the home of all, we equally stress that there must be no loss of our respective national and cultural heritages and certainly no domination of any group by any other but a full equality, total trust and truly Christian brotherhood. As we send you the peace and love of our First Council as the Orthodox Church in America, we assure you that we understand ourselves first and foremost as the servants of the full unity of the Church in the freedom, love and mutual respect of all churches and dioceses of our Orthodox Church in the World and in this blessed land of America.

Glory to our Lord Jesus Christ, with the Father and the Holy Spirit, unto ages of ages. Amen.

Orthodoxy and Roman Catholicism

Even while attempting to mend deep divisions within its own theological household, the Eastern "half" of Christendom has opened doors long shut (for nearly a thousand years) toward the Western "half." Late in 1979 Pope John Paul II, a highly peripatetic leader of the Western church, journeyed to Constantinople to meet with Patriarch Demetrios I of the Greek Orthodox Church. Explaining the reason for his making a long trip to a dangerous and often hostile part of the world, the pope stated: "I must go for ecumenical reasons. Love is stronger than danger." Both patriarch and pope attended the same mass even if, with the two great churches still in an official state of schism, it was not possible for them to celebrate the mass together. But as the "Joint Statement" below indicates, both looked toward that day "when we will finally be able to concelebrate the Divine Eucharist." Both would agree that much needed yet to be done before that day arrives, but these two pilgrims stood ready to begin the journey.

We, Pope John Paul II and Ecumenical Patriarch Demetrios I, thank God who has granted that we meet to celebrate together the feast of the apostle Andrew, the first called and the brother of the apostle Peter. "Praised be the God and Father of our Lord Jesus Christ, who has bestowed on us in Christ every spiritual blessing in the heavens" (Eph. 1:3).

It is in seeking the sole glory of God through the accomplishment of his will that we affirm anew our firm will to do all that is possible to hasten the day when full communion between the Catholic Church and the Orthodox Church will be reestablished and when we will finally be able to concelebrate the Divine Eucharist.

We are grateful to our predecessors, Pope Paul VI and Patriarch Athenagoras I for all they have done to reconcile our churches and to make them progress in unity.

The progress made in the preparatory stage permits us to announce that the theological dialogue is going to begin and to make public the list of members of the mixed Orthodox-Catholic commission which will be entrusted with it.

This theological dialogue has as its goal not only to progress toward the reestablishment of full communion between the Orthodox and Catholic sister Churches, but further to contribute to the many dialogues which are going on in the Christian world in quest of its unity.

The dialogue of charity (cf. Jn. 13:34; Eph. 4:1−7), rooted in a complete fidelity to the one Lord Jesus Christ and to his church (cf. Jn. 17:21), has opened the way to a better understanding of mutual theological positions and, from there, to new approaches to theological work and to a new attitude

[Source: *Greek Orthodox Theological Review*, 25 (Summer, 1980), 129−30.]

toward the common past of our churches. This purification of the collective memory of our churches is an important fruit of the dialogue of charity and an indispensable condition of future progress. This dialogue of charity must continue and be intensified in the complex situation which we have inherited from the past and which constitutes the reality in which our effort must go on today.

We desire that progress in unity may open new possibilities for dialogue and collaboration with believers of other religions and with all men of good will, so that love and brotherhood may win over hatred and opposition between men. We hope thus to contribute to the coming of a true peace in the world. We implore this gift from him who was, who is and who is to come, Christ our only Lord and our true peace.

Phanar, on the feast of St. Andrew, 1979.

3. SOCIETY AND ITS CONFLICTS

Communism and the Churches

"Reds and Our Churches"

In 1953 an article appearing in the American Mercury *began with this sentence: "The largest single group supporting the Communist apparatus in the United States today is composed of Protestant clergymen." For openers, that sweeping assertion would be hard to beat. Its author, J. B. Matthews (b. 1894) of Kentucky Methodist background, had in the early 1930s been attracted to communism and to the Soviet Union. By the end of the decade, he had become quite disillusioned with communism and with much else besides. With the zeal of the convert, he now began a new career as vigorous anticommunist and chief investigator for the House of Representatives committee charged with investigating "Un-American Activities." A portion of his inflammatory article follows.*

The largest single group supporting the Communist apparatus in the United States today is composed of Protestant clergymen.

Since the beginning of the First Cold War in April, 1948, the Communist Party of this country has placed more and more reliance upon the ranks of the Protestant clergy to provide the party's subversive apparatus with its agents, stooges, dupes, front men, and fellow-travelers.

Clergymen outnumbered professors two to one in supporting the Communist-front apparatus of the Kremlin conspiracy. In the May issue of the AMERICAN MERCURY, we pointed out that during the past seventeen years the Communist Party has enlisted the support of at least thirty-five hundred professors — many of them as dues-paying members, many others as fellow-travelers, some as out-and-out espionage agents, some as adherents of the

[Source: J. B. Matthews, "Reds and Our Churches," *American Mercury,* 77 (July, 1953), 3, 4–5, 13.]

party line in varying degrees, and some as the unwitting dupes of subversion. During the same seventeen-year period, the Communist Party has enlisted the support of at least seven thousand Protestant clergymen in the same categories — party members, fellow-travelers, espionage agents, party-line adherents, and unwitting dupes. . . .

The People's Institute of Applied Religion — a Communist school which is run, sponsored, and subsidized by Protestant clergymen — publishes a handbook which says: "True religion uses the class struggle as the most effective weapon of constructive social change in a class society. It recognizes from its study of our religious heritage that the class struggle, while it is not a permanent weapon of the people, is the historic weapon."

The People's Institute defines salvation, in its handbook, as follows: "Salvation is the result of the collective effort of the workers and other victims of this [the capitalist] world system to save *themselves* from the oppressors."

On the subject of Protestantism, the People's Institute offers the following viewpoint: "Protestant church religion came into being to enhance the rise of capitalism. It proclaimed the divine right of property. It deified [spelled *defied* in the original] the kings of finance, the lords of commerce and the captains of industry. Today this church religion is directed by remote control from the Chamber of Commerce, the National Association of Manufacturers and the offices of cartel imperialists. With these it has economic investments in the capitalist exploits of the whole world."

Any casual student of Communism will recognize the party line in these quotations from the published handbook of the People's Institute of Applied Religion. More about the Communist training school for clergymen presently!

Our next witness is the Director of the Federal Bureau of Investigation. In testimony before the Congressional Committee on Un-American Activities, on March 26, 1947, J. Edgar Hoover — who speaks with the highest authority on the subject of Communism — said: "I confess to a real apprehension so long as Communists are able to secure ministers of the Gospel to promote their evil work and espouse a cause that is alien to the religion of Christ and Judaism." . . .

Preachers, too, are people. As such, they are citizens to be held responsible for their civic and political acts. If professors and government employees are held to strict accountability for collaboration with the Communist-front apparatus, why not clergymen? Do clergymen have their own little Yalu River — their professional status — beyond which they have sanctuary? Why should they be allowed to participate, without investigation and exposure, in the "campaign to disarm and defeat the United States"? The Communist Party counts heavily on this immunity which cowardly politicians would grant to ministers of the Gospel. . . .

Why, one often hears, is it a matter of any great concern that ministers of the Gospel join, sponsor, or otherwise support the Communist-front apparatus? The answer to that question is that the Communist-front apparatus is an integral part of the whole nefarious Communist conspiracy to destroy us; that it is assigned as definite a role as the Communist Party itself, the espionage cells, the Communist training schools, and the Communist press. In the May issue of AMERICAN MERCURY, the multiple uses of the Communist-front apparatus were set forth in some detail. The reader is invited to refer to that discussion in my article on "Communism and the Colleges."

It hardly needs to be said that the vast majority of American Protestant clergymen are loyal to the free institutions of this country, as well as loyal to their solemn trust as ministers of the Gospel. In a sense, this overwhelming majority is embarrassed by the participation of the minority in the activities of the most sinister conspiracy in the history of the world.

The international Communist conspiracy aims at the total obliteration of Judeo-Christian civilization. Communist dogma is diametrically opposed to every tenet of Judeo-Christian theology and philosophy. It is, therefore, nothing short of a monstrous puzzle that some seven thousand Protestant clergymen have been drawn during the past seventeen years into the network of the Kremlin's conspiracy. Could it be that these pro-Communist clergymen have allowed their zeal for social justice to run away with their better judgment and patriotism?

A partial explanation of these thousands of clergymen who have collaborated in one way or another with the Communist-front apparatus may be found in the vogue of the "social gospel" which infected the Protestant theological seminaries more than a generation ago. Many graduates of the "liberalized" Protestant seminaries abandoned religion altogether in favor of the "social gospel."

The Rev. Walter Rauschenbusch,* with his *Christianizing the Social Order*, and the Rev. Harry F. Ward,** with his *The New Social Order*, pioneered the "social gospel" in the years before World War I, the former a Baptist and the latter a Methodist. In the generation which followed, these two men recruited through their teaching and writings thousands of younger clergymen who began to fancy themselves as modern editions of the Eighth Century Prophets — Amos, Hosea, Isaiah, and Micah. They forgot that these Prophets were as passionately concerned with individual human freedom as they were with social justice.

*See above, pp. 120ff.
**See above, p. 277.

"I Protest"

Among the Protestant clergymen who found themselves persistently under attack was Methodist Bishop G. Bromley Oxnam (1891–1963). A highly respected and highly visible Methodist, Oxnam served as president of the Federal Council of Churches from 1944 to 1946 and as president of the World Council of Churches from 1948 to 1954. The Un-American Activities Committee repeatedly released "unevaluated" reports implying that Oxnam either sympathized with the Communist party or allowed himself to be used by it. The same hard choice was offered in those days to many Americans inside the churches and out: confess either to treason or to treasonable stupidity. Oxnam was not summoned to appear before the committee; rather, he demanded to be heard. He protested "against procedures that are in effect the rule of men and not of law; procedures subject to the prejudices, passions and political ambitions of Committeemen; procedures designed less to elicit information than to entrap; procedures that cease to be investigation and become inquisition and intimidation."

. . . So with but fifteen minutes allotted, I turned to what I believed to be the fundamentals.

The room became silent. I said:

When I declare, "I believe in God, the Father Almighty," I affirm the theistic faith and strike at the fundamental fallacy of communism, which is atheism. I thereby reaffirm the basic conviction upon which this republic rests, namely, that all men are created by the Eternal and in His image, beings of infinite worth, members of one family, brothers. We are endowed by the Creator with certain inalienable rights. The State does not confer them; it merely confirms them. They belong to man because he is a son of God. When I say, "I believe in God," I am also saying that moral law is written into the nature of things. There are moral absolutes. Marxism, by definition, rules out moral absolutes. Because I believe the will of God is revealed in the Gospel of Christ, I hold that all historically conditioned political, economic, social, and ecclesiastical systems must be judged by the Gospel, not identified with it. This is to say I reject communism, first, because of its atheism.

There was a puzzled expression upon the faces of some Committeemen. I continued:

When I declare, "I believe in Jesus Christ, His only Son, our Lord," I am affirming faith in a spiritual view of life. By so doing, I repudiate the philosophy of materialism upon which communism is based, and thereby undermine it. I reject the theory of social development that assumes social institutions and even morality are determined by the prevailing mode of production. When I accept the law of love taught by Christ and revealed in

[Source: G. B. Oxnam, *I Protest* (New York: Harper & Brothers, 1954), pp. 35–37.]

His person, I must, of necessity, oppose to the death a theory that justifies dictatorship with its annihilation of freedom. I am not an economist, but have studied sufficiently to be convinced that there are basic fallacies in Marxian economics. Believing as I do that personality is a supreme good and that personality flowers in freedom, I stand for the free man in the free society, seeking the truth that frees. I hold that the free man must discover concrete measures through which the ideals of religion may be translated into the realities of world law and order, economic justice, and racial brotherhood.

As a result of long study and of prayer, I am by conviction pledged to the free way of life and opposed to all forms of totalitarianism, left or right, and to all tendencies toward such practices at home or abroad. Consequently, I have been actively opposed to communism all my life. I have never been a member of the Communist Party. My opposition to communism is a matter of public record in books, numerous articles, addresses, and sermons, and in resolutions I have drafted or sponsored in which powerful religious agencies have been put on record as opposed to communism. It is evidenced likewise in a life of service and the sponsorship of measures designed to make the free society impregnable to communist attack.

Loyalty to my family, my church, and my country are fundamental to me; and when any man or any Committee questions that loyalty, I doubt that I would be worthy of the name American if I took it lying down.

I then proceeded to certain considerations that I stated "I desire to lay before this Committee":

Bishop G. Bromley Oxnam (1891–1963)
(Methodist Information Services)

First, this Committee has followed a practice of releasing unverified and unevaluated material designated as "information" to citizens, organizations, and Members of Congress. It accepts no responsibility for the accuracy of the newspaper clippings recorded and so released; and insists that the material does not represent an opinion or a conclusion of the Committee. This material, officially released on official letterheads and signed by an official clerk, carried no disclaimer, in my case, and the recipient understandably assumed it did represent a conclusion. I am here formally to request that this "file" be cleaned up, that the Committee frankly admit its inaccuracies and misrepresentations, and that this matter be brought to a close.

It is alleged that the Committee has "files" on a million individuals, many of whom are among the most respected, patriotic, and devoted citizens of this nation. This is not the proper place to raise question as to the propriety of maintaining such vast "files" at public expense; but it is the proper place, in my case, to request that the practice of releasing unverified and unevaluated material, for which the Committee accepts no responsibility, cease. It can be shown that these reports are the result of inexcusable incompetence or of slanted selection, the result being the same in either case, namely, to question loyalty, to pillory or to intimidate the individual, to damage reputation, and to turn attention from the communist conspirator who pursues his nefarious work in the shadows, while a patriotic citizen is disgraced in public. The preparation and publication of these "files" puts into the hands of irresponsible individuals and agencies a wicked tool. It gives rise to a new and vicious expression of Ku-Kluxism, in which an innocent person may be beaten by unknown assailants who are cloaked in anonymity and at times immunity, whose whips are cleverly constructed lists of so-called subversive organizations and whose floggings appear all too often to be sadistic in spirit rather than patriotic in purpose.

Civil Rights and the Churches

Martin Luther King, Jr. (1929–68)

The modern world is short of prophets, not of men and women who predict but of men and women who pronounce, pronounce with awful clarity the demand that God's justice run down like waters and righteousness as a mighty stream. Martin Luther King, Jr., quoted those words from the prophet Amos as well as many other prophetic voices from Old Testament and New. Thus he sought to stir the conscience even of a nation, to move the ponderous

[Sources: (1) M. L. King, Jr., *Why We Can't Wait* (New York: Harper & Row, 1963), pp. 77–79, 81, 83–84. (2) Leon Friedman, ed., *The Civil Rights Reader* (New York: Walker & Co., 1967), pp. 112–13.]

and resistant machinery of government. His cause was civil rights, human freedom, divine justice. King, a Baptist minister in Montgomery, Alabama, gave inspiration to his own black brothers and sisters as he counseled resistance, not violent resistance, but a strong, steady, loving, believing resistance. Right up to the night in April, 1968, when he was assassinated, King never wavered in his own assurance that "We Shall Overcome." Two documents, both King's and both from 1963, reflect the depth and height of emotional intensity at this time. (1) The first comes from a Birmingham jail in April of that year; King had been arrested for leading a protest march in which whites and blacks, Protestants, Catholics, Orthodox, and Jews had all participated. (2) The following August tens of thousands marched to Washington where on the mall near the Washington Monument and beside the Lincoln Memorial King delivered his finest speech.

1.

I think I should indicate why I am here in Birmingham, since you have been influenced by the view which argues against "outsiders coming in."* I have the honor of serving as president of the Southern Christian Leadership Conference, an organization operating in every southern state, with headquarters in Atlanta, Georgia. We have some eighty-five affiliated organizations across the South, and one of them is the Alabama Christian Movement for Human Rights. Frequently we share staff, educational and financial resources with our affiliates. Several months ago the affiliate here in Birmingham asked us to be on call to engage in a nonviolent direct-action program if such were deemed necessary. We readily consented, and when the hour came we lived up to our promise. So I, along with several members of my staff, am here because I was invited here. I am here because I have organizational ties here.

But more basically, I am in Birmingham because injustice is here. Just as the prophets of the eighth century B.C. left their villages and carried their "thus saith the Lord" far beyond the boundaries of their home towns, and just as the Apostle Paul left his village of Tarsus and carried the gospel of Jesus Christ to the far corners of the Greco-Roman world, so am I compelled to carry the gospel of freedom beyond my own home town. Like Paul, I must constantly respond to the Macedonian call for aid.

Moreover, I am cognizant of the interrelatedness of all communities and states. I cannot sit idly by in Atlanta and not be concerned about what happens in Birmingham. Injustice anywhere is a threat to justice everywhere. We are caught in an inescapable network of mutuality, tied in a single garment of destiny. Whatever affects one directly, affects all indirectly. Never again can we afford to live with the narrow, provincial "outside agitator" idea. Anyone

*This letter was written in response to eight Alabama clergymen who signed a statement protesting the march.

who lives inside the United States can never be considered an outsider any-where within its bounds.

You deplore the demonstrations taking place in Birmingham. But your statement, I am sorry to say, fails to express a similar concern for the conditions that brought about the demonstrations. I am sure that none of you would want to rest content with the superficial kind of social analysis that deals merely with effects and does not grapple with underlying causes. It is unfortunate that demonstrations are taking place in Birmingham, but it is even more unfortunate that the city's white power structure left the Negro community with no alternative. . . .

You may well ask: "Why direct action? Why sit-ins, marches and so forth? Isn't negotiation a better path?" You are quite right in calling for negotiation. Indeed, this is the very purpose of direct action. Nonviolent direct action seeks to create such a crisis and foster such a tension that a community which has constantly refused to negotiate is forced to confront the issue. It seeks so to dramatize the issue that it can no longer be ignored. My citing the creation of tension as part of the work of the nonviolent-resister may sound rather shocking. But I must confess that I am not afraid of the word "tension." I have earnestly opposed violent tension, but there is a type of constructive non-violent tension which is necessary for growth. . . .

We have waited for more than 340 years for our constitutional and God-given rights. The nations of Asia and Africa are moving with jetlike speed toward gaining political independence, but we still creep at horse-and-buggy pace toward gaining a cup of coffee at a lunch counter. Perhaps it is easy for those who have never felt the stinging darts of segregation to say, "Wait." But when you have seen vicious mobs lynch your mothers and fathers at will and drown your sisters and brothers at whim; when you have seen hate-filled policemen curse, kick and even kill your black brothers and sisters; when you see the vast majority of your twenty million Negro brothers smothering in an airtight cage of poverty in the midst of an affluent society; when you suddenly find your tongue twisted and your speech stammering as you seek to explain to your six-year-old daughter why she can't go to the public amusement park that has just been advertised on television, and see tears welling up in her eyes when she is told that Funtown is closed to colored children, and see ominous clouds of inferiority beginning to form in her little mental sky, and see her beginning to distort her personality by developing an unconscious bitterness toward white people; when you have to concoct an answer for a five-year-old son who is asking: "Daddy, why do white people treat colored people so mean?"; when you take a cross-country drive and find it necessary to sleep night after night in the uncomfortable corners of your automobile because no motel will accept you; when you are humiliated day in and day out by nagging signs reading "white" and "colored"; when your first name becomes "nigger," your middle name becomes "boy" (however old you are) and your last name becomes "John," and your wife and mother are never given the respected title "Mrs."; when you are harried by day and haunted by night by the fact that you are a Negro, living constantly at tiptoe stance, never quite knowing what to expect next, and are plagued with inner fears and outer resentments; when you are forever fighting a degenerating sense of "nobodiness" —then you will understand why we find it difficult to wait. There comes a time when the cup of endurance runs over, and men are no longer willing to be plunged into the abyss of despair. I hope, sirs, you can understand our legitimate and unavoidable impatience.

2.

I say to you today, my friends, that in spite of the difficulties and frustrations of the moment I still have a dream. It is a dream deeply rooted in the American dream.

I have a dream that one day this nation will rise up and live out the true meaning of its creed: "We hold these truths to be self-evident; that all men are created equal."

I have a dream that one day on the red hills of Georgia the sons of former slaves and the sons of former slaveowners will be able to sit down together at the table of brotherhood.

I have a dream that one day even the state of Mississippi, a desert state

Martin Luther King and the march on Selma, Alabama, in 1965
(Religious News Service)

sweltering with the heat of injustice and oppression, will be transformed into an oasis of freedom and justice.

I have a dream that my four little children will one day live in a nation where they will not be judged by the color of their skin but by the content of their character.

I have a dream today.

I have a dream that one day the state of Alabama, whose governor's lips are presently dripping with the words of interposition and nullification, will be transformed into a situation where little black boys and black girls will be able to join hands with little white boys and white girls and walk together as sisters and brothers.

I have a dream today.

I have a dream that one day every valley shall be exalted, every hill and mountain shall be made low, the rough places will be made plains, and the crooked places will be made straight, and the glory of the Lord shall be revealed, and all flesh shall see it together.

This is our hope. This is the faith with which I return to the South. With this faith we will be able to hew out of the mountain of despair a stone of hope. With this faith we will be able to transform the jangling discords of our nation into a beautiful symphony of brotherhood. With this faith we will be able to work together, to pray together, to struggle together, to go to jail together, to stand up for freedom together, knowing that we will be free one day.

This will be the day when all of God's children will be able to sing with new meaning "My country 'tis of thee, sweet land of liberty, of thee I sing. Land where my fathers died, land of the pilgrim's pride, from every mountainside, let freedom ring."

And if America is to be a great nation this must become true. So let freedom ring from the prodigious hilltops of New Hampshire. Let freedom ring from the mighty mountains of New York. Let freedom ring from the heightening Alleghenies of Pennsylvania!

Let freedom ring from the snowcapped Rockies of Colorado!

Let freedom ring from the curvaceous peaks of California!

But not only that; let freedom ring from Stone Mountain of Georgia!

Let freedom ring from Lookout Mountain of Tennessee!

Let freedom ring from every hill and mole hill of Mississippi. From every mountainside, let freedom ring.

When we let freedom ring, when we let it ring from every village and every hamlet, from every state and every city, we will be able to speed up that day when all of God's children, black men and white men, Jews and Gentiles, Protestants and Catholics, will be able to join hands and sing in the words of the old Negro spiritual, "Free at last! free at last! thank God almighty, we are free at last!"

Black Manifesto, 1969

*The year after King's death the religious institutions of America found them-
selves challenged roughly by a group of black leaders identified with the
National Black Economic Development Conference (Detroit, April 1969).
Under the leadership of James Forman (b. 1928), the Conference adopted
a manifesto addressed "To the White Christian Churches and the Synagogues
in the United States of America and to All Other Racist Institutions." The
rhetoric had grown sharper and the demand for justice had received a price
tag: 500 million dollars in reparations "to the black people in this country."
This amounts only to about fifteen dollars per black in America and is but
"a beginning of the reparations due us as people who have been exploited and
degraded, brutalized, killed and persecuted." The concluding section of the
manifesto follows.*

Brothers and sisters, we are no longer shuffling our feet and scratching our
heads. We are tall, black and proud.

And we say to the white Christian churches and Jewish synagogues, to the
government of this country and to all the white racist imperialists who compose it, there is only one thing left that you can do to further degrade black
people and that is to kill us. But we have been dying too long for this country.
We have died in every war. We are dying in Vietnam today fighting the
wrong enemy.

The new black man wants to live, and to live means that we must not
become static or merely believe in self-defense. We must boldly go out and
attack the white Western world at its power centers. The white Christian
churches are another form of government in this country, and they are used
by the government of this country to exploit the people of Latin America,
Asia and Africa, but the day is soon coming to an end. Therefore, brothers
and sisters, the demands we make upon the white Christian churches and the
Jewish synagogues are small demands. They represent fifteen dollars per black
person in these United States. We can legitimately demand this from the
church power structure. We must demand more from the United States
Government.

But to win our demands from the church, which is linked up with the
United States Government, we must not forget that it will ultimately be by
force and power that we will win.

We are not threatening the churches. We are saying that we know the
churches came with the military might of the colonizers and have been sustained by the military might of the colonizers. Hence, if the churches in
colonial territories were established by military might, we know deep within
our hearts that we must be prepared to use force to get our demands. We are

[Source: R. S. Lecky and H. E. Wright, eds., *Black Manifesto: Religion, Racism, and
Reparations* (New York: Sheed & Ward, 1969), pp. 125–26.]

not saying that this is the road we want to take. It is not, but let us be very clear that we are not opposed to force and we are not opposed to violence. We were captured in Africa by violence. We were kept in bondage and political servitude and forced to work as slaves by the military machinery and the Christian Church working hand in hand.

We recognize that in issuing this Manifesto we must prepare for a long-range educational campaign in all communities of this country, but we know that the Christian churches have contributed to our oppression in white America. We do not intend to abuse our black brothers and sisters in black churches who have uncritically accepted Christianity. We want them to understand how the racist white Christian church with its hypocritical declarations and doctrines of brotherhood has abused our trust and faith. An attack on the religious beliefs of black people is not our major objective, even though we know that we were not Christians when we were brought to this country, but that Christianity was used to help enslave us. Our objective in issuing this Manifesto is to force the racist white Christian church to begin the payment of reparations which are due to all black people, not only by the church but also by private business and the United States government. We see this focus on the Christian church as an effort around which all black people can unite.

Black Manifesto spokesman James Forman seized office space belonging to the National Council of Churches and United Presbyterian Board of Missions, New York City, 1969. *(Religious News Service)*

Response to Racism & Manifesto

Among other things, the Black Manifesto urged that on Sunday, May 4, 1969, blacks around the country "commence the disruption of the racist churches and synagogues throughout the United States." This was confrontation of the most direct sort, with James Forman himself disrupting the services of New York's Riverside Church. Institutional response to this tactic was uniformly negative. The Roman Catholic Archdiocese of New York replied that "we do not endorse the 'Black Manifesto' and its demands." The Synagogue Council of America declared: "We find the demands and the tactics objectionable on both moral and practical grounds." And Riverside Church let it be known that "we have received from the courts a Civil Restraining Order that could place any individual in contempt of court who interfered with our worship of Almighty God or otherwise sought to render the Riverside Church inoperative." All of the above institutions, however, separated the immediate challenge from the underlying and persisting problem of racism. And all pledged themselves to renewed effort to alleviate that "degradation and hopelessness that still afflict the lives of so many of our fellow citizens." A portion of the Synagogue Council statement (together with the National Jewish Community Relations Advisory Council) follows, the statement being dated May 12, 1969.

Two separate issues have been raised by the "Black Manifesto": one by the substance of the demands, the other by the tactics employed to advance them. We find the demands and the tactics objectionable on both moral and practical grounds.

(1) The Demands

It is evident that much remains to be done if the racial discrimination that has shamed our American past is to be wiped out. We believe that it is entirely in order for our religious and communal institutions — no less than other segments of our society — to be challenged, both from within and from without, to face up to their own shortcomings and responsibilities. The gap between principle and performance is lamentably large; we have fallen short of our responsibilities in working for racial and economic justice.

We submit, on the other hand, that the demands for reparations by the Black Economic Development Conference is not an answer to the inequities and injustices of our society. It is clear that even if these demands were met in full, these inequities and injustices would not be rectified. . . .

What is required is massive government action in the areas of employment, housing, education, health and welfare. To say this is not to shirk personal

[Source: R. S. Lecky and H. E. Wright, eds., *Black Manifesto: Religion, Racism, and Reparations* (New York: Sheed & Ward, 1969), pp. 141, 142–43.]

or organizational responsibility, for such action can come about only if we as citizens declare and press our determination to pay the substantial costs that are involved. . . .

The Synagogue Council of America, through its newly established division of urban affairs, the National Jewish Community Relations Advisory Council and their national constituent agencies are prepared to assist synagogues and communal institutions in the implementation of these goals.

(2) The Tactics

The tactics resorted to by spokesmen for the Black Economic Development Conference in advancing their demands must also receive our serious attention, for these tactics involve disruption of divine services, demands for "ransom," and threats of violence.

We recognize that Americans "can no longer speak of 'violence' and 'extremism' without the terrible knowledge that their most destructive manifestation in American life is to be found in the violence done to the lives, the hopes and aspirations of our Negro citizens" (SCA policy statement March 6, 1968). It is equally true, however, that even in pursuit of desirable ends, violence does not contribute to the fashioning of a better society; violence only breeds more violence and nourishes repression, not justice.

We further express our conviction that the values by which men's actions and goals are judged are not subject to the exigencies of time and certainly not to those of race. The "revolution" in our cities and on our campuses does not create its own morality. The exegesis which enables some religious leaders to suspend biblical injunctions against violence, arson and murder and to invest these with a special grace when committed in the name of the "revolution" has no sanction in Jewish tradition.

If we speak up at this time, it is not only to clarify our position in regard to the demands and the tactics of the Black Economic Development Conference, but to urge that reprehensible actions not be permitted to divert our attention from the hard tasks which require our efforts and resources if our moral and religious professions are to be taken seriously. By implementing the specific actions outlined above, synagogues and communal institutions will give tangible expression of their commitment to the elimination of the poverty, degradation and hopelessness that still afflict the lives of so many of our fellow citizens.

Politics and Religion

"A Roman Catholic for President?"

The question of a Catholic president raised memories of 1928 (see above, p. 271) and fears of unknown tomorrows. In both 1928 and 1960, the question sometimes met with reason and careful argument, at other times with passion and prejudice unchecked. A singularly well-informed authority, John C. Bennett (b. 1902), professor and president at Union Theological Seminary in New York City, wrote from the vantage point of one thoroughly versed in Christian ethics. Bennett was also keenly attuned to the rapidly beating pulse of a non-Catholic public facing the direct issue of a Catholic president in the person of John F. Kennedy.

The issue raised by the possibility of a Roman Catholic candidate for the Presidency is the most significant immediate problem that grows out of the confrontation of Roman Catholicism with other religious communities in the United States. There are a great many Protestants of influence who are inclined to say that they would never vote for a Roman Catholic for President. Many of them refuse to say this with finality, but there is a strong trend in this direction. Our guess is that it may be stronger among the clergy and among official Protestant spokesmen than among the laity.

Aside from crude forms of prejudice and a reluctance to accept the fact that this is no longer a Protestant country, there are two considerations behind this position that have some substance. The first is that the traditional teaching of the Catholic Church is at variance with American conceptions of religious liberty and of church-state relations. There is a fear that a Catholic President might be used by a politically powerful Catholic Church to give that church the preferred position to which, according to its tradition, it believes itself entitled.

The other consideration is that there are a few specific issues on which there is a Catholic position, and, short of any basic change in our institutions, the nation's legislation and policy might be deflected by a Catholic President toward these known positions of his church. One example that is not often mentioned is the intransigent view of the problems of the cold war that was expressed in the American Catholic Bishops' statement late in 1959. (We would not vote for any man, Protestant or Catholic, who takes such a view.)

On matters of this kind most Catholics are more likely to be affected by the position taken by the authorities of their church than would a Protestant.

[Source: J. C. Bennett, in *Christianity & Crisis* (Mar. 7, 1960), reprinted in W. H. Cowan, ed., *Witness to a Generation* (Indianapolis: Bobbs-Merrill, 1966), pp. 62–63, 64–65.]

Even though they may not agree with the bishops, it would be embarrassing to oppose them publicly. Catholic bishops do their debating privately; American Catholicism on the hierarchical level, therefore, gives the impression of a united front that no Protestant churches are able to give.

We want to direct three comments to those who take a negative view concerning a possible Roman Catholic President:

(1) If the American people should make it clear that a Catholic could never be elected President, this would be an affront to 39,500,000 of our fellow citizens, and it would suggest that full participation in American political life is denied to them as Catholics. This would be true even though Catholics are governors, senators, congressmen and Supreme Court justices. We believe that this situation would wound our common life and damage our institutions more grievously than it would be possible for a Catholic President to do even if he chose to. We are shocked that so many Protestants seem unwilling to give any weight to this.

(2) We are justified in ascertaining what view of church-state relations and of the basis of religious liberty a particular Catholic candidate holds. We may learn this without grilling him, for his record of public service and its implications would be an open book.

There are two main views of religious liberty that are held among Catholics. The traditional view regards as normative the idea of a Catholic state with the church in a privileged position and with at least a curtailment of the liberties of non-Catholics. This view is an inheritance from an earlier period of history, and many Catholic theologians and ecclesiastical leaders now reject it. They believe in religious liberty for non-Catholics on principle and not merely as a matter of pragmatic adjustment to the American situation.

This more liberal view is not limited to this country; it is held widely in Western Europe. It is one view held in Vatican circles. Those who hold this view believe that Pius XII was at least open to it, and they are even more sure that this is true of his generous-minded successor. . . .

(3) So far as the specific issues on which there is a known Catholic position are concerned, there are very few that come to the desk of the President. More of them are dealt with by mayors and governors, and the Republic has survived many Catholic mayors and governors. And on many issues within the purview of the President, the Catholic community is divided — even, for example, on the appointment of an ambassador to the Vatican. (It was a Baptist who made the latest appointment to the Vatican.) Furthermore, a President is subjected to so many pressures and counterpressures that he is less vulnerable to any one form of pressure than most other public servants.

There is the vexing problem of birth control. As a domestic problem it belongs chiefly to the states, and it is fortunate that many Catholics, while they do not reject their church's position on birth control in terms of morals and theology, do not believe there should be a civil law that imposes the Catholic moral teaching upon non-Catholics. . . .

We should like to add to these considerations a more positive note: a Catholic President who is well instructed in the moral teachings of his church would have certain assets. (It is chiefly in the areas of sex and medicine that the Protestant finds elements of an intolerable legalism in Catholic moral teaching.) If he is of an essentially liberal spirit he may absorb the best in the real humanism of Catholic thought.

A Catholic President might have a better perspective on the issue of social justice than many Protestants. He might be guided by the ethical inhibitions present in Catholic views of the just war so as to resist the temptation to make military necessity paramount in all matters of national strategy. He might have a wiser and more seasoned understanding of the claims of the person in relation to the community than many a one-sided Protestant individualist.

We are not now speaking of any particular Catholic candidate, and there are elements in Catholic moral doctrine that we reject. When these are interpreted by the narrower type of ecclesiastic, we often find them repellent. But Catholic teaching has its better and more humane side, and it is the repository of much wisdom that could stand a Catholic President in good stead.

"It Is My Job to Face It . . ."

"The religious issue," as John F. Kennedy noted, would not go away in the campaign for the presidency in 1960. It was raised as Kennedy sought the nomination of the Democratic party, then raised more widely and vociferously once that nomination was his. Ignoring the issue did not dispose of it. Kennedy therefore concluded that it was his job "to face it frankly and fully." He did so on three occasions: in Washington, D. C., in April before the Society of American Newspaper Editors; in Los Angeles in July after winning the Democratic nomination; and in Houston before the Ministerial Association in September, less than two months before the election. The remarks below are from the first of the three occasions.

I have decided, in view of current press reports, that it would be appropriate to speak with you today about what has widely been called "the religious issue" in American politics.

The phrase covers a multitude of meanings. There is no religious issue in the sense that any of the major candidates differ on the role of religion in our political life. Every Presidential contender, I am certain, is dedicated to the separation of church and state, to the preservation of religious liberty, to an

[Source: Moses Rischin, ed., *Immigration and the American Tradition* (Indianapolis: Bobbs-Merrill, 1976), pp. 414–15, 416–17, 418–19, 420–21.]

end to religious bigotry, and to the total independence of the officeholder from any form of ecclesiastical dictation.

Nor is there any real issue in the sense that any candidate is exploiting his religious affiliation. No one's candidacy, by itself, raises a religious issue. And I believe it is inaccurate to state that my "candidacy created the issue."

Nor am I appealing, as is too often claimed, to a so-called Catholic vote. Even if such a vote exists — which I doubt — I want to make one thing clear again: I want no votes solely on account of my religion. Any voter, Catholic or otherwise, who feels another candidate would be a superior President should support that candidate. I do not want any vote cast for me for such illogical and irrelevant reasons.

Neither do I want anyone to support my candidacy merely to prove that this nation is not bigoted — and that a Catholic can be elected President. I have never suggested that those opposed to me are thereby anti-Catholic. . . .

For the past month and years I have answered almost daily inquiries from the press about the religious issue. I want to take this opportunity to turn the tables — and to raise some questions for your thoughtful consideration.

First: Is the religious issue a legislative issue in this campaign?

There is only one legitimate question underlying all the rest: Would you, as President of the United States, be responsive in any way to ecclesiastical pressures or obligations of any kind that might in any fashion influence or interfere with your conduct of that office in the national interest? I have answered that question many times. My answer was — and is — "No."

Once that question is answered there is no legitimate issue of my religion, but there are, I think, legitimate questions of public policy — of concern to religious groups which no one should feel bigoted about raising, and to which I do not object answering. But I do object to being the only candidate required to answer those questions.

Federal assistance to parochial schools, for example, is a very legitimate issue actually before the Congress. I am opposed to it. I believe it is clearly unconstitutional. I voted against it on the Senate floor this year, when offered by Senator Morse. But interestingly enough, I was the only announced candidate in the Senate who did so. Nevertheless, I have not yet charged my opponents with taking orders from Rome.

An Ambassador to the Vatican could conceivably become a real issue again. I am opposed to it, and said so long ago. But even though it was last proposed by a Baptist President, I know of no other candidate who has been even asked about this matter.

The prospects of any President ever receiving for his signature a bill providing foreign aid funds for birth control are very remote indeed. It is hardly the major issue some have suggested. Nevertheless, I have made it clear that I would neither veto nor sign such a bill on any basis except what I considered to be the public interest, without regard to my private religious views. I have said the same about bills dealing with censorship, divorce, our relations with Spain or any other subject.

These are legitimate inquiries about real questions which the next President may conceivably have to face. But these inquiries ought to be directed equally to all candidates.

Secondly, can we justify analyzing voters as well as candidates strictly in terms of their religion? I think the voters of Wisconsin objected to being categorized simply as either Catholics or Protestants in analyzing their political choices. I think they objected to being accosted by reporters outside of political meetings and asked one question only — their religion — not their occupation or education or philosophy or income — only their religion. . . .

The voters are more than Catholics, Protestants or Jews. They make up their minds for many diverse reasons, good and bad. To submit the candidates to a religious test is unfair — to apply it to the voters themselves is divisive, degrading and wholly unwarranted.

Third and finally: Is there any justification for applying special religious tests to one office only? The Presidency? Little or no attention was paid to my religion when I took the oath as Senator in 1953 — as a Congressman in 1947 — or as a naval officer in 1941. Members of my faith abound in public office at every level except the White House. What is there about the Presidency that justifies this constant emphasis upon a candidate's religion and that of his supporters?

The Presidency is not, after all, the British crown, serving a dual capacity in both church and state. The President is not elected to be protector of the faith — or guardian of the public morals. His attendance at church on Sunday should be his business alone, not a showcase for the nation.

On the other hand, we are in no danger of a one-man Constitutional upheaval. The President, however intent he may be on subverting our institutions, cannot ignore the Congress — or the voters — or the courts. And our highest court, incidentally, has a long history of Catholic justices, none of whom, as far as I know, was ever challenged on the fairness of his ruling on sensitive church-state issues. . . .

If there is bigotry in the country, then so be it — there is bigotry. If that bigotry is too great to permit the fair consideration of a Catholic who has made clear his complete independence and his complete dedication to separation of church and state, then we ought to know it.

But I do not believe this is the case. I believe the American people are more concerned with a man's views and abilities than with the church to which he belongs. I believe that the founding fathers meant it when they provided in Article VI of the Constitution that there should be no religious test for public office — a provision that brought not one dissenting vote, only the comment of Roger Sherman that it was surely unnecessary — "the prevailing liberality being a sufficient security against such tests." And I believe that the American people mean to adhere to those principles today.

But regardless of the political outcome, this issue is here to be faced. It is my job to face it frankly and fully. And it is your job to face it fairly, in perspective and in proportion.

I am confident that the press and the other media of this country will recognize their responsibilities in this area — to refute falsehood, to inform the ignorant, and to concentrate on the issues, the real issues in this hour of the nation's peril.

The Supreme Court has written that as public officials "we are neither Jew nor gentile, neither Catholic nor agnostic. We owe equal attachment to the Constitution and are equally bound by our obligation, whether we derive our citizenship from the earliest or latest immigrants to these shores . . . (for) religion is outside the sphere of political government."

We must all — candidates, press, and voters alike — dedicate ourselves to these principles, for they are the key to a free society.

Moral Responsibility and Religion

The Great Society

Following the assassination of John F. Kennedy in November of 1963, Vice President Lyndon B. Johnson upon assuming the presidency moved quickly in urging Congress to pass major civil rights legislation as a memorial to the fallen leader. Johnson thereafter pressed his war against poverty as an additional step toward what he called "the Great Society." Some churches concluded that it was their responsibility to enlist in that "war," while others saw this emphasis as more the affair of politics or of governmental agencies. A Methodist perspective is provided below.

As a nation, we have the wealth, income, technical know-how and productive capacity to reduce drastically the incidence of poverty in America — serious social, economic, political, and cultural deprivations of individuals and families.

As a nation, we clearly have the capacity to achieve this degree of social justice in our time. What we need is national commitment — a dedication to the task on the part of people, local communities, private organizations (including churches), labor, business, and public authorities at every level of government.

With the passage of Economic Opportunity Act (Public Law 88-452), the Federal Government initiated a national attack on poverty. That government pledged its resources to combat domestic poverty. Under the Act, an Office

[Source: *Concern* (published by the General Board of Christian Social Concerns of The Methodist Church), Dec. 1, 1965, p. 14.]

of Economic Opportunity (OEO) was established to administer national programs. . . .

These OEO programs confront churches with both a challenge and an opportunity. Churches are challenged to commit a substantial portion of their institutional resources to coordinated national, state, and local programs to combat poverty. More important, perhaps, is the unparalleled opportunity the churches now have to demonstrate what love, brotherhood, and human dignity really mean in the context of a responsible society. In imaginative, creative, and sacrificial ways, churches can help establish social, economic, and political relationships which will restore to the poor the satisfaction of belonging to a community in which they can find security and significance. The church will, of course, include the impoverished in all efforts to develop Christian fellowship.

It seems unlikely that churches can either fully meet the challenge or take advantage of the opportunity offered by OEO programs to combat poverty without becoming more involved in formal relations with government, particularly at the local level. Therefore, the General Board of Christian Social Concerns recommends:

1. That national agencies, annual conferences, and local congregations of The Methodist Church cooperate with and supplement the efforts of agencies of government to eradicate poverty, through means such as:

   a. serving as participants in policy-shaping and project-implementation where community anti-poverty programs are under way;

   b. acting as a catalyst in the initiation of anti-poverty programs in communities where such programs have not yet been undertaken;

   c. supporting the involvement of the poor in anti-poverty policy and program development;

   d. working for the strengthening and improvement of the legislative framework for the struggle against poverty.

2. That, if churches find it desirable to enter into contractual relationships with government and to accept public funds, the following principles should govern that relationship:

   a. Churches should seek no self-aggrandisement.

   b. The Methodist Church and its local congregations should seek out other religious and secular institutions in the community with which to cooperate in the development of comprehensive programs.

   c. The decisions to cooperate should rest with the official governing body of the institution, but this body may find it desirable to establish a non-profit organization to implement its purposes. Where such organizations are established, churches should make careful provisions for continuing liaison.

   d. Before entering into any such contractual relationship, the official governing body of the church or agency should become familiar with the governmental principles and regulations involved as stated in Public Law 88-452 and the regulations pertaining thereto.

We believe that The Methodist Church and its congregations should support the officially stated objectives of the War on Poverty. At the same time, we urge churches and church-related organizations to give careful and continuing consideration to the possibility that religious principles or the integrity of government may be compromised in such supportive arrangements as may be evolved. Such a result must be avoided. We urge The Methodist Church and all of its agencies to maintain a continuing responsibility for assuring that the stated purposes of the Act are adhered to faithfully at the same time that every effort is made to insure the greatest possible effect in eradicating poverty.

The Betrayed Society

On August 9, 1974, for the first time in America's history a president of the United States resigned from that high office. The word "Watergate" had by then come to symbolize corruption, cover-up, and abuse of power. Richard M. Nixon, said the House of Representatives Judiciary Committee, "has acted in a manner contrary to his trust as President and subversive of constitutional government, to the great prejudice of the cause of law and justice and to the manifest injury of the people of the United States." Words such as "trust" and "justice" and phrases such as Breach of Faith (Theodore White, 1975) suggested an ethical element, perhaps even a religious element in this national tragedy. Where the repentance, the atonement, the reconciliation? Where or what was the moral hidden away in this long national nightmare (as newly inaugurated President Gerald Ford had called it)? Chair of the Senate Select Committee to investigate the sorry episode, Sam J. Ervin, Jr. (1896–1985), in submitting the committee's final report added his own "Meditations." Ervin, Presbyterian layman and "simple country lawyer" (Harvard bachelor of law in 1922), took a long look into the lessons of history and a deep gaze into the nature of man.

Unlike the men who were responsible for Teapot Dome, the presidential aides who perpetrated Watergate were not seduced by the love of money, which is sometimes thought to be the root of all evil. On the contrary, they were instigated by a lust for political power, which is at least as corrupting as political power itself.

They gave their allegiance to the President and his policies. They had stood for a time near to him, and had been entrusted by him with great governmental and political power. They enjoyed exercising such power, and longed for its continuance.

[Source: Sam J. Ervin, Jr., *The Whole Truth: The Watergate Conspiracy* (New York: Random House, 1980), pp. 310–11, 312.]

They knew that the power they enjoyed would be lost and the policies to which they adhered would be frustrated if the President should be defeated.

As a consequence of these things, they believed the President's reelection to be a most worthy objective, and succumbed to an age-old temptation. They resorted to evil means to promote what they conceived to be a good end.

Their lust for political power blinded them to ethical considerations and legal requirements; to Aristotle's aphorism that the good of man must be the end of politics; and to Grover Cleveland's conviction that a public office is a public trust.

They had forgotten, if they ever knew, that the Constitution is designed to be a law for rulers and people alike at all times and under all circumstances; and that no doctrine involving more pernicious consequences to the commonweal has ever been invented by the wit of man than the notion that any of its provisions can be suspended by the President for any reason whatsoever.

On the contrary, they apparently believed that the President is above the Constitution, and has the autocratic power to suspend its provisions if he decides in his own unreviewable judgment that his action in so doing promotes his own political interests or the welfare of the nation. As one of them testified before the Senate Select Committee, they believed that the President has the autocratic power to suspend the Fourth Amendment whenever he imagines that some indefinable aspect of national security is involved.

I digress to reject this doctrine of the constitutional omnipotence of the President. As long as I have a mind to think, a tongue to speak, and a heart to love my country, I shall deny that the Constitution confers any autocratic power on the President, or authorizes him to convert George Washington's America into Gaius Caesar's Rome.

The lust for political power of the presidential aides who perpetrated Watergate on America blinded them to the laws of God as well as to the laws and ethics of man.

As a consequence, they violated the spiritual law which forbids men to do evil even when they think good will result from it, and ignored these warnings of the King James version of the Bible:

1. "There is nothing covered, that shall not be revealed; neither hid, that shall not be known."

2. "Be not deceived; God is not mocked: For whatsoever a man soweth, that shall he also reap."

I find corroboration for my conclusion that lust for political power produced Watergate in words uttered by the most eloquent and learned of all the Romans, Marcus Tullius Cicero, about 2100 years ago. He said:

"Most men, however, are inclined to forget justice altogether, when once the craving for military power or political honors and glory has taken possession of them. Remember the saying of Ennius, 'When crowns are at stake, no friendship is sacred, no faith shall be kept.' " . . .

Since politics is the art or science of government, no man is fit to participate in politics or to seek or hold public office unless he has two characteristics.

The first of these characteristics is that he must understand and be dedicated to the true purpose of government, which is to promote the good of the people, and entertain the abiding conviction that a public office is a public trust, which must never be abused to secure private advantage.

The second characteristic is that he must possess that intellectual and moral integrity, which is the priceless ingredient in good character.

When all is said, the only sure antidote for future Watergates is understanding of fundamental principles and intellectual and moral integrity in the men and women who achieve or are entrusted with governmental or political power.

4. REVIVALISM AND RETREAT

Postwar Revivalism: Billy Graham

Postwar recovery seemed to include a recovery for organized religion in America: church membership increased, attendance improved, prosperity returned. The 1950s were good years —stable, peaceful, with return to the traditional values of family (the baby boom), of decency (the Eisenhower years), of church (the Billy Graham revivals). Graham (b. 1918), North Carolina native and Baptist evangelist, rose to national prominence in the early fifties, particularly after a successful revival meeting or "crusade" in Los Angeles at the very end of the previous decade. "To me it was like a bolt of lightning out of a clear sky," Graham wrote ten years later of his swift rise to fame. "I was bewildered, challenged and humbled by the sudden avalanche of opportunities that deluged me." In 1960, looking back over that exciting decade and his own large part in it, Graham reflected upon his development and growing confidence.

The lessons of this decade have been staggering. Many of my original concepts and convictions have become more certain; others have been amplified, enlarged and changed.

First, I recognize more clearly today than I did ten years ago the narrow limits assigned to the evangelist. I take as my definition of evangelism the classic one formed by the Archbishop of Canterbury's Committee of 1918: "To evangelize is so to present Christ Jesus in the power of the Holy Spirit that men shall come to put their trust in God through Him, to accept Him as their Savior and serve Him as their King in the fellowship of His Church."

One of the best definitions of evangelism is that formulated by representatives of 30 Protestant communions at the 1946 meeting in Columbus, Ohio, of the executive committee of the old Federal Council of Churches. It reads: "Evangelism is the presentation of the good news of God in Jesus Christ so

[Source: Billy Graham, "What Ten Years Have Taught Me," *Christian Century*, Feb. 17, 1960, pp. 186, 187, 188, 189.]

that men are brought through the power of the Holy Spirit to put their trust in God, accept Jesus Christ as their Savior from the guilt and power of sin, to follow and serve Him as their Lord in the fellowship of the church and in the vocations of the common life."

The evangel is the good news that God was in Christ, reconciling the world to himself. The word *evangelism* comes from the word *evangel*, which means "good news" or "gospel." The evangelist is the *keryx*, or the proclaimer of this message. The Scriptures indicate that when Christ gave gifts to his church, one of the gifts was that of the evangelist (Eph. 4:11). Philip was called an evangelist, and Paul told Timothy to do the work of an evangelist. Yet some in the church refuse — to the detriment of the church — to recognize this particular gift that has been given to some men.

The message of the evangelist is "narrow." It does not spread-eagle out into the broad ramifications of a total theology or sociology. Contrary to the opinion of some, the evangelist is not primarily a social reformer, a temperance lecturer or a moralizer. He is simply a *keryx*, a proclaimer of the good news, which in capsule form is "Christ died for our sins according to the Scriptures; . . . was buried, and . . . rose again the third day, according to the Scriptures" (I Cor. 15:3f.). This terse proclamation stretches over the broad frame of man's basic need. It declares that man is a sinner, that Christ is the only Savior, that Christ lives evermore and that the Scriptures are trustworthy. . . .

A second lesson of the past decade: I have come to face realistically the results of mass evangelism. I am convinced that mass evangelism is not the most ideal method of evangelism. There are many methods that the church can effectively use, and mass evangelism is only one of them. Yet it is an important one.

My associates and I have spent a great deal of time and effort in studying the results of our crusades. Personally I am sick of statistics. How can one translate a reconciled home, a transformed drunkard or a new selfless attitude into a cold statistic? The only reason we keep statistics at all is for the sake of accuracy. If no statistics were kept, the press would exaggerate out of all proportion the number of those who respond to the appeal. For several years we spoke of the responses of the people who came forward in our crusades as "decisions," but we have even stopped doing that, for only God knows how many have made a definite commitment to Christ. Now we simply call them "inquirers" — people whose interest is sufficiently strong to cause them to make further inquiry about the Christian life. But of course each of these persons is dealt with as an earnest seeker of salvation, as indeed most of them turn out to be. . . .

In the third place, my faith in earlier theological concepts has deepened. For example, the years have brought a deepening conviction that the Word of God is quick and powerful and a discerner of the thoughts and intents of the heart.

The church has been effective only when it has spoken with authority. Truth begets its own authenticity; if we allow the truth to become adulterated and weakened by rationalisms it loses its power. At one time I grappled with the problem of the authority of the Scriptures. But the problem resolved itself when I finally said, "Lord, I take the Scriptures as thy revealed Word — by faith!" That ended my doubts. From that day to this the Scriptures have been like a rapier in my hand and I am sure that I would be shorn of any effectiveness I may have if this authority were taken from me. Someone will cry "Bibliolatry," but a soldier need not worship his sword to wield it effectively. I have learned with Jeremiah: "Is not my word like as a fire? saith the Lord; and like a hammer that breaketh the rock in pieces?" (Jer. 23:29). I am convinced that the reason some ministers are cracking up is that they have no authority. I am thankful that there is a return to biblical preaching in America. The Scriptures are beginning to return to their rightful place as the authority in the church.

A fourth change is to be seen in the fact that during the past ten years my concept of the church has taken on greater dimension. Ten years ago my concept of the church tended to be narrow and provincial, but after a decade of intimate contact with Christians the world over I am now aware that the family of God contains people of various ethnological, cultural, class and

Evangelist Billy Graham and presidential nominee Richard Nixon in
Pittsburgh, Pennsylvania, in 1968
(Religious News Service)

denominational differences. I have learned that there can even be minor disagreements of theology, methods and motives but that within the true church there is a mysterious unity that overrides all divisive factors.

In groups which in my ignorant piousness I formerly "frowned upon" I have found men so dedicated to Christ and so in love with the truth that I have felt unworthy to be in their presence. I have learned that although Christians do not always agree, they can disagree agreeably, and that what is most needed in the church today is for us to show an unbelieving world that we love one another. To me the church has become a great, glorious and triumphant organism. It is the body of Christ, and the humblest member is an important part of that body. I have also come to believe that within every visible church there is a group of regenerated, dedicated disciples of Christ.

A fifth change: my belief in the social implications of the gospel has deepened and broadened. I am convinced that faith without works is dead. I have never felt that the accusations against me of having no social concern were valid. Often the message of the evangelist is so personal that his statements on social matters are forgotten or left out when reports are made. It is my conviction that even though evangelism is necessarily confined within narrow limits the evangelist must not hedge on social issues. The cost of discipleship must be made plain from the platform. I have made the strongest possible statements on every social issue of our day. In addition, in our crusades we have tried to set an example. (Naturally, there are some statements that I made a few years ago on sociopolitical affairs that I would like to retract.)

Yet I am more convinced than ever before that we must change men before we can change society. The international problems are only reflections of individual problems. Sin is sin, be it personal or social, and the word *repent* is inseparably bound up with evangelism. Social sins, after all, are merely a large-scale projection of individual sins and need to be repented of by the offending segment of society. But the task of the evangelist is not merely to reform but to stimulate conversion, for conversion puts man in a position where God can do for him, and through him, what man is incapable of doing for or by himself.

Sixth, I have an increasing confidence in the ultimate triumph of the kingdom of God. I am convinced that history is not wandering aimlessly, but that there is a plan and purpose in what often seems to us hopeless confusion. God has intervened more than once in history, and there is every reason to believe that he will intervene again. Man may build his towers of Babel, as he always has, and the world may marvel at his genius and his ability to make progress even apart from God, but history shows that ultimately man comes down from his tower in confusion and chaos, disillusioned and frustrated. The Scriptures declare that there is only One whose kingdom shall never end. I believe that when our Lord prayed, "Thy kingdom come, Thy will be done on earth as it is in heaven," he prayed a prayer which is going to be answered. This will come about not by man's efforts within history itself but by a direct, climactic intervention of the sovereign God.

Seventh, the past decade has been a period of ripening tares and ripening wheat. During this interval we have seen a strange paradox that often confused and bewildered me. We have seen a revival of religious interest throughout the United States but an acceleration of crime, divorce and immorality. Within the church there is a new depth of commitment, a new sense of destiny and a spirit of revival, yet in the world there is an intensification of the forces of evil. Crime is on the increase. Fear haunts the council halls of the nations. Wars, hot and cold, are being spawned across the world. Family life is threatened by evil forces. And in many places there is a stark lack of social concern. The tares of evil flourish even in the same field with the growing grain of righteousness. But we forget that Christ said: "In the time of harvest I will say to the reapers, Gather ye first the tares and bind them in bundles and burn them; but gather the wheat into my barn" (Matt. 13:30). The wheat and the tares are destined to grow side by side; when wheat is sown, the Devil sows tares. But a day of separation, an ultimate triumph for truth and righteousness, is coming.

Theological Retreat

Peace and Positive Thoughts

Once the conquest of Hitler's, Hirohito's, and Mussolini's forces was accomplished, religious leaders gave their attention to a conquest of inner turmoil and doubt. Turning from catechism to comfort, popular religion offered assurance that peace can be achieved not only on the battlefield but as well in the recesses of mind and soul. Rabbi Joshua Loth Liebman led off in 1946 with his widely read Peace of Mind, *observing that "it remains only for man to hearken to these divine reverberations in his own soul." The Reverend Norman Vincent Peale (see above, p. 253) provided* A Guide to Confident Living *in 1948, this to be followed four years later by the spectacularly successful* Power of Positive Thinking. *Dr. Billy Graham also entered the list with his* Peace with God *(1953), declaring therein: "In Christ we are relaxed and at peace in the midst of confusions, bewilderments, and perplexities of this life. The storm rages, but our hearts are at rest." On national television, few if any could compete with the dramatic "presence" of Monsignor Fulton J. Sheen (1895 – 1979) on the "Catholic Hour" and, in the 1950s, on a program entitled "Is Life Worth Living?" In 1949, Sheen published both* Way to Happiness *and* Peace of Soul. *An excerpt from the latter describes this peace as one of the several effects of conversion.*

[Source: F. J. Sheen, *Peace of Soul* (New York: McGraw Hill, 1949), pp. 286– 89.]

The new certitude of the convert, then, is a precious thing and very different from the abandonment of will and intellect some imagine it to be. But the full tale of the benefits from conversion is not ended. We must speak of another christening gift — *peace of soul*. There is a world of difference between peace of mind and peace of soul. Peace of mind is the result of bringing *some* ordering principle to bear on discordant human experiences; this may be achieved by tolerance, or by a gritting of one's teeth in the face of pain; by killing conscience, or denying guilt, or by finding new loves to assuage old griefs. Each of these is an integration, but on a very low level. This kind of peace Our Lord calls false, and He likens it to living under the dominion of Satan: "When a strong man armed keepeth his court, those things are in peace which he possesseth" (Luke 11:21). It is the peace of those who have convinced themselves they are animals; the peace of the stone-deaf whom no word of truth can pierce; the peace of the blind who guard themselves against every ray of heavenly light. It is the false peace of the slothful servant who had the same talent at the end as at the beginning because he ignored the judgment which would demand an account of his stewardship. It is the false peace of the man who built his house on the shifting road, so that it vanished with the floods and the storms. With such false peace of mind, Satan tempts his victims; he makes it seem refined to the refined, sensual to the sensual, and coarse to the coarse.

Conversion brings the soul out of either chaos or this false peace of mind to true peace of soul. "Peace I leave with you, my peace I give unto you: not as the world giveth, do I give unto you. Let not your heart be troubled, nor let it be afraid" (John 14:27). This true peace is born of the tranquillity of order, wherein the senses are subject to the reason, the reason to faith, and the whole personality to the Will of God. The true peace that follows conversion is deepened, not disturbed, by the crosses, checks, and disquietudes of the world, for they are all welcomed as coming from the hands of the Loving Father. This true peace can never come from adjustment to the world, for if the world is wicked, adjustments to wickedness make us worse. It comes only from identification of one's own will with the Will of God.

The peaceful soul does not seek, now, to live morally, but to live for God; morality is only a by-product of the union with Him. This peace unites the soul with his neighbor, prompting him to visit the sick, to feed the hungry and clothe the naked; for by loving another soul one gives to God.

The only real pain the convert now has is his inability to do more for the love of God. It is easy to fulfill the claims of lesser ideals, such as Humanism, and their disciples very quickly become complacent; they are already as virtuous as their code asks them to be. It is very easy to be a good Humanist, but it is very hard to be a true follower of Christ. Yet it is not the memory of *past* sins which creates this pain amid the peace, but present shortcomings: because he loves so much, the convert feels as if he had done nothing. What gift can ever be an expression of this new love? If he could give God the universe, even that would not be enough.

All the energy that was previously wasted in conflict — either in trying to find the purpose of life or in trying alone and futilely to conquer his vices — can now be released to serve a single purpose. Regret, remorse, fears, and the anxieties that flowed from sin now completely vanish in repentance. The convert no longer regrets what he might have been; the Holy Spirit fills his soul with a constant presentiment of what he can become through grace. This spiritual recuperation is accompanied by hope, at no matter what age the change occurs — although the convert always regrets that he waited so long. As St. Augustine said, "Too late, O ancient beauty, have I loved thee." But since grace rejuvenates, it quickens even the old to consecrated service.

And there are many other ways in which peace of soul will manifest itself after conversion: it makes somebodies out of nobodies by giving them a service of Divine Sonship; it roots out anger, resentments, and hate by overcoming sin; it gives the convert faith in other people, whom he now sees as potential sons of God; it improves his health by curing the ills that sprang from a disordered, unhappy, and restless mind; for trials and difficulties, it gives him the aid of Divine power; it brings him at all times a sense of harmony with the universe; it sublimates his passions; it makes him fret less about the spiritual shortcomings of the world because he is engrossed in seeking his own spiritualization; it enables the soul to live in a constant consciousness of God's presence, as the earth, in its flight about the sun, carries its own atmosphere with it. In business, in the home, in household duties, in the factory, all actions are done in the sight of God, all thoughts revolve about His Truths. The unreasoning blame, the false accusations, the jealousies and bitterness of others are borne patiently, as our Lord bore them, so that love might reign and that God might be glorified in the bitter as in the sweet. Dependence on Him becomes strength; one no longer fears to undertake good works, knowing He will supply the means. But above all else, with this deep sense of peace, there is the gift of perseverance, which inspires us never to let down our guard, or to shrink from difficulties, or to be depressed as the soul presses on to its supernal vocation in Christ Jesus, Our Lord.

The Death of God

The 1960s, turbulent and antiauthority in so many ways, made no exception for that normally staid and stodgy discipline of theology. With free speech movements, political protests, anti-Vietnam riots, and televised trials, the "death of God" theology took its place. For a few years, theology was again suitable for public discussion, though the discussion now concerned the futility or marginality of the hoary discipline. As William Hamilton (b. 1924) noted in 1966, the theologian in America today is "a man without faith, without hope, with only the present, with only love to guide him." Hamilton, at that time on the faculty of Colgate Rochester Divinity School, joined with such others as Thomas J. Altizer, Paul Van Buren, A. J. Robinson, Gabriel Vahanian, Richard Rubenstein, and Leslie Dewart to explain this new and somewhat unnerving stance with respect to the current task of theology — or at least of "radical theology." In the excerpt below, Hamilton responds to specific questions about this theology whose object of investigation no longer survives.

Question 1: What God is referred to in the phrase the "death of God"?

The "death of God," as the radicals use it, does not mean that some ways of thinking or talking about God in traditional Christianity are done for. It means that no ways are possible. The "God" meant in the phrase "death of God" is the God in the phrase "I believe in God the Father Almighty, Maker of heaven and earth." The God whose death is believed in is the Christian God. "Death of God" does not refer to a disappearance of a psychological capacity. Let me put it this way. Faith in God in the classical Christian tradition has always meant this: an act of passionate, personal daring and courage can be made, and when it is made, a real other is made known, over against man, making demands and making Himself known. This is the meaning of faith in God. It is this God of faith, known in this way (as against the God of religion or culture) who is no more.

Question 2: Are radical theologians Christians?

Yes, because the "death of God" is now (mainly but not entirely) being talked about by Christians. Yes, because it is the Christian God that is referred to in the phrase. Yes, because the "death of God" is an affirmation that does not disable or block, but acts as enabling things, making possible Christian allegiance not possible along other lines. But what is the proper definition of a Christian in this context? Two answers can be given. In one sense, the Christian is defined by his choice of comrades. Whom does he seek out?

[Source: J. L. Ice and J. J. Carey, *The Death of God Debate* (Philadelphia: Westminster Press, 1967), pp. 213–15.]

Whose questions and answers are his? Who makes the noises he wishes to make? "Death of God" is a Christian affirmation in this sense. The Christian is also a man in relation to Jesus, and the radical theologian affirming the "death of God" claims to be Christian in this second sense as well.

Question 3: Would the radical theologians call themselves agnostics, or atheists, or antitheists?

"Atheist" would be the closest. Agnostic suggests maybe, and "death of God" is not a maybe theology. Antitheism suggests an aggressiveness about others' views that the radicals don't have. But if they are atheists, they are atheists with a difference. Perhaps the difference can be put in this way. Traditional atheism believes that there is now no God and that there never has been, beliefs in God of the past being deception, ignorance, fear. Radical theology believes that there was once a time (Bible, sixteenth century, for example) when having a god was appropriate, possible, even necessary. But now is not such a time. There was once, and is not now. The present of the radical is like that of the atheist, but the memories are different. The radical can say yes to the Christian past; the atheist cannot.

Question 4:   Isn't radical theology just another form of humanism?

It is humanism, if humanism means a belief that there are no viable objects of loyalty beyond man, his values, his communities, his life. But it is a Christian humanism.

Question 5: Why have you insisted on the phrase "death of God"? Just because it gives offense?

It is an offensive phrase, but we have not chosen it to give offense. We have chosen it partly because we wish to relate to the tradition of religious thought in the past century that has made use of it, but primarily because it expresses exactly what we wish to express — the sense of a possession that has been taken away, a possession we do not expect to be made good, to come back. Thus, the traditional words — absence of God, or silence, or disappearance, or eclipse — all live within the world of a loss that is temporary, short-ranged, soon to be removed. And whatever we expect or hope for, the object of hope is not the Christian God.

Religious Humanism

In 1933 a Humanist Manifesto declared that "the quest for the good life is still the central task of mankind." In that quest, old theologies, outworn creeds, and the "outward forms of religion" play little part, or perhaps even an obstructive part —according to this perspective. Yet, it is important that religion survive, for "religions have always been the means for realizing the highest values of life." A generation later an effort to update and rewrite that Manifesto failed, but a personal statement issued in the wake of the Death of God theology retained the characteristic emphases of religious humanism. ". . . It is important to the survival of mankind, and indeed of life itself, that religion does not die with God." This statement comes from William S. Fisk, lay president of a Unitarian-Universalist fellowship in Ohio.

But out of his necessity, man created more than gods. He created religion, too; and these are not co-equal. For religion pervaded men's lives, ordered their societies, set the patterns of behavior, set the goals of men's desires. Religion provided, and still provides, a repository for the highest and best of man's thoughts and aspirations. In many forms, this is cloaked in divine sanction as a means of enforcement and promulgation, but basically, all of man's hopes for his future, all of what he has learned on how to live and prosper, all the essence of centuries of trial and error are found in the values of the religions of the world. . . .

Our age has seen what can happen when the great values of religion were brushed aside, and the weakened faith in a man-made God could not support them. The gas chambers at Dachau are evidence enough; the mass removal of dissidents to Siberian work camps adds continuing evidence. The willingness of men to conceive of, and prepare for, a nuclear war in which civilization might well die, is only the final proof.

Humanist Alternative

Liberal religion, humanistic religion, stands as living evidence of another alternative. We meet in our churches, yet there is no excommunication if we do not attend. We possess, and will defend, firm ideals which have grown out of the great religious traditions; yet we do not believe we will live forever in fire if we fail a few times in living up to those ideals. Nor will most of us defend those ideals on any supernatural or divine basis, for many of us would agree that there is no proof of a God who speaks and acts in the world of men. Yet we meet in a church and we speak of our religion. Is this a clue to the future?

[Source: W. S. Fisk, " 'God is Dead'—Long Live Religion!" *Religious Humanism*, 1 (Winter, 1967), 12–13.]

The concept of God may well be powerless in the future, but it is important to the survival of mankind, and indeed of life itself, that religion does not die with God. Let us remember that man created God, and man created religion, in the image of his necessity. Let us hold on firmly to that which is still needed; to the values that man has built, not received as a gift of divine revelation — but built painstakingly over the ages of mistakes. Let us hold on to the great empirical truths from all religious systems. Truths — a strong word, but used in this sense: we believe that they work in improving the relations of man to man, and as long as they work, let us act as if.they were true. The Golden Rule is not a revelation from on high, nor is it a one-shot bright idea from some past historic pen. It is a universal axiom which developed in every great religion: treat other men in the way that you want to be treated. Its greatness lies in its simplicity and in its changeability. Each man decides for himself, in his own time and with his own knowledge of things, of science, or whatever, how he wants to be considered, and then applies it to others. These kinds of ideals must not die.

Suggested Reading
(Chapter Eleven)

Pacifism flourished in the 1930s but quickly waned during the years of World War II (1941 – 45). Two general treatments display the shifting sentiments: J. T. Addison, *War, Peace, and the Christian Mind* (1953); and R. L. Moellering, *Modern War and the American Churches* (1956). On the secret development and swift use of the atomic bomb, and on the religious responsibilities pertinent thereto, two reports sponsored by the Federal Council of Churches merit attention: *Atomic Warfare and the Christian Faith* (1946) and *The Christian Conscience and Weapons of Mass Destruction* (1950). Also see Edward L. Long, *The Christian Response to the Atomic Crisis* (1950). The literature on the Holocaust is vast, and still growing. Recent volumes include the following: Arthur Cohen, *The Tremendum: A Theological Interpretation of the Holocaust* (1981); H. J. Cargas, *A Christian Response to the Holocaust* (1981) and a volume edited by Cargas, *When God and Man Failed: Non-Jewish Views of the Holocaust* (1981); Yehuda Bauer, *A History of the Holocaust* (1982); and Azriel Eisenberg, *The Lost Generation: Children in the Holocaust* (1982). The relationship between the Holocaust and Zionism is explored in Jacob Neusner's *Stranger at Home* (1981). Other treatments of Zionism include Arthur Hertzberg, *The Zionist Idea* (1959) and Abraham Heschel, *The Earth is the Lord's* (1966). For Protestantism's involvement with this part of the world as well as with the "Zionist idea," see Robert T. Handy, ed., *The Holy Land in American Protestant Life, 1800 – 1948* (1981). In the period of the Vietnam War, religious no less than political protest reached new heights. The degree of Roman Catholic resistance to or condemnation of that conflict was especially striking. On this confrontation, these studies are revealing: T. E. Quigley, ed., *American Catholics and Vietnam*

(1968); R. F. Drinan, S. J., *Vietnam and Armageddon: Peace, War, and the Christian Conscience* (1970); William O'Rourke, *The Harrisburg 7 and the New Catholic Left* (1972); and on the most conspicuous Catholic dissenters of that period, Stephen Halpert and Tom Murray, *Witness of the Berrigans* (1972). More general treatments of religious protest include Homer A. Jack, ed., *Religion and Peace* (1966); and M. P. Hamilton, ed., *The Vietnam War: Christian Perspectives* (1967).

For a comprehensive view of ecumenical developments after World War II, one should begin with the systematic survey edited by Harold E. Fey, *History of the Ecumenical Movement, Vol. 2, 1948–68* (1970). Robert McAfee Brown's *Ecumenical Revolution* (rev. ed., 1969) traces the many fast-breaking developments of the 1960s. Details of the Consultation on Church Union can best be followed in the Proceedings and Digests of the consultations themselves; an excellent point of departure is in two small booklets published by COCU: *Principles of Church Union* and *The Reports of the Four Meetings,* both issued in 1966. An informed discussion of the Lutheran Church—Missouri Synod crisis comes from the journalist pen of James E. Adams, *Preus of Missouri and the Great Lutheran Civil War* (1977). Vatican II had many journalistic reporters, none superior to Xavier Rynne whose several letters, first appearing in the *New Yorker* and later issued in a series of paperbacks, helped satisfy a large public appetite for the "goings-on" in Rome. The permanent work of the council appeared in a convenient and valuable format under the general editorship of Walter M. Abbott, S. J.: namely, *Documents of Vatican II,* "with notes and comments by Catholic, Protestant, and Orthodox authorities." Published in 1966, the year after the close of the council, this book was itself an ecumenical event: released simultaneously by Catholic and Protestant houses, broadly based in its commentaries and interpretation, refreshingly open in its discussion and documentation. Earlier, *Pacem in Terris* had led to broad public comment and analysis, one witness to that being the February 13, 1965, issue of *Saturday Review* which was given over entirely to a discussion of Pope John's impressive encyclical. John Courtney Murray, S. J., introduced the Declaration on Religious Freedom in the Abbott volume noted above, but one may also turn to a wide range of commentary in Murray's edited work, *Religious Liberty: An End and a Beginning* (1966). Since the Bible has so often divided Protestant and Catholic, Christian and Jew, in America's history, it is important to note one other ecumenical product of this busy decade: *The Bible Reader* (1969). The Jesuit father, W. M. Abbott, also played a major role in the production of this impressive work, as did Jewish and Protestant scholars as well. Deliberately interfaith and carefully nondivisive, *The Bible Reader* represented a major step toward a common Bible, with cultural commentary from which all could learn. On Eastern Orthodoxy, Alexander Schmemann has written on the "Problems of Orthodoxy in America" in a series of articles for *St. Vladimir's Seminary Quarterly,* 8 and 9 (1964, 1965). Also, the great interpreter of East to West, Georges Florovsky, has provided these valuable books: *Bible, Church, Tradition: An Eastern Orthodox View* (1972); *Christianity and Culture* (1974); and *Aspects of Church History* (1975).

A Roman Catholic perspective on *Christianity and Communism* is provided by Henri Chambre, S. J. (1960), while John C. Bennett writes from a Protestant perspective in his *Christianity and Communism,* also published in 1960. The confrontational aspect of these two forces or ideologies in America is delineated in detail in Ralph L.

Roy's *Communism and the Churches* (1960). Roy also provided a useful bibliographical essay along with more than thirty pages of notes. On Martin Luther King, one can profitably read King himself in several readily available paperbacks (or even listen to a record of his major speeches). A full biography has been provided by Stephen B. Oates: *Let the Trumpet Sound: The Life of Martin Luther King* (1982). See also James Forman, *The Making of Black Revolutionaries* (1972), as well as the older forays into civil rights: Louis Lomax, *The Negro Revolt* (1962), and James Baldwin, *The Fire Next Time* (1963). A valuable source on John F. Kennedy has been compiled by N. A. Schneider, *Religious Views of President John F. Kennedy in His Own Words* (1965). For a Protestant debate on the wisdom of electing a Catholic president, the debate being aired only two weeks before the election, see *Christian Century*, Oct. 26, 1960. Watergate has had almost as many interpreters as perpetrators, but among the best books on this sad subject are Anthony Lukas, *Nightmare* (1976); Jonathan Schell, *The Time of Illusion* (1976); and Leon Jaworski, *The Right and the Power* (1976).

The life and thought of Billy Graham, as in the case of Martin Luther King, can be followed in many of his own books, but biographical treatments serve as a useful supplement. The ablest study is by William G. McLoughlin, *Billy Graham* (1960). This was preceded by the sympathetic portrayal of Stanley High, *Billy Graham* . . . (1956) and followed by the more critical appraisals of Joe E. Barnhart, *The Billy Graham Religion* (1972) and Marshall Frady, *Billy Graham: A Parable of American Righteousness* (1979). McLoughlin's *Revivals, Awakenings and Reform* (1978) offers an interpretive thesis for understanding the vital role of revivals in American history and culture. Donald B. Meyer's *Positive Thinkers* (1965), previously cited, affords excellent background for the "peace books" of the postwar world. Radical theology is unfolded by two of its exponents in T. J. J. Altizer and William Hamilton, *Radical Theology and the Death of God* (1966). A Jewish voice also suggests that the theological enterprise is over: Richard Rubenstein, *After Auschwitz* (1966). And for a Roman Catholic perspective, one may turn to Leslie Dewart's *Future of Belief* (1966). On nontheistic religion in the twentieth century, see Mason Olds, *Religious Humanism in America* . . . (1977).

TWELVE:

E Pluribus ... Unum?

The 1970s and 1980s continued to show signs of social strain, even if not in the stridently confrontational manner of the 1960s. Consensus proved elusive, and variety blossomed into magnificent if often bewildering diversity. Many gloried in that value which the American scene so extravagantly revealed: religious freedom. Some questioned whether that value could also be compatible with a unified support for other worthy social ends. This nation was "conceived in liberty, and dedicated to the proposition that all men are created equal," Lincoln had pointed out. The question in the 1980s as in the 1860s was how long that nation "or any nation so conceived, and so dedicated," could endure.

PLURALISM PLUS

While religious and cultural variety is as American as apple pie and as old as the kachina doll, few would deny that in the second half of the twentieth century such variety reached dizzying new heights. One no longer needed to be told of such diversity, for it confronted even the most casual observer upon the streets, at the airports, in the media, and sometimes most poignantly within the family. The new burst of Oriental religious practice and proselytizing was especially striking. Transcendental Meditation and its persuasive guru, Maharishi Mahesh Yogi, seemed for a time a Vedic stream so wide and swift as to saturate all levels of American society, including the public schools. Hare Krishna, or more properly the International Society of Krishna Consciousness, presented modern Hinduism in even more dramatic form: yellow robes, shaved heads, black topknots, obtrusive methods of fund raising, and authoritarian communal living. Buddhism was no longer only the exotic visitor at the World Parliament of Religions or merely a Japanese import into the Hawaiian Islands: it moved onto mainstreet America and into middle-class suburbia. Westerners accustomed to divisions and factions in their own religious traditions learned that Buddhism too came in many guises, in many richly varied manifestations. And the Unification Church, the followers of Sun Myung Moon, combined East and West as it mixed (in the words of Robert Ellwood) "the traditional shamanism of the Korean countryside" with "missionary Christianity." While in most cases the number of converts to Oriental religions remained modest, the presence of these "new religions" could no longer be regarded as a momentary rebellion or fascination of the young which would soon fade away.

Some of the nation's emphatic variety bore no denominational label, reflected clearly no ancient tradition of either East or West. Successful promoters, charismatic healers, convincing stage managers, and magnetic pulpiteers gathered around themselves large followings whose commitment was to little more than the magic of a powerful personality. In tiny communes or sprawling congregations, in rustic wildernesses or showy cathedrals, among the "haves" but even more potently among the "have-nots," people found answers and assurances, authority and control. The tragedy is that some, as in Jonestown, also found manipulation, exploitation, abuse, and final destruction.

The "radical left," here understood as a conscious return to or revival of demonology, witchcraft, and "pagan religion," made its presence felt in many ways, including that most powerful of modern media — the Hollywood movie. From the *Exorcist* and *Rosemary's Baby,* through *Omen I* and *II* and *Amityville I* and *II,* to *Poltergeist* and no doubt far beyond, Americans revealed a great appetite for preternatural phenomena, for covens and curses, for bad seeds and demonic possession. Salem, Massachusetts (see Vol. I, pp. 135–40) never seemed so near. Again, the numbers involved in any organized form of neopaganism were not large, but the tug upon the popular imagination was surprisingly strong. The gods of neopaganism were many, the incantations and liturgies diverse, the satisfactions found within the circles and in the practice of the Craft of several sorts. A real religious left, proudly anti-Christian and anti-Judaic and generally aloof to the ancient wisdom of the East, accentuated the religious pluralism of contemporary America.

If the media gave significant attention to the radical left, it pulled out all stops with respect to the radical right: the Moral Majority, the Christian Voice, the Christian Voter's Victory Fund, the National Christian Action Coalition, the Faith and Freedom Foundation, the Praise the Lord (PTL) television network, and many more. It is a *Holy Terror,* asserted authors Flo Conway and Jim Siegelman in 1982, this "fundamentalist war on America's freedoms in religion, politics, and our private lives." Even Billy Graham expressed concern about the possible "wedding between religious fundamentalists and the political right." Whatever the merits of these evaluations, the "New Christian Right" seemed both more visible and more powerful in the 1980s than ever before. And the electronic church, often its major vehicle of communication and persuasion, challenged the traditional ways of worship, the caring and intimate congregation, substituting in its stead a religion by kilowatt and cancelled check.

LIBERATION/ALIENATION

In the 1950s and 1960s the struggle for human rights and minority recognition was largely a matter of power politics and ecclesiastical pressures. By the 1970s and 1980s, theology itself stood on the front lines. Theology no longer spoke in the quiet and assured tones of unchallenged establishment but in the strident voices of the oppressed. A liberation theology, either with Christianity or against Christianity, contended that poverty, hunger, injustice, and oppression were theological problems; dependence and discrimination and domination required theological solutions. Among America's blacks, some sought solution in the tradition of Israel's ancient prophets (Amos and Isaiah, for example) or in the tradition of this nation's more recent ones (Rauschenbusch and Niebuhr, for example). Others, however — and the Black Muslims constitute the most conspicuous example — saw Christianity as so thoroughly entangled in white domination and Western imperialism as to require that the black man reject "the devil white man" and his exploiting, enslaving religion.

Other minorities in America hungered for words and deeds that would liberate. Pope John Paul II in his 1979 visit to the United States sought out several such groups in order to tell them (as he did the Ukrainians in Philadelphia) that the Church knew of their suffering, of "the countless Ukrainian martyrs . . . who gave up their lives rather than abandon their faith." To Chicago's Poles, the pope spoke of "their toil, efforts, struggles and sufferings," of the pain and poverty that forced them to cross a great ocean: "all the price of love they had to part with in order to look here anew for multiplied family, social and all human threads." And to the Spanish-speaking people of the South Bronx, this Catholic pilgrim offered encouragement and pastoral concern "on behalf of so many who experience inner anxiety and material deprivation." Liberation or even recognition came tardily to the Hispanic community within Roman Catholicism. Not until 1970 did the American church appoint its first Hispanic bishop: Patricio F. Flores. And in 1977, this Bishop of San Antonio declared that the Hispanic community, "which has been oppressed, excluded and discriminated against, harbors no ill will. It is eager to contribute. . . ." Suffering, Flores added, is the common bond that unites Puerto Ricans, Cubans, Central and South Americans, and Mexican-Americans. "We also believe that God is present among all who suffer. Slaves and oppressed persons will liberate themselves and in so doing will liberate their oppressors."

Indians in modern America, having long since despaired of genuine liberation, fought for the right, at the very least, to practice their own version of sacramental Christianity. The Native American Church, chartered in Oklahoma in 1918, declared its purpose "to foster and promote religious believers in Almighty God and the customs of the several Tribes throughout the United States in the worship of a Heavenly Father and to promote morality, sobriety, industry, charity, and right living. . . ." Such purposes suggested nothing controversial or inimical to the public good — except for the fact that for this Church the body of Christ in communion was peyote. That food provided a spiritual liberation and offered a means of divine communication.

Liberation was most visible in connection with the new feminism. Churches and synagogues faced issues of female participation and ordination, of female oppression and discrimination. In 1972 Sally Priesand was ordained rabbi by Hebrew Union College — Jewish Institute of Religion (Reform) in Cincinnati, Ohio, and in 1983 the faculty of Jewish Theological Seminary (Conservative) of New York City voted to ordain its qualified women graduates. In Orthodox Judaism, the question was not even put to a vote. In 1976 the Episcopal Church ruled that women could be ordained as priests, and the following year a dozen or more churches broke away from the parent church to form a separate diocese for those who "wish to remain faithful to the traditional Church." As one of the dissidents explained, "The nature of the priesthood itself is a continuation of the priesthood of Christ, a man."

In 1976 hundreds of Roman Catholic women organized a Women's Ordination Conference to protest against "a priesthood that is elitist, hierarchical, racist, classist"; the conference championed the cause of "equal *rites* for women." In 1977 the Vatican issued a "Declaration on the Question of the Admission of Women to the Ministerial Priesthood," affirming that the Church's longstanding limitation of the priesthood to males was based on Christ's clear intent and could not be changed. "Never has an official Vatican declaration been so roundly rejected and even ridiculed," wrote theologian Rosemary Ruether in 1979, "by both theological authorities and the general populace." Sexist language in liturgy and scripture fell before feminist challenges. Phyllis Trible wrote on "Depatriarchalizing the Bible," Sarah B. Doely on *Women's Liberation and the Church*, and Margaret S. Ermarth on *Adam's Fractured Rib*. Books, articles, conferences, and congresses pointed to a liberation movement of broadest sweep.

LITIGATION/DIVISIONS

Prior to World War II, the United States Supreme Court heard very few cases relating to religion in the century-and-a-half of the nation's existence. Since World War II the Court has been inundated with dozens of such cases, as religious divisions and differences have been exposed for all the world to see. Pluralism was taking its case to court, over and over, aided in that enterprise by the high Court's judgment in 1940 that the First Amendment clauses on religion were applicable, via the Fourteenth Amendment, to all fifty states. Religious litigation also found itself frequently assisted by the good offices of the American Civil Liberties Union, the American Jewish Congress, Americans United for Separation of Church and State, and other such entities.

The area of education proved the most troublesome. In public schools, the issues concerned what might be taught, recited, sung, or prayed; in private schools, the issues concerned fiscal support for buildings, salaries, services, or supplies. Since 1947 (*Everson* v. *Board of Education*) the Court has repeatedly confronted the complex questions of public monies applied, directly or indirectly, to private school ends. And since 1948 (*McCollum* v. *Board of Education*) the Court has attempted, amid ever growing controversy, to determine the precise location of that "wall of separation" between church and state. Rarely has the Supreme Court been unanimous in any of these decisions, while on some occasions the dissent has been so forceful or bitter as to dash hopes of greater unanimity in the future. The problem, of course, is not that the Court is divided, but that its divisions accurately reflect fissures deep within American society itself.

Conscientious objection to war has always been the occasion for disagreement and discord (see, for example, Vol. I, pp. 230–37, and above, pp. 148–53). Through most of the nation's history, moreover, religion has been the focal issue. In the dissenting days of Vietnam, however, the Supreme Court saw "conscience" and "religious commitment" as separable entities. Again, divisions appeared in Court and congress, in synagogue and church. In 1982 as national registration for military service was again required, the historic peace churches — notably young men from the Church of the Brethren and the Mennonites — were once more the first to draw down upon themselves the penalties provided by law.

The most passionate social issues of all, however, were also the most private: the use of contraceptives to prevent fertilization, and the resort to abortion procedures following fertilization. On these subjects nearly everyone had an opinion and nearly every opinion was held with tenacity and unshakable conviction. The crisis over contraception was particularly severe within the Roman Catholic Church. With regard to abortion, an entire nation found itself caught in a storm that showed little sign of abating, as moral issues also loomed as constitutional issues. On such questions as these, the "pluribus" was all too evident, the "unum" all too elusive.

EROSIONS/AFFIRMATIONS

The remaining and overarching question concerned not this specific public debate or that, this particular court case or that proposed constitutional amendment. Rather, it concerned the wholeness of the nation, of its people, and of its purposes. What was the role of religion in national life? or was there any such legitimate role? What part did religion play, what part did the nation play, in the future course of civilization? As technology grew more sophisticated and the engines of destruction more awesome, were religiously affiliated Americans reduced more and more to the status of mere observers, of innocent (if vulnerable) bystanders? And if religion were removed altogether from the public agenda, did this mean that self-seeking was the only thing left to seek? In 1776 a group of like-minded Americans, determining to chart

a new course for a new nation, began by asserting: "We hold these truths.
. . ." Truth was deemed relevant to politics and war, to fortunes and sacred
honor, to communal resolve and cooperative undertaking. As the twentieth
century drew toward a close, it grew more difficult to specify with assurance
those truths held in common or to locate those links that bound faith to action.
Affirmations seemed more tentative, anxieties more colossal.

1. PLURALISM PLUS

The Orient in America: Zen Buddhism

The two great streams of Oriental religious thought and practice, Hinduism and Buddhism, first flowed into the public consciousness of Americans during the World Parliament of Religions in 1893 (see above, pp. 85–86). More than two generations were to pass, however, before the Orient became part of America's "street scene" and before the esoteric language of Eastern religion entered into casual conversation. Satori and ashram, guru and mantra, koan and zazen were no longer totally foreign words, as East and West began to become better acquainted. No Oriental religion had greater impact or broader appeal than Zen Buddhism: austere, simple, disciplined, and paradoxical — full and empty, ignorant and wise, godly and godless. A further paradox was that Zen seemed so totally un-Western, and yet the West seemed so eager to receive it. (1) Alan Watts (1915–73), lecturer, writer, sometime Episcopal minister, effectively interpreted and popularized The Way of Zen *(1957); a portion of its preface appears below. (2) Gary Snyder (b. 1930), prize-winning poet, conservationist, and careful student of the Orient, commented in 1976 (at a meeting at Swarthmore College) on the "Zen of Humanity."*

1.

During the past twenty years there has been an extraordinary growth of interest in Zen Buddhism. Since the Second World War this interest has increased so much that it seems to be becoming a considerable force in the intellectual and artistic world of the West. It is connected, no doubt, with the prevalent enthusiasm for Japanese culture which is one of the constructive results of the late war, but which may amount to no more than a passing fashion. The deeper reason for this interest is that the viewpoint of Zen lies so close to the "growing edge" of Western thought.

The more alarming and destructive aspects of Western civilization should

[Sources: (1) Alan Watts, *The Way of Zen* (New York: Vintage Books, 1957), pp. ix–xi. (2) Gary Snyder, *The Real Work: Interviews & Talks, 1964–1979* (edited by W. S. McLean) (New York: New Directions, 1980), pp. 83–84.]

not blind us to the fact that at this very time it is also in one of its most creative periods. Ideas and insights of the greatest fascination are appearing in some of the newer fields of Western science — in psychology and psychotherapy, in logic and the philosophy of science, in semantics and communications theory. Some of these developments might be due to suggestive influences from Asian philosophy, but on the whole I am inclined to feel that there is more of a parallelism than a direct influence. We are, however, becoming aware of the parallelism, and it promises an exchange of views which should be extremely stimulating.

Western thought has changed so rapidly in this century that we are in a state of considerable confusion. Not only are there serious difficulties of communication between the intellectual and the general public, but the course of our thinking and of our very history has seriously undermined the commonsense assumptions which lie at the roots of our social conventions and institutions. Familiar concepts of space, time, and motion, of nature and natural law, of history and social change, and of human personality itself have dissolved, and we find ourselves adrift without landmarks in a universe which more and more resembles the Buddhist principle of the "Great Void." The various wisdoms of the West, religious, philosophical, and scientific, do not offer much guidance to the art of living in such a universe, and we find the prospects of making our way in so trackless an ocean of relativity rather frightening. For we are used to absolutes, to firm principles and laws to which we can cling for spiritual and psychological security.

This is why, I think, there is so much interest in a culturally productive way of life which, for some fifteen hundred years, has felt thoroughly at home in "the Void," and which not only feels no terror for it but rather a positive delight. To use its own words, the situation of Zen has always been —

> *Above, not a tile to cover the head;*
> *Below, not an inch of ground for the foot.*

Such language should not actually be so unfamiliar to us, were we truly prepared to accept the meaning of "the foxes have holes, and the birds of the air have nests; but the Son of Man hath not where to lay his head."

I am not in favor of "importing" Zen from the Far East, for it has become deeply involved with cultural institutions which are quite foreign to us. But there is no doubt that there are things which we can learn, or unlearn, from it and apply in our own way. It has the special merit of a mode of expressing itself which is as intelligible — or perhaps as baffling — to the intellectual as to the illiterate, offering possibilities of communication which we have not explored. It has a directness, verve, and humor, and a sense of both beauty and nonsense at once exasperating and delightful. But above all it has a way of being able to turn one's mind inside out, and dissolving what seemed to be the most oppressive human problems into questions like "Why is a mouse when it spins?" At its heart there is a strong but completely unsentimental

"Walking meditation" (*kinhin*) of Zen Buddhists in Los Angeles
(Zen Center of Los Angeles)

compassion for human beings suffering and perishing from their very attempts to save themselves.

2.

I stay with Zen, because sitting, doing zazen,* is a primary factor. Sitting is the act of looking-in. Meditation is fundamental, you can't subtract anything from that. It's so fundamental that it's been with us for forty or fifty thousand years in one form or another. It's not even something that is specifically Buddhist. It's as fundamental a human activity as taking naps is to wolves, or soaring in circles is to hawks and eagles. It's how you contact the basics and the base of yourself. And Zen has cut away a lot of frills, to keep that foremost.

Now the completion of this is understood very clearly in the Tibetan tradition when they speak of the three mysteries: body, speech, and mind. This is fundamental Buddhism to me; it's fundamental to existence itself, and Buddhism is about existence. The three things that are closest to us — our bodies, our minds, and our language — are the three things we know least about, that we pay least attention to, that we use as our tools throughout our lifetimes to various relatively limited ends, including survival, but there's very little attention to the fact of existence of this in its own right. A simple message of the teaching is that much of the pain, suffering, confusion, and contradiction you encounter in your own life is simply caused by not paying attention to what you have closest to you from the beginning and then using it well: body, speech, and mind. The three practices are then: sitting meditation, for exploring the mind; singing or chantings or poetry or mantras, for exploring speech and voice; and yoga, or dance, or hoeing the garden and gathering firewood, for the exploration of the body. We all do all these things, so all that needs to be added to that is a real awareness and attention in the doing, and a realization of the marvelousness, the mysteriousness, of all these simple acts, which again comes back to the sitting meditation, because it's at that point that you can really nurture and contact the marvelousness — and also the tiresomeness [in your life]. . . .

For myself personally all I would add to that are some very ancient and to me beautiful and useful ways of handling things: attention to place; gratitude to the physical universe and to all the other beings for what they exchange with you; good health, good luck, good crops. Basic old-style religion.

*Meditation, usually while seated in lotus position.

Personality Cults: Jonestown

Much of American religion in the 1960s and 1970s seemed to be akin to the child's game of "follow the leader." The largest advertisements on the religion pages of major metropolitan dailies testified to the prowess and salesmanship of the preacher-performer, the pied piper of new life-styles, the announcer of millenniums to come, or the midwife of millenniums at hand. Denominations and recognizable institutional affiliations counted for little. In no sense typical of such cults but, on the contrary, atypical in its abnormality and tragedy, the group led by the Reverend James Warren (Jim) Jones (1931–78) shocked the sensibilities of the nation. On November 18, 1978, in far-off Guyana over nine hundred followers of Jones joined him in mass suicide. Jones, from a midwestern and Disciples of Christ background, emerged in California as a messiah to the poor and oppressed, to the empty and confused, to those searching for authority and assurance. As the object of unquestioning trust Jones came to see himself as worthy of such trust, as more than the announcer of divine things but as the very embodiment of the divine. His faithful followed him from northern rural California to San Francisco, and from there to the steamy jungles of Guyana where a Marxist-Christian utopia was to arise from the earth. The darkest side of that grim tragedy was the number of children and young people led to their doom. The document below comes from distraught parents and relatives who, seven months before that November day, wrote an open letter to Jones, begging for the right to see their children and to communicate freely with them.

We, the undersigned, are the grief-stricken parents and relatives of the hereinafter-designated persons you arranged to be transported to Guyana, South America, at a jungle encampment you call "Jonestown." We are advised there are no telephones or exit roads from Jonestown, and that you now have more than 1,000 U.S. citizens living with you there.

We have allowed nine months to pass since you left the United States in June 1977. Although certain of us knew it would do no good to wait before making a group protest, others of us were willing to wait to see whether you would in fact respect the fundamental freedoms and dignity of our children and family members in Jonestown. Sadly, your conduct over the past year has shown such a flagrant and cruel disregard for human rights that we have no choice as responsible people but to make this public accusation and to demand the immediate elimination of these outrageous abuses.

II. Summary of Violations

We hereby accuse you, Jim Jones, of the following acts violating the human rights of our family members:

[Source: Kenneth Wooden, *The Children of Jonestown* (New York: McGraw Hill Book Co., 1981), pp. 210–12, 213–14.]

People's Temple leader, Jim Jones, in Georgetown, Guyana, 1978
(Religious News Service)

1. Making the following threat calculated to cause alarm for the lives of our relatives: "I can say without hesitation that we are devoted to a decision that it is better even to die than to be constantly harassed from one continent to the next."
2. Employing physical intimidation and psychological coercion as part of a mind-programming campaign aimed at destroying family ties, discrediting belief in God, and causing contempt for the United States of America.
3. Prohibiting our relatives from leaving Guyana by confiscating their passports and money and by stationing guards around Jonestown to prevent anyone escaping.
4. Depriving them of their right to privacy, free speech, and freedom of association by:
    a. Prohibiting telephone calls;
    b. Prohibiting individual contacts with "outsiders";
    c. Censoring all incoming and outgoing mail;
    d. Extorting silence from relatives in the U.S. by threats to stop all communication;
    e. Preventing our children from seeing us when we travel to Guyana.

The "1,000 U.S. citizens" you claim to have brought to Guyana include our beloved relatives who are "devoted to a decision that it is better to die." We frankly do not know if you have become so corrupted by power that you would actually allow a collective "decision" to die, or whether your letter is simply a bluff designed to deter investigations into your practices. . . .

We hereby give you the opportunity now to publicly repudiate our interpretation of your threat. If you refuse to deny the apparent meaning of your letter, we demand that you immediately answer the following questions:

1. When you refer to "a decision that it is better even to die than to be constantly harrassed," has this "decision" already been made or is it to be made in the future? If made, when and where? Were our relatives consulted? Did anybody dissent? By what moral or legal justification could you possibly make such a decision on behalf of minor children?
2. When you say you are "devoted" to this decision, does it mean it is irreversible? If irreversible, at what point will the alleged "harassment" have gotten so great as to make death "better"? Would it be an International Human Rights Commission investigation, or an on-premise investigation of your operations by the U.S. Government? Who besides you will decide when that point "to die" is reached?

We know your psychological coercion of the residents of Jonestown to be so "totalitarian" that nobody there, including adults, could possibly make such a decision to die freely and voluntarily. The evidence is that our relatives are in fact hostages, and we hereby serve notice that should any harm befall them, we will hold you and People's Temple church responsible and will employ every legal and diplomatic resource to bring you to justice.

Radical Left: Neopaganism

Neopaganism sees itself as a revival of ancient pre-Christian religion: the old nature religions of Greece and Rome, and of the wandering Teutonic tribes and others as well. Beyond that, neopaganism may be identified by what it is not: neither Christian nor Judaic, neither monotheistic nor agnostic, neither Oriental nor humanistic. A revived polytheism, it is hardly a mass movement in modern America; nevertheless, it is no longer a movement totally underground or scarcely visible. A recent volume offers, in the words of its subtitle, an explication of "Witches, Druids, Goddess Worshippers, and Other Pagans in America Today." The document below suggests some of the attraction which neopaganism holds.

[Source: Margot Adler, *Drawing Down the Moon* (New York: Viking Press, 1979), pp. 14–16.]

How do people become Neo-Pagans? This question assumes great importance when we consider that Neo-Pagan groups rarely proselytize and certain of them are quite selective. There are few converts. In most cases, word of mouth, a discussion between friends, a lecture, a book, or an article provides the entry point. But these events merely confirm some original, private experience, so that the most common feeling of those who have named themselves Pagans is something like "I finally found a group that has the same religious perceptions I always had." A common phrase you hear is "I've come home," or, as one woman told me excitedly after a lecture, "I always knew I had a religion, I just never knew it had a name."

Alison Harlow, a systems analyst at a large medical research center in California, described her first experience this way:

"It was Christmas Eve and I was singing in the choir of a lovely church at the edge of a lake, and the church was filled with beautiful decorations. It was full moon, and the moon was shining right through the glass windows of the church. I looked out and felt something very special happening, but it didn't seem to be happening inside the church.

"After the Midnight Mass was over and everyone adjourned to the parish house for coffee, I knew I needed to be alone for a minute, so I left my husband and climbed up the hill behind the church. I sat on this hill looking at the full moon, and I could hear the sound of coffee cups clinking and the murmur of conversation from the parish house.

"I was looking down on all this, when suddenly I felt a 'presence.' It seemed very ancient and wise and definitely female. I can't describe it any closer than that, but I felt that this presence, this being, was looking down on me, on this church and these people and saying, 'The poor little ones! They mean so well and they understand so little.'

"I felt that whoever 'she' was, she was incredibly old and patient; she was exasperated with the way things were **goi**ng on the planet, but she hadn't given up hope that we would start making some sense of the world. So, after that, I knew I had to find out more about her."

Harlow is now a priestess in the Craft, working in a self-created tradition that deals mostly, but not exclusively, with women. As a result of her experience, she began a complex journey to find out about the history and experience of goddess worship. This search led her, through various readings, into contact with a number of Craft traditions, until she ended up writing a column on feminism and Witchcraft for the Neo-Pagan magazine *Nemeton* (now defunct). It is perhaps only fair, at this point, to describe my own entry into this same world.

When I was a small child, I had the good fortune to enter an unusual New York City grammar school (City and Country) that allowed its students to immerse themselves in historical periods to such an extent that we often seemed to live in them. At the age of twelve, a traditional time for rites of passage, that historical period was ancient Greece. I remember entering into the Greek myths as if I had returned to my true homeland.

My friends and I lived through the battles of the *Iliad*; we read the historical novels of Mary Renault and Caroline Dale Snedeker and took the parts of ancient heroes and heroines in plays and fantasy. I wrote hymns to gods and goddesses and poured libations (of water) onto the grass of neighboring parks. In my deepest and most secret moments I daydreamed that I had become these beings, feeling what it would be like to be Artemis or Athena. I acted out the old myths and created new ones, in fantasy and private play. It was a great and deep secret that found its way into brief diary entries and unskilled drawings. But like many inner things, it was not unique to me.

I have since discovered that these experiences are common. The pantheons may differ according to circumstances, class, ethnic and cultural background, opportunity, and even chance. There are children in the United States whose pantheons come from "Star Trek," while their parents remember the days of Buck Rogers. The archetypal images seem to wander in and out of the fantasies of millions of children, disguised in contemporary forms. That I and most of my friends had the opportunity to take our archetypes from the rich pantheon of ancient Greece was a result of class and opportunity, nothing more.

What were these fantasies of gods and goddesses? What was their use, their purpose? I see them now as daydreams used in the struggle toward my own becoming. They were hardly idle, though, since they focused on stronger and healthier "role models" than the images of women projected in the late 1950s. The fantasies enabled me to contact stronger parts of myself, to embolden my vision of myself. Besides, these experiences were filled with power, intensity, and even ecstasy that, on reflection, seem religious or spiritual.

Radical Right: Electronic Fundamentalism

Two developments brought the radical religious right to the attention of the American public in dramatic fashion. Successful exploitation of new technology, initially radio and then television, then television networks, was the first significant step. The second was the strong alliance with political causes and political candidates, these alliances also often involving campaigns to defeat those of opposing views or stances. Historian and scholar of revivalism, the charismatic movement, and southern sects, David E. Harrell, Jr. (b. 1930), treats below both aspects of the new fundamentalism in American life: its technological sophistication and its political participation.

[Source: D. E. Harrell, Jr., *Occasional Papers* (Collegeville, Minn.: Institute for Ecumenical and Cultural Research, 1981), pp. 3–4, 4–5, 5–7.]

By the 1970s conservative American religion had bred a new generation of leaders, leaders with unparalleled financial power and communications resources. Some of them were evangelists of the old school who admired Billy Graham and Billy Sunday, but others rarely preached; they were religious television personalities, the products of the modern media revolution.

Threatened by science, conservative religion has always been fascinated by technology, from neon signs to satellite television. Revivalism has been religion's Wild West; it beckoned bold entrepreneurs and speculators. Since the time of the early 100,000 watt radio stations in Chicago and Del Rio, Texas, independent evangelists have played a game of revival of the fittest. They skillfully built clienteles and experimented with every new communications advance. When cable and satellite television made relatively cheap programming possible, the fundamentalists and charismatics were miles ahead in knowing how to market their product.

By 1980, the power and breadth of the electronic church, composed mostly of independent ministries, was staggering. An estimated 130 million Americans tuned in a religious television program each week, approximately forty-seven per cent of the population, while only forty-one per cent attended church services. Of the 8,000 radio stations in the United States, 1,400 are religious; 30 of the nation's 800 television stations and 66 of the 800 cable systems are religious. Including small local ministries, radio and television evangelists probably take in over one billion dollars each year, the largest being Oral Roberts at $60 million, Pat Robertson at $58 million, Jim Bakker at $51 million, Jerry Falwell at about $50 million, Rex Humbard at $25 million and Jimmy Swaggart at $20 million. With a touch of braggadocio, Ben Armstrong, executive secretary of the National Religious Broadcasters, reported in 1980 that "broadcast religion touches more people than all the churches combined."

Curious as it seems, the growth of the electronic church took place outside the attention of most Americans, certainly most American intellectuals. It is true that the preachers were there when one spun the television dial (Gary Trudeau lingered long enough to do a couple of Doonesbury strips on Jimmy Swaggart), but they seemed relatively irrelevant. Then, early in 1979, Jerry Falwell formed the Moral Majority. He caught the attention of the news media, increasing numbers of politicians, and some suggest as many as four million voters. When the postmortem began in November, 1980, the Moral Majority claimed to have been crucial not only in the election of Ronald Reagan, but to have cleansed the Senate of the likes of Gravel of Alaska, McGovern of South Dakota, Bayh of Indiana, Church of Idaho, Culver of Iowa and Nelson of Wisconsin. They clearly swayed state elections, especially in the South. Alabama elected its first Republican senator in 100 years and first Catholic ever, former POW Jeremiah Denton; Birmingham voters unseated Congressman James Buchanan, a Republican and the only Southern Baptist minister in Congress, because he had voted "immorally" on several women's rights and civil rights issues. The Moral Majority intended for 1980 to be a trial run, preparation for an all-out assault in 1984. Even they were astonished by their success. . . .

Most visible in the religious right are evangelists from the fundamentalist tradition. Their acknowledged leader is Jerry Falwell, pastor of Thomas Road Baptist Church in Lynchburg, Virginia, an independent Baptist church with 17,000 members, an elementary and high school, a college, seminary, an alcoholic treatment center, a summer camp and a foreign mission. In addition, Falwell broadcasts "The Old Time Gospel Hour" over 324 television outlets to an estimated audience of fifty million viewers. His ministry employs 950 people and has an operating budget of just over one million dollars a week. Cherubic and rosy-cheeked in the pulpit, Falwell is tough and articulate. Born into a family of "brawlers," Falwell was a good student and excelled on his high school football team. Jerry found the Lord in 1952. After four years in Bible School he returned to Lynchburg to establish a new congregation in an abandoned pop factory. Since that time, Falwell has had every reason to believe that God liked what he was doing and it was clear that many Americans did. By 1981 he was receiving support from three and one-half million families.

Probably the second most visible of the fundamentalist evangelists is Southern Baptist revivalist James Robison, whose crusade ministry has been second only to Billy Graham's for two decades. Robison is Texas-born and based and his style is tough and abrasive. "That's how I witnessed," says Robison, "tear 'em up. I'd have truck drivers push back their beer and start crying and say 'tell me more.' " In 1980 Robison's ministry reportedly employed 125 people and was growing; he budgeted $15 million for prime-time television specials during 1981. Robison is a key figure in the conservative push to control the Southern Baptist Convention. Since the mid-1970s he has turned increasingly political and is a leader in the Religious Roundtable and the Moral Majority.

The charismatic wing of the electronic church, which is by far the largest segment, has been far less committed to the political right. Conspicuously absent from almost all of the coalition meetings have been Oral Roberts, Rex Humbard and Jimmy Swaggart. The main links of the charismatics to the religious right have been Jim Bakker and Pat Robertson, the powerful hosts of PTL and The 700 Club.

Bakker's support for the right has been strong and consistent. An Assemblies of God minister, Bakker first gained fame as Robertson's employee, but in the mid-1970s he broke to establish his own Christian network. Bakker has received constant criticism both because of his unsophisticated theology and because of chronic financial difficulties and high pressure money-raising techniques. All through 1979 and 1980 Bakker fought a running battle with the FCC over the alleged misuse of funds. Critics suggested that PTL (originally signifying Praise the Lord or People that Love) should be christened Please Throw a Lifesaver or Pay the Lawyer. But in spite of this "shaky

Electronic church host Jim Bakker (PTL Club) interviews his wife about the conquest of spiritual problems, 1981. *(Religious News Service)*

public image," in 1980 Bakker's two-hour talk show was aired daily on over 200 television stations, his headquarters was contacted daily by 20,000 people and he received monthly support from 700,000 contributors. Deeply angered by his legal bouts with government agencies, Bakker apparently gave his full support to the new political right.

Pat Robertson, host of the theologically more serious 700 Club and founder of the Christian Broadcasting Network, gave important but more limited support to the new right. Robertson, a charismatic Baptist minister whose father was a senator from Virginia, has consistently denied any direct political interest and publicly avowed that "God isn't a right-winger or a left-winger." Robertson was one of the major sponsors of the Washington for Jesus Rally which drew about 200,000 Christian demonstrators to Washington in April, 1980. The charismatic-dominated organizers of the event were "careful to avoid identification with New Right politics or specific controversial causes," a stand which probably accounted for Falwell's inability to fit the rally into his schedule. One prominent charismatic leader privately expressed the belief that Robertson later regretted the limited support he had given to the political right. And yet Robertson's influence was important to the conservatives. The Washington for Jesus Rally featured such militant conservatives as James Robison and Southern Baptist Convention president Adrian Rogers; Robertson's 700 Club was a litany of support for conservative causes, if not candidates (particularly a millennialistic backing for military spending and support of Israel). He also reportedly supported several of the new religious right organizations, particularly the Christian Voice. . . .

Three areas of concerns are generally shared by the religious right and political candidates are graded in each area.

One set of religious right issues has to do with the preservation of traditional moral values. Specific concerns include curbing abortion, opposition to ERA, gay rights and other alternate lifestyles as destructive of the family unity, and banning pornography. The pro-life issue comes closer than any other to being, especially for Catholics, what the *Christian Century* has called "one of the most intense 'single issues' yet to plague the American political system." At the huge Convocation '81 rally held by religious conservatives in Washington in February, 1981, the pro-life groups seemed particularly confident that they were the "vital element of the whole New Right package deal." Several pro-life constitutional amendments have been proposed, all aimed generally at defining life as beginning at conception.

If pro-life is the most important single issue in the coalition, the most hysterical moral issue for most fundamentalists is the open flaunting of alternate lifestyles. Fundamentalism is a masculine movement, its language filled with militant, aggressive imagery. "Men are the key to a moral revolution in America," wrote Falwell. "Men have led women and children a long way; now it is time for an 'army' of spiritually concerned men to lead America the right way." The Equal Rights Amendment is seen as a threat to traditional sex roles; Falwell has warned that it would allow homosexual marriages. But it is gay rights which receives their most severe abuse; fundamentalist sermons are filled with attacks on "homosexual perverts." James Robison's politicization can be dated from a legal confrontation with a Dallas television station in the summer of 1979 when his program was cancelled because of his withering attacks on homosexuals. Homosexuality quite obviously disgusts fundamentalists, and a recent critic of the religious right charges that "while Falwell piously informs us that it is our duty to love homosexuals, he makes it clear that God wants them killed." In general, this set of issues symbolizes what conservatives believe is a pervasive decay in the moral fiber of American society.

The second set of issues which unites the religious right concerns schools, and, at least partly, reflects old doctrinal concerns. At the center is the still unresolved issue of teaching evolution. Nell Seagraves and her son Kelly, of recent television fame, have led an attack in California for the past eighteen years through their San Diego-based Creation Science Research Center to require that textbooks specifically acknowledge that evolution is a theory and not a fact. Most anti-evolutionist plans are more ambitious. While it is clear that laws prohibiting the teaching of evolution are unconstitutional (the Supreme Court finally ruling in 1968 that the 1927 Arkansas law violated the First Amendment), most recent efforts have tried to force the teaching of creationism. A 1973 Tennessee law requiring teachers to explain the Genesis account was declared unconstitutional because it gave preferential treatment to a particular faith. Creationists have since pressed for the teaching of "scientific creationism" in schools where evolution is taught. In more than thirty states legislation is now pending on that subject. A bill which almost surely will be introduced in Congress this year would require equal federal funding for creationist research, equal federal allocations for creationists' museum exhibits, and restrict evolutionary teaching in the schools. Despite a string of judicial setbacks, the creationist assault has had its impact. Many widely used textbooks now approach evolution with great caution and many school boards, in order to avoid confrontation with the fundamentalists, have either de-emphasized evolution or omitted it entirely. "Quite likely," writes one critic, "many students graduating from today's schools have no knowledge of evolution."

More emotional is the effort to nullify the 1963 Supreme Court decision banning prayer in the public schools. Angered by this symbol of the secularization of the school system, the issue has become a test case for fundamentalists. In recent testimony before the House Judiciary Committee, James Robison charged that banning prayer in the schools was followed by "plagues" which included "acceleration of the Vietnam war, escalation of crime, disintegration of families, racial conflict, teenage pregnancies and venereal disease." Senator Jesse Helms introduced a bill in 1980 which would have banned federal court review of any case involving prayer in the schools; other conservatives favored a constitutional amendment guaranteeing that right. . . .

The third set of issues uniting the religious right includes support for military spending, an aggressive foreign policy, and, especially, vigorous support for Israel. It is at this point that the conservative alliance is probably weakest, since many conservative businessmen favor an accommodation with the Arabs. It is also at this point that the religious right seems to its critics to be least Christian. And yet, the militant pro-Israel foreign policy of the religious right is probably the issue most directly related to its doctrinal beliefs. More ominously, as several critics have observed, this is the point at which the religious right might well make its largest contribution toward the dramatic world-ending cataclysm they are confident is rapidly approaching.

Such, then, are the general outlines of the rise of the religious right.

2. LIBERATION/ALIENATION

Blacks

Liberation Theology

The Third World, the persecuted and oppressed, the hungry and the poor all found in theology, or at least in some theology, a message of emancipation and liberation. For many of these persons, Christianity had a new relevance, a new dynamism, even a new revolutionary power. For blacks in America, the strongest theological voice was that of James Cone (b. 1938), professor of theology at Union Theological Seminary in New York City. Cone published Black Theology and Black Power *in 1969,* A Black Theology of Liberation *in 1970, and edited (with G. S. Wilmore) an enormously valuable documentary history of* Black Theology *in 1979. In the excerpt below, Cone explains why liberation is at the heart of theology and why black theology may at present be the only theology possible in America.*

Christian theology is a theology of liberation. It is *a rational study of the being of God in the world in light of the existential situation of an oppressed community, relating the forces of liberation to the essence of the gospel, which is Jesus Christ.* This means that its sole reason for existence is to put into ordered speech the meaning of God's activity in the world, so that the community of the oppressed will recognize that their inner thrust for liberation is not only *consistent* with the gospel but *is* the gospel of Jesus Christ. There can be no Christian theology which is not identified unreservedly with those who are humiliated and abused. In fact, theology ceases to be a theology of the gospel when it fails to arise out of the community of the oppressed. For it is impossible to speak of the God of Israelite history, who is the God who revealed himself in Jesus Christ, without recognizing that he is the God *of* and *for* those who labor and are heavy laden.

Unfortunately, American white theology has not been involved in the

[Source: J. H. Cone, *A Black Theology of Liberation* (Philadelphia: J. B. Lippincott, 1970), pp. 17–18, 22–24.]

struggle for black liberation. It has been basically a theology of the white oppressor, giving religious sanction to the genocide of Indians and the enslavement of black people. From the very beginning to the present day, American white theological thought has been "patriotic," either by defining the theological task independently of black suffering (the liberal northern approach) or by defining Christianity as compatible with white racism (the conservative southern approach). In both cases theology becomes a servant of the state, and that can only mean death to black people. It is little wonder that an increasing number of black religionists are finding it difficult to be black and also to be identified with traditional theological thought forms.

The appearance of Black Theology on the American scene then is due exclusively to the failure of white religionists to relate the gospel of Jesus to the pain of being black in a white racist society. It arises from the need of black people to liberate themselves from white oppressors. Black Theology is a theology of liberation because it is a theology which arises from an identification with the oppressed blacks of America, seeking to interpret the gospel of Christ in the light of the black condition. It believes that the liberation of black people *is* God's liberation.

The task of Black Theology then is to analyze the nature of the gospel of Jesus Christ in the light of oppressed black people so they will see the gospel as inseparable from the necessary power to break the chains of oppression. This means that it is a theology of and for the black community, seeking to interpret the religious dimensions of the forces of liberation in that community.

There are two reasons why Black Theology is Christian theology and possibly the only expression of Christian theology in America. First, there can be no theology of the gospel which does not arise from an oppressed community. This is so because God in Christ has revealed himself as a God whose righteousness is inseparable from the weak and helpless in human society. The goal of Black Theology is to interpret God's activity as he is related to the oppressed black community.

Second, Black Theology is Christian theology because it centers on Jesus Christ. There can be no Christian theology which does not have Jesus Christ as its point of departure. Though Black Theology affirms the black condition as the primary datum of reality which must be reckoned with, this does not mean that it denies the absolute revelation of God in Jesus Christ. Rather it affirms it. Unlike white theology which tends to make the Christ-event an abstract, intellectual idea, Black Theology believes that the black community itself is precisely where Christ is at work. The Christ-event in twentieth-century America is a black-event, that is, an event of liberation taking place in the black community in which black people recognize that it is incumbent upon them to throw off the chains of white oppression by whatever means they regard as suitable. This is what God's revelation means to black and white America, and why Black Theology may be the only possible theology in our time.

Muslim Theology

Black Muslims — or the Nation of Islam — in the 1960s represented not merely a rejection of the white man's theology but of Christianity itself. What was evident initially was not so much an embrace of worldwide Islam as a thrusting away of a religion that was seen as only another instrument in the hands of whites for keeping blacks suppressed, dependent, and haunted by a sense of their own inferiority. Malcolm X (1925 – 65) preached the Black Muslim gospel of the black's inherent and historical superiority, a truth that has been deliberately concealed from him for centuries. In 1963 and after, Malcolm X began to moderate his rhetoric and pull away from the dogmatic certainties handed down by Elijah Muhammad and other leaders in the Black Muslim movement. This moderation was seen as defection, and on February 21, 1965, Malcolm X was assassinated. That violent act robbed the United States of a major voice and a much-needed voice of reconciliation. The document below, however, comes from his earlier phase as loyal spokesman for Black Muslims and for Allah as perceived by that group.

"The true knowledge," reconstructed much more briefly than I received it, was that history had been "whitened" in the white man's history books, and that the black man had been "brainwashed for hundred of years." Original Man was black, in the continent called Africa where the human race had emerged on the planet Earth.

The black man, original man, built great empires and civilizations and cultures while the white man was still living on all fours in caves. "The devil white man," down through history, out of his devilish nature, had pillaged, murdered, raped, and exploited every race of man not white.

Human history's greatest crime was the traffic in black flesh when the devil white man went into Africa and murdered and kidnapped to bring to the West in chains, in slave ships, millions of black men, women, and children who were worked and beaten and tortured as slaves.

The devil white man cut these black people off from all knowledge of their own kind, and cut them off from any knowledge of their own language, religion, and past culture, until the black man in America was the earth's only race of people who had absolutely no knowledge of his true identity.

In one generation, the black slave women in America had been raped by the slavemaster white man until there had begun to emerge a homemade, handmade, brainwashed race that was no longer even of its true color, that no longer even knew its true family names. The slavemaster forced his family name upon this rape-mixed race, which the slavemaster began to call "the Negro."

This "Negro" was taught of his native Africa that it was peopled by

[Source: *The Autobiography of Malcolm X* (New York: Grove Press, 1964), pp. 163 – 64.]

heathen, black savages, swinging like monkeys from trees. This "Negro"
accepted this along with every other teaching of the slavemaster that was
designed to make him accept and obey and worship the white man.

And where the religion of every other people on earth taught its believers
of a God with whom they could identify, a God who at least looked like one
of their own kind, the slavemaster injected his Christian religion into this

Martin Luther King and Malcolm X met in Washington, D.C., in 1964; the next
year Malcolm X was slain, and three years later, King. *(Religious News Service)*

"Negro." This "Negro" was taught to worship an alien God having the same blond hair, pale skin, and blue eyes as the slavemaster.

This religion taught the "Negro" that black was a curse. It taught him to hate everything black, including himself. It taught him that everything white was good, to be admired, respected, and loved. It brainwashed this "Negro" to think he was superior if his complexion showed more of the white pollution of the slavemaster. The white man's Christian religion further deceived and brainwashed this "Negro" to always turn the other cheek, and grin, and scrape, and bow, and be humble, and to sing, and to pray, and to take whatever was dished out by the devilish white man; and to look for his pie in the sky, and for his heaven in the hereafter, while right here on earth the slavemaster white man enjoyed *his* heaven.

Many a time, I have looked back, trying to assess, just for myself, my first reactions to all this. Every instinct of the ghetto jungle streets, every hustling fox and criminal wolf instinct in me, which would have scoffed at and rejected anything else, was struck numb. It was as though all of that life merely was back there, without any remaining effect, or influence. I remember how, some time later reading the Bible in the Norfolk Prison Colony library, I came upon, then I read, over and over, how Paul on the road to Damascus, upon hearing the voice of Christ, was so smitten that he was knocked off his horse, in a daze. I do not now, and I did not then, liken myself to Paul. But I do understand his experience.

Chicanos

Response to Enculturation
If for most of America's blacks, theological adjustment was a Protestant problem, for most of the nation's Hispanics, such adjustment was a Roman Catholic problem. And the adjustment came slowly not only in theology but also in ecclesiastical recognition and representation. Although about one-quarter of this nation's Roman Catholics are of Latin American descent, their representation in the offices of priest and bishop has often been less than one percent. The challenge to the Church has been one of "enculturation," argued Frank Ponce (b. 1941), Chicano priest and Associate Director of the Secretariat for Hispanic Affairs for the National Conference of Catholic Bishops. To the challenge, "the Church has responded ambiguously. . . ."

How has the Church responded to the challenge of enculturation? On the one hand, the Church has responded ambiguously, in many ways out of a

[Source: Frank Ponce, in *New Catholic World*, July/Aug., 1980, pp. 164–65.]

fear that allowing cultural diversity would wound the Church's unity, and also because applying the Gospel in a given culture is extremely complex. On the other hand, there are hopeful signs that a greater consciousness regarding the demands of enculturation is arising. But on the whole, the Church's failures have often been more impressive than its successes.

For example, one need only look closely at the ethnic, racial, and cultural make-up of our parishes. Especially in dioceses or regions where Blacks, Hispanics, American Indians, or other minorities predominate, we need to ask: How are these groups represented — not merely in a token way — in parish councils, in diocesan pastoral councils? And if parishes — the particular "local Churches" imaging the universal Church — truly breed vocations, why are our seminaries pathetically bereft of Blacks, Hispanics, or American Indians? (The seminaries of religious orders fare better here than diocesan seminaries perhaps because of the "missions" influence.) More importantly, in their evangelizing efforts, do our parishes continue to "save the saved," or are bold, creative efforts made to reach out to the alienated, the disaffected, the marginal — most of them the very groups excluded by our lack of cultural sensitivity? How we answer these questions as Church will help us gauge our efforts at enculturation.

The picture becomes clearer — or muddier, depending on one's perspective — when we look at the Church's national leadership. To be sure, there are now eight Hispanic bishops, when in 1970 there was only one. And to be sure, there are now five Black bishops, when ten years ago there were none. Yet, given the centuries-old presence of these two groups in the United States (and that there are approximately 320 bishops), is not the record rather dismal? And what of the (lack of) presence of American Indians? They have a saint, Kateri Tekakwitha, but it is odd that the mystery of episcopal divine election has not yet alighted on any American Indian for the bishop's office. Now one should not dwell on the "numbers game," but statistics do tell us part of the problem and gives us part of the solution.

As one who participated in the Detroit "Call to Action" in 1976, I could not help but be gratified by the number of racial, cultural, and ethnic groups there represented. I was not inspired, however, by the lack of similar representation at the "Call to Action" follow-up, "To Do the Work of Justice," held in Washington, D.C., this past March. This national workshop asked bishops to send their diocesan personnel to learn skills enabling them to carry out the mandate of the Detroit meeting. The conclusion: few dioceses have — or are willing to involve — Blacks, Hispanics, American Indians, Asian Americans, or other minorities in responsible, diocesan decision-making positions.

We trumpet loudly the importance of a Catholic press in forming and informing our faithful. Yet I could not help swallowing hard when the excellent paper, *Impact,* published by the National Organization of Black Catholics (NOBC) reported in its December 1978 issue that only two Black journalists work in the Catholic press, which has 470 publications. Certainly these figures are little better among Hispanics, American Indians, or Asian Americans.

On everyone's lips these days, especially after the tragic Jonestown events, is the meteoric rise of cults. One of these, the so-called "Moonies," is alive and well among Hispanics. In Brooklyn the "Moonies" have bought a large storefront building, offered various health services, staffed their offices with bilingual personnel (the director is a Cuban ex-priest), and provided food for families. Hispanics flock there by the hundreds. How many are converted is unknown. But this much is known: Hispanics are respected, they are served cheerfully — and in *their own language.* How many Catholic schools, churches, and agencies can boast the same? Of course I could recount numerous stories about Hispanic services being relegated to Church basements, Blacks discriminated against in numerous seminaries, derision of American Indian religious beliefs in Catholic publications, perduring stereotypes of "inscrutable Eastern" orientals and such. But you get the idea: we've a long way to go making enculturation a fact, not a fiction, in our Catholic Church.

Unity in Pluralism

In 1977 the second National Pastoral Hispanic Conference (Encuentro) met at Trinity College in Washington, D.C. The very fact of such a gathering (the first had been held in 1972) dramatized the growing recognition of this large and largely ignored minority within the Catholic community. But the proceedings themselves were also dramatic as the 850 delegates passed resolutions relating to human rights, education, political responsibility, and the conduct of the Church. The Cuban bishop-in-exile, Eduardo Boza Masvidal (b. 1915), spoke of what Latins had to give to North American culture and vice-versa. In seeking "unity in pluralism" the choice for Hispanics — whether north or south of the border — was not between capitalism and Marxism, but between a prophetic Church and an indifferent one.

The Second National Hispanic Pastoral Encuentro, which has called together representatives from the various Hispanic communities residing in the United States, does not seek to isolate Hispanics from the mainstream, neither does it seek to encourage mistaken ideas of nationalism. Its objective, rather, is to accomplish the opposite: to create unity in pluralism and thereby to bear witness to the marvelous plan by which God made us all brothers, members of the large human family which is subject to His universal fatherhood.

[Source: E. B. Masvidal, in *Proceedings of the Segundo Encuentro Nacional Hispano de Pastoral* (Washington, D. C.: U. S. Catholic Conference, 1978), pp. 58 – 59.]

However, at the same time, He has made us all different, each with our own physical and spiritual identity.

God, in His infinite wisdom, did not ordain that each of us be a "standard" type, each cut with the same mold, uniform. Rather, He willed that individuals as well as nations retain their own identity, their language, their values, their customs, their history, their qualities and also their defects, that is to say, all those aspects which constitute their own culture. Thus, even among the Hispanic nations, there exists a great deal of diversity. This diversity neither destroys, nor does it go contrary to the unity which God intended for mankind, because unity is different from uniformity. It is compatible with diversity in the same manner that each member of a family has his own personality. This in no way destroys the unity of the family. Yet no member can take upon himself the right of absorbing another so as to make of the other a replica of himself.

Great enrichment is possible whenever two cultures come together in a spirit of mutual respect, each contributing some of its values. This constitutes a healthy integration, and both benefit. However, the opposite occurs whenever one culture absorbs the other, because then the assimilated culture has lost its own identity and its values. It is no longer itself. It is dead. . . .

I have observed that many Cubans, with whom I am in close personal contact, though I suppose the same to occur among other nationalities, present this dilemma: What must I do: integrate myself into the mainstream or continue to feel Cuban? I believe this "either-or" premise to be false; one must do both things. We must become a part of the country in which we live, love it, feel its problems, give it our best effort. At the same time we must continue to be what we are. We must not lose our own identity.

This unity in pluralism must be lived at many different levels. It must exist, first of all, within the Church. The Church is one and the same throughout the world. Wherever we go, the bishop of that diocese becomes our pastor. We must feel that that local Church is our own. In his letter to the Ephesians, St. Paul enunciates the fundamental reasons for our unity: we all have "but one Lord, one faith, one baptism, one God and Father."

Christ's message is for all peoples, yet each people must live this message within the framework of its own culture. The Second Vatican Council points this out very clearly in its *Decree on the Church's Missionary Activity*. It states: "Particular traditions, together with the individual patrimony of each family of nations, can be illumined by the light of the Gospel and then be taken up into Catholic unity" (*Ad Gentes*, 22).

Secondly, this unity in pluralism must be visible in the Church's attitude toward the exterior world. It must be open to all the peoples of the world, to their anxieties and to their problems. In this same letter to the Ephesians, St. Paul tells us that Christ, by means of His death, tore down the wall of hatred which separated men, that He came to draw close all those who were far away from God. For this reason the Second Vatican Council begins its

Mariachi band accompanies Requiem Mass for slain Franciscan father
Reynaldo Rivera in front of St. Francis Cathedral, Santa Fe, New Mexico, 1982.
(Photo by Peggy Gaustad)

Pastoral Constitution on the Church in the Modern World with these words:
"The joys and the hopes, the griefs and the anxieties of the men of this age,
especially those who are poor or in any way afflicted, those too are the joys
and hopes and the griefs and anxieties of the followers of Christ. Indeed
nothing genuinely human fails to raise an echo in their hearts" (*Gaudium et
Spes*, 1).

Today, more than ever, Christians must reject the temptation to isolate themselves in closed groups. If Christ called us to be "leaven" we have to be in the midst of all. Nevertheless, we must continue to be different, so that instead of adopting the principles and criteria of the world, we will be able to infuse it with Christian values. Our pluralism is not a confusion of ideas. It is not apathy, neither is it moral relativism. Our criteria and ideas must be very clearly delineated in our minds, even while we respect those held by others. Only in this way will our light shine before all men, so that they in turn will give glory to our Father in heaven.

We must be open to all men, but above all we must be committed to the plight of the poor and oppressed. We must follow the example of Christ, who, while loving all people, showed a preference for the weak and needy. For this reason He said: "Come unto me all you who toil and are laden." At present many of our brothers throughout Latin America and the rest of the world are forced to live in very harsh circumstances. Many are oppressed, many hungry, many unjustly imprisoned, many tortured under dictatorship both of the right and of the left, by regimes which are either Marxist or capitalist. We cannot be indifferent to any of these sorrows. For this reason an open Church is a prophetic Church which denounces evil wherever it exists. We cannot be harsh with one system or ideology and complacent of another, as unfortunately some Christians do today, because our commitment is not to a system but to Christ, to justice and to truth. It is necessary for Christians to refute the false premise which others seek to impose upon them, that one is either a capitalist or a Marxist. We are with the poor and oppressed of the world from the East and West, from North and South. We seek redemption by uniting with Christ for the salvation of the world, which begins in the heart of each man when he seeks liberation from sin. We strive to build a society in which the dignity of man as child of God is respected, as well as his God-given rights; where men are not divided by hatred or class struggle, but united by love; and where the human person will not be oppressed by the state, or by the oligarchics, but rather, we will be builders of our own destiny in a society in which liberty will not be an empty word. . . .

Indians: Native American Church

The Native American Church, first chartered by Oklahoma in 1918, had received charters by 1960 from a dozen states. Even the Indian, exiled and cheated where he had not been exterminated, had a right to his own religious institutions and practices (a right formally recognized in the Indian Religious Freedom Act of 1978). But that right was not won without challenge. The Native American Church employed the peyote button as a regular part of

[Source: *People* v. *Woody*, in *California Reporter*, 40 (Apr. 24, 1964), pp. 72–74, 77–78.]

its sacramental ritual, as a way of establishing communion with God or with other spirits. In 1962 three Navajo Indians were arrested near Needles, California, for using peyote in their religious rite. Charged with violating the state's narcotics act, the three were found guilty. The case of People v. Woody *was appealed to the California Supreme Court, which reversed the finding of the lower court, contending that "the varying currents of the subcultures that flow into the mainstream of our national life give it depth and beauty."*

The plant Lophophora williamsii, a small, spineless cactus, found in the Rio Grande Valley of Texas and northern Mexico, produces peyote, which grows in small buttons on the top of the cactus. Peyote's principal constituent is mescaline. When taken internally by chewing the buttons or drinking a derivative tea, peyote produces several types of hallucinations, depending primarily upon the user. In most subjects it causes extraordinary vision marked by bright and kaleidoscopic colors, geometric patterns, or scenes involving humans or animals. In others it engenders hallucinatory symptoms similar to those produced in cases of schizophrenia, dementia praecox, or paranoia. Beyond its hallucinatory effect, peyote renders for most users a heightened sense of comprehension; it fosters a feeling of friendliness toward other persons.

Peyote, as we shall see, plays a central role in the ceremony and practice of the Native American Church, a religious organization of Indians. Although the church claims no official prerequisites to membership, no written membership rolls, and no recorded theology, estimates of its membership range from 30,000 to 250,000, the wide variance deriving from differing definitions of a "member." As the anthropologists have ascertained through conversations with members, the theology of the church combines certain Christian teachings with the belief that peyote embodies the Holy Spirit and that those who partake of peyote enter into direct contact with God.

Peyotism discloses a long history. A reference to the religious use of peyote in Mexico appears in Spanish historical sources as early as 1560. Peyotism spread from Mexico to the United States and Canada; American anthropologists describe it as well established in this country during the latter part of the nineteenth century. Today, Indians of many tribes practice Peyotism. Despite the absence of recorded dogma, the several tribes follow surprisingly similar ritual and theology; the practices of Navajo members in Arizona practically parallel those of adherents in California, Montana, Oklahoma, Wisconsin, and Saskatchewan.

The "meeting," a ceremony marked by the sacramental use of peyote, composes the cornerstone of the peyote religion. The meeting convenes in an enclosure and continues from sundown Saturday to sunrise Sunday. To give thanks for the past good fortune or find guidance for future conduct, a member will "sponsor" a meeting and supply to those who attend both the peyote and the next morning's breakfast. The "sponsor," usually but not always the "leader," takes charge of the meeting; he decides the order of events and the amount of peyote to be consumed. Although the individual leader exercises an absolute control of the meeting, anthropologists report a striking uniformity of its ritual.

A meeting connotes a solemn and special occasion. Whole families attend together, although children and young women participate only by their presence. Adherents don their finest clothing, usually suits for men and fancy dresses for the women, but sometimes ceremonial Indian costumes. At the meeting the members pray, sing, and make ritual use of drum, fan, eagle bone, whistle, rattle and prayer cigarette, the symbolic emblems of their faith. The central event, of course, consists of the use of peyote in quantities sufficient to produce an hallucinatory state.

At an early but fixed stage in the ritual the members pass around a ceremonial bag of peyote buttons. Each adult may take four, the customary number, or take none. The participants chew the buttons, usually with some difficulty because of extreme bitterness; later, at a set time in the ceremony

Blackfoot Indian Father Ksistaki-Poka. The first western Indian to be ordained as a Roman Catholic priest here blesses fellow tribesmen along with Flathead and Coeur D'Alene Indians. *(Religious News Service)*

any member may ask for more peyote; occasionally a member may take as many as four more buttons. At sunrise on Sunday the ritual ends; after a brief outdoor prayer, the host and his family serve breakfast. Then the members depart. By morning the effects of the peyote disappear; the users suffer no aftereffects.

Although peyote serves as a sacramental symbol similar to bread and wine in certain Christian churches, it is more than a sacrament. Peyote constitutes in itself an object of worship; prayers are directed to it much as prayers are devoted to the Holy Ghost. On the other hand, to use peyote for nonreligious purposes is sacrilegious. Members of the church regard peyote also as a "teacher" because it induces a feeling of brotherhood with other members; indeed, it enables the participant to experience the Deity. Finally, devotees treat peyote as a "protector." Much as a Catholic carries his medallion, an Indian G.I. often wears around his neck a beautifully beaded pouch containing one large peyote button.

The record thus establishes that the application of the statutory prohibition of the use of peyote results in a virtual inhibition of the practice of defendants' religion. To forbid the use of peyote is to remove the theological heart of Peyotism.

We have weighed the competing values represented in this case on the symbolic scale of constitutionality. On the one side we have placed the weight of freedom of religion as protected by the First Amendment; on the other, the weight of the state's "compelling interest." Since the use of peyote incorporates the essence of the religious expression, the first weight is heavy. Yet the use of peyote presents only slight danger to the state and to the enforcement of its laws; the second weight is relatively light. The scale tips in favor of the constitutional protection.

We know that some will urge that it is more important to subserve the rigorous enforcement of the narcotic laws than to carve out of them an exception for a few believers in a strange faith. They will say that the exception may produce problems of enforcement and that the dictate of the state must overcome the beliefs of a minority of Indians. But the problems of enforcement here do not inherently differ from those of other situations which call for the detection of fraud. On the other hand, the right to free religious expression embodies a precious heritage of our history. In a mass society, which presses at every point toward conformity, the protection of a self-expression, however unique, of the individual and the group becomes ever more important. The varying currents of the subcultures that flow into the mainstream of our national life give it depth and beauty. We preserve a greater value than an ancient tradition when we protect the rights of the Indians who honestly practiced an old religion in using peyote one night at a meeting in a desert hogan near Needles, California.

The judgment is reversed.

Women

Judaism

If civil rights dominated the 1950s and 1960s, women's rights and feminist movements dominated the 1970s. Religion of course did not, could not remain aloof to this "liberation," anymore than it had to those already considered. Questions arose concerning the ordination of women ministers, priests, and rabbis; concerning full participation in the liturgies and on the governing boards of local or national churches; and concerning masculinely loaded theological and biblical language —"the rhetoric of sexuality." Even in Orthodox Judaism, seemingly impervious to the feminist movement (in any case, impervious to the ordination of women rabbis), the wedge of women's liberation entered. In the engaging autobiographical account below, one follows the slowly dawning realization that male domination in Orthodox Judaism had been total.

I was born into a strongly traditional family. With all the structure this entails, it was quite natural to be socialized early into the proper roles. I knew my place and I liked it — the warmth, the rituals, the solid, tight parameters. I never gave a thought as to what responsibilities I did or didn't have as a female growing up in the Orthodox Jewish community. It was just the way things were — the most natural order in the world.

My friends and I shared the same world of expectation. I remember the year of the bar mitzvahs of our eighth-grade male friends. We girls sat up in the women's section of the synagogue and took great pride in "our boys." If we thought about ourselves at all, it was along the lines of "thank God we are females and don't have to go through the public ordeal." Quite remarkably, there never was any envy of what the boys were doing, never a thought of "why not us?" Perhaps it was because we knew that our big moment would come: as proper young ladies growing up in the modern Orthodox community in the 1950s, *our* puberty rite was the Sweet Sixteen.

My short-lived encounter with daily prayer ended when I was fourteen. I had graduated from a local yeshiva in Far Rockaway, New York, and had begun commuting to a girls' yeshiva high school in Brooklyn. This meant getting up an hour earlier to catch the 7:18 Long Island train, so prayer was the first thing to go. I had it down to a science: if I laid out my clothes in exactly the right order the night before, I could set the alarm for 6:52, get up, wash, dress, eat the hot breakfast without which, my mother insisted, a person could not face the world each day, and still have time to walk briskly

[Source: Blu Greenberg, *On Women and Judaism: A View from Tradition* (Philadelphia: Jewish Publication Society of America, 1981), pp. 21–22, 25–26, 27–29.]

Rabbi Sally Priesand (center), ordained as first female rabbi in the United
States, Temple Emanu-El, New York City, 1972
(Religious News Service)

to the train. I would reserve a four-seater in the same car each day. Just as
the train started to pull out, my friends who were attending the boys' yeshiva
would come dashing down the platform and fling themselves onto the slowly
moving train. I knew that they had been up since six o'clock to allow enough
time for *shaharit*, the mandatory morning prayers. There they were, a little
bleary-eyed, already spent at 7:18, with just a package of Sen-Sen for breakfast. Those were wonderful, funny trips. Though I laughed with the boys
each morning, I certainly didn't envy their more rigorous regimen. . . .

After my marriage in the late 1950s, my feelings of contentment and
fulfillment were enhanced rather than diminished. The ways of a traditional
Jewish woman suited me just fine. All those platitudes about building a
faithful Jewish home were not nearly as pleasant as the real thing itself.
Moreover, none of those obligations ruled out graduate studies and plans for
a career. It was a time of peaceful coexistence between the traditional roles
and the initial stirrings of self-actualization for women. I considered myself
very lucky to have a husband to care for me and I for him — a man, moreover,
who encouraged me to expand my own horizons.

The religious role of a married woman was also perfect in my eyes. I found the clear division of labor, and its nonnegotiable quality, most satisfying. It never crossed my mind that experiencing certain mitzvot* vicariously was anything less than the real thing. Quite the reverse. When my husband had to be away on the Sabbath, the act of my reciting the blessings over the wine and the bread for our small children only served to heighten my sense of loneliness for him.

The real thing, then, was for him to perform his mitzvot and for me to attend to mine. I wasn't looking for anything more than I had, certainly not in the way of religious obligations or rights. On those bitter cold Sabbath mornings I was absolutely delighted to linger an hour longer in a nice warm bed and play with the kids rather than to have to brave the elements. I could choose to go to the synagogue when I wanted or pray at home when I wanted; for my husband there was no choice.

The *mehitzah*** separating men from women in the synagogue served to symbolize the dividing line. Although there were certain things about sitting behind the *mehitzah* that I didn't exactly appreciate, none seemed an attack on my womanhood. Not only did I not perceive the *mehitzah* to be a denigration of women in the synagogue, but I couldn't understand why some Jews felt that way. At some level, to me the *mehitzah* symbolized the ancient, natural, immutable order of male and female. One didn't question such things. . . .

And then came feminism. In 1963, I read Betty Friedan's *Feminine Mystique,* still the classic text of the women's movement. I was a little intimidated by its force and had trouble with what seemed to me a portent of friction between the sexes, but the essential idea, equality of women, was exciting, and mind-boggling, and very just. Still, correct or not, it didn't mean me, nor did it apply to women in Judaism. On that score I was defensive, resistant, and probably just plain frightened. It must have threatened my status quo.

And yet . . . Once I had tasted of the fruit of the tree of knowledge, there was no going back. The basic idea had found a resting spot somewhere inside me. Little by little, and with a good deal of prodding from my husband, I became sensitized to issues and situations that previously had made no impression on me. Some of my complacency was eroded; my placidity churned up. In place of blind acceptance, I slowly began to ask questions, not really sure if I wanted to hear the answers. Because I was so satisfied, because I had no sense of injustice, some of the new thinking, including my own, came to me as a shock. Things that had run right past me before I now had to grab hold of, for a still moment, to examine under the white light of equality.

I began to think not just about the idea, but about myself as a woman — in relation to people, to a place in the larger society, to a career, and finally to Judaism. I did not look back over my past and say it was bad. In fact, I

*Commandments, duties.
**Curtain.

knew it was very good. What I did begin to say was that perhaps it could have been better. Again, it was not a case of closing my eyes and thinking hard. Instead, it was a series of incidents, encounters, a matter of timing; it was also memories and recollections, a review in which isolated incidents began to emerge as part of a pattern. This pattern now had to be tested against a new value framework.

It was almost ten years before I began systematically to apply the new categories to my Jewishness. As I reviewed my education, one fact emerged — a fact so obvious that I was stunned more by my unresponsiveness to it over the years than by the fact itself. It was this: the study of Talmud, which was a primary goal in my family and community, consistently was closed off to me. Beginning with elementary school, the girls studied Israeli folk dancing while the boys studied Talmud. In the yeshiva high school, the girls' branch had no course of study in Talmud; the boys' branch had three hours a day. In Israel, in the Jewish studies seminar, all of the classes were coeducational except Talmud. The girls studied laws and customs on one day and enjoyed a free period the other four days.

And then there was my father. The great love of his life, beyond his family, was not his business; it was his study of the Talmud. Every day, before he left for work, he would spend an hour studying Talmud with a rabbi friend. In fact, he had not missed a day of study in his life, even during family vacations or times of stress. Yet although he reviewed religious texts regularly with his daughters, it was never Talmud. He even would collar my dates, while I was getting ready, for a few minutes of Talmud discussion. That we didn't participate in those years more directly in our father's passion for Talmud study was not a willful denial on his part; he simply was following the hallowed custom. As a result of all this, when I began to study rabbinic literature in graduate school in my late twenties, I realized that my male fellow students all had the edge of fifteen or twenty years of Talmud study behind them.

Gradually, too, I became aware of the power of conditioning and how early in life it takes place. On the last Sabbath that my husband served as rabbi of a congregation, the children and I decided to surprise him. Moshe, then ten and a half, prepared the haftarah reading, David, nine, the *An'im Zemirot* prayer, and J.J., six, the *Adon Olam*. It was a real treat for their father and for the entire congregation; it seemed to the boys as if the whole world was proud of them. On the following Sunday morning, their grandparents visited and gave each of the boys two dollars for doing such a fine job. When the boys told Deborah, then eight, that they each had been given two dollars, she complained that it wasn't fair. At which point Moshe retorted, with the biting honesty of a ten year old: "Well, so what, you can't even do anything in the synagogue!" Click, click, I thought to myself, another woman radicalized.

Oddly enough, until that moment it never had occurred to me that it could or should be otherwise, that perhaps it wasn't "fair" to a little girl. Even more astounding was the fact that with all the weeks of secret practice, all the fuss I had made over the boys beforehand, and all the compliments they received afterward, Deborah never once had complained. It was only the two dollars that finally got to her; to everything else she had already been conditioned . . . to expect nothing.

Mormonism

The Equal Rights Amendment (ERA) proposed that just as the rights of citizens could "not be denied or abridged . . . on account of race, color, or previous condition of servitude," so those rights could not be violated on grounds of gender. The amendment, requiring the endorsement by two-thirds of the states, failed to win ratification in 1982. What it did win was both passionate support and passionate opposition. Many religious bodies endorsed the amendment, some opposed it, and some held themselves aloof. The Church of Jesus Christ of Latter Day Saints through its leadership spoke against the amendment as a threat to traditional family life and moral values. One member of that church, Sonia Johnson, openly and strongly supported ERA. When neither she nor the church authorities backed away from an inevitable confrontation, Sonia Johnson was formally tried and excommunicated in December of 1979. Below, the excommunicated Mormon gives her version of the summons to trial in Virginia before the court presided over by Bishop Jeff Willis.

I read the letter again. This was Wednesday night [Nov. 14, 1979] — late by now. The trial was set for early Saturday morning. Slowly I began to understand the strategy behind it all. They were giving me only two days! Two days to prepare my defense, to prepare myself spiritually, psychologically, two days to find witnesses. *Only two days!* The cruelty of that and the already clear judgment it revealed that had been made about my guilt struck me like a heavy fist in the face. They did not intend to give me a real trial at all! They were not even going to give me a real chance to defend myself. I had been found guilty and now they were only going through the formalities. . . .

Press coverage of the trial had begun.

Thursday, November 15. I tried all day to reach Jeff [Willis]. Judy told me he was on jury duty (ironies never ceased) and could not be reached all day. Frantically, I explained to her that I had only two days before the trial and that I did not even know what the charges were. Would she please help

[Source: Sonia Johnson, *From Housewife to Heretic* (New York: Doubleday & Co., 1981), pp. 276, 278– 80.]

me get in touch with Jeff. Finally, she made an appointment for me with him at 8 P.M. that night at the Sterling Park Ward chapel. One whole precious day wasted. In the end, I drove out to Sterling Park Ward alone, and at 8 P.M. sat for the last time alone with Jeff Willis in that office.

As I recall, the first question I asked him was, "Who is my accuser?" "I am," he answered. "Who is my judge, then?" "I am," he said again. "But how can you be both my accuser and my judge? For heaven's sake, Jeff, I've been an American too long to feel comfortable with that. I'm accustomed to

Three Episcopal women ordained in 1974 celebrate the Eucharist in Riverside Church, New York City. *(Religious News Service)*

at least the appearance of due process. If you've decided I'm guilty — and you must have, since you're willing to accuse me — how can you bring an impartial decision?" "Don't worry, Sonia," he assured me. "I will receive the correct decision through inspiration from our Heavenly Father. The courts of the church are courts of love." Ignoring the love nonsense, I asked, "How do you expect to be able to hear God's will over the roar of your own conviction that I'm guilty? What exactly do you expect him to do, Jeff? Hit you over the head with a lightning bolt? Knock you down on the road to Langley?"

I was not mollified. I was as prayerful a person as I had ever known (except for my mother), and I knew how hard it is to get answers. I had heard mission presidents say that they could not tell whether or not someone had negroid ancestry no matter how hard they prayed. I very much suspected that Jeff was more influenced by what his superiors told him *they* had heard from God than he was from what he had personally managed to glean. "Wait just a second, God. I have to check it out with the Big Boys." But I was determined not to view the situation as hopeless — though I know now that it was from the beginning.

"What are the charges against me, Jeff? Please write them down so we will each know this is what you said, and so I won't make a mistake when I tell my witnesses what they need to respond to."

He refused to write anything down. That's what comes of working for the CIA — deep distrust as a first response. So I asked him if he would dictate the charges to me. He agreed to do that. Perhaps because they were not in his handwriting, he could forever deny that they had come from him. I cannot imagine why else he refused to write them himself. These are his exact words as I took them down on the night of November 15, 1979:

"You have broken the covenants you made in the temple, specifically:

1. evil speaking of the Lord's anointed;
2. the law of consecration;
3. your general attitude and expression."

I protested. Where have I spoken evil of the Lord's anointed? I asked. In your APA speech, he answered. Show me the place, I demanded. "You call them chauvinistic," he shot back. "That's not evil; that's true!" I replied. "And what's this about the law of consecration?" You promised in the temple to give your time, your talents, all the Lord has blessed you with and all he may yet bless you with to the upbuilding of the church and to the establishment of Zion."

"Jeff, I pay a full tithing and have all my life. I'm the ward organist and spend many extra hours practicing alone and with the choir. I teach the cultural refinement lesson in Relief Society, I am a visiting teacher [in the Relief Society], I attend church, we hold family home evenings, I attend the temple. If you're going to excommunicate everybody in the ward who is doing this much or less, you won't have anybody left in the congregation when you're through!

"And tell me how I'm going to defend myself against your annoyance at my 'general attitude and expression.' What does that even mean? Just because men in the church don't like uppity women, does that mean we should all be *excommunicated?*" I thought but held my tongue: "Do we have to have an attitude of hero worship and awe even when our male leaders do little or nothing to deserve it? Why should we be in awe? Because you're *male?*"

3. LITIGATION/DIVISION

Public Education

*The question of religion and the public schools, a curricular and a consti-
tutional issue, has threatened the unity of towns, school boards, churches, and
courts. In the nineteenth century, passions had been aroused in New York
City, Cincinnati, San Francisco, and elsewhere (see above, pp. 39, 50,
and 52). But in the 1960s and beyond, passions were inflamed all across
the nation. (The debate grew warm again in the 1980s when President
Ronald Reagan joined those proposing a constitutional amendment that would
permit individual or group prayer in public schools or other public buildings.)
In 1962 (*Engel v. Vitale*) the U. S. Supreme Court declared unconstitutional the use of a prayer written by New York's Board of Regents in the
public schools. The outcry greeting that decision revealed the country's deep
divisions and this issue's capacity to arouse intense emotion. Francis Cardinal
Spellman responded to the decision by saying that he was "shocked and
frightened." Bishop James A. Pike declared that "the Supreme Court has
just deconsecrated the nation." Others saw in the decision a communist conspiracy or found it merely "asinine" and "stupid." On the other hand,
theologians writing in the* Christian Century *argued that the decision "protects the integrity of the religious conscience and the proper function of religious
and governmental institutions." And the president of the Southern Baptist
Convention at that time, Herschel H. Hobbs, concluded that the Court had
"struck one of the most powerful blows in our lifetime . . . for the freedom
of religion in our Nation." Justice Hugo Black (1886 – 1971) wrote the
opinion of the Court, a portion of which follows.*

We think that by using its public school system to encourage recitation of
the Regents' prayer, the State of New York has adopted a practice wholly
inconsistent with the Establishment Clause. There can, of course, be no doubt
that New York's program of daily classroom invocation of God's blessing as
prescribed in the Regents' prayer is a religious activity. It is a solemn avowal

[Source: R. T. Miller and R. B. Flowers, *Toward Benevolent Neutrality: Church, State,
and the Supreme Court*, rev. ed. (Waco, Texas: Baylor University Press, 1982), pp. 332,
333, 334 – 35.]

of divine faith and supplication for the blessings of the Almighty. The nature of such a prayer has always been religious, none of the respondents has denied this and the trial court expressly so found:

"The religious nature of prayer was recognized by Jefferson and has been concurred in by theological writers, the United States Supreme Court and State courts and administrative officials, including New York's Commissioner of Education. A committee of the New York Legislature has agreed.

"The Board of Regents as *amicus curiae,* the respondents and intervenors all concede the religious nature of prayer, but seek to distinguish this prayer because it is based on our spiritual heritage. . . ."

The petitioners contend among other things that the state laws requiring or permitting use of the Regents' prayer must be struck down as a violation of the Establishment Clause because that prayer was composed by governmental officials as a part of a governmental program to further religious beliefs. For this reason, petitioners argue, the State's use of the Regents' prayer in its public school system breaches the constitutional wall of separation between Church and State. We agree with that contention since we think that the constitutional prohibition against laws respecting an establishment of religion must at least mean that in this country it is no part of the business of government to compose official prayers for any group of the American people to recite as a part of a religious program carried on by government.

It is a matter of history that this very practice of establishing governmentally composed prayers for religious services was one of the reasons which caused many of our early colonists to leave England and seek religious freedom in America. The Book of Common Prayer, which was created under governmental direction and which was approved by Acts of Parliament in 1548 and 1549, set out in minute detail the accepted form and content of prayer and other religious ceremonies to be used in the established, tax-supported Church of England. The controversies over the Book and what should be its content repeatedly threatened to disrupt the peace of that country as the accepted forms of prayer in the established church changed with the views of the particular ruler that happened to be in control at the time. Powerful groups representing some of the varying religious views of the people struggled among themselves to impress their particular views upon the Government and obtain amendments of the Book more suitable to their respective notions of how religious services should be conducted in order that the official religious establishment would advance their particular religious beliefs. Other groups, lacking the necessary political power to influence the Government on the matter, decided to leave England and its established church and seek freedom in America from England's governmentally ordained and supported religion. . . .

By the time of the adoption of the Constitution, our history shows that there was a widespread awareness among many Americans of the dangers of a union of Church and State. These people knew, some of them from bitter personal experience, that one of the greatest dangers to the freedom of the individual to worship in his own way lay in the Government's placing its official stamp of approval upon one particular kind of prayer or one particular form of religious services. They knew the anguish, hardship and bitter strife that could come when zealous religious groups struggled with one another to obtain the Government's stamp of approval from each King, Queen, or Protector that came to temporary power. The Constitution was intended to avert a part of this danger by leaving the government of this country in the hands of the people rather than in the hands of any monarch. But this safeguard was not enough. Our Founders were no more willing to let the content of their prayers and their privilege of praying whenever they pleased be influenced by the ballot box than they were to let these vital matters of personal conscience depend upon the succession of monarchs. The First Amendment was added to the Constitution to stand as a guarantee that neither the power nor the prestige of Federal Government would be used to control, support or influence the kinds of prayer the American people can say — that the people's religions must not be subjected to the pressures of government for change each time a new political administration is elected to office. Under that Amendment's prohibition against governmental establishment of religion, as reinforced by the provisions of the Fourteenth Amendment, government in this country, be it state or federal, is without power to prescribe by law any particular form of prayer which is to be used as an official prayer in carrying on any program of governmentally sponsored religious activity.

There can be no doubt that New York's state prayer program officially establishes the religious beliefs embodied as the Regents' prayer. The respondents' argument to the contrary, which is largely based upon the contention that the Regents' prayer is "nondenominational" and the fact that the program, as modified and approved by state courts, does not require all pupils to recite the prayer but permits those who wish to do so to remain silent or be excused from the room, ignores the essential nature of the program's constitutional defects. Neither the fact that the prayer may be denominationally neutral nor the fact that its observance on the part of the students is voluntary can serve to free it from the limitations of the Establishment Clause. . . .

It has been argued that to apply the Constitution in such a way as to prohibit state laws respecting an establishment of religious services in public schools is to indicate a hostility toward religion or toward prayer. Nothing, of course, could be more wrong. The history of man is inseparable from the history of religion. And perhaps it is not too much to say that since the beginning of that history many people have devoutly believed that "More things are wrought by prayer than this world dreams of." It was doubtless largely due to men who believed this that there grew up a sentiment that caused men to leave the cross-currents of officially established state religions and religious persecution in Europe and come to this country filled with the hope that they could find a place in which they could pray when they pleased to the God of their faith in the language they chose. And there were men of this same faith in the power of prayer who led the fight for adoption of our Constitution and also for our Bill of Rights with the very guarantees of religious freedom that forbid the sort of governmental activity which New York has attempted here. These men knew that the First Amendment, which tried to put an end to governmental control of religion and of prayer, was not written to destroy either. They knew rather that it was written to quiet well-justified fears which nearly all of them felt arising out of an awareness that governments of the past had shackled men's tongues to make them speak only the religious thoughts that government wanted them to speak and to pray only to the God that government wanted them to pray to. It is neither sacrilegious nor anti-religious to say that each separate government in this country should stay out of the business of writing or sanctioning official prayers and leave that purely religious function to the people themselves and to those the people choose to look to for religious guidance.

Private Education

*Religion and private education presented problems that were chiefly financial: how much in tax monies, if any, may be used in support of schools (directly or indirectly) that are private and often sectarian. If money cannot be given directly to such a school, can the public treasury be used for the support of auxiliary services, or for the purchase of instructional materials, or for conducting state-mandated tests, or for constructing buildings where no religious instruction will take place, or . . . ? Litigation in this complex area has forced the U. S. Supreme Court to move beyond the language of the First Amendment in order to apply other tests by which to reach a determination. For example, is the benefit granted primarily to the child, or to the school? Does the law in question have primarily a secular purpose? Is the effect of this particular law such as neither to advance nor inhibit religion? By the operation of this law, is government excessively entangled with religion? Is American society further divided and polarized? By the time all the questions are raised, the test may not be so clear, and the justices are most unlikely to be of one opinion. In a famous 1947 case (*Everson v. Board of Education*), the Court decided on a 5 to 4 vote that public money could be used to pay for the transportation of school children —all school children, public or private —to their respective institutions. It was a close vote and dissents were strong. Justice Black wrote the majority opinion. Twenty-one years later, however, in a case involving the free loan of textbooks to private schools in New York, Black found himself strongly op-*

[Source: R. T. Miller and R. B. Flowers, *Toward Benevolent Neutrality: Church, State, and the Supreme Court,* rev. ed. (Waco, Texas: Baylor University Press, 1982), pp. 458– 59.]

posed —and in the minority. Again, the vote was split (6 to 3), a pattern that repeated itself with monotonous regularity. Black's dissent in this case (Board of Education v. Allen [1968]) protests against a decision which, he wrote, "bodes nothing but evil to religious peace in this country."

Mr. Justice BLACK, dissenting.

The Court here affirms a judgment of the New York Court of Appeals which sustained the constitutionality of a New York law providing state tax-raised funds to supply school books for use by pupils in schools owned and operated by religious sects. I believe the New York law held valid is a flat, flagrant, open violation of the First and Fourteenth Amendments which together forbid Congress or state legislatures to enact any law "respecting an establishment of religion." For that reason I would reverse the New York Court of Appeals' judgment. . . .

The *Everson* and *McCollum** cases plainly interpret the First and Fourteenth Amendments as protecting the taxpayers of a State from being compelled to pay taxes to their government to support the agencies of private religious organizations the taxpayers oppose. To authorize a State to tax its residents for such church purposes is to put the State squarely in the religious activities of certain religious groups that happen to be strong enough politically to write their own religious preferences and prejudices into the laws. This links state and churches together in controlling the lives and destinies of our citizenship—a citizenship composed of people of myriad religious faiths, some of them bitterly hostile to and completely intolerant of the others. It was to escape laws precisely like this that a large part of the Nation's early immigrants fled to this country. It was also to escape such laws and such consequences that the First Amendment was written in language strong and clear barring passage of any law "respecting an establishment of religion."

It is true, of course, that the New York law does not as yet formally adopt or establish a state religion. But it takes a great stride in that direction and coming events cast their shadows before them. The same powerful sectarian religious propagandists who have succeeded in securing passage of the present law to help religious schools carry on their sectarian religious purposes can and doubtless will continue their propaganda, looking toward complete domination and supremacy of their particular brand of religion. And it nearly always is by insidious approaches that the citadels of liberty are more successfully attacked.

I know of no prior opinion of this Court upon which the majority here can rightfully rely to support its holding this New York law constitutional.

*The *McCollum* case (1948) concerned a program of released time for religious instruction in the public schools of Champaign, Illinois. By a vote of 8 to 1, the program was found to be unconstitutional.

Public school students receiving "released time" religious education in mobile classroom parked just off school grounds in Fort Wayne, Indiana. *(Religious News Service)*

In saying this, I am not unmindful of the fact that the New York Court of Appeals purported to follow *Everson* v. *Board of Education,* in which this Court, in an opinion written by me, upheld a New Jersey law authorizing reimbursement to parents for the transportation of children attending sectarian schools. That law did not attempt to deny the benefit of its general terms to children of any faith going to any legally authorized school. Thus, it was treated in the same way as a general law paying the streetcar fare *of all school children,* or a law providing midday lunches for all children or all school children, or a law to provide police protection for children going to and from school, or general laws to provide police and fire protection for buildings, including, of course, churches and church school buildings as well as others.

As my *Brother DOUGLAS** so forcefully shows, in an argument with which I fully agree, upholding a State's power to pay bus or streetcar fares for school children cannot provide support for the validity of a state law using tax-raised funds to buy school books for a religious school. The First Amendment's bar to establishment of religion must preclude a State from using

*Justice William O. Douglas (1898-1980)

funds levied from all of its citizens to purchase books for use by sectarian schools, which, although "secular," realistically will in some way inevitably tend to propagate the religious views of the favored sect. Books are the most essential tool of education since they contain the resources of knowledge which the educational process is designed to exploit. In this sense it is not difficult to distinguish books, which are the heart of any school, from bus fares, which provide a convenient and helpful general public service. With respect to the former, state financial support actively and directly assists the teaching and propagation of sectarian religious viewpoints in clear conflict with the First Amendment's establishment bar; with respect to the latter, the State merely provides a general and non-discriminatory service in no way related to substantive religious views and beliefs.

This New York law, it may be said by some, makes but a small inroad and does not amount to complete state establishment of religion. But that is no excuse for upholding it. It requires no prophet to foresee that on the argument used to support this law others could be upheld providing for state or federal government funds to buy property on which to erect religious school buildings or to erect the buildings themselves, to pay the salaries of the religious school teachers, and finally to have the sectarian religious groups cease to rely on voluntary contributions of members of their sects while waiting for the Government to pick up all the bills for the religious schools. Arguments made in favor of this New York law point squarely in this direction, namely, that the fact that government has not heretofore aided religious schools with tax-raised funds amounts to a discrimination against those schools and against religion. . . .

I still subscribe to the belief that tax-raised funds cannot constitutionally be used to support religious schools, buy their school books, erect their buildings, pay their teachers, or pay any other of their maintenance expenses, even to the extent of one penny. The First Amendment's prohibition against governmental establishment of religion was written on the assumption that state aid to religion and religious schools generates discord, disharmony, hatred, and strife among our people, and that any government that supplies such aids is to that extent a tyranny. And I still believe that the only way to protect minority religious groups from majority groups in this country is to keep the wall of separation between church and state high and impregnable as the First and Fourteenth Amendments provide. The Court's affirmance here bodes nothing but evil to religious peace in this country.

Conscientious Objection

The long years of protest against the Vietnam War forced the courts to reexamine the whole question of conscientious objection to military service. In the process of that reexamination, difficult questions were posed: what is religion? what is "conscientious" —and must it be religious? can one, in good conscience, object only to a particular war? what does the national interest demand when free exercise of religion is involved? These hard queries were not all resolved, to be sure, but the U. S. Supreme Court found itself wrestling with every one of them. The national congress (in Article 6j of the Universal Military Training and Service Act of 1948) had allowed for conscientious objection only "by reason of religious training and belief," further stating that this meant "an individual's belief in relation to a Supreme Being . . ." and did not include "essentially political, sociological, or philosophical views or a merely personal moral code." Religion, and theistic religion at that, was thus given special status in the matter of conscientious objection. But in the case of the United States v. Seeger *(1965), the Court in a wide-ranging opinion spoke only of "sincere belief." Surely congress did not intend to limit exemptions only to those who acknowledged the Judeo-Christian God! In a case five years later, however, the Court (in* Welsh v. United States*) is less sure about what it meant, and presumably also less sure about what congress meant. A divided vote (5 to 3) was cast in favor of the petitioner, with Justice John Marshall Harlan (1899–1971) writing a long and troubled concurring opinion. Harlan declared that many difficulties lay ahead when one began to play semantic games, when one defined "words so as to change policy." And while he had voted with the majority in* Seeger, *"today's decision convinces me that in doing so I made a mistake. . . ." Removing the clear theistic requirement for conscientious objection was, he added, "a remarkable feat of judicial surgery."*

Candor requires me to say that I joined the Court's opinion in *United States* v. *Seeger* only with the gravest misgivings as to whether it was a legitimate exercise in statutory construction, and today's decision convinces me that in doing so I made a mistake which I should now acknowledge.

In *Seeger* the Court construed §6(j) of the Universal Military Training and Service Act so as to sustain a conscientious objector claim not founded on a theistic belief.

Today, the prevailing opinion makes explicit its total elimination of the statutorily required religious content for a conscientious objector exemption. The prevailing opinion now says: "If an individual deeply and sincerely holds beliefs that are *purely ethical* or *moral* in source and content but that never-

[Source: R. T. Miller and R. B. Flowers, *Toward Benevolent Neutrality: Church, State, and the Supreme Court,* rev. ed. (Waco, Texas: Baylor University Press, 1982), pp. 191–93.]

theless impose upon him a duty of conscience to refrain from participating in any war at any time" (emphasis added), he qualifies for a §6(j) exemption.

In my opinion, the liberties taken with the statute both in *Seeger* and today's decision cannot be justified in the name of the familiar doctrine of construing federal statutes in a manner that will avoid possible constitutional infirmities in them. There are limits to the permissible application of that doctrine, and, as I will undertake to show in this opinion, those limits were crossed in *Seeger*, and even more apparently have been exceeded in the present case. I therefore find myself unable to escape facing the constitutional issue that this case squarely presents: whether §6(j) in limiting this draft exemption to those opposed to war in general because of theistic beliefs runs afoul of the religious clauses of the First Amendment. For reasons later appearing I believe it does, and on that basis I concur in the judgment reversing this conviction, and adopt the test announced by Mr. Justice Black, not as a matter of statutory construction, but as the touchstone for salvaging a congressional policy of long standing that would otherwise have to be nullified. . . .

I

Against this legislative history it is a remarkable feat of judicial surgery to remove, as did *Seeger*, the theistic requirement of §6(j). The prevailing opinion today, however, in the name of interpreting the will of Congress, has performed a lobotomy and completely transformed the statute by reading out of it any distinction between religiously acquired beliefs and those deriving from "essentially political, sociological, or philosophical views or a merely personal moral code. . . ."

Unless we are to assume an Alice-in-Wonderland world where words have no meaning, I think it fair to say that Congress' choice of language cannot fail to convey to the discerning reader the very policy choice that the prevailing opinion today completely obliterates: that between conventional religions that usually have an organized and formal structure and dogma and a cohesive group identity, even when nontheistic, and cults that represent schools of thought and in the usual case are without formal structure or are, at most, loose and informal associations of individuals who share common ethical, moral, or intellectual views.

II

When the plain thrust of a legislative enactment can only be circumvented by distortion to avert an inevitable constitutional collision, it is only by exalting form over substance that one can justify this veering off the path that has been plainly marked by the statute. Such a course betrays extreme skepticism as to constitutionality, and, in this instance, reflects a groping to preserve the conscientious objector exemption at all cost.

I cannot subscribe to a wholly emasculated construction of a statute to avoid facing a latent constitutional question, in purported fidelity to the salutary doctrine of avoiding unnecessary resolution of constitutional issues, a principle to which I fully adhere. . . .

III

The constitutional question that must be faced in this case is whether a statute that defers to the individual's conscience only when his views emanate from adherence to theistic religious beliefs is within the power of Congress. Congress, of course, could, entirely consistently with the requirements of the Constitution, eliminate *all* exemptions for conscientious objectors. Such a course would be wholly "neutral" and, in my view, would not offend the Free Exercise Clause. . . .

The "radius" of this legislation is the conscientiousness with which an individual opposes war in general, yet the statute, as I think it must be construed, excludes from its "scope" individuals motivated by teachings of non-theistic religions, and individuals guided by an inner ethical voice that bespeaks secular and not "religious" reflection. It not only accords a preference to the "religious" but also disadvantages adherents of religions that do not worship a Supreme Being. The constitutional infirmity cannot be cured, moreover, even by an impermissible construction that eliminates the theistic requirement and simply draws the line between religious and nonreligious. This in my view offends the Establishment Clause and is that kind of classification that this Court has condemned. . . .

The policy of exempting religious conscientious objectors is one of long-standing tradition in this country and accords recognition to what is, in a diverse and "open" society, the important value of reconciling individuality of belief with practical exigencies whenever possible. It dates back to colonial times and has been perpetuated in state and federal conscription statutes. That it has been phrased in religious terms reflects, I assume, the fact that ethics and morals, while the concern of secular philosophy, have traditionally been matters taught by organized religion and that for most individuals spiritual and ethical nourishment is derived from that source. It further reflects, I would suppose, the assumption that beliefs emanating from a religious source are probably held with great intensity.

When a policy has roots so deeply embedded in history, there is a compelling reason for a court to hazard the necessary statutory repairs if they can be made within the administrative framework of the statute and without impairing other legislative goals, even though they entail, not simply eliminating an offending section, but rather building upon it. Thus I am prepared to accept the prevailing opinion's conscientious objector test, not as a reflection of congressional statutory intent but as patchwork of judicial making that cures the defect of underinclusion in §6(j) and can be administered by local boards in the usual course of business. Like the prevailing opinion, I also conclude that petitioner's beliefs are held with the required intensity and consequently vote to *reverse* the judgment of conviction.

Contraception and Abortion

Humanae Vitae: A "Defect" and "Tragedy"?

If Vatican II can be styled as Pope John's revolution, Humanae Vitae *(1968) may be regarded as Pope Paul's counterrevolution. This important encyclical, contrary to wide expectations, reaffirmed the historic opposition of the Roman Catholic Church to any form of birth control except that of the "natural" rhythm method and, of course, abstinence. The papal letter stated that "every action which either in anticipation of the conjugal act, or in development of its natural consequences, purposes to render procreation impossible" is absolutely prohibited. ". . . Each and every marriage act must remain open to the transmission of life." Before* Humanae Vitae *was issued, surveys conducted among America's Catholics showed that the Church's teaching on contraception was a most troublesome one for the faithful and that, further, it was being widely ignored. The encyclical proved more of a shock because it had been widely rumored that the papal commission advising Pope Paul VI would recommend some modification in the long-standing condemnation of all artificial means of birth control. Thus, when* Humanae Vitae *was proclaimed on July 29, 1968, it provoked protests, outcries, and defiance. More was at stake than a single moral teaching: the whole question of papal authority came under urgent and critical review. Two statements follow: (1) Roman Catholic theologians at the Catholic University of America, one day after the encyclical was published, issued a declaration which spoke of the "defects" in* Humanae Vitae; *(2) Protestant theologian and leading ecumenist Robert McAfee Brown (b. 1920) was invited by Charles E. Curran (b. 1934), professor of moral theology at Catholic University, to offer "a Protestant reaction" to the papal pronouncement.*

1.

1. As Roman Catholic theologians we respectfully acknowledge a distinct role of hierarchical *magisterium* (teaching authority) in the Church of Christ. At the same time, Christian tradition assigns theologians the special responsibility

[Sources: (1) Charles E. Curran and Robert E. Hunt, *Dissent In and For the Church: Theologians and Humanae Vitae* (New York: Sheed & Ward, 1969), pp. 24–26. (2) Charles E. Curran, ed., *Contraception: Authority and Dissent* (New York: Herder and Herder, 1969), pp. 193–94, 201–7.]

of evaluating and interpreting pronouncements of the magisterium in the light of the total theological data operative in each question or statement. We offer these initial comments on Pope Paul VI's Encyclical on the Regulation of Birth.

2. The Encyclical is not an infallible teaching. History shows that a number of statements of similar or even greater authoritative weight have subsequently been proved inadequate or even erroneous. Past authoritative statements on religious liberty, interest-taking, the right to silence, and the ends of marriage have all been corrected at a later date.

3. Many positive values concerning marriage are expressed in Paul VI's Encyclical. However, we take exception to the ecclesiology implied and the methodology used by Paul VI in the writing and promulgation of the document: they are incompatible with the Church's authentic self-awareness as expressed in and suggested by the acts of the Second Vatican Council itself. The Encyclical consistently assumes that the Church is identical with the hierarchical office. No real importance is afforded the witness of the life of the Church in its totality; the special witness of many Catholic couples is neglected; it fails to acknowledge the witness of the separated Christian churches and ecclesial communities; it is insensitive to the witness of many men of good will; it pays insufficient attention to the ethical import of modern science.

4. Furthermore, the Encyclical betrays a narrow and positivistic notion of papal authority, as illustrated by the rejection of the majority view presented by the Commission established to consider the question, as well as by the rejection of the conclusion of a large part of the international Catholic theological community.

5. Likewise, we take exception to some of the specific ethical conclusions contained in the Encyclical. They are based on an inadequate concept of natural law: the multiple forms of natural law theory are ignored and the fact that competent philosophers come to different conclusions on this very question is disregarded. Even the minority report of the papal commission noted grave difficulty in attempting to present conclusive proof of the immorality of artificial contraception based on natural law.

6. Other defects include: overemphasis on the biological aspects of conjugal relations as ethically normative; undue stress on sexual acts and on the faculty of sex viewed in itself, apart from the person and the couple; a static worldview which downplays the historical and evolutionary character of humanity in its finite existence, as described in Vatican II's *Pastoral Constitution on the Church in the Modern World*; unfounded assumptions about 'the evil consequences of methods of artificial birth control'; indifference to Vatican II's assertion that prolonged sexual abstinence may cause 'faithfulness to be imperiled and its quality of fruitfulness to be ruined'; an almost total disregard for the dignity of millions of human beings brought into the world without the slightest possibility of being fed and educated decently.

7. In actual fact, the Encyclical demonstrates no development over the

teaching of Pius XI's *Casti Connubii* [1930] whose conclusions have been called into question for grave and serious reasons. These reasons, given a muffled voice at Vatican II, have not been adequately handled by the mere repetition of past teaching.

8. It is common teaching in the Church that Catholics may dissent from authoritative, noninfallible teachings of the magisterium when sufficient reasons for so doing exist.

9. Therefore, as Roman Catholic theologians, conscious of our duty and our limitations, we conclude that spouses may responsibly decide according to their conscience that artificial contraception in some circumstances is permissible and indeed necessary to preserve and foster the values and sacredness of marriage.

10. It is our conviction also that true commitment to the mystery of Christ and the Church requires a candid statement of mind at this time by all Catholic theologians.

2.

In recent years it has been the rule of ecumenical encounter not to engage in vigorous criticism of the "other" side. The proper ecumenical stance has been to concentrate on the failings of our own confessional family and to appreciate the good qualities of our ecumenical counterparts. On the whole, this is a good principle. But to assume in relation to *Humanae Vitae* a judicious silence, when so much is at stake, not only for ecumenism but for the whole family of man, is no way to contribute to the ecumenical future. If my own denomination, or the World Council of Churches, made a mistake as monumental as I feel *Humanae Vitae* to be, I would want every Catholic who would to join the chorus of criticism, so that we might collectively forestall the repetition of such an error in the future. So the ecumenically responsible thing to do is not to say, "Wasn't *Populorum Progressio* forward looking?", but to ask, "How can the harm of *Humanae Vitae* be undone?"

Ecumenical responsibility demands personal honesty, and it is therefore only fair to forewarn readers at the start that the underlying presupposition of the following pages is that *Humanae Vitae* is a tragedy for the Catholic Church and for the contemporary world. It is not only its content that upsets me, although I think it objectively wrong on almost every score, from its lack of contact with the modern world to its limited understanding of the psychology of marriage and its faulty understanding of the place of sexual intercourse in that relationship. It is also the manner of its issuance that upsets me; it not only fails to produce convincing arguments to support its thesis and to go counter to the overwhelming majority opinion of the papal commission that was presumably to guide its final content, but it also flies in the face of collegial principle that I thought had been established by Vatican II and implies, possibly by intent, that papal authority is once again to be understood along the most reactionary lines of nineteenth-century Catholic thought.

It grieves me to write such words, for I know that to many Catholics they will seem shrill and lacking in the ecumenical charity all of us have been trying to establish. But if our goal is to speak the truth in love, we must remember that sometimes in the name of love we are forced to speak in terms that initially hurt. And if out of hurt can come healing, then perhaps out of the total episode of *Humanae Vitae* — both its presentation and reception — some good may yet come. . . .

An article in *Observatore Romano,* that bastion of orthodoxy, appearing in late August 1968, suggested that Catholics should accept the teaching of *Humanae Vitae* unquestioningly, since the Pope knows best, just as a patient unquestioningly accepts the diagnosis of a doctor because of the doctor's superior wisdom, or a foot soldier unhesitatingly carries out the command of his superior officer because of the officer's greater knowledge of military tactics. Even on the basis of these very dubious analogies it could be argued that a doctor might diagnose wrongly, and a military tactician make an unwise decision. So too, pressing the analogy, might a pope be incorrect. Conservatives as well as progressives have conceded that the encyclical is not infallible. Since the opposite of infallibility is fallibility, it might be presumed that one could question the conclusions of a fallible document, and that, of course, is precisely what the dissenters have done.

But the ecclesiastical authorities have questioned this right. They have demanded ecclesiastical loyalty oaths from those who dared to differ, and have begun engaging in punitive measures against those who do not fall into line. This, I assume, is because papal encyclicals up to now have enjoyed a kind of "practical infallibility," so that although one might have inward doubts, he did not voice them, lest scandal be caused to the faithful.

At all events, earlier papal encyclicals have been accorded a high degree of authority. But this has not been true of *Humanae Vitae.* From the moment of its release it has been the object of strong dissent by many of the most able Catholic theologians of our time, as well as priests and laymen. The authority of the pope, in other words, has been seriously questioned.

The type of questioning, I believe, is of an order different from past questioning. When the dogma of the assumption was promulgated in 1950, for example, many Catholics said that they questioned the "opportuneness" of the definition, but not that they questioned its substantive truth. Today, the disaffection over *Humanae Vitae* is not merely with the "opportuneness" but with the substantive claims. The Pope, so say the Catholic dissenters, is wrong. Rome has spoken, but the case is *not* closed. On the contrary, it remains open, and hundreds of theologians have said in effect that although the Pope has denied to Catholics the right to use contraceptives, Catholics can for good and sufficient reasons use them anyhow.

What does this do to the notion of papal authority? It obviously compromises it in very serious terms, and means that drastic overhauling of traditional views of authority is urgent, with no guarantee provided that the overhauling will be rapid enough to overtake the disintegrating process. . . .

I see no way in which this crisis of authority can be resolved without great damage to the Roman Catholic Church. The priests, theologians, and lay people are not going to accept *Humanae Vitae* with the dutiful docility the curia expects, and the Pope is not about to admit that he was wrong. (A papacy that cannot yet be quite sure if a mistake was made about Galileo will be in no hurry to acknowledge that a mistake has been made about birth control.) In the past, of course, such an *impasse* was solved by time. Catholics can now look at *Unam Sanctam* [1302] and dismiss it as time-bound, and they can employ the same procedure with the *Syllabus of Errors* [1864] or Pius IX's characterization of the notion of religious liberty as a "nightmare." In these and dozens of other instances, there has been time for the church to adjust. With *Humanae Vitae* there is not. For not only does it appear in an age of instant communication, but it appears in an age where, if its teachings were widely followed, many well-informed people believe that the consequences in terms of population explosion could well destroy man's future.

Can one then do no more than throw up his hands in dismay? I believe there are other options and that the most important one centers around the pressing of the very principle the encyclical appears to have bypassed, the principle of collegiality. Heiko Oberman, a Protestant observer at Vatican II, stated that while it had affirmed the collegiality of the bishops, it might take Vatican III to affirm the collegiality of the pope. The crisis of authority in the church today indicates that even more than this will be needed, and that it will be needed considerably sooner than Vatican IV. What will be needed is an extension of the principle of collegiality to include the collegiality of the whole people of God, for example the drawing into the highest councils and decisions of the church of the priests, theologians and laity. Such an extension could be justified on the controversy over birth control alone, for it is clear that the wisdom of the laity in this matter has exceeded the wisdom of the bishops, the bishop of Rome included. (Joseph Noonan has a cartoon in the *National Catholic Reporter*, August 21, 1968, p. 4, which shows a woman saying, "I keep asking myself 'Do I really have a better understanding of the matter than the Pope?' And I keep answering 'Yes.' ")

The church could learn from the experience of the reception of *Humanae Vitae* that the full exercise of teaching authority cannot rest with the bishop of Rome alone, nor even with the college of bishops alone, but must include the priests, theologians, and laity as well. Informally, the principle has long been acknowledged: the teaching of the church must correspond to the *sensus fidelium*. But the *sensus fidelium* in recent years has been highly elusive, particularly to inhabitants of Vatican City, to be intuited perhaps but never validated by a head count. Surely now, however, some kind of structure must emerge by means of which subsequent articulations of the Catholic faith can take account of the charisms that Vatican II insisted were not the exclusive prerogative of the hierarchy. The reception of *Humanae Vitae* is a grim reminder that when the hierarchy speaks without "consulting the faithful in matters of doctrine," it paints itself into awkward corners.

Abortion: A Religious War?

No issue divided American society more sharply than did abortion. What might appear to some to be a very private question in fact became a noisy, clamorous, public one as the opposing armies took to the streets: "right to life" versus "freedom of choice." Churches found themselves whipped around in the maelstrom along with courts, legislatures, welfare agencies, and medical clinics. In a major U. S. Supreme Court case, Roe v. Wade (1973), the high Court finally dealt with —but surely did not dispose of—the issue of abortion's constitutionality. Justice Harry Blackmun (b. 1908) indicated that the Court well knew what a tangled thicket it entered: "We forthwith acknowledge our awareness of the sensitive and emotional nature of the abortion controversy, of the vigorous opposing views . . . and of the deep and seemingly absolute convictions that the subject inspires. One's philosophy, one's experiences, one's exposure to the raw edges of human experience, one's religious training, one's attitude toward life and family and their values, and the moral standards one establishes and seeks to observe, are all likely to influence and to color one's thinking and conclusions about abortion." With that prelude, the Court (in a 7 to 2 vote) concluded that the state could not interfere with a woman's decision to have an abortion during the first three months of her pregnancy —a decision widely interpreted by abortion's opponents as the functional equivalent of "abortion on demand." In 1976 the Hyde Amendment prohibited the use of federal funds for any such abortions, that amendment to a federal appropriations bill being narrowly upheld (5 to 4) by the Supreme Court in 1980 (Harris v. McRae). Proposals for a constitutional amendment to prohibit abortions, whether federally funded or not, and "single-issue" campaigns to elect selected candidates or defeat others kept the issue alive and society divided. The religious community was likewise divided, not along a simple Protestant-Catholic split, though that element was often present. A public "Call to Concern" issued by a large number of professors of religious ethics supported "abortion rights." The "Call" met with a "Reply" by Notre Dame's James T. Burtchaell (b. 1934), professor of theology and Holy Cross Father. The Catholic aspect of the "religious war" is addressed directly in his statement.

[Source: "A Call and a Reply," advertisement in *Christian Century*, Nov. 16, 1977, pp. 1074–75.]

(This is in response to an earlier paid advertisement entitled "A Call to Concern" and reproduces its text in entirety.)

A CALL AND A REPLY

A Call to Concern
      The increasing urgency of the issue of abortion rights requires us as teachers and writers of religious ethics to speak out.

A Reply

"A Call to Concern" is not a professional position paper by ethicists. It is a political manifesto, and its rhetoric is not very professional. Opposition to abortion is described as "absolutist," "rigid," "relentless," "extreme," "inflexible," "blind," "denial," "dangerous." The signers' position is sanctified with a different vocabulary: "sound," "moral," "responsible," "affirmation," "candor," "conscience," "professional responsibility," "deeply held convictions." In a Bronx election one might expect this kind of cant, but it is hardly the way philosophers and theologians should go about their business.

> Abortion is a serious and sometimes tragic procedure for dealing with fetal life. It raises important ethical issues and cannot be blandly legitimized by the mere whim of an individual. Nevertheless, it belongs in that large realm of often tragic actions where circumstances can render it a less destructive procedure than the rigid prolongation of pregnancy.

What is more destructive than death? The only serious ground for abortion being tragic is that it deals with fetal life by terminating it. On any less serious view of abortion there can be no substantial tragedy. And if one accepts the tragic view, then what misfortunes can possibly follow from birth which are arguably more destructive than the extermination of a fellow human? Those who regard abortion as life-taking do not foreclose this question; indeed, it is more often they who pose it.

> We support the Supreme Court decisions of 1973 which had the effect of removing abortion from the criminal law codes. The Court did not appeal to religion or ethics in arriving at its judgment, but we believe the decision to have been in accord with sound ethical judgment. Taking note of the fact that theologians, as well as other experts, disagree on the fundamental moral question of when human life begins, the Court decided that the law ought not to compel the conscience of those who believe abortion to be in harmony with their moral convictions.

Quite true: in WADE and BOLTON the Court said that, absent complete agreement whether human life begins before birth, the interests of the mother may overbear those of the offspring. Just as truly, those who understand life to begin before birth (and this is not really an ethical judgment, nor one upon which biologists quarrel as do divines) dissent from these decisions and continue to press for legal protections for the unborn comparable to those we ourselves enjoy.

> In the last four years, however, those decisions have been subjected to a relentless attack from those who take the absolutist position that it is always wrong to terminate a pregnancy at any time after the moment of conception. Those who take this absolutist position have not hesitated to equate abortion at any stage of pregnancy with murder or manslaughter. From such an extreme viewpoint, all legal means are considered justified if they limit abortions, no matter what the human consequences for poor women and others — as in the recent efforts to deny Medicaid funds and to prohibit use of public hospitals for abortion services.

Ethicists are expected to restrain themselves from misrepresenting positions with which they disagree. The position against abortion is both more simple and less silly than here portrayed. It is that human life begins when the human organism is first definitively composed; that destruction of a living human before birth is therefore homicide (a neutral term, not an absolutist one); and that ethical judgments about such termination of life must be consistent with all other deliberations about life-taking. The position, then, is not that abortion must always be morally wrong, but that anyone undertaking it bears the burden of justifying it. One can argue for justifiable homicide in war, in self-defense, in abortion, in criminal penalties. But when one hears no consistent or justifying arguments, and sees instead a straightforward desire to be rid of a fellow human who is an annoyance or a burden (as so often in war and in criminal punishment), then one quite reasonably says that most of this homicide is unjustified: hence, murder or manslaughter. What is more proper than for citizens of this mind to oppose the payment of tax moneys for purposes they regard as homicidal? To acknowledge that in many cases the birth of a child conceived will impose heavy burdens is not to treat those burdens lightly, but to say that burdens brought by the innocent young will hardly justify extermination. . . .

> We are saddened by the heavy institutional involvement of the bishops of the Roman Catholic Church in a campaign to enact religiously based anti-abortion commitments into law, and we view this as a serious threat to religious liberty and freedom of conscience. We acknowledge the legal right of all individuals and groups, both religious and secular, to seek laws that reflect their religious and ethical beliefs. But the institutional mobilization of Roman Catholic dioceses, including massive financial contributions by those dioceses to the National Committee for a Human Life Amendment, is inappropriate on this issue. If successful, it would violate the deeply held religious convictions of individual members and official bodies of many other religious groups about when human personhood begins, the relative rights of a woman and a fetus, and responsible family life. This is particularly a problem when there is no clear majority opinion on these fundamental issues

nor an adequate social base of consensus for legitimate and enforceable legislation.

The explicit effort of the Catholic bishops to protect the lives of unborn children is as "religiously based" and as threatening to freedom of religion and conscience as were their legislative programs for prison reform, for the right of farm laborers to organize, for recognition of conscientious objection, for racial justice, and for an end to the Vietnam War.

As for their "massive contributions" to the NCHLA, these amount to about $280,000 this year: half a cent per Catholic; an average contribution of $1,590 per diocese; less than one half of one per cent of what they budget for Catholic Charities alone, not to mention health care, inner-city schools, overseas relief, etc.

And as for the Catholics imposing a minority view on the nation, this is nonsense. It is well known — at least it should be well known to scholars who do their homework — that the elected legislatures and executives of 46 States chose laws restricting abortion, and that in every single statewide referendum held on this issue the people rejected abortion on demand. A clear majority of Americans have expressed the opinion that: 1) human life begins at conception or at quickening, and the unborn are persons before birth; 2) there

Antiabortion protest, Washington, D.C., 1978
(Religious News Service)

should be legal restraints on abortion; 3) abortion should be lawful if the mother's health is endangered or if the child will likely be deformed, but not if the child is simply unwanted; 4) abortion should in any case be unlawful after the third month; 5) it should also be unlawful without the husband's consent; 6) and it should be lawful only in hospitals. Each of these views is held invariably by a majority of both Catholics and non-Catholics, both men and women, as shown in surveys commissioned by pro-abortionists and conducted by Gallup before and after the Court decisions of 1973. It is these views that had been embodied in State laws. This is no Catholic peculiarity.

Catholics have no unanimity of opinion about abortion, morally or politically. In fact they disagree strenuously among themselves. What they do agree on is what the majority of Americans agree on with them: that unborn children are not to be sacrificed at the whim of their elders.

Those Catholics who disagree with the decision imposed by the Court, who prefer to live according to the national will as expressed by the common law and the statutes of the States, who are willing to put their convictions to the proof by working to amend the Constitution, which would require a more massive consent than any other undertaking in the American political process — these Catholics are understandably exasperated and injured when accused of being a backward minority coercively imposing their religious structures on an unwilling country. The accusation is simply bigotry, and "A Call to Concern" is infected with it.

If American leaders of all religious and humanitarian persuasions succeed in rallying the massive public support needed for a constitutional amendment which would leave the Congress and States free once again to enact publicly desired laws protecting the unborn, it is they who will be serving the public will, in supporting a policy which already at this time enjoys a very wide "social base of consensus."

> We call upon leaders of religious groups supporting abortion rights to speak out more clearly and publicly in response to the dangerously increasing influence of the absolutist position. There may be some ecumenical risks in such candor, but those risks have already been assumed by those who have pressed the absolutist position on religious grounds. In the long run, the true test of ecumenical authenticity is the ability to sustain dialogue and friendship in spite of sharp disagreements on matters of substance.

A "Call to Concern" is a political statement by ethical scholars. Ethically, it simply fails to address what is a serious ethical position: that the unborn deserve protection of their rights as do we all, and that the laws of the land ought not allow them to be put to death for our convenience. Politically, it vilifies those who strive in the political process to win recognition of a widely held human and civil right. In any case, this manifesto hardly represents the best that ethical scholars can contribute to this or any other national debate. It is not fair. It is not generous. It is not true.

4. EROSIONS/AFFIRMATIONS

Isolation and Community

"Pursuit of Loneliness"

"We seek more and more privacy," wrote sociologist Philip Slater (b. 1927) in 1970, "and feel more and more alienated and lonely when we get it." Slater's small but important book, The Pursuit of Loneliness, *carried as its subtitle the bald assertion: American Culture at the Breaking Point. A major reason why this culture stood at the breaking point was its scanty opportunity for community, for living "in trust and fraternal cooperation with one's fellows in a total and visible collective entity." We compete rather than cooperate; we avoid rather than engage; we play it cool, thereby "making [the] world a little colder." In contemporary America, Slater concluded, "the moral unity is gone."*

We are so accustomed to living in a society that stresses individualism that we need to be reminded that "collectivism" in a broad sense has always been the more usual lot of mankind, as well as of most other species. Most people in most societies have been born into and died in stable communities in which the subordination of the individual to the welfare of the group was taken for granted, while the aggrandizement of the individual at the expense of his fellows was simply a crime.

This is not to say that competition is an American invention — all societies involve some sort of admixture of cooperative and competitive institutions. But our society lies near or on the competitive extreme, and although it contains cooperative institutions I think it is fair to say that Americans suffer from their relative weakness and peripherality. Studies of business executives have revealed, for example, a deep hunger for an atmosphere of trust and fraternity with their colleagues (with whom they must, in the short run, engage in what Riesman calls "antagonistic cooperation"). The competitive

[Source: Philip Slater, *The Pursuit of Loneliness* (Boston: Beacon Press, 1976), pp. 9–11, 13.]

life is a lonely one, and its satisfactions are very short-lived indeed, for each race leads only to a new one.

In the past, as so many have pointed out, there were in our society many oases in which one could take refuge from the frenzied invidiousness of our economic system — institutions such as the extended family and the stable local neighborhood in which one could take pleasure from something other than winning a symbolic victory over one of his fellows. But these have disappeared one by one, leaving the individual more and more in a situation in which he must try to satisfy his affiliative and invidious needs in the same place. This has made the balance a more brittle one — the appeal of cooperative living more seductive, and the need to suppress our longing for it more acute.

In recent decades the principal vehicle for the tolerated expression of this longing has been the mass media. Popular songs and film comedies have continually engaged in a sentimental rejection of the dominant mores, maintaining that the best things in life are free, that love is more important than success, that keeping up with the Joneses is absurd, that personal integrity should take precedence over winning, and so on. But these protestations must be understood for what they are: a safety valve for the dissatisfactions that the modal American experiences when he behaves as he thinks he should. The same man who chuckles and sentimentalizes over a happy-go-lucky hero in a film would view his real-life counterpart as frivolous and irresponsible, and suburbanites who philosophize over their back fence with complete sincerity about their "dog-eat-dog-world," and what-is-it-all-for, and you-can't-take-it-with-you, and success-doesn't-make-you-happy-it-just-gives-you-ulcers-and-a-heart-condition — would be enraged should their children pay serious attention to such a viewpoint. Indeed, the degree of rage is, up to a point, a function of the degree of sincerity: if the individual did not feel these things he would not have to fight them so vigorously. The peculiarly exaggerated hostility that hippies tend to arouse suggests that the life they strive for is highly seductive to middle-aged Americans. . . .

It is easy to produce examples of the many ways in which Americans attempt to minimize, circumvent, or deny the interdependence upon which all human societies are based. We seek a private house, a private means of transportation, a private garden, a private laundry, self-service stores, and do-it-yourself skills of every kind. An enormous technology seems to have set itself the task of making it unnecessary for one human being ever to ask anything of another in the course of going about his daily business. Even within the family Americans are unique in their feeling that each member should have a separate room, and even a separate telephone, television, and car, when economically possible. We seek more and more privacy, and feel more and more alienated and lonely when we get it. What accidental contacts we do have, furthermore, seem more intrusive, not only because they are unsought but because they are unconnected with any familiar pattern of interdependence.

"The Mandate to Congregate"

Church historian Martin E. Marty (b. 1928), resisting the modern tendency to split off into ever narrowing confines of private interest, argued for the centrality of the congregation, and therefore of community, in American religious life. The only alternative, it would appear, "is a world in which there will be as many religions as there are people." Marty writes of "the public church," those churches "especially sensitive to the res publica, *the public order that surrounds and includes people of faith. The public church is a communion of communions. . . ." Affirmations of community are the antidotes for lost weekends (or decades) of isolation.*

The public church is a communion of communions and these, in turn, are also communities of communities. Most participants would regard the local congregation to be the basic expression of Christian community. While efforts to establish an essential form of communal life for Christians everywhere may be futile and may limit imagination, *something like* the local assembly will remain fundamental. The public church properly develops other forms to enhance the local gatherings, but it is not likely to settle for less than these. These congregations will take on varied colorings in different times or cultures, but in every case they serve to perpetuate embodiment, which is essential in the whole church.

Shortly after mid-century, the congregation suffered eclipse during a moment when experimenters promoted larger forms of community. Seminarians who were entering office characteristically told poll-takers that they aspired to ministries in agencies that promised more power and drama than did the local church. If only they could be mass communicators, workers for government, ecumenical field workers, or representatives of secular community organizations, they might be nearer the utopia of which the young must dream: that they might almost singlehandedly reshape a world. At least they could thus join hands with other people who had immediate access to networks of power.

Where universal or cosmopolitan forms of ministry seemed beyond reach, lay and clerical leaders, still despairing over the local church, were determined to set up parallel agencies of any sort to replace them. For a certain period these took the form of metropolitan parishes, paracongregations, chaplaincies to ill-defined respondents, nomadic apartment ministries, rural retreat communities, intentional congregations, or similar elites. Most of them did serve and their survivors still do serve as parables or exemplars for the more mundane congregations that remained prevalent. When these innovations failed and died, few mourned them, though many should have. In any case, in the present unfolding of forms, these para-parishes do not flourish and do

[Source: Martin E. Marty, *The Public Church: Mainline, Evangelical, Catholic* (New York: Crossroad, 1981), pp. 45–47, 53–54.]

not seem to be on the verge of doing so. The vast majority of participants put their communal energies into some form of local congregation.

Today instead of being assaulted or displaced by larger forms or mirror-image communities, the congregation suffers chiefly from a challenge to the communal ideal itself. A negative impulse often lies behind such rejection, for the congregation is an institution and modern religion abhors organized religion. The spirit of William James, a pioneer in modernity, has made its way. For him, religion was only the moment of incandescent stirring in the soul of the individual, the isolated mystic or saint. When two people linked up and set out to embody a spiritual experience through two seconds of time, the character of religion, he thought, began to be compromised.

The attack on the congregation as institution came from many sources. During a period of youth revolt the change derived from a spirit of anti-institutionalism. The churches were perceived as part of the power structure. People invested in them. Believers settled congregational affairs more or less democratically, which meant that they took votes, or creatively dragged their feet if they disagreed with the orders of the bishop. And if there was democracy, it was said, there could be neither prophecy nor purity. Religious institutions stifled the spirit and played into the hands of other grasping establishments. They were boring and lifeless, dulling to the spirit of adventurers, clouders of vision, promoters of mediocrity. The fact that there was and remains much truth to all these criticisms ought to keep the partisans of the parish from becoming complacent. But anti-institutionalism and the crisis of legitimacy together did not account for the whole of the assault on the congregation.

Instead, agents of modernity . . . consider that a contradiction exists between the religious spirit and social form, *any* social form. They celebrate and make a virtue of "the pluralization of life worlds." These moderns despair of any possibility of bringing such diverse personal worlds into confluence for positive purposes. They carry the chopping up of life and choice to the final degree. Religion becomes "invisible," says Thomas Luckmann, a "private affair," something which is an accidental and quiet footnote to one's biography but not something of social significance. To sociologist Bryan Wilson sacrality would be apparent only if a whole culture would live by a single set of sacred symbols. Subcommunities in a society do not count. So each individual who cares for the holy must be a steadfast eccentric who builds a private castle or fortress inside the mind. In the mental stronghold the last and only shrine survives, and from it individuals may draw strength, but they can never share this strength, only live off it.

The consequence of this tendency is a world in which there will be as many religions as there are people. I am told that if two people would set out to move chess pieces through all the variations that the first eleven moves on each side allow, the possibilities would be nearly infinite. "If all the people now alive had been playing a game every few minutes since Christ was born

. . .", they would not have exhausted these possibilities. Employing that sort of mathematics, one can imagine the varieties of, say, eleven component "private religions." . . .

In the primal documents that lie behind the life of the public church the social and communal dimensions are prime no matter what cultural shifts occur. Creation is a social act. God engages in an act of process by forming responsive universes, worlds, and humans. Creation establishes communion. The fall, that great mystery, is a corporate act. Whether the fall transmits itself through history, ontological fault, or broken personal responsibility, it is somehow corporate. The divine address to the fall is the promise of a people. Its first prefigurement is the *Qahal Yahweh,* the congregation of Yahweh. "Once you were not a people, but now you are a people."

In the covenant in Christ, which is grafted to the original one, the plan remains one of the congregants. The choice by Jesus of The Twelve replicates and affirms the tribes of Israel. A new covenant associates the old promise with the new people. Here imagery and reality of Christ as head of a body is in place. The New Testament knows of no consumerist or clientele religion, but always it is the congregation that seeks to transcend caucuses of male and female, causes of bond and free, or coteries of Jew and Greek.

Triviality and Responsibility

"Transcendental Self-Attention"

The turning of one's attention inward has in recent years become a national preoccupation. Self-help is the only help worth reading about or writing about or engaging in. In a provocative 1978 book about our "age of diminishing expectations," historian Christopher Lasch (b. 1932) spoke of America as a "narcissistic society" that has no interest in the past because it "cannot face the future." Persons in such a society avoid personal relations or "getting involved," avoid making "too large an investment in love and friendship" in order to "stay loose," ever free to do one's own thing in the momentary present. Such a culture manages to trivialize everything as it offers "solutions" that turn out to be self-defeating and empty.

As the twentieth century approaches its end, the conviction grows that many other things are ending too. Storm warnings, portents, hints of catastrophe haunt our times. The "sense of an ending," which has given shape to so much of twentieth-century literature, now pervades the popular imagination as well.

[Source: Christopher Lasch, *The Culture of Narcissism* (New York: W. W. Norton, 1978), pp. 3–6.]

The Nazi holocaust, the threat of nuclear annihilation, the depletion of natural resources, well-founded predictions of ecological disaster have fulfilled poetic prophecy, giving concrete historical substance to the nightmare, or death wish, that avant-garde artists were the first to express. The question of whether the world will end in fire or in ice, with a bang or a whimper, no longer interests artists alone. Impending disaster has become an everyday concern, so commonplace and familiar that nobody any longer gives much thought to how disaster might be averted. People busy themselves instead with survival strategies, measures designed to prolong their own lives, or programs guaranteed to ensure good health and peace of mind.

Those who dig bomb shelters hope to survive by surrounding themselves with the latest products of modern technology. Communards in the country adhere to an opposite plan: to free themselves from dependence on technology and thus to outlive its destruction or collapse. A visitor to a commune in North Carolina writes: "Everyone seems to share this sense of imminent doomsday." Stewart Brand, editor of the *Whole Earth Catalogue,* reports that "sales of the *Survival Book* are booming; it's one of our fastest moving items." Both strategies reflect the growing despair of changing society, even of understanding it, which also underlies the cult of expanded consciousness, health, and personal "growth" so prevalent today.

After the political turmoil of the sixties, Americans have retreated to purely personal preoccupations. Having no hope of improving their lives in any of the ways that matter, people have convinced themselves that what matters is psychic self-improvement: getting in touch with their feelings, eating health food, taking lessons in ballet or belly-dancing, immersing themselves in the wisdom of the East, jogging, learning how to "relate," overcoming the "fear of pleasure." Harmless in themselves, these pursuits, elevated to a program and wrapped in the rhetoric of authenticity and awareness, signify a retreat from politics and a repudiation of the recent past. Indeed Americans seem to wish to forget not only the sixties, the riots, the new left, the disruptions on college campuses, Vietnam, Watergate, and the Nixon presidency, but their entire collective past, even in the antiseptic form in which it was celebrated during the Bicentennial. Woody Allen's movie *Sleeper,* issued in 1973, accurately caught the mood of the seventies. Appropriately cast in the form of a parody of futuristic science fiction, the film finds a great many ways to convey the message that "political solutions don't work," as Allen flatly announces at one point. When asked what he believes in, Allen, having ruled out politics, religion, and science, declares: "I believe in sex and death — two experiences that come once in a lifetime."

To live for the moment is the prevailing passion — to live for yourself, not for your predecessors or posterity. We are fast losing the sense of historical continuity, the sense of belonging to a succession of generations originating in the past and stretching into the future. It is the waning of the sense of historical time — in particular, the erosion of any strong concern for poster-

ity—that distinguishes the spiritual crisis of the seventies from earlier out-
breaks of millenarian religion, to which it bears a superficial resemblance. . . .

. . . [Jim] Hougan notes* that survival has become the "catchword of the
seventies" and "collective narcissism" the dominant disposition. Since "the
society" has no future, it makes sense to live only for the moment, to fix our
eyes on our own "private performance," to become connoisseurs of our own
decadence, to cultivate a "transcendental self-attention."

"Broken Covenant"

*If neither moral unity nor moral purpose can currently be found, why is it
that the American present differs so markedly in this regard from the American past? Sociologist Robert Bellah (b. 1927) explains that disparity in
terms of a covenantal understanding that prevailed for so long, but prevails
no longer. This covenant called for mutual obligation and responsibility, and
it rested upon "a common set of moral understandings" which in turn "rest
upon a common set of religious understandings." Any society requires such
commonalities, Bellah argued, in order to be legitimate, in order to have
integrity, in order to survive. Such "civil religion," religion beyond but not
irrelevant to denominational particularity, has now broken down or is in
utter disarray. "The major tendency in the society at large seems to be
erosion," and the urgent need is for a "rebirth of imaginative vision."*

To those who say the answer to our present need is no control at all, let the
impulses run free, natural man is at heart innocent and good, I would with
Melville reply: "Well, well, one hears the kettledrums of hell." The great
antinomies of human life are never solved by grasping one polarity and
forgetting the other. Our problem is not to get rid of control in any absolute
sense but to find a new kind of control that will allow a wider freedom. It
is hard for this generation to understand a phrase like "those wise restraints
that make men free," perhaps because such phrases too often have been used
as part of a con game to get youth to buy the illusions of middle age. But
short of the Apocalypse, there is no freedom without constraint. The great
urge at the moment, and rightly so in my opinion, is liberation. But without
a new order, without a new system of control, liberation cannot become
liberty and quickly becomes depotism. As when some superliberated youth
jumps into the arms of a totalitarian religious or political sect.

With respect to the human personality, the deepest ordering of impulse is

[Source: Robert N. Bellah, *The Broken Covenant: American Civil Religion in Time of
Trial* (New York: Seabury Press, 1975), pp. 84–86.]

*In a book entitled *Decadence: Radical Nostalgia, Narcissism, and Decline in the Seventies*
(New York: William Morrow & Co., Inc., 1975).

cultural, is religious, occurs in myth and ritual. America began when the great new mythic ordering of the Protestant Reformation was still vital and alive. That pattern combined with the newer myth of republican liberty sustained and reinvigorated us in our first and second times of trial. But now our cultural crisis is deeper. The single vision that has been on the rise since the 18th century is now more than ever the dominant cultural orientation. A profound experience of conversion, of the reordering of the deepest levels of the personality in the light of a transcendent vision, is not absent in America, but it is harder than ever to integrate with the dominant cultural mood. The established structures of economic and political power seem perversely set on maximizing wealth and power regardless of the cost to the society or the natural environment. Under these circumstances we should not be surprised if efforts at liberation, revolution, and counterculture seem fragmented and chaotic. Anarchy and antinomianism are always present in the effort to change a social order that has become too constricting.

But the dominant American cultural and social system can put up with a certain amount of anarchy and antinomianism, can even encourage it. A highly private "freedom" in certain restricted spheres can go together with the dominance of purely technical control at the center of social power. From this point of view the mere rejection of the established order, even if flamboyantly symbolized, has a strictly limited utility. If we are to transcend the limitations of American culture and society it can only be on the basis of an imaginative vision that can generate an experience of inner conversion and lead to a new form of covenant. Liberation without any sense of constitution will surely be self-defeating. The perils of late 20th-century America will not be overcome by everyone doing his or her "own thing," but through the discovery of cultural and social forms that can give the disciplined basis for a new degree of moral freedom.

Affirmations

Hartford

Early in 1975 a broad range of theologians —liberal and conservative, Orthodox and Roman Catholic, hierarchical and low church —met in Hartford, Connecticut to call for "theological affirmation." The organizers of the gathering, sociologist Peter L. Berger and pastor-editor Richard J. Neuhaus, both happened to be Lutherans, but the resulting Hartford Appeal was in no sense a narrowly sectarian document. It was, rather, an effort to escape being "imprisoned in modernity" (as Berger noted), or (as Jesuit Avery Dulles wrote) an attempt to "confront the dominant cultural patterns" and

[Source: "An Appeal for Theological Affirmation," in *Against the World/For the World*, by Peter L. Berger and Richard J. Neuhaus (New York: The Seabury Press, 1976), pp. 1–5.]

not merely to bow before them. Hartford, "a totally unauthorized gathering,"
represented no ecumenical structure and was responsible to no watchful con-
stituency. It was, rather, a personal effort to identify what was wrong or
missing in the nation's major theological tradition ("themes false and debil-
itating") and to press for a "renewal of Christian witness and mission."

The renewal of Christian witness and mission requires constant examination
of the assumptions shaping the Church's life. Today an apparent loss of a
sense of the transcendent is undermining the Church's ability to address with
clarity and courage the urgent tasks to which God calls it in the world. This
loss is manifest in a number of pervasive themes. Many are superficially
attractive, but upon closer examination we find these themes false and debil-
itating to the Church's life and work. Among such themes are:

Theme 1. *Modern thought is superior to all past forms of understanding reality,*
    and is therefore normative for Christian faith and life.
In repudiating this theme we are protesting the captivity to the prevailing
thought structures not only of the twentieth century but of any historical
period. We favor using any helpful means of understanding, ancient or modern, and insist that the Christian proclamation must be related to the idiom
of the culture. At the same time, we affirm the need for Christian thought
to confront and be confronted by other world views, all of which are necessarily provisional.

Theme 2. *Religious statements are totally independent of reasonable discourse.*
The capitulation to the alleged primacy of modern thought takes two forms:
one is the subordination of religious statements to the canons of scientific
rationality; the other, equating reason with scientific rationality, would remove
religious statements from the realm of reasonable discourse altogether. A
religion of pure subjectivity and nonrationality results in treating faith statements as being, at best, statements about the believer. We repudiate both
forms of capitulation.

Theme 3. *Religious language refers to human experience and nothing else, God*
    being humanity's noblest creation
Religion is also a set of symbols and even of human projections. We
repudiate the assumption that it is nothing but that. What is here at stake is
nothing less than the reality of God. *We did not invent God; God invented us.*

Theme 4. *Jesus can only be understood in terms of contemporary models of*
    humanity.
This theme suggests a reversal of "the imitation of Christ"; that is, the
image of Jesus is made to reflect cultural and countercultural notions of human
excellence. We do not deny that all aspects of humanity are illumined by

First pontiff to visit the nation's capital, Pope John Paul II met with President Jimmy Carter to discuss issues of peace and war, and of human rights (1979). *(Religious News Service)*

Jesus. Indeed, it is necessary to the universality of the Christ that he be perceived in relation to the particularities of the believers' world. We do repudiate the captivity to such metaphors, which are necessarily inadequate, relative, transitory, and frequently idolatrous. Jesus, together with the Scriptures and the whole of the Christian tradition, cannot be arbitrarily interpreted without reference to the history of which they are part. The danger is in the attempt to exploit the tradition without taking the tradition seriously.

Theme 5. *All religions are equally valid; the choice among them is not a matter of conviction about truth but only of personal preference or life style.*

We affirm our common humanity. We affirm the importance of exploring and confronting all manifestations of the religious quest and of learning from the riches of other religions. But we repudiate this theme because it flattens diversities and ignores contradictions. In doing so, it not only obscures the meaning of Christian faith, but also fails to respect the integrity of other faiths. Truth matters; therefore differences among religions are deeply significant.

Theme 6. *To realize one's potential and to be true to oneself is the whole meaning of salvation.*
Salvation contains a promise of human fulfillment, but to identify salvation with human fulfillment can trivialize the promise. We affirm that salvation cannot be found apart from God.

Theme 7. *Since what is human is good, evil can adequately be understood as failure to realize potential.*
This theme invites false understanding of the ambivalence of human existence and underestimates the pervasiveness of sin. Paradoxically, by minimizing the enormity of evil, it undermines serious and sustained attacks on particular social or individual evils.

Theme 8. *The sole purpose of worship is to promote individual self-realization and human community.*
Worship promotes individual and communal values, but it is above all a response to the reality of God and arises out of the fundamental need and desire to know, love, and adore God. We worship God because God is to be worshiped.

Theme 9. *Institutions and historical traditions are oppressive and inimical to our being truly human; liberation from them is required for authentic existence and authentic religion.*
Institutions and traditions are often oppressive. For this reason they must be subjected to relentless criticism. But human community inescapably requires institutions and traditions. Without them life would degenerate into chaos and new forms of bondage. The modern pursuit of liberation from all social and historical restraints is finally dehumanizing.

Theme 10. *The world must set the agenda for the Church. Social, political, and economic programs to improve the quality of life are ultimately normative for the Church's mission in the world.*
This theme cuts across the political and ideological spectrum. Its form remains the same, no matter whether the content is defined as upholding the values of the American way of life, promoting socialism, or raising human consciousness. The Church must denounce oppressors, help liberate the op-

pressed, and seek to heal human misery. Sometimes the Church's mission coincides with the world's programs. But the norms for the Church's activity derive from its own perception of God's will for the world.

Theme 11. *An emphasis on God's transcendence is at least a hindrance to, and perhaps incompatible with, Christian social concern and action.*

This supposition leads some to denigrate God's transcendence. Others, holding to a false transcendence, withdraw into religious privatism or individualism and neglect the personal and communal responsibility of Christians for the earthly city. From a biblical perspective, it is precisely because of confidence in God's reign over all aspects of life that Christians must participate fully in the struggle against oppressive and dehumanizing structures and their manifestations in racism, war, and economic exploitation.

Theme 12. *The struggle for a better humanity will bring about the Kingdom of God.*

The struggle for a better humanity is essential to Christian faith and can be informed and inspired by the biblical promise of the Kingdom of God. But imperfect human beings cannot create a perfect society. The Kingdom of God surpasses any conceivable utopia. God has his own designs which confront ours, surprising us with judgment and redemption.

Theme 13. *The question of hope beyond death is irrelevant or at best marginal to the Christian understanding of human fulfillment.*

This is the final capitulation to modern thought. If death is the last word, then Christianity has nothing to say to the final questions of life. We believe that God raised Jesus from the dead and are ". . . convinced that there is nothing in death or life, in the realm of spirits or superhuman powers, in the world as it is or in the world as it shall be, in the forces of the universe, in heights or depths — nothing in all creation that can separate us from the love of God in Christ Jesus our Lord" (Romans 8:38f.).

Seattle

If Hartford sought to escape the prison of modernity, Seattle sought to limit its terror. In the 1980s nuclear arms multiplied and international negotiations on limiting such arms faltered. Government officials also began to talk of nuclear war as a genuine option, of "first strike" capability, even of a "winnable" nuclear war. The jargon of sophisticated weapons systems and the calculus of how many millions might survive the many million annihilated could turn an entire citizenry numb. Perhaps it should all be left to the experts. Increasingly, however, major religious voices and forces called for

[Source: *National Catholic Reporter*, Feb. 12, 1982, p. 43.]

some limits, some "moral norms." Not just the "peaceniks" and professional
dissenters spoke out, but great segments of America's mainline churches. The
National Conference of Catholic Bishops sought an immediate multilateral
freeze on the production and deployment of nuclear weapons. Southern Bap-
tists launched in 1981 a quarterly paper, Baptist Peacemaker, *published*
on "four major calendar dates: Christmas, Easter, Pentecost, Hiroshima."
Peace conferences were held, peace sermons preached, and books on Nuclear
Holocaust and Christian Hope *written. In Seattle a mass demonstration,*
"Target Seattle," gathered in 1982 to press for nuclear restraint and spiritual
responsibility. This followed the pastoral letter of Seattle's Archbishop Ray-
mond G. Hunthausen (b. 1921) written earlier in the year, asserting that
"The very existence of humanity is at stake."

Dear People of God:

As you all know, I have spoken out against the participation of our country
in the nuclear arms race because I believe that such participation leads to
incalculable harm. Not only does it take us along the path toward nuclear
destruction, but it also diverts immense resources from helping the needy.
As Vatican II put it, "The arms race is one of the greatest curses on the human
race and the harm it inflicts on the poor is more than can be endured" (*The
Church in the Modern World,* n. 81).

I believe that as Christians imbued with the spirit of peacemaking expressed
by the Lord in the Sermon on the Mount, we must find ways to make known
our objections to the present concentration on further nuclear arms buildup.
Accordingly, after much prayer, thought, and personal struggle, I have decided to withhold 50 per cent of my income taxes as a means of protesting
our nation's continuing involvement in the race for nuclear arms supremacy.

I am aware that this action will provoke a variety of responses. Many will
agree with me and support me as they have done in the past. Other conscientious people will be puzzled, uncomprehending, resentful and even angry.
For the sake of all, I shall clarify what I am attempting and not attempting
to do by my tax-withholding action. I do so in the prayerful hope that all
continue to discuss this nuclear arms issue in a spirit of mutual openness and
charity. How ironic if we as Christians were to discuss the issue of disarmament for peace in a warlike fashion!

I am not attempting to say that there is but one way of dealing with the
problem of the arms race and the nuclear holocaust toward which it leads. I
recognize the need for a number of different strategies for the promotion of
arms reduction. Accordingly, I welcome the diverse efforts of many individuals and groups, including the efforts of some of my fellow bishops, to call
attention to the seriousness of this matter and to suggest practical ways of
acting with regard to it.

I am not attempting to divide the Christian community. I pray that because
of our openness and respect for one another, we can grow together by our

concentration on the goal of world peace and the eventual elimination of nuclear arms despite our disagreements over the best way to achieve such goals.

I am not suggesting that all who agree with my peace and disarmament views should imitate my action of income tax withholding. I recognize that some who agree with me in their hearts find it practically impossible to run the risk of withholding taxes because of their obligations to those personally dependent upon them. Moreover, I see little value in imitating what I am doing simply because I am doing it. I prefer that each individual come to his or her own decision on what should be done to meet the nuclear arms challenge.

I am not pointing a finger of accusation at those who disagree with what I plan to do. I would hope, however, that such persons will respect those whose views differ from theirs. No one has answers that are absolutely certain in such complex matters. I am suggesting that we must maintain a continuing and open dialogue. . . .

I believe that the present issue is as serious as any the world has faced. The very existence of humanity is at stake.

I am not encouraging those who wish to avoid paying taxes to use my action as a justification for their own personal gain. I plan to deposit what I withhold in a fund to be used for charitable peaceful purposes. There come to mind the needs of those workers who will require assistance should they decide to leave their nuclear war-related jobs, the bona fide peace movements, the Academy of Peace and Conflict Resolution or programs for the aid of pregnant women who have chosen not to terminate their pregnancies by abortion.

I am saying by my action that in conscience I cannot support or acquiesce in a nuclear arms buildup which I consider a grave moral evil.

I am saying that I see no possible justification for the willingness to employ nuclear weapons capable of destroying humanity as we know it.

I am saying that everyone should think profoundly and pray deeply over the issue of nuclear armaments. My words and my action of tax-withholding are meant to awaken those who have come to accept without thinking the continuation of the arms race, to stir even those who disagree with me to find a better path than the one we now follow, to encourage all to put in first place not the production of arms but the production of peace.

I urge all of you to pray and to fast, to study and to discuss, and then to decide what you shall do to combat the evil of the nuclear arms race. *I cannot make your decision for you. I can and do challenge you to make a decision.*

May God be with you. His joy. His peace. His love.

Suggested Reading
(Chapter Twelve)

Even the most superficial observer could not remain oblivious to the burst of "new religions" upon the American scene in the 1970s and 1980s. Jacob Needleman and George Baker edited a helpful guide to *Understanding the New Religions* (1978), with chapters by dozens of authorities on one phase or another of the mazelike phenomena. *Religious Movements in Contemporary America* (1974), a massive work edited by I. I. Zaretsky and M. P. Leone, also brought together many experts along with a variety of methodologies and perspectives to interpret the "current religious renaissance." In *Religious and Spiritual Groups in Modern America* (1973), Robert S. Ellwood, Jr., offered to the student clear and knowledgeable introductions, ephemeral documents, extensive bibliography, and even the names and addresses of fugitive groups ranging from the Amalgamated Flying Saucer Club of America to the Tibetan Nyingmapa Meditation Center. Ellwood in a later book, *Alternative Altars: Unconventional and Eastern Spirituality in America* (1979), gave special attention to Spiritualism, Theosophy, and Zen Buddhism. Specific treatments of Zen include the classic by D. T. Suzuki, *Zen Buddhism* (1956), this to be supplemented by Shunryu Suzuki, *Zen Mind, Beginner's Mind* (1970), and Roshi Kapleau, *Zen: Dawn in the West* (1979).

When the new religions first came to the public's attention, the initial reaction was confusion, resentment, fright. More reflective sociological analyses have recently been provided by Steven M. Tipton, *Getting Saved from the Sixties* (1982), and by D. G. Bromley and A. D. Shupe, Jr., *Strange Gods: The Great American Cult Scare* (1982). The power of specific personalities (e.g., Robert Schuller, Oral Roberts, Pat Boone, Bob Dylan) is explored in Richard Quebedeaux's *By What Authority? The Rise of Personality Cults in American Christianity* (1982), while Sun Myung Moon is the focus of Bromley and Shupe's *The Moonies in America* (1979). Autobiographical accounts by ex-Moonies include Christopher Edwards, *Crazy for God* (1979), and the mother-daughter story told by Barbara and Betty Underwood, *Hostage to Heaven* (1979). Jonestown of course evoked extensive reporting and commenting: for example, George Klineman et al., *The Cult that Died* (1980); M. S. Yee et al., *In My Father's House* (1981); and James Reston, Jr., *Our Father Who Art in Hell* (1981). The recent upsurge of neopaganism, sometimes mixed with elements of feminism, is the subject of Zee Budapest, *The Feminist Book of Light and Shadows* (1976), as well as Merlin Stone, *When God Was a Woman* (1978), and Naomi Goldenberg, *The Changing of the Gods: Feminism and the End of Traditional Religion* (1979). The Dominican Richard Woods explores *The Occult Revolution* (1971) along with its implications for the Christian churches.

Books on the radical right are almost as numerous as its adherents. Those concerned particularly with the political alliances and implications include the following: Erling Jorstad, *The Politics of Moralism: The New Christian Right in America* (1981); S. S. Hill and D. E. Owen, *The New Religious Political Right in America* (1982); Peggy L. Shriver, *The Bible Vote: Religion and the New Right* (1981); and Flo

Conway and Jim Siegelman, *Holy Terror* . . . (1982). The following authors pay special attention to the electronic church: J. K. Haddam and C. E. Swann, *Prime Time Preachers* (1981); Virginia S. Owens, *The Total Image, or Selling Jesus in the Modern Age* (1980); and Jerry Sholes, *Give Me that Prime Time Religion* (1979). Insider accounts include Ben Armstrong, *The Electronic Church* (1979); Jerry Falwell, *Listen, America!* (1980); Charles F. Stanley, *Stand Up, America* (1980); Richard A. Viguerie, *The New Right: We're Ready to Lead* (1980); and James C. Roberts, *The Conservative Decade* (1980), with an introduction by Ronald Reagan.

Liberation theology moved beyond the limits of class, country, race, and sex, but often found its most eloquent or poignant expression in intimate association with one or more of the above. A broad survey edited by Dale Richeson and Brian Mahan, *The Challenge of Liberation Theology* (1981), offers an excellent starting point. Also see Robert M. Brown, *Theology in a New Key: Responding to Themes of Liberation* (1978). *Black Nationalism in America* (1970), by John H. Bracey and others, may be supplemented by Peter Goldman's biography, *The Death and Life of Malcolm X* (1972) and by Albert B. Cleage, *Black Christian Nationalism* (1972). The Paulist journal, *New Catholic World*, devoted its July-August, 1980, issue entirely to "The Hispanic Church," a subject still underreported and under-analyzed. Shifting from the North American scene to South America, one follows the Roman Catholic Church's course (and the involvement of the United States) in Penny Lernoux, *Cry of the People* (1980).

Feminism and the religious dimensions thereof have, like the radical right, received a full press. One of the best historic surveys is that of Rosemary Ruether and Eleanor McLaughlin, *Women of Spirit: Female Leadership in the Jewish and Christian Traditions* (1979). James A. Coriden, ed., in *Sexism and Church Law* (1977) examines the Catholic tradition specifically, as do Leonard and Arlene Swidler in *Women Priests: A Catholic Commentary on the Vatican Declaration* (1977). Rabbi Sally Priesand has told her own story and what it portends for her religious tradition in *Judaism and the New Woman* (1975). For the application of acute biblical scholarship to some of the new questions which feminism has raised, see Phyllis Trible, *God and the Rhetoric of Sexuality* (1978).

Because of the current abundant litigation in church-state matters, "suggested readings" rapidly grow obsolete. One may keep abreast of developments through such organs as the *Journal of Church and State* edited by James E. Wood, Jr., and the annual *Supreme Court Review* edited by Philip B. Kurland. A recent symposium at the University of Southern California, *Freedom of Religion in America* (1982), explored that large subject from several disciplinary points of view. Jay Mechling's volume on *Church, State, and Public Policy* (1978) discusses the "new shape" of today's confrontation, while the legal activism characteristic of the contemporary scene is neatly unfolded in Frank J. Sorauf's *Wall of Separation* (1976). With respect to religion and public education, the following volumes summarize much of the discussion of the last two decades: Theodore Sizer, ed., *Religion and Public Education* (1967); David E. Engel, *Religion in Public Education* (1974); and Paul J. Will, ed., *Public Education Religion Studies: An Overview* (1981). Concerning religion and private education, the following monographs offer guidance but also contrasting points of view: Neil G. McCluskey, *Catholic Education in America*

(1964); P. R. Moots and E. M. Gaffney, Jr., *Church and Campus: Legal Issues in Religiously Affiliated Education* (1979); P. J. Weber and D. A. Gilbert, *Private Churches and Public Monies* (1981); and Gaffney again, as editor, *Private Schools and Public Good* (1981). Recent conscientious objection issues are treated more in articles than books, but two studies do concern themselves with the Vietnam years: J. D. Finn, ed., *A Conflict of Loyalties: The Case for Selective Conscientious Objection* (1968); and M. Q. Sibley, *The Obligation to Disobey: Conscience and the Law* (1970). On the intersection of biology with theology, see John T. Noonan, ed., *The Morality of Abortion* (1970); Daniel Callahan, *Abortion: Law, Choice and Morality* (1970); and Paul Ramsey, *Ethics at the Edges of Life* (1978).

Issues raised in the final section often impinge on what has been named "civil religion" or the "religion of the republic." Convenient collections pertinent to these subjects may be found in Elwyn A. Smith, ed., *The Religion of the Republic* (1971); R. E. Richey and D. G. Jones, eds., *American Civil Religion* (1974); Sidney E. Mead, *The Nation with the Soul of a Church* (1975); and Robert N. Bellah and Phillip E. Hammond, eds., *Varieties of Civil Religion* (1980). On other religious currents in contemporary America, see *Daedalus*, Winter, 1982, or the expanded book version also published by the American Academy of Arts and Sciences (1983). In *Theology Today*, 36 (January, 1980), Sydney E. Ahlstrom presented in revised form an earlier *Daedalus* article: "The Traumatic Years: American Religion and Culture in the '60s and '70s." Jonathan Schell's best-selling, *The Fate of the Earth* (1982), originally appearing in the *New Yorker* magazine, greatly heightened public awareness of and anxiety concerning nuclear catastrophe. But see also Dale Aukerman, *Darkening Valley: A Biblical Perspective on Nuclear War* (1981); D. B. Kraybill, *Facing Nuclear War* (1982), published by a Mennonite house; and R. J. Sider and Richard Taylor, *Nuclear Holocaust and Christian Hope* (1982), released jointly by Catholic and Protestant publishers.

INDEX